EXPLORATIONS IN THE ARTS

reproduced on the cover:
I.M. Pei. National Gallery of Art, East Wing, Washington, D.C.
Photograph by Bill Carter/The Image Bank, New York.

Painting
Sculpture
Architecture
Photography
Literature
Music
Theatre
Film
Opera
Dance

EXPLORATIONS IN THE ARTS

An Introduction to the Humanities

G. M. Pinciss
Marlies K. Danziger
Peter Basquin
Wayne R. Dynes

all of Hunter College
of the City University of New York

Holt, Rinehart and Winston, Inc.
Fort Worth Chicago San Francisco Philadelphia Montreal Toronto
London Sydney Tokyo

Publisher Susan Katz
Acquisitions Editor Karen Dubno
Picture Editor Joan Scafarello
Senior Picture Researcher Marion Geisinger
Special Projects Editors Pamela Forcey, Jeanette Ninas Johnson
Production Manager Nancy Myers
Art Director Louis Scardino
Book Design Caliber Design Planning, Inc.
Cover Design Louis Scardino
Composition and camera work York Graphic Services
Color separations The Lehigh Press, Inc.
Printing and binding R. R. Donnelley & Sons Co.

Library of Congress Cataloging in Publication Data
Main entry under title:

Explorations in the arts.

Includes index.
1. Arts—Addresses, essays, lectures.
I. Pinciss, G. M.
NX60.E96 1985 700 84-19224

ISBN 0-03-062939-X

Address Editorial correspondence to:
301 Commerce St.
Fort Worth, TX 76102

Printed in the United States of America
9012 039 9 8 7 6 5

Holt, Rinehart and Winston, Inc.
The Dryden Press
Saunders College Publishing

Preface

Explorations in the Arts is intended for introductory, interdisciplinary Humanities courses that integrate the study of the various visual, verbal, and performing arts. This broad perspective fosters awareness of the elements common to all the arts as well as of the distinctive characteristics of each art form.

Rather than presenting a chronological survey of the arts or discussing each art form separately, *Explorations in the Arts* groups the arts into three broad categories: the spatial (painting, sculpture, architecture, photography), the temporal (music poetry, prose narrative), and the composite (theater, film, dance, opera) This organization enables us both to introduce the basic elements of each art form and to show what the arts within each group have in common. Furthermore, we have linked the well-known concepts of perspective and point of view to demonstrate how artists shape their material, and we have used comparable terms in discussing how performers reshape a work as they interpret it. We have, moreover, considered works of art in several broader contexts: in relation to certain major cultural traditions, to genres, and to several historical periods. Finally, we take up the knotty problem of evaluation, giving attention to a number of criteria for judging works of art and suggesting to what degree these are useful. Here, as elsewhere in the text, we test these theoretical principles by applying them to specific works.

Explorations in the Arts is basically a self-sufficient text that includes over 200 illustrations, two short stories, a number of poems, and two reviews of actual performances. In the earlier chapters we discuss a variety of works rather briefly; later, we consider a few works in depth. Throughout, we offer vivid examples—some well-known and some unusual—to illustrate basic concepts.

We have tried to make *Explorations in the Arts* as understandable and useful as possible. We have adopted a level of writing and chosen examples that are, we hope, appropriate for students whether they come with traditional preparation or with more limited experience and whether they are enrolled in two- or four-year colleges. Although our text is written for students of widely varying backgrounds, it has several distinctive features that will be of benefit to all. The "Questions for Study and Discussion" at the end of each chapter encourage students to consolidate their understanding of the material and to apply what they have learned to new situations. Occasional bars of music are reproduced in the text as visual guides and require no ability to read notes. Technical terms are identified by bold-faced lettering and carefully defined in the chapters in which they first appear; they are, moreover, redefined in the Glossary. An appendix offers a brief review of musical notation for those students who are asked to deal with this more technical material. In addition, the specially prepared cassette (available for student purchase) allows students to hear some of the music they are reading about; it also describes and demonstrates the key musical terms.

We have presented the subject matter in such a way that the course can be successfully taught not only by a team of specialists but also by a single instructor. For those who prefer to teach each of the arts separately, we have supplied an Alternate Table of Contents arranged by art forms. The separate Instructor's Manual offers step-by-step guidance for each class meeting over an entire semester as well as providing alternative examples, answers to the "Questions for Study and Discussion," short-answer test questions (with answers), and suggestions for further reading.

A book that attempts to synthesize so many fields could have been written only with the help of many colleagues and friends, both at Hunter College and beyond. Our text owes its inception to the encouragement of Dr. Gerald Freund, formerly Dean of Humanities and the Arts at Hunter, whose continued interest in our venture we acknowledge with pleasure. An outgrowth of a course initiated with funding from the Mellon Foundation, whose assistance was crucial in the early stages, our text has profited from classroom use at Hunter. We are grateful to our students for allowing us to test our ideas and to the administration of the College for its efforts to ease our writing.

We should like to give special thanks to our many friends who have read the manuscript in part or as a whole and who have offered helpful suggestions. Among our colleagues at Hunter, the late Professor Claireve

Grandjouan and Professors Harriet Johnson, Mildred Kuner, Vera Roberts, Jane Roos, Steven Ross, Edwin Wilson, and Joel Zuker have been especially generous with their time and knowledge. We are also deeply indebted to Don McDonagh, ballet critic, and William D. Quesenbery, Jr., of ABC Television for sharing with us their wisdom and practical good sense; and to Professors Emeriti Morton N. Cohen of the City University of New York and Richard N. Swift of New York University for their continuing encouragement. In addition, Professors Dora Zaslavsky of the Manhattan School of Music and William E. Nelson of Carleton College have demonstrated, by their example, the intimate connection between the analysis and performance of music. Guy Weill has chosen our illustration of a Chinese scroll with exceptional care and has photographed it with great skill and sensitivity; Stephen Schneiderman has kindly translated our selection from *The Iliad;* and Janet Hulstrand greatly helped with our manuscript.

We are particularly grateful to Professor Lewis Falb of The New School for Social Research, an inexhaustible source of useful information, for his patient and enduring faith in our project; and to Dr. Kurt Mitchells of London for his thoughtful, painstaking, and invaluable reading of our manuscript in various stages. We should also like to acknowledge the contribution of Katie Basquin, who added a note of harmony, and of Tony Crickmay, Charles Danziger, and Wendy Warnken, Associate Curator of the Theater Collection of the Museum of the City of New York, who indefatigably and cheerfully located illustrations and photographs. Dennis Paoli of Hunter College, with the encouragement and help of Heidi Paoli, wrote the Instructor's Manual; drawing on his experience in teaching the course, he brought to his task both inventiveness and a sharp eye for the multiple possibilities of the text.

Others who read our manuscript at various stages of its development and offered helpful comments are: Harrison M. Davis, Brigham Young University, Provo, Utah; Homer Edwards, Jr., Wayne State University, Detroit; Diane M. Fairchild, City College of San Francisco, Calif.; Ronald Ham, Ferris State College, Big Rapids, Mich.; William A. Lozano, Johnson County Community College, Overland Park, Kan.; Moylen Mills, Ogontz Campus of The Pennsylvania State University; Linda Ostrander, Bunker Hill Community College, Charlestown, Mass.; Michael Tesh, Miami Dade Community College, Miami.

Finally, we record our admiration and appreciation for the talents and ingenuity of those at Holt, Rinehart and Winston who have been indispensable in providing advice and assistance. We were most fortunate to have Karen Dubno as our general editor: she found us, nurtured us, and has remained our mentor to the end. Her rigorous thinking and well-timed nudging greatly improved our work; we are grateful for her support and her friendship. We have also benefitted from the enthusiasm, knowledge, and organizational skills of Joan Scafarello, our picture editor, and from the tireless researching of Marion Paone Geisinger, who relentlessly pursued all leads until she found exactly the right picture. Our manuscript profited from the professional skills of Pamela Forcey, who with unflappable composure transformed our typescript into carefully designed galleys, and of Jeanette Ninas Johnson, who oversaw the final stages of production, solving last-minute problems with sympathetic understanding.

Contents

PART TWO

The Context of Tradition and Genres

PART THREE

The Context of Historical Periods

PART FOUR

Approaches to Appreciating and Evaluating the Arts

Alternate Table of Contents
Arranged by Art Forms

Painting, Drawing, and Printmaking

Dance

Poetry

Prose Narrative

Introduction: The World of the Arts

A study of the humanities is basic in any education, for these are the disciplines that record and transmit the traditions and values of our civilization. Only by gaining some familiarity with such subjects as history, philosophy, and the arts can we truly come to understand ourselves and our society. By providing a broader frame of reference, by enabling us to hold a more comprehensive view of life, this knowledge frees us from the constraints of the present moment.

Formerly, the humanities were associated by educators with the legacy of the Ancient World, especially the creations of the finest minds of classical Greece and Rome. Although educators today have a broader conception of the humanities, these still deal with fundamental and enduring themes. Indeed, all the subjects now considered "humanistic" share this quality of lasting importance, permanent value. They will not be outmoded by scientific or technological advances.

Among the humanities, the arts have a particularly important role, for they express and transmit with special vividness what we have gained from the past. In this book, we shall consider the various branches of the arts—painting, sculpture, architecture, photography, music, poetry, fiction, theater, film, opera, and dance. The terms *art* and *artist* will be used here in their broadest sense, applying to all these fields, rather than just to the visual arts.

We shall begin our explorations by examining the basic elements of each art form, the possibilities of each medium, and the similarities and differences among them. We will go on to consider both how artists shape their material—with emphasis on their choice of a particular point of view—and how performers reshape a work of art as they interpret it. We will also look at some of the ways in which cultural traditions and artistic genres can contribute to an artist's work. In a section on historical periods, we will focus on three recent ones—neoclassicism, romanticism, and modernism—and identify the thematic and technical elements distinctive of each. Finally, we shall explore several critical approaches to the arts as well as various criteria for judging individual works.

All of us have had the experience of appreciating the subtleties of a work of art only after becoming thoroughly familiar with it. With this greater understanding, we will be able to avoid the overly simple gut reaction of "I know what I like, but I can't tell you why," which suggests that further knowledge cannot enhance and may even destroy our enjoyment. We will also be able to avoid the even more closed-minded response of "I know what I like—and I don't like this!" which suggests an immediate rejection of the new and unfamiliar. Most of us, after all, hope to deepen our intellectual understanding and heighten our emotional responses to works of art, thereby intensifying our enjoyment.

We are all familiar with the enjoyment we gain from certain works of art, usually of our own time. To such art we often have a personal and possibly even a possessive reaction. We are also familiar with the feelings of confusion or even repulsion aroused by other works, usually of earlier times but possibly also of very recent date. An increased knowledge of artistic techniques and traditions can enable us to respond to highly complex works of different ages. We can understand the attraction of works both ancient and modern, because art organizes and reinterprets commonly shared human experiences with freshness and profundity. Birth and death, nature, love and other emotions provide constant subject matter for art because in the most fundamental ways the human condition and the range of our responses remain unchanged.

The rewards of increasing our understanding of the arts can be a lifetime of enjoyment. As an appropriate starting point for our explorations, we should raise questions about the definition of art, the possible classifications of the arts, the relationship among creator and work and audience, and the function of art. Although we cannot expect definitive answers to these complex questions, we will, at least, be clarifying some basic issues.

What Is Art?

Perhaps the most immediate truth about art is that it is always made by people and by humanity alone, for no other animal has attained anything comparable. Natural wonders such as the Matterhorn or the Grand Canyon, even though they strike us as magnificent and awe inspiring, do not qualify. They do not have in their creation a shaping human intelligence. This distinction is easily made, but others are less clear-cut. For example, can both a painting and a photograph of water lilies qualify as art? Both works can exhibit a "shaping human intelligence" in their composition, in their selectivity, and in their presentation. Simply because one of these uses scientific or mechanical methods as a means of creation should not disqualify it. But other questions remain. For instance, is photography a lesser or more restricted medium, or is it as subtle and responsive a medium of artistic expression as paint?

Another truth about art is that its creators need not think of themselves as artists. Often they are amateurs who create primarily for themselves. Folk sculptors, Sunday painters, or country diarists who intend their work for their own pleasure and self-expression may produce works of universal artistic significance. For instance, Henri Rousseau (1849–1910), a customs officer, began as a nonprofessional but is now widely acknowledged as an artist of merit [1].

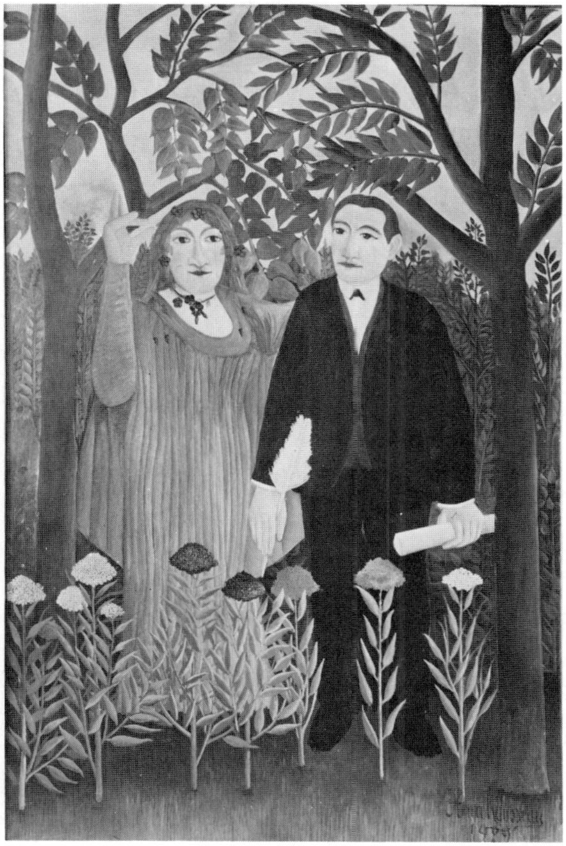

1 Henri Rousseau. *The Muse Inspiring the Poet.* 1909. Oil on canvas, 4′9″ × 3′1⅞″ (1.46 × .97 m). Öffentliche Kunstsammlung, Basel. The flatness of the figures and the crudeness of the drawing reveal Rousseau's lack of formal training. The ordinariness of the two figures contrasts with the luxuriant flowers, foliage, and trees, combining a sense of the everyday and the exotic.

On the other hand, a work of art is not worthwhile simply because someone called an artist made it. The intention of the maker does not determine the value of the creation. The work's real value lies in its ability to express something significant in a coherent and distinctive manner. This ability is what often allows it to withstand changes in taste, manners, and sensibility that may affect its critical reception. An important work of art manages to transcend the restrictions of time, country, and language.

To help us define what is and is not a work of art, we can consider two illustrations that deal with a similar subject: the Brooklyn Bridge [2 and 3]. Both present an image of the roadway and tower design, and both create geometric patterns and have a clear organization. Yet we would agree that *The Bridge* by Joseph Stella (1880–1946) is a work of art, whereas Roebling's technical drawing is not. The Stella painting exhibits some of the elements we expect to find in all works of art: not only organization of the material but also conscious selection and a distinctive interpretation of reality. Indeed, with its patterns which are partly regular and partly irregular, and with its abstract shapes which suggest the New York City skyline framed within the arches of the bridge, the painting brings out the immensity, the rhythm, and the soaring

below: 2 Joseph Stella. *The Bridge,* from the series *New York Interpreted.* 1922. Oil on canvas, 4′6″ × 7′4¼″ (1.37 × 2.24 m). Newark Museum, Felix Fuld Bequest Fund, 1937.

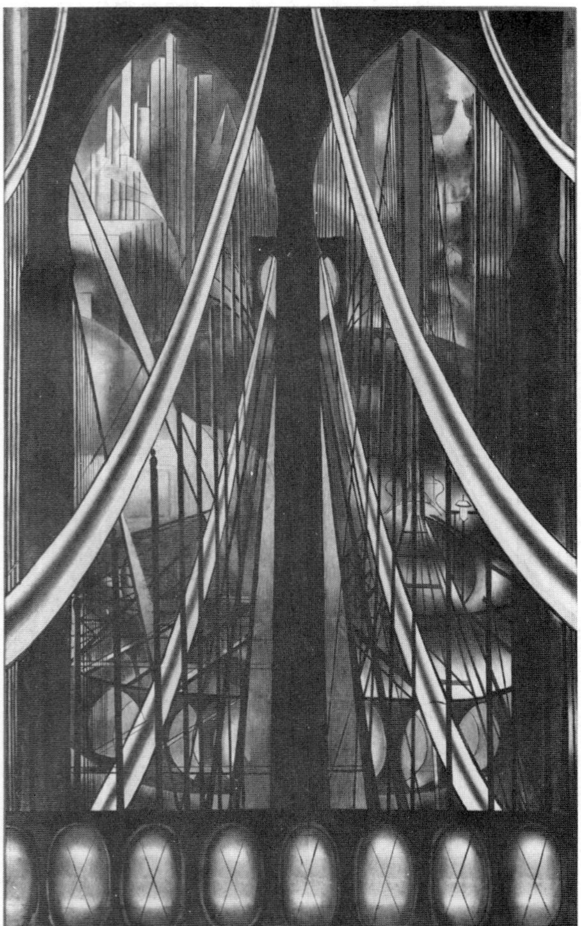

3 John Augustus Roebling. Front elevation of tower, East River Bridge. 1869. Pencil and ink, 23 × 15″ (58 × 38 cm). Rensselaer Polytechnic Institute Archives, Troy, N.Y.

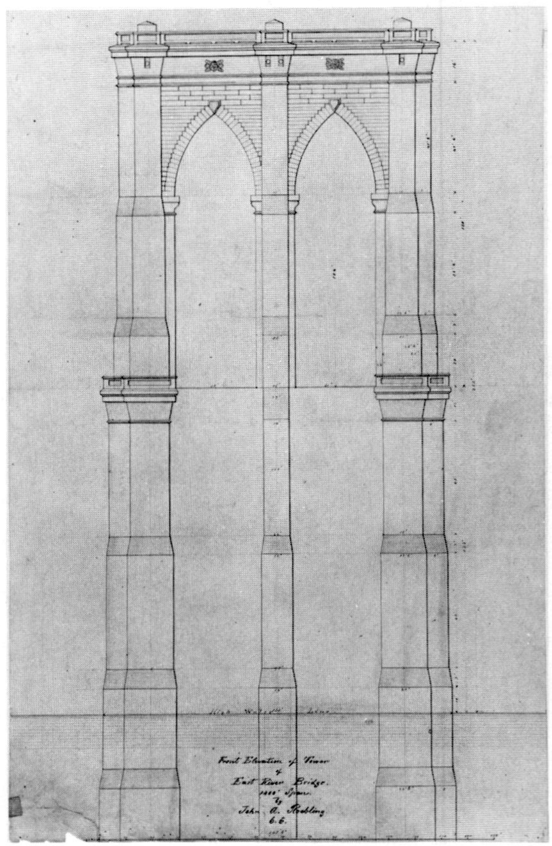

and inspiring power that are characteristic of this extraordinary structure. The drawing, in contrast, records the position of the roadway and the towers with their intersecting supports. It presents no imaginative reinterpretation of the material.

An even more important distinction between these two works is that the painting is an end in itself, existing for its own sake, whereas the drawing serves as a means of helping us to grasp the location of the structure. This is not to deny that art can have a useful function—architecture has. But in general we usually distinguish between the fine arts and the applied or practical arts, and we value all art for itself rather than for any practical use it may have.

Now that we have started to distinguish between art and non-art, we should become aware of a further distinction: what makes one work better than another. To focus on this question of quality, we can consider two more illustrations that deal with a similar subject: ideal images of women. The *Venus de Milo* [4], a Greek statue, and the photograph of Marilyn Monroe (1926–1962) [5] are both widely known and admired. Their common subject matter makes the differences in treatment particularly revealing. We should

below left: 4 *Venus de Milo.* c. 150–100 B.C. Marble, height approx. 6′10″ (2.08 m). Louvre, Paris.

below right: 5 Tom Kelley. *Golden Dreams* (Marilyn Monroe). 1949. Photograph. © Tom Kelley.

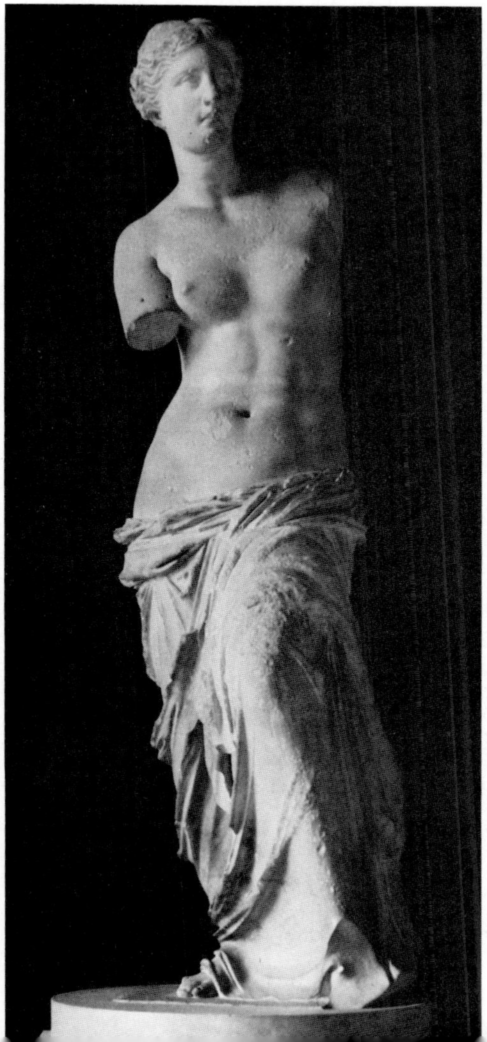

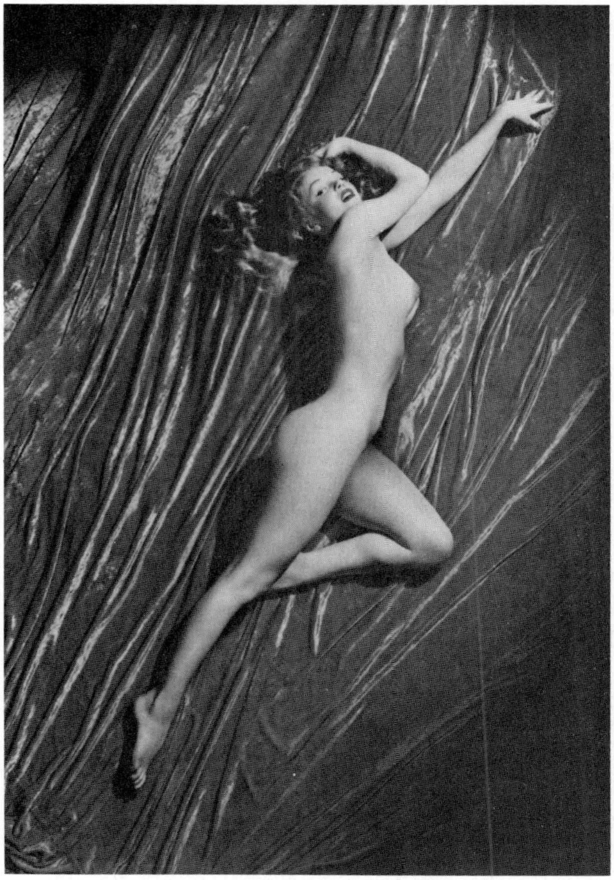

note that both might be considered as erotic, that is, intended to arouse sexual interest; indeed, the line between erotica and art is sometimes hard to determine. We, however, shall be considering both works as objects of art.

Let us begin with the Venus. The most striking aspect of this marble statue is its size: it is almost seven feet high. We are not accustomed to finding an idealized image of femininity represented in such generous proportions. Along with this unexpected size, the sculptor has presented the body with its weight unevenly distributed. The left leg is thrust quite noticeably ahead of the right and the torso is twisted, conveying an impression of direct, forward motion. Since the carver could more easily have presented the figure at rest, with the weight of the body balanced on the lower frame, we must consider how these deliberate elements of size and motion affect our response to the work.

First, we should recall the subject. Venus is not a mortal; she is the goddess of love. This larger-than-life-size presentation is appropriate for a resident of Mount Olympus. Furthermore, her graceful, effortless movement suggests that love is not idle: it can be irresistible and overwhelming. The emotion that Venus embodies may be pleasant and rewarding, but it need not be. Her expression of absolute assurance and imperturbability conveys a sense of her pride, fierceness, and strength. We can well believe that, as ancient myths relate, Venus could drive some people mad and destroy those foolish enough to deny her power.

Now let us turn to the photograph [see Figure 5, page 5]. Although we are looking at a picture of a real woman, it is not more life-like than the statue. In the full-color original, the image is overly warm and rich, lush and soft. The shades of color are highly exaggerated. The strong lighting intensifies the flesh color of the body while the red velvet fabric used as the background heightens the contrast of texture as well as color. But even the black-and-white reproduction of the photograph stresses what is most important—the passivity of the nude. Instead of emphasizing strength and power, as does the *Venus de Milo,* the female in the photograph suggests purely erotic pleasure, embodied in an exquisite but sleepy sensualist. Paradoxically, the young, yielding, totally nude woman, although more bold and forthright as sex object, may be less intriguing than the mature, vigorous, semiclothed Venus.

Finally, we should consider the placement of the figure in relation to the viewer. The sculptor's *Venus de Milo*—with its height, mass, grace, and power—is impressive: literally and figuratively, we look up to it. The reverse is true of the photograph: here we look down on the subject. In effect, the spectator is cast as the sexually dominant partner, and the nude sprawling beneath us is seen from a perspective that clearly dictates her subordinate role. As a study in sensuality that presents a superb female form in a pose of complete passivity, the photograph is outstandingly successful. But that does not resolve the issue of quality. Although the photograph of Marilyn Monroe is a splendid work of its kind, it is not a work that attempts to present a variety of subtle, complicated, and symbolic meanings. Yet this is exactly the strength of the *Venus de Milo,* a work that conveys with immediacy and power something unique and forceful but much less easily defined. The statue is a richer, more complex work, and for this reason will probably be admired longer.

From this analysis we can also gain a few procedural principles for examining a work of art. For instance, we can learn to isolate for special consideration the elements or characteristics that strike us as especially important; to use the title as a clue to a work's meaning; and to bring to bear in our interpretation some of the relevant cultural and intellectual associations. Although sculptors, photographers, and other artists do not tell us what they intend, their works of art speak for themselves.

Classifying the Arts

The two works we have just examined, a sculpture and a photograph presenting ideal images of women, both belong to the realm of the *visual arts.* For the present, let us simply note that the two works are perceived solely through the sense of sight and that we can take in the whole image more or less in a single act of looking. Instead of these two examples, we might have chosen to present the concept of woman in words, as in Eudora Welty's "Circe," reprinted in Chapter 4. This short story is an instance of the *verbal* or *literary arts,* which use language as the medium of expression and which are experienced over a period of time. Still other art forms are not tied to specific subject matter. *Music,* a third major category of art, employs sounds arranged in complex patterns that are also experienced over a period of time. This division into three major categories—visual, verbal, and musical—is one of several traditional ways of classifying the arts.

A classification more useful for our purposes divides the arts into those experienced in space and those experienced over time. This fundamental classification more readily allows us to recognize significant similarities and differences among the arts. The *arts of space* include painting, sculpture, architecture, and photography; the *arts of time,* music and literature (poetry and prose narrative). A third group, which we will call the *composite arts,* includes theater, opera, dance, and film—art forms that draw on both the arts of space and of time.

Another useful way of categorizing the arts divides them into *nonperforming* and *performing arts.* In general, we might say that the nonperforming arts—particularly the spatial ones such as architecture, painting, or sculpture—exist as distinct or concrete objects. On the other hand, the performing arts—music, theater, and dance—are incomplete without performance. The musical score, dramatic text, and notation for dance movement are not themselves the work of art, but merely give directions for realizing it. In such cases, there is not a single work of art, but various interpretations of it. For instance, the same opera sounded noticeably different when conducted by Arturo Toscanini, who was famous for the rapid pace he set his orchestra, and by Wilhelm Furtwängler, who preferred a slow and deliberate pace. In spite of these differences, the interpretations are not, and should not be, so far apart that the work is no longer recognizable.

Finally, we should focus on the distinction between the *fine arts* and the *applied* or *practical arts,* which we observed in discussing the two renderings of the Brooklyn Bridge [see Figures 2 and 3, page 4]. The fine arts are created for their own sake and traditionally include painting, sculpture, music, poetry (including dramatic poetry), and even architecture. But as we saw in considering the diagram of the bridge, architecture can also be regarded as a practical art—one that has a specific useful purpose. Other practical or applied arts, all of which serve an end beyond themselves, include commercial posters, furniture design, and quilt making. The distinctive feature of these art forms is that they are intended to fulfill a specific function, and their design is determined largely by this function. A concert hall must have good acoustics, and its interior plan may well be dictated by this requirement. A poster must provide essential information about the product it is advertising. Yet these art forms may also be important in their own right. We shall consider some of the applied arts in Chapter 7, focusing on qualities that they share with the fine arts.

A more fundamental question arises when we consider that some works of art exist as *single and unique objects,* while others can be reproduced in *multiple and more or less identical copies.* A building or painting is unique, but a novel or other printed text is equally authentic in all the copies available to the readers. Each copy is as valid a presentation of the novel as all other copies, assuming that the printing is free of error. Each copy reproduces the author's original words and, therefore, meaning. Different editions may vary in typography, but all do justice to the work of literature as art because the artistic value does not depend on the typography but on the author's language.

Musical recordings are another example of this copy-original relationship, since each recording is identical with all other recordings of the same performance. We should notice, however, that one performance will differ from other performances of the same work because performances by their nature are different interpretations of the original musical score.

A few of the spatial arts also exist not as unique objects but as copies of an original. When a work of sculpture consists of a cast made from a mold, additional casts can be produced from the original mold. Rodin's *Thinker* [6] can be seen in various places, for several casts were made from the same mold. Perhaps its multiple existence has even contributed to its fame. However, engravings may well differ subtly from each other—as copies of the same novel or recording of the same musical performance do not—in that earlier casts or prints are likely to be clearer and sharper than later ones. The situation is still more complicated in photography, in which different prints can be made from the same negative. Here again, prints may differ in clarity and sharpness, but the earlier ones may not necessarily be better.

Interestingly, the commercial value of a particular cast, engraving, or book is determined by its closeness to the hand of its creator, even when this closeness does not affect the quality of the work. In other words, one of the first prints made from a plate or a first edition has greater commercial value than later copies.

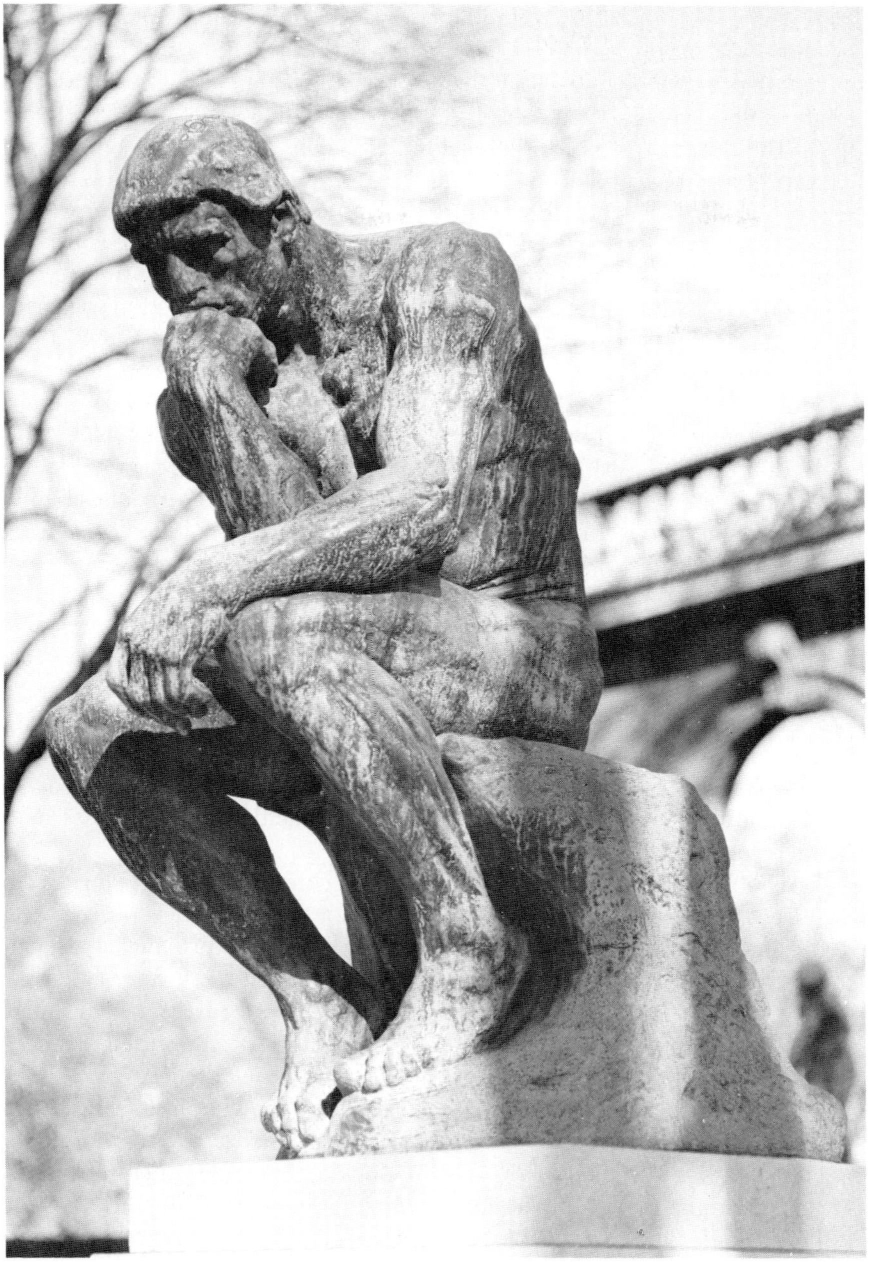

6 Auguste Rodin. *The Thinker.* 1880–1885. Bronze, 6′7″ × 4′3¼″ × 4′7¼″ (1.9 × 1.2 × 1.37 m). Rodin Museum, Philadelphia. Gift of Jules E. Mastbaum.

Transmitting Art from Artist to Audience

Although our primary concern as we proceed will be with the actual works of art, we should not overlook the fact that art also involves production, on the one hand, and appreciation, on the other. In a fundamental sense, art is part of a process of communication between artists and their audience.

The creative process usually involves an *artist*—the painter, sculptor, or writer—*working alone and in private.* However, all the arts can also be the result of *collaborative effort.* Teams of artisans, often anonymous, worked on the architecture, sculpture, and stained-glass windows of medieval cathedrals. The original poets of folk ballads are usually unknown, and their lines were probably changed as these songs were passed from generation to generation. Moreover, some arts require collaboration, notably theater, opera, ballet, and film. Even in recent works, the relative contributions of collaborators are sometimes impossible to determine. In the case of the film *Citizen Kane* (1940), critics have debated whether the greater contribution was made by Orson Welles (b. 1915) as director or Herman J. Mankiewicz (1898–1953) as script writer.

Since the artist is the initiator in this communication process, we might assume that no one is more knowledgeable about the meaning or value of the work of art than the person who created it. Ironically, this is not necessarily the case. Even when artists have left explicit statements—manifestoes or prefaces—their conscious intentions may not have been fulfilled or, alternatively, the creators may have done better than they realized. Artists are often so close to their work that they cannot really judge what they have achieved. For instance, the poet Vergil (70–19 B.C.) considered his great epic *The Aeneid* unfinished and left instructions to have it destroyed. Shakespeare (1564–1616) never concerned himself with the publication of any of his plays, evidently considering them inferior to his long poems, whose printing he carefully supervised. In short, although we can hardly fail to acknowledge the importance of the creator or creators as the original source of the work of art, we should be careful not to allow the artist's stated intention to determine our interpretation of the artwork.

The interpretation of a work is further complicated in art forms that require *performers.* Unlike a painter, novelist, or poet, who can speak directly to the audience, a dramatist, composer, or choreographer usually has to communicate through actors, musicians, or dancers. These performers interpret the work as they execute it, and it can be said that there are as many Hamlets as there are actors who have played the role. Performers, then, serve as intermediaries between the original creator and the audience.

The members of the *audience,* who act as receivers in the process of communication, can experience the work of art either singly, as when reading a novel, or collectively, as when attending a play, film, concert, or ballet. Not all the members of the audience will approach the work with the same skill and understanding. All of us may at times be limited by our inexperience, preconceptions, or prejudices. Challenging and complicated works may seem to be willful, boring, and possibly even demented. In such cases, we may have to make ourselves sensitive to the special qualities of each work, remembering that what at first seems strange and bewildering often later becomes readily understandable.

Since the range of audience reaction is wide and since audience taste can easily change, the value of a work is not necessarily determined by its public acceptance, any more than by the intention of the creator. Still, the audience has an essential part in the process of artistic communication. We should strive to become informed and responsive members of this audience, for great art flourishes most when encouraged by a receptive public.

The Function of the Arts

Some philosophers claim that one purpose of the arts is to create a *special kind of satisfaction* more refined than purely sensory pleasure. At times we can experience this satisfaction in the delightful melodies of a piece of music or the powerful scenes of a favorite painter. At other times, our pleasure is more complex and may be mingled with pain. The suspense we experience in seeing an Alfred Hitchcock thriller is both exciting and distressing, and the terrible revelations in any tragedy are profoundly disturbing. Nevertheless, the artistry of such works makes our total experience ultimately pleasurable.

Since classical times philosophers have also claimed that another function of art is to provide *moral or social improvement.* Literature has been thought of as a source of instruction as well as pleasure. The ancient Roman poet Horace (65–8 B.C.) summarized this idea in the maxim that art should both teach and delight. Some ages have given more emphasis than others to the so-called teaching, or didactic, function of art. In ancient Egypt, for example, most art works served to affirm the accepted values of the society, the satisfactions of life achieved under the just rule of the pharaoh, and the expectation of a prosperous life to come. In many past cultures, art has been closely involved with communicating political or religious concepts; and in our own time, the films, ballets, and posters of the People's Republic of China are designed to convey the positive values of a new society. Whether we accept this role for art, we must be aware of the complicated question of the relationship of the arts to the purposes of society as a whole.

Rather than upholding established moral or social standards, a great deal of North American and European art seeks to oppose or at least to question established pieties. Some people, uncomfortable with this *gadfly role* of art, tend to resist such works. But we should recognize that such art can make us more sensitive to the ambiguities of the world in which we live.

Finally, we may also come to agree with those philosophers who hold that art need have no function other than to exist in and of itself, *for its own sake.* In denying that the didactic or political impact of a work of art on the audience is important, this view draws attention back to the work itself. Although we cannot ignore the fact that some art is created to fulfill particular functions, we should make the effort to view and value all works of art as self-sufficient entities.

Questions for Study and Discussion

1. If art is made only by human beings, what are some of the motives that lead human beings to create works of art?

2. Compare the definitions of *art* given in three different encyclopedias. What are the most important elements of art according to these definitions?
3. What are the chief classifications of the arts, on what basis are they determined, and are they mutually exclusive? What are the limitations of these systems of classifying the arts?
4. Draw a diagram of the transmission of a work of art from the artist to the audience. Does this process of transmission differ from other forms of person-to-person communication? Where on this diagram could one indicate that a work is by a single artist or is a collaborative effort, that it requires performers, and that it is experienced individually or collectively?
5. To demonstrate the possible functions of the arts, consider specific works of painting, sculpture, architecture, music, literature, or film that you have recently experienced. Find examples that illustrate the use of art for social, political, or moral improvement; as gadfly; and as existing for its own sake.

PART ONE

The Elements of the Arts

A fundamental distinction can be made between the arts of space and the arts of time. A painting occupies a definite physical space and may even suggest the illusion of space within itself. We are free to apprehend the painting at once. All the visual arts—painting, sculpture, architecture, and photography—to some degree permit this freedom of contemplation by the viewer. Although we can generally take in the entire work at a glance, we shall want to examine its basic elements and details with great care. Chapter 1, "Components of the Arts of Space," introduces the elements of the spatial arts.

But such immediate presentation is not the case in all art forms. A symphony, for example, cannot be experienced in a single moment; we must listen to the movements, one after another, as they follow a definite sequence. The piece unfolds in time. All the arts that depend on sound require time for their presentation. Music and literature—poems or stories, whether spoken or read—belong to the temporal arts. Chapter 2, "Components of the Arts of Time," describes the basic elements of these arts.

These clear-cut distinctions between the spatial and temporal arts, however, need some qualification. As we shall see, poems are not simply words on a page but may also be visual arrangements. More importantly, some art forms exist both in space and in time. Theater, film, and dance, for example, are both spatial and temporal arts. Chapter 3, "Components of the Composite Arts," discusses the basic elements of these.

All three types of art—spatial, temporal, and composite—may adopt special points of view. Chapter 4, "Point of View: Shaping the Work of Art," analyzes the approaches—perspectives or narrative voices—available in different art forms. Finally, Chapter 5, "Performance: Interpreting the Work of Art," considers the elements involved in the actual performing of works of music, theater, film, and dance.

CHAPTER 1

Components of the Arts of Space

The arts normally regarded as the arts of space are painting, sculpture, architecture, and photography. Being in space, they are apprehended in inches or yards, not in minutes or hours. Our eyes have the capacity to perceive a painting or photograph as a single image, grasping the whole more or less simultaneously. A single glance may not be sufficient to appreciate sculptures or works of architecture, for we have to look at their sides consecutively, but even these can be grasped as a whole almost immediately, once we have walked around them. In all the spatial arts, our eyes can also distinguish colors and textures directly.

Because they exist before our eyes, the spatial arts require a special mental habit. This consists of observing all that is happening in front of us—outlines, details, the unity and diversity of each piece. The mental habit of prolonged observation, of close *attention* to the object before us, is required by these arts.

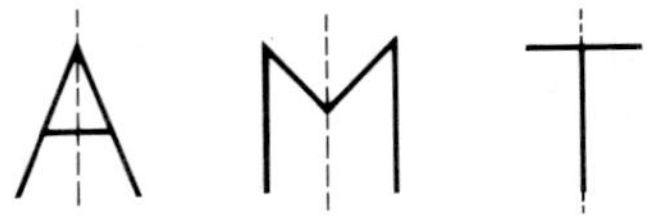

7 Symmetrical balance.

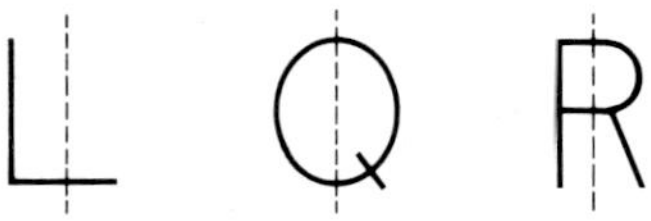

8 Dynamic balance.

Painting, Sculpture, Architecture, and Photography

To help us focus our attention, we shall first consider the larger question of organization or composition in the spatial arts, using the principles of symmetrical balance, dynamic balance, and overall patterning. Then we shall look at the individual elements from which the spatial arts are created—color, line, volume, and texture. We shall examine how color is produced in painting and how line is produced in the graphic arts. In addition, we shall give some thought to the choice of moment in painting, sculpture, and photography and to the choice of location in architecture. Finally, in dealing with architecture, we shall analyze some basic building techniques that have evolved over the centuries. This brief survey of the components of the spatial arts will provide the terminology necessary for interpreting them more accurately and appreciating them more fully.

Composition

As we take in the whole of an art object, we are aware of the organization of the material within the space available. This ordering of the material is common to all art forms. In the spatial arts it is known as *composition,* a term used for the actual organization of a work of art (the same term is used in a different sense for the act of creating in music and literature). In art objects of all kinds, composition involves the arrangement of the components to form a unified work.

One of the most fundamental organizing principles of composition is *symmetry.* We can recognize this by looking for the **axis of symmetry**. For example, if we take such capital letters of the alphabet as A, M, T, and draw a dotted line through them from top to bottom [7], we notice that the two halves of the letter match exactly. They reflect each other with a mirror-like precision. If we were to take the same letters, cut them in two along the dotted lines with scissors, and throw one half away, we would be able to reconstruct the other half by looking at what is left. If we now take the capital letters L, Q, and R [8], we notice that the two halves do not match and we cannot supply the missing half with certainty. These two different types of letters illustrate two basic categories of composition: **symmetrical balance*** (A, M, T) and **dynamic balance** (L, Q, R).

Symmetrical balance The Japanese Nōh mask [9] is a good example of symmetrical balance. When there is only one feature, such as the nose or mouth, it is placed squarely in the center; when there are two, such as the eyes or cheeks, they are carefully balanced on either side. We are all familiar with this principle of distribution from our own bodies, and the constant reminder of it in the bodies that we see gives symmetrical balance its abiding interest.

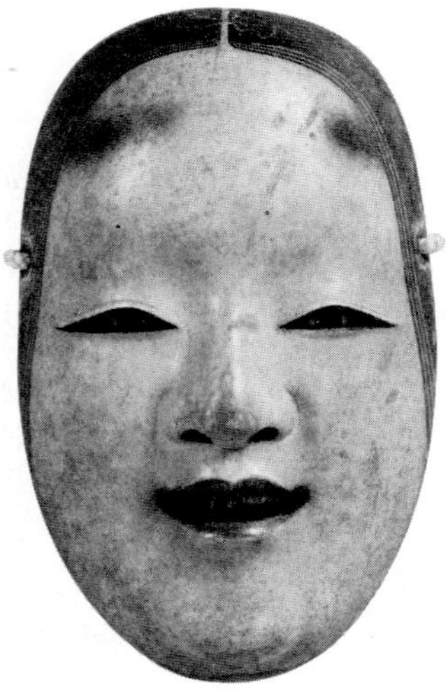

9 Ko-Omote (Nōh mask of noble young woman). Muromachi Period, 15th century. Painted wood, height 8⅜″ (21 cm). National Museum, Tokyo.

*Terms in boldface are defined in the Glossary of Terms at the end of the book.

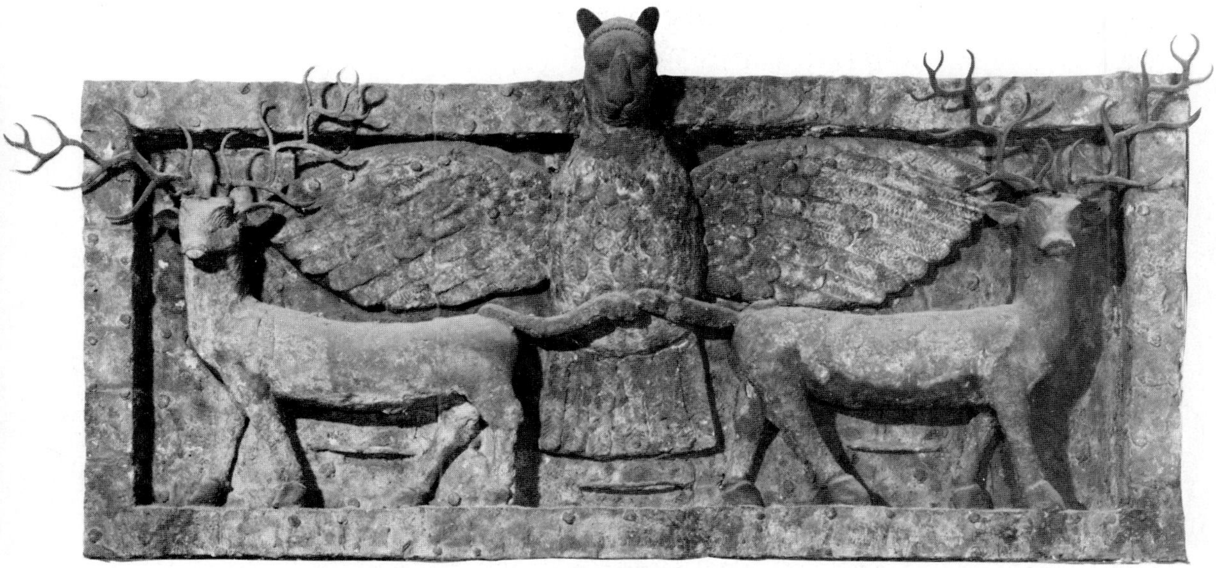

10 Lion-headed eagle Im-Dugud between two stags, from the Temple of Ninkhursag at Al 'Ubaid. Sumerian, c. 2000 B.C. Copper relief on bitumen, mounted on mosaic columns; 3′6″ × 8′6″ (1.07 × 2.59 m). British Museum, London (reproduced by courtesy of the Trustees).

The Im-Dugud plaque from Iraq [10] is more complex than the Japanese mask, for it presents three animals. Still, the basic method of arrangement is the same. One-of-a-kind things are placed in the middle. When there are two of a kind, they are balanced, so that the antlers appear in the upper right and upper left corners, respectively. However, a closer look suggests some discrepancies in the Im-Dugud plaque: the details of the antlers are not quite the same, and the tail of one four-legged beast overlaps the tail of the other. Most strikingly, the beasts' legs do not correspond. These seeming oversights are deliberate, for the artist has sought to lend vitality to his work by introducing small variations. Indeed, very few works slavishly follow the principle of symmetrical balance.

Dynamic balance The complementary principle of asymmetrical or dynamic balance can be seen in the Siberian gold belt buckle [11]. In this instance, drawing our axis of symmetry does not single out any important central element toward which the things shown to right or left gravitate in echoing fashion. Still, dividing the panel mentally into two parts is helpful because we notice a correspondence, even if it is not a symmetrical one. The compact low forms on the left are in balance with the tall open forms on the right. To overstate the case a trifle, a pound of feathers equals a pound of iron on the scales, though the former is much bulkier. At first sight, we might have been tempted to call this Siberian object a bungled work of art, since it violates the criterion of symmetrical balance. But once we have adjusted our expectations and view it in the light of the different but equally valid principle of dynamic balance, we can find this object quite satisfying.

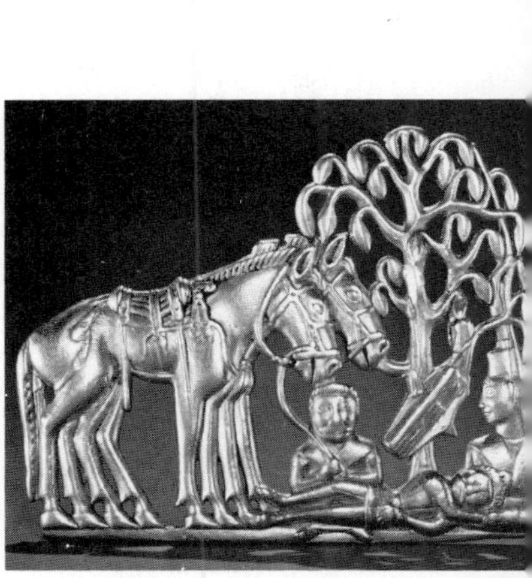

11 Scene of a warrior resting, belt plate from the collection of Peter the Great. Siberian, 4th–3rd century B.C. Gold, length 6⅜″ (16 cm). Hermitage, Leningrad.

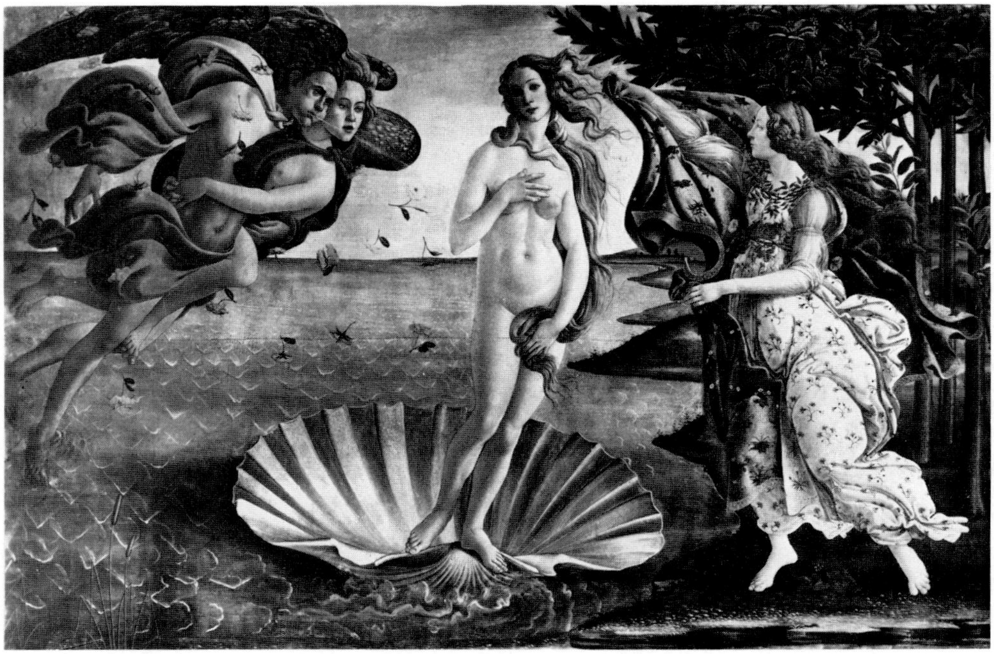

12 Sandro Botticelli. *The Birth of Venus.* 1480. Tempera on canvas, 6′7″ × 9′2″ (2.01 × 2.79 m). Uffizi, Florence.

Many works of art achieve their effects by pursuing a middle path between symmetrical and dynamic balance. In the *Birth of Venus* [12] by Sandro Botticelli (1447–1510), the nude figure of the goddess standing on the shell establishes the visual center, which is close to but not precisely at the picture's axis of symmetry. Appropriately, the goddess is flanked by attendants on either side. The two flying zephyrs on the left are matched by a single standing figure personifying Spring on the right. In order to compensate for the numerical imbalance—two against one—Spring holds the fluttering drapery intended for Venus and is backed by a landscape with three slender trees and other plants. While the zephyrs float at the upper left of the canvas, Spring stands on the lower right. The composition is subtly balanced to create a remarkably harmonious whole.

We can also contrast symmetrical and dynamic balance in architecture. The Petit Trianon [13] is organized according to symmetrical balance in that the main part in the center with the four columns projects slightly, so that it is set apart from the two equal wings on either side. If we drew a line through the center of the whole building, we would see that there are the same number of columns and windows in identical placement in both halves. Such balance is definitely not the case in the main front of the Crane Memorial Library [14]. Here the vertical emphasis and richness of forms on the right are deliberately counterposed with the horizontal simplicity on the left. Cutting the building in half and demolishing one side would prevent us from reconstructing the original arrangement—at least without other aids. This library is a good example of dynamic balance, which, in this respect, corresponds visually to the Siberian plaque.

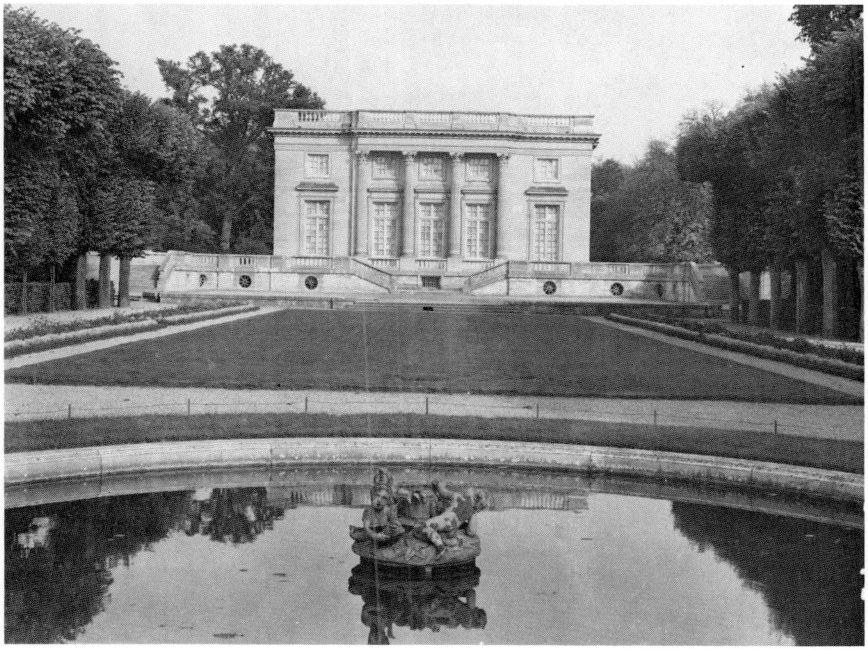

above: 13 Ange-Jacques Gabriel. The Petit Trianon, Versailles. 1762–1768.

below: 14 Henry Hobson Richardson. Crane Memorial Library, Quincy, Mass. 1883.

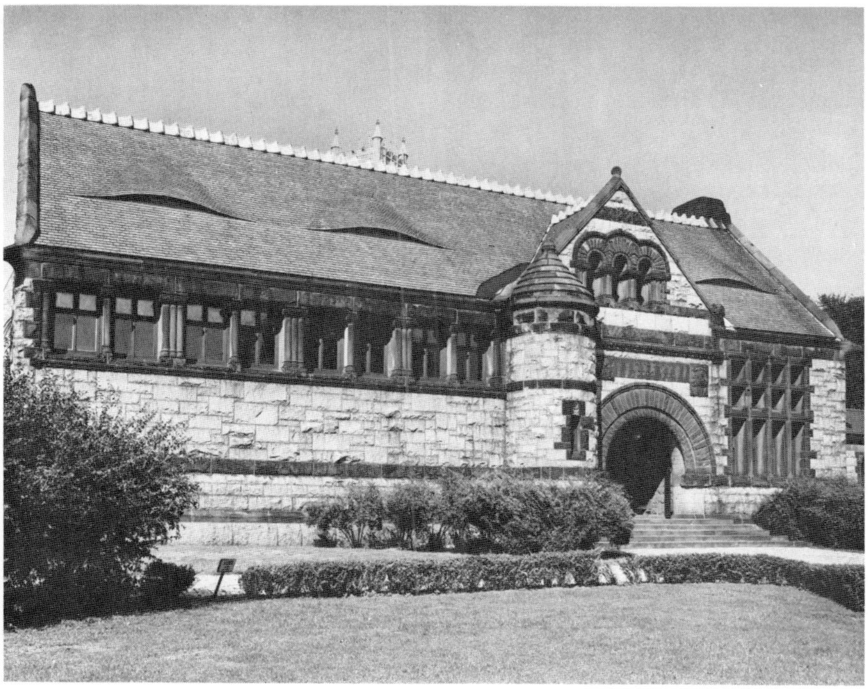

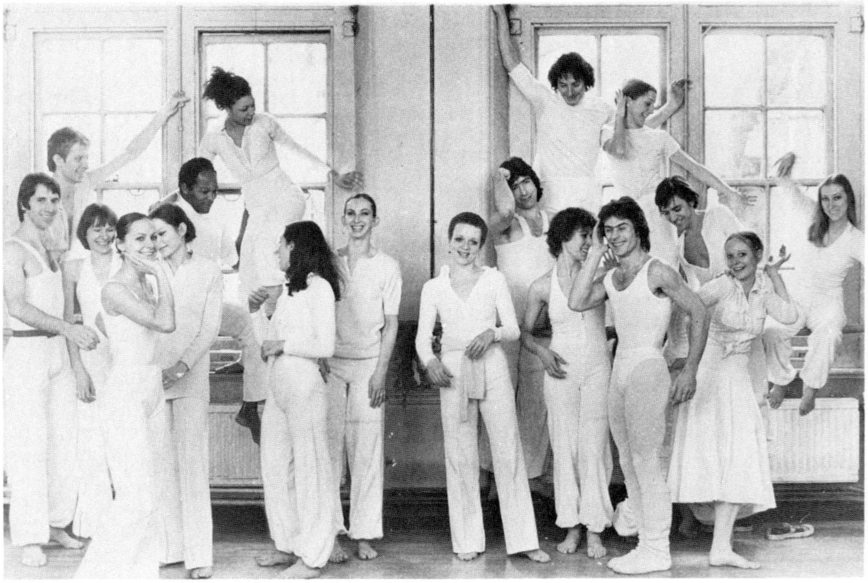

15 Anthony Crickmay. The London Contemporary Dance Company, March 17, 1977. Photograph.

The principles of symmetrical and dynamic balance are also used in photography. Although snapping a photograph takes far less time than painting a picture or constructing a building, the arrangement of the photographic subject may be the result of careful planning and deliberate choice. For instance, in the group portrait of the London Contemporary Dance Theatre [15], Anthony Crickmay (b. 1937) has arranged what seem to be casually placed figures in a dynamically balanced pattern that juxtaposes the groups at the left windows with those at the right, both in their placement and individual gestures.

16 Prehistoric cave painting of bison, from the "Salon," Niaux Cave, Ariège, France. c. 10,000 B.C.

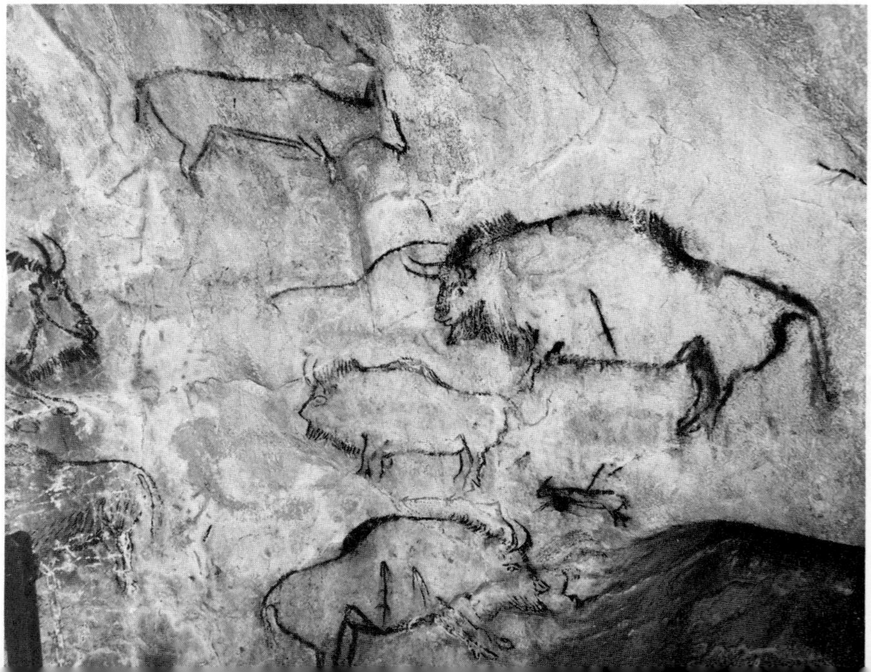

Overall patterning A third type of composition is less frequently encountered than the other two: **overall patterning.** It is found in some very ancient works of art, such as the murals in the Niaux Cave in France [16], created some 12,000 years ago in the Paleolithic or Old Stone Age. Here we see a succession of animal forms, which just seem to flow on and on. To try to apply the axis of symmetry in this instance would make no sense; we would not know where to put it. This principle of overall patterning can be seen in craftwork, too, such as weaving, wallpaper, and domestic pottery. The Native American mortar, a kitchen container for mashing grain or spices with a pestle, is decorated with notches, zigzags, and hooks in a pattern that has no determinable beginning or end [17]. As a rule, overall design achieves its purpose by avoiding external boundaries or frames, which would enable us to place our axis of symmetry by halving the distance between boundaries on either side. In some works with more definite boundaries, artists have also tried to exploit this principle. In *Convergence* [18], Jackson Pollock (1912–1956) gives the impression that the drip forms can easily continue in any or all directions. The painting seems to offer itself as a segment of a much larger whole, which follows the overall patterning principle.

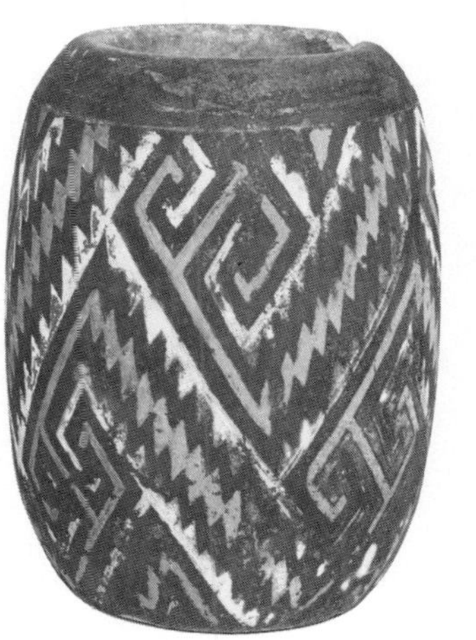

17 Mortar with painted geometric design, from Pueblo Bonito, Chaco Canyon, N.M. c. 1200. Sandstone, height 8″ (20 cm). Museum of the American Indian, Heye Foundation, New York.

below: 18 Jackson Pollock. *Convergence.* 1952. Oil on canvas, 7′9½″ × 12′11″ (2.37 × 3.94 m). Albright-Knox Art Gallery, Buffalo (gift of Seymour H. Knox).

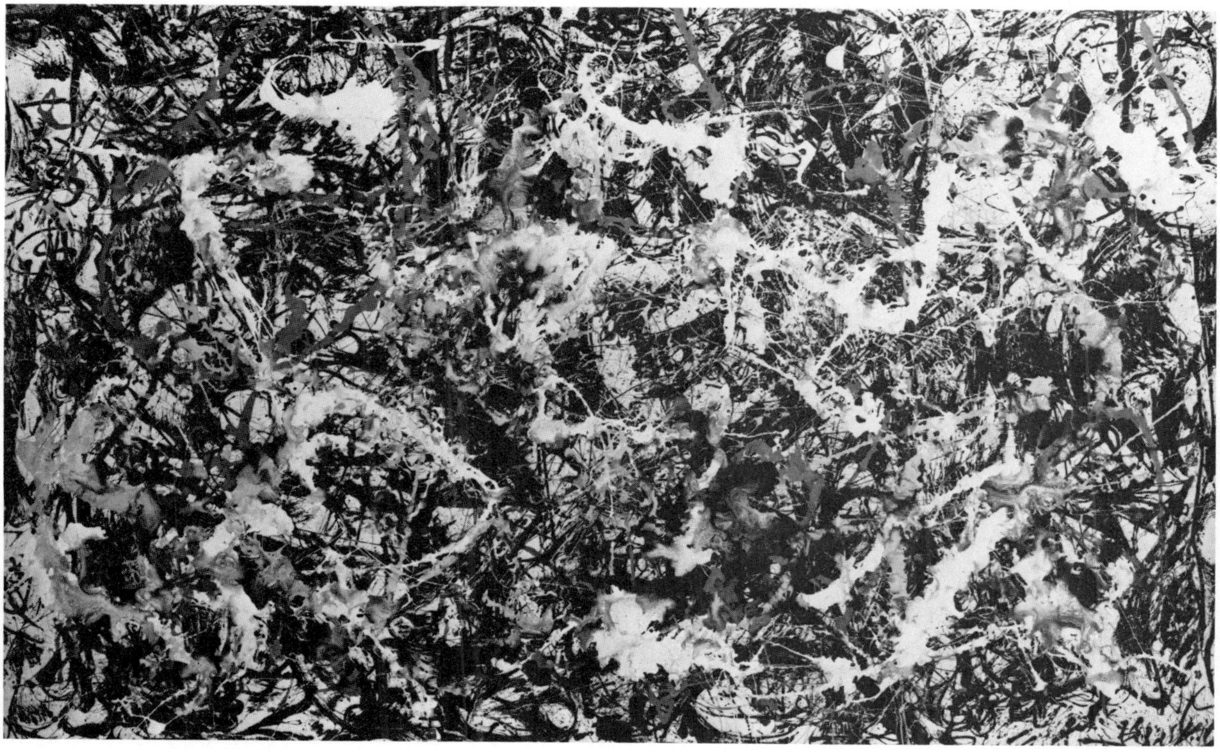

Color

The second important element of the spatial arts is *color.* So complicated is this subject that experts do not always agree in analyzing color, yet our eyes have developed a phenomenal ability to discriminate among subtle differences. Here, we can only mention some of the most striking aspects of the use of color in art.

We may begin by asking "What color is it?" This question seems straightforward, and the answer may be simply "green" or "red." But if it is green, is it Kelly or apple green? if red, a Venetian or Chinese red? Our ability to distinguish different reds and greens from one another reflects the fact that colors, measured by scientists in angstrom units, shift gradually from one to another. In this way, a red may tilt toward the purple segment of the spectrum or toward the orange segment. Similarly, green may go either in the direction of yellow or blue.

Some traditional color theorists have assigned a special role to three colors—red, blue, and yellow—called the *primary colors.* From these three, all other colors can be derived. Although scientists concerned with visual perception tend to regard this singling out of primary colors as overly simple, many artists have accepted it. Mondrian, in particular, restricted his mature paintings to pure or unmixed colors, along with black and white, which he did not regard as colors properly speaking [Plate 1, page 33]. For him, this restriction, together with severely limited shapes, was the result of a conscious effort to reduce art to its barest fundamentals.

By mixing the primary colors, one can create a whole range of other colors—yellow and blue produce green; red and yellow, orange; red and blue, purple. And by a further extension we can produce reddish orange and yellowish green. All these varieties belong to the general category called **hue**. In fact, hue is the first major variable or sub-element in the study of color; it is what many people think of as color pure and simple—a red hue or a green hue.

In addition to hue, however, we often recognize that there are differences of **shade**. Two reds may be equally red, but have different shades. The hue does not vary, something else does. According to color specialists, what we call shade is actually made up of two separate variables: **value** and **intensity** [19]. Value reflects the degree of a mixture of white or black. By adding white paint to a blue that may strike us as too dark, we can get a pale blue, changing the value. If it is too light, we can add black, changing the color's value in the other direction. The colors in *The Nightwatch* [Plate 2, page 34] by Rembrandt van Rijn (1606–1669) display a remarkable range of value. The red of the rifleman's suit at the left of the canvas consists of bright scarlet highlights, apparently dappled by the sun, and a much deeper red that has been darkened by adding black. Rembrandt further demonstrates his control of color values by the precision with which he has painted the shadow on the pale yellow suit of the man near the center—a shadow cast by the extended left hand of the man with the red sash.

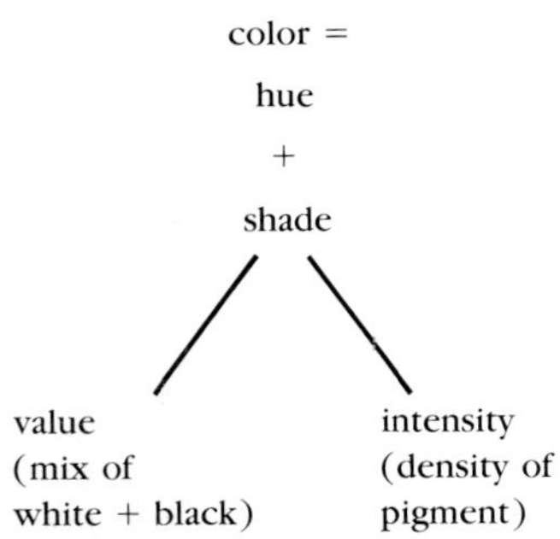

19 Relationship of color, hue, and shade.

Instead of value, shade often refers to intensity. Some red paints have a higher density of pigment or color particles than others: they are more intense. We can all recognize the contrast between a screaming red and a dull red. This is mainly a difference in intensity between the two, though value may play a role as well, since a red that does not have black in it may seem a redder red than one which does. Medieval painting in general and the *Annunciation* [Plate 3, page 35] by Duccio di Buoninsegna (c. 1255–c. 1319) in particular are noteworthy for their bright, clear colors. Duccio achieves his principal effects by creating broad areas of intense red and gold. The total impression is very different from that of Rembrandt's *Nightwatch,* in which contrasts of color value are predominant and are expressed through the use of light and shade. Duccio's work has no cast shadows and very little shading in the color.

From this very basic discussion of the three variables of color—hue, value, and intensity (remember that shade = value + intensity)—we can begin to grasp how the human eye can distinguish so many different variations of color, far more than we have names to give. Over the centuries, artists have developed distinctive approaches to color, which are sometimes culturally determined and sometimes highly personal. Artists' color preferences are called their "palette," after the oval board or tablet in which many painters mix their pigments.

Certain colors have acquired special meanings or associations in particular cultures. For the Romans, purple was identified with power, and its use was reserved for the emperor. In some Islamic countries today, the color blue is thought to help ward off evil; for this reason, blue is often used in decorating the exterior walls of houses. Traditional Chinese culture stressed a relationship between red and black, which were associated with the two major parts of the country—the south and the north—and often also with other aspects of life such as the female and male principle, humidity and dryness, and sunlight and darkness. Because of this complex symbolism, the costumes of Chinese sorcerers were red and black, suggesting their control over cosmic powers. Even today the interiors of Chinese buildings are often dominated by a red-and-black color scheme.

Some recent European painters have worked out a color symbolism that is personal to them rather than culturally determined. For instance, Vincent van Gogh (1853–1890) said that, in painting *The Night Café* [Plate 4, page 36], he

> tried to express the terrible passions of humanity by means of red and green. The room is blood red and dark yellow with a green billiard table . . . . Everywhere there is a clash and contrast of the most disparate reds and greens in the figures of little sleeping hooligans in the empty dreary rooms, in violet and blue.

On the other hand, Henri Matisse (1869–1954) chose a rich red of uniform intensity in *The Red Studio* [Plate 5, page 37] to suggest the energy and warmth of his combined living and working quarters. Matisse was one of a group of artists called *Les Fauves* ("the wild beasts") because they used startling colors and distorted forms in untraditional ways. In *The Red Studio,* Matisse makes no distinction between the floor and walls, and he displays miniature versions of his other canvases whose colors contrast strongly with the vibrant red that dominates this work. At about the same time, Picasso restricted his palette to shades of blue. In his Blue Period (1901–1904) he used it as the dominant color to suffuse his paintings with an atmosphere of gentle melancholy suited to the outcasts and bohemians who were his subjects.

The relationship between a color and a mood suggests that colors may have what some critics call "emotional values." Yet such a relationship is difficult to establish, since the emotional overtones of colors may be culturally determined or may merely be the private associations of an individual painter.

Color media and techniques Color in painting is often strongly affected by the artist's choice of medium. In the **fresco** technique, the colors are applied directly to the plaster of walls as it dries. As a result, the color effects are somewhat soft and lack intensity when viewed in detail. Frescoed murals make up for this limitation by their generally large size. A favorite medium in the Middle Ages and Renaissance, the fresco has been revived recently, in particular by the Mexican muralists of the 20th century. Michelangelo's greatest paintings, those in the Sistine Chapel of the Vatican (1508–1512), are frescoes. In **tempera**, also popular in the Middle Ages, the colors are suspended in an egg-based medium, giving them a brilliant effect often high in intensity. Tempera is applied over a binder which fixes it to a wooden panel. The brightness of Duccio's *Annunciation* [see Plate 3, page 35] could be achieved only through his mastery of the tempera technique.

Oil painting, in which the pigment is mixed with oil, is a more flexible medium, which can combine the opaque brilliance achieved by tempera with transparent glazes. It is usually executed on canvas. Developed with great virtuosity in northern Europe and Venice from the 15th to the 17th centuries, oil painting enabled artists to achieve remarkable gradations of value through light and shade. *The Nightwatch* [see Plate 2, page 34] could hardly have attained its subtle yet glowing colors in any other medium. In **watercolor**, pigments are mixed in water soluble gum and applied in broad strokes, or washes, on white paper; the unstained areas stand out as highlights. This much more delicate effect can be seen in *Italian Mountains* [Plate 6, page 38] by Albrecht Dürer (1471–1528). Here we find very few intense colors, but soft flowing hues that define the vague shapes of a landscape in the early morning hours. The pale diluted colors possible in this medium enable the artist to suggest that the mountain at the right is still enveloped in dawn mists. Finally, 20th-century technology has introduced new paints, notably **acrylic**, which have been widely adopted. A synthetic product, in which the pigment is combined with an acrylic polymer, this medium sometimes appears garish but can be used to achieve many different effects.

In photography, early pictures had to be confined to black and white; they lacked color because the technological process for reproducing color had not yet been invented. Many excellent photographers still continue to work in black and white, probably because they can achieve more subtle gradations of shading than is possible with color film. These effects are accomplished through the technology involved both in the taking of the picture—choice of lenses and shutter speed—and in the printing—choice of developing fluid and printing paper. The developing of the negative can greatly affect the final image: overdeveloping lightens the image, underdeveloping darkens it.

Line

Another important element of the visual arts is *line,* the visible link between two or more points in space. It has been said that lines do not occur in nature, which prefers smooth transitions to sharp boundaries. Like most generalizations, this one has exceptions, such as the veins of leaves or the sharp scalloping of shells. Nonetheless, line is much more evident in parts of our environment that have been actively shaped by human intervention; for instance, many straight lines appear in the windows and doors of a building, and in roads and highways cutting paths across the landscape. While the contrast between unlined nature and highly lined human products is not absolute, the use of lines is an important and omnipresent sign of the way in which human beings have transformed the world. The artist's use of line turns out to be a special case of a basic human inclination.

Sometimes line alone can make up a work of art. The witty line drawing [20] by Ben Shahn (1898–1969) gives the impression of an entire orchestra. The artist cleverly uses line in at least two distinct ways. On the one hand he uses it to represent the shafts of the music stands as well as the legs and frames of the chairs. On the other hand, he uses line simply to indicate the contours of the tops and bottoms of the music stands as well as the shapes of the seats and backs of the chairs. Furthermore, an imaginative viewing of this sketch reveals a third use of line, for the legs of some chairs are like the stems of musical notes whose heads are simultaneously the hinges of the folding chairs. Indeed, if we follow these suggested notes across the page, we might hear the "silent music" of the title.

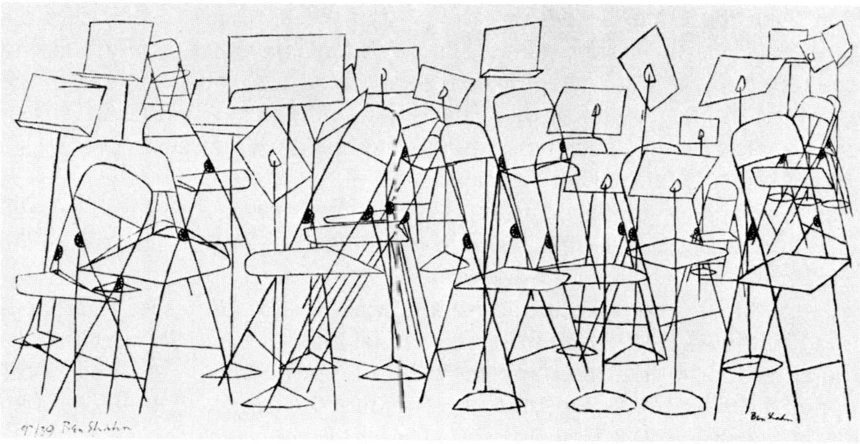

20 Ben Shahn. *Silent Music.* 1950. Serigraph, 17⅛ × 35⅜" (43.5 × 89 cm). Museum of Modern Art, New York.

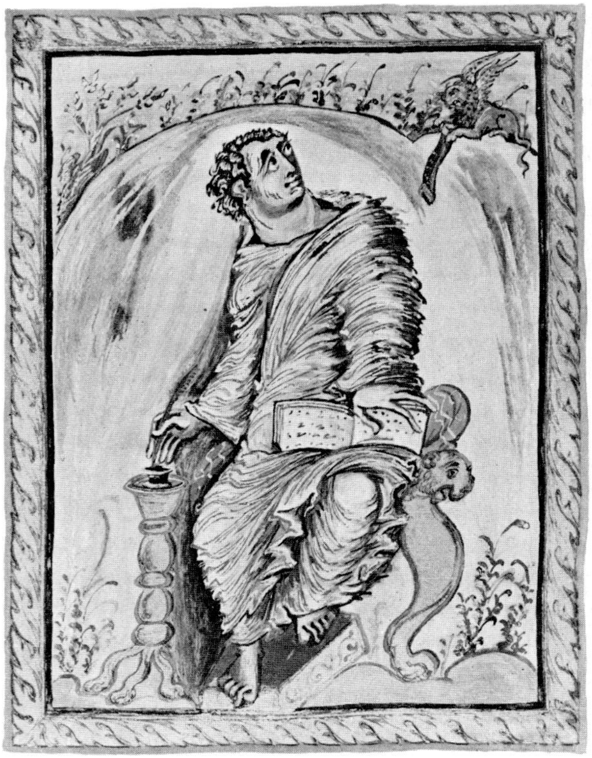

above: 21 *Saint Mark,* from the Gospel Book of Bishop Ebbo. 816–835. Manuscript illumination. Bibliothèque Municipale, Epernay.

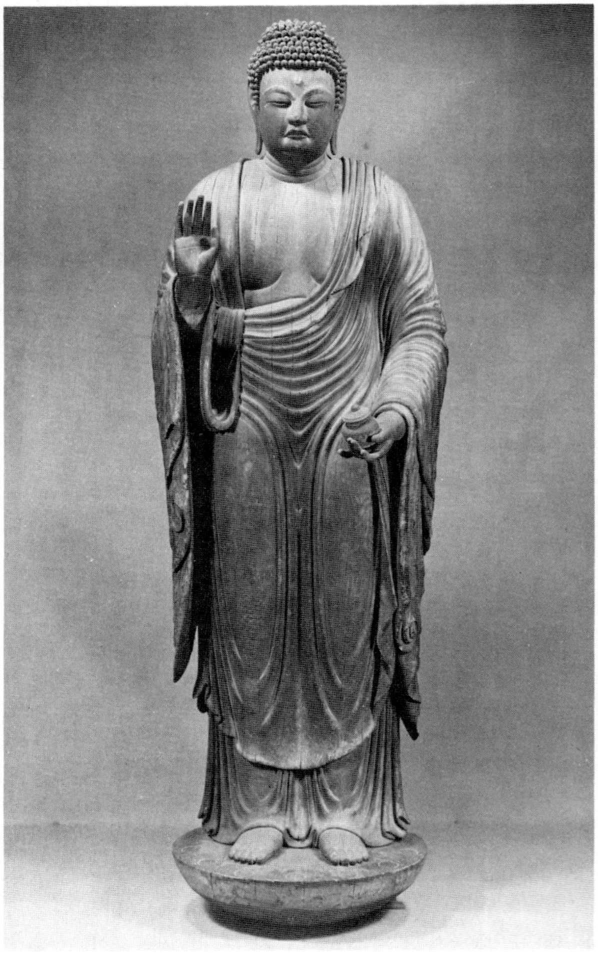

right: 22 *Yakushi (Bhaishajyaguru).* c. 794–897. Early Heian Period. Wood, height 5′4½″ (1.66 m). Gangōji Temple, Nara, Japan.

Line can also be used to express emotions, as in the medieval illumination from the Ebbo Gospel (c. A.D. 835). In the portrait of Saint Mark the Evangelist [21], the vibrating lines of the garment convey a powerful sense of ecstatic energy as the evangelist strives to capture every nuance of the divine word transmitted to him by the winged lion in the upper right-hand corner. Such a use of line is sometimes called "expressionist" because it conveys a strong sense of emotional experience.

One way or another, line appears in many paintings. It is used to striking effect in Botticelli's *Birth of Venus* [see Figure 12, page 18] to outline the shell and even the hair and features of the various figures. Line may also play an important role in sculpture and architecture. In Japanese statues [22] line is often an indispensable feature, as seen in the folds of the torso, which attract the eye to follow their sinuous paths, contrasting with the smooth areas of the upper chest and thighs. Line may even occur in the façades of buildings, as in the horizontal and vertical patterning on the Palazzo Rucellai [23].

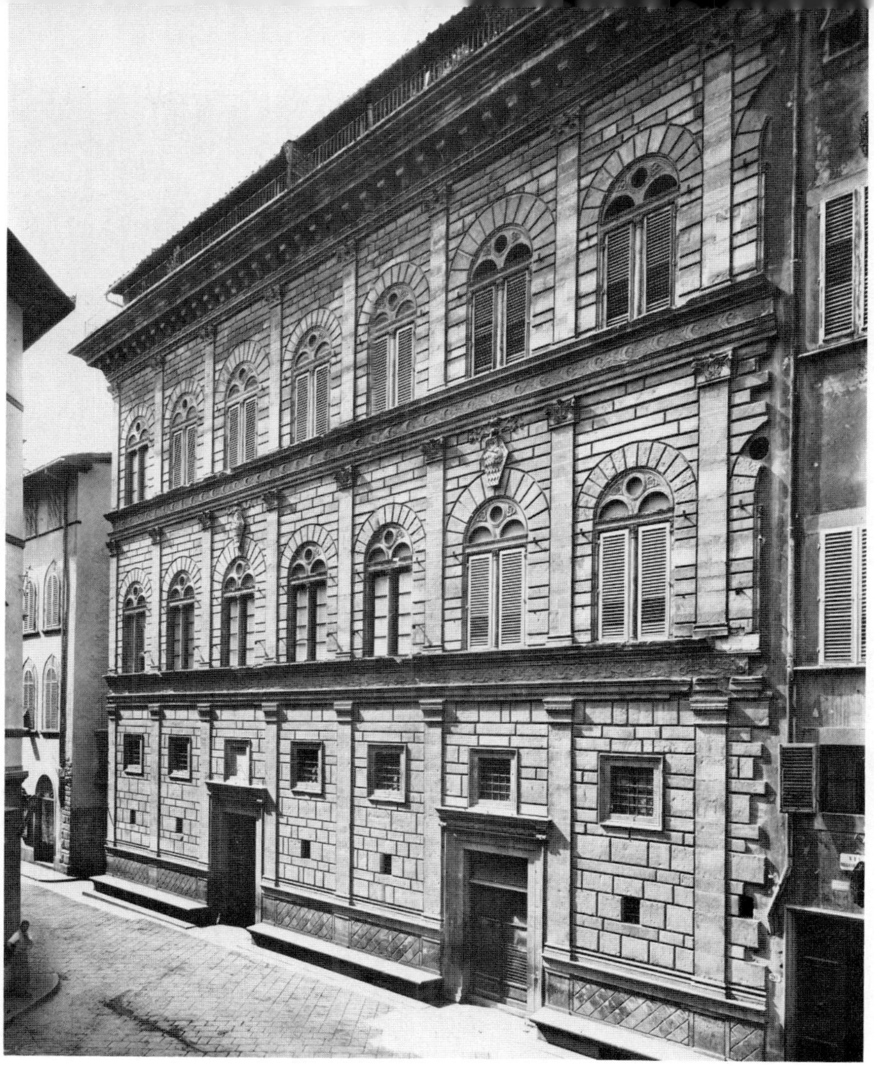

23 Leon Battista Alberti. Palazzo Rucellai. Florence. 1446.

On the other hand, some 17th- and 18th-century painters such as Rembrandt [see Plate 2, page 34] have tried to efface boundary lines where we would expect them to appear. The colors used by these artists modulate gently so that one shade merges imperceptibly with the next. Others even attempt to exclude line altogether by presenting their images through masses of color. But these exceptions should not cause us to undervalue line. Indeed, we might argue that its importance is proven by the extraordinary care such artists take to avoid it.

Media and techniques in the graphic arts Line is especially significant not only as outline or contour but also as the actual means of creating visual images in the *graphic arts.* In these, designs composed basically of lines are cut into a durable flat surface that is then inked to print multiple copies. Each of the graphic arts uses a slightly different technique for creating its lines.

In **engraving,** the artist cuts a pattern of tiny furrows onto the surface of a metal plate with a special tool called a burin. Dürer's compassionate engrav-

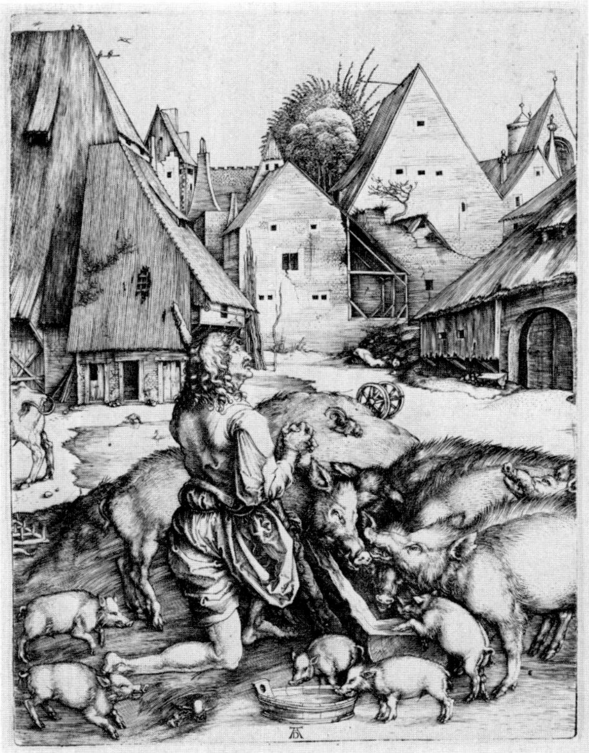

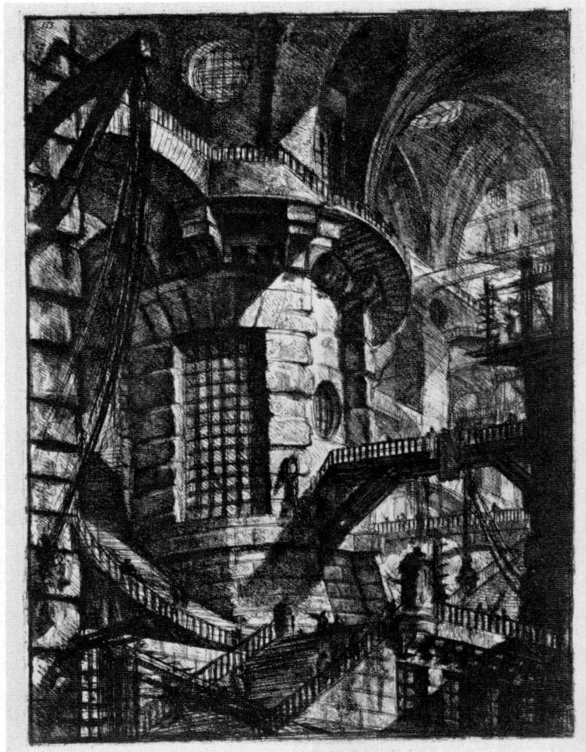

above left: 24 Albrecht Dürer. *The Prodigal Son.* c. 1496. Engraving, 9¾ × 7½″ (25 × 19 cm). National Gallery of Art, Washington (Rosenwald Collection).

above right: 25 Giovanni Battista Piranesi. *Carceri (Prisons),* Plate III. 1748–1750. Etching, 21½ × 16⅜″ (55 × 42 cm). National Gallery of Art, Washington (Rosenwald Collection).

ing *The Prodigal Son* [24] shows such a pattern of lines clearly. The repentant figure, kneeling among the swine, expresses a yearning for the comfortable security represented by the family dwellings in the background. In fact, the background and foreground are linked by the feathery pattern of the lines to which the engraving technique lends itself. In an **etching**, the sharp lines of an engraving are softened by suspending the metal plate in a series of acid baths. Giovanni Battista Piranesi (1720–1778) in his *Prison* series [25] uses the blurring of the lines that results from this process to create an impression of gloom, suggesting psychological as well as physical incarceration. Finally, **woodcut** uses the opposite procedure from engraving. By cutting away the background, the artist leaves a network of thick lines that stand out in relief. *The Way to Emmaus* [26] by Karl Schmidt-Rottluff (1884–1976) is a modern artist's experiment in this traditional technique which produces an effect of great emotional starkness. The artist has used this medium in a deliberately old-fashioned manner, simplifying forms. His figures express the feelings of pathos, shock, and exhaustion as Christ, just risen from the dead, appears unexpectedly between two of his disciples. Perhaps the desolate landscape in the background suggests not only the suffering Christ has experienced but also the devastation Europe was experiencing during World War I (1914–1918). Line, then, is a basic and remarkably versatile element of the spatial arts.

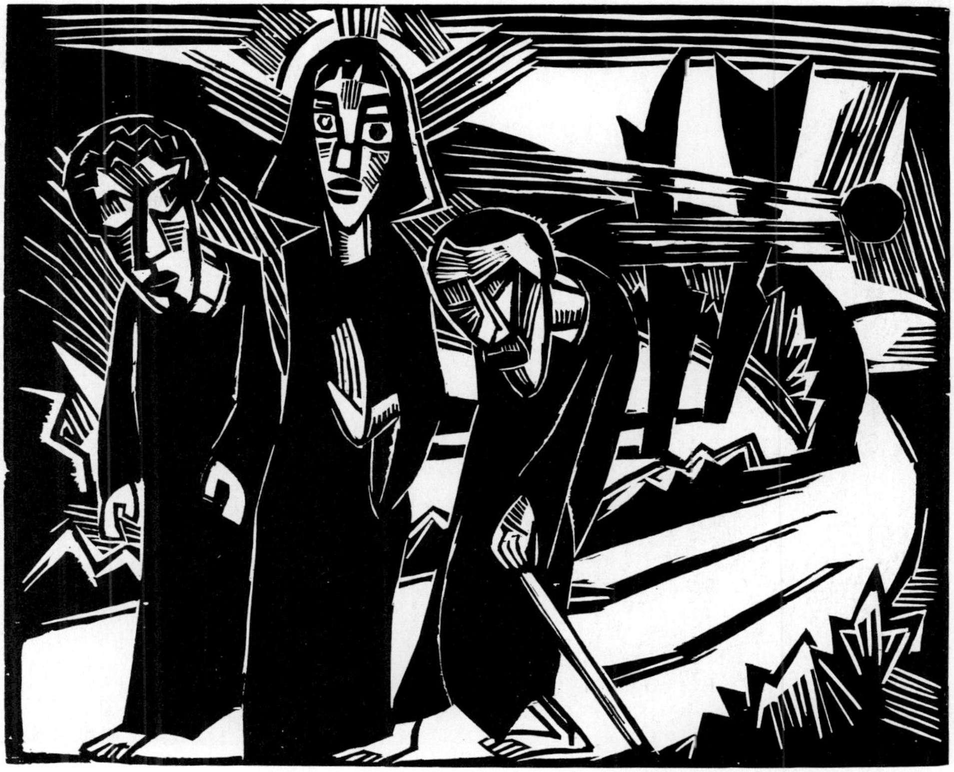

above: 26 Karl Schmidt-Rottluff. *The Way to Emmaus.* 1918. Woodcut, 15½ × 19½″ (39 × 50 cm). Fogg Art Museum, Harvard University, Cambridge, Mass. (purchase, Francis Calley Gray Fund).

Volume

Another significant element of design in at least some of the visual arts is *volume.* In the 3rd century B.C., Archimedes, the Greek scientist, devised a simple test to measure volume when he was required to calculate the volume of gold needed to make an intricate crown. Getting into his bath one day, he realized that his body was displacing the amount of water equal to his volume, whereupon he uttered the famous exclamation "Eureka!" ("I have found it!"). Art objects that can be given the bathtub test have volume. Even though we might not want to execute this maneuver for many reasons, we can estimate volume through the use of our eyes, drawing on our previous experience. Volume is perhaps most evident in sculpture, from small figurines to huge colossi, and is exemplified in the curved shape of the Japanese figure [see Figure 22, page 26] just discussed, which is about life-size. Volume occurs in architecture because all buildings are three-dimensional.

Over the centuries sculptors have been able to choose between two ways of creating volume. One is to build up the form from an initial core, adding material such as clay or plaster. The other is to remove superfluous material from a single mass of stone or wood, leaving the desired shape. Michelangelo (1476–1564), who preferred the second method, believed that he was liberating figures that he thought of as imprisoned in the block of

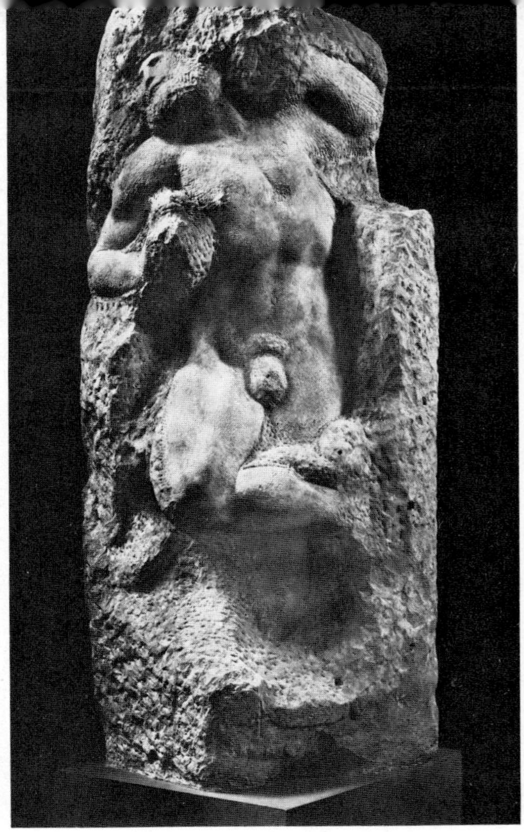

right: 27 Michelangelo. *Boboli Captive.* 1527–1528. Marble, height 7′6½″ (2.3 m). Accademia, Florence.

below: 28 Donatello. *The Miracle of Saint Anthony.* Relief, bronze. Basilica of San Antonio, Padua.

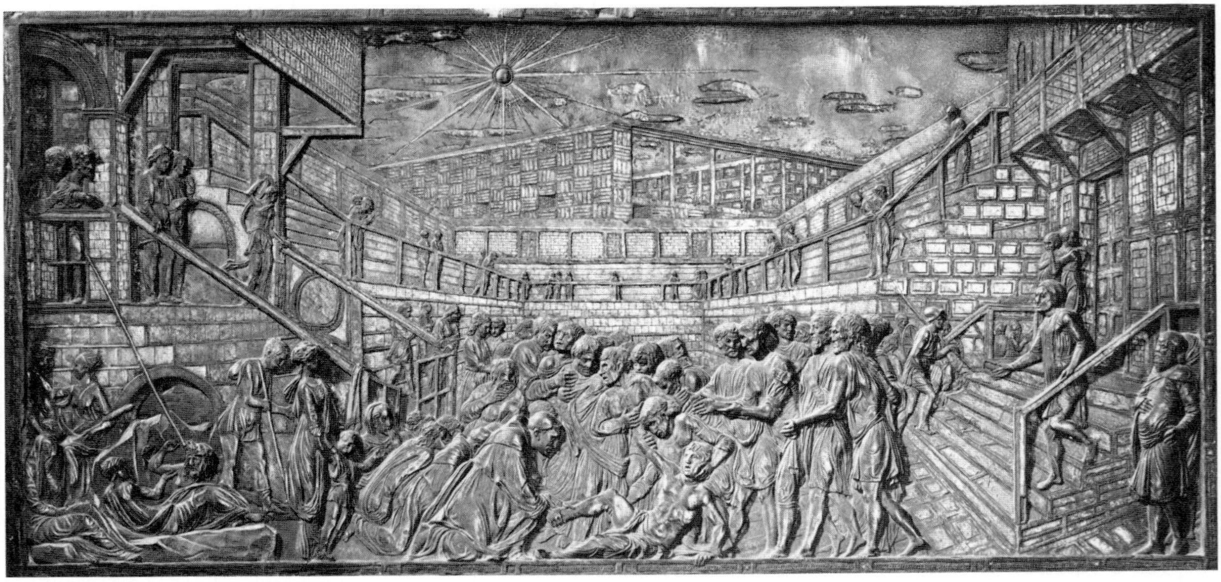

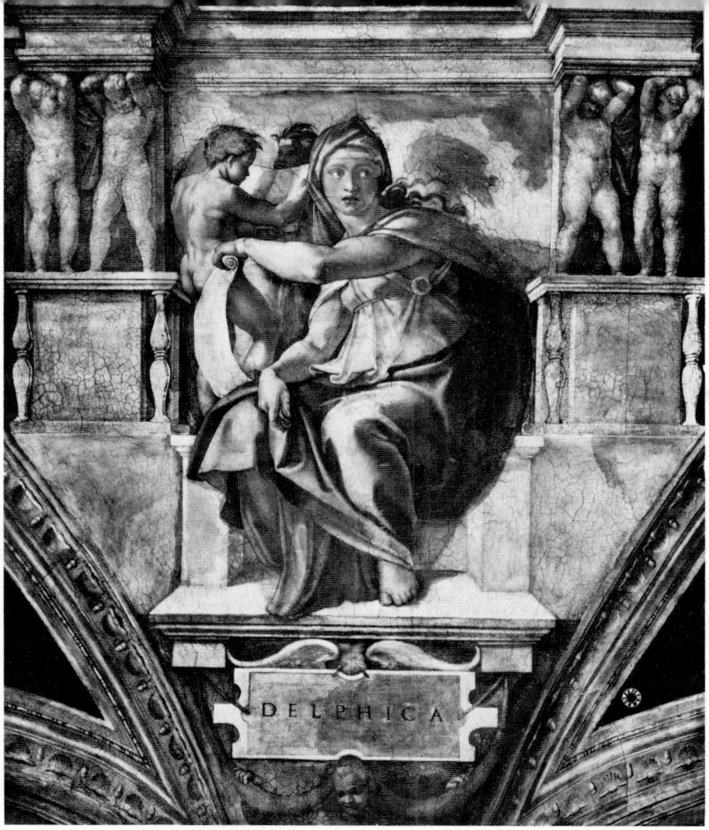

29 Michelangelo. *Delphic Sibyl,* detail of Sistine Chapel ceiling. 1509. Fresco. Vatican, Rome.

stone. In some of his sculptures the figures seem to be emerging from chunks of unfinished marble [27].

Different degrees of volume can be achieved in sculpture. *Free-standing* figures, which can be seen entirely in the round, have the greatest volume. Much less volume occurs in various forms of **relief**: in **high relief** the figures emerge substantially from their background, appearing almost three dimensional; in *low relief,* also known as **bas relief,** they remain rather flat. In his *Miracle of Saint Anthony* [28], a bas relief, Donatello (1386–1466) introduces some variations of volume. The figures in the foreground involved in the miraculous healing of a young man stand out most distinctly. The minor figures and the buildings in the rear are lower in relief. Donatello provides a remarkably detailed setting with steps, balconies, and even a sun in the sky. In fact, bas relief with its panel-like format is closer to painting than other kinds of sculpture and accordingly can offer more setting and atmosphere.

Does volume occur in painting? At first we might say no, at least for practical purposes, since the variations on the surface are usually negligible. Volume is a function of three-dimensionality, which the picture surface of paintings normally lacks. However, in some paintings, as in a portion of Michelangelo's Sistine Chapel ceiling [29], we may encounter a strong illusion of volume. Through masterful contrasts of light and shade, Michelangelo makes

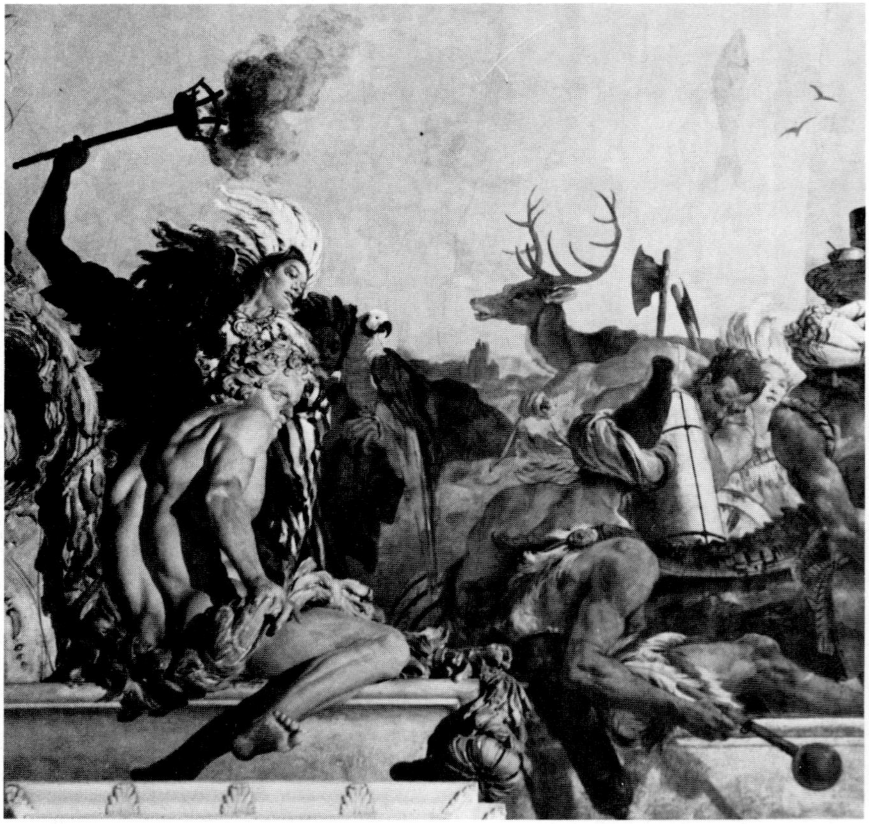

30 Giovanni Battista Tiepolo. *The American Continent,* detail. 1753. Fresco. Residenz, Würzburg.

the monumental figure of the Sibyl seem to stand out against the architectural background. In actual fact, of course, the painting is entirely flat.

The capacity of the artist to deceive the eye, sometimes called by the French term **trompe l'oeil**, is often found in European and American paintings. Michelangelo's Sybil is an example of such *simulated volume,* for the surface is flat and smooth, and only the artist's skill makes us "see" volume where there is none. In the illusionistic ceiling paintings of some 17th- and 18th-century churches and palaces, artists blend the simulated volume effects of painted figures with actual sculptural elements in plaster or stucco. In a detail from the ambitious ceiling painting depicting the continent of America [30], by Giovanni Battista Tiepolo (1696–1770), a stucco figure of a muscular young man intrudes upon the painted figures of three Native Americans. The sculptured figure seems to be thrusting himself into the two-dimensional world of the painting, while the parallel painted figure in the turban on the right seems to be leaning out of the two-dimensional into the three-dimensional space. The sculpture provides a transition or link between the world in which we live and the imaginary world on the ceiling.

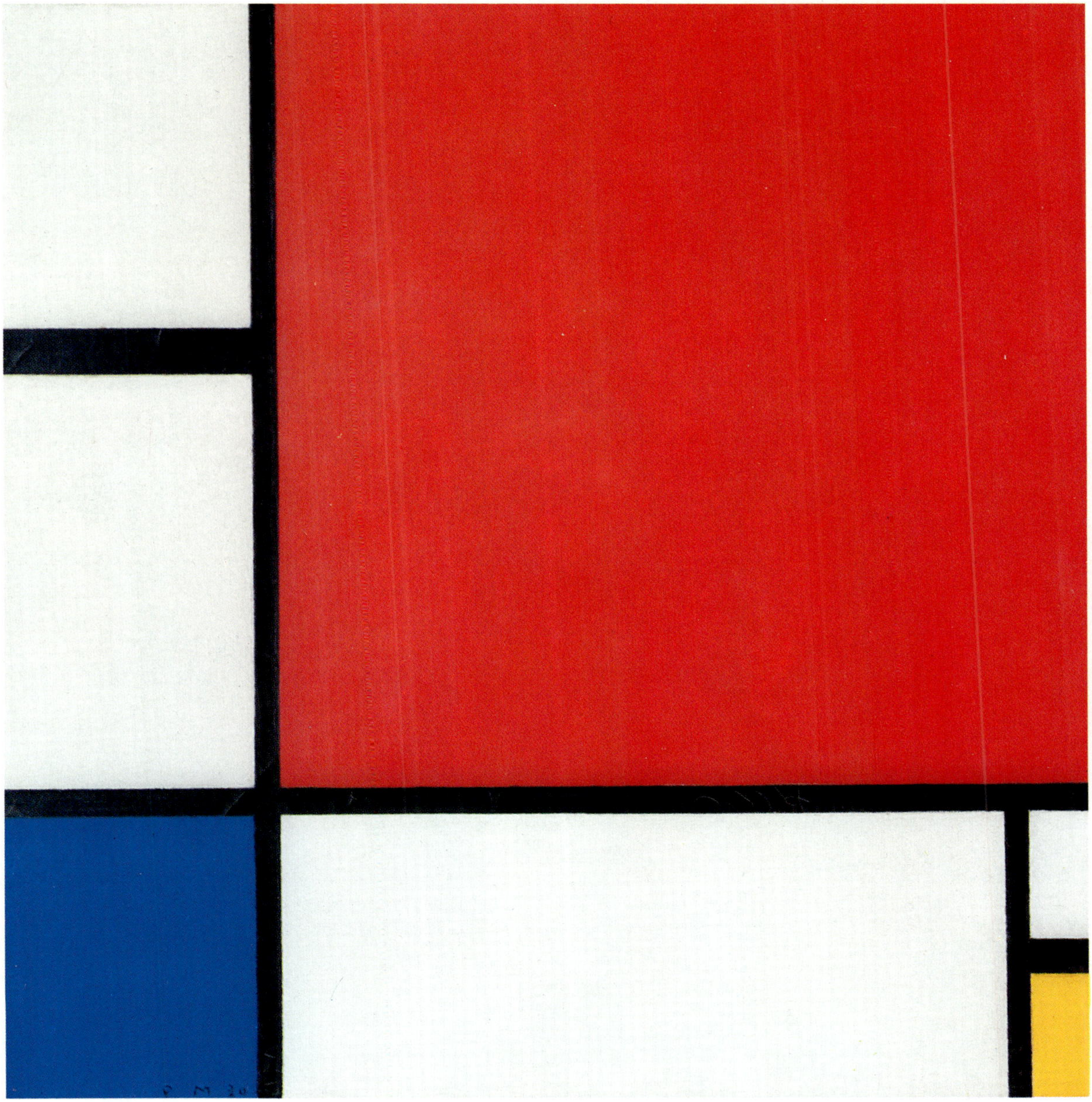

Plate 1 Piet Mondrian. *Composition with Red, Blue, and Yellow.* 1930. Oil on canvas, 20″ (51 cm) square. Private collection.

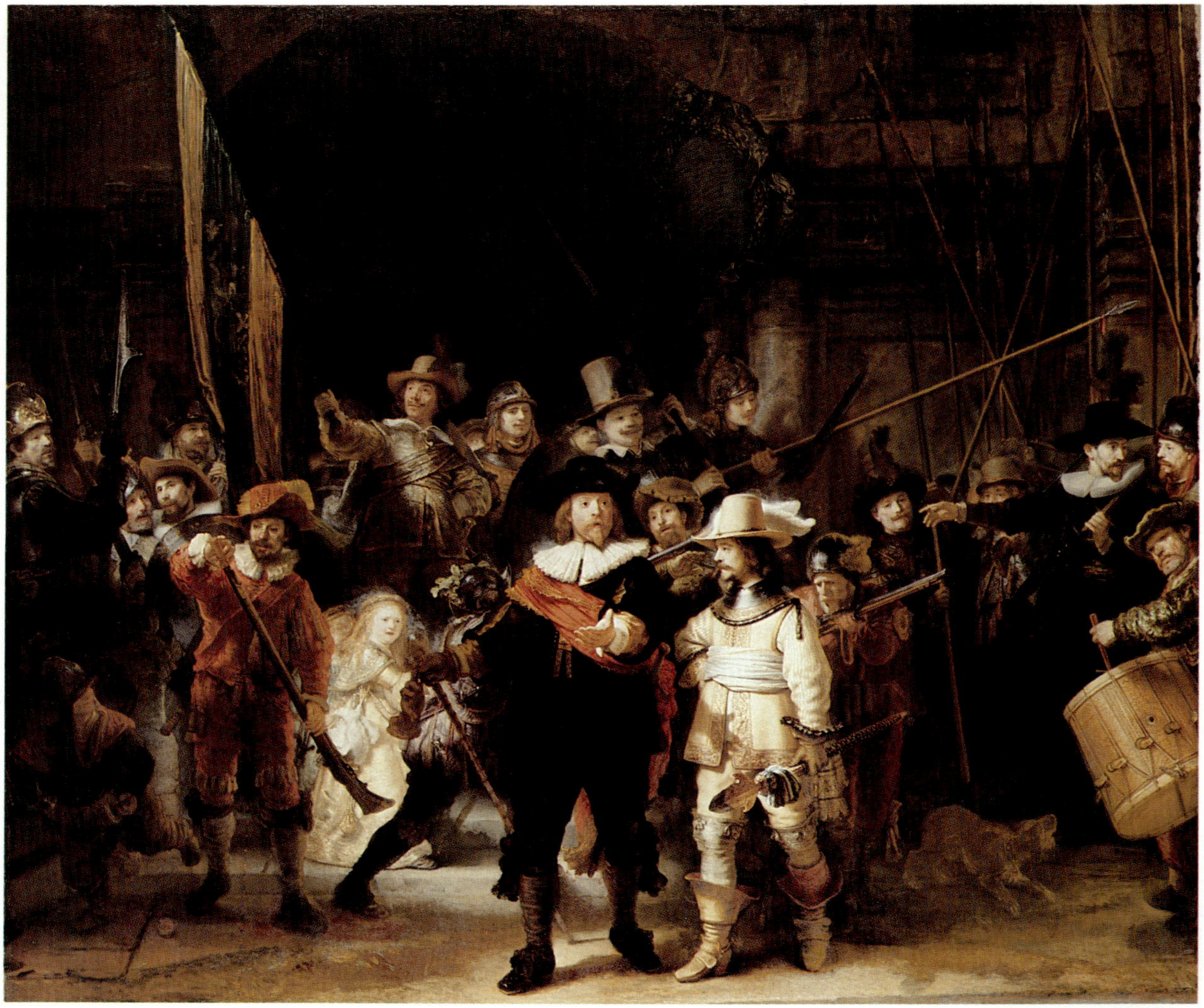

Plate 2 Rembrandt van Rijn. *The Nightwatch (The Company of Captain Frans Banning Cocq and Lieutenant Willem van Ruytenburch).* 1642. Oil on canvas, 11′9½″ × 14′2½″ (3.63 × 4.37 m). Rijksmuseum, Amsterdam.

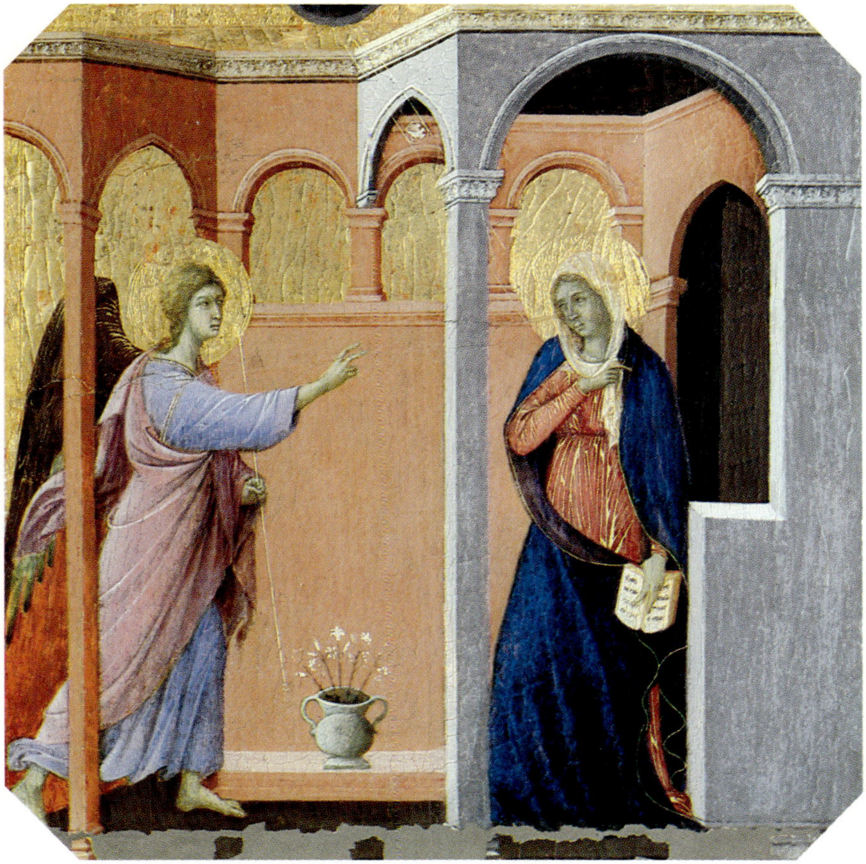

Plate 3 Duccio di Buoninsegna. *Annunciation,* from the *Maestà Altar.* 1308–1311. Tempera on wood, 16¾ × 17⅛″ (43 × 44 cm). National Gallery, London (reproduced by courtesy of the Trustees). Duccio's bold colors are in keeping with the straightforward setting of the scene. The Virgin, who has been reading a work of religious devotion, stands in a small alcove on the right, while the angel advances respectfully in the arcaded gallery to the left.

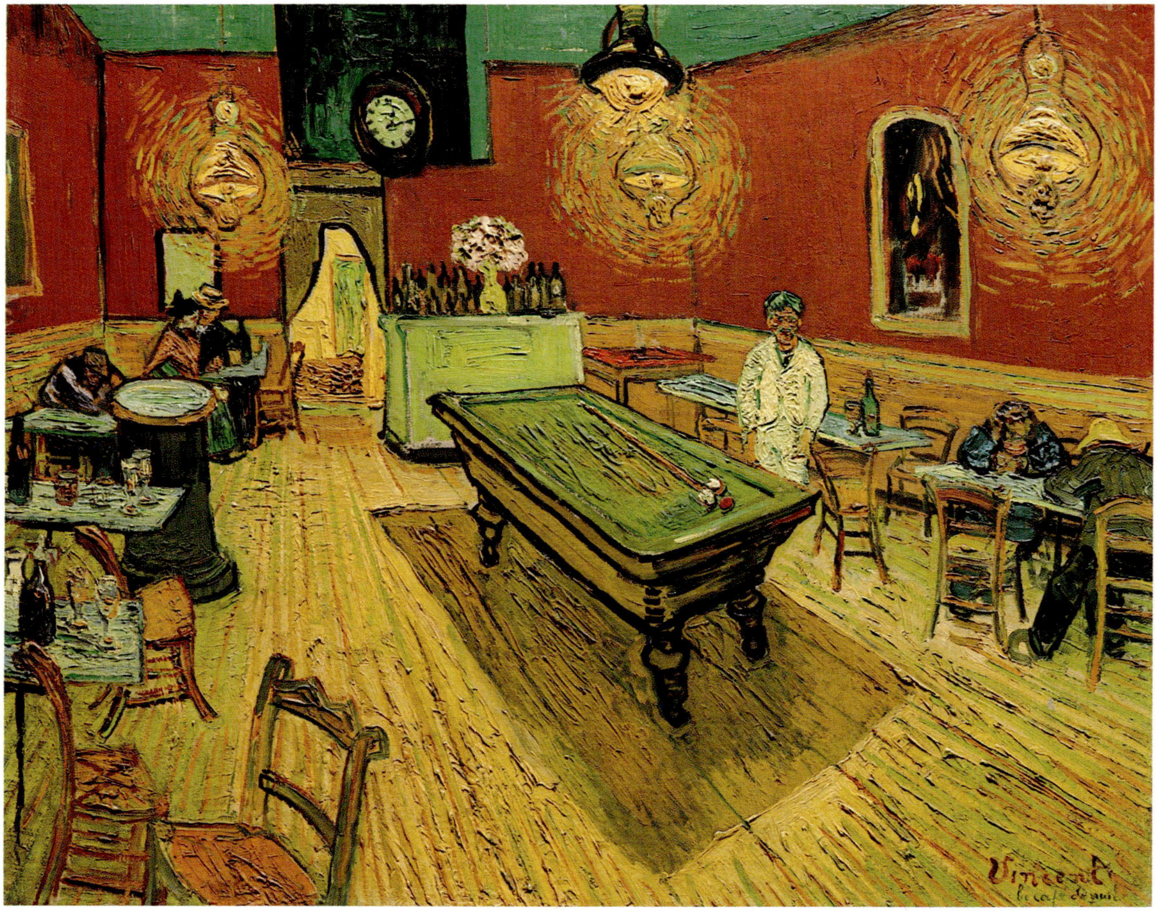

Plate 4 Vincent van Gogh. *The Night Café.* 1888.
Oil on canvas, 28½ × 36¼″ (72 × 92 cm).
Yale University Art Gallery
(bequest of Stephen Carlton Clark, B.A. 1903).

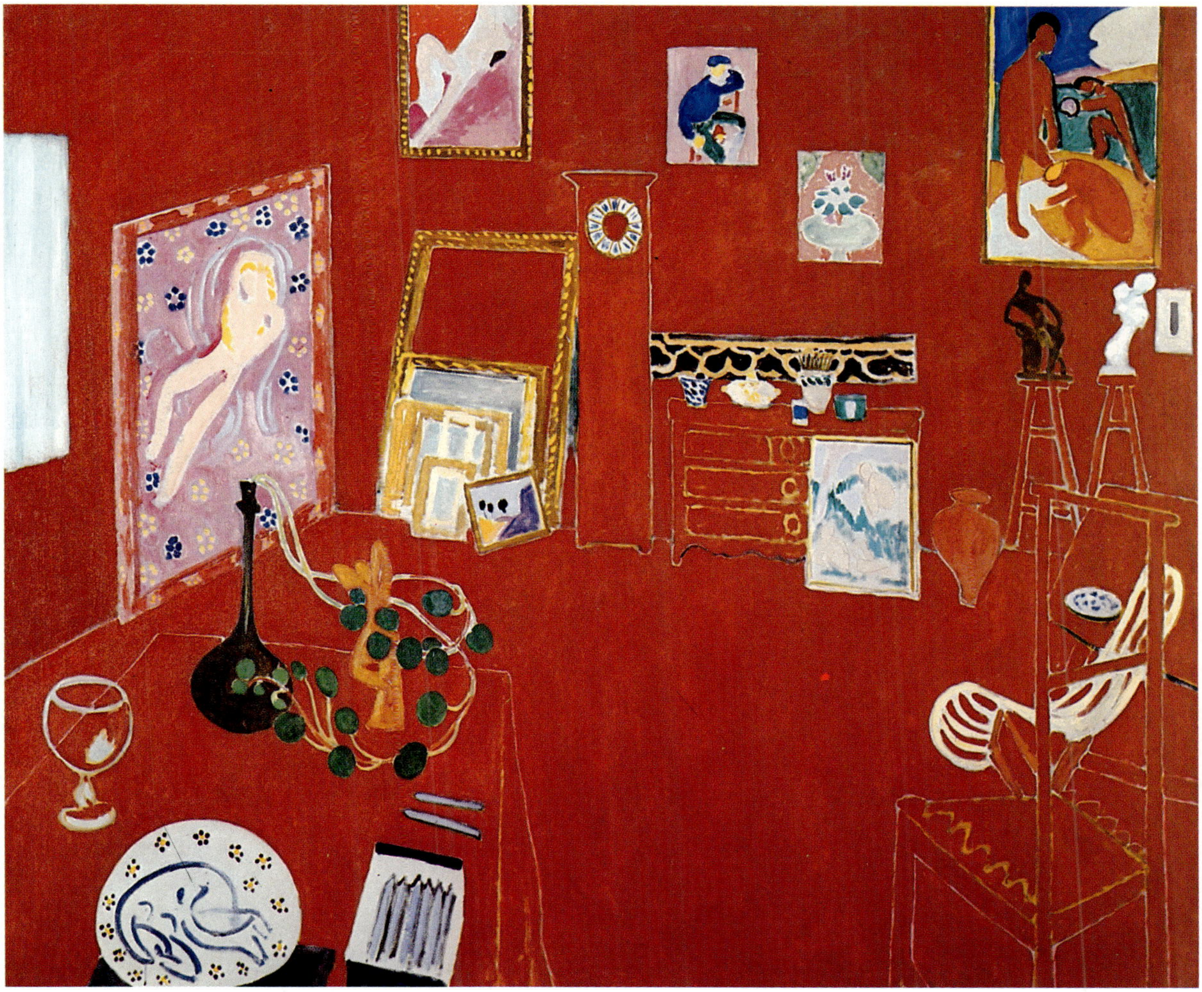

Plate 5 Henri Matisse. *The Red Studio*. 1911. Oil on canvas, 5′11¼″ × 7′2¼″ (1.81 × 2.19 m). Museum of Modern Art, New York (Mrs. Simon Guggenheim Fund).

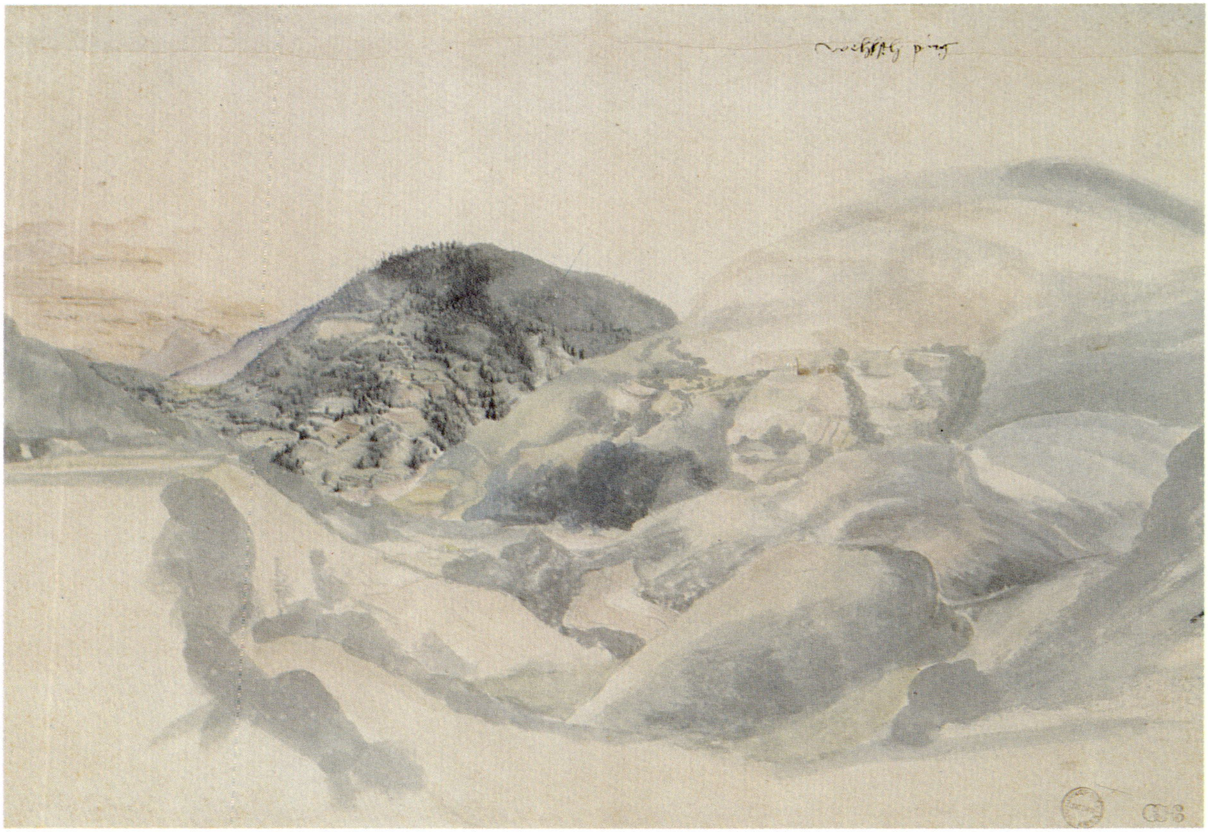

Plate 6 Albrecht Dürer. *Italian Mountains.* c. 1495. Brush drawing in watercolor and body color on white paper, 8¼ × 12¼″ (21 × 31 cm). Ashmolean Museum, Oxford.

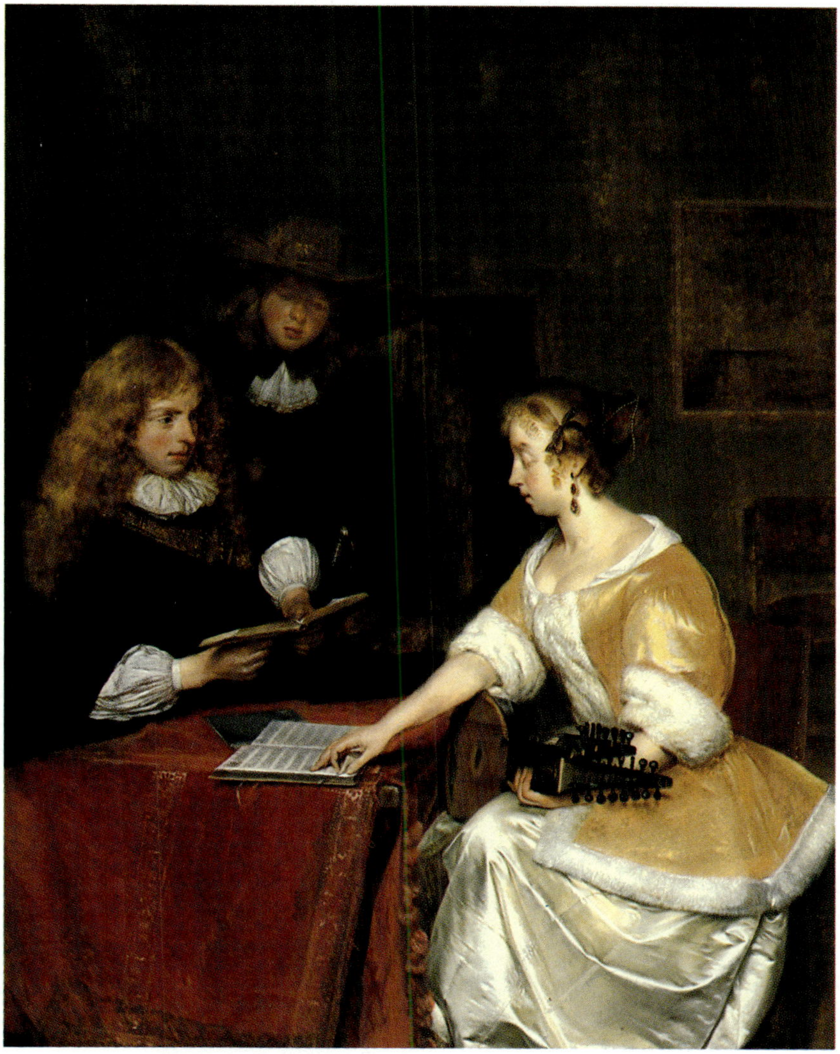

Plate 7 Gerard Terborch. *A Music Party*. c. 1675. Oil on wood panel, 22⅞ × 18⅝″ (15 × 47 cm). Cincinnati Art Museum (bequest of Mary M. Emery).

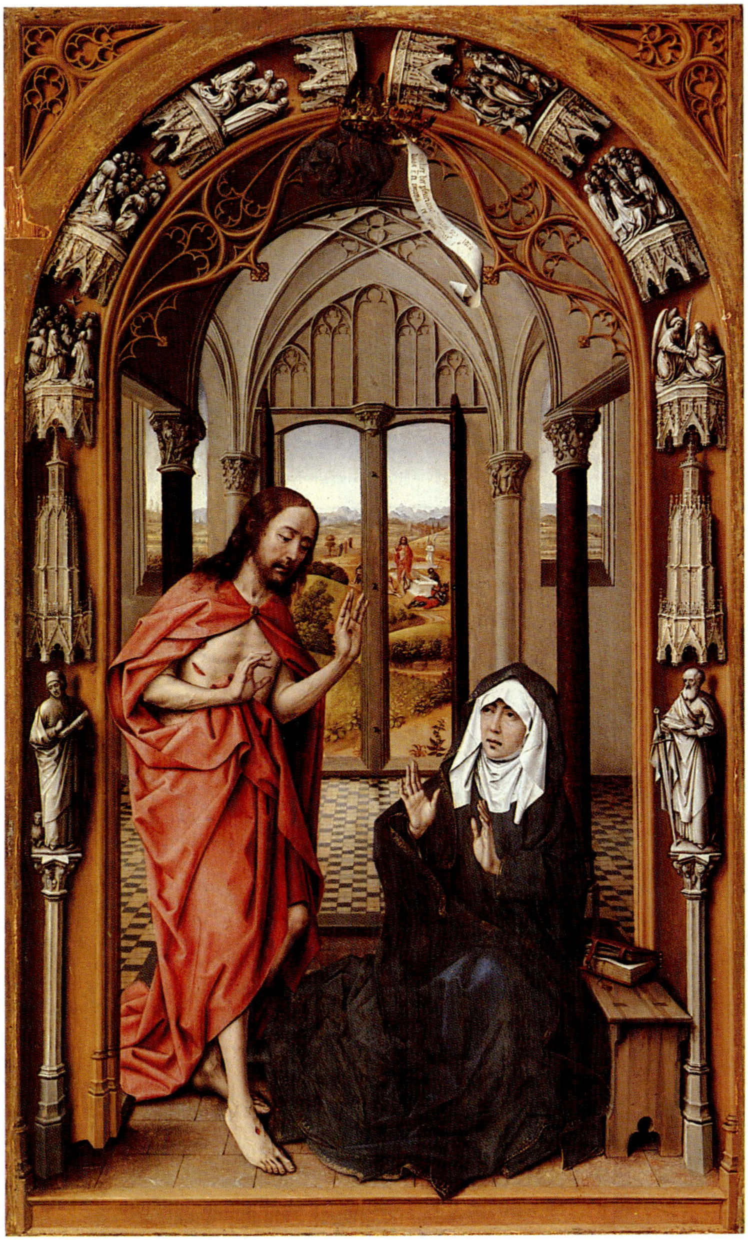

Plate 8 Rogier van der Weyden. *Christ Appearing to His Mother,* right wing of a triptych from the Chapel Royal, Granada Cathedral. c. 1440–1444. Tempera and oil on panel, 25 × 15″ (64 × 38 cm). Metropolitan Museum of Art, New York (bequest of Michael Dreicer, 1921, Michael Dreicer Collection). Van der Weyden has restricted his use of color to emphasize the importance of the two principal figures. Christ's red robe symbolically suggests his past suffering and passion; Mary's traditional blue dress symbolically suggests her eventual Assumption into heaven. Continuing the story into the future, the scenes on the archway are deliberately presented in the neutral tones of sculpture.

Texture

Whereas volume refers to the three-dimensionality of some art objects, **texture**, another significant element in visual design, refers to the treatment of the surface. The bronze head from West Africa [31] offers a good example of textural contrast, for the patterning of the head covering, the hair, and the neckpiece all afford different contrasts with the smooth skin. Smoothness is also texture. Our perception of textural contrasts tempts us to reach out and touch a work of art. Although we are usually forbidden to touch, we can form a pretty good estimate of the degree of roughness and smoothness with our eyes. Texture also occurs in architecture, as we can see by contrasting the rough surface of the Crane Memorial Library [see Figure 14, page 19] with the smoother one of the Florentine palace [see Figure 23, page 27].

Texture might seem to be more important in sculpture and architecture than in painting, which is confined to flat surfaces. Yet we often encounter a simulation of texture that resembles the simulation of volume just mentioned. In *The Music Lesson* [Plate 7, page 39] by Gerard Terborch (1617–1681), the satiny texture of the woman's dress contrasts with the rough texture of the rug. Moreover, the dress captures our attention not only through its sheen but also through its intensity. The brilliance of its silvery and golden colors differs sharply from the relatively muted shades surrounding it. Yet the texture of neither the dress nor the rug is a property of the paint surface, which is smooth as glass. Instead, the artist has used his skill to create the illusion of considerable textural variation within the imaginary space of the painting. In other paintings, such as those of Vincent van Gogh [see Plate 4, page 36], variations in texture are achieved by applying actual blobs of thick paint to the surface, making it rugged.

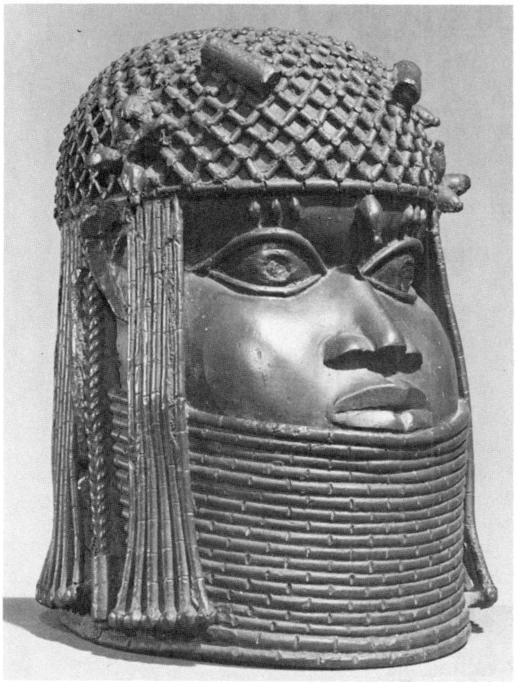

31 Head, from Court of Benin, Nigeria. Bini tribe, c. 1550–1680. Bronze, height 10¾″ (27 cm). Metropolitan Museum of Art, New York (Michael C. Rockefeller Memorial Collection of Primitive Art).

Choice of Moment

Because the arts we have been considering exist in space and can present only one moment at a time, the choice of moment becomes extraordinarily important. Far from making a random selection, artists take great pains to single out the precise scene they wish to depict. When Rembrandt painted his *Nightwatch* [see Plate 2, page 34], which was commissioned as a group portrait, he avoided the stiff and formal presentation usual in such works by depicting men in the process of spilling out onto the street. Moreover, by unexpectedly introducing the young girl in the foreground, he gained the

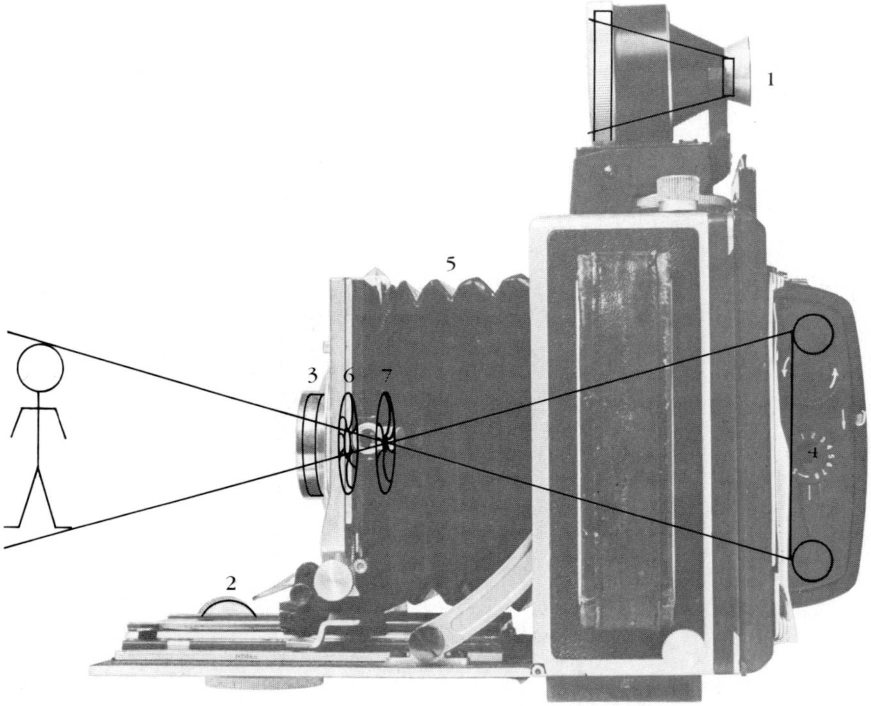

32 Basic components of the camera. Photographers, like other artists, must not only select a significant moment but must also control their medium. All cameras operate basically in the same way. Once the subject is located in the *viewer* (1), the image is focused by adjusting a focusing knob (2) to alter the distance between the *lens* (3) and the *focal plane* (4), where film records the image. In this camera, such an adjustment is made by sliding the *collapsible lens box* (5) away from or toward the focal plane. The image recorded on the film is affected both by the amount of light that reaches the film, which is controlled by the *aperture* or *diaphragm* (6), and by the length of time that such light is allowed to reach the film, which is controlled by the *shutter* (7). In most cameras, three adjustments are possible. Focusing sharpens the image by changing the distance between the lens and the film until it relates to the distance between the camera and the subject. Changing the aperture size and altering the shutter speed allow the photographer to take into account the amount of illumination in the scene, the movement of the subject, and the depth of field—that is, the extent to which objects in the foreground and background remain in sharp focus.

opportunity to contrast youth with age and femininity with masculinity as well as to reinforce the casual informality of the whole. In terms of composition, Rembrandt created a dynamic balance between the bright figures in the center and the darker figures surrounding them.

In photography, the deliberate selection of a particular moment or scene—as well as the control of the camera itself [32]—distinguishes the photograph from a mere record. The seemingly casual dancers in Anthony Crickmay's picture [see Figure 15, page 20] were carefully posed. But even when an object or a scene is not consciously "staged," it has been recognized and appreciated by the photographer as an image worth recording. The three women in the photograph [33] by Weegee (Arthur Fellig) (1899–1968) were clearly not posed, but the artist realized that the juxtaposition of the two haughty bejeweled ladies on the left with the abject figure on the right would make a significant social comment.

Often artists choose not the moment we might consider the most dramatic but one immediately preceding the climax—one that implies the crisis and its resolution but leaves these to the viewer's imagination. A famous example of this **pregnant moment** is the sculpture of the Old Testament David [34] by Gianlorenzo Bernini (1598–1680). Here the young man is

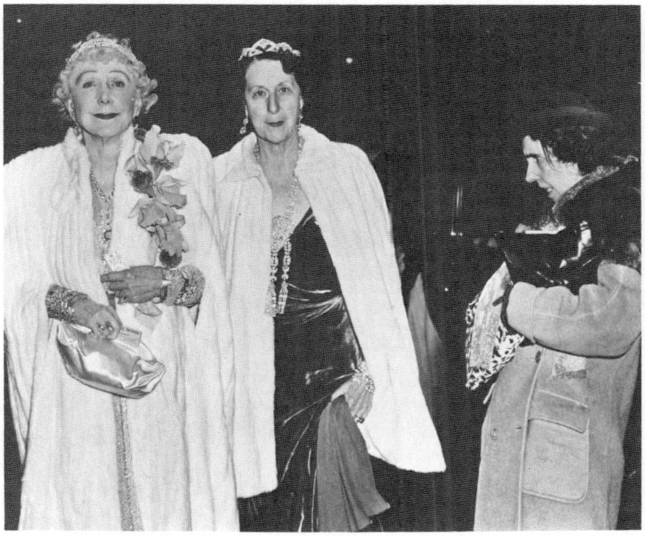

above: 33 Weegee (Arthur Fellig). *The Critic (Opening Night at the Opera).* 1943. Gelatin-silver print, 12⅝ × 10⅝" (32 × 27 cm). Museum of Modern Art, New York.

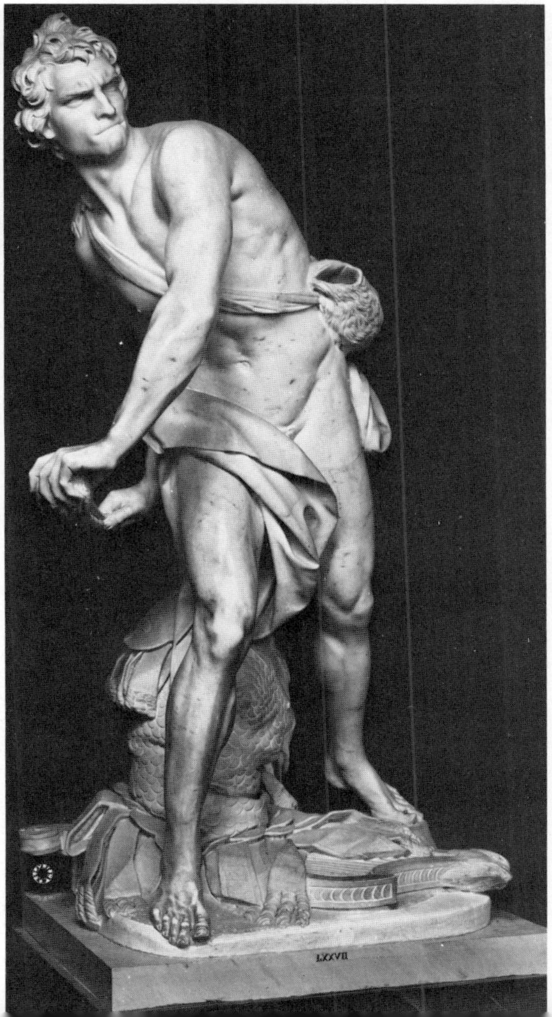

right: 34 Gianlorenzo Bernini. *David.* 1623–1624. Marble, height 5′6¼″ (1.7 m). Borghese Gallery, Rome.

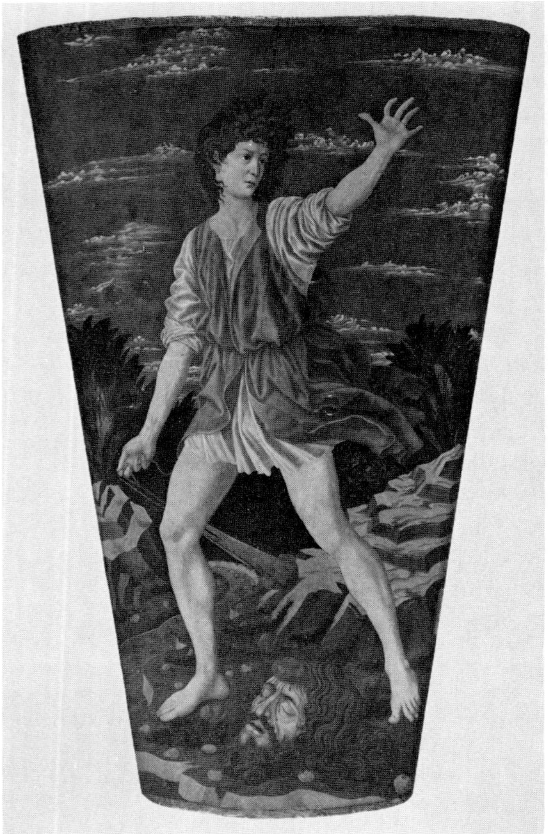

above: 35 Andrea del Castagno. *The Youthful David.* c. 1450. Leather, 45½ × 30¼″ (116 × 77 cm). National Gallery of Art, Washington, D.C. (Widener Collection).

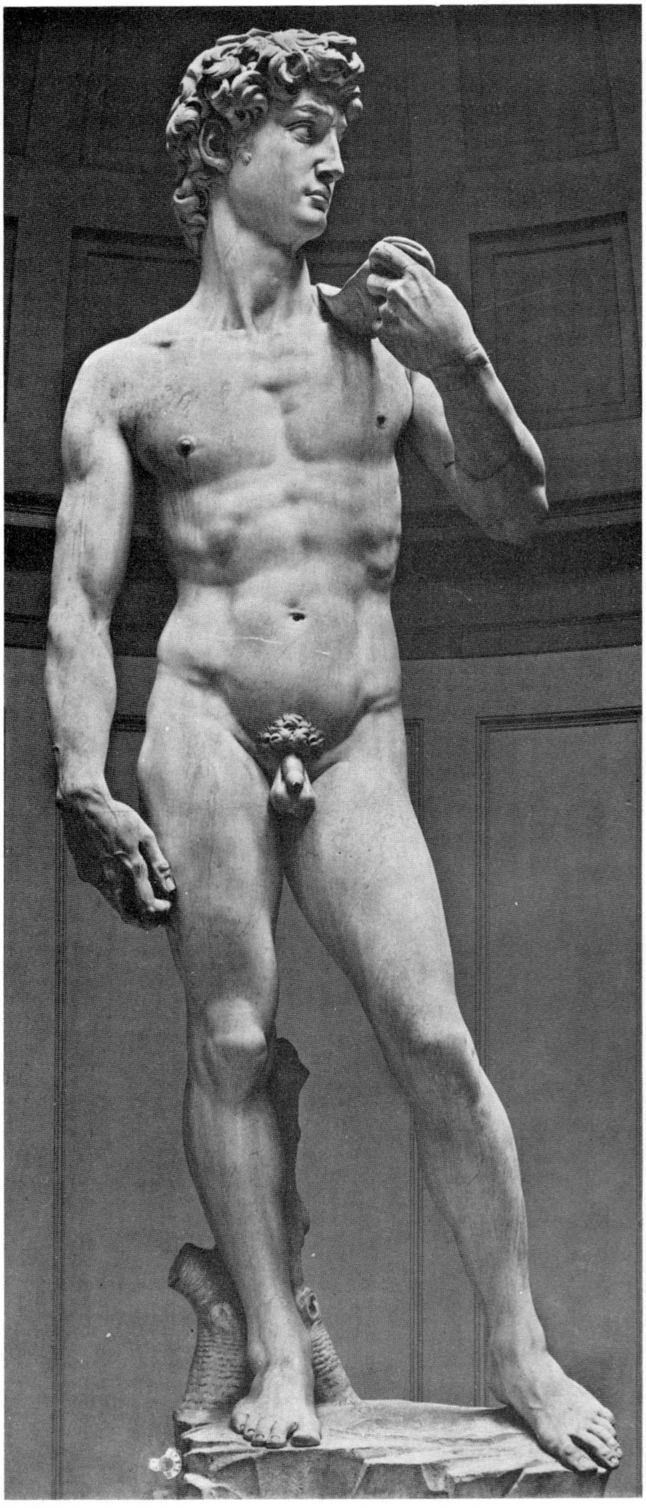

right: 36 Michelangelo. *David.* 1501–1504. Marble, height 18′ (5.49 m). Accademia, Florence.

about to heave the stone that will kill the giant, and his determined look suggests his intense concentration. Bernini has clearly chosen the moment just before the climax, which is the actual slaying of Goliath. But as our other illustrations of David reveal [35, 36], artists have also chosen different moments in the story to present powerful images of this hero.

The device of choosing the moment before the climax has become so familiar that Roy Lichtenstein (b. 1923), who specializes in modern pop art, makes fun of it in his *I Know How You Must Feel, Brad!* [37]. Adapting the cartoon style used in comic strips, the artist mocks the facile sentiments found in these as well as in modern soap operas. To keep the audience interest alive, both comic strips and soap operas present a series of pregnant moments that are never fully resolved, and so Lichtenstein consciously offers no clue about what has preceded the outcry in the balloon or what will follow.

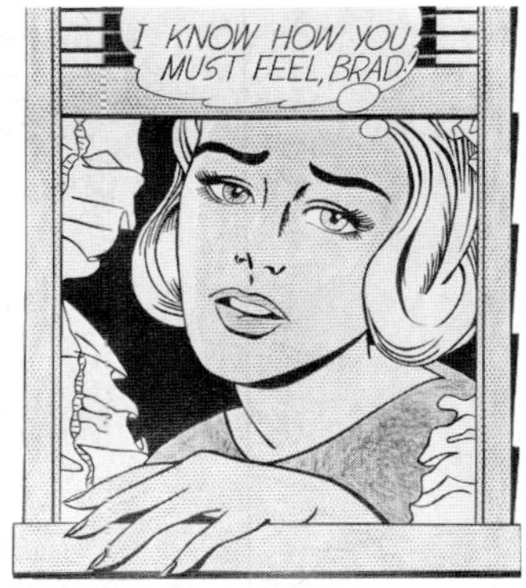

37 Roy Lichtenstein. *I Know How You Must Feel, Brad!* 1963. Pencil and tusche on paper, 30 × 22½" (76 × 57 cm). Collection Mrs. Vera List, New York.

Artists have naturally tried to overcome the innate limitation of space to represent only a single moment. In China, artists have painted horizontal scrolls which, unfolded from right to left, give the viewer the impression of following a story through time. Opening *Farewell at the Bridge* [38] section by section, we would first see a hilly, wooded landscape, then the leavetaking at the bridge shown below, and finally the open waters into which the boat with the departing friend is heading.

38 Wen Cheng-ming. *Farewell at the Bridge.* 1510. Chinese handscroll; ink and color on paper, 13⅝ × 53⅜" (35.1 × 135.2 cm). Private collection, New York. This scroll continues on both sides of the image shown here. Such scrolls were not intended for the public but for quiet contemplation by a few viewers at a time.

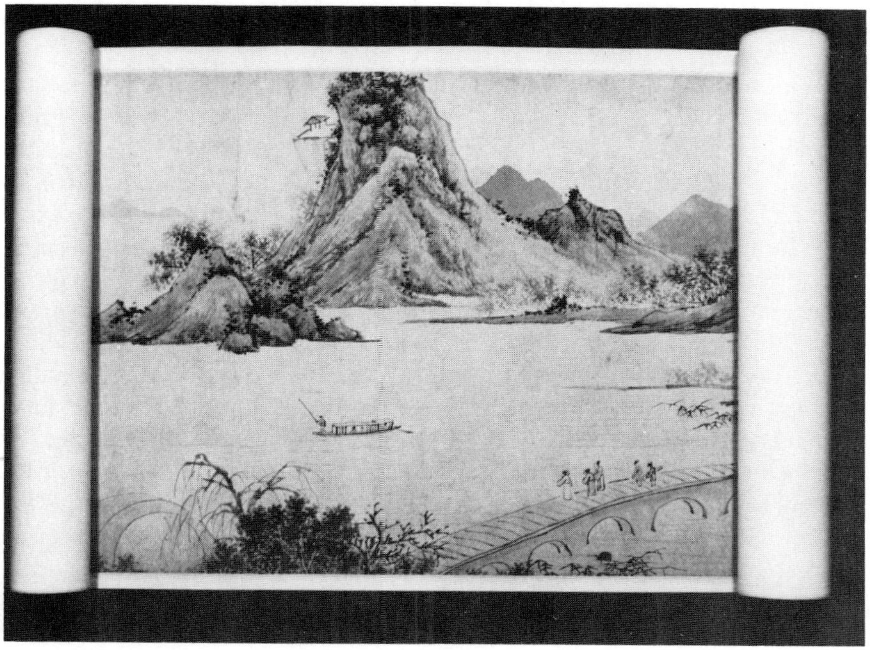

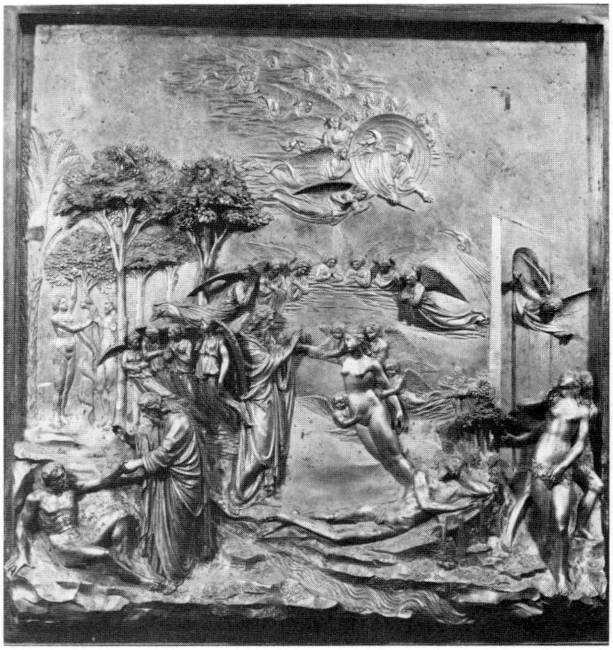

above: 39 Lorenzo Ghiberti.
The Story of Adam and Eve, detail of east doors, Baptistry, Florence. c. 1435.
Gilded bronze, 31¼″ (79 cm) square.

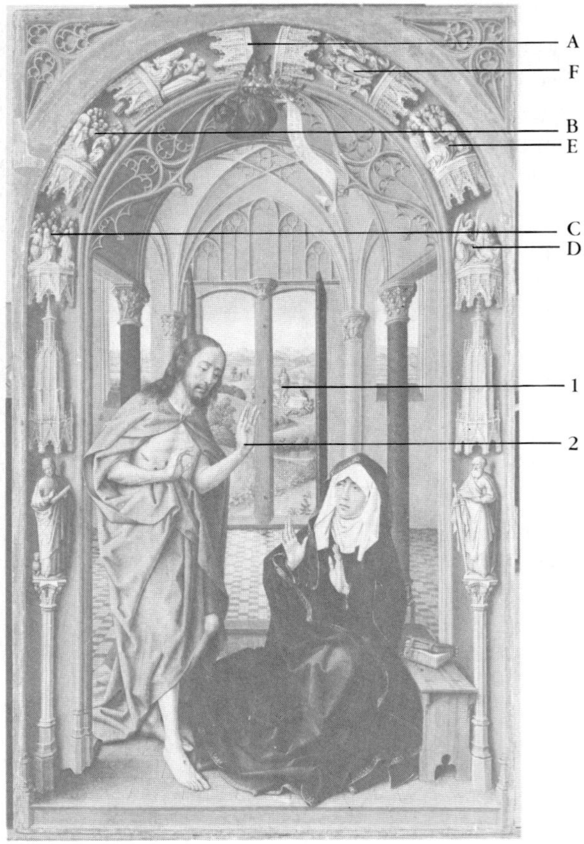

above right: 40 Time sequences in Rogier van der Weyden's *Christ Appearing to His Mother* [see Plate 8, page 40]. Key to scenes in order of time:
1 Center background: Resurrection of Christ from his tomb. *2* Center foreground: Appearance of resurrected Christ to Mary.
A The holy women at the tomb.
B Ascension of Christ. *C* Pentecost: appearance of the Holy Spirit as a dove to Mary and the twelve disciples. *D* Angel appearing to Mary with news of her last sleep and assumption. *E* Disciples assembled at the death of Mary.
F Coronation of Mary in heaven.

Some Western artists have managed to present within one work several incidents occurring at different times. Lorenzo Ghiberti (1378–1455), for instance, depicts a number of separate episodes from Genesis in a single panel [39]: The Creation of Adam (bottom, lower left), the Creation of Eve (center), the Temptation (far left above the Creation of Adam), and the Expulsion from Eden (extreme right). Rogier van der Weyden (1400?–1464) in his altarpiece panel of *Christ Appearing to His Mother* [40 and Plate 8, page 40] offers an even more elaborate solution to the problem of how to present more than a single moment of time in a single space. The main focus is the foreground scene of Christ's appearance. Here Mary is startled by the sudden presence of her son, who has risen from the grave and bears the stigmata, or wounds, of his Crucifixion. He is holding out his hands to reassure her. But far in the background Christ is just rising from his tomb—an event that occurs before he appears to Mary. In addition, the smaller scenes on the arch tell of several other events in Mary's life, most of which take place after the appearance of the risen Christ. All of these are arranged chronologically, beginning at the top left and proceeding counterclockwise to the top right. Van der Weyden distinguishes these moments from the central events by

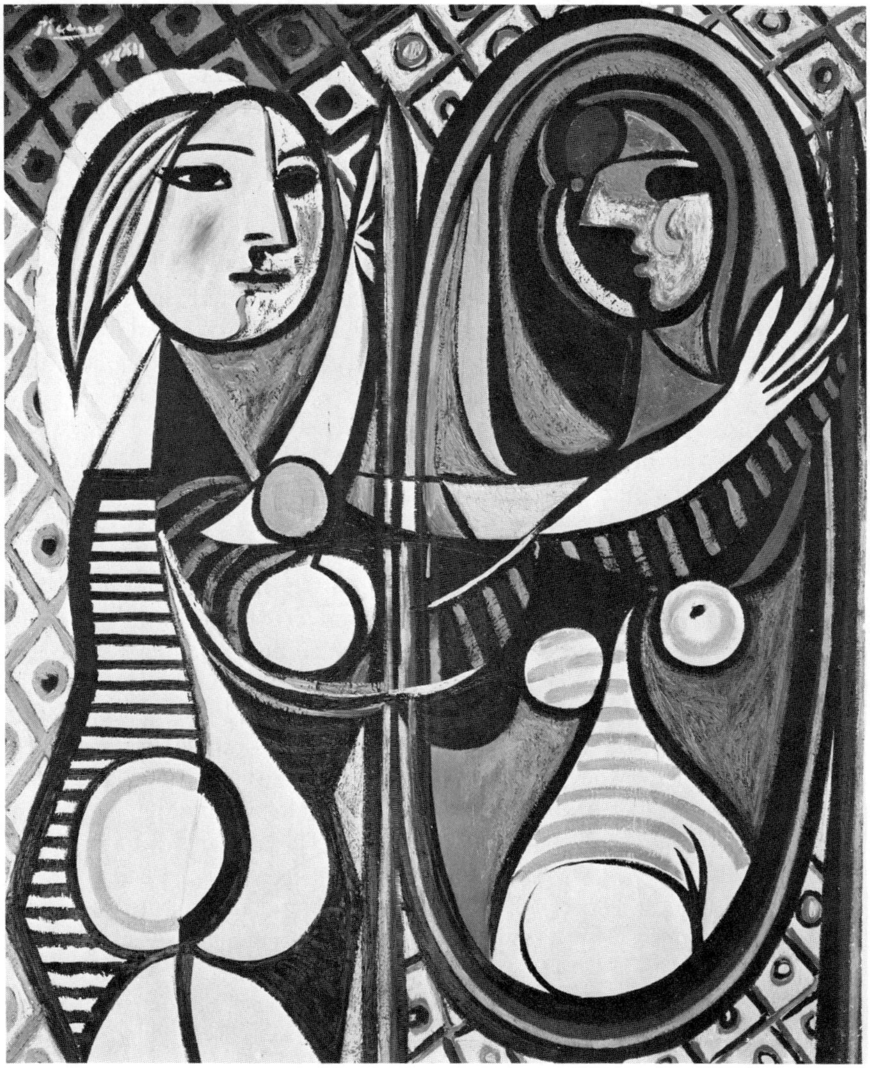

41 Pablo Picasso.
Girl Before a Mirror. 1932.
Oil on canvas,
5′4″ × 4′3¼″ (1.63 × 1.3 m).
Museum of Modern Art, New York
(gift of Mrs. Simon Guggenheim).

using a uniform color that has no variations in hue or intensity, but only changes in value to produce the effect of highlights and shadows.

Modern artists have tried to overcome the temporal restrictions of painting by experimenting even more radically with their medium. In his *Girl Before a Mirror* [41] Pablo Picasso (1881–1973) sets the profile head in the upper left within an oval that contains both a second eye and a continuation of the mouth. In this way, he fuses the profile and frontal views of the girl. Below, her torso appears as both nude and clothed. The practice of breaking up and recombining images—a hallmark of the revolutionary movement in modern painting known as **Cubism**—allows the artist to present more than one moment of time within a single composition. Picasso is doing the opposite of what Van der Weyden does when he presents a series of separate images in one altarpiece. Picasso's combining of several angles is, perhaps, an effort to capture in painting something approximating the sequence of images we see as we examine any three-dimensional object from different viewing positions.

Choice of Location and Design

The consequences of existing in space are even more evident in architecture, which is three-dimensional. Buildings—whether small or large, plain or ornate—have two related features that distinguish them from other art forms. They are fixed to the ground at a specific spot or *site,* and they enclose a space that human beings can enter.

The location of a building strongly influences the design. The physical properties of the site can inspire planning that takes advantage of the available light, air, or other spatial assets. Alternatively, the site can present great difficulties, especially when natural features or existing buildings cramp the space. The fact that buildings enclose space for human use is of even greater importance, for it affects their scale and need for stability. In addition, the practical function or purpose of a work of architecture fundamentally influences its design; residences, churches, and office buildings have their own special requirements. Nonetheless, architecture shares with all the arts the need for the careful selection and arrangement of parts into a visually coherent whole. To provide appropriate space that offers both shelter and structural stability for our various activities calls for careful planning. Except perhaps for small cottages, designers cannot improvise buildings as they go along. Unlike painters, architects cannot change their minds without drastic consequences.

The structural features of a building and its relationship to its site are projected in graphic representations—blueprints in many cases—which are completed before any construction is begun. Such graphic representations are of two kinds: **plans** and **elevations**. A plan shows the layout at some particular level. Every building needs a plan at ground level, or groundplan, and possibly plans for each floor. The elevation complements the horizontal plan, for it shows the vertical arrangement of the structure, how it "grows up" into the air. Again, several elevations may be necessary: elevations of each side of the building are required if the sides differ, and cutaway elevations, sometimes called *sections,* may be used to reveal the interior organization.

One of the earliest examples of monumental architecture, the ancient Egyptian Temple of Khonsu [42], the moon god (12th century B.C.), was planned with great care. The temple's exterior boundaries are determined by massive walls that slope inward toward the top. Such outer walls are more significant in religious structures than in ordinary buildings, for they mark the difference between the profane space of everyday life and the sacred enclosure within.

The organization of the building reflects the religious ceremonies conducted in secrecy within it. The outer wall is especially imposing on the main

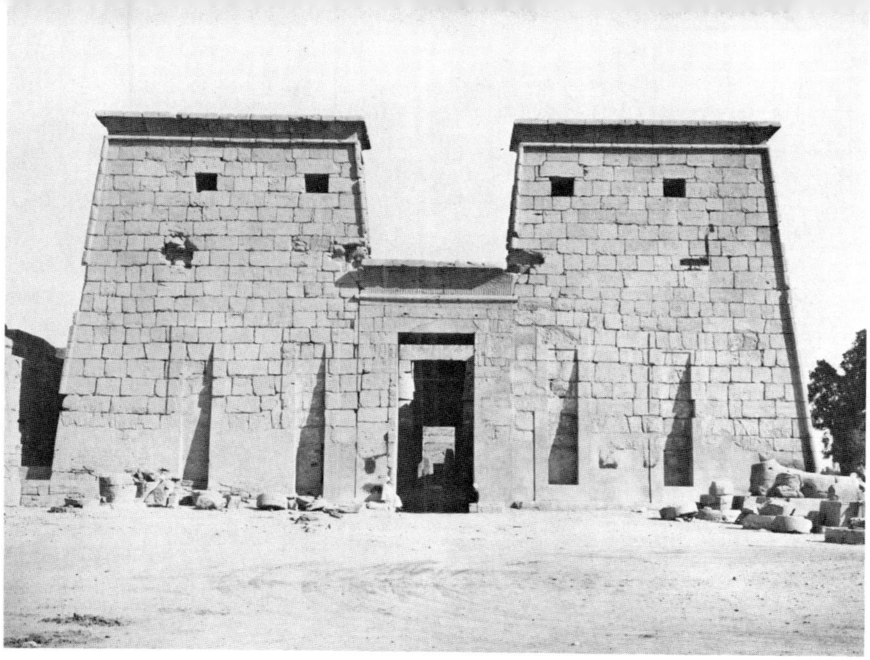

42 Temple of Khonsu, Karnak. 12th century B.C.

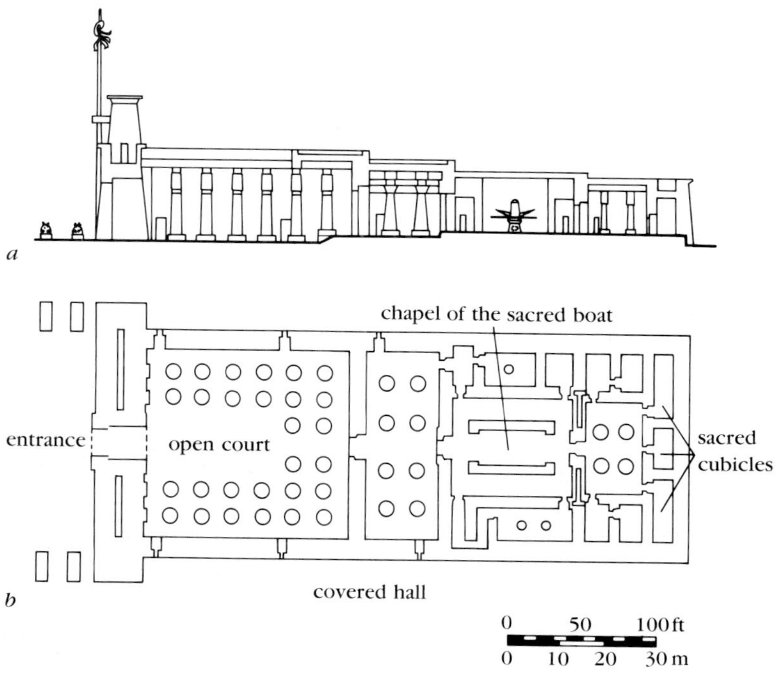

43 Section *(a)* and groundplan *(b)* of Temple of Khonsu.

entrance side [43a]. The gateway opens into a court, the first of a succession of spaces that formed the processional route of the ancient priests [43b]. This route is flanked by **columns** of various sizes. The Egyptians were the first people, it seems, to introduce rows of regular columns, a structural device that continued, with changes and refinements, among the Greeks, Romans, and Europeans of later times.

The basic aim of the design is to create a single path from the entrance to the shrine area at the back. This central path is known as the *axis*—a term used in a sense similar to that of the *axis of symmetry* (see page 16). Following the axis, one moves from the open court to the covered hall, then to a special chapel holding a sacred boat, and finally to the obscure and sacred cubicles that housed the images of the god. Each area or room along the axis becomes progressively darker and smaller. When the temple was used for worship, the public was never allowed into the most sacred areas, but could see the god on ceremonial occasions when his statue was brought out on his sacred boat.

No longer excluded from any part of the Egyptian temple, modern visitors can wander through the building at their own pace, following the axis or straying from it as they grasp the details that will enable them to form a unified impression of the whole. This experience is significant, for unlike our experience of hearing a symphony or watching a play, we are not required in architecture to follow the axial path undeviatingly or at any particular tempo.

Building Techniques

Architecture, such as the Temple of Khonsu, which employs columns or posts serving as vertical supports and beams serving as horizontal supports for the walls and roofs, is known as **post-and-lintel construction**. Such a building consists, when all is said and done, of rather elementary construction—a grid of verticals and horizontals.

The same post-and-lintel construction is used with very different effect in the temples of ancient Greece. In these, too, columns support horizontal beams that carry the weight of the roof. But the rows of columns create a sharply defined, perfectly proportioned rectangular building. Indeed, the total impression given by the Parthenon [44], the most universally admired of the Greek temples, is one of grace rather than of forbidding massiveness.

44 Ictinus and Callicrates.
The Parthenon, Athens. 447–432 B.C.
Height of columns 34′ (10.36 m).

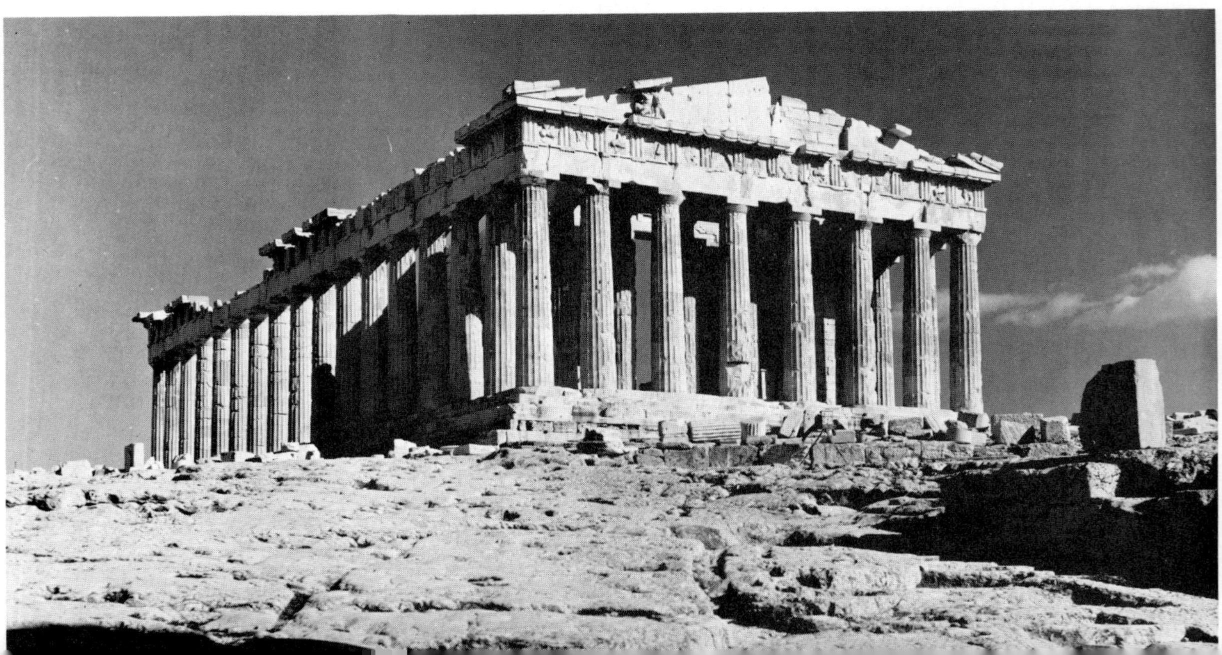

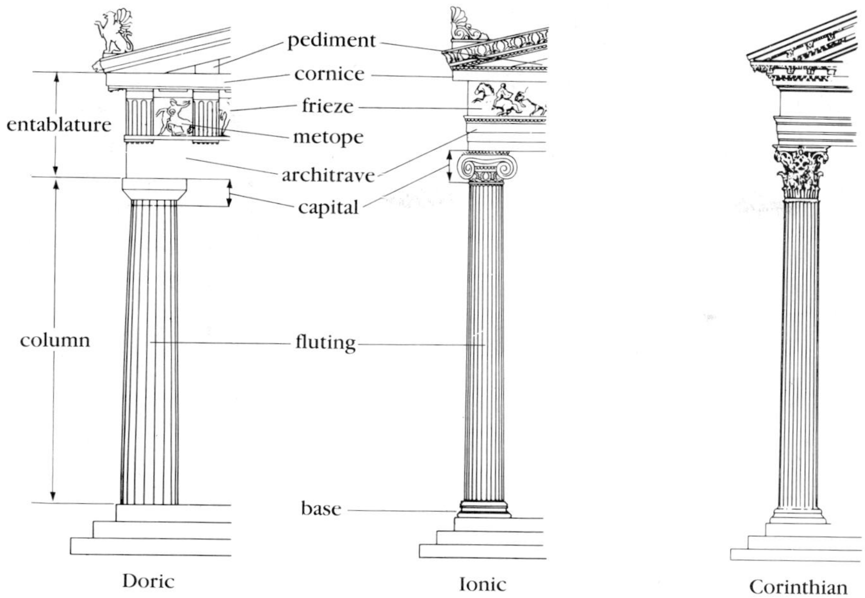

45 The three classical orders.

In the Greek temples in general and the Parthenon in particular, both the horizontal lintels and the upright posts or columns follow well-defined patterns [45]. The horizontal beams that constitute the upper part form what is known as the **entablature**. They are arranged in three layers: the **architrave**, the **frieze**, and the **cornice**. While the architrave, the lowest of the three levels, is plain, the frieze is decorated with shallow sculptures called **metopes**. The cornice at the top, jutting out beyond the frieze, provides a sharp boundary that helps to define the shape of the temple. At the east and west end of the building, the entablature is surmounted by a triangular gable known as the **pediment**, which often contains sculptured figures [46].

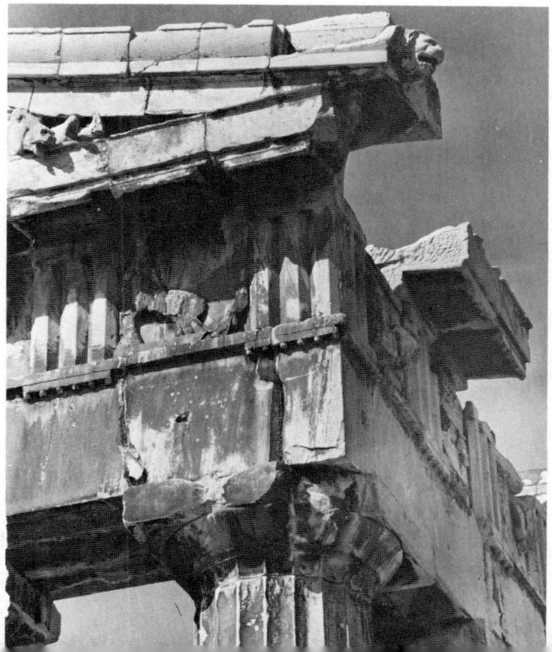

46 Northeast corner of Parthenon. This detailed view shows the upper part of a fluted column with its capital surmounted by the entablature and pediment. Sculptural decorations appear in the metopes, a series of rectangular blocks forming part of the entablature, and in the pediment.

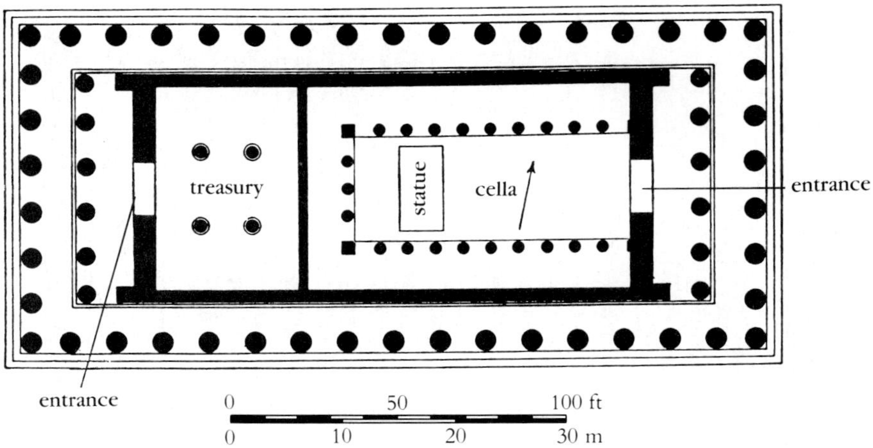

47 Groundplan of the Parthenon.

Each column characteristically ends in a decorated top, or **capital.** The Greeks designed three basic combinations of capitals and their columns: the Doric, Ionic, and Corinthian [see Figure 45, page 51]. This fixed arrangement of elements together with the entablature is called an **order.** Each of the classical orders has a distinctive shape of column and capital as well as of base and **fluting**—the shallow grooves that run the entire height. *Doric* columns are the plainest of the three. Their height is about five-and-a-half times the diameter, they have no separate base, and they taper slightly as they rise. Their capitals consist of a flared circular segment set under a square stone that rests against the architrave. The fluting is usually made up of twenty shallow channels, which emphasize the texture of the marble. In contrast, *Ionic* columns have more delicate proportions, for their height is about eight to ten times the diameter. They have a definite base which raises the lower end of the column from the floor. The distinctive Ionic capital is composed of two spiral swirls that are joined across the front of the column. Ionic fluting has twenty-four narrow and deep channels, each separated by a narrow strip. Finally, the *Corinthian* order combines the slender height of the Ionic column with a type of unified circular capital. Larger than the other two, the Corinthian capital is carved in a stylized foliage pattern often showing two rows of the leaves of the Greek acanthus plant.

The Parthenon, devoted to the worship of the goddess Athena, demonstrates the building techniques of the Greeks at their most subtle. They chose an imposing site at the top of a hill called the Acropolis in the center of Athens. The appearance of lightness and grace for which the temple is famous is due largely to the treatment of the Doric columns, the careful attention the architects gave to the relationship between the height of the columns and their thickness and also to the spacing between the columns. Although most of them are a little more than eight feet apart, those at the corners are slightly closer together, with a little more than six feet between them. The general impression of harmony and ease is further enhanced by the shapes of the

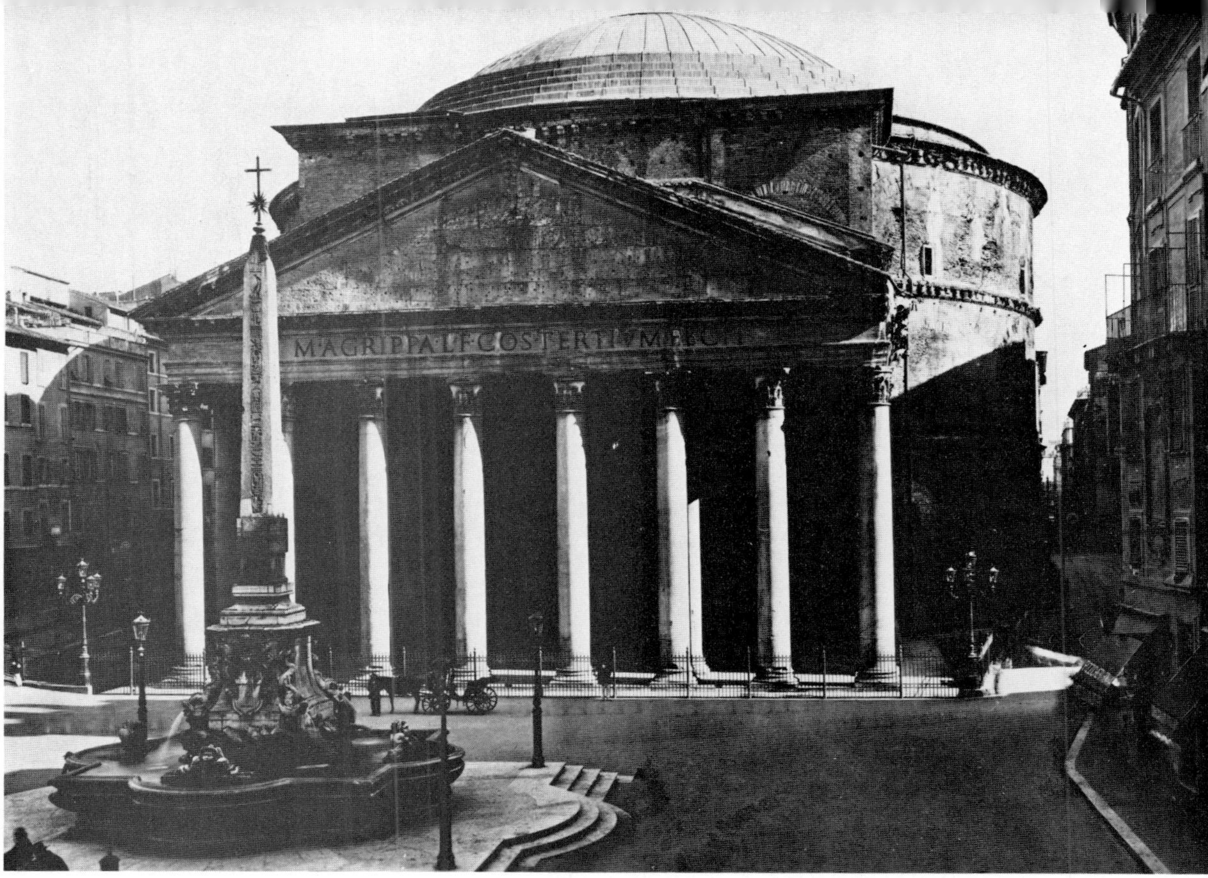

48 Pantheon, Rome. c. 126 A.D. Height of portico 59′ (17.98 m).

columns themselves. Because they each have fluting and are painstakingly tapered, they appear remarkably slender and delicate.

Like the Khonsu temple [see Figure 42, page 49], the Parthenon housed a sacred image that was tended by priests but was not normally accessible to the general public. A colossal statue of Athena, made of ivory and gold, and about forty feet high, dominated the large inner chamber known as the **cella**. But as the groundplan [47] shows, the building was not constructed with a continuous axial path. The only other room in the interior, the treasury, was not connected with the cella. The two chambers—the cella and the treasury—each had a separate entrance at the short end of the building, and those permitted to enter had to choose one of the two paths that, though on the same axis, did not join. Still, the entrances at each end were identical, and this symmetry contributes to the sense of proportion, grace, and harmony of the whole.

A later religious building, the Pantheon [48], constructed in Rome in the early 2nd century A.D., combines post and lintel with other structural principles. The entrance porch features a festive row of Corinthian columns [see Figure 45, page 51]. But the glory of this temple is the interior, which is surmounted by a great **dome** with a small opening to the sky that lets light

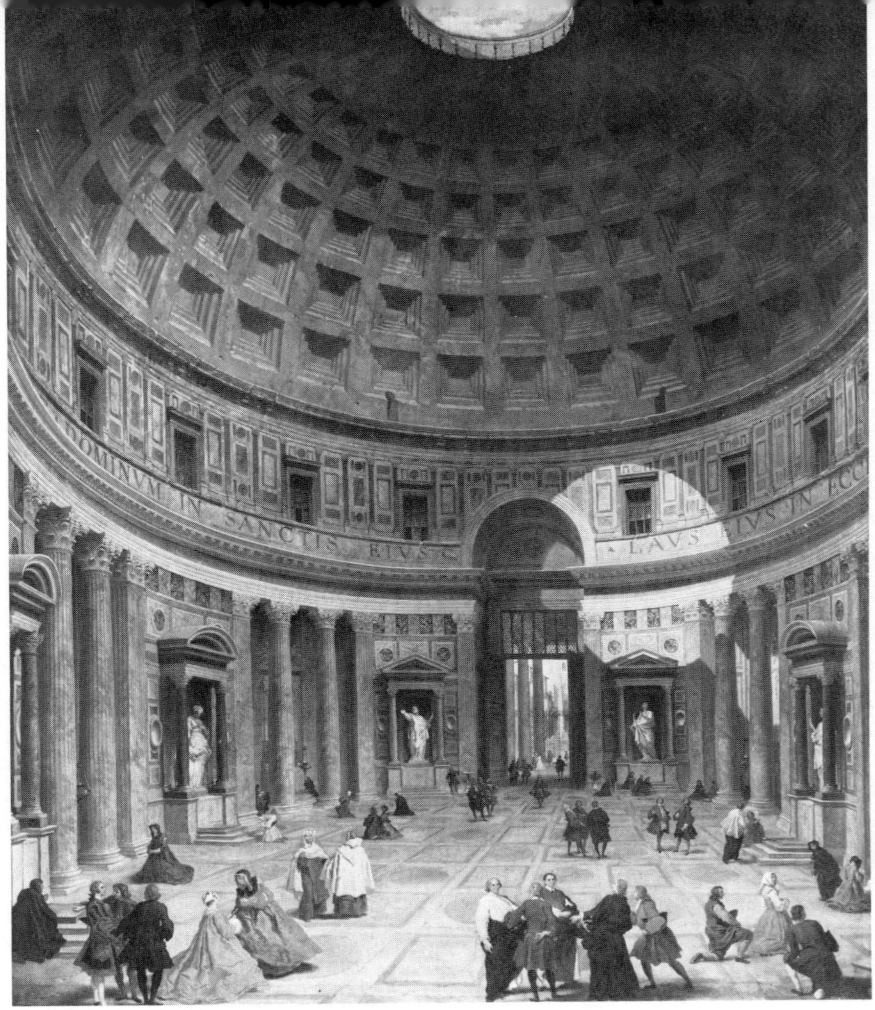

49 Giovanni Paolo Panini. *Interior of the Pantheon.* c. 1750. Oil on canvas, 4′2½″ × 3′3″ (1.28 × .99 m). National Gallery of Art, Washington (Samuel H. Kress Collection).

into the building [49]. In fact, without entirely discarding the post-and-lintel construction of Egyptian and Greek architecture, the Romans fully developed a building procedure using curves, as in the dome of the Pantheon and in the rounded **arches** that are so prominent in many of their designs. Domes and arches are actually related, for a dome can really be thought of as a series of arches placed one behind another that first increase and then decrease in height. In addition to their visual properties, arches permit greater enclosed spaces. They are able to do so because they transmit the load or stress created by the weight of the masonry more efficiently to the ground.

The use of these curved forms was continued in a different way in medieval cathedrals such as the famous Notre Dame of Paris [50], with the soaring pointed arches of **Gothic** architecture. Furthermore, medieval architects sought to increase the area of glass in the upper parts of the building. When they found that this lightening of the structure weakened the building's

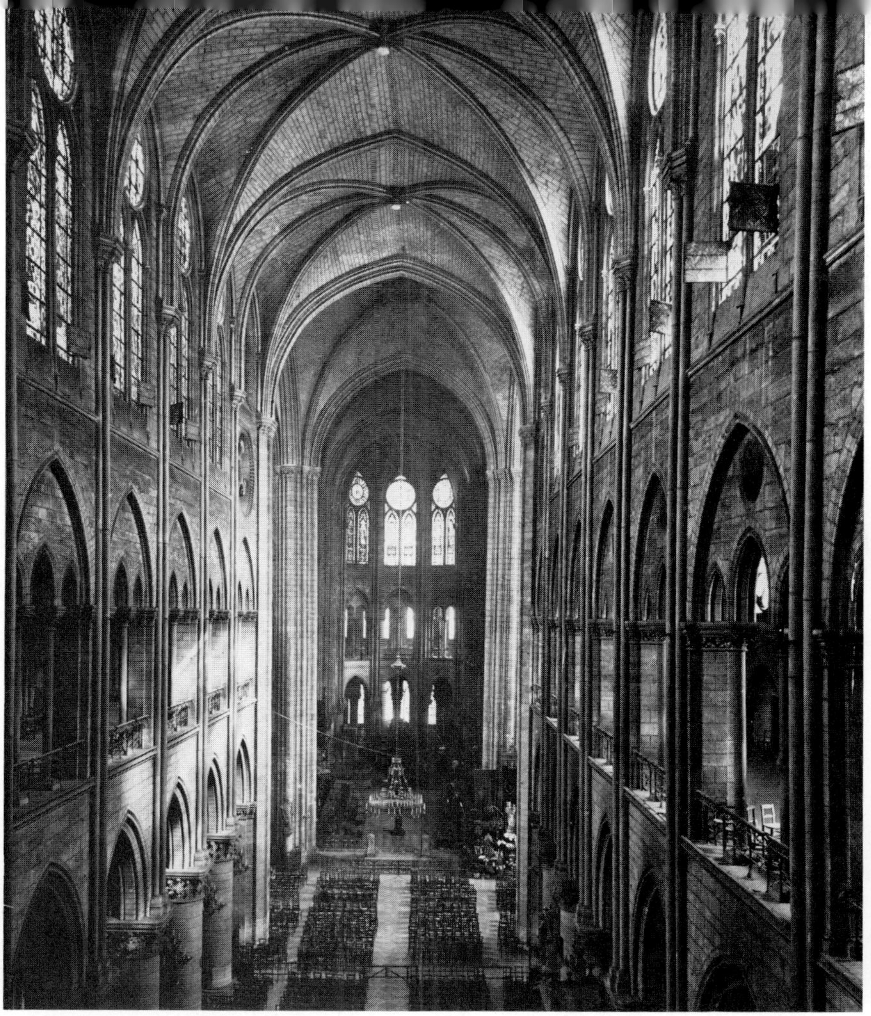

50 Interior of the Cathedral of Notre Dame, Paris. c. 1163–c. 1250. The pointed arches and the many verticals of the nave and choir convey the soaring sense of space characteristic of Gothic cathedrals.

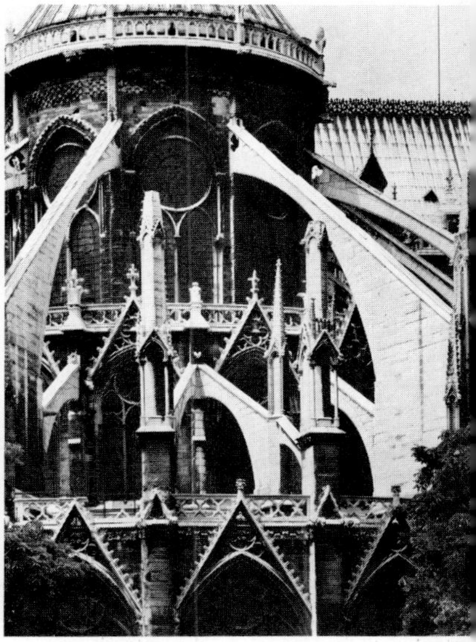

51 Exterior of the Cathedral of Notre Dame, showing flying buttresses.

stability, they devised a new version of the arch in the form of **flying buttresses** [51], half-arches that prop up the building from the outside. Perhaps their name comes from the fact that these arches leap from one part of the building to another so as to prevent the walls from buckling outward.

In the succeeding centuries, both the post-and-lintel and the arch constructions continued to be used, either separately or in combination. The façade of the Palazzo Rucellai [see Figure 23, page 27] combines a strictly vertical-horizontal grid with curved arches over the windows.

Technological advances in the later 19th century offered designers new materials and techniques. Preeminent among these was the use of concrete reinforced with iron and steel. Reinforced concrete sometimes lends itself to striking effects such as the **cantilever**—an extension into space such as a balcony or canopy that appears not to be supported, but is actually maintained by hidden steel girders linking it to the main part of the structure.

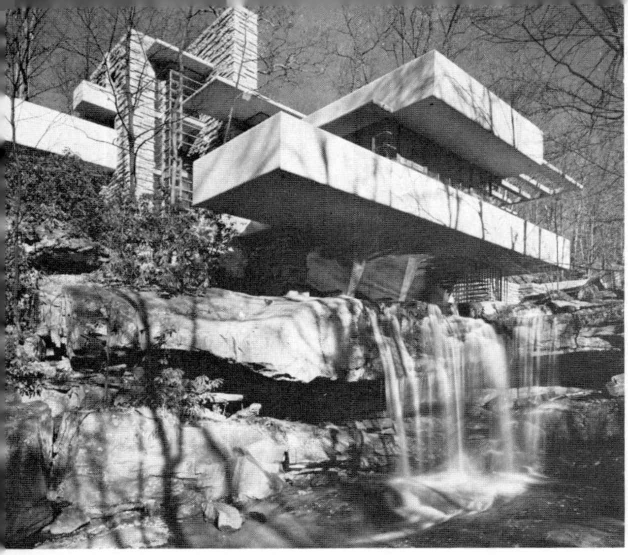

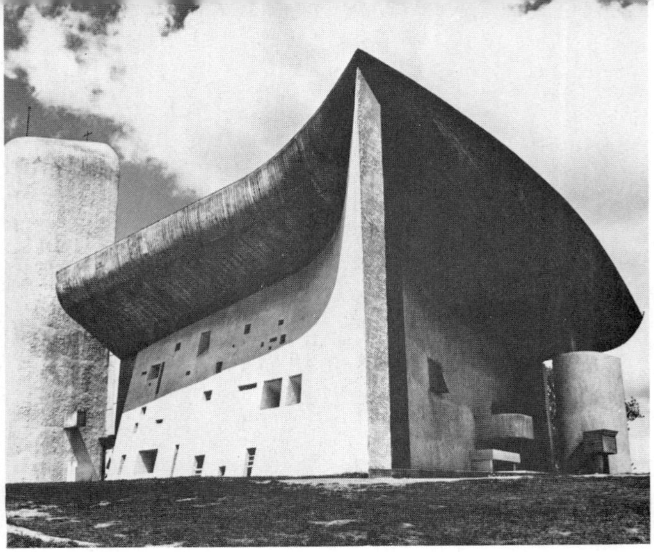

above left: 52 Frank Lloyd Wright. Falling Water (Kaufman House), Bear Run, Pa. 1936–1937.

above right: 53 Le Corbusier. Notre Dame du Haut, Ronchamp, France. 1950–1955.

below: 54 Eero Saarinen. Trans World Airlines Flight Center, Kennedy International Airport, New York. 1962. Ezra Stoller © ESTO.

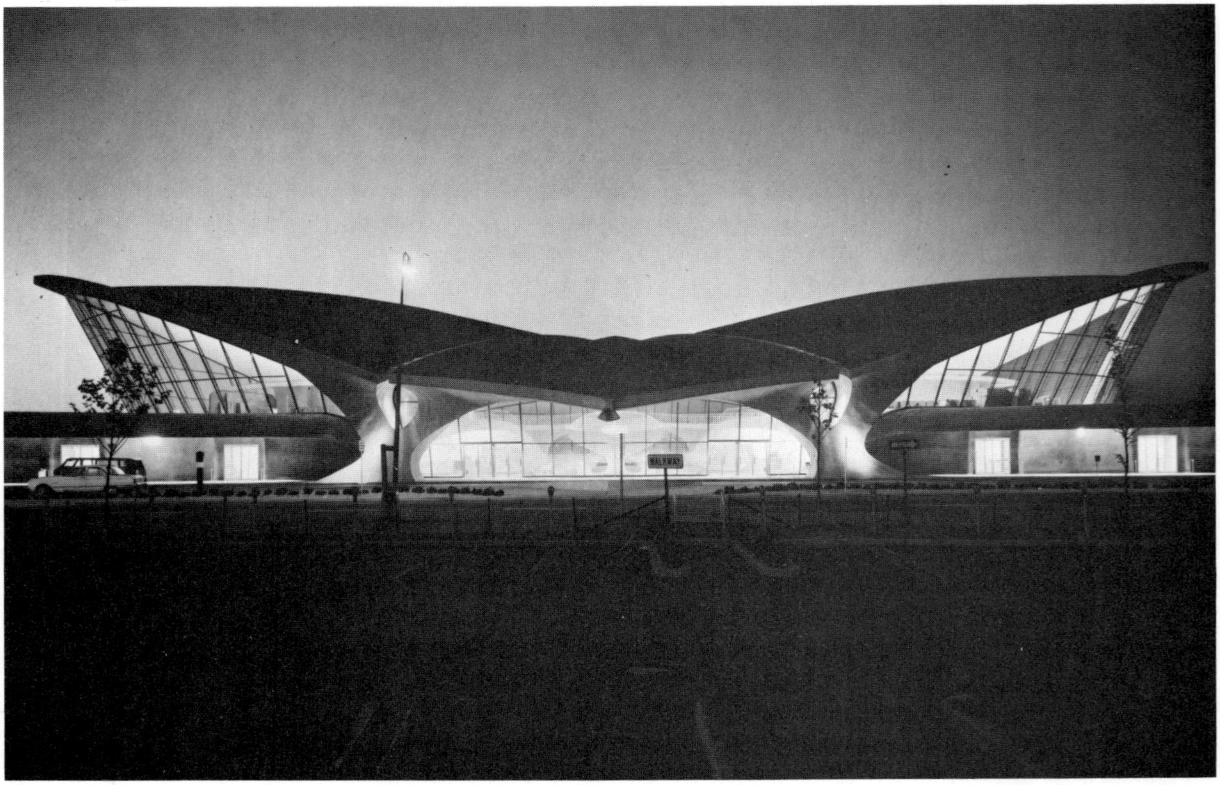

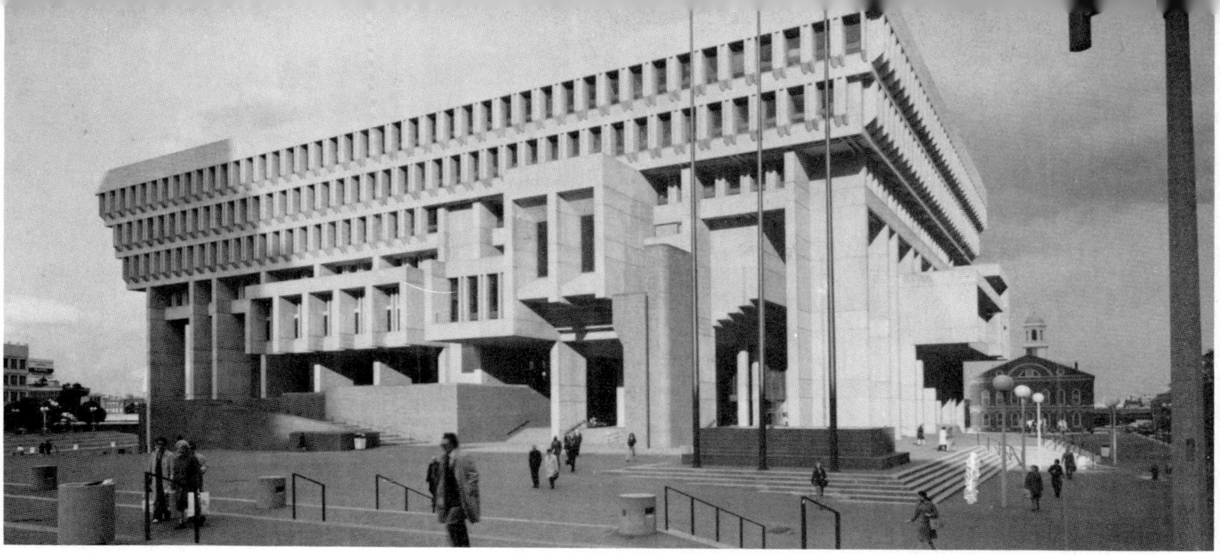

55 Kallmann, McKinnell & Knowles, in association with Campbell, Aldrich & Nulty. Boston City Hall. 1968. Ezra Stoller © ESTO.

Falling Water [52], a private residence designed by Frank Lloyd Wright (1885–1959), is a brilliant and influential example of the use of this technique in domestic architecture. In this residence Wright has dramatically juxtaposed three levels of cantilevering that project in two directions. The whole building seems to float above the stream that gives the house its name.

At the turn of the century, architects were reluctant to exploit modern technological advances for striking effects. They preferred to disguise their new methods by covering them with traditional ornament. The designs of modern architecture that became popular in the 1920s finally revealed in their straightforward simplicity the new forms made possible by technology. Although such designs led to a controversy over the esthetic merits of the "new nakedness" which continues to this day, some architects have used the new methods to achieve highly dramatic effects. The famous church of Notre Dame du Haut at Ronchamp [53] in eastern France designed by Le Corbusier (1887–1965) seems more like a sculpture than a building. It does not adhere to the grid of the post-and-lintel tradition, nor does it display the regular curved features of the arch and dome. Its billowing forms were designed just for this building, giving it a previously inconceivable expressiveness. A little later, a similar but more regularly shaped set of billowing forms was chosen by Eero Saarinen (1912–1960) for an airline terminal [54]. Here the wing-like shapes prepare passengers for the experience of flight. Yet another contemporary building, the Boston City Hall [55] by Gerhard Kallmann (b. 1915), Michael McKinnell (b. 1935), and Edward Knowles (b. 1929) is in the post-and-lintel mode, but uses cantilevering so that the upper stories jut out beyond the lower ones. The arrangement of the lower box-like units is irregular or asymmetrical, appropriate for the variety of functions that a modern city administration must fulfill. In addition, the architects, taking advantage of their site at the center of the Boston government complex, have cleverly designed the mayor's private office to look out on 18th-century Faneuil Hall, visible at the far right. Closely identified with the American Revolution, this hall serves as a constant reminder of the roots of American democracy.

Questions for Study and Discussion

1. What are the chief differences between the arts of space and the arts of time? What kinds of works are exceptions to this basic classification?
2. How does the total composition—the use of symmetrical and dynamic balance in the arrangement of the figures—contribute to the impression of motion and rest in Botticelli's *The Birth of Venus* [see Figure 12, page 18]? What effect of motion or rest is created by blocking from view the figures on both the left and the right of the goddess? What different effect is created by blocking out only the right-hand third of the painting?
3. Contrast the hue, value, and intensity of color as well as the general color scheme of Botticelli's *The Birth of Venus* [see Figure 12, page 18] and Van Gogh's *The Night Café* [see Plate 4, page 36]. How important are the differences in establishing the mood of the two paintings? What would be achieved if *The Night Café,* an oil painting, used the hue, value, and intensity of the colors in Dürer's *Italian Mountains* [see Plate 6, page 38], a watercolor?
4. How important is line in the Niaux Cave painting [see Figure 16, page 20], Jackson Pollock's *Convergence* [see Figure 18, page 21], Mondrian's *Composition with Red, Blue, and Yellow* [see Plate 1, page 33], and Duccio's *Annunciation* [see Plate 3, page 35]? Is Duccio's use of line closer to Botticelli's [see Figure 12, page 18] or to Rembrandt's *Nightwatch* [see Plate 2, page 34]—two artists who use line in totally different ways?
5. Describe the characteristic effects created by each of the graphic arts—engraving, etching, and woodcut. Could Piranesi's prison scene [see Figure 25, page 28] be presented as a woodcut, and what would be the effect if one tried?
6. In what sense does each of the three images of David [see Figures 34, 35, and 36, pages 43, 44] represent a *pregnant moment?* How do the facial expressions and physical poses suggest different interpretations of David's character?
7. Some art critics have suggested that modern artists are less likely than earlier ones to be interested in the pregnant moment. If so, what does this fact suggest about modern conceptions of life, particularly our notions about the possibility of significant action which will determine an inevitable course of events?
8. Examine the treatment of time in the various scenes of Rogier van der Weyden's *Christ Appearing to His Mother* [see Figure 40, page 46]. What is the time relationship between the center background and the center foreground? What is unexpected in the placing of scenes A to F on the arch above? What religious ideas are emphasized by this treatment of time in space?
9. Locate examples of post and lintel, columns with various types of capitals, arches, domes, and cantilever construction in the buildings of your community. To what extent is the technique used related to the function of the building and the period in which it was constructed? Do these buildings harmonize with the surrounding space?

CHAPTER 2

Components of the Arts of Time

Unlike the arts of space, music and literature exist in time and appeal to the ear or directly to the mind rather than to the eye. They are apprehended in minutes and hours, not in inches and yards. Music is experienced in a strictly temporal sequence, for we do not have control over the order in which we receive our impressions. Music is also a purely *auditory* form, which requires a different effort of concentration for most of us, for whom vision is the primary sense. Spoken literature is also an auditory form, but much of the time we enjoy poetry, prose, and plays silently through reading. In this case, we have some control over the sequence—if we miss something, we can go back and reread it.

Again unlike the spatial arts, which require the mental habit of close attention to the object before us, the temporal arts require at least two additional mental habits: memory and anticipation. Indeed, *memory, attention,* and *anticipation* (or expectation) parallel our concept of time, which consists of past, present, and future. As a piece of music or novel unfolds in time, we need to remember what has happened, attend closely to what is happening at the moment, and anticipate what is going to happen next. All three are necessary, for if we just stay with the tiny point of consciousness that is *now,* the piece will not make much sense. For someone who follows music with a full awareness of what has gone before and what may follow, listening becomes an active process quite different from the passive awareness of background music. Similarly, the active reader will recall the events narrated early in the novel to give meaning to the later course of the plot. We may say that without memory, attention, and anticipation, works of music or literature would have little coherence and give little pleasure.

Music

Most of us have found that our awareness as well as our pleasure in music are increased by knowing its basic components. Music has **notes**, **rhythm**, **melody**, **harmony**, **tone color** or **timbre**, and **tonality**. It also has a larger form or structure, whether divided into movements or not. We have a basic human tendency to segment a work when it is unfolding in time, just as we segment time into minutes, hours, days, and weeks. And so we should learn to perceive the individual parts and at the same time to comprehend the whole of a piece of music as it unfolds.

Notes

In the same way as we might discuss time by beginning with the smallest units, considering perhaps the second as the smallest normal subdivision, so we may analyze the elements of music by beginning with the smallest units. First, music is composed of sounds—individual *notes*—and of silences or *rests* which occupy the spaces between the notes. Most music seems to conceal this simple fact because composers want to draw us to their particular expressions and make us aware of the flow of the music. Some contemporary music, however, calls attention to the individual notes and silences. For example, the Pulitzer Prize–winning composer Charles Wuorinen (b. 1938) in his *Time's Encomium* (1969) uses an electronic synthesizer and magnetic recording tape to manipulate individual notes in a highly ordered way. This organization may not be self-evident, since Wuorinen has consciously avoided most patterns that sound like traditional kinds of melody. The notes give a disjointed impression and are more than usually conspicuous as individual elements.

What is immediately apparent in a work of this kind is that the notes vary in several specific ways, which we may consider the fundamental qualities of sound. These qualities have been given the following names:

- Pitch = How high or low?
- Duration = How long or short?
- Intensity (dynamics, sound volume) = How loud or soft?
- Tone color, timbre = What quality of sound?

We should realize that in and of themselves, these individual tonal characteristics seem to convey almost nothing (although a loud sound may convey alarm). Normally, to have meaning, these fundamental qualities must be combined in various ways.

Rhythm

Since music is an art of time, rhythm, the subject that deals with all aspects of musical time, is obviously fundamental. Just as a human heart beats at a steady rate, so most music has a steady pulse, or *beat.* But *rhythm* is actually a complex term that includes, besides the underlying pulse and its speed, the pattern of note durations.

Let us begin by combining several notes of equal **duration**, but systematically varying the **intensity**. If we simply say "LOUD soft LOUD soft LOUD soft," we have created a simple musical rhythm. Rhythm is often considered the most basic element of music, since it can exist even without notes of specific pitch.

As in our "LOUD soft" example, steady beats are grouped in repeated patterns of greater and lesser *stress,* or emphasis. Each stress group is a measure or bar of music. The most common patterns are those in which the beats are repeated in stress-groups of two, three, or four. For example, a two-beat rhythm is strong on beat 1, weaker on beat 2. In a three-beat rhythm, the first beat is again the strongest, while in a four-beat pattern, the main stress is on beat 1 with a secondary stress on beat 3. This repeated pattern of stressed and unstressed beats is called the **meter** of the music, a term that is used in a very similar way in describing the rhythm of poetry. In practice, we can easily call to mind the meter of some rhythmic pieces such as "The Stars and Stripes Forever" march (two beats) and the "Blue Danube" waltz (three beats).

Pieces such as these have a very strongly marked beat and a very regular rhythm. Other pieces, such as *Time's Encomium,* are very irregular in rhythm, and cannot be counted in simple twos and threes. However, we can still tell that some portions of such a piece are fast or slow. The *speed* of a piece (or the speed of the beat in metrical music) is called the **tempo**. Human beings seem to react to tempo by a kind of automatic association with the rate of breathing and of the heartbeat. That is, a fast piece seems to make a listener feel literally breathless, while a slow one tends to calm a listener down and to slow the heart rate. A moderate tempo is felt when the beat is about seventy per minute, roughly the same as the average adult heart rate.

Traditionally, composers indicate the tempo at the beginning of a piece of music. These tempo markings are generally written in Italian. They were first used only by Italian opera composers, but gradually the Italian words

Tempo Indications

Italian	*English*
largo	broadly, very slow
adagio	quite slow
lento	slow
andante	moderately slow
moderato	moderate, medium speed
allegretto	moderately fast
allegro	fast (originally "cheerful")
vivace	lively, faster than *allegro*
presto	very fast

were adopted by composers of other nations. Some of these terms suggest the general character of the piece as well as indicating its speed. The list of common tempo indications given here is arranged from slowest to fastest.

Musical rhythm involves more than just meter and tempo. What we hear as the rhythm of the music is the variation in the time values (durations) and stress (intensity) of the many notes that make up a piece, against a background of the underlying beat. In a piece like "The Entertainer" (1902) by Scott Joplin (1868–1917), the contrast between the rhythm and the meter is made particularly obvious by the device called **syncopation.** This is created by placing a strong stress on a normally weak beat, or part of a beat, or by omitting the expected stress on a strong beat.

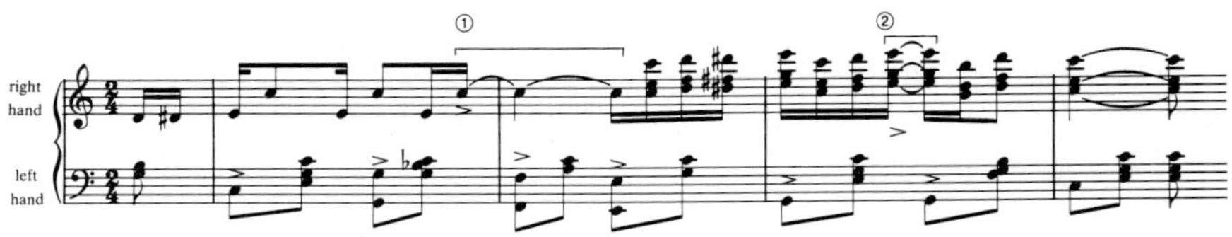

Example 1 Scott Joplin. *"The Entertainer."*

At ① and ② of Example 1, this effect of syncopation can be seen graphically, even by those of us who do not read music. The left hand, as the accent mark (>) shows, plays a steady beat, two stresses to each measure. The right hand plays its stressed notes (>) at moments that do not coincide with the left-hand beat. These notes are stressed and made more emphatic by the lack of a melody note on the strong beat. The curved line, called a *tie* (⌒), shows that a note is sustained but not struck again. (The Appendix describes the system of musical notation in greater detail.)

Syncopated effects predominate in jazz and rock music, but are also fairly common in the works of some traditional composers such as Bach and Beethoven, whose music has a strong rhythmic component.

Melody

After rhythm, perhaps the most important musical element is *melody.* In any tune we can remember, melody results when we combine the element of pitch with rhythm. Melodies are enormously varied, ranging from simple tunes with only a few different pitches such as "My Country, 'Tis of Thee" or "Happy Birthday" to complex and wide-ranging ones. Melodies can be partially described in everyday language as simple, complex, expressive, charming, or mysterious. But a few technical terms help to make the description more exact. The musician notices the **intervals** between different pairs of **pitches**; two notes that are close together in pitch differ by a *step,* wider intervals are described as *skips* or *leaps* in the melody line. A melody that varies very little between its lowest and highest notes has a *narrow range,* or *compass,* as is seen in the melody line of "My Country, 'Tis of Thee" [Example

2]. This familiar melody, originally English and still sung in Great Britain as "God Save the King" (or "Queen"), covers a range of only seven notes from the F-sharp of "'tis" to the E of "Let."

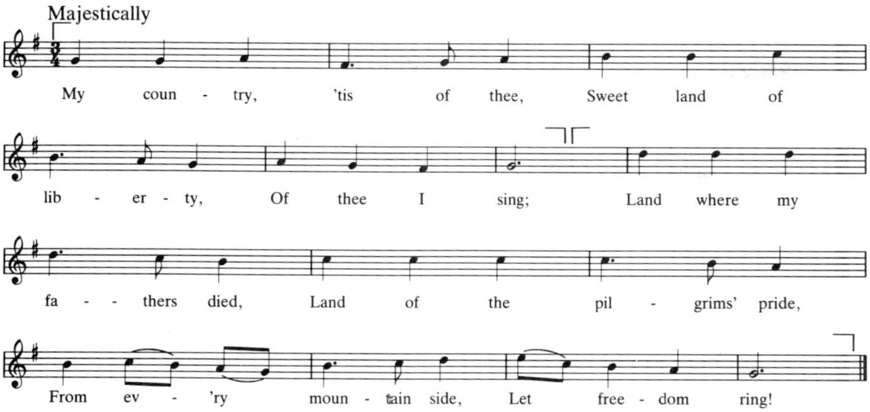

Example 2 "My Country, 'Tis of Thee."

Melodies of any length are divided by brief resting points, called **cadences**, into segments called **phrases**. For example, "My Country, 'Tis of Thee" has two cadences and consequently two phrases. The first phrase ends at "Of thee I sing"; the second phrase ends at "Let freedom ring!" Paired brackets have been added in Example 2 to show the beginnings and ends of phrases.

In contrast to the simple melody we have been considering, a far more complicated one can be found in the opening notes [Example 3] of *Ein Heldenleben* ("A Life of a Hero") by Richard Strauss (1864–1949).

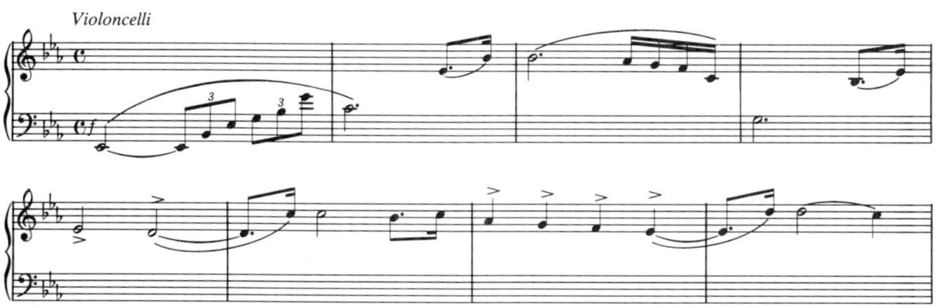

Example 3 Richard Strauss. *Ein Heldenleben* (reduction), main theme.

As can be seen from the placement of the notes, this melody varies greatly between its lowest and highest notes and so has a wide range or compass. Its complexity is also evident in its many skips and leaps—the great variety of its melodic intervals.

The most important concept about melody for understanding music as a whole is the idea of the *melodic curve*. This concept permits us to discuss the melody as a unit of emotional expression, for it leads us to examine both the rhythm of the melody and its rise and fall in pitch. Higher notes in the melody line seem to have greater tension and are, as a general rule, found at or near the climax of the melodic curve. Lower pitches usually begin and end the melodic curve.

For instance, the spiritual "Swing Low, Sweet Chariot" has a memorable melodic curve that echoes the words. The curve descends to a lower pitch with the words "Swing low" and ascends with the important words "coming for to carry me home," suggesting salvation in heaven. At the same time, the rhythmic rise and fall and the slow tempo reinforce the general mood of consolation.

In a more complex melody such as the duet "Bess, You Is My Woman Now," which George Gershwin (1898–1937) wrote for his opera *Porgy and Bess* (1935), the melodic curve includes many smaller rises and falls, many subsidiary climaxes. It seems to express far more than the words alone—yearning, desire, excitement, joy, and even the undercurrent of tragedy inherent in the story of the opera. Exactly how music expresses what it does, remains something of a mystery, but almost anyone accustomed to Western music will feel that Gershwin's melody expresses passionate emotion.

Harmony

The third important element of music after rhythm and melody is *harmony*. The term is used for the way in which different pitches sound together. When three or more different pitches are arranged to sound simultaneously, they form a **chord**. When they sound one after another in close succession, they form a **broken chord**. Harmony may, in fact, be defined as the structure and movement of chords.

Harmony may be the most complex element of music. When a composer writes a series of chords, a listener will normally hear only one note of each chord—the highest note—as the melody note. Since note succeeds note in performance, the listener is aware not simply of chords but also, over a period of time, of a melodic and rhythmic progression. In listening, we cannot isolate the harmony and deal with it as if it were independent of other musical elements.

Chords can be described by the *intervals*, the distance between pairs of pitches, that constitute each chord. This distance is expressed as an ordinal number (second, third, fourth, and so on), which can be quickly read on the musical staff by counting lines and spaces [see Example 4]. We must remember to count all the lines and spaces that are occupied by and are between each note of the interval.

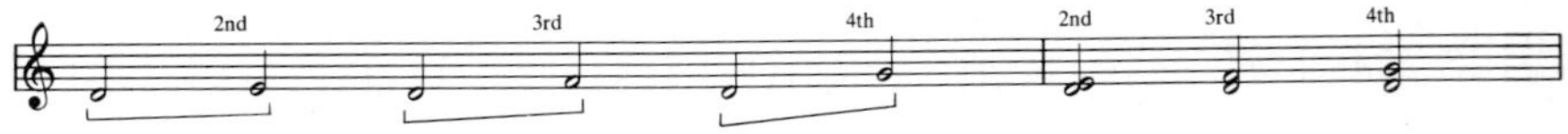

Example 4 Some musical intervals.

Since a chord consists of at least three distinct pitches, it includes a minimum of three intervals: between the two lower notes, between the two upper notes, and between the highest and lowest notes [Example 5]. For

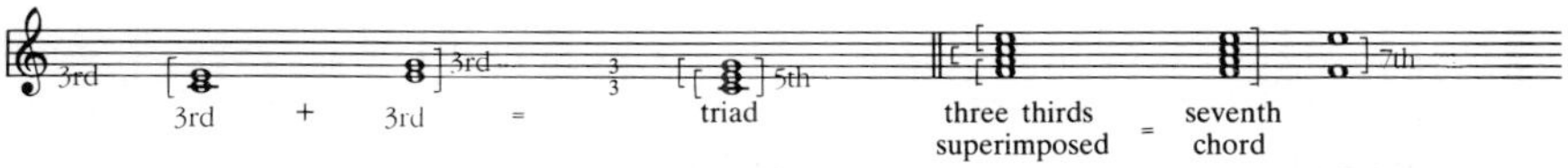

Example 5 Triads.

instance, a three-note chord, made up of two thirds and the outer fifth, is a **triad.** A four-note chord, consisting of three thirds, is commonly called a *seventh* chord because the interval from lowest to highest note is a seventh [Example 6].

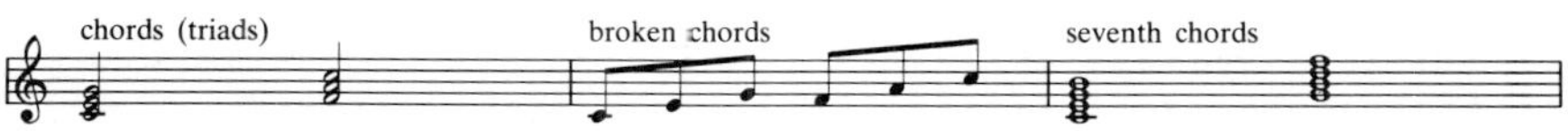

Example 6 Triads, broken chords, and seventh chords.

To the listener, the most important aspect of chords is not their individual construction, but the way in which one chord follows another. This is termed *chord progression.* Designating chords by their fundamental or lowest note, called the *root* of the chord, is helpful in analyzing chord progression. The basic triad consisting of C-E-G has the C as its fundamental note or root. And so a shorthand designation for the entire chord is "C-triad" or "C-chord" [Example 7].

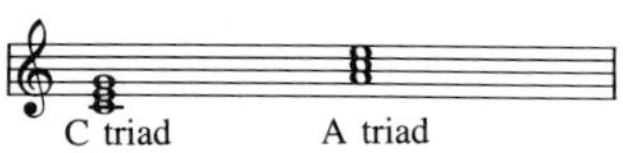

Example 7 Triads and roots.

In Western music, the most important chord progression usually occurs between two chords with roots that are the interval of a fifth apart. Thus, the chord G-B-D (root G) progresses to the chord C-E-G (root C), since G is a fifth from C (C-D-E-F-G). In the same way, the A-chord progresses to the D-chord since A is five notes above D (D-E-F-G-A), the C-chord to the F-chord (F-G-A-B-C), and so on through the various keys [Example 8]. Traditional

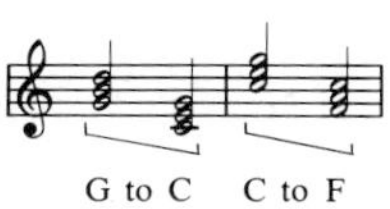

Example 8 Two progressions: G Major to C Major and C Major to F Major.

terms are used to define this interval relationship. The fundamental note of any key is its **tonic**; the note a fifth above is the **dominant.** The same terms also refer to the chords built on these notes. Summarizing our discussion, we can speak of a progression from dominant to tonic. This is, in fact, the most important harmonic progression in Western music.

The tonic and dominant chords are most commonly paired to reinforce a melodic **cadence**, a resting point or relaxation of tension in a musical phrase. And the movement from the dominant to the tonic is often called a harmonic cadence. We can hear it accompanying the last two melody notes of each phrase of "My Country, 'Tis of Thee" as well as accompanying the final notes of "The Star-Spangled Banner" and "Happy Birthday." Most compositions end with this cadence, and many internal cadences use it, also.

Normally, the melodic cadence is strongly confirmed and reinforced by the appropriate chord progression. Indeed, in any key, only the tonic chord provides a truly satisfying point of rest, and all other chords are heard as to some extent transitional. At the same time, each simple triad is composed of three notes that harmonize. To express this relationship in musical terms, we can say that the three notes of a common triad are *consonant* with one another, with no harshness or tension arising from the juxtaposition of the tones.

Composers may, however, use groupings of tones that are not consonant. In this case, a melody note whose relation to an underlying chord is not harmonious will be heard as a source of tension. A note of such **dissonance** must sooner or later find its **resolution** in a consonant chord. And some chords, such as seventh chords, include dissonant intervals and are themselves dissonant chords. In other words, a musical dissonance is a combination of harmonic tones that must resolve to a consonance, and the consonant chord functions as a point of rest in the composition. By using a satisfying proportion of consonant and dissonant harmonies, a composer achieves a balance between the need for calm, satisfying sounds and the equally great need for sounds that are unsettled and propelling. Dissonance should not be confused with discord; the former is an essential part of all harmonic music.

Harmony may be not only the most abstract element in music but also the newest. The complexity of the harmonic system is one of the distinguishing features of Western music. No other civilization has developed this element of music to such an extent. Composers today continue to experiment with new chord combinations, exploiting dissonant chord progressions to the point where the sound is uncomfortable to some listeners. Indeed, the extensive use of dissonance prevents many people from enjoying 20th-century music. Nevertheless, we must remember that dissonance provides the driving energy for our sense of harmonic progression and that music consisting only of consonant sounds would be dull and lifeless.

Tone Color, or Timbre

Tone color, also known by the French word **timbre**, is one of the fundamental distinctions between different sounds. The term refers to the special qualities of a particular note as it is produced by different instruments or voices. To most people, the tone color is one of the most obvious aspects of sound. If the identical note, C, is played first by a flute and then by a trumpet, few people have any difficulty identifying which instrument is which. Even when these two instruments play at the same volume of sound (dynamics), they have a particular tone color that is created by their material (wood, silver, or brass), by their construction, and by the manner in which the player's lips produce the sound.

A more technical explanation of why a note played on the flute and the same note played on the trumpet are distinctive in tone color is that each has its own mix of component pitches. Called *overtones* or **harmonics**, these pitches can be most easily demonstrated with stringed instruments. When we lightly touch a vibrating string at specific points, we force the principal pitch to stop sounding and allow one or more of the harmonics to emerge. Although the listener cannot distinguish these multiple pitches or harmonics, they are crucial in determining the tone color.

To a limited degree, different tonal qualities can be produced on a single instrument. The human voice offers an especially rich variety of timbres. But the greatest resource of tone color for today's composer is the variety of instruments available in a symphony orchestra.

The orchestra To the composer, the orchestra is what palette and oils are to the painter—a collection of different hues and tints waiting for an artist to reveal their expressive potential.

So important for tone color are the possibilities of the various instruments that we should become familiar with the great range of these in an orchestra. We can best appreciate this range if we are aware of the components of a modern symphony orchestra, noticing how each group produces its distinctive sounds and even how the groups are usually placed on stage. The approximately one hundred players of such an orchestra are subdivided into four groups—strings, woodwinds, brass, and percussion.

1. Strings: Violins
Violas
Violoncelli (cellos)
Double-basses (bass viols)
Harp
2. Woodwinds: Flutes (and piccolo)
Oboes (and English horn)
Clarinets (and bass clarinet)
Bassoons (and contra-bassoon)
3. Brass(winds): Trumpets
French horns (or simply, horns)
Trombones
Tuba
4. Percussion: Tympani (or kettledrums)
Snare drum
Bass drum
Cymbals
Triangle
Xylophone
Various other instruments that are struck to produce sound

The instruments in each group share similar means of sound production. The *string instruments,* for instance, create sound when the player causes the strings to vibrate. Each of the bowed string instruments, such as the violin, viola, cello, and bass viol, has four sounding strings made of gut or wire which produce a tone when a bow made of wood and horsehair is drawn across them. The sound is amplified by the wooden box, shaped and varnished by methods discovered in the 17th century by Italians such as Stradivarius (1644–1737) to produce a tone of great beauty. The harp, another orchestral string instrument, is played not by bowing but by plucking its fifty-six strings with the fingers.

The *wind instruments* create sound when the player's wind supply vibrates a flexible material of some kind. For the oboe, clarinet, and bassoon, this material is a piece of carefully shaped cane called "the reed." The *brass instruments* all use the player's lips as the vibrating "reed." Only the flute, with its larger and smaller cousins the alto flute and the piccolo, works without a vibrating solid. Instead, the player's breath passes over an oval hole and produces a tone exactly in the way one can produce a sound by blowing across the mouth of a bottle.

The *percussion section* produces sound when the player strikes a vibrating part of the instrument. This section has many subcategories: instruments that have pitch, such as the xylophone, and those that do not, such as the bass drum; those that have a stretched membrane, such as the drums, and those made of metal, such as cymbals and the triangle. Even the piano, with strings

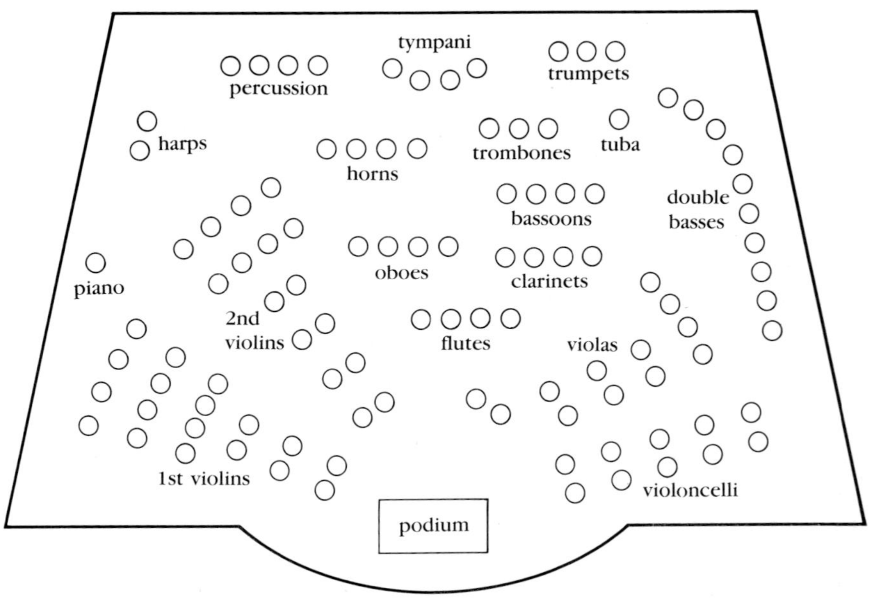

56 Seating plan of a modern symphony orchestra.

struck by felt-covered hammers, is considered a percussion instrument in the orchestra.

The performers of these instruments are seated on stage in roughly the same arrangement at most concerts [56]. The number of players of each instrument varies considerably in order to balance the volume and the tone color of the four sections. To create this balanced sound, the violinists always outnumber the other performers.

The tonal resources of the orchestra are so great and the possibilities for different and intriguing combinations so many that an entire field of study for the composer that is called *orchestration* is now devoted to their exploration.

Tonality

One of the central organizing principles of Western music is *tonality*. Each section of a piece is in a specific key, which is determined by the principal pitches (melodic notes) to be used. These pitches can be arranged from low to high, forming a **scale.** Beginning with any of the twelve fundamental pitches, the composer can erect either a *major* or a *minor scale,* so that the total number of keys available is twenty-four. The key chosen for the opening and closing of the piece is normally the principal tonality which determines the key of the piece. The keys chosen for the various other sections are related in specific ways to the principal tonality.

J. S. Bach (1685–1750), one of the first composers to exploit this scale system in a rigorously systematic way, wrote two volumes of preludes and **fugues** for keyboard instruments, called the *Well-Tempered Clavier*. For each volume, he wrote a prelude and a fugue in each key, arranging them in order beginning on C major, so that each volume has twenty-four preludes and twenty-four fugues (the first in C major, the second in C minor, the third in C-sharp major, and so on).

In listening to any of these preludes or fugues, we become aware of the difference in character that the differing major or minor modes give each piece. Major is heard most often as bright, cheerful, noble, or calm; minor is, by contrast, somber, sorrowful, tragic, or agitated and angry. This traditional key system has been avoided by many modern composers, but is by no means obsolete, since an appreciation of these associative qualities is taken for granted in almost all music commonly heard.

To understand why the major and minor scales sound so different, we must realize that the distances between the pitches of the major scale are different from those of the minor. These distances, which can be whole or half-steps, are marked by *sharps* (♯) and *flats* (♭). A sharp is a symbol for raising the pitch of a note by a half-step; a flat is a symbol for lowering the pitch a half-step. The distance from C to D is one whole step (or whole tone), while the distance from C to C-sharp (C ♯) or from C-sharp to D is a half-step.

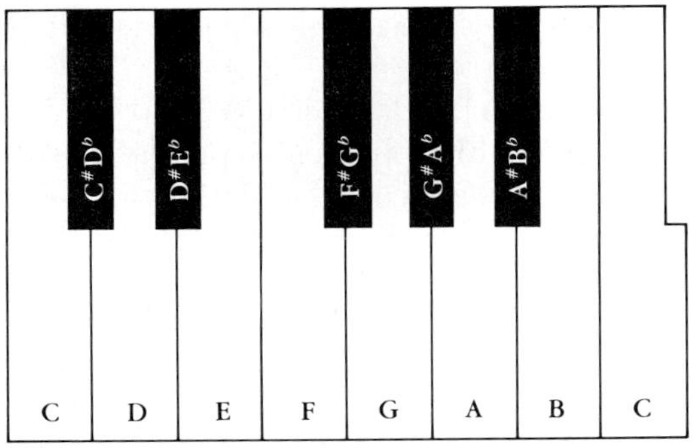

57 One octave of the piano keyboard.

On the piano keyboard [57], the half-step is immediately recognizable as the distance between two adjacent piano keys; a whole step has one additional piano key between its two pitches. On a fretted string instrument such as the guitar [58], a whole step requires the player's finger to move up two frets; a half-step, only one fret. In all major scales, half-steps occur between the third and fourth, and again between the seventh and eighth, pitches or degrees. The remaining steps of the major scale are all whole steps. In contrast, minor scales follow several patterns, but all have a half-step between the second and third pitches or degrees. For example, the C-major scale begins with the notes C, D, E; whereas the C-minor scale begins with the notes C, D, E-flat (E♭). How astonishing that the slight change of one or two half-steps can so fundamentally affect the sound and mood created by the two scales!

Form

In music, we are aware of form on at least two different levels—in small units and in the larger organization. We have already discussed form at the phrase level by using terms such as *cadence, phrase,* and **melodic curve**—all basic elements of musical form. An additional small-scale feature of musical form is the **motive.** This term is used to define a small group of notes,

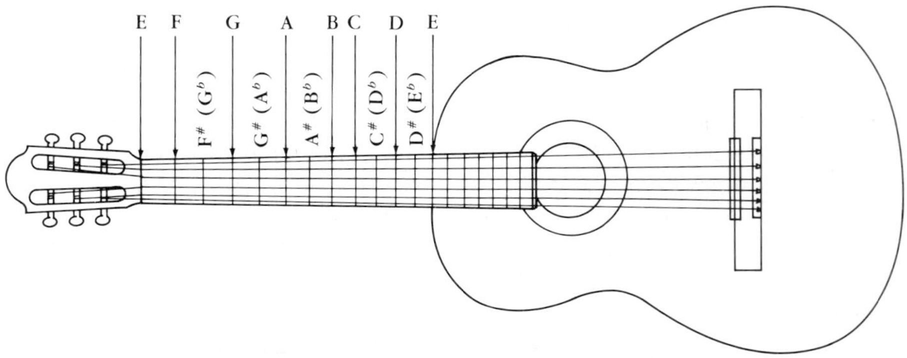

58 Guitar pitches on an E string.

shorter than a phrase, repeated in either melody or rhythm and used as a building block by the composer. For example, a *melodic motive* can be heard in "My Country, 'Tis of Thee" where the first three notes are repeated two steps higher in the third measure at the words "Sweet land of." A *rhythmic motive* can be heard in the same song at measures 2, 4, 8, 10, and 12, where the same rhythm occurs: ♩. ♪ ♩ [see Example 2, page 63]. Although these measures are melodically different, the identical rhythm creates a rhythmic motive.

The large-scale organization of a musical work relies on the recognition of sections, which may be repeated or varied; on tonality or key, which may be emphasized or altered; and on *theme.* Short pieces are often cast in simple sectional forms, designated by capital letters that symbolize the main sections. "My Country, 'Tis of Thee" is a two-part form, because the first phrase differs from the second, and two phrases are all there are. A two-part form can also be called *binary* and may be symbolized by the letters A–B. A song that repeats its first section to create a more rounded feeling is a three-part, *ternary* form, or A–B–A form. "Old Folks at Home" and many similar popular and **folk songs** are in three-part form, which is consequently sometimes called "song-form." More complex kinds of formal organization will be considered in later chapters.

Another way of talking about form in music is to emphasize the process by which the composer moves from one idea to another. A composer can choose one of four basic methods: *repetition, contrast, variation,* and *through-composition.* The first three terms are self-explanatory; the last refers to sections that unfold with continuously new material.

The fundamentals of music briefly described here will become clearer as we continue to listen to music in a concentrated way. As we experience more complex pieces of music, our attention may shift from one component to another. We can increase our awareness by consciously singling out first one component and then another at each hearing.

A good example for this purpose is the minuet from *Symphony No. 104 in D Major* (1794–1795), one of the London symphonies of Franz Josef Haydn (1732–1809). At first we may be struck by the lively rhythm. Not so fast as a *presto,* it is an *allegro.* The meter is ¾ time—a three-beat rhythm or triple meter—that is characteristic of many dances, including the minuet. The rhythm of the melody, played primarily by the violins, repeats the fundamental beat-note, here a quarter-note, until the first cadence, which alters the rhythmic pattern.

When we consider the melody, we will probably find the combination of repeated notes memorable, but will not hear a pronounced melodic curve. However, in the middle section of what is basically an A–B–A form, a more curving, lyrical melodic line is presented. In this middle, or B, section, the dynamic level is reduced, the timbre of the instruments changes as the oboe and bassoon emerge, and the key changes from D to B-flat (B♭). Such a key change is known as **modulation.**

If we now focus on the harmony, we can hear the characteristic dominant-to-tonic cadence throughout this piece. In the repeated eight-bar phrase at the beginning, we find almost no other chord than this dominant-to-tonic progression. Haydn consciously chose such a simple and even elementary progression to create the hearty, cheerful mood.

In sum, all of the basic components we have been studying are present in Haydn's minuet, as indeed in almost all music. By repeated listening, we can increase our awareness until we can hear and enjoy all of them, both as individual elements and as part of a coherent whole.

Poetry

We have said that literature also exists in time. The verbal art closest to music is poetry, especially **lyric** poetry, which has a particularly song-like quality. All poetry, like music, has a definite rhythm or meter. In addition, poetry can use its words to introduce **rhyme** and other sound effects. Moreover, being a verbal art, it depends on careful choice of diction and often also on **imagery**, including similes, metaphors, and **symbols**. Interestingly, a poem can be set on the page in such a way that it even has some of the qualities of the spatial arts as well.

Rhythm and Meter

As in music, rhythm and meter in poetry are established by stress—by stressed or unstressed syllables, also known as accented or unaccented syllables. Again as in music, poetry may have rests or pauses, called *caesurae* (singular, **caesura**), to break the flow of a line.

We can be aware of rhythm even if we do not know the technicalities of scansion, or counting the meter. Here, for instance, is a blithe little love poem by Nikki Giovanni (b. 1943) with a very pronounced modern beat:

Nikki Giovanni

KIDNAP POEM

ever been kidnapped
by a poet
if i were a poet
i'd kidnap you
put you in my phrases and meter
you to jones beach
or maybe coney island
or maybe just to my house
lyric you in lilacs
dash you in the rain
blend into the beach
to complement my see
play the lyre for you
ode you with my love song
anything to win you

wrap you in the red Black green
show you off to mama
yeah if i were a poet i'd kid
nap you

(1970)

The strong but irregular rhythm that changes from line to line makes this poem **free verse**, an adaptable experimental form especially suitable for the exuberant rush of affection the poet is trying to express.

Much of modern poetry is in free verse. Until the 20th century, however, poems were usually written according to a traditional system whereby each line is subdivided into feet, and each foot is determined by the stressed (′) and related unstressed (˘) syllables. Normally, only one stressed syllable can appear in any one foot. We should bear in mind that a syllable is a unit of sound; *párt | éd,* for instance, has two syllables, but *lovĕd* has only one.

In English, the most frequently used foot and the one best suited to the language is the *iamb* (˘′). This basic pattern can be heard in the lines

Come LIVE | with ME | and BE | my LOVE,
And WE | will ALL | the PLEA | sures PROVE
That HILLS | and VALL | eys, DALE | and FIELD,
And ALL | the CRAG | gy MOUN | tains YIELD!

Christopher Marlowe, "The Passionate Shepherd to His Love" (pub. 1600)

The three other traditional kinds of feet appear in the following passages:

Trochee (′˘):

CHLoe | FOUND a | MYNtas | LYing
ALL in | TEARS u | PON the | PLAIN
SIGHing | TO him | SELF, and | CRYing
WRETched | I, to | LOVE in | VAIN!
KISS me, | DEAR, u | PON my | DYing;
KISS me | ONCE, and | EASE my PAIN.

John Dryden, "Rondelay" (1693)

Anapest (˘˘′):

The AsSYR | ian came DOWN | like a WOLF | on the FOLD
And his CO | horts were GLEAM | ing in PUR | ple and GOLD
And the SHEEN | of their SPEARS | was like STARS | in the SEA
When the BLUE | wave rolls NIGHT | ly on DEEP | GalliLEE.

Lord Byron, "Destruction of Sennacherib" (1814–1815)

Dactyl (′˘˘):

AFter the | PANGS of a | DESperate | LOVer
WHEN day and | NIGHT I have | SIGHED all in | VAIN
AH what a | PLEAsure it | IS to dis | COVer
IN her eyes | PITy, who | CAUses my | PAIN.

John Dryden, "Song" (1668)

As can be seen by the vertical slash (|) that separates the feet, each of these passages is written in four-foot, or *tetrameter,* lines. An even more widely used pattern in English is the five-foot, or *pentameter* line. But poets may use shorter lines such as *trimeter* (three feet), *dimeter* (two feet), and *monometer* (one foot). On the other hand, they may use *hexameter* (six feet), a line that sounds very long and emphatic in English, but is common in 17th-century French poetry.

Many readers find it difficult to scan poems according to the system just described, and with good reason. This system was developed for Greek or Latin poems of classical antiquity, in which the long and short syllables were clearly defined and much more easily recognizable than the stressed and unstressed syllables of English. Indeed, some of the rough scanning we have just done to review the traditional kinds of feet might well be questioned. Should the last line quoted be scanned as "ín her̆ eyĕs | píty̆" or "in̆ her̆ eyés | píty̆"? In spite of such uncertainties, a knowledge of the basic metrical patterns will make us more sensitive to the complexities of the poems we read.

Such knowledge will also make us more aware of the substitution of one kind of foot for another, a device poets use very freely, partly to avoid a monotonous beat and partly to emphasize a special phrase. We can, for instance, recognize the slight metrical variations in the opening speech of *Twelfth Night* (1600) by William Shakespeare. The lovesick Duke is calling for music to heighten, then calm, his passionate mood:

Ĭf MÚ | sĭc BÉ | thĕ FÓOD | ŏf LÓVE, | plăy ÓN;
GÍVE mĕ | ĕxCÉSS | ŏf ÍT, | thăt SÚR | feĭtÍNG
Thĕ ÁP | pĕTÍTE | măy SÍCK | ĕn ÁND | sŏ DÍE.
Thăt STRÁIN | ăGÁIN! | Ĭt HÁD | ă DÝ | ĭng FÁLL;
Ó, ĭt | căme Ó'ER | my̆ EÁR | lĭke thĕ | SWÉET SOÚND
Thăt BREÁTHES | ŭPÓN | ă BÁNK | ŏf VÍ | ŏLÉTS.

The basic pattern of this speech, as so often in Shakespeare, is iambic pentameter. But in the second line the pattern is broken by the trochee "Gíve mĕ," which emphasizes the Duke's yearning for music and for love. In line 5, Shakespeare introduces two other feet often used as substitutes—the *spondee* (′ ′), a very strong foot with two stressed syllables, and the *pyrrhic* (˘˘), an unobtrusive foot with two unstressed syllables. The emphasis on the spondee "swéet soúnd" is intensified by the pyrrhic "lĭke thĕ" that immediately precedes it. Or, to take a more extreme example, we can be aware of the fact that in her "Kidnap Poem" (see page 72), Nikki Giovanni achieves the jazzy, syncopated rhythm by going against the usual, expected iambic pattern (˘′˘′˘′), using, instead, irregular combinations of trochees ("dásh yŏu," "pláy thĕ," "wráp yŏu," "óde yŏu,") followed by anapests ("ĭn thĕ ráin," "ĭn thĕ réd") or a dactyl ("lýre fŏr yŏu") or even a pyrrhic and spondaic foot ("wĭth mĭy lóve sóng").

Obviously, our awareness both of the basic rhythm and of variations from it requires the habits of mind we mentioned earlier in connection with the temporal arts: *memory,* as we recall the beat established earlier; *attention,* as we grasp the beat we are currently hearing; and *anticipation,* as we listen for either a repetition of or a deviation from the basic metrical pattern. And here, most fundamentally, our awareness depends upon a sensitive ear.

Rhyme and Other Sound Effects

Playing with sounds as does music, poems may—but need not—use *rhyme,* an echoing of sound that usually links the last syllable or last two syllables of nearby lines. Rhyme is not an essential of poetry; indeed, the iambic pentameter used by Shakespeare and many other English poets is not rhymed. Unrhymed iambic pentameter is called **blank verse**—not to be confused with *free verse,* which is far more irregular and follows no predetermined pattern. However, rhyme is used charmingly in Dryden's two little love poems. For instance, in "After the pangs of a desperate lover," *lover* rhymes with *discover* in a *feminine rhyme* (so called because two syllables rhyme, the second one unaccented), and *vain* echoes *pain* in a *masculine,* or single-syllable, *rhyme.* Although rhymes in English often sound light-hearted and sometimes downright comic, they can also be used for serious purposes, as they are in Alexander Pope's horrifying glimpse of injustice, presented in the concentrated form of two lines that rhyme called a **couplet**:

The hungry judges soon the sentence sign,
And wretches hang, that jurymen may dine.

The Rape of the Lock, III, 21–22 (1714)

Here the rhyme forces together the intensely serious *sign,* marking the conviction of the accused, and the trivial *dine,* pointing to the desire to have lunch that makes the jury hurry to reach its verdict. The pause or caesura in the middle of the second line is carefully placed to emphasize the plight of the wretches, trapped between the hungry (or bloodthirsty) judge and the equally hungry jury. Rhymes need not occur in successive lines, as they do in Pope's couplets (which are marked aabbccdd—each new sound indicated by a new letter of the alphabet) but can appear in far more elaborate patterns. Dryden's rhymes are abab, and in Keats's "Ode to a Nightingale," which we will discuss in Chapter 11, the pattern ababcdecde recurs in each stanza, creating a very subtle repetition of sounds.

Not only conventional rhymes but other *sound effects* are also frequently explored by poets. W. H. Auden (1907–1973) does so brilliantly in a poem whose speaker tries to capture a certain scene, a seascape, by urging a companion to take it in through the eyes and ears and thereby to make the transient moment more permanent:

W. H. Auden
LOOK, STRANGER

Look, stranger, on this island now
The leaping light for your delight discovers,
Stand stable here
And silent be,
That through the channels of the ear
May wander like a river
The swaying sound of the sea.

Here at the small field's ending pause
When the chalk wall falls to the foam and its tall ledges
Oppose the pluck
And knock of the tide,
And the shingle scrambles after the sucking surf
And the gull lodges
A moment on its sheer side.

Far off like floating seeds the ships
Diverge on urgent voluntary errands
And the full view
Indeed may enter
And move in memory as now these clouds do,
That pass the harbor mirror
And all the summer through the water saunter.

(1936)

Here Auden uses *internal rhyme*—rhyme that occurs within rather than at the end of the lines ("light" and "delight"). He uses *slant rhyme,* which subtly echoes but does not precisely repeat the sound ("water" and "saunter"). Apart from numerous examples of *alliteration*—the repetition of consonants at the beginning of words ("leaping light"; "delight discovers"), he introduces *assonance,* the repetition of vowel sounds ("chalk wall falls"; "diverge" and "urgent"). And he tries to suggest the actual sound of the surf ("pluck" and "knock"; "shingle scrambles")—not by *onomatopoeia,* the choice of a word that imitates the sound it represents, a rare occurrence except in a few words such as *buzz* or *sizzle,* but by the overtones or associations of the words and the rhythm of the lines. Through these various devices, Auden manages to create an effect of *euphony,* pleasant melodiousness, in the first stanza, and a contrasting effect of *cacophony,* rugged harshness, in the second. The many sound effects contribute to the poem's meaning—or rather, they carry it. For as everything echoes and reechoes everything else, Auden is implying that there is a basic harmony in nature that will draw in the "stranger" and make him less estranged if he will allow the natural scene to enter his consciousness. We should remember that sound effects in a poem are hardly ever merely decorative but rather serve to express or emphasize the meaning. We should bear in mind that these devices create their effect cumulatively, over a period of time. We as readers must use not only our inner ear but also our memory and attention to recognize their workings.

Diction

A poem consists of more than rhythm and sounds. It expresses its meaning through aspects of language that differ from music—through its **diction**, the choice of words, and usually also through imagery, the sense impressions created by the words. Like music and unlike the visual arts, poetry presents these, too, consecutively, in time, and so again requires memory, attention, and anticipation.

In their choice of words, poets not only try to express their meaning as precisely as possible but also often wish to startle us into attention. They may use a condensed, elliptical, shorthand style, omitting words that would be necessary in a prose statement. Nikki Giovanni's "put you in my phrases and meter/you to jones beach," would have to be expanded in normal prose to "capture you in the phrases of my poem and mail you to Jones Beach." Poets may also use wordplay, or *puns,* as Nikki Giovanni does with the double meaning of *meter.* In the passage just quoted, *meter* has the sense of sending by mail but also of capturing the beloved in the meter of the poem. Furthermore, poets are likely to develop patterns of diction over a number of lines, as Auden does in "Look, stranger" with a whole series of words associated with channels and tides.

Poets may even coin new words to express their meaning. In "Adam's Task" John Hollander (b. 1929) has proved how enjoyable and useful this act of word invention, of creating neologisms, can be. He imagines the moment when Adam fulfills the exhausting task mentioned in Genesis of naming all the creatures around him.

John Hollander

ADAM'S TASK

"And Adam gave names to all cattle, and to the fowl of the air, and to every beast of the field . . ."—Gen. 2:20

Thou, paw-paw-paw; thou, glurd; thou, spotted
   Glurd; thou, whitestap, lurching through
The high-grown brush; thou, pliant-footed,
   Implex; thou, awagabu.

Every burrower, each flier
   Came for the name he had to give
Gay, first work, ever to be prior,
   Not yet sunk to primitive.

Thou, verdle; thou, McFleery's pomma;
   Thou; thou; thou—three types of grawl;
Thou, flisket; thou, kabasch; thou, comma-
   Eared mashawk; thou, all; thou, all.

Were, in a fire of becoming,
   Laboring to be burned away,

Then work, half-measuring, half-humming,
Would be as serious as play.

Thou, pambler; thou, rivarn; thou, greater
Wherret, and thou, lesser one;
Thou, sproal; thou, zant; thou, lily-eater.
Naming's over. Day is done.

(1971)

Hollander obviously has fun spoofing the process of naming. Throughout, he displays a delightfully playful attitude toward words, even though these are, after all, a serious concern for a poet. For instance, Hollander chooses terms that suggest each animal's identity by the very sound ("glurd," "flisket"). He also mocks the scientific practices of naming either by the discoverer ("McFleery's pomma") or by classification ("thou, greater/Wherret, and thou, lesser one"). As this example suggests, poetry tends to be a more concentrated and more heightened form of expression than prose.

Yet poems do not necessarily sound "poetic" or different from prose. The diction in W. H. Auden's "Musée des Beaux Arts" ("Museum of Fine Arts") is remarkably prosaic. Here the speaker, apparently inspired by the paintings he has seen in a museum, reflects on how human beings often fail to respond to or even notice the suffering of their fellow human beings.

W. H. Auden
MUSÉE DES BEAUX ARTS

About suffering they were never wrong,
The Old Masters: how well they understood
Its human position; how it takes place
While someone else is eating or opening a window or just walking dully along;
How, when the aged are reverently, passionately waiting
For the miraculous birth, there always must be
Children who did not specially want it to happen, skating
On a pond at the edge of the wood:
They never forgot
That even the dreadful martyrdom must run its course
Anyhow in a corner, some untidy spot
Where the dogs go on with their doggy life and the torturer's horse
Scratches its innocent behind on a tree.

In Brueghel's *Icarus,* for instance: how everything turns away
Quite leisurely from the disaster; the ploughman may
Have heard the splash, the forsaken cry,
But for him it was not an important failure; the sun shone
As it had to on the white legs disappearing into the green
Water; and the expensive delicate ship that must have seen
Something amazing, a boy falling out of the sky,
Had somewhere to get to and sailed on.

(1940)

Although by the same poet as "Look, stranger," this poem avoids internal or end rhymes and other pronounced sound effects. Its rhythms and diction are those of 20th-century colloquial speech: "how it takes place/While someone else is eating or opening a window or just walking dully along"; "Where the dogs go on with their doggy life"; "Had somewhere to get to and sailed on." Through this diction, Auden emphasizes the ordinariness of the occurrence and the bitterness of his conclusion. In all ages—at the time when the three Magi were waiting for the miraculous birth of Christ, at the time when Pieter Brueghel the Elder (c. 1525–1569) painted the fall of the mythological Icarus from the sky, and even in our own time when torture or pain are inflicted—we are inclined thoughtlessly or callously to ignore the suffering of others and go on with our own affairs.

Images

"Musée des Beaux Arts" works primarily through *images,* a flexible term that includes vivid concrete details as well as similes, metaphors, and other figures of speech. Most images are *visual,* as they are in this Auden poem when the focus is on specific pictorial details, such as children skating on a pond or a horse scratching itself on a tree. The visual images are even stronger in the second stanza, which evokes the most significant details of Brueghel's *The Fall of Icarus* [59]: the farmer plowing, the sun, the falling boy,

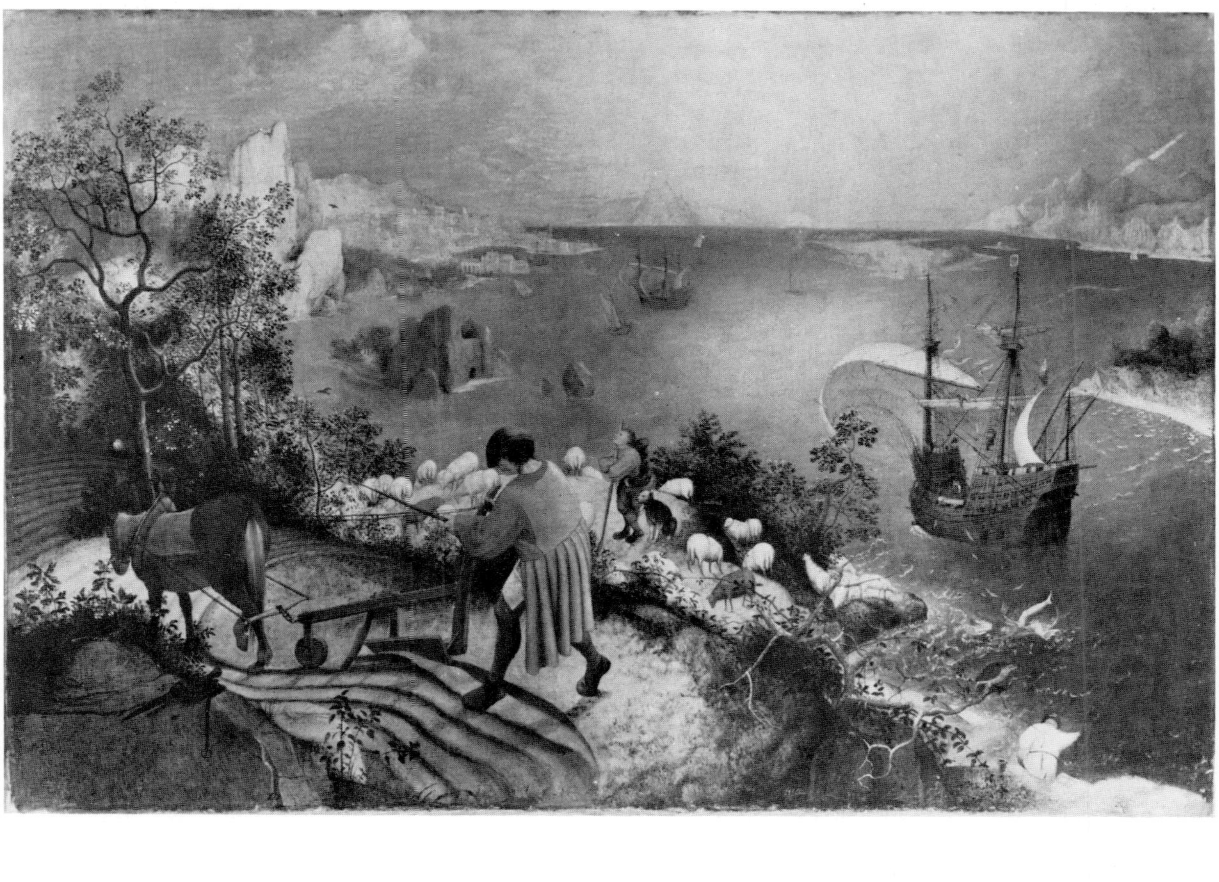

59 Pieter Brueghel the Elder. *The Fall of Icarus.* c. 1555. Oil panel transferred to canvas, 28½ × 43¾" (72 × 111 cm). Musée des Beaux-Arts, Brussels.

the ship. Yet poetic images need not be exclusively visual: they can also invoke the other senses. Auden uses *images of hearing* in the splash and the "forsaken cry" of the boy Icarus, just as he uses auditory as well as visual images when he conjures up the sounds along with the sight of the sea in "Look, stranger." *Images of touch* and even of *smell* can also be found in poetry. Moreover, some poets, especially those writing in the 19th and 20th centuries, like to mingle different sensory images, thereby creating what is called **synaesthesia.** When John Keats writes of "pale and silver silence," he is combining images of color and sound. And when Nikki Giovanni cries "lyric you in lilacs," she links sound with color and possibly also with smell, a lilac being one of the most delightfully scented bushes of the spring.

As for the other types of images or imagery, *similes* and *metaphors* are closely related in that they both present comparisons. Similes introduce such comparison with "as" or "like," and metaphors only imply the comparison. Alexander Pope uses the various kinds of images to describe the cycle of life—indeed, the recycling of life—in the universe:

See dying vegetables life sustain,
See life dissolving vegetate again:
All forms that perish other forms supply,
(By turns we catch the vital breath, and die).
Like bubbles in the sea of matter born.
They rise, they break, and to that sea return.

Essay on Man, III, 15–20 (1733–1734)

The poet begins with the visual image of vegetables dying to nourish other living beings; these, in turn, die and nourish new life—"vegetate again." In line 5, Pope introduces a simile—"like bubbles" that rise, break, and fall—to suggest the fragility and brevity of human life. He adds the metaphor "sea of matter" for the vast universe of which we are a part and from which bubbles, made of water, can appropriately come as well as return. Another metaphor, "the vital breath," suggests the short span of our life and also prepares for the image of bubbles, which are, after all, formed by human breath. Altogether, the images permit Pope to express very complicated ideas—not only the recurring cycle of life in the universe but also the interrelationship among all living beings and the transitory quality of human life—with extraordinary conciseness and vividness. That Pope feels free to mingle the various types of images, whether specific details, similes, or metaphors, is not unusual. Poets frequently do so, extending the range of their language and the meanings they can present in a highly concentrated way.

Poets can also use a special kind of image, the *symbol.* This can be defined as an image, object, or action that stands for some idea or feeling or experience beyond itself. By describing an object with great vividness or intensity, poets can give it special associations or overtones that convey further significance. Indeed, symbols are much more open-ended than other forms of comparison and are therefore not easily definable. Usually carrying a whole range of meanings, they are among the most valuable poetic devices. Symbols are not confined to poetry, but can be found in other writing and in the spatial arts as well.

In the following poem by William Blake (1757–1827), the rose is not so much a metaphor, or implied comparison with something else, as a symbol—a genuine flower that suggests more than that flower.

William Blake
THE SICK ROSE

O Rose, thou art sick.
The invisible worm
That flies in the night
In the howling storm

Has found out thy bed
Of crimson joy,
And his dark secret love
Does thy life destroy.
(1794)

Not only is the rose an actual flower here but it also brings to mind the qualities often associated with it—beauty, love, femininity, fragility, and brevity of existence. Moreover, this rose is unusual. It is also "sick," and it has a "bed/Of crimson joy" that suggests far more than just its color. And the flower is being threatened, indeed destroyed, by a worm. This creature might be just a caterpillar that blights the petals, but its invisibility and its involvement with the "night" and the "storm" turn it into a sinister, evil, and destructive force. In addition, "worm" is another name for Satan, or the serpent whose form Satan took in the garden of Eden. In using the rose and the worm as symbols, Blake is suggesting powerfully and hauntingly that mysterious, corrupting forces can destroy even the most beautiful living thing.

Blake introduces a further meaning through the references to "night," "bed," and "crimson joy." In this context, the relationship between the rose and the worm is sexual and closely relates love with death. Perhaps Blake is hinting at the terrifying notion that even the most life-giving of forces, love, is subject to life-destroying forces. All of these complex meanings are only implied. Indeed, we cannot be more precise in our interpretation because symbols by their very nature always work through suggestions and associations rather than definite statements.

The symbols Blake uses in the poem are of two different kinds. The rose is a largely *traditional symbol,* for its overtones of beauty and love are qualities generally thought of in relation to such a flower. As readers, we immediately grasp these overtones because they are customarily associated with roses. At the same time, the rose and the worm are *universal symbols,* for they derive their meaning from the natural world. We can also, then, grasp at least some of the significance of the two symbols because they represent unchanging aspects of nature.

Modern poets, in particular, like to use still another kind of symbol that tends to be much more personal and idiosyncratic. Such *private* or *arbitrary symbols* do not derive their meaning from traditional associations nor from the universal aspects of nature, but from the poet's own special experiences or personal associations. For instance, in "The Circus Animals' Desertion" (1939), W. B. Yeats (1865–1939) introduces an image of the circus in the first stanza:

My circus animals were all on show,
Those stilted boys, that burnished chariot,
Lion and woman and the Lord knows what.

Actually, Yeats is not writing about circus animals at all, but about his own earlier poems and plays. The "stilted boys" are probably the mythic Irish heroes of Yeats's early poetry; "that burnished chariot" may well recall the elaborate carriage used in his play *The Unicorn and the Stars;* a "lion" is mentioned in many of his poems; and a "woman," often suggesting Maud Gonne, the firebrand who rejected him, appears in much of Yeats's verse.

These connections between the circus animals and Yeats's poetic creations are highly personal. Accordingly, we as readers must make a great effort to grasp the meaning either by understanding the context or by learning about the poet's life. Although more difficult to grasp, private symbols should not be regarded as less effective than traditional or universal ones. In Yeats's poem, the circus figures have a complex and important function. By presenting his early works as mere carnival or sideshow creatures, Yeats conveys his ambivalent attitude toward them, an attitude that is self-deprecating but also, perhaps, appreciative.

We must emphasize again that all the various possibilities of language—rhythm, rhyme, and images—can be explored or presented only in time, sequentially, one by one. This point becomes especially clear when we recognize that Auden, in the second stanza of "Musée des Beaux Arts," is describing Brueghel's painting. But Auden can give only a consecutive account of the various details—the ploughman, the sun, the boy, the ship—while the painting [see Figure 59, page 79] presents these simultaneously, next to each other in space, accessible at a single glance. On the other hand, the meaning can be only implied by the visual details of the painting, while it can be made more explicit in the language of the poem. More important still, in the painting the meaning tends to be restricted to the case of Icarus, but in the poem it can be generalized more easily to many kinds of human suffering and to the perception of many other artists ("About suffering they were never wrong,/The Old Masters . . ."). This is not to say that one art form is superior to the other, but that poetry and the visual arts have different possibilities, and some of these possibilities are inherent in whether the art form exists primarily in time or whether it exists primarily in space.

Spatial Aspects of Poetry

Finally, we must acknowledge that poems also exist in space. Except for oral poetry—poetry that is only sung or recited—poems are written in *lines* on a page. Precisely this trait distinguishes poetry from prose. The lack of capitals and of a final period in Nikki Giovanni's "Kidnap Poem" (see page 72) contributes a meaning of its own. This device suggests a breaking in on the speaker in the middle of a thought and a leaving off before the rush of feeling has come to an end.

Some poets make even more obvious use of the spatial possibilities of their art. The 17th-century religious poet George Herbert (1593–1633), for instance, wrote his deeply felt "Easter Wings" in the shape of wings:

George Herbert

EASTER WINGS

Lord, who createdst man in wealth and store,[1]
Though foolishly he lost the same,
Decaying more and more,
Till he became
Most poor:
With thee
O let me rise
As larks, harmoniously,
And sing this day thy victories:
Then shall the fall further the flight in me.

My tender age in sorrow did begin;
And still with sicknesses and shame
Thou didst so punish sin,
That I became
Most thin.
With thee
Let me combine,
And feel this day thy victory;
For, if I imp[2] my wing on thine,
Affliction shall advance the flight in me.

(1633)

1 goods
2 to add or graft feathers to the wings of hunting birds to increase their speed and power

Not only does the shape of the poem correspond with the title but the length of each line echoes and emphasizes the sense. As Herbert dwells on man's weakness, the lines decrease to a monometer (a one-foot line); as Herbert dwells on man's possibility of rising toward God, the lines expand again. The general pattern also echoes the Christian doctrines of the Fall and the Redemption—especially appropriate in a poem written for Easter, which celebrates Christ's death and Resurrection. Although few poems work with shape and space in such a pronounced fashion, those that do serve to remind us that one cannot make hard and fast distinctions between the arts of time and space. Poems exist not only in time but also in space; paintings, conversely, exist not only in space but also, in a sense, in time.

Prose Narrative

Unlike short poems, which can exist in space as well as time, longer narratives exist primarily in time. For writers of short stories or novels, this temporal aspect of their medium presents a particular difficulty, since they cannot express simultaneously everything they would like their reader to know. And so they must decide in what order to relate their material, paying particular attention to plot and character, setting, and treatment of time. The decisions they make are crucial in determining the total effect of the narrative.

Laurence Sterne (1713–1768) in *Tristram Shandy* (1759–1767) expresses the frustrations of a writer grappling with the problem of how to order his material—how to set down both the many different events happening concurrently and the background necessary to understand these events. In trying to explain the life and character of Tristram Shandy, Sterne takes so long in describing the circumstances of Tristram's conception and birth, the events that immediately preceded it, and the characters and opinions of those involved, that his hero is born only in Book IV of a seven-book novel that was never completed—and could, in fact, never be completed! Of course, Sterne delighted in the opportunity to bring in more and more supposed digressions which actually further his narrative, for he was really not interested in external events or logical plot development: "My work is digressive, and it is progressive too,—and at the same time." (I, chapter 22).

Plot and Character

Most prose writers are, however, interested in their plot and in the characters who enact it. In working with these two basic components of prose narrative, they must accept the fact that their narrative can only unfold sequentially in time. *Plot* is the term used not just for the story material but for the way this material has been shaped. Some writers are interested in intricate plots involving surprises, twists, reversals, coincidences, and even shock endings. Adventure stories, detective stories, Gothic horror novels, and science fiction all tend to use such highly patterned plots. Other writers prefer loosely structured plots that create a mood, give a glimpse of life, or provide a momentary insight into a distinctive society or personality. Such writers do not feel compelled to mold their material into artificial patterns.

Character refers to the personality of those involved in the plot. Characters may be *types* or *individuals;* that is, they may have traits that identify them with members of a group or traits that distinguish them from a group. For instance, Scrooge in *A Christmas Carol* (1843) by Charles Dickens (1812–1870) is a type character who reveals the traits of a miser: penny pinching, hard-heartedness, cheerlessness, and excessive concern for the safety of his property. We ourselves, if we were to be featured in a prose narrative, would expect to be depicted as individuals. For we are aware of our own uniqueness, complexity, and even idiosyncracies, and do not consider ourselves as reducible to the common denominator that defines a type.

In addition, characters may be presented—to use the terms of the novelist E. M. Forster—as *flat* or as *round.* Flat characters, as the term suggests, reveal only one or two sides of their personality. Round characters, in contrast, are shown as many-sided and complex. Although we may think that type characters are likely to be flat and individual characters are likely to be round, these categories are not mutually exclusive. That is, a type character, especially in a longer narrative, may be presented so as to reveal a number of traits. Scrooge, for instance, is shown to have been an unhappy child, a disappointed lover, and—though long a hard-hearted miser—eventually capable of learning charity. Still, individual characters are likely to be presented as round rather than flat, since their complexity and uniqueness must be demonstrated.

But to talk separately of plot and character is to make an artificial distinction. For plot and character can be revealed only simultaneously; a writer cannot create a plot without characters, and characters do not exist apart from their actions in the plot. And both plot and character can be revealed only step by step in the time span chosen by the writer. These interrelationships are vividly illustrated in the short story "Roman Fever" by Edith Wharton (1862–1937).

Edith Wharton's story focuses on two older women, central characters who are clearly defined from the start as having contrasting personalities. Mrs. Slade is self-assured and domineering; Mrs. Ansley is reticent and rather passive. Their seemingly trivial conversation leads to a plot revelation concerning earlier experiences that are not only surprising but also full of passionate intensity.

Edith Wharton

ROMAN FEVER

I

From the table at which they had been lunching two American ladies of ripe but well-cared-for middle age moved across the lofty terrace of the Roman restaurant and, leaning on its parapet, looked first at each other, and then down on the outspread glories of the Palatine and the Forum, with the same expression of vague but benevolent approval.

As they leaned there a girlish voice echoed up gaily from the stairs leading to the court below. "Well, come along, then," it cried, not to them but to an invisible companion, "and let's leave the young things to their knitting"; and a voice as fresh laughed back: "Oh, look here, Babs, not actually *knitting*—" "Well, I mean figuratively," rejoined the first. "After all, we haven't left our poor parents much else to do. . . ." and at that point the turn of the stairs engulfed the dialogue.

The two ladies looked at each other again, this time with a tinge of smiling embarrassment, and the smaller and paler one shook her head and colored slightly.

"Barbara!" she murmured, sending an unheard rebuke after the mocking voice in the stairway.

The other lady, who was fuller, and higher in color, with a small determined nose supported by vigorous black eyebrows, gave a good-humored laugh. "That's what our daughters think of us!"

Her companion replied by a deprecating gesture. "Not of us individually. We must remember that. It's just the collective modern idea of Mothers. And you see—" Half-guiltily she drew from her handsomely mounted black handbag a twist of crimson silk run through by two fine knitting needles. "One never knows," she murmured. "The new system has certainly given us a good deal of time to kill; and sometimes I get tired just looking—even at this." Her gesture was now addressed to the stupendous scene at their feet.

The dark lady laughed again, and they both relapsed upon the view, contemplating it in silence, with a sort of diffused serenity which might have been borrowed from the spring effulgence of the Roman skies. The luncheon hour was long past, and the two had their end of the vast terrace to themselves. At its opposite extremity a few groups, detained by a lingering look at the outspread city, were gathering up guidebooks and fumbling for tips. The last of them scattered, and the two ladies were alone on the air-washed height.

"Well, I don't see why we shouldn't just stay here," said Mrs. Slade, the lady of the high color and energetic brows. Two derelict basket chairs stood near, and she pushed them into the angle of the parapet, and settled herself in one, her gaze upon the Palatine. "After all, it's still the most beautiful view in the world."

"It always will be, to me," assented her friend Mrs. Ansley, with so slight a stress on the "me" that Mrs. Slade, though she noticed it, wondered if it were not merely accidental, like the random underlinings of old-fashioned letter writers.

"Grace Ansley was always old-fashioned," she thought; and added aloud, with a retrospective smile: "It's a view we've both been familiar with for a good many years. When we first met here we were younger than our girls are now. You remember?"

"Oh, yes, I remember," murmured Mrs. Ansley, with the same undefinable stress. "There's that headwaiter wondering," she interpolated. She was evidently far less sure than her companion of herself and of her rights in the world.

"I'll cure him of wondering," said Mrs. Slade, stretching her hand toward a bag as discreetly opulent-looking as Mrs. Ansley's. Signing to the headwaiter, she explained that she and her friend were old lovers of Rome, and would like to spend the end of the afternoon looking down on the view—that is, if it did not disturb the service? The headwaiter, bowing over her gratuity, assured her that the ladies were most welcome, and would be still more so if they would condescend to remain for dinner. A full-moon night, they would remember. . . .

Mrs. Slade's black brows drew together, as though references to the moon were out of place and even unwelcome. But she smiled away her frown as the headwaiter retreated. "Well, why not? We might do worse. There's no knowing, I suppose, when the girls will be back. Do you even know back from *where?* I don't!"

Mrs. Ansley again colored slightly. "I think those young Italian aviators we met at the Embassy invited them to fly to Tarquinia for tea. I suppose they'll want to wait and fly back by moonlight."

"Moonlight—moonlight! What a part it still plays. Do you suppose they're as sentimental as we were?"

"I've come to the conclusion that I don't in the least know what they are," said Mrs. Ansley. "And perhaps we didn't know much more about each other."

"No; perhaps we didn't."

Her friend gave her a shy glance. "I never should have supposed you were sentimental, Alida."

"Well, perhaps I wasn't." Mrs. Slade drew her lids together in retrospect; and for a few moments the two ladies, who had been intimate since childhood, reflected how little they knew each other. Each one, of course, had a label ready to attach to the other's name; Mrs. Delphin Slade, for instance, would have told herself, or anyone who asked her, that Mrs. Horace Ansley, twenty-five years ago, had been exquisitely lovely—no, you wouldn't believe it, would you? . . . though, of course, still charming, distinguished. . . . Well, as a girl she had been exquisite; far more beautiful than her daughter Barbara, though certainly Babs, according to the new standards at any rate, was more effective—had more *edge,* as they say. Funny where she got it, with those two nullities as parents. Yes; Horace Ansley was—well, just the duplicate of his wife. Museum specimens of old New York. Good-looking, irreproachable, exemplary. Mrs. Slade and Mrs. Ansley had lived opposite each other—actually as well as figuratively—for years. When the drawing-room curtains in No. 20 East 73rd Street were renewed, No. 23, across the way, was always aware of it. And of all the movings, buyings, travels, anniversaries, illnesses—the tame chronicle of an estimable pair. Little of it escaped Mrs. Slade. But she had grown bored with it by the time her husband made his big *coup* in Wall Street, and when they bought in upper Park Avenue had already begun to think: "I'd rather live opposite a speakeasy for a change; at least one might see it raided." The idea of seeing Grace raided was so amusing that (before the move) she launched it at a woman's lunch. It made a hit, and went the rounds—she sometimes wondered if it had crossed the street, and reached Mrs. Ansley. She hoped not, but didn't much mind. Those were the days when respectability was at a discount, and it did the irreproachable no harm to laugh at them a little.

A few years later, and not many months apart, both ladies lost their husbands. There was an appropriate exchange of wreaths and condolences, and a brief renewal of intimacy in the half-shadow of their mourning; and now, after another interval, they had run across each other in Rome, at the same hotel, each of them the modest appendage of a salient daughter. The similarity of their lot had again drawn them together, lending itself to mild jokes, and the mutual confession that, if in old days it must have been tiring to "keep up" with daughters, it was now, at times, a little dull not to.

No doubt, Mrs. Slade reflected, she felt her unemployment more than poor Grace ever would. It was a big drop from being the wife of Delphin Slade to being his widow. She had always regarded herself (with a certain conjugal pride) as his equal in social gifts, as contributing her full share to the making of the exceptional couple they were: but the difference after his death was irremediable. As the wife of the famous corporation lawyer, always with an international case or two on hand, every day brought its exciting and unexpected obligation: the impromptu entertaining of eminent colleagues from abroad, the hurried dashes on legal business to London, Paris or Rome, where the entertaining was so handsomely reciprocated; the amusement of hearing in her wake: "What, that handsome woman with the good clothes and the eyes is Mrs. Slade—*the* Slade's wife? Really? Generally the wives of celebrities are such frumps."

Yes; being *the* Slade's widow was a dullish business after that. In living up to such a husband all her faculties had been engaged; now she had only her daughter to live up to, for the son who seemed to have inherited his father's gifts had died suddenly in boyhood. She had fought through that agony because her husband was there, to be helped and to help; now, after the father's death, the thought of the boy had become unbearable. There was nothing left but to mother her daughter; and dear Jenny was such a perfect daughter that she needed no excessive mothering. "Now with Babs Ansley I don't know that I *should* be so quiet," Mrs. Slade sometimes half-enviously reflected; but Jenny, who was younger than her brilliant friend, was that rare accident, an extremely pretty girl who somehow made youth and prettiness seem as safe as their absence. It was all perplexing—and to Mrs. Slade a little boring. She wished that Jenny would fall in love—with the wrong man, even; that she might have to be watched, out-maneuvered, rescued. And instead, it was Jenny who watched her mother, kept her out of drafts, made sure that she had taken her tonic. . . .

Mrs. Ansley was much less articulate than her friend, and her mental portrait of Mrs. Slade was slighter, and drawn with fainter touches. "Alida Slade's awfully brilliant; but not as brilliant as she thinks," would have summed it up; though she would have added, for the enlightenment of strangers, that Mrs. Slade had been an extremely dashing girl; much more so than her daughter, who was pretty, of course, and clever in a way, but had none of her mother's—well, "vividness," someone had once called it. Mrs. Ansley would take up current words like this, and cite them in quotation marks, as unheard of audacities. No; Jenny was not like her mother. Sometimes Mrs. Ansley thought Alida Slade was disappointed; on the whole she had had a sad life. Full of failures and mistakes; Mrs. Ansley had always been rather sorry for her. . . .

So these two ladies visualized each other, each through the wrong end of her little telescope.

II

For a long time they continued to sit side by side without speaking. It seemed as though, to both, there was a relief in laying down their somewhat futile activities in the presence of the vast Memento Mori which faced them. Mrs. Slade sat quite still, her eyes fixed on the golden slope of the Palace of the Caesars, and after a while Mrs. Ansley ceased to fidget with her bag, and she too sank into meditation. Like many intimate friends, the two ladies had never before had occasion to be silent together, and Mrs. Ansley was slightly embarrassed by what seemed, after so many years, a new stage in their intimacy, and one with which she did not yet know how to deal.

Suddenly the air was full of that deep clangor of bells which periodically covers Rome with a roof of silver. Mrs. Slade glanced at her wristwatch. "Five o'clock already," she said, as though surprised.

Mrs. Ansley suggested interrogatively: "There's bridge at the Embassy at five." For a long time Mrs. Slade did not answer. She appeared to be lost in contemplation, and Mrs. Ansley thought the remark had escaped her. But after a while she said, as if speaking out of a dream: "Bridge, did you say? Not unless you want to. . . . But I don't think I will, you know."

"Oh, no," Mrs. Ansley hastened to assure her. "I don't care to at all. It's so lovely here; and so full of old memories, as you say." She settled herself in her chair, and almost furtively drew forth her knitting. Mrs. Slade took sideway note of this activity, but her own beautifully cared-for hands remained motionless on her knee.

"I was just thinking," she said slowly, "what different things Rome stands for to each generation of travelers. To our grandmothers, Roman fever; to our moth-

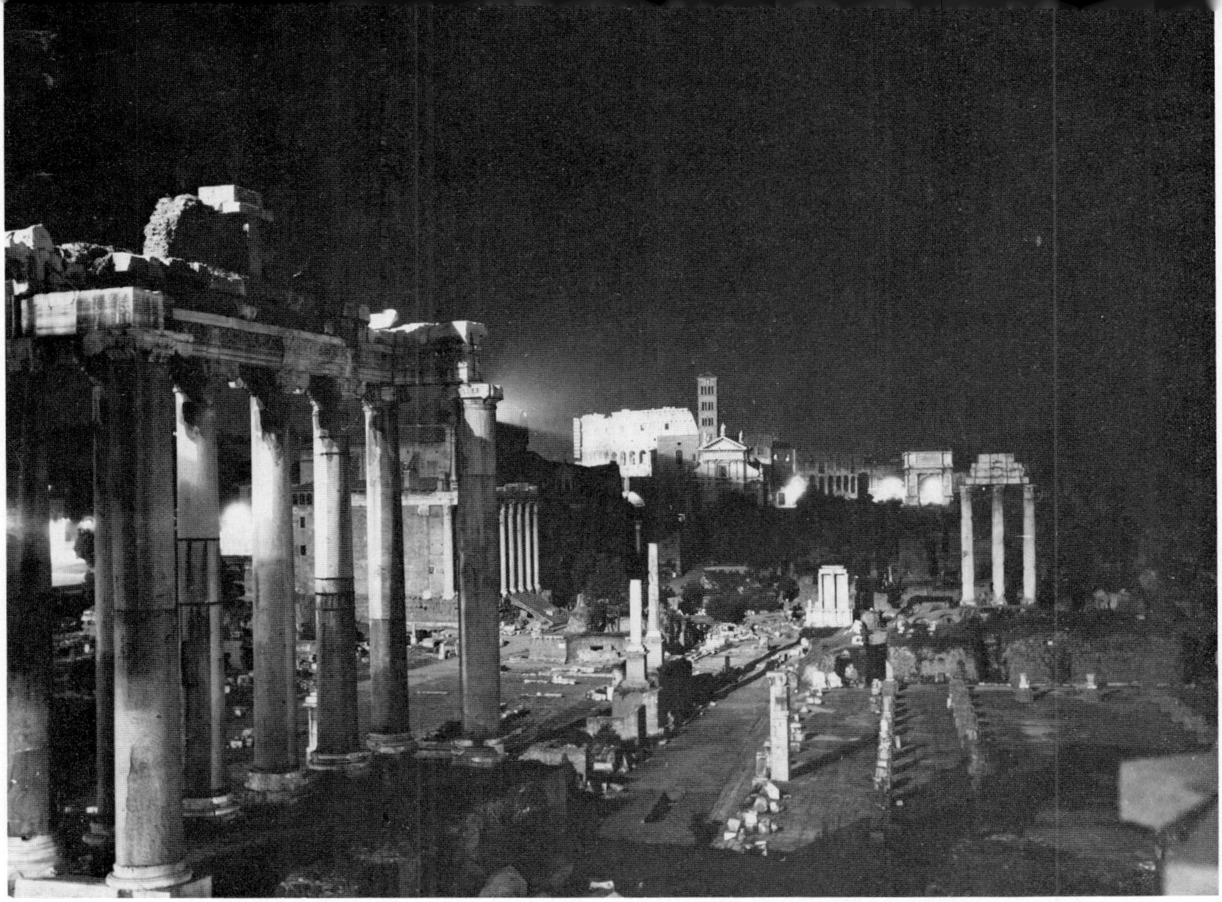

ers, sentimental dangers—how we used to be guarded!—to our daughters, no more dangers than the middle of Main Street. They don't know it—but how much they're missing!"

The long golden light was beginning to pale, and Mrs. Ansley lifted her knitting a little closer to her eyes. "Yes; how we were guarded!"

"I always used to think," Mrs. Slade continued, "that our mothers had a much more difficult job than our grandmothers. When Roman fever stalked the streets it must have been comparatively easy to gather in the girls at the danger hour; but when you and I were young, with such beauty calling us, and the spice of disobedience thrown in, and no worse risk than catching cold during the cool hour after sunset, the mothers used to be put to it to keep us in—didn't they?"

She turned again toward Mrs Ansley, but the latter had reached a delicate point in her knitting. "One, two, three—slip two; yes, they must have been," she assented, without looking up.

Mrs. Slade's eyes rested on her with a deepened attention. "She can knit—in the face of *this!* How like her. . . ."

Mrs. Slade leaned back, brooding, her eyes ranging from the ruins which faced her to the long green hollow of the Forum [60], the fading glow of the church fronts beyond it, and the outlying immensity of the Colosseum. Suddenly she thought: "It's all very well to say that our girls have done away with sentiment and moonlight. But if Babs Ansley isn't out to catch that young aviator—the one

60 The Roman Forum at night. Beyond the ruins of the Forum, a church front, a bell tower, and the brightly lit curved wall of the Colosseum are visible in the distance.

who's a Marchese—then I don't know anything. And Jenny has no chance beside her. I know that too. I wonder if that's why Grace Ansley likes the two girls to go everywhere together? My poor Jenny as a foil—!" Mrs. Slade gave a hardly audible laugh, and at the sound Mrs. Ansley dropped her knitting.

"Yes—?"

"I—oh, nothing. I was only thinking how your Babs carries everything before her. That Campolieri boy is one of the best matches in Rome. Don't look so innocent, my dear—you know he is. And I was wondering, ever so respectfully, you understand . . . wondering how two such exemplary characters as you and Horace had managed to produce anything quite so dynamic." Mrs. Slade laughed again, with a touch of asperity.

Mrs. Ansley's hands lay inert across her needles. She looked straight out at the great accumulated wreckage of passion and splendor at her feet. But her small profile was almost expressionless. At length she said: "I think you overrate Babs, my dear."

Mrs. Slade's tone grew easier. "No; I don't. I appreciate her. And perhaps envy you. Oh, my girl's perfect; if I were a chronic invalid I'd—well, I think I'd rather be in Jenny's hands. There must be times . . . but there! I always wanted a brilliant daughter . . . and never quite understood why I got an angel instead."

Mrs. Ansley echoed her laugh in a faint murmur. "Babs is an angel too."

"Of course—of course! But she's got rainbow wings. Well, they're wandering by the sea with their young men; and here we sit . . . and it all brings back the past a little too acutely."

Mrs. Ansley had resumed her knitting. One might almost have imagined (if one had known her less well, Mrs. Slade reflected) that, for her also, too many memories rose from the lengthening shadows of those august ruins. But no; she was simply absorbed in her work. What was there for her to worry about? She knew that Babs would almost certainly come back engaged to the extremely eligible Campolieri. "And she'll sell the New York house, and settle down near them in Rome, and never be in their way . . . she's much too tactful. But she'll have an excellent cook, and just the right people in for bridge and cocktails . . . and a perfectly peaceful old age among her grandchildren."

Mrs. Slade broke off this prophetic flight with a recoil of self-disgust. There was no one of whom she had less right to think unkindly than of Grace Ansley. Would she never cure herself of envying her? Perhaps she had begun too long ago.

She stood up and leaned against the parapet, filling her troubled eyes with the tranquilizing magic of the hour. But instead of tranquilizing her the sight seemed to increase her exasperation. Her gaze turned toward the Colosseum. Already its golden flank was drowned in purple shadow, and above it the sky curved crystal clear, without light or color. It was the moment when afternoon and evening hang balanced in mid-heaven.

Mrs. Slade turned back and laid her hand on her friend's arm. The gesture was so abrupt that Mrs. Ansley looked up, startled.

"The sun's set. You're not afraid, my dear?"

"Afraid—?"

"Of Roman fever or pneumonia? I remember how ill you were that winter. As a girl you had a very delicate throat, hadn't you?"

"Oh, we're all right up here. Down below, in the Forum, it does get deathly cold, all of a sudden . . . but not here."

"Ah, of course you know because you had to be so careful." Mrs. Slade turned back to the parapet. She thought: "I must make one more effort not to hate her." Aloud she said: "Whenever I look at the Forum from up here, I remember that story about a great-aunt of yours, wasn't she? A dreadfully wicked great-aunt?"

"Oh, yes; great-aunt Harriet. The one who was supposed to have sent her young sister out to the Forum after sunset to gather a night-blooming flower for her album. All our great-aunts and grandmothers used to have albums of dried flowers."

Mrs. Slade nodded. "But she really sent her because they were in love with the same man—"

"Well, that was the family tradition. They said Aunt Harriet confessed it years afterward. At any rate, the poor little sister caught the fever and died. Mother used to frighten us with the story when we were children."

"And you frightened *me* with it, that winter when you and I were here as girls. The winter I was engaged to Delphin."

Mrs. Ansley gave a faint laugh. "Oh, did I? Really frightened you? I don't believe you're easily frightened."

"Not often; but I was then. I was easily frightened because I was too happy. I wonder if you know what that means?"

"I—yes . . ." Mrs. Ansley faltered.

"Well, I suppose that was why the story of your wicked aunt made such an impression on me. And I thought: 'There's no more Roman fever, but the Forum is deathly cold after sunset—especially after a hot day. And the Colosseum's even colder and damper'."

"The Colosseum—?"

"Yes. It wasn't easy to get in, after the gates were locked for the night. Far from easy. Still, in those days it could be managed; it *was* managed, often. Lovers met there who couldn't meet elsewhere. You knew that?"

"I—I dare say. I don't remember."

"You don't remember? You don't remember going to visit some ruins or other one evening, just after dark, and catching a bad chill? You were supposed to have gone to see the moon rise. People always said that expedition was what caused your illness."

There was a moment's silence; then Mrs. Ansley rejoined: "Did they? It was all so long ago."

"Yes. And you got well again—so it didn't matter. But I suppose it struck your friends—the reason given for your illness, I mean—because everybody knew you were so prudent on account of your throat, and your mother took such care of you. . . . You *had* been out late sight-seeing, hadn't you, that night?"

"Perhaps I had. The most prudent girls aren't always prudent. What made you think of it now?"

Mrs. Slade seemed to have no answer ready. But after a moment she broke out: "Because I simply can't bear it any longer—!"

Mrs. Ansley lifted her head quickly. Her eyes were wide and very pale. "Can't bear what?"

"Why—your not knowing that I've always known why you went."

"Why I went—?"

"Yes. You think I'm bluffing, don't you? Well, you went to meet the man I was engaged to—and I can repeat every word of the letter that took you there."

While Mrs. Slade spoke Mrs. Ansley had risen unsteadily to her feet. Her bag, her knitting and gloves, slid in a panic-stricken heap to the ground. She looked at Mrs. Slade as though she were looking at a ghost.

"No, no—don't," she faltered out.

"Why not? Listen, if you don't believe me. 'My one darling, things can't go on like this. I must see you alone. Come to the Colosseum immediately after dark tomorrow. There will be somebody to let you in. No one whom you need fear will suspect'—but perhaps you've forgotten what the letter said?"

Mrs. Ansley met the challenge with an unexpected composure. Steadying herself against the chair she looked at her friend, and replied: "No; I know it by heart too."

"And the signature? 'Only *your* D.S.' Was that it? I'm right, am I? That was the letter that took you out that evening after dark?"

Mrs. Ansley was still looking at her. It seemed to Mrs. Slade that a slow struggle was going on behind the voluntarily controlled mask of her small quiet face. "I shouldn't have thought she had herself so well in hand," Mrs. Slade reflected, almost resentfully. But at this moment Mrs. Ansley spoke. "I don't know how you knew. I burnt that letter at once."

"Yes; you would, naturally—you're so prudent!" The sneer was open now. "And if you burnt the letter you're wondering how on earth I know what was in it. That's it, isn't it?"

Mrs. Slade waited, but Mrs. Ansley did not speak.

"Well, my dear, I know what was in that letter because I wrote it!"

"You wrote it?"

"Yes."

The two women stood for a minute staring at each other in the last golden light. Then Mrs. Ansley dropped back into her chair. "Oh," she murmured, and covered her face with her hands.

Mrs. Slade waited nervously for another word or movement. None came, and at length she broke out: "I horrify you."

Mrs. Ansley's hands dropped to her knee. The face they uncovered was streaked with tears. "I wasn't thinking of you. I was thinking—it was the only letter I ever had from him!"

"And I wrote it. Yes; I wrote it! But I was the girl he was engaged to. Did you happen to remember that?"

Mrs. Ansley's head drooped again. "I'm not trying to excuse myself . . . I remembered. . . ."

"And still you went?"

"Still I went."

Mrs. Slade stood looking down on the small bowed figure at her side. The flame of her wrath had already sunk, and she wondered why she had ever thought there would be any satisfaction in inflicting so purposeless a wound on her friend. But she had to justify herself.

"You do understand? I'd found out—and I hated you, hated you. I knew you were in love with Delphin—and I was afraid; afraid of you, of your quiet ways, your sweetness . . . your . . . well, I wanted you out of the way, that's all. Just for a few weeks; just till I was sure of him. So in a blind fury I wrote that letter. . . . I don't know why I'm telling you now."

"I suppose," said Mrs. Ansley slowly, "it's because you've always gone on hating me."

"Perhaps. Or because I wanted to get the whole thing off my mind." She paused. "I'm glad you destroyed the letter. Of course I never thought you'd die."

Mrs. Ansley relapsed into silence, and Mrs. Slade, leaning above her, was conscious of a strange sense of isolation, of being cut off from the warm current of human communion. "You think me a monster!"

"I don't know. . . . It was the only letter I had, and you say he didn't write it?"

"Ah, how you care for him still!"

"I cared for that memory," said Mrs. Ansley.

Mrs. Slade continued to look down on her. She seemed physically reduced by the blow—as if, when she got up, the wind might scatter her like a puff of dust. Mrs. Slade's jealousy suddenly leapt up again at the sight. All these years the woman had been living on that letter. How she must have loved him, to treasure the mere memory of its ashes! The letter of the man her friend was engaged to. Wasn't it she who was the monster?

"You tried your best to get him away from me, didn't you? But you failed; and I kept him. That's all."

"Yes. That's all."

"I wish now I hadn't told you. I'd no idea you'd feel about it as you do; I thought you'd be amused. It all happened so long ago, as you say; and you must do me the justice to remember that I had no reason to think you'd ever taken it seriously. How could I, when you were married to Horace Ansley two months afterward? As soon as you could get out of bed your mother rushed you off to Florence and married you. People were rather surprised—they wondered at its being done so quickly; but I thought I knew. I had an idea you did it out of *pique*—to be able to say you'd got ahead of Delphin and me. Girls have such silly reasons for doing the most serious things. And your marrying so soon convinced me that you'd never really cared."

"Yes. I suppose it would," Mrs. Ansley assented.

The clear heaven overhead was emptied of all its gold. Dusk spread over it, abruptly darkening the Seven Hills. Here and there lights began to twinkle through the foliage at their feet. Steps were coming and going on the deserted terrace—waiters looking out of the doorway at the head of the stairs, then reappearing with trays and napkins and flasks of wine. Tables were moved, chairs straightened. A feeble string of electric lights flickered out. Some vases of faded flowers were carried away, and brought back replenished. A stout lady in a dust coat suddenly appeared, asking in broken Italian if anyone had seen the elastic band which held together her tattered Baedeker. She poked with her stick under the table at which she had lunched, the waiters assisting.

The corner where Mrs. Slade and Mrs. Ansley sat was still shadowy and deserted. For a long time neither of them spoke. At length Mrs. Slade began again: "I suppose I did it as a sort of joke—"

"A joke?"

"Well, girls are ferocious sometimes, you know. Girls in love especially. And I remember laughing to myself all that evening at the idea that you were waiting around there in the dark, dodging out of sight, listening for every sound, trying to get in— Of course I was upset when I heard you were so ill afterward."

Mrs. Ansley had not moved for a long time. But now she turned slowly toward her companion. "But I didn't wait. He'd arranged everything. He was there. We were let in at once," she said.

Mrs. Slade sprang up from her leaning position. "Delphin there? They let you in?— Ah, now you're lying!" she burst out with violence.

Mrs. Ansley's voice grew clearer, and full of surprise. "But of course he was there. Naturally he came—"

"Came? How did he know he'd find you there? You must be raving!"

Mrs. Ansley hesitated, as though reflecting. "But I answered the letter. I told him I'd be there. So he came."

Mrs. Slade flung her hands up to her face. "Oh, God—you answered! I never thought of your answering. . . ."

"It's odd you never thought of it, if you wrote the letter."

"Yes. I was blind with rage."

Mrs. Ansley rose, and drew her fur scarf about her. "It is cold here. We'd better go . . . I'm sorry for you," she said, as she clasped the fur about her throat.

The unexpected words sent a pang through Mrs. Slade. "Yes; we'd better go." She gathered up her bag and cloak. "I don't know why you should be sorry for me," she muttered.

Mrs. Ansley stood looking away from her toward the dusky secret mass of the Colosseum. "Well—because I didn't have to wait that night."

Mrs. Slade gave an unquiet laugh. "Yes; I was beaten there. But I oughtn't to begrudge it to you, I suppose. At the end of all these years. After all, I had everything; I had him for twenty-five years. And you had nothing but that one letter that he didn't write."

Mrs. Ansley was again silent. At length she turned toward the door of the terrace. She took a step, and turned back, facing her companion.

"I had Barbara," she said, and began to move ahead of Mrs. Slade toward the stairway.

(1934)

Edith Wharton's story is remarkable for its tight plot construction. It proceeds by a series of fascinating revelations. These reverse our view of both characters, and their view of each other, for first Mrs. Slade and then Mrs. Ansley proves to be the stronger of the two. Indeed, every detail in the story leads to an *ironic reversal*—the opposite of the expected—that shows how Mrs. Ansley, in her own quiet way, has had far greater success as a young woman than the patronizing Mrs. Slade ever imagined. Why, for instance, does Mrs. Slade admire Babs more than her own daughter? Why is Mrs. Ansley's great-aunt Harriet introduced (and why is she not Mrs. Slade's aunt)? What is the nature of Mrs. Slade's triumph when she reveals that she wrote the letter inviting her rival to the dangerous Colosseum? And how profoundly does Mrs. Ansley's revelation about what she did on receiving the letter top Mrs. Slade's triumph, so that Mrs. Ansley can finally say "I'm sorry for you"? How, finally, is the last line *foreshadowed,* prepared for, by the opening, in which the two young girls leave their mothers in the restaurant? This link between the beginning and the ending emphasizes the highly structured nature of the plot.

To appreciate fully the ironic reversal so carefully constructed in this story, we must be alert to the interrelationship between the incidents being revealed and the nature of the two main characters. At first, these seem to be merely flat types—elderly tourists reduced to being detached observers of life while their daughters rush off to an exciting rendezvous with eligible young men. Although Mrs. Slade and Mrs. Ansley remain types—wealthy Americans enjoying a life of ease—they become more complex as the plot unfolds. They are surely presented more in the round than, say, their two daughters, though not from as many sides as the figures in longer novels tend to be. Mrs. Slade and Mrs. Ansley seem relatively complex because the plot revelations not only bring to light the past—fascinating as that is—but also result in profound psychological changes in the present. The two women are not mere observers of life, but are involved in a drama of their own. The misconceptions they have about each other, their changed perceptions, and especially the final recognition of an unexpected and unwelcome truth by the condescending Mrs. Slade—these are the aspects of characterization brought about by the plot incidents. Agents and actions are, then, inseparable. W. B. Yeats has summed up such interdependence in his intriguing rhetorical question: "How can we know the dancer from the dance?"

Setting

When writers wish to include descriptions of the *setting*—that is, the place and perhaps also the time in which the action unfolds—they must make conscious decisions about where and at what length in the sequential narrative to introduce such material. Edith Wharton in "Roman Fever" places her two characters in a hillside restaurant overlooking the ancient Roman Forum and Colosseum—the very place where the significant incident of their youth occurred. She gives a brief description of the Palatine and Forum in the opening paragraph and only later in part II, focuses on the Colosseum. Moreover, she refers intermittently to the time of day, from early afternoon to the moonlit night in which the ladies' conversation takes place, but which also parallels the time of the crucial experience being revealed. There is significance, too, in the relative positions of the terrace restaurant and the Colosseum—high and low, detached and involved—and even in the fact that the Colosseum is associated with fever, both physical and emotional. As so often in narrative, then, the setting becomes symbolic, reinforcing the main action. Although unobtrusive, the various elements of the setting, placed with great skill, serve to enrich the story.

Treatment of Time

Perhaps the first conscious decision facing all writers is at what point in the story to begin. Since they can tell their stories only over time, they must decide which moment they will use as opening. They might follow Humpty Dumpty's advice to Alice and "begin at the beginning and go right on till you come to the end: then stop." Or they might find that a less strictly chronological method permits them to develop their material in more subtle or ironic ways. The choice they make has important consequences. Readers who follow the events in the order of their occurrence will respond differently from readers who know the outcome from the very beginning. While suspense can be maintained if we are kept guessing, irony is created when we know more than the characters at any point in the story.

An intermediate device in storytelling—one that neither follows strict chronology nor announces the outcome at the start—is known as *in medias res* ("in the middle of things"). Beginning in midstream, the storyteller draws attention to events nearing a climax, but then moves back in time to earlier events that led up to that climax. This device is as old as the classical epic. Vergil, for instance, begins the *Aeneid* with his hero's stay in Carthage midway on his journey from Troy to Rome and then focuses on the destruction of Troy that led to Aeneas's journey.

More recently, Joseph Conrad (1857–1924) set the opening scene of the *Heart of Darkness* (1902) in London on a boat on which the central character, Marlow, tells of his adventures in Africa. As Marlow talks, Conrad gives the impression that we are actually witnessing Marlow's story as it unfolds. At the conclusion, however, Conrad returns to the original setting, which allows him to compare the supposedly civilized life of London with the primitive life of the Congo. Many 20th-century writers have become especially interested in beginning **in medias res** because they are influenced by the flashback technique that is, as we shall see, frequently used in motion pictures.

In short, narratives have the advantage of being able to use time flexibly, going back into the past, dwelling on the present, or going forward into the future. Charles Dickens in *Great Expectations* (1860–1861) uses the time element with the utmost subtlety. As Pip's life unfolds from boyhood to maturity, Dickens moves from the present forward so as to trace his hero's *development.* This organizational pattern is typical of the **Bildungsroman**, the type of novel that focuses on the growth to maturity of the central character. At the same time, Dickens also drops a series of clues about Pip's mysterious benefactor and the parentage of the novel's heroine, so that our attention is drawn to past events in a pattern of *revelation* that is typical of the mystery story. In effect, Dickens is able to move his narrative both forward and backward in time.

In any narrative, writers must decide what verb tenses are most appropriate for their purposes. Although most narratives are written in the past, this is a "timeless" tense which often has the effect of seeming to be in the present. Such an effect is vividly exemplified in the opening scene of *Great Expectations,* in which young Pip is confronted by a terrifying convict:

> "Hold your noise!" cried a terrible voice, as a man started up from among the graves at the side of the church porch. "Keep still, you little devil, or I'll cut your throat!"

The basic tense is simple past ("cried," "started up"), yet the impression, achieved mainly by the convict's speech, is immediate.

Changes in time can be indicated in a narrative by subtler means than the choice of verb tenses. Indeed, Dickens in *Great Expectations* gives us the impression, without changing the tense, that the narrator functions at two different times. At one moment, young Pip seems to be recounting experiences he has just had, and at the next moment, an older Pip is reflecting on these same experiences. When the simple blacksmith Joe visits Pip in London and embarrasses him by his awkward manners, this double time focus is especially clear:

Then he fell into such unaccountable fits of meditation, with his fork midway between his plate and his mouth; had his eyes attracted in such strange directions; was afflicted with such remarkable coughs; sat so far from the table, and dropped so much more than he ate, and pretended that he hadn't dropped it; that I was heartily glad when Herbert [a London friend] left us for the city. I had neither the good sense nor the good feeling to know that this was all my fault, and that if I had been easier with Joe, Joe would have been easier with me. I felt impatient of him, and out of temper with him; in which condition he heaped coals of fire [i.e., of embarrassment] on my head.

(chap. 27)

Although the basic tense of this passage remains the simple past, the first part makes Joe's coughs and sloppiness seem a recent occurrence to Pip, whereas the next part of the passage gives the more mature reflection of an older Pip at a later time.

Our discussion of how writers can manipulate the time sequence of their narrative should make us realize how much attention goes into the creation of plot, character, and setting. To appreciate a writer's artistry, especially in a piece of prose fiction that unfolds over a long period of time, we must again cultivate our memory, attention, and anticipation. And if we take into account the writer's images, speech rhythms, and the like, we will also have to cultivate our ear, just as we do with music and poetry.

Questions for Study and Discussion

1. Choosing as an example a popular song with a pronounced melody, such as Paul McCartney's "Yesterday," consider the following:
   a. Is the beat strong and clear, is it only somewhat easy to hear, or is it barely audible?
   b. By tapping the beat, can you determine the repeated beat pattern and hence the meter? Is there more than one possible pattern?
   c. Is the tempo relatively fast or slow?
   d. Does the song change either the meter or the tempo during its course?
   e. Does the melody consist of notes held for different lengths of time? Try tapping out the melodic rhythm while singing to yourself. Are there dramatic skips at certain points in the melody?
   f. How would you describe the melodic curve? Do the high points of the melodic line seem to emphasize certain words in the text?
   g. Are different melodic patterns used for key words in the song? For instance, in the McCartney song, what is the difference in the melodic pattern used for the word "yesterday" at the beginning of the principal phrase and at its end? What is the effect of these two slightly different pitch sequences?
   h. Listening to a record of a favorite song, determine whether the chords that support the melody are unsurprising, unobtrusive, noticeable in and of themselves, or subtly unusual. Try to describe the effect in your own words.

    i. By comparing the melody at different times, try to recognize different sections of your chosen song. Then try to determine whether it is organized in binary form (A–B), ternary form (A–B–A), or some other sectional arrangement.

2. Listen to an orchestral piece and try to recognize the tone color, or timbre, of the various sections: strings, woodwinds, brass, percussion. Then try to identify the tone color of individual instruments. What tone colors, or timbres, predominate in contemporary rock music, in classical Indian music, and in jazz of the "swing" era?
3. What is the technical name for the number of feet in each line of George Herbert's "Easter Wings" (see page 83)?
4. What is the general meter of the poem? How is the usual metrical pattern not followed in line 1 and what is emphasized by this irregularity?
5. What special diction does Herbert use in the first five lines of each stanza to suggest the weakness or decline of human beings without God?
6. What images, including similes and metaphors, does Herbert use in the second half of each stanza to suggest hope of salvation?
7. How are the sound effects of alliteration and assonance used to emphasize the meaning, especially in the last lines of each stanza?
8. How is the title symbolic? What is the difference between a symbol and a simile or metaphor?
9. What is achieved by the particular placement of the lines on the page?
10. At what point in the experiences of Mrs. Ansley and Mrs. Slade does Edith Wharton choose to begin the story "Roman Fever" (see page 85)? What different effect would have been achieved if the story had begun with the two women's first stay in Rome?
11. In what sense are the two mothers and their daughters type characters? What details in the story gradually make the two older women round rather than flat characters?
12. As the plot unfolds, what three revelations skillfully placed in part II lead up to the culminating revelation in the last line? What ironies can one see in the reversal—i.e., the total change—in the way in which the main characters perceive each other, and how is this prepared for?
13. How does the setting contribute to the ironies of the story? Why, for instance, does Mrs. Ansley agree with Mrs. Slade's statement that the view is "the most beautiful view in the world"?
14. In what sense can the Colosseum be regarded as a symbol? What does it suggest?

CHAPTER 3

Components of the Composite Arts

Unlike the arts we have been considering, which exist primarily either in space or in time, the theater and film belong to the *composite arts,* which are both spatial and temporal. Theater and film unfold before our eyes in a defined playing space or on a screen, sharing many of the qualities we associate with the spatial arts. In addition, they relate a story over time, have a plot enacted through the dialogue and movement of its characters, and therefore share many qualities associated with the temporal arts. They require our attention to the individual stage or screen images, as well as our use of memory and anticipation, the mental habits necessary for understanding a narrative.

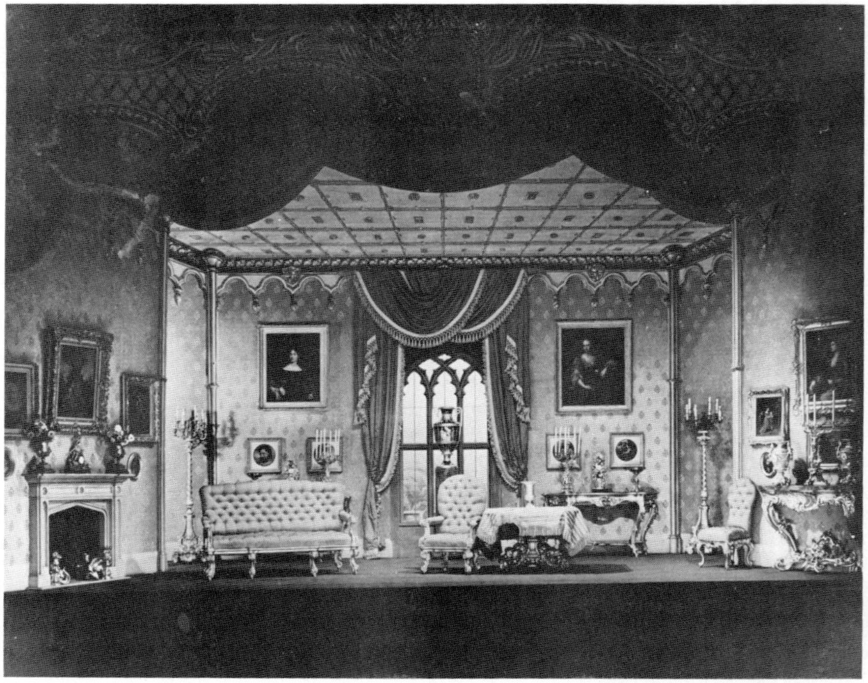

61 Stage set, Act I, Scene 2, for *Victoria Regina,* 1935. Designed by Rex Whistler. This box set with its overstuffed furniture, heavy draperies, numerous pictures, and elaborate ceiling gives the appearance of a mid-19th-century English parlor.

Theater

In addition to the components of the spatial and temporal arts we have already discussed, theater has several distinctive features. Most fundamentally, it consists of an actual performance, enabling us to witness the events as they occur; we are observers of the action as it happens. Furthermore, theater has a special playing space and a special kind of stage time.

The Stage as Playing Space

The playing area, the spatial component of the theater, is in many cases defined by the proscenium arch, which surrounds the opening of the stage and separates it from the auditorium. In effect, this arch is a frame, setting off the playing space as if it were a picture. Theaters with a **proscenium stage** are usually designed to accommodate fairly elaborate sets. Using backdrops, wings, and even false ceilings, the **box set** [61] can create the illusion of reality, of looking into a room as if a wall had been removed. The plays of Henrik Ibsen (1828–1906) and George Bernard Shaw (1856–1950), with their detailed directions for locales and furnishings, were written for this type of theater. However, such elaborate sets limit the number of locations that can be shown in one play.

The playing space of a theater can also be less precisely defined. Shakespeare wrote his plays for a much more flexible stage, one that did not attempt to recreate specific locations through scenery. Because Shakespeare and his contemporaries used only a few movable objects—such as a throne or a bed—they relied on language to paint the setting of each scene. As a result, Renaissance English playwrights were free both to vary the locales of their drama and to change their settings rapidly. Moreover, the bareness of the stage encouraged the writing of glorious, descriptive blank verse.

The fluid staging of the Elizabethan theater makes greater demands on the audience's imagination than is usual in a proscenium theater. But audiences are capable of exercising a good deal of imagination, and they are usually not troubled by indeterminate or unlocalized scenes. The audience may not know or care where the action is supposed to be occurring, since this information may not matter. Samuel Beckett (b. 1906) in *Waiting for Godot* (1952), for example, calls for a single tree on an otherwise bare stage; that is the only visual indication of place.

Such flexible use of the playing space is accomplished less easily in proscenium houses than in modern *experimental theaters*. Here the spectators often sit on three or even four sides, surrounding the playing area. This arrangement limits the painted scenic effects that can be used, but has the advantages of permitting actors to enter or exit from various sides and of creating an intimate relationship between the audience and the play being performed. Although we associate such seating with the post–World War II theater, it is derived, in fact, from patterns established by the **amphitheaters** and coliseums of ancient Greece and Rome.

Regardless of how precisely or vaguely defined the playing area is, the audience must use its imagination. For the playing space is hardly ever identical with the place called for by the playwright. No matter how many trees and even live rabbits are placed on the stage, for instance, we must still supply the imaginative act that transforms these into the forest of Arden in Shakespeare's *As You Like It.* Some theorists believe that we, as spectators, experience what Samuel Taylor Coleridge calls "the willing suspension of disbelief"—that we ignore the reality of the stage and its sets. Most of us actually have a double experience, simultaneously appreciating the physical reality of the theater and enjoying the fictional world of the play. Indeed, *play*—with its double connotation of "imaginative playfulness" and of "drama"—is the appropriate word for what we experience in the theater.

Stage Time

But theater, we have said, is an art of time as well as of place. Just as space or place has two meanings in theater productions—being both the physical stage and the fictional location for the action—so time has a double significance. It refers to both the actual time taken by the performance of a play and the fictional time experienced by the characters in the plot.

The actual time of a performance is limited. In this respect, plays differ from novels, which may vary according to the wishes of the author. A more significant difference between experiencing a novel and a play is that a performance cannot be interrupted at the spectator's will. A novel can be picked up and put down, and can also be reread. A play in the theater can be experienced only in the order in which it is performed. Consequently, we as spectators cannot go back and must rely even more heavily on our memory and attention than we do as readers. In general, theater provides a more concentrated experience than novel reading, perhaps because we are caught in the excitement of witnessing an actual performance. We are called upon to use the same mental habits and we feel the same excitement when we watch such related arts as opera and ballet.

Unlike real time, stage time can be either longer or shorter than the duration of the actual performance. In most plays the action is compressed so that the events cover a greater span than the time taken to show them on stage. For example, in only three hours of playing time, *The Tragedy of Dr. Faustus* (1592) by Christopher Marlowe (1564–1593) presents incidents that occur during the twenty-four years of Faustus's pact with the Devil. Then, at the end, the play takes only a few minutes to present Faustus's agonizing last hour. Indeed, this last hour is compressed into one soliloquy: "Now, Faustus, hast thou but one bare hour to live." The preparation for this moment, the intensity of Faustus's emotion, and the brilliance of Marlowe's poetry make the audience forget that far fewer than sixty minutes are elapsing.

A still more flexible use of stage time can be found in *Waiting for Godot.* The audience cannot know whether the second act of this two-act play really occurs, as the stage directions claim, "Next day. Same time." Although the characters talk as if only one night has passed, the tree, bare in Act I, has sprouted leaves; one character has gone blind; and another character has become dumb. This ambiguous treatment of time is used deliberately by Beckett to suggest at once the monotony and the radical changes brought by life.

Some experiments in stage time resemble those made by novelists, who can freely manipulate the time sequence of their narrative. The American playwright George S. Kaufman (1889–1961) in *Merrily We Roll Along* (1934) and the English dramatist Harold Pinter (b. 1930) in *Betrayal* (1978) both begin their plays at the end of the story and move backward in time in the succeeding scenes. The effect is strong dramatic irony, for the audience sees the characters play out the resolution, and then watches them at earlier moments in their lives when they are still ignorant of their futures.

Like other storytellers, playwrights have also adopted the device of beginning **in medias res**, "in the middle of things," moving backward in some scenes while still generally moving forward in their plot development. But stage scenes, unlike those in prose fiction, present their material before our very eyes and exist, so to speak, only in the present tense. In this regard, they resemble film. Some modern playwrights have, in fact, taken over a cinematographic device for dramatizing earlier moments in time—the **flashback.** This device, which we will consider at greater length in the next section, is used with special effectiveness in *Death of a Salesman* by Arthur Miller (b. 1915). Although the main action occurs at the end of the life of Willy Loman, a frustrated and pathetic traveling salesman, earlier moments are introduced as Willy remembers them. One powerful scene dramatizes the time years earlier

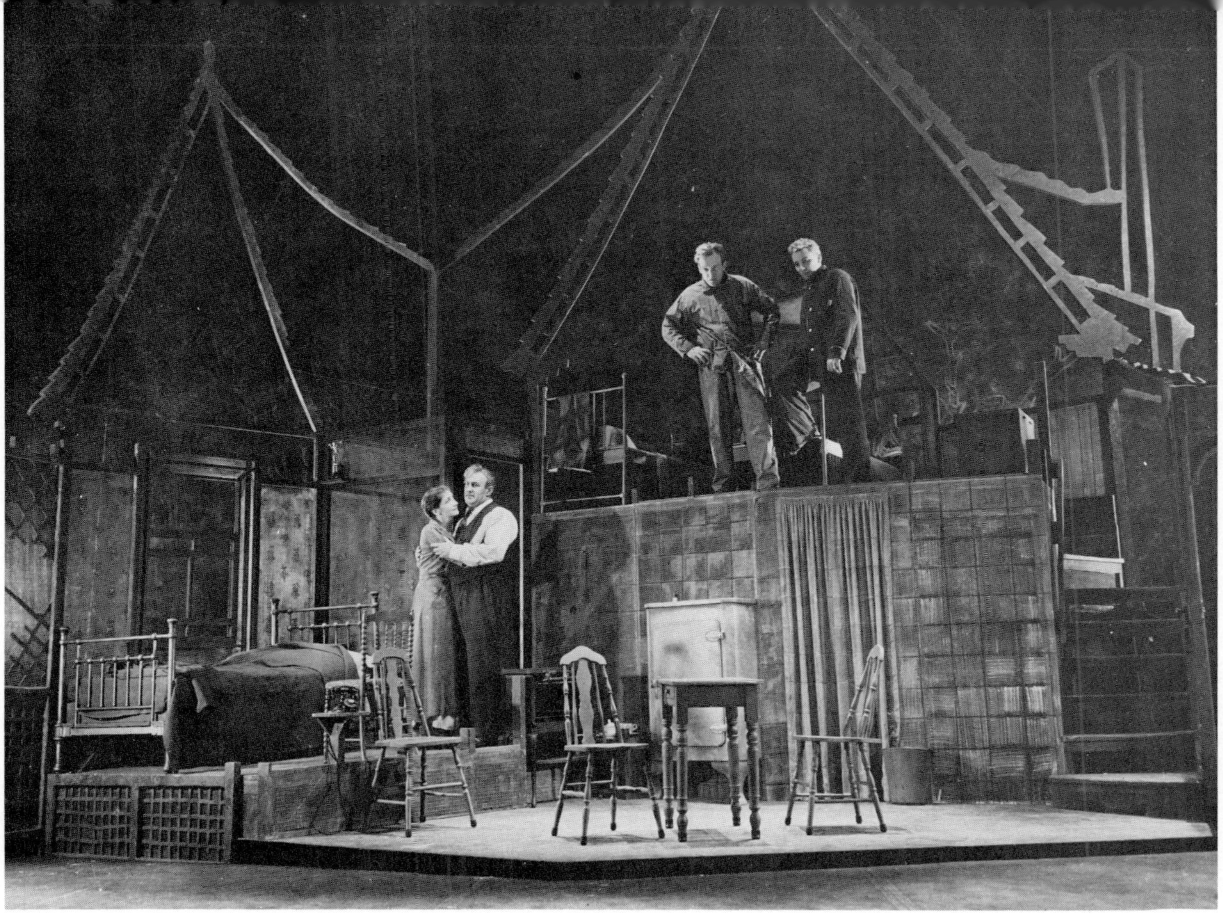

when Biff, Willy's son, discovers Willy committing adultery. The set, which presents two levels of a house, helps the audience to understand the differences in time. When the action takes place in the present, the characters move through conventional door openings. But when the action takes place in Willy's memory, the characters move through wall areas that are only suggested by the framework of the house [62]. Interestingly, the time of the various scenes is indicated by the way in which the space is used. This example reminds us of how intimately space and time are related in the theater.

62 Scene from *Death of a Salesman* by Arthur Miller, with Mildred Dunnock and Lee J. Cobb as Willy Loman and his wife and Arthur Kennedy and Cameron Mitchell as their sons, 1949. Directed by Elia Kazan. Setting and lighting by Jo Mielziner.

Film

Although the theater, along with opera and dance, can present space and time with considerable flexibility, film is a still more fluid and flexible medium. Like the theater, film provides visual images and can also dramatize events in space over a period of time. After 1928, when the sound track was invented, speech, music, and other sound effects could be included, bringing this medium still closer to the theater.

In a crucial respect, however, theater and film differ. The theater presents an actual performance by actors on the stage, and even the same company of actors will inevitably present slightly different performances from night to night. Motion pictures, on the other hand, present a filmed performance by actors on the screen, and the actors' performance can never vary because it is recorded. All copies of any film are basically the same.

In its use of cameras to record the action, film is also related to and an outgrowth of still photography. As such, it shares some of the technical advantages of the latter art form. But as the term *motion picture* implies, film differs from still photography in being able to present movement.

Indeed, the distinctive feature of film is that it can record motion by showing us characters moving from one place to another over a period of time. In doing so, it gives a vivid impression of how we actually experience time and space in our own lives—simultaneously. We are, after all, always conscious of motion, and we measure it at once spatially, in a physical setting, and chronologically, by the clock. That is, we measure motion by both the distance and the time it takes to get from one point to another—"It's a two-hour trip." By recording motion that shows space and time operating simultaneously, film comes closer than the other arts, including theater, to recreating reality as we normally experience it.

Yet film is not limited to recording aspects of reality. Like the theater, it has the capacity to manipulate space and time. And it has the additional capacity to create images representing thoughts or dreams. Indeed, film can present images that are imaginary or fantastic. Moreover, the fact that we can watch the images, often larger than life, while sitting passively in the dark makes our experience of film close to dreaming.

That motion pictures can create an illusion either of reality or of fantasy is amazing if we consider that the camera can take only two-dimensional shots, while we see the world in three dimensions because of our binocular vision. The camera, with its single opening, cannot as readily record depth as can our brain, which combines images entering at different angles through our two eyes. But by skillful use of technical devices, the director can overcome the limitations of the camera in order to fashion the entire film into a coherent and artistically meaningful whole.

Treatment of Space

The technical devices film can use to capture both space and time in motion are so numerous that only the most important can be considered here. In terms of space, the size of objects or people can be determined by the distance between them and the camera: the closer they are to the camera, the larger they will appear. In *Notorious* (1946), for instance, Alfred Hitchcock (1899–1980) photographs a cup of drugged coffee first with normal dimensions but then menacingly larger as the camera moves closer. The term *close-up* is used for the shot of an object or even just a part of an object taken at such close range that it fills the screen. In *Apocalypse Now* (1979), Francis

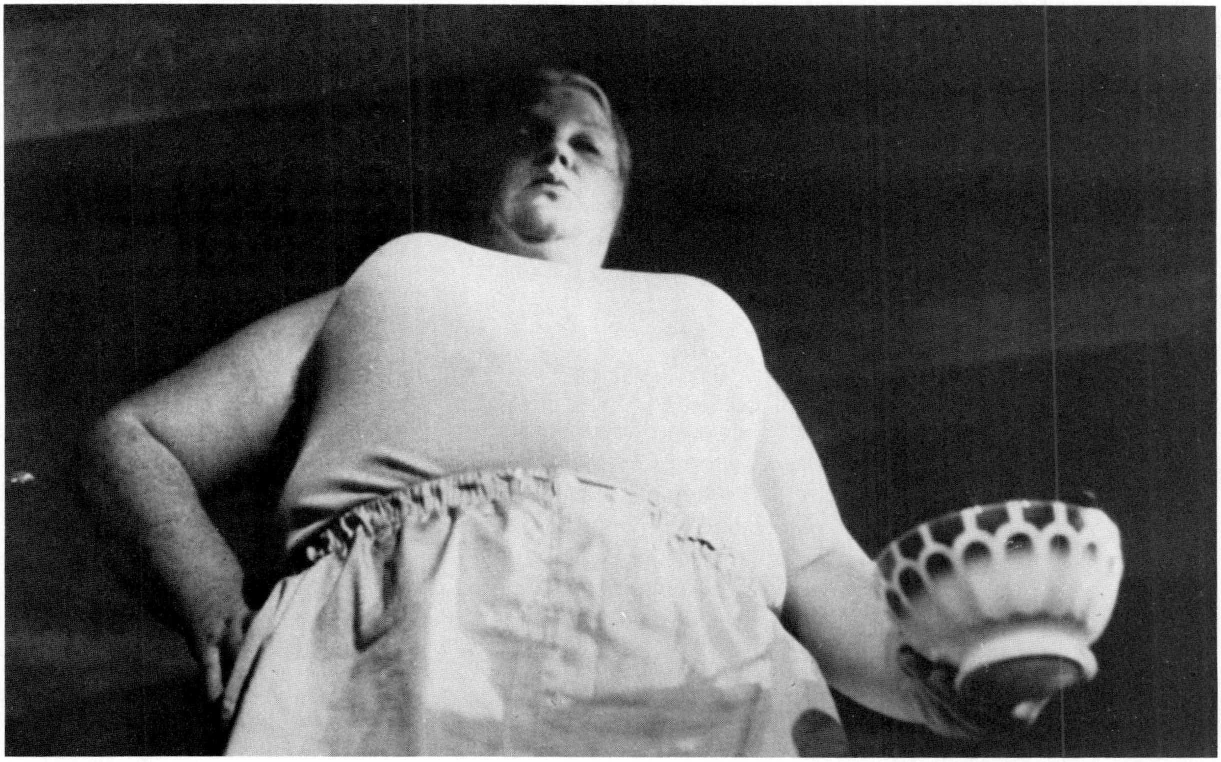

63 Scene from *Seven Beauties,* with Shirley Stoller as the sadistic commandant of the concentration camp, 1976. Directed by Lina Wertmüller.

Ford Coppola (b. 1933) at crucial moments emphasizes the harshness of the American colonel in Vietnam by focusing only on his stern and brutal face, which looms gigantically before us.

Size can also be determined by the angle from which an object or person is photographed. An upward shot makes the image appear large; a downward shot makes it appear small. In *Seven Beauties,* directed by Lina Wertmüller (b. 1930), the sadistic concentration camp guard Hilde is photographed at a sharp angle from below so as to appear monumental and threatening [63]. Conversely, her pathetic victim is photographed from above so as to appear smaller and helpless. Crowd scenes must be taken at a downward angle in order to include a sufficient number of people, and the individuals in such crowds always appear tiny.

Depth in motion pictures—the troubling problem of creating the illusion of three-dimensionality even though the camera can only record two dimensions—can be achieved not only by camera angles but also by the lighting of a scene and even by the choice of lenses. Although the focusing of the camera is usually taken for granted by the audience, only the technological advances of the 1930s have made it possible to establish an extensive "depth of field"—that is, the amount of space including both foreground and background that is kept in sharp focus. Mike Nichols (b. 1931) in *The Graduate* is able to capture not only the silhouette of the young hero in the balcony of the church but also the figures at the altar and even the natural setting beyond [64].

The choice of camera angles and focus as well as lighting are all available to still photography and motion pictures alike, but the latter have the additional possibility of creating depth through movement. In the technique called **panning**, the camera can film in an uninterrupted horizontal sweep by rotating from a fixed pivot. In the technique called **tracking**, the camera films while itself in motion. For instance, panning can record the progress of a train through a landscape by photographing the train from a fixed location; tracking can record it by moving with the moving train. Both techniques enable the camera to move about, capturing various aspects of a scene and throwing objects into relief. In addition, these techniques allow the audience to become participants in the space, not mere spectators as in the theater.

While simulating motion, film also presents a series of isolated images in space because everything is seen within the rectangular shape of the screen. The darkness that surrounds the screen can serve as a frame—just like the frame of a picture or like the arch that separates the proscenium stage from the theater audience. In the movies, we are so absorbed in the action that we are usually not conscious of such a "frame," but directors use the device of **framing** to organize their shots. They can select and order their material as if it were a painting, paying attention to symmetrical and dynamic

left: 64 Scene from *The Graduate,* 1968. Dustin Hoffman is shown at the church trying to stop the marriage of the woman he loves (Katharine Ross) to Brian Avery. Directed by Mike Nichols.

right: 65 Scene from *Ivan the Terrible,* Part I, with Nikolai Cherkassov in the title role, 1943–1946. Screenplay and direction by Sergei Eisenstein. This shot, carefully composed, uses framing to balance the close-up of the tsar's profile on the right with the queue of Russian peasants at the left. Here the size of the figures is directly related to their closeness to the camera.

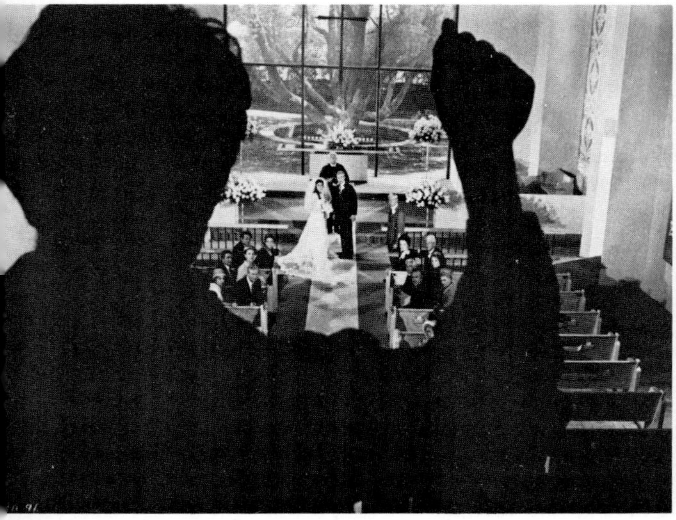

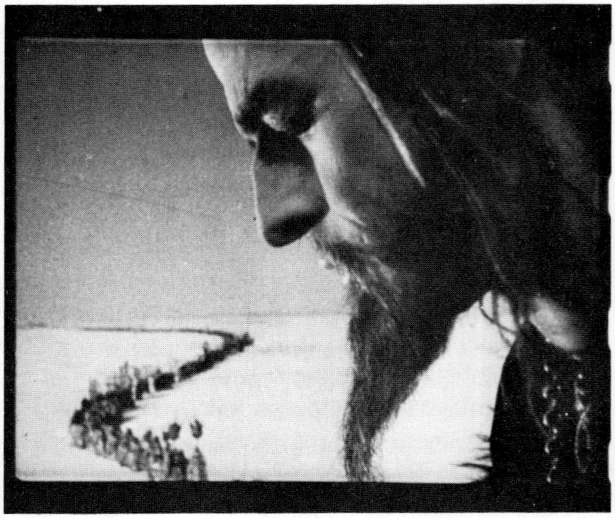

balance, light and shadow, and other patterns of composition we have observed in the spatial arts. By lingering over such shots—for instance, the brooding face of the tsar with the masses of Russian peasants behind him at the end of *Ivan the Terrible* [65]—Sergei Eisenstein (1898–1948) gives tremendous emphasis to the scene, which sums up the relationship between the fatherly ruler and the Russian people.

Treatment of Time

The director can manipulate the time elements of a film with as much freedom as the spatial elements. For one thing, film is always highly selective, moving quickly from one significant moment to the next. In Alfred Hitchcock's *Spellbound* (1945), we see the heroine in a sanitorium in Vermont, reading a letter that mentions a Manhattan hotel; and in the very next shot, we see her in the lobby of that hotel. Her intervening trip is omitted.

Large spans of time are also frequently omitted in films that record such factual happenings as a process of growth. Using a technique called *lapse time,* the camera may photograph flowers only at set intervals of, say, four hours. When shown uninterruptedly, such shots make us ignore the omitted time and actually give the impression that the flower is unfolding before our eyes.

The abrupt transition from one significant moment to the next, known as **cutting**, is one of the most common devices used in motion pictures. So common that we are usually not aware of it, cutting can be used quite deliberately for dramatic effect. It is especially memorable when it takes the form of **cross-cutting**, or the back-and-forth movement between shots. In *Apocalypse Now,* Coppola juxtaposes shots of the murder of the American colonel, who has become a tribal chieftain and demigod, with shots of the sacrificial slaying of a water buffalo. These two bloody acts are shown alternately in quick succession, indicating that they occur simultaneously and implying a close parallel. The skillful combining or juxtaposing of images is known as **montage**, a term derived from the French *monter,* "to mount" or put into place.

More gradual and less abrupt transitions between scenes than those made possible by cutting can be achieved by the devices known as **dissolves** and **fades.** In a dissolve the image disappears gradually while a new image emerges; for a brief moment the two images are superimposed on one another. In a **fade-out** the image gradually dims and finally disappears into blankness; in a **fade-in** a new image gradually appears out of the blankness. Early in the action of Orson Welles' *Citizen Kane,* as the camera focuses on Kane on his deathbed, the script calls for both devices:

[Scene No. 14] The Foot of Kane's Bed
The camera very close. Outlined against the shuttered window, we can see a form—the form of a nurse as she pulls the sheet up over [Kane's] head. The camera follows this action up the length of the bed and arrives at the face after the sheet has covered it.

Fade Out

Fade In
[Scene No. 15] Int[erior] of a Motion Picture Projection Room.
Herman J. Mankiewicz and Orson Welles, *The Citizen Kane Book: The Shooting Script*

The rest of Scene No. 15 focuses on the newsreels that give background material on Kane, whose life story is the basis of the film. This example suggests how well the fade-out, fade-in technique can be used to mark a change in both place and time.

The motion picture also can manipulate time quite literally by reversing, stopping (or *freezing*), speeding up, or slowing down the action. Keystone Cops movies use *accelerated motion* in their chase sequences to intensify the excitement, crowding far more activity into a short time than is humanly possible. In the frolic sequence in *Hard Day's Night* (1964) Richard Lester (b. 1932) shows the Beatles running at impossible speeds, leaping up and then floating back to earth with a languor that defies gravity. Both the fast and the slow motion delightfully capture the mood of exuberance.

The director can not only manipulate relatively short periods of time by expanding, contracting, and even on occasion stopping the film, but can also manipulate larger units of time in telling a story. Such treatment is often necessary because film narrative can depict action only in the present tense, since the action always unfolds before our eyes. In this respect, film is more limited than prose narrative, which tends to be expressed in the past tense, but can also use the present and future tenses. Film does not even have a cinematographic means of including time references such as "Earlier that day," "In the meantime," or "Later on."

To overcome this limitation in treating time, film can use the device of the flashback, breaking the chronology of the narrative by shifting to a scene set at an earlier time. This earlier scene, however, unfolds in the present tense. Such a scene is often introduced not by an abrupt cut, but by a dissolve or a fade-out and fade-in calling attention to shifts in time. When the chronology shifts to the future rather than the past, the scene is known as a *flashforward.*

Michael Curtiz (1888–1962) uses flashback memorably in *Casablanca* (1942) when the tough adventurer Rick, played by Humphrey Bogart, sits drunk in his Casablanca nightclub and recalls his earlier meetings with the beautiful refugee Ilsa, played by Ingrid Bergman. The script reads:

> The camera closes in on Rick. From his expression you know that he is thinking of the past. Slowly the sounds of an orchestra join into Sam's [the club pianist's] playing as the scene dissolves.
>
> It is Paris in spring. A shot of the Arc de Triomphe is followed by one of Rick driving a small, open car along the boulevard. Close beside him, with her arm linked in his, sits Ilsa.
>
> On an excursion boat on the Seine. At the rail of the boat stand Rick and Ilsa. They are transported by each other. Ilsa laughs.
>
> Inside Rick's Paris apartment, Ilsa fixes flowers at the window. Rick opens champagne. Ilsa joins him.

These quick visual flashbacks, introduced by a dissolve, are followed by scenes of dialogue in Paris in which Ilsa promises to elope with Rick in order to escape from the invading Nazis. The sequence ends at the train station as Rick learns that she will not join him. Transition back to the Casablanca nightclub is achieved by a dissolve as "the steam from the engine clouds over the scene."

Ingmar Bergman (b. 1918) uses a more elaborate flashback in *Wild Strawberries* (1957), in which two different times in one man's life are presented simultaneously. The central figure, an elderly widower, indulges in memories of his youth. Flashbacks show the girl he loved as young as she was at the time he is remembering, but show him in the same shot as old as he is now. This flashback goes beyond the bounds of human possibility by combining two different times in the same image. It demonstrates that film can convey complicated psychological experiences in direct visual terms.

Not only can film record events or memories of events but it can also focus on the workings of a character's mind. In the nightmare sequence of Hitchcock's *Spellbound,* the camera presents an actual dream as if we were witnessing the processes of the hero's unconscious. As we shall see in the section on stream of consciousness (in Chapter 4), our minds, especially in a dream, function in visual images, and a film-maker can present the workings of the mind directly in those visual images.

Films, especially on science-fiction subjects, can even make us witness totally fantastic spectacles. Stanley Kubrick (b. 1928) in *2001: A Space Odyssey* [66] and George Lucas (b. 1945) in *Star Wars* (1977), can make us feel that we are traveling on futuristic space ships and engaging in epic battles beyond the solar system. By enlarging photographs of miniature models and using computers, mirrors, and other means of achieving special visual effects, film-makers can make the most implausible scenes seem real. The accompanying sound—overwhelmingly loud, clear, stereophonic or even quadrophonic—often intensifies the experience in such films.

66 Scene from *2001: A Space Odyssey,* 1966. Keir Dullea (unseen, in space exploration vehicle) attempts to retrieve the body of Gary Lockwood. Produced and directed by Stanley Kubrick. Screenplay by Stanley Kubrick and Arthur C. Clarke, based on Clarke's story "The Sentinel."

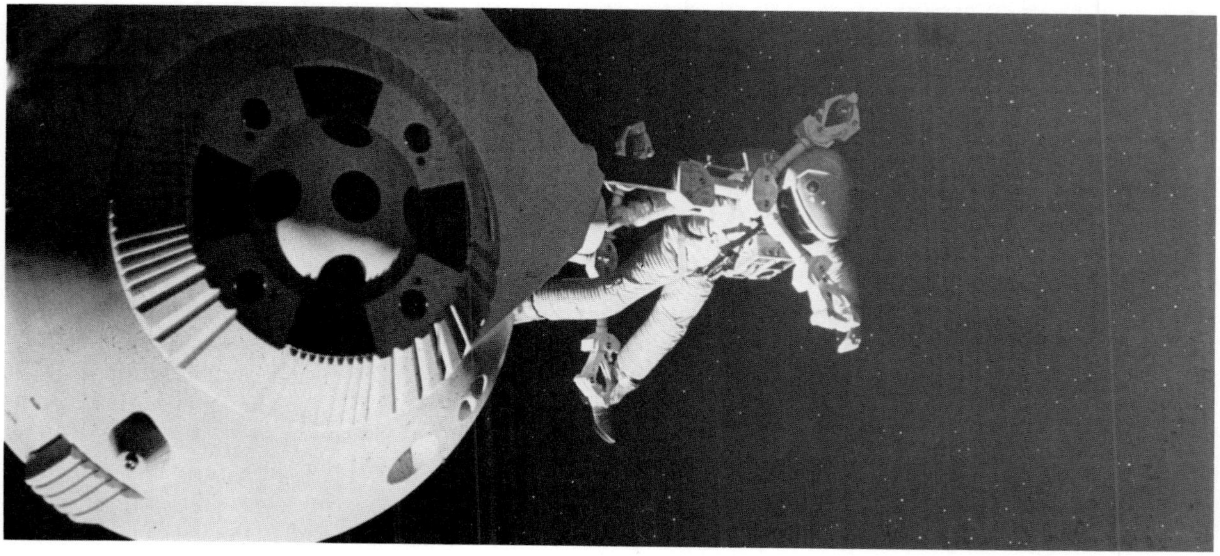

Sound

Sound is an important component in many modern films. This later addition to film technology, which became practicable only after the development of the sound track in 1928, makes possible the synchronizing of the image with spoken words, special sound effects, and music. Some critics have suggested that sound is not as essential to the film medium as are the visual images. We might argue, however, that it certainly enriches the art form. Especially in the dialogue, through which much of the story is usually told, words and facial expressions can reinforce each other, as is vividly demonstrated in *The African Queen* (1952) directed by John Huston (b. 1906). When Humphrey Bogart as Mr. Allnut flippantly asks Katharine Hepburn why she has come to such "a God-forsaken place," her indignant retort that "God has not forsaken this place" is emphasized by her tone as well as by her disdainful look.

No less than in the case of visual images, film has special devices for manipulating sound. Because the sound track operates separately from the images on the screen, a voice can be heard without our seeing the lips of the speaker. This technique is called **voice-over.** The voice need not be that of the person we see on the screen, but can belong to a narrator. *Citizen Kane* opens with a disembodied voice commenting on the newsreel shots that depict Kane's life.

Voice-over is especially useful as a means of expressing the character's innermost thoughts. Known also as **interior monologue**, this device uses the sound track to let us listen in on the character's thinking while allowing the camera to show that the actor is not speaking. In doing so, film can express private thoughts more believably than a play, for in drama such thoughts can be delivered only in a **soliloquy**, a monologue spoken by an actor alone on the stage. Appropriately, Laurence Olivier [67] used voice-overs to translate the soliloquies of both Hamlet and Henry V to the screen.

Again because the sound track can be separated from the visual image, voices can be *dubbed;* that is, someone else's voice can be synchronized with an actor's lip movements. This device is useful not only in translating films from one language into another but also in substituting the voice of a professional singer for that of a nonsinging actor. In *My Fair Lady* (1964), George Cukor (1899–1983) gave the visually enchanting Audrey Hepburn the appearance of delivering songs that were actually recorded by the singer Marni Nixon.

The sound track also makes it possible to enrich a film with special sound effects. We are all familiar with the shrieks, groans, and echoing footsteps in horror movies—all of which may either accompany an image or merely be audible while the camera focuses on a frightened face. A much subtler use of sound detached from the image occurs in the film *In Which We Serve* (1941) about the British navy in World War II written and directed by Noel Coward (1899–1973). As we watch the English captain picnicking peacefully with his family while on leave, we hear the ominous sounds of fighting planes offscreen and realize that the war is beginning in earnest.

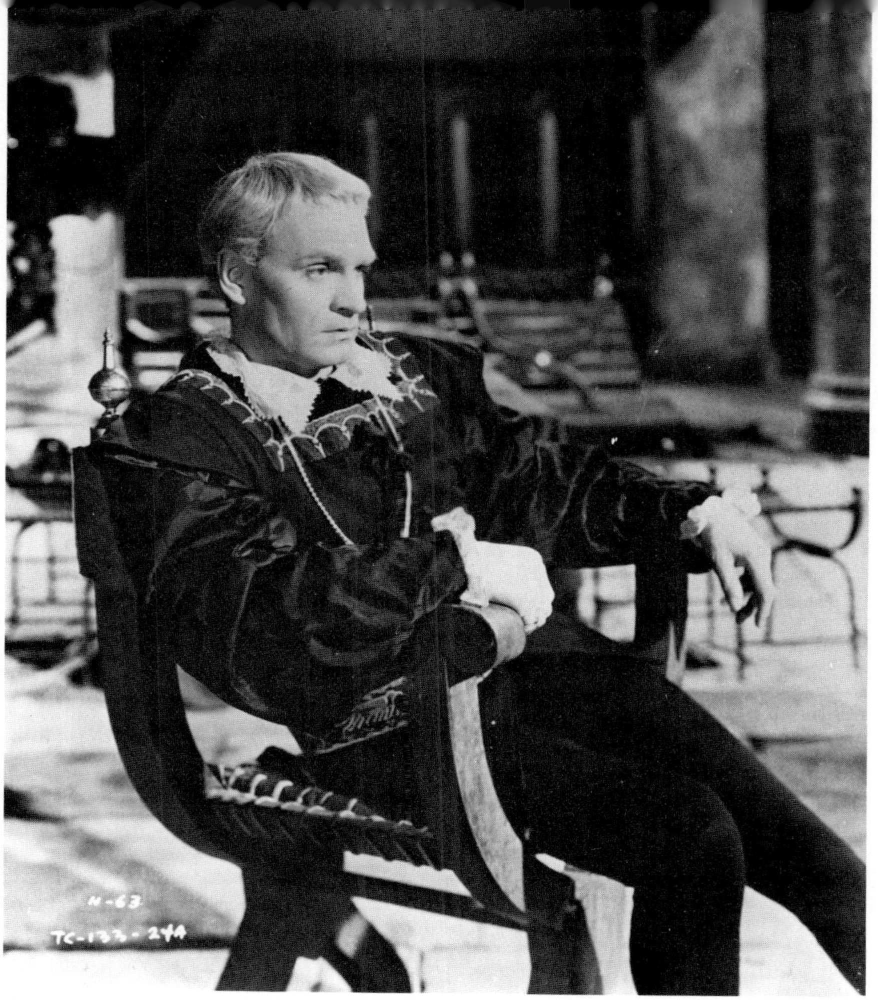

67 Scene from *Hamlet,* with Laurence Olivier, 1948. Olivier sits immobile in deep contemplation as his voice is heard delivering a soliloquy. Produced and directed by Laurence Olivier.

One of the most frequently used sound effects consists of music that is written especially to accompany some of the action. Often such music becomes the theme song of the film and is totally identified with the characters. "As Time Goes By" is inseparable from Rick and Ilsa's love relationship in *Casablanca,* just as Paul Simon and Art Garfunkel's "Mrs. Robinson" is identified with the older woman in *The Graduate.* These theme songs do much to establish or intensify the mood, as does orchestral music adapted or especially composed for a film.

Varied effects can be achieved by either paralleling or contrasting the music with the visual images. The delicate lyricism of Mozart's *Piano Concerto No. 21 in C Major, K. 467,* contributes to the idyllic background of the poignant and poetic love story in *Elvira Madigan* (1967) directed by Bo Widerberg (b. 1930). On the other hand, the equally lyrical excerpt from Mozart's opera *Cosi Fan Tutte* forms an ironic counterpoint to the irresolvable love relationship in *Sunday, Bloody Sunday* (1971), directed by John

Schlesinger (b. 1926), in which the two main characters can never achieve the balance and harmony established at the end of Mozart's opera.

From this discussion, we can understand that film draws on all the elements of both the spatial and the temporal arts and can unite these in unique and complex ways. In fact, film is probably the richest and most flexible of the composite arts. No wonder it is so popular in our day.

To sum up, both plays and films can manipulate space and time in distinctive ways. The stage need not define precisely the location for the action, and the plot of the play need not unfold in simple chronological fashion. Stage place and stage time can even be interrelated by the staging. Film is still freer in treating space and time. With its special devices of the close-up, panning, and tracking, film can alter the size and spatial relationships of objects on the screen. With its special devices of cutting, cross-cutting, montage, and flashback, it can also rearrange the time sequence of the story. Although theater and film have much in common—since both present narratives in space as well as time—each of these art forms has distinctive possibilities of its own.

Two other art forms closely related to theater also exist in both space and time. Opera combines drama with music, vocal as well as orchestral; dance combines bodily movement with music. Both of these art forms unfold before our eyes in a defined playing space. They develop narratives or, in the case of some ballets, abstract patterns over time. And they share the distinctive feature of the theater in that they exist in performance. Rather than analyze their components further here, we will consider opera in Chapter 9, on genres, and dance in Chapter 5, on performance.

Questions for Study and Discussion

1. For a dramatization of Edith Wharton's "Roman Fever" (see page 85), what stage designs would be appropriate in a proscenium house and what different designs for theater-in-the-round?
2. In a dramatization of "Roman Fever," what problems of stage time—if any—would have to be solved? If the play version begins exactly when the story begins, how could a playwright dramatize the earlier events that Edith Wharton conveys through the reflections of her characters?
3. In a film version of "Roman Fever," what special devices—such as close-up, angle shots, panning, tracking, framing, cutting, cross-cutting, dissolves, fade-out, fade-in, freezing, accelerated motion, flashback, flash-forward—could be used? What sound effects—voice-over, off-screen sounds, theme music—could be included?
4. Because "Roman Fever" takes place in only one setting and in a short period of time, it seems to lend itself more readily to dramatization as a stage play than as a film. Agree or disagree.
5. In the next motion picture you see, find examples of as many of the special devices of film—such as close-ups or angle shots—as possible. In each case, consider what the use of the device contributes to the film.

CHAPTER 4

Point of View: Shaping the Work of Art

When we see a finished work, we are tempted to think that it could not be different from what it is. However, the finished creation is the result of definite choices not only about what to include but also about what to exclude. These choices, in turn, frequently depend on the **point of view** from which the material is to be presented—various types of **perspective** in some of the spatial arts and various kinds of narrators in some of the temporal arts. Naturally, we, as audience, can see and understand the work only in the terms chosen by the artist.

Painting, Sculpture, Architecture

In looking at works that belong to the spatial arts, we must be aware of the ways in which space affects the presentation of the work. These include the vantage point, which determines the distance or relationship between the viewer and the art object; the treatment of space within the object itself, often through the use of perspective; and the demarcation of space between the work and its surroundings by means of a frame.

Vantage Points

In sculpture, spatial relationships are particularly evident. Sculptors intend their works to be seen from a certain distance—too close, and we will be unable to relate the parts to the whole; too far, and even the whole becomes blurry. We normally take this element of scale for granted, and it causes little difficulty. Yet sometimes in museums, miniature works are placed too high or too far away to be studied properly. Then we become aware of how scale matters.

More important is the sculptor's choice of how much to show. To put it differently, the sculptor invites us to take a certain position in relation to the statue or carving. In Donatello's *The Miracle of Saint Anthony* [see Figure 28, page 30] we are aware of the need for this frontal vantage point. We are also

left: 68 *Chefren.* Giza, c. 2560 B.C. Dark green diorite, height 5′ (1.52 m). Egyptian Museum, Cairo.

right: 69 *Chefren.* Side view.

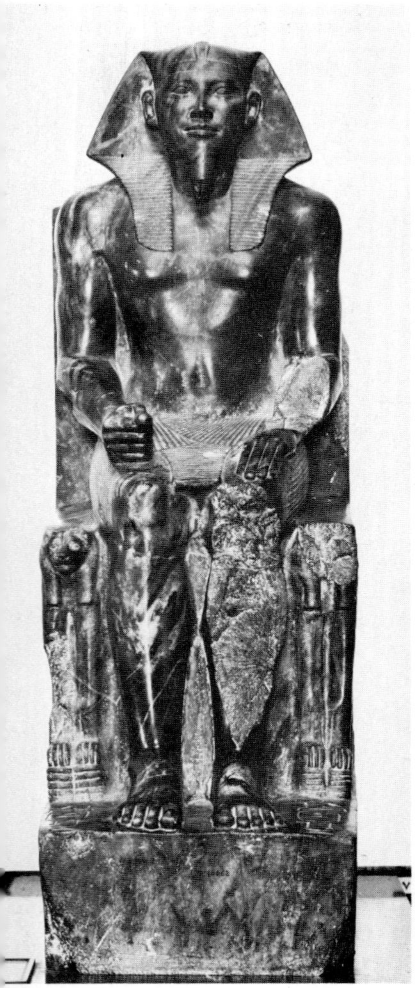

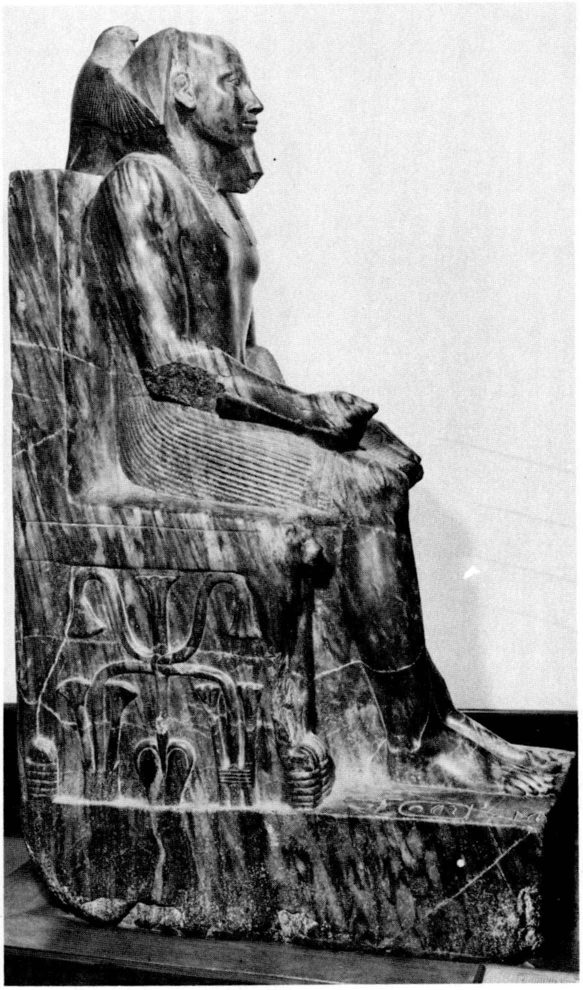

aware that the architectural setting suggests further vistas behind the closed-off walls to the right and left, but we realize that it would be useless to come closer to the work in order to peek into the wings.

A three-dimensional sculpture allows the artist and the spectators more complicated vantage points. In the seated figure of a ruler of the Old Kingdom in Egypt [68], the main impression of a handsome and majestic king is certainly gained by viewing the work from the front. At the same time, additional information can be gained by walking around and looking at the statue from the side [69]. In fact, only the side view clearly shows the protective bird perched on the nape of the king's neck. In this instance, a dominant *front view* is supplemented by side, or *lateral,* views. Similar vantage points that permit some view of the sides but still focus attention primarily on the front are offered by early Greek sculpture and by much Chinese and Japanese sculpture.

Some types of sculpture offer no single dominant view to which the others are subordinated. The free-standing *Rape of the Sabines* by Giovanni Bologna (1529–1608) [70] can only be properly understood by circling

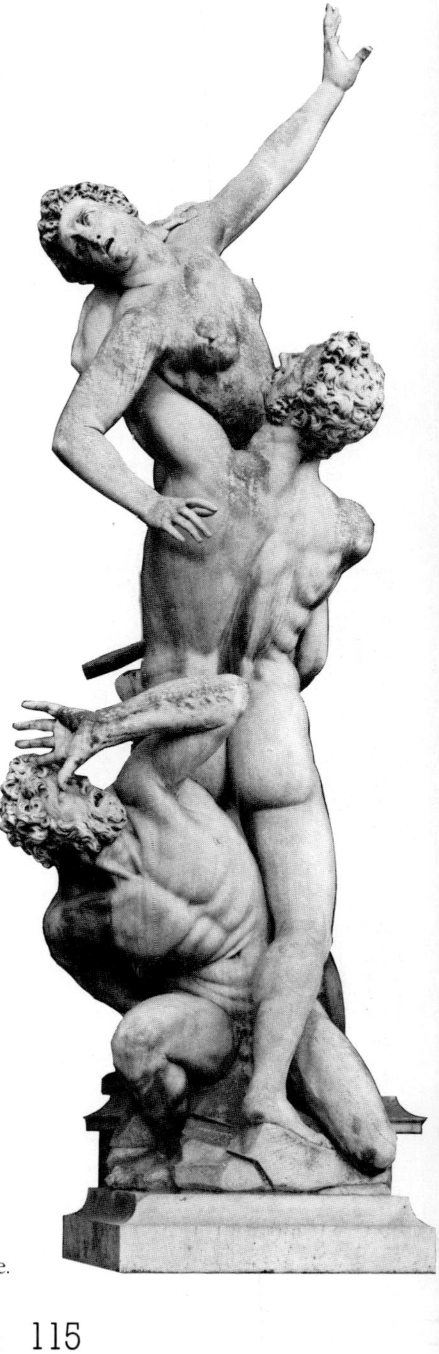

70 Giovanni Bologna. *The Rape of the Sabines.* 1583. Marble, height 13′4″ (4.1 m). Loggia dei Lanzi, Florence.

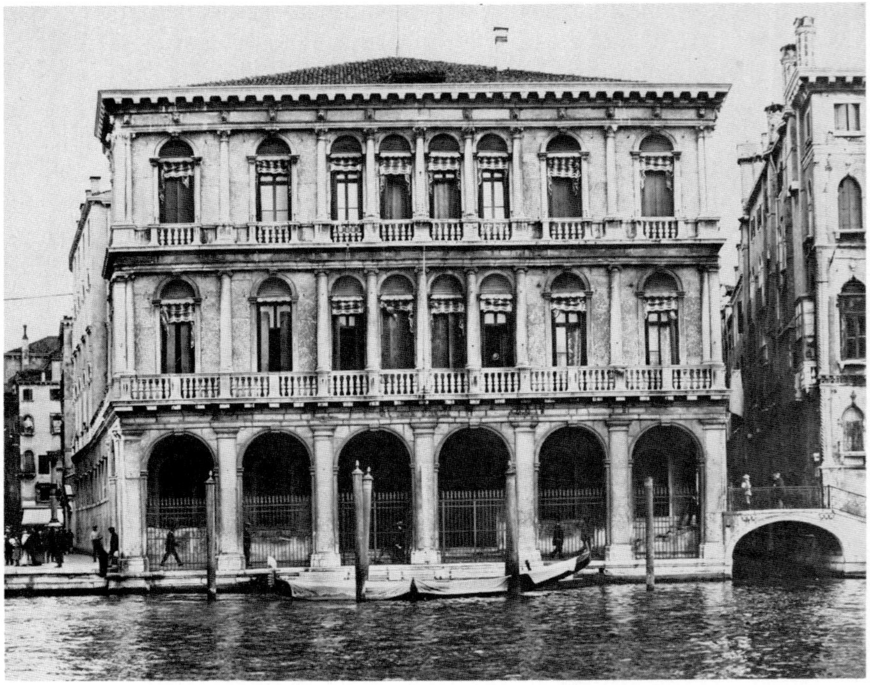

71 Jacopo Sansovino.
Palazzo Manin, Venice. c. 1535.

around it, so that our idea of the object's wholeness depends on the many "mental snapshots" we have taken of it.

In fact, sculpture may be seen from one of three points of view: the *unitary,* as in Donatello's *bas relief;* the *unitary-subordinate,* as in the Egyptian figure; and the *plural,* as in Bologna's group. In each case, we must bear in mind that the ways we view the work are determined by its creator, who has selected the particular vantage point or points for the work.

Architecture presents a similar range of vantage points. A few buildings, such as the Renaissance Palazzo Rucellai [see Figure 23, page 27], are of interest only as **façades** and are meant to be viewed essentially in one dimension; that is, from a unitary vantage point. Here there are no artistically shaped walls of importance to left or right, and the interior of the building no longer has great interest, if it ever had any. Most people who are concerned with this building are satisfied with studying it as we see it in the photograph, in effect as a bas relief.

But architecture is usually concerned with more than one dimension or one vantage point. Most of the structures that we find interesting are plural with respect to point of view. In typical Renaissance buildings, the architect presents a showy major façade with subordinate ones on either side [71]. And complex buildings such as Le Corbusier's church in Ronchamp [see Figure 53, page 56] or the Boston City Hall [see Figure 55, page 57] ask to be viewed from many different angles from the outside and, appropriately, from several additional vantage points on the inside as well.

Perspective

When we turn to paintings, we discover that we must view them much as we view relief sculptures. The artist invites us to place ourselves at a certain distance in order to see the painting from a unitary point of view. But as we explore the painted canvas, we find that many paintings also seem to contain some inner space. They present the illusion of space as if it were spread out behind the surface. This illusory space—presenting objects such as buildings and mountains, people and furniture—complements the space between us and the painting, extending it into the distance as if the picture surface were a window through which we can peer into still further space.

Painters often achieve this illusion of depth and three-dimensionality by manipulating the lines in their picture. For instance, a table appears to be three-dimensional when the lines defining its sides converge slightly toward one another as they move "back," that is, up on the canvas. When the lines diverge rather than converge, as in the drawing of the table on the right in Figure 72, a less convincing impression of depth results. In fact, definite rules govern the arrangement of lines that give an impression of depth.

The arrangement of lines we have been observing creates **perspective.** This term is used for the method of creating an illusion of three-dimensional space or depth on a flat, two-dimensional surface. Artists have long known how to present this impression of depth in individual objects. In Roman times, for instance, artists peppered the surface with many small, isolated objects, each of which individually seems to be three-dimensional [73]. But only in 15th-century Italy was a consistent system worked out for organizing an entire painting into a coherent, seemingly three-dimensional whole. Such coherent perspective was achieved through the discovery of definite mathematical principles that govern the placing of the lines.

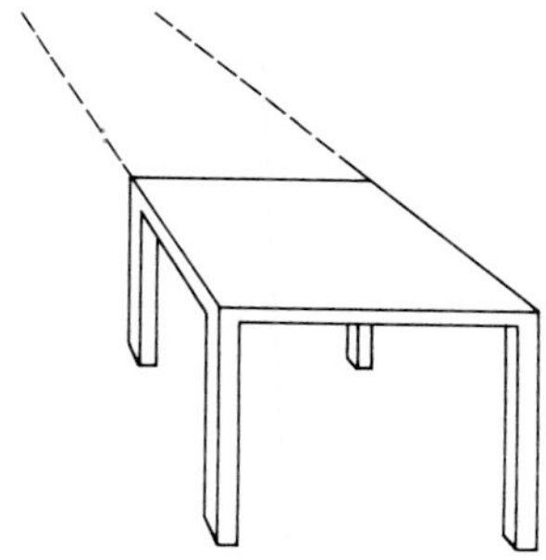

a

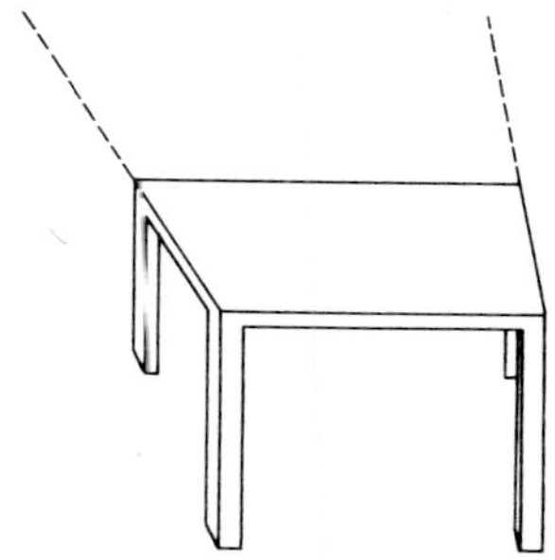

b

72 Converging lines suggest depth (a), and diverging lines fail to suggest depth (b).

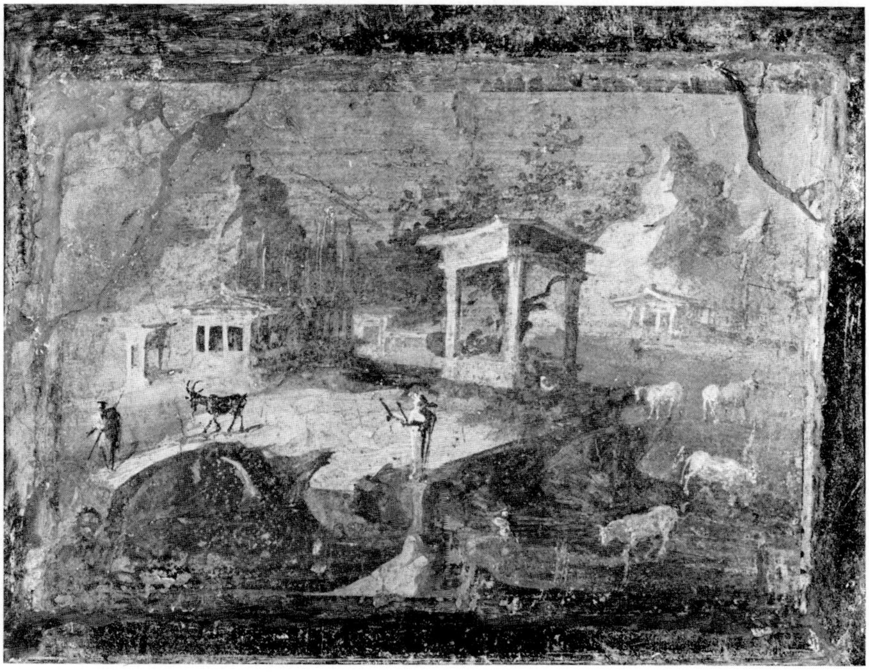

73 Landscape painting, from Pompeii. 1st century. Fresco, 11″ × 15″ (28 × 38 cm). Museo Nazionale, Naples.

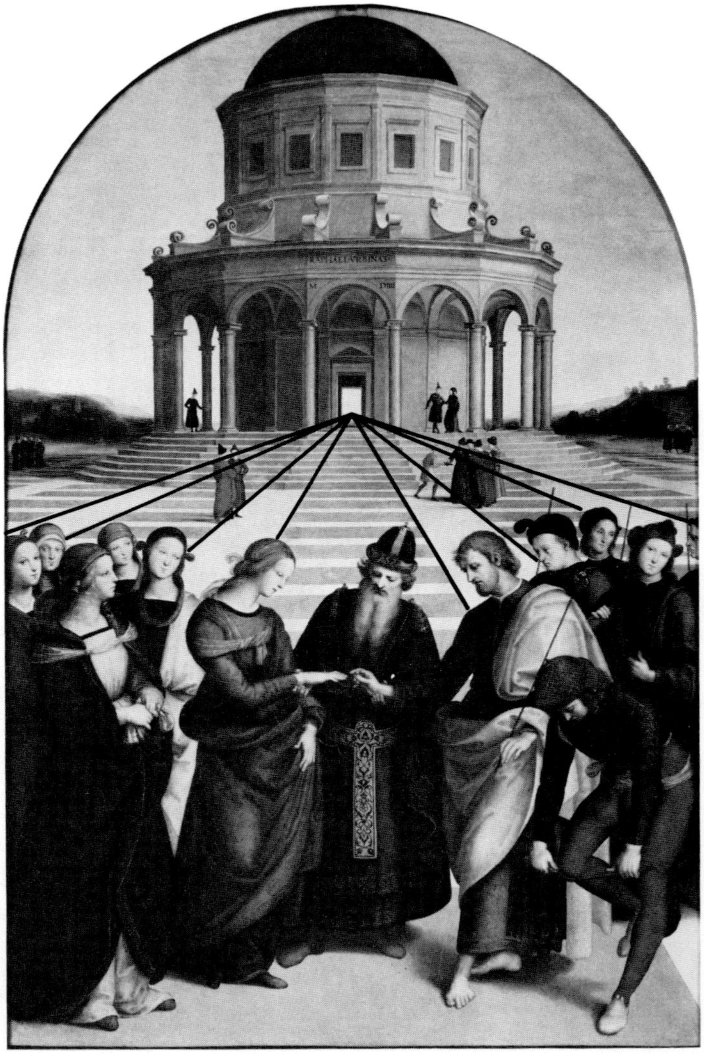

74 Analysis of Raphael's *The Marriage of the Virgin* [see Plate 9, Page 121] showing single-point perspective.

In the *Marriage of the Virgin* [74 and Plate 9, page 121] by Raphael (1483–1520), the grid pattern of the paving stones establishes a scheme which determines the relative size of all the elements in the painting. Raphael has created a network of these stones which diminish geometrically in size. He has then used this pattern to determine the size of the figures in the painting. Like the paving stones, the figures closest to the viewer are largest while those in the middle and background are progressively smaller. Moreover, the sides of the stones form converging lines, and if we imagine these continuing beyond the building at the back, we would find them eventually coming together at a single point. This method is appropriately called **single-point perspective**. The single point where all converging lines meet is also known as the **vanishing point**, and it is often placed at the eye level of the

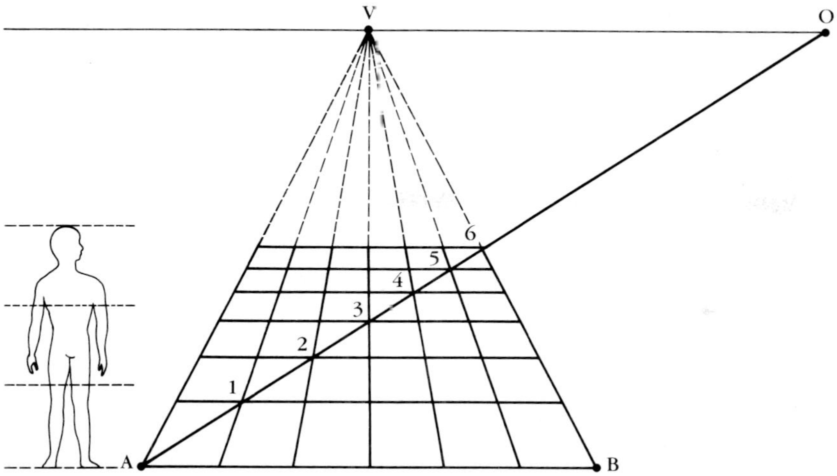

75 Diagram showing the Renaissance method of determining perspective.

person seeing the painting. As we face the *Marriage of the Virgin,* we seem to be placed slightly above the figures in the foreground, on a level with the entranceway to the chapel at the rear.

The geometric principles that determine perspective and the vanishing point in Renaissance paintings are highly complicated but can be visualized in Figure 75. As in the Raphael picture, all the vertical lines converge at the vanishing point, V. To determine the distance between these vertical lines, an artist had to decide on the height of a human figure as if this were painted at the base line AB. The height was then divided into three equal parts and the base line was marked off at distances equal to one of these points. The vanishing point was set directly above the midpoint of the picture, where lines from these markings all converge.

To determine the distances between the horizontal lines, the artist imagined the distance between the viewer and the painting, and noted this point O on the diagram on a line level with vanishing point V. The artist then linked point O with the left front of the picture (point A). At the points where line AO intersects with the converging vertical lines (1, 2, 3, 4, 5, 6) the artist could now draw horizontal lines parallel with the base line, thereby creating squares of diminishing size that give us the impression of depth. Even though these calculations seem cumbersome, artists used them for centuries to achieve perspective. They did so either by setting up an actual gridwork in the painting, as Raphael does, or by sketching one in at a preliminary stage.

The effort of setting up such a gridwork is rewarding because this device can be used as a model for any surface. Turned on its side, the diagram can serve as a model for a wall; turned upside down, it can serve as a model for a ceiling. Once we become aware of this gridwork, we can find it in countless paintings from the Renaissance through the 19th century. Used on floors, walls, or ceilings, it helps to establish perspective and the illusion of depth.

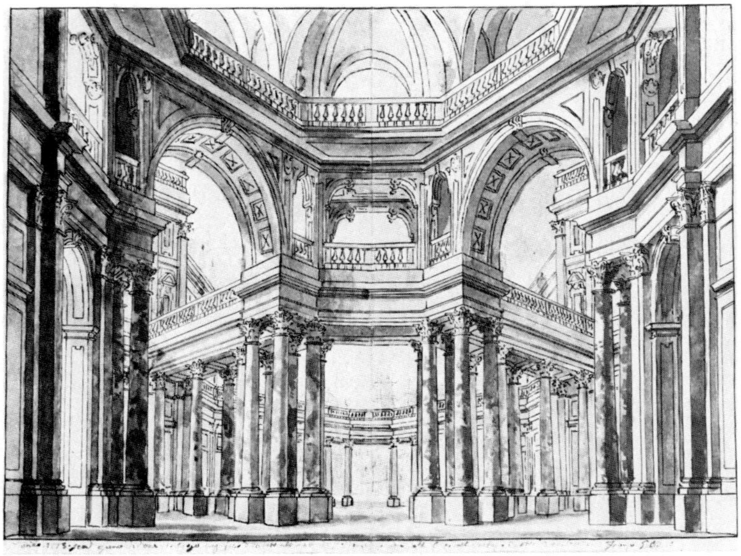

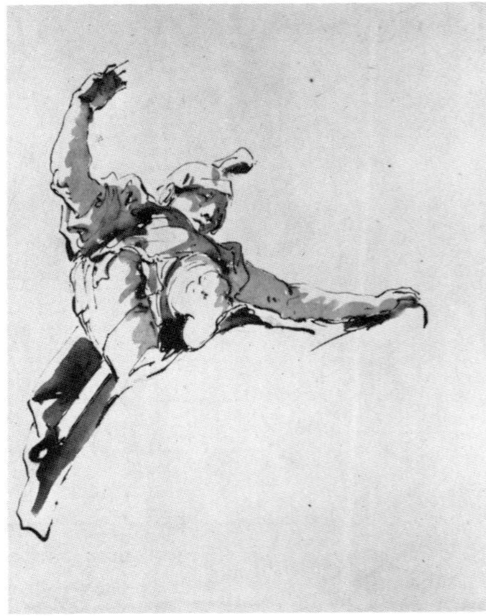

above left: 76 Fabrizio Galliari. Royal palace, set for *Didone,* 1773.
Pen and ink with sepia wash, 12⅜″ × 17¾″ (32 × 46 cm).
Museo Teatrale alla Scala, Milan.

above right: 77
Giovanni Battista Tiepolo.
Warrior Standing on Clouds.
Pen and wash on white paper, 8⅜″ × 6¾″ (22 × 18 cm).
British Museum, London (reproduced by courtesy of the Trustees).

For some time after its invention, the artists who adopted perspective used it in an uncomplicated, almost simplistic manner. They did so much like someone who is learning to take photographs and who just aims the camera straight at the scene without attempting any intricate effects. But such a direct approach to perspective need not be unskillful. In the *Marriage of the Virgin* Raphael establishes a sense of depth by using the principles of single-point perspective in a straightforward yet convincing manner.

These principles came to be treated with greater freedom and daring by later artists. Theater designers of the 17th and 18th centuries were especially adept at conveying the impression of vast architectural spaces on stage simply with a painted backcloth. By carefully presenting the architectural details of his setting, Fabrizio Galliari (1709–1790) seems to have different vanishing points [76], although, in fact, the principle of a single vanishing point, at the low center of the picture, is retained.

Gradually, artists also learned to take advantage of other striking effects made possible by perspective. Many of these effects are based on the principle of **foreshortening**, drawing objects so that they drastically diminish in size according to the laws of perspective. For instance, in painting a human figure, the artist will make the part of the body closest to the viewer appear proportionately larger than the parts of the body further away from the viewer [77]. Foreshortening may be found in whole paintings, as we see in the "worm's-eye view," in which the scene is depicted, so to speak, from the ground up. This effect is created when figures are painted on the ceiling of a palace, municipal building, or church. The feet of such figures are actually painted larger than their heads to suggest that their feet are closer to the viewer. Conversely, the artist may show a scene that is viewed from a great height—from a tower or mountain top. Here again, the parts closest to the viewer will be made largest.

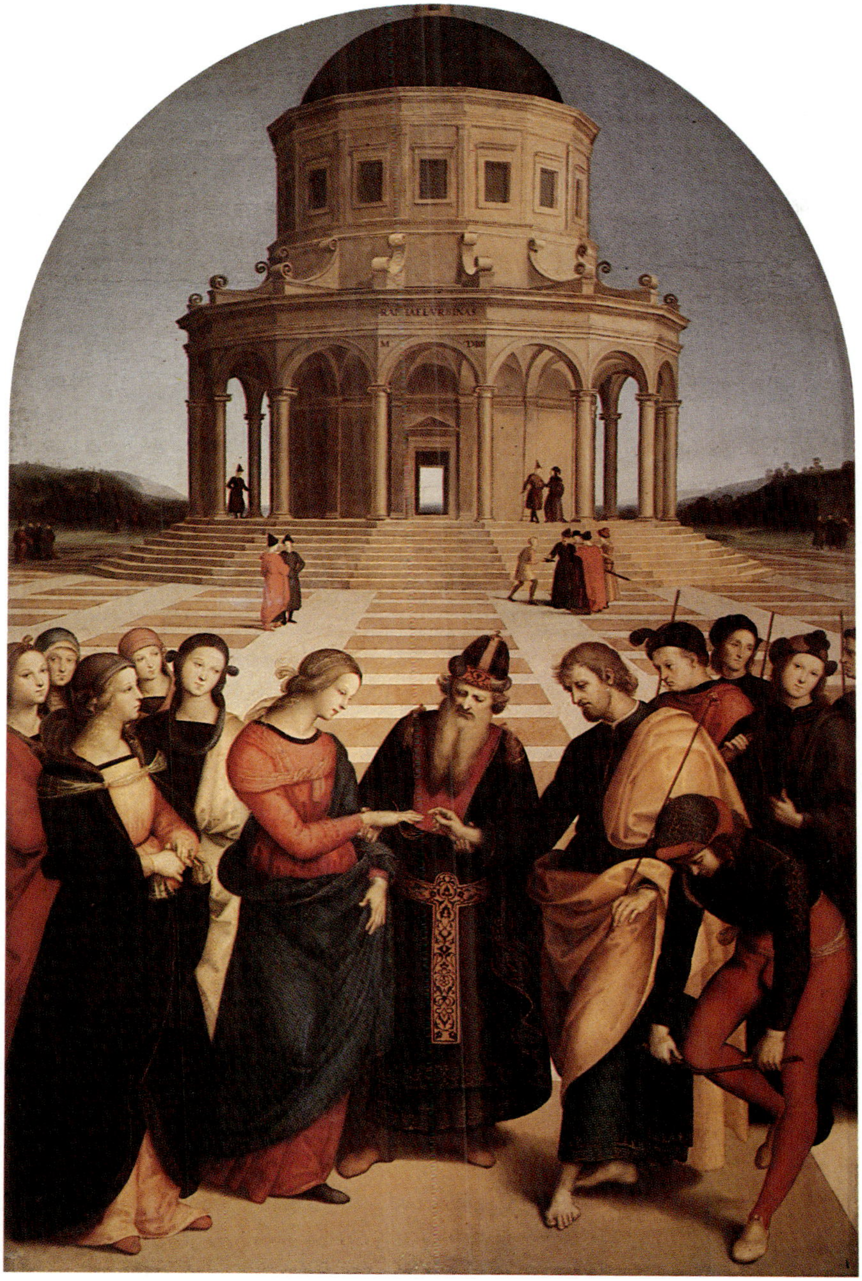

Plate 9 Raphael. *The Marriage of the Virgin.* 1504. Oil on panel, 5′7″ × 3′11½″ (1.7 × 1.2 m). Pinacoteca di Brera, Milan. All of Mary's suitors on the right carry rods, indicating their candidacy as potential husbands. Joseph holds a rod that has flowered—the sign that he has been chosen—while a rejected suitor in the right foreground breaks his rod across his knee in disappointment.

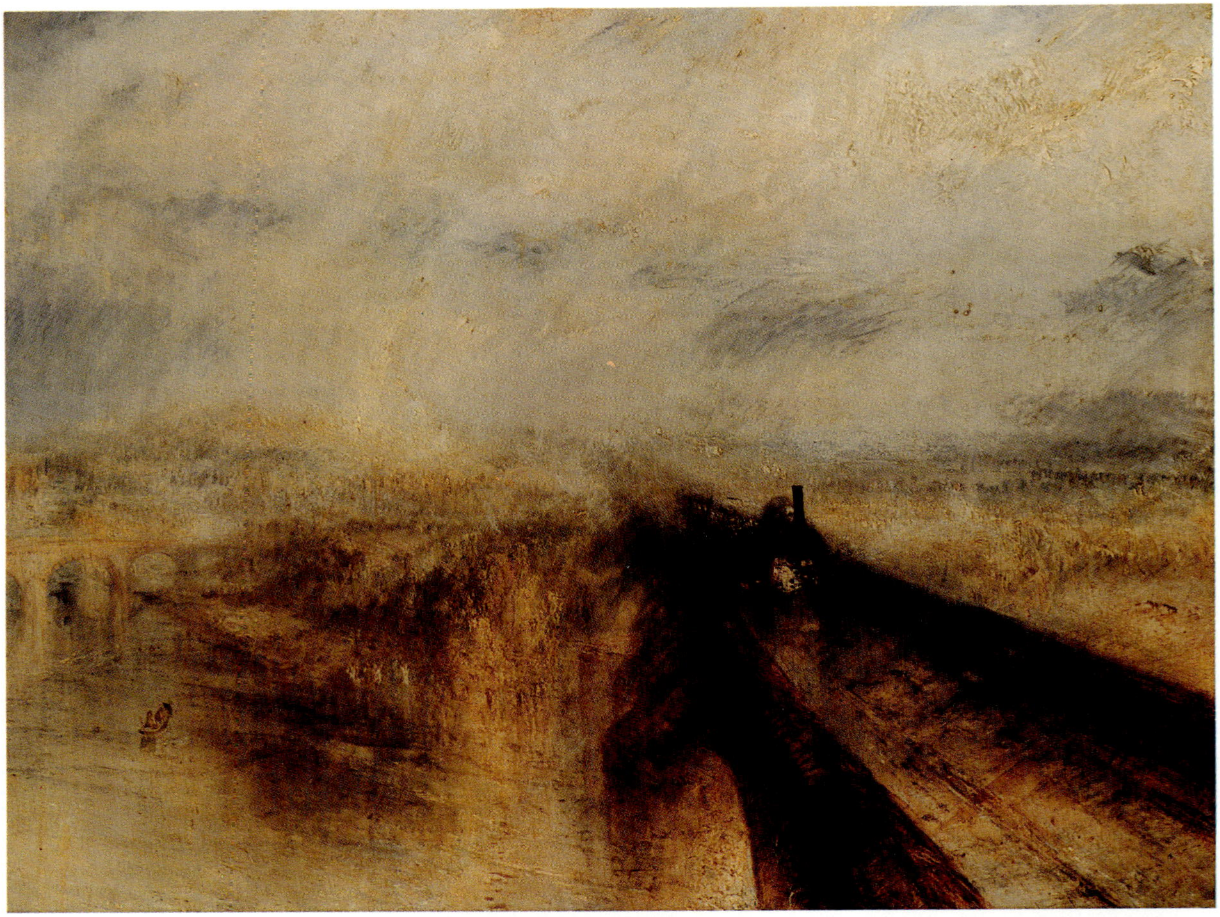

Plate 10 Joseph Mallord William Turner. *Rain, Steam, and Speed.* 1844. Oil on canvas, 3 × 4′ (.91 × 1.22 m). National Gallery, London (reproduced by courtesy of the Trustees).

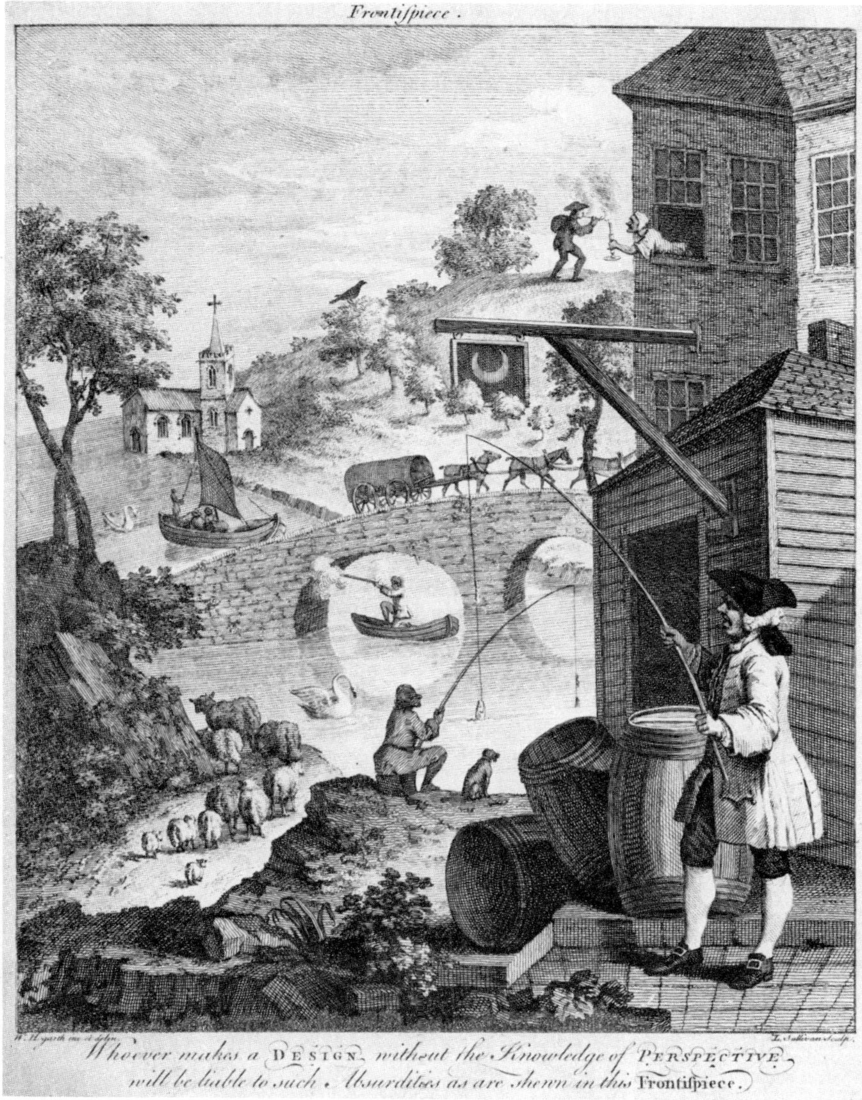

78 Engraving by Luke Sullivan after William Hogarth. *Frontispiece Dr. Brook Taylor's Method of Perspective Made Easy* by John Joshua Kirby. 1754. Engraving, $8\frac{5}{16} \times 7\frac{1}{16}''$ (23×18 cm). Yale Center for British Art, New Haven (Paul Mellon Collection).

The English artist William Hogarth (1697–1764) uses perspective in a playful, humorous fashion, stretching its possibilities to the limit—and beyond. In his drawing [78], the frontispiece to a book on how to create perspective, Hogarth exaggerates and distorts lines to demonstrate what can happen when an artist does not know the laws of perspective. For instance, the monstrous sign on the building at the right has a flag that nestles perversely behind tiny trees far away. The figures are placed in impossible combinations, particularly the obliging man with a candlestick leaning from the window who offers a light to a traveler on a distant hill. These tricks result from exaggerating the possibilities inherent in perspective.

In some paintings mathematically determined linear perspective can look rigid and mechanical. A freer and more flexible approach for suggesting depth on a two-dimensional surface is created by **aerial perspective.** This is achieved not only by manipulating converging lines and vanishing points but also by controlling light, shading, and color intensity; blurring outlines; and introducing haze into the background. An early example of aerial perspective can be found in the triangular slivers of landscape that Raphael has included on either side of the temple in his *Marriage of the Virgin* [see Plate 9, page 121]. This landscape extends far into the distance not only because, beyond the darkish forest, the lighter bluish gray mountains appear covered in haze but also because their outlines are only dimly perceptible.

A more extensive use of aerial perspective can be seen in *Rain, Steam,*

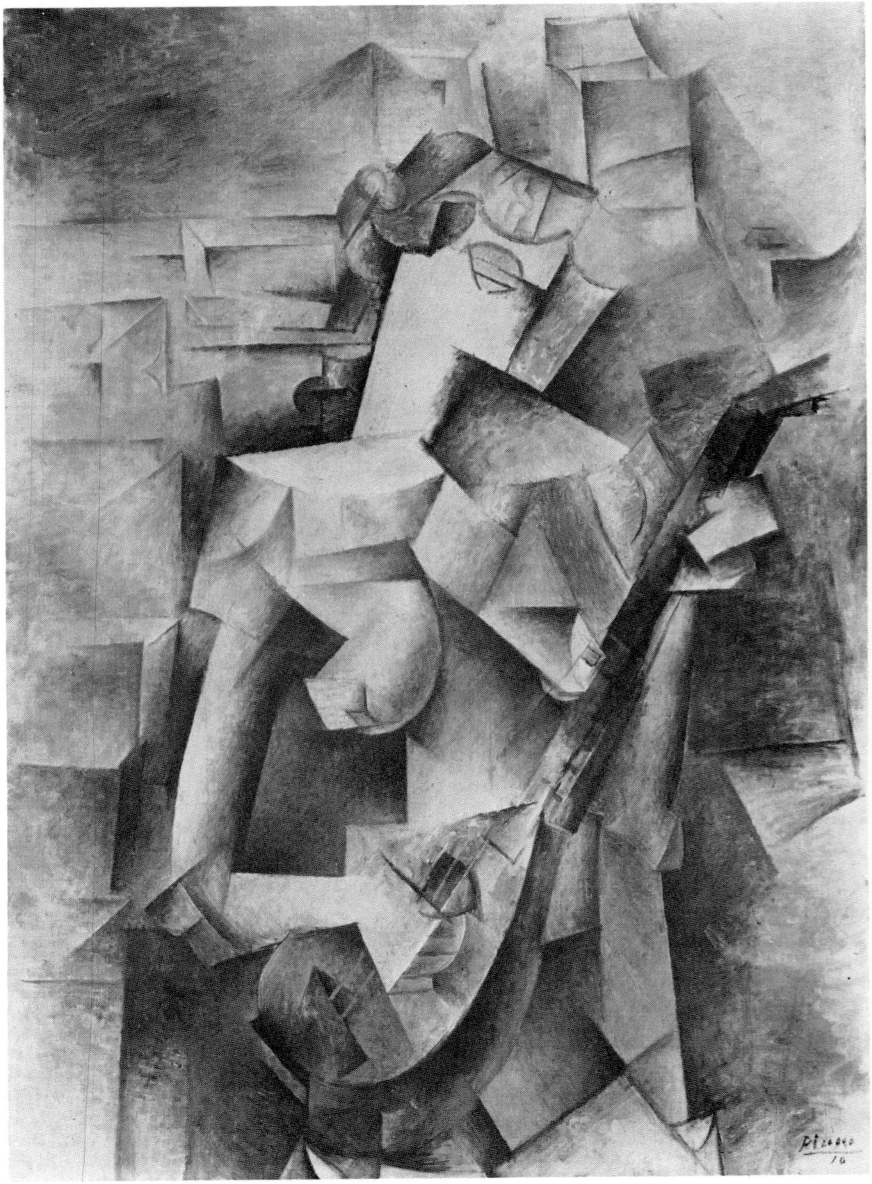

79 Pablo Picasso. *Girl with a Mandolin (Fanny Tellier).* 1910. Oil on canvas, 39½ × 29″ (100 × 74 cm). Museum of Modern Art, New York (Nelson A. Rockefeller Bequest).

and Speed [Plate 10, page 122] by J. M. W. Turner (1775–1851). In this painting of a train moving through the fog over a railway bridge, we are again struck by the powerful sense of depth. This is created primarily by the increasing haziness and the lightening of the blues and browns toward the horizon, although the converging black lines of the bridge at the right also contribute to the three-dimensional impression. Turner enjoyed showing how the shapes of objects are dissolved through the effects of light and atmosphere, leaving the mere suggestion of the train, the ships on the river, and the buildings in the distance.

Both linear and aerial perspective try to capture the impression of depth and three-dimensionality we all experience when we see objects in space. In the late 19th century, a few daring artists began to experiment by tilting or flattening objects in an unrealistic manner to present a different sense of reality. Their innovations led to still more radical distortions of space by Cubist and Expressionist painters. These deliberately fragmented perspective in order to create a new and challenging image of reality. In Picasso's *Girl with a Mandolin* [79], we can still detect remnants of the older tradition, particularly in the converging lines on the edges of the cube-like parts. Yet the lines do not form a single grid, nor do they lead to a vanishing point. It is as if perspective were a panel of glass: Picasso has shattered it and given us the splinters. To him, the old, traditional way of presenting space no longer seemed valid.

In the 20th century, continued experimentation has moved painting still further away from traditional treatments of space. In the nonobjective art of Jackson Pollock, the idea of perspective, and even of space itself, has become irrelevant. When we look at a Pollock painting, we can speak of point of view in the sense of an ideal distance from which to view the painting, but we cannot speak of point of view in the sense of an imaginary three-dimensional space provided by perspective within the painting. Jackson Pollock's *Convergence* [see Figure 18, page 21] is a painting, but not a picture.

Frame

However differently traditional and nonobjective paintings may treat space, they have one spatial element in common: they are limited at the edges by a definite boundary. The frame, which sets the picture off from its surroundings, defines the size and shape of the work, helping us concentrate on its organization or composition. Most of the paintings we know are rectangular or square, although some, such as Raphael's *Marriage of the Virgin* [see Plate 9, page 121], may have circular variations on one or more sides. Through **framing**, the painter controls a specific zone of reality set off from every other part of reality—including the space we occupy. Insofar as we value a work, we make its zone of reality into a sacred enclosure, an area to be admired but not intruded upon or modified. This quality of being set apart exists whether the painting has a real frame of gilt, wood, or metal, or just stops at the edges of the canvas. Some painters have found the frame so important that they have even painted their own frame on the canvas.

Georges Seurat (1859–1891), for instance, made little patterns of dots all along the inner edges of *Port-en-Bessin, Entrance to the Harbor* [80] and other of his works.

Although paintings offer the most obvious example of framing, other arts of space also use framing devices occasionally. In statues the base can perform a role similar to the frame in painting, although the work's own power is often sufficient to guarantee that it will be seen within its own zone of reality. The outlines of buildings can be set off by bases and also sometimes by *cornices,* the decorative elements placed along the roof line [see Figure 45, page 51]. The theater, another art form that exists at least partially in space, uses the proscenium arch as a frame to separate the stage from the audience. And in motion pictures a beam of light cuts off a segment of reality from the surrounding darkness, framing the images on the screen. In addition, as we have noted in Chapter 3, directors can consciously organize individual shots by the device appropriately known as *framing* [see Figure 65, page 106]. Not surprisingly, some of the early pioneers of cinematography made a close study of easel paintings as a guide to their own compositions.

Prose Narrative

Just as sculptors or painters can consciously shape their material by choosing a special vantage point or perspective, so writers can shape their narratives by choosing a special point of view. When we refer to point of view in literary narratives, we are talking about the voice that we hear telling the story. In fact, various "voices" or points of view are available to the storyteller. Each has an impact on the story, shaping it in a particular way, and each has its own advantages.

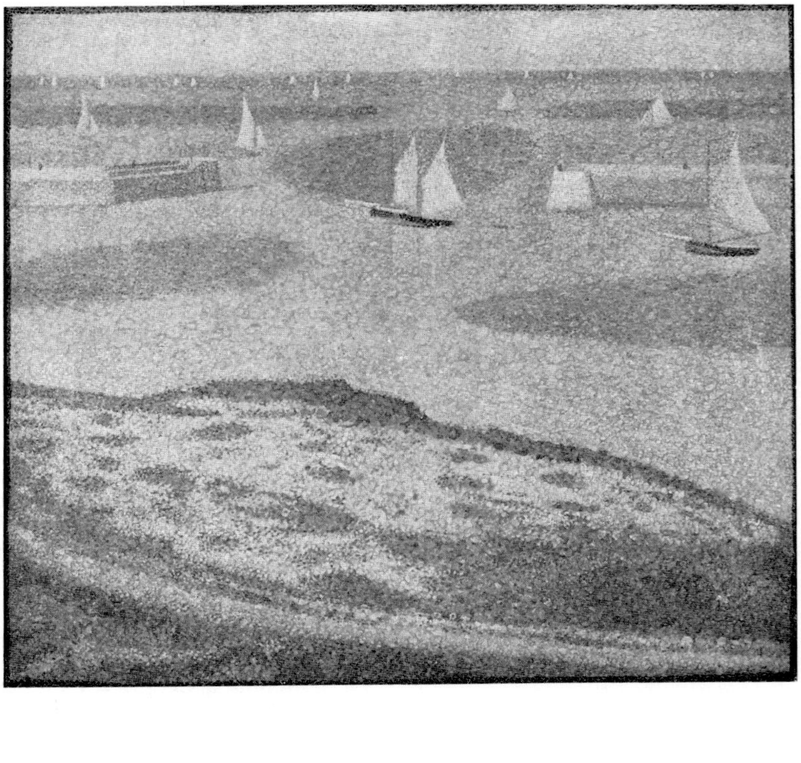

80 Georges Seurat. *Port-en-Bessin, Entrance to the Harbor.* 1888. Oil on canvas, 21⅝ × 25⅝" (55 × 65 cm). Museum of Modern Art, New York (Lillie P. Bliss Collection).

Omniscient Narrator

One of the most common points of view is that of an omniscient author or narrator. Such narrators know what is happening everywhere and what each character is thinking. They are *omniscient*—all knowing—as a god might be all-knowing about human events. The first sentence of "Roman Fever" (see page 85) is spoken by an omniscient narrator who sets the stage on the terrace high above Rome and who, as the story progresses, knows what Mrs. Slade and Mrs. Ansley think about each other. This point of view is perhaps the most flexible, since the writer can introduce whatever information is desirable at any point in the story. Such flexibility does not, however, make the storytelling as easy as it sounds. As we have seen in Edith Wharton's "Roman Fever," considerable skill is necessary to drop subtle hints, withhold crucial information, and shape the material to achieve the greatest impact.

Often omniscient narrators are unobtrusive, so that we are hardly aware of their presence. But sometimes they can be quite conspicuous. Henry Fielding (1707–1754) is so in a charmingly chatty way, breaking into the narrative and talking directly to the reader:

> We are now, Reader, arrived at the last stage of our journey. As we have, therefore, traveled together through so many pages, let us behave to one another like fellow-travelers in a stage-coach, who have passed several days in the company of each other, and who, notwithstanding any bickerings or little animosities which may have occurred on the road, generally make all up at last, and mount, for the last time, into their vehicle with cheerfulness and good humor; since after this one stage, it may possibly happen to us, as it commonly happens to them, never to meet more.
>
> *Tom Jones,* XVIII, chap. 1 (1749)

Fielding reveals so wise and benevolent a personality as narrator of his novel *Tom Jones* that we feel regret on coming upon this "Farewell to the Reader."

First-Person Narrator

Another common point of view available to the storyteller is that of the *first-person narrator.* This "voice" differs radically from that of an omniscient narrator in being limited to a single perspective. The "I" knows only what an individual can observe and may not quite understand all that is happening. Sometimes diary entries or letters are used, but more often first-person narrators speak directly about their experiences. The first sentences of Charles Dickens' *Great Expectations* take us directly into the mind of the small Pip just at the moment when he is becoming conscious of the threatening world around him and of his own identity.

> My father's family name being Pirrip, and my christian name Philip, my infant tongue could make of both names nothing longer or more explicit than Pip. So, I called myself Pip, and came to be called Pip.
>
> I give Pirrip as my father's family name, on the authority of his tombstone and my sister—Mrs. Joe Gargery, who married the blacksmith. As I never saw my father or my mother, and never saw any likeness of either of them (for their days were long before the days of photographs), my first fancies regarding what they were like, were unreasonably derived from their tombstones. The shape of the

letters on my father's, gave me an odd idea that he was a square, stout, dark man, with curly black hair. From the character and turn of the inscription, *Also Georgiana Wife of the Above,* I drew a childish conclusion that my mother was freckled and sickly. To five little stone lozenges, each about a foot and a half long, which were arranged in a neat row beside their grave, and were sacred to the memory of five little brothers of mine—who gave up trying to get a living, exceedingly early in that universal struggle—I am indebted for a belief I religiously entertained that they had all been born on their backs with their hands in their trousers-pockets, and had never taken them out in this state of existence.

Ours was the marsh country, down by the river, within, as the river wound, twenty miles of the sea. My first most vivid and broad impression of the identity of things, seems to me to have been gained on a memorable raw afternoon towards evening. At such a time I found out for certain, that this bleak place overgrown with nettles was the churchyard; and that Philip Pirrip, late of this parish, and also Georgiana wife of the above, were dead and buried; and that Alexander, Bartholomew, Abraham, Tobias, and Roger, infant children of the aforesaid, were also dead and buried; and that the dark flat wilderness beyond the churchyard, intersected with dykes and mounds and gates, with scattered cattle feeding on it, was the marshes; and that the low leaden line beyond, was the river; and that the distant savage lair from which the wind was rushing, was the sea; and that the small bundle of shivers growing afraid of it all and beginning to cry, was Pip.

As we have seen, this novel uses the first-person narrative in a more complex fashion than usual. In this case, the voice of the young Pip, involved in the action, merges with the voice of the older Pip, who, in retrospect, is able to judge his behavior in more mature terms. However, Dickens carefully maintains the limitations of the first-person narrative by not allowing Pip fully to understand those around him, particularly his idol Estella. Such limitations are far closer to our normal experience than is the knowledge of the omniscient narrator. For, locked into our own consciousness, we can see the world only from our individual point of view. We seldom know with certainty what other people are experiencing or thinking.

Third-Person Limited Narrator

Still another limited point of view is possible in fiction—that of a *third-person limited* narrator. In this case, all the characters, including the narrator, are presented in the third person, but the author introduces a single consciousness through whose eyes the experiences are seen. The third-person limited point of view is used in an intriguing and radical way in *A Portrait of the Artist as a Young Man* (1916), by James Joyce (1882–1941). In the opening passage the main character, Stephen Dedalus, is shown as a very young child, who, like Dickens' Pip, is first experiencing self-awareness.

Once upon a time and a very good time it was there was a moocow coming down along the road and this moocow that was down along the road met a nicens little boy named baby tuckoo. . . .

His father told him that story: his father looked at him through a glass: he had a hairy face.

He was baby tuckoo. The moocow came down the road where Betty Byrne lived: she sold lemon platt.

> O, the wild rose blossoms
> On the little green place.

He sang that song. That was his song.

> O, the green wothe botheth.

When you wet the bed, first it is warm then it gets cold. His mother put on the oilsheet. That had the queer smell.

His mother had a nicer smell than his father. She played on the piano the sailor's hornpipe for him to dance. He danced . . .

Since Stephen is just becoming conscious of the world around him and especially since he is to become an artist, Joyce gives great emphasis to the child's varied perceptions of his surroundings. These perceptions involve each of Stephen's senses in turn—hearing (the story his father tells), sight (his father's face), taste (the lemon candy), touch (the wet bed), and smell (the oilsheet). Appropriately for an incipient artist, too, Stephen begins to compose a poem, altering reality by creating a "green rose." Although Joyce provides a very intimate view of the workings of the child's mind, the third-person pronoun "he" is used, as it is throughout the novel, to present the character in a somewhat more detached and nonsubjective way than through a first-person narrator.

Stream of Consciousness

Another point of view, which has become particularly popular among modern writers, attempts to show the mind of a character in action. A voice expresses the very thoughts as they take shape. When these thoughts are presented in a polished and coherent form, the technique is called an **interior monologue**, as it is in film (see Chapter 3), and resembles a soliloquy in a play. However, when these thoughts are presented more loosely, in ways that are not logical in the ordinary sense, the technique is called **stream of consciousness**. This attempts to show the mind working in idiosyncratic ways—by personal associations or sense impressions or even subconscious impulses. The result may seem more or less chaotic, but, in fact, has a logic of its own.

Perhaps the most famous and elaborate example of such stream of consciousness appears in the last chapter of Joyce's *Ulysses* (1922), in which Molly Bloom, the wife of one of the main characters, indulges in a half-conscious reverie. To imitate the fluid wanderings of her mind, Joyce omits all punctuation for some fifty pages of printed text. Toward the end of this tour de force Molly thinks about atheists and their guilty consciences, and then suddenly remembers the hot summer day when her husband proposed to her:

> why dont they go and create something I often asked him atheists or whatever they call themselves go and wash the cobbles off themselves first then they go howling for the priest and they dying and why why because theyre afraid of hell on account of their bad conscience ah yes I know them well who was the first person in the universe before there was anybody that made it all who ah that they dont know neither do I so there you are they might as well try to stop the sun

from rising tomorrow the sun shines for you he said the day we were lying among the rhododendrons on Howth head in the grey tweed suit and his straw hat the day I got him to propose to me yes first I gave him the bit of seedcake out of my mouth and it was leapyear like now yes 16 years ago my God after that long kiss I near lost my breath yes he said I was a flower of the mountain yes so we are flowers all a womans body yes that was one true thing he said in his life and the sun shines for you today yes that was why I liked him because I saw he understood or felt what a woman is and I knew I could always get round him and I gave him all the pleasure I could leading him on till he asked me to say yes and I wouldnt answer first only looked out over the sea and the sky I was thinking of so many things he didnt know of Mulvey and Mr Stanhope and Hester and father and old captain Groves and the sailors playing all birds fly and I say stoop and washing up dishes they called it on the pier and the sentry in front of the governors house with the thing round his white helmet poor devil half roasted and the Spanish girls laughing in their shawls and their tall combs and the auctions in the morning

At first glance, Molly's thinking seems purely personal and chaotic, and consequently hard to follow. But a closer look shows that a definite association links one thought with the next. For example, Molly's challenge that atheists can no more explain who started the universe than they can "stop the sun from rising" leads her to think of another sun which, her husband gallantly said, "shines for you." This association in turn leads Molly to recall the details of his actual proposal. She remembers not only the incident but also her private thoughts at that moment—memories within memories. This device, a kind of mental shorthand, has the advantage of compressing a great deal of material into a brief passage. In addition, it can present a series of sense impressions—the seedcake, the hot sun—with both spontaneity and concreteness.

As a 20th-century technique, stream of consciousness has had the advantage of the insights of modern psychology. Writers who use this device have drawn especially on Sigmund Freud (1856–1939) and Carl Jung (1875–1961), who emphasized the significance of subconscious and even unconscious mental activity. Some stream-of-consciousness passages, as we shall see shortly, present a series of images or even whole dreams that may or may not be decipherable to the character but that are certainly significant to the reader.

Stream of consciousness is not exclusively a modern invention. Its possibilities were already explored by Laurence Sterne (1713–1768) in *Tristram Shandy*. Describing the process of Tristram's birth, Sterne was aware of the fact that "millions" of thoughts float in everyone's mind and that only a few rise to consciousness at any one moment.

Great wits jump: for the moment Dr. Slop cast his eyes upon his bag (which he had not done till the dispute with my uncle Toby about midwifery put him in mind of it)—the very same thought occurred.—'Tis God's mercy, quoth he (to himself) that Mrs. Shandy has had so bad a time of it,—else she might have been brought to bed seven times told, before one half of these knots could have got untied.—But here you must distinguish—the thought floated only in Dr. Slop's mind, without sail or ballast to it, as a simple proposition; millions of which, as

> your worship knows, are every day swimming quietly in the middle of the thin juice of a man's understanding, without being carried backwards or forwards, till some little gusts of passion or interest drive them to one side.
>
> III, chap. 9 (1761)

In this scene the male midwife, Dr. Slop, who was summoned to help at Tristram's birth but who has become involved in a lengthy conversation, chances to notice his medical bag, which has just been brought to him, and suddenly remembers why he was called to the house in the first place. The bag has been tied up in many knots by an overly conscientious servant. The difficulty of untying these in time to help with the delivery of the child begins to strike the ineffectual doctor. This passage gives the reader insight into Dr. Slop's sluggish mind, but it does so less by a direct presentation of his thought processes than by Tristram's recreation of these, as he tries to reconstruct the incidents just prior to his birth.

As a matter of fact, although we tend to expect stream of consciousness to mimic the thought processes directly, as it does in Molly Bloom's reverie, such processes are often presented through another narrative voice that guides the stream. Joyce uses such an approach in *Portrait of the Artist* when he presents Stephen's terrifying nightmare, the consequence of a hellfire-and-brimstone sermon the adolescent boy has just heard. The passage begins as if Stephen's own consciousness were given directly, but then returns to Joyce's usual third-person limited point of view.

> Creatures were in the field; one, three, six: creatures were moving in the field, hither and thither. Goatish creatures with human faces, horny browed, lightly bearded and grey as indiarubber. The malice of evil glittered in their hard eyes, as they moved hither and thither, trailing their long tails behind them. A rictus [gaping mouth] of cruel malignity lit up greyly their old bony faces. One was clasping about his ribs a torn flannel waistcoat, another complained monotonously as his beard stuck in the tufted weeds. Soft language issued from their spittleless lips as they swished in slow circles round and round the field, winding hither and thither through the weeds, dragging their long tails amid the rattling canisters. They moved in slow circles, circling closer and closer to enclose, to enclose, soft language issuing from their lips, their long swishing tails besmeared with stale shite, thrusting upwards their terrific faces. . .
>
> Help!
>
> He flung the blankets from him madly to free his face and neck. That was his hell. God had allowed him to see the hell reserved for his sins: stinking, bestial, malignant, a hell of lecherous goatish fiends. For him! For him!

The excerpt once again shows how stream of consciousness presents images as they cross the mind of a character. The first paragraph gives a series of vivid visual, auditory, and tactile images as Stephen dreams of the loathsome creatures, who are obviously devils. At the same time, the workings of Stephen's subconscious, his unacknowledged guilt feelings, are strongly suggested, for "goatish creatures" traditionally symbolize lust or lasciviousness. Before Stephen consciously understands this significance, we can link Stephen's nightmare with his recent visits to the brothels of Dublin, for the slow circles described in the dream echo Stephen's earlier prowling of the narrow back alleys of the city in search of pleasure.

This excerpt differs from Molly Bloom's stream of consciousness, however, in that it is much more coherently presented. Normal sentence structure and punctuation are retained. This greater coherence is largely due to the controlling third-person limited point of view, which is especially apparent in the last paragraph. Here Stephen is referred to in a detached manner: "He flung the blankets from him. . . ." But then Joyce returns to a somewhat more subjective presentation, though still using the third-person pronoun: "That was his hell. . . . For him! For him!" Most stream-of-consciousness passages are written in this restrained and controlled manner, usually because they are presented through a third-person rather than a first-person point of view.

Stream of consciousness is rarely used exclusively in a work of any length. Often it is combined with other narrative points of view. Indeed, in our last excerpt from *Portrait of the Artist,* "Help!" is an exclamation made in the first person, the voice of the frantic Stephen awakening terrified from his dream. Joyce shifts to the first-person point of view because it sounds more immediate. The impact from this change in point of view is especially strong, since only this single word separates the two passages that use the third-person limited perspective.

Another, more elaborate, use of varied points of view can be found in *The Sound and the Fury* (1929) by William Faulkner (1897–1962). This novel consists of three first-person narratives incorporating moments of stream of consciousness, followed by a final third-person limited narrative. The first three sections present the thoughts of three siblings of widely differing character as they recall the critical moments of their lives; the last section gives another perspective, that of the family servant.

Faulkner is highly conscious of the technical possibilities of the different narrative points of view. Like many other writers, he is also keenly aware of the implications of using such differing points of view. Because the characters describe the same experiences so differently, we are led to question how much of the truth each character has understood. More fundamentally, we question where the truth lies and whether any single truth can be said to exist.

The question of the relativity of truth has been an important theme in the novel from its beginning. Cervantes (1547–1616) in his *Don Quixote* (1605) delighted in contrasting the widely differing perceptions of the idealistic knight Quixote and his practical squire Sancho Panza. And Samuel Richardson (1689–1761) wrote both *Pamela* (1740) and *Clarissa* (1747–1748) as a series of letters, giving each correspondent a limited perspective as well as a different bias. For modern novelists the theme of the relativity of truth has become especially important because it embodies current scientific and philosophical ideas about relativity, the concept that no absolute truth can be determined.

Two Narratives

The opening and closing of some narratives may provide additional variety in the point of view. Special narrators may be invented simply to repeat a story told to them. This story, which is the heart of the matter, may use a totally different point of view and is usually set in an entirely different time or place. Such framing is especially effective in Conrad's *Heart of Darkness* (see page 96). Here the opening and closing segments are told by a nameless Londoner, one of five gentlemen on a boat on the Thames. But the main story, which has taken place years before in Africa, is told to him by another member of the group, Marlow, who speaks in the first person. This literary frame is comparable to the frame enclosing a painting, contrasting it with the surrounding space and defining its boundaries. Conrad's frame contrasts London and the Thames with Africa and the Congo and, more profoundly, Western civilized life with the more primitive. Still, this elaborate narrative framing is much rarer in literature than frames are in paintings.

To help us appreciate the importance of the point of view, we can compare the first-person narrators in two versions of the same material: an episode from Homer's *Odyssey* (late 8th century B.C.) and a short story by Eudora Welty (b. 1909). Both narratives relate the episode in which Odysseus, on his way home from Troy to Ithaca, encounters and escapes from the immortal Circe, an enchantress who turns men into swine.

The following prose translation of Homer's poetic narrative gives a vivid impression of his approach.

Homer

"CIRCE" FROM *THE ODYSSEY*

"We travelled on in utter dejection, thankful to have escaped alive, but grieving for the good comrades we had lost. In due course we came to the island of Aeaea, the home of the beautiful Circe, a formidable goddess, though her voice is like a woman's. She is the sister of the wizard Aeetes, both being children of the Sun who lights the world, by the same mother, Perse the Daughter of Ocean. We approached the coast of this island and brought our ship into the shelter of the haven without making a sound. Some god must have guided us in. And when we had disembarked, for two whole days and nights we lay on the beach, suffering not only from exhaustion but from the horrors we had been through. The third day was heralded by a lovely dawn. When the sun was up I took my spear and sword, slipped away from the ship, and struck inland, making for a coign of vantage from which I might look out for signs of human industry or hear men's voices. I climbed a rocky height which promised a wide view, and on reaching the top I was able to see the smoke rising from the distant spot where Circe's house lay screened by the dense oak-scrub and forest trees. That glimpse I had of ruddy smoke left me in two minds whether or not to press forward and reconnoitre. After some hesitation I thought the better course would be to return first to my ship on the beach, give my men a meal and send out an exploring party. . . .

"I numbered them off into two well-armed parties with a commander for each. Of one, I myself took charge; the other I gave to an officer of noble birth called Eurylochus; and without more ado we shook lots in a bronze helmet. Out came the gallant Eurylochus' lot, and so he went off with his two-and-twenty men, a tearful company, leaving us, who stayed behind, in no better case. In due course they came upon Circe's house, which was built of dressed stone and stood in the middle of a clearing in a forest dell. Prowling about the place were mountain wolves and lions, actually the drugged victims of Circe's magic, for they not only refrained from attacking my men, but rose on their hind legs to caress them, with much wagging of their long tails, like dogs fawning on their master, as he comes from table, for the tasty bits they know he always brings. But these were wolves and lions with great claws that were gambolling in this way round my men. Terrified at the sight of the formidable beasts, they shrunk away and took refuge in the porch of the fair goddess' castle. From there they could hear Circe within, singing in her beautiful voice as she went to and fro at her great and everlasting loom, on which she was weaving one of those delicate, graceful, and dazzling fabrics that goddesses love to make.

"Polites, one of my captains and the man in my party whom I liked and trusted most, now took the lead. 'Friends,' he said, 'there is someone in the castle working at a loom. The whole place echoes to that lovely voice. It's either a goddess or a woman. Let us waste no more time, but give her a shout.'

"So they shouted to attract attention, and the next moment Circe came out, opened the polished doors, and invited them to enter. In their innocence, the whole party except Eurylochus followed her in. But he suspected a trap and stayed outside. Circe ushered the rest into her hall, gave them settles and chairs to sit on, and then prepared them a mixture of cheese, barley-meal, and yellow honey flavoured with Pramnian wine. But into this dish she introduced a powerful drug, to make them lose all memory of their native land. And when they had emptied the bowls in which she had served them, she struck them with her wand [81], drove them off and penned them in the pig-sties. For now to all appearance they were swine: they had pigs' heads and bristles, and they grunted like pigs; but their minds were as human as they had been before the change. Indeed, they shed tears in their sties. But Circe flung them some mast, acorns, and cornel-berries, and left them to eat this pigs' fodder and wallow in the mud.

"Meanwhile Eurylochus came back to the good black ship to report the catastrophe his party had met with. He was in such anguish that for all his eagerness to tell us he could utter not a single word; his eyes were filled with tears, and the rising sobs stuck in his throat. Aghast at the sight, we all bombarded him with questions, till at length the story of his comrades' fate came out.

"'My lord Odysseus,' he said, 'we followed your orders. We made our way through the oaklands and in a clearing in a glade we came to a well-built castle of dressed stone. Someone was working at a great loom inside and singing in a clear voice—either a goddess or a woman. My men gave a shout to attract her attention. In a moment she came out, opened the polished doors and invited us in. Not knowing better, the men followed her into the house in a body. But I stayed where I was, for I thought it might be a trap. And now the whole party have vanished. Not a single man showed up, though I sat there a long time and kept a sharp lookout.'

"When I heard this story I slung my bow over my shoulder, and my big bronze sword in its silver scabbard, and I told Eurylochus to take me back with him by the way he had come. But he threw his arms round my knees in supplication and broke into a pitiful appeal.

"'My king,' he said, 'leave me behind and don't force me to go with you there. You will never come back yourself and you won't rescue a man of your crew. I am certain of it. Let us get away quickly with those that are left here. We might still save our skins.'

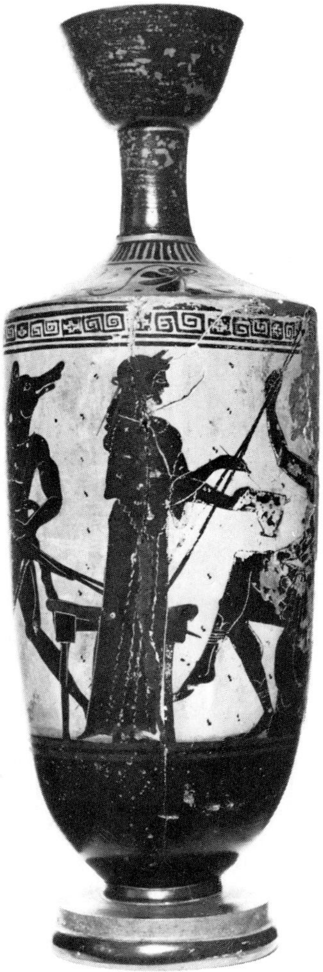

81 The Athena Painter. Circe on a Grecian urn. c. 490–480 B.C. Pottery. National Archaeological Museum, Athens. The enchantress offers her potion to the figure on the right, while the figure on the left has already been transformed.

"'Very well, Eurylochus,' I replied; 'stay where you are, and eat and drink by the black ship's hull. But I shall go. It is my plain and bounden duty.'

"With this, I turned my back on the ship and the sea, and struck inland. But as I was threading my way through the enchanted glades that led to the witch's castle, whom should I fall in with but Hermes, god of the golden wand, who came up to me just before I reached the house, looking like a young man at that most charming age when the beard first starts to grow. He took my hand in his and greeted me amiably.

"'Where are you off to now, my poor fellow,' he said, 'wandering alone through the wilds in unknown country, with your friends there in Circe's house penned like pigs in their crowded sties? I suppose you have come here to free them, though I think you are more likely to stay with them yourself and never see your home again. However, I am coming to the rescue and will see you through. Look; here is a drug of real virtue that you must take with you into Circe's palace to save yourself from disaster. But I must explain how she works her black magic. She will begin by mixing you a pottage, into which she will put her poison. But even with its help she will be unable to enchant you, for this antidote that I am going to give you and describe will rob it of its power. When Circe strikes you with her long wand, you must draw your sword from your side and rush at her as though you meant to take her life. She will shrink from you in terror and invite you to her bed. Nor must you hesitate to accept the goddess' favours, if you want her to free your men and treat you kindly. But make her swear a solemn oath by the blessed gods not to try on you any more of her tricks, or when she has you stripped she may rob you of your courage and your manhood.'

"Then the Giant-killer handed me a herb he had plucked from the ground, and showed me what it was like. It had a black root and a milk-white flower. The gods call it Moly, and it is an awkward plant to dig up, at any rate for a mere man. But the gods, after all, can do anything.

"Hermes went off through the island forest, making for high Olympus, while I with a heart oppressed by many dark forebodings pursued my way to Circe's home, till I found myself at the doors of the lovely goddess' palace. Here I halted and gave a shout. Circe heard my call, came out at once, and opening the polished doors invited me in. Filled with misgivings, I followed her indoors and was asked to sit down on a beautiful chair with silver decorations and a stool for my feet, while she prepared some pottage in a golden bowl for me to drink, and for her own evil purposes threw in some poison. When I had taken the bowl from her and drained it, but without suffering any magic effects, she touched me with her wand and sharply ordered me to be off to the pigsties and lie down with my friends. Whereupon I snatched my sword from my hip and rushed on Circe as though I meant to kill her. But with a shriek she slipped below my blade, fell at my knees and burst into tears.

"'Who on earth are you?' she asked. 'What parents begot, what city bred such a man? I am amazed to see you take my poison and suffer no magic change. For never before have I known a man who could resist that drug once he had taken it and swallowed it down. You must have a heart in your breast that is proof against all enchantment. I am sure you are Odysseus, the man whom nothing defeats, the man whom the Giant-slayer with the golden wand always told me to expect here on his way back from Troy in his good black ship. But I beg you now to put up your sword and come with me to my bed, so that in love and sleep we may learn to trust one another.'

"'Circe,' I answered her, 'how can you expect me to be gentle with you, who have turned my friends into pigs here in your house, and now that you have me too in your clutches are inveigling me to your bedroom and inviting me to your bed, to make a coward and a weakling of me when you have me stripped? Nothing, goddess, would induce me to sleep with you, unless you can bring yourself to swear a solemn oath that you have no other mischief in store for me.'

"Circe complied and swore that she had no evil intentions. So when she had given me her word with due solemnity, I went with the goddess to her beautiful bed.

"Meanwhile the four maids who do the housework for Circe were busying themselves in the palace. They are the daughters of Springs and Groves and the sacred Rivers that flow out into the sea. One of them threw covers over the chairs and spread fine purple rugs on top. Another drew silver tables up to the chairs and placed golden baskets upon them; while the third was mixing the sweet and mellow wine in a silver bowl and setting out the golden cups; and the fourth fetched water and lit up a great fire under the big cauldron so that the water grew warm.

"When the bright copper was boiling, she sat me down in a bath and washed me with water from the great cauldron mixed with cold to a comfortable heat, sluicing my head and shoulders till all the painful weariness was gone from my limbs. My bath done, she rubbed me with olive oil, clothed me in a tunic and a splendid cloak, and conducted me to the hall, where she seated me in a beautiful chair with silver decorations and a footstool below. Next came another maid with water in a splendid golden ewer. She poured it out over a silver basin so that I could rinse my hands, and then drew up a polished table to my side. A staid housekeeper brought some bread, which she put by me with a variety of dainties; and after helping me liberally to all she had brought she invited me to fall to. But I had no heart for eating. I sat there heedless, engrossed in my cares.

"When Circe saw me sitting so quiet and not helping myself to the food, she knew that I had some serious trouble on my mind. So she faced me and came straight to the point.

"'Odysseus,' she said, 'why are you sitting here like this as though you were dumb, and feeding on your own thoughts instead of helping yourself to meat and wine? Do you suspect another trap? You need have no fears: I have given you my solemn word to do you no more harm.'

"'Circe,' I answered her, 'could any honest man in my position bear to taste food and drink before he had freed his men and seen them face to face? If you really mean me to eat and drink, give them their liberty and let me set eyes on my loyal followers.'

"Wand in hand, Circe went straight out of the hall, threw open the pigsty gate and drove them out, looking exactly like full-grown swine. And there they stood and faced her. She went in among them and smeared them each in turn with some new salve she had. Whereupon the bristles which her first deadly potion had made them sprout dropped off their limbs, and they not only became men again but looked younger and much handsomer and taller than before. They recognized me now, and one after the other ran up and seized my hand. We were so moved that we all wept for happiness. It was a strange sound for those walls to echo. Even the goddess was touched.

"Presently she came up to me and said: 'Royal son of Laertes, you have shown your infinite resource. Go down now to your ship and the sea-shore, drag her straight up onto dry land, stow your belongings and all the ship's tackle in a cave, and then come back yourself with the rest of your loyal company.'

"I could not refuse this challenge to my adventurous spirit. So off I went to the ship and the sea-shore. I found my good fellows by the ship in a woebegone state, with the tears streaming down their cheeks. Indeed I was reminded of the scene at a farm when a drove of cows come home full-fed from the pastures to the yard and are welcomed by all their frisking calves, who burst out from the pens to gambol round their mothers and fill the air with the sound of their lowing. For my men no sooner caught sight of me than they were all round me in a weeping throng. They were as deeply moved as if they had reached their homeland and were standing in the streets of their own town in rugged Ithaca, where they were born and bred.

"'Royal master,' they said between their sobs, 'we are as happy to see you back as we should be to set foot in our own island of Ithaca. But tell us how our comrades met their end.'

"I gave them a cheerful reply. 'Our first business,' I said, 'is to drag up the ship on dry land and stow our cargo and the tackle in a cave. Then you must get ready and all come along with me yourselves, if you wish to see your friends eating and drinking in Circe's enchanted palace, where I tell you they have enough to last them for ever.'

"The rest were quick to fall in with my suggestion. But not Eurylochus, who, by infecting them with his fears, did his best to keep the whole company back.

"'Where are we poor wretches off to now?' he cried. 'Are you so keen on trouble that you must seek out the Witch in her stronghold, and all be turned into pigs or wolves or lions, and forced to keep watch in that great house of hers? We have had all this before, with the Cyclops, when our friends found their way into his fold with this dare-devil Odysseus for company. It was this man's reckless folly that cost *them* their lives.'

"Now when Eurylochus said that, I had half a mind, though he was a close kinsman of my own, to draw the long sword from my side and lop his head off to roll in the dust. But I was checked by a chorus of remonstrance from my men, who took a milder view.

"'Sir,' they said, 'it is for you to give the order; but why not leave this fellow here by the ship on guard, while we follow your lead to Circe's enchanted castle?'

"So we turned our backs on the ship and the sea and struck inland. And Eurylochus came with us after all. He was not going to be left by the ship, and was afraid of the stinging rebuke I might give him.

"Circe had been spending the interval in hospitable care for the party in her house. She bathed and anointed them with olive-oil, and gave them all tunics and warm cloaks to wear, so that on our arrival we found them enjoying a comfortable dinner in the hall. When the two companies came face to face and each man recognized his friends, they burst into tears and the whole house echoed to their sobs, till the goddess herself, coming up and addressing me by my royal titles, appealed to me to check this fit of weeping.

"'I know as well as you,' she said, 'all you have gone through on the fish-infested seas and suffered at the hands of savages on land. But now I want to see you enjoying your food and putting down your wine, till you are once more the men you were when first you sailed from your homes in rugged Ithaca. You are worn out now and depressed: you cannot forget the buffetings you have had. And your sufferings have been so continuous that you don't know what it is to have a merry heart.'

"My gallant company were not difficult to persuade. In fact we stayed on day after day for a whole year, feasting on meat galore and mellow wine. But when the year was out, and the seasons began to repeat their round, my good friends called me aside one day and said reproachfully: 'Master, if you are ever going to escape and get back to your old home in your own country, it's high time you thought of Ithaca again.' This was enough: my proud heart was convinced.

"For the rest of that day till sunset we sat and banqueted on the meat and mellow wine that were provided in such abundance. When the sun sank and night fell, my men settled down for sleep in the darkened hall. But I went to the beautiful bed where Circe lay and there clasped the goddess' knees in prayer, while she listened to my eager words:

"'Circe,' I said, 'I beseech you to keep that promise which you made me once to send me home. I am eager now to be gone, and so are all my men. They wear me out and pester me with their complaints whenever you are not about.'

"'Royal son of Laertes, Odysseus of the nimble wits,' the goddess answered me, 'I am not going to keep you in my house against your wishes. But before I can send you home you have to make a journey of a very different kind, and find your way to the Halls of Hades and Persephone the Dread, to consult the soul of Teiresias, the blind Theban prophet, whose understanding even death has not impaired. For dead though he is, Persephone has left to him, and him alone, a mind to reason with. The rest are mere shadows flitting to and fro.'

"This news broke my heart. I sat down on the bed and wept. I had no further use for life, no wish to see the sunshine any more. But when at last I grew tired of tears and of tossing about on the bed, I began to question her:

"'But tell me, Circe, who is to guide me on the way? No-one has ever sailed a black ship into Hell.'

"'Odysseus,' the goddess answered me, 'don't think of lingering on shore for lack of a pilot. Set up your mast, spread the white sail and sit down in the ship. The North Wind will blow her on her way; and when she has brought you across the River of Ocean, you will come to a wild coast and to Persephone's Grove, where the tall poplars grow and the willows that so quickly shed their seeds. Beach your boat there by Ocean's swirling stream and march on into Hades' Kingdom of Decay. There the River of Flaming Fire and the River of Lamentation, which is a branch of the Waters of Styx, unite round a pinnacle of rock to pour their thundering streams into Acheron. This is the spot, my lord, that I bid you to seek out. Once there, dig a trench about a cubit long and a cubit in breadth. Around this trench pour offerings to all the dead, first with honey mixed with milk, then with sweet wine, and last of all with water. Over all this sprinkle white barley and then begin your prayers to the helpless ghosts of the dead. Promise them that once you are in Ithaca you will sacrifice in your palace a barren heifer, the best that you have, and will heap the pyre with treasures and make Teiresias a separate offering of the finest jet-black sheep to be found in your flock. When you have finished your invocations to the glorious fellowship of the dead, sacrifice a young ram and a black ewe, holding their heads down towards Erebus while you turn your own aside, as though about to recross the River of Ocean. Then the souls of the dead and departed will come up in their multitudes and you must bid your men make haste to flay the sheep that are lying there slaughtered by your blade, and burn them up while they pray to the gods, to mighty Hades and august Persephone. Sit still yourself meanwhile, with your drawn sword in your hand, and do not let any of the helpless ghosts come near the blood till you have had speech with Teiresias. Presently the prophet himself will come to you, my lord king. And he will lay down for you your journey and the distances to be covered, and direct you home across the fish-delighting seas.'

"Circe finished, and soon after the Dawn enthroned herself in gold. The Nymph clothed me in my tunic and cloak and dressed herself in a long robe of silvery sheen, light in fabric and charming to the eye. She put a veil on her head, and round her waist she fastened a splendid golden belt. Then I walked through the palace and made the round of my men, rousing them each with a cheerful word.

"'Wake up,' I said, 'and bid your pleasant dreams farewell. We must be off. My lady Circe has given me our sailing orders.'

"My gallant band made no demur. But not even now did I get them all off without a casualty. There was one called Elpenor, the youngest of the party, not much of a fighting man nor very strong in the head. This young fellow of mine had got drunk, and longing for fresh air had left his friends in the enchanted palace and gone to sleep by himself. Roused in the morning by the bustle and din of their departure, he leapt up suddenly, and forgetting to go to the long ladder and take the right way down, he toppled headlong from the roof. He broke his neck and his soul went down to Hades.

"When the rest of the party joined me I took them into my confidence. 'You no doubt imagine,' I said, 'that you are bound for home and our beloved Ithaca. But Circe has marked out for us a very different route, to the Halls of Hades and Persephone the Dread, where we must seek advice of the soul of Theban Teiresias.'

"When I told them this they were heart-broken. They sat down where they were and wept and tore their hair. But they might have spared themselves their lamentations for all the good they did.

"We made our way to our ship and the beach in a sorry mood and with many tears. Meanwhile Circe, after taking leave of us, had tethered a young ram and a black ewe by the ship. She had slipped past us with ease; and when a god wishes to remain unseen, what eye can observe his coming or his going?"

Homer tells this episode through the eyes of Odysseus, whose concerns are those of a hero and leader of men. Full of courage and loyalty, Odysseus is willing to risk his own safety to save his companions, though he also cleverly follows the instructions of the god Hermes. Yet Odysseus remains with Circe after his men have been restored to their human form, for he finds the whole situation a "challenge to my adventurous spirit." Even though Odysseus stays with Circe for a year, he seems to feel little for his hostess. Circe remains a shadowy figure. Her feelings for Odysseus are hardly made clear, and she expresses little regret when he announces his departure. As Odysseus tells it, the episode first provides an exciting adventure and then a moment of luxury and ease that contrasts with the hardship and suffering described elsewhere in this long poem.

Although primarily told in the first person, Homer's episode has a flexible point of view. When Odysseus describes the scene in which Circe transforms the advance party into pigs, he presents details he could not have witnessed. Momentarily, an omniscient narrator seems to be speaking. Yet the total impression remains that of a first-person narrator.

In Eudora Welty's story, the same episode is told not from the point of view of Odysseus, but from another first-person point of view—Circe's. The shift from the masculine to the feminine perspective makes possible a radically different interpretation of the experience and a different kind of story.

Eudora Welty

CIRCE

Needle in air, I stopped what I was making. From the upper casement, my lookout on the sea, I saw them disembark and find the path; I heard that whole drove of mine break loose on the beautiful strangers. I slipped down the ladder. When I heard men breathing and sandals kicking the stones, I threw open the door. A shaft of light from the zenith struck my brow, and the wind let out my hair. Something else swayed my body outward.

"Welcome!" I said—the most dangerous word in the world.

Heads lifted to the smell of my bread, they trooped inside—and with such a grunting and frisking at their heels to the very threshold. Star-gazers! They stumbled on my polished floor, strewing sand, crowding on each other, sizing up the household for gifts (thinking already of sailing away), and sighted upwards where the ladder went, to the sighs of the island girls who peeped from the kitchen door. In the hope of a bath, they looked in awe at their hands.

I left them thus, and withdrew to make the broth.

With their tear-bright eyes they watched me come in with the great winking tray, and circle the room in a winding wreath of steam. Each in turn with a pair of black-nailed hands swept up his bowl. The first were trotting at my heels while the last still reached with their hands. Then the last drank too, and dredging their snouts from the bowls, let go and shuttled into the company.

That moment of transformation—only the gods really like it! Men and beasts almost never take in enough of the wonder to justify the trouble. The floor was swaying like a bridge in battle. "Outside!" I commanded. "No dirt is allowed in this house!" In the end, it takes phenomenal neatness of housekeeping to put it through the heads of men that they are swine. With my wand seething in the air like a broom, I drove them all through the door—twice as many hooves as there had been feet before—to join their brothers, who rushed forward to meet them now, filthily rivaling, but welcoming. What tusks I had given them!

As I shut the door on the sight, and drew back into my privacy—deathless privacy that heals everything, even the effort of magic—I felt something from behind press like the air of heaven before a storm, and reach like another wand over my head.

I spun round, thinking, O gods, it has failed me, it's drying up. Before everything, I think of my power. One man was left.

"What makes you think you're different from anyone else?" I screamed; and he laughed.

Before I'd believe it, I ran back to my broth. I had thought it perfect—I'd allowed no other woman to come near it. I tasted, and it was perfect—swimming with oysters from my reef and flecks of golden pork, redolent with leaves of bay and basil and rosemary, with the glass of island wine tossed in at the last: it has been my infallible recipe. Circe's broth: all the gods have heard of it and envied it. No, the fault had to be in the drinker. If a man remained, unable to leave that magnificent body of his, then enchantment had met with a hero. Oh, I know those prophecies as well as the back of my hand—only nothing is here to warn me when it is *now*.

The island girls, those servants I support, stood there in the kitchen and smiled at me. I threw kettle and all at their withering heels. Let them learn that unmagical people are put into the world to justify and serve the magical—not to smile at them!

I whirled back again. The hero stood as before. But his laugh had gone too, after his friends. His gaze was empty, as though I were not in it—I was invisible. His hand groped across the rushes of a chair. I moved beyond him and bolted the door against the murmurous outside. Still invisibly, I took away his sword. I sent his tunic away to the spring for washing, and I, with my own hands, gave him his bath. Then he sat and dried himself before the fire—carefully, the only mortal man on an island in the sea. I rubbed oil on his shadowy shoulders, and on the rope of curls in which his jaw was set. His rapt ears still listened to the human silence there.

"I know your name," I said in the voice of a woman, "and you know mine by now."

I took the chain from my waist, it slipped shining to the floor between us, where it lay as if it slept, as I came forth. Under my palms he stood warm and dense as a myrtle grove at noon. His limbs were heavy, braced like a sleep-walker's who has wandered, alas, to cliffs above the sea. When I passed before him, his arm lifted and barred my way. When I held up the glass he opened his mouth. He fell among the pillows, his still-open eyes two clouds stopped over the sun, and I lifted and kissed his hand.

It was he who in a burst of speech announced the end of day. As though the hour brought a signal to the wanderer, he told me a story, while the owl made comment outside. He told me of the monster with one eye—he had put out the eye, he said. Yes, said the owl, the monster is growing another, and a new man will sail along to blind it again. I had heard it all before, from man and owl. I didn't want his story, I wanted his secret.

When Venus leaned at the window, I called him by name, but he had talked himself into a dream, and his dream had him fast. I now saw through the cautious herb that had protected him from my broth. From the first, he had found some way to resist my power. He must laugh, sleep, ravish, he must talk and sleep. Next it would be he must die. I looked an age into that face above the beard's black crescent, the eyes turned loose from mine like the statues' that sleep on the hill. I took him by the locks of his beard and hair, but he rolled away with his snore to the very floor of sleep—as far beneath my reach as the drowned sailor dropped out of his, in the tale he told of the sea.

I thought of my father the Sun, who went on his divine way untroubled, ambitionless—unconsumed; suffering no loss, no heroic fear of corruption through his constant shedding of light, needing no story, no retinue to vouch for where he has been—even heroes could learn of the gods!

Yet I know they keep something from me, asleep and awake. There exists a mortal mystery, that, if I knew where it was, I could crush like an island grape. Only frailty, it seems, can divine it—and I was not endowed with that property. They live by frailty! By the moment! I tell myself that it is only a mystery, and mystery is only uncertainty. (There is no mystery in magic! Men are swine: let it be said, and no sooner said than done.) Yet mortals alone can divine where it lies in each other, can find it and prick it in all its peril, with an instrument made of air. I swear that only to possess that one, trifling secret, I would willingly turn myself into a harmless dove for the rest of eternity!

When presently he leapt up, I had nearly forgotten he would move again—

as a golden hibiscus startles you, all flowers, when you are walking in some weedy place apart.

Yes, but he would not dine. Dinner was carried in, but he would not dine with me until I would undo that day's havoc in the pigsty. I pointed out that his portion was served in a golden bowl—the very copy of that bowl my own father the Sun crosses back in each night after his journey of the day. But he cared nothing for beauty that was not of the world, he did not want the first taste of anything new. He wanted his men back. In the end, it was necessary for me to cloak myself and go down in the dark, under the willows where the bones are hung to the wind, into the sty; and to sort out and bring up his friends again from their muddy labyrinth. I had to pass them back through the doorway as themselves. I could not skip or brush lightly over one—he named and counted. Then he could look at them all he liked, staggering up on their hind legs before him. Their jaws sank asthmatically, and he cried, "Do you know me?"

"It's Odysseus!" I called, to spoil the moment. But with a shout he had already sprung to their damp embrace.

Reunions, it seems, are to be celebrated. (I have never had such a thing.) All of us feasted together on meat and bread, honey and wine, and the fire roared. We heard out the flute player, we heard out the story, and the fair-haired sailor, whose name is now forgotten, danced on the table and pleased them. When the fire was black, my servants came languishing from the kitchen, and all the way up the ladder to the beds above they had to pull the drowsy-kneed star-gazers, spilling laughter and songs all the way. I could hear them calling away to the girls as they would call them home. But the pigsty was where they belonged.

Hand in hand, we climbed to my tower room. His cheeks were grave and his eyes black, put out with puzzles and solutions. We conversed of signs, omens, premonitions, riddles and dreams, and ended in fierce, cold sleep. Strange man, as unflinching and as wound up as I am. His short life and my long one have their ground in common. Passion is our ground, our island—do others exist?

His sailors came jumping down in the morning, full of themselves and stories. Preparing the breakfast, I watched them tag one another, run rough-and-tumble around the table, regaling the house. "What did *I* do? How far did *I* go with it?" and in a reckless reassurance imitating the sounds of pigs at each other's backs. They were certainly more winsome now than they could ever have been before; I'd made them younger, too, while I was about it. But tell me of one that appreciated it! Tell me one now who looked my way until I had brought him his milk and figs.

When he made his appearance, we devoured a god's breakfast—all, the very sausages, taken for granted. The kitchen girls simpered and cried that if this went on, we'd be eaten out of house and home. But I didn't care if I put the house under greater stress for this one mortal than I ever dreamed of for myself—even on those lonely dull mornings when mist wraps the island and hides every path of the sea, and when my heart is black.

But a stir was upon them all from the moment they rose from the table. Treading on their napkins, tracking the clean floor with honey, they deserted me in the house and collected, arms wound on each other's shoulders, to talk beneath the sky. There they were in a knot, with him in the center of it. He folded his arms and sank his golden weight on one leg, while every ear on the island listened. I stood in the door and waited.

He walked up and said, "Thank you, Circe, for the hospitality we have enjoyed beneath your roof."

"What is the occasion for a speech?" I asked.

"We are setting sail," he said. "A year's visit is visit enough. It's time we were on our way."

Ever since the morning Time came and sat on the world, men have been on the run as fast as they can go, with beauty flung over their shoulders. I ground my teeth. I raised my wand in his face.

"You've put yourself to great trouble for us. You may have done too much," he said.

"I undid as much as I did!" I cried. "That was hard."

He gave me a pecking, recapitulating kiss, his black beard thrust at me like a shoe. I kissed it, his mouth, his wrist, his shoulder, I put my eyes to his eyes, through which I saw seas toss, and to the cabinet of his chest.

He turned and raised an arm to the others. "Tomorrow."

The knot broke and they wandered apart to the shore. They were not so forlorn when they could eat acorns and trot quickly where they would go.

It was as though I had no memory, to discover how early and late the cicadas drew long sighs like the playing out of all my silver shuttles. Wasn't it always the time of greatest heat, the Dog Star running with the Sun? The sea the color of honey looked sweet even to the tongue, the salt and vengeful sea. My grapes had ripened all over again while we stretched and drank our wine, and I ordered the harvest gathered and pressed—but this wine, I made clear to the servants, was to store. Hospitality is one thing, but I must consider how my time is endless, how I shall need wine endlessly. They smiled; but magic is the tree, and intoxication is just the little bird that flies in it to sing and flies out again. But the wanderers were watching the sun and waiting for the stars.

Now the night wind was rising. I went my way over the house as I do by night to see if all is well and holding together. From the rooftop I looked out. I saw the vineyards spread out like wings on the hill, the servants' huts and the swarthy groves, the sea awake, and the eye of the black ship. I saw in the moonlight the dance of the bones in the willows. "Old, displeasing ones!" I sang to them on the wind. "There's another now more displeasing than you! Your bite would be sweeter to my mouth than the soft kiss of a wanderer." I looked up at Cassiopeia, who sits there and needs nothing, pale in her chair in the stream of heaven. The old Moon was still at work. "Why keep it up, old woman?" I whispered to her, while the lions roared among the rocks; but I could hear plainly the crying of birds nearby and along the mournful shore.

I swayed, and was flung backward by my torment. I believed that I lay in disgrace and my blood ran green, like the wand that breaks in two. My sight returned to me when I awoke in the pigsty, in the red and black aurora of flesh, and it was day.

They sailed from me, all but one.

The youngest—Elpenor was his name—fell from my roof. He had forgotten where he had gone to sleep. Drunk on the last night, the drunkest of them all—so as not to be known any longer as only the youngest—he'd gone to sleep on the rooftop, and when they called him, his step went off into air. I saw him beating down through the light with rosy fists, as though he'd never left his mother's side till then.

They all ran from the table as though a star had fallen. They stood or they crouched above Elpenor fallen in my yard, low-voiced now like conspirators—as indeed they were. They wept for Elpenor lying on his face, and for themselves, as *he* wept for them the day they came, when I had made them swine.

He knelt and touched Elpenor, and like a lover lifted him; then each in turn held the transformed boy in his arms. They brushed the leaves from his face, and smoothed his red locks, which were still in their tangle from his brief attempts at love-making and from his too-sound sleep.

I spoke from the door. "When you dig the grave for that one, and bury him in the lonely sand by the shadow of your fleeing ship, write on the stone: 'I died of love.'"

I thought I spoke in epitaph—in the idiom of man. But when they heard me, they left Elpenor where he lay, and ran. Red-limbed, with linens sparkling, they sped over the windy path from house to ship like a rainbow in the sun, like new butterflies turned erratically to sea. While he stood in the prow and shouted to them, they loaded the greedy ship. They carried off their gifts from me—all unappreciated, unappraised.

I slid out of their path. I had no need to see them set sail, knowing as well as if I'd been ahead of them all the way, the far and wide, misty and islanded, bright and indelible and menacing world under which they all must go. But foreknowledge is not the same as the last word.

My cheek against the stony ground, I could hear the swine like summer thunder. These were with me still, pets now, once again—grumbling without meaning. I rose to my feet. I was sickened, with child. The ground fell away before me, blotted with sweet myrtle, with high oak that would have given me a ship too, if I were not tied to my island, as Cassiopeia must be to the sticks and stars of her chair. We were a rim of fire, a ring on the sea. His ship was a moment's gleam on a wave. The little son, I knew, was to follow—follow and slay him. That was the story. For whom is a story enough. For the wanderers who will tell it—it's where they must find their strange felicity.

I stood on my rock and wished for grief. It would not come. Though I could shriek at the rising Moon, and she, so near, would wax or wane, there was still grief, that couldn't hear me—grief that cannot be round or plain or solid-bright or running on its track, where a curse could get at it. It has no heavenly course; it is like mystery, and knows where to hide itself. At last it does not even breathe. I cannot find the dusty mouth of grief. I am sure now grief is a ghost—only a ghost in Hades, where ungrateful Odysseus is going—waiting on him.

(1955)

Even though, like Homer, Welty uses a first-person point of view, the effect created in her loosely constructed character sketch is strikingly different from Homer's. Circe is a far more complex, or "round," character than Odysseus. The narrative emphasizes her dual nature, combining the mortal with the immortal. Emotionally, Circe for the first time seems to be experiencing human passion. But being immortal, she cannot fully give way to her feelings; she simultaneously envies human emotions and holds them in contempt. Unlike Elpenor, she will never have an epitaph—let alone one that states "I died of love." Moreover, because events are told from her point of view and because, as an immortal, Circe has no sense of the momentary, the passage of time is never made explicit. Circe is surprised, as is the reader, when Odysseus suddenly says "A year's visit is visit enough."

Despite her superhuman qualities, Circe is very much a housewife, proud of her cleanliness and good cooking. She is modern in her practical view of life, independent spirit, and outspoken nature.

"Outside!" I commanded. "No dirt is allowed in this house!" In the end, it takes phenomenal neatness of housekeeping to put it through the heads of men that they are swine.

Indeed, through Circe's acerbic comments, Welty playfully changes the story of the transformation of men into swine into a symbol of a woman's perception of uncouth masculine behavior. In doing so, Welty has reinterpreted Homer's story and given it a recognizably modern twist.

Because Welty's story is presented strictly from Circe's point of view, with no momentary omniscient interjection, the whole piece might be called an interior monologue. We are very much aware of Circe's distinctive voice throughout, as she reveals her innermost thoughts. In contrast to Homer, who emphasizes his hero's adventures, Welty concentrates on Circe's psychological experiences. From the first poetic sentence to the last, Welty has created a uniquely intense and poignant character sketch.

Although we may be tempted to identify some of Circe's responses with Welty's own view of life, we should be aware that authors seldom speak in their own voice. With the variety of approaches available in narrative writing, authors consciously choose their narrative point of view. We might ask whether we ever really know when authors of fictional works speak in their own voice. We should rarely, if ever, assume that the voice of a first-person or even an omniscient narrator is the author's own.

Poetry

In general, the same points of view, or "voices," we have been observing in prose narrative can be found in poetry. The poet, too, makes conscious choices and uses point of view to shape the material. Since we, as readers, may regard poetry as an especially challenging art form, we may find that asking from what point of view the text was written is a particularly useful way to begin our reading of any poem. In other words, we might start with the question: "Who is the speaker of the words on the page?"

Omniscient Speaker

Some poems use an omniscient speaker. Narrative poems often use such a point of view to tell their story. With this approach, the poet can easily reveal both what is happening and what will happen in the future, as well as what various characters are thinking. Shorter poems such as William Blake's "The Sick Rose" (see Chapter 2) can also have an omniscient speaker who knows—apparently better than the rose—what malevolent force is destroying her.

In descriptive poems, the voice of the speaker may be hard to identify. This voice may be impersonal, as in W. H. Auden's "Musée des Beaux Arts" (see Chapter 2), or in the following poem by Alfred, Lord Tennyson (1809–1892):

Alfred, Lord Tennyson

THE EAGLE

FRAGMENT

He clasps the crag with crooked hands;
Close to the sun in lonely lands,
Ringed with the azure world, he stands.

The wrinkled sea beneath him crawls;
He watches from his mountain walls,
And like a thunderbolt he falls.

(1851)

The splendid image of the eagle is presented by a disembodied voice. Nonetheless, we can say that a speaker in this poem is watching and describing the eagle, first as it clasps the mountain crags and then as it swoops down to the sea. Whether this voice is closer to the omniscient narrator or to a first-person speaker is a question that really cannot be answered.

First-Person Speaker

The first-person speaker is, in fact, found more often in poetry than the omniscient speaker, especially in shorter poems. Among the examples we considered in Chapter 2, Nikki Giovanni's "Kidnap Poem" and George Herbert's "Easter Wings" both have this point of view. So frequent is the use of the first-person voice in poetry that we as readers may be tempted to identify the voice with the poet. After all, Nikki Giovanni makes her speaker into a poet, refers to New York locations, and capitalizes the word "Black"—all details directly related to her own life. And in "Easter Wings," the speaker's sense of his own unworthiness, coupled with his faith in divine love, certainly conveys Herbert's known piety.

Deep and intense feelings, expressed through a first-person voice, are especially characteristic of the Romantic poetry of the early 19th century. "My heart aches, and a drowsy numbness pains / My sense" are the opening words of John Keats's "Ode to a Nightingale" (1819), which we shall consider in detail in Chapter 11. Even more highly subjective poetry is being created by certain modern poets, who consciously write "confessional" pieces that come directly out of their own private lives. "Of Suicide" (1970), by John Berryman (1914–1972), begins:

Reflections on suicide, & on my father, possess me.
I drink too much. My wife threatens separation.
She won't 'nurse' me. She feels 'inadequate.'
We don't mix together.

In these few lines Berryman reveals not only highly personal hostilities toward his father and wife but also his problem with alcoholism.

Still, we should not assume that the "I" of the poem is identical with the poet, any more than we assume that a first-person narrator in a story or novel is identical with the author. Even in highly subjective poems, the first-person speaker reveals only a facet of the poet's personality, usually expressing one mood—exuberant love in "Kidnap Poem," devotion in "Easter Wings," and despair in "Of Suicide." Moreover, in the act of committing the poem to paper, the poet does not just express naked emotions, but gives them shape. And once on paper, the poem takes on a life of its own. We should bear in mind that the voice of the first-person speaker is invented by the writer as a means of expression. By using the term *speaker* instead of the name of the poet, we can keep the distinction between the two clearly in mind.

Other first-person speakers, less obviously autobiographical, are more easily distinguished from the poet. They are voices of more or less fully defined characters, and are close to the first-person narrators who are characters in stories or novels. A striking example is presented in "My Last Duchess," by Robert Browning (1812–1889). Here the "I," far from being identical with Browning, is an historical figure, the Duke of Ferrara, who is describing the portrait of his late wife.

Robert Browning

MY LAST DUCHESS

Ferrara

That's my last Duchess painted on the wall,
Looking as if she were alive. I call
That piece a wonder, now: Frà Pandolf's hands
Worked busily a day, and there she stands.
Will't please you sit and look at her? I said
"Frà Pandolf" by design, for never read
Strangers like you that pictured countenance,
The depth and passion of its earnest glance,
But to myself they turned (since none puts by
The curtain I have drawn for you, but I)
And seemed as they would ask me, if they durst,
How such a glance came there; so, not the first
Are you to turn and ask thus. Sir, 'twas not
Her husband's presence only, called that spot
Of joy into the Duchess' cheek: perhaps
Frà Pandolf chanced to say "Her mantle laps
Over my lady's wrist too much," or "Paint
Must never hope to reproduce the faint
Half-flush that dies along her throat": such stuff
Was courtesy, she thought, and cause enough
For calling up that spot of joy. She had
A heart—how shall I say?—too soon made glad,
Too easily impressed; she liked whate'er
She looked on, and her looks went everywhere.
Sir, 'twas all one! My favor at her breast,
The dropping of the daylight in the West,
The bough of cherries some officious fool
Broke in the orchard for her, the white mule
She rode with round the terrace—all and each
Would draw from her alike the approving speech,
Or blush, at least. She thanked men,—good! but thanked

Somehow—I know not how—as if she ranked
My gift of a nine-hundred-years-old name
With anybody's gift. Who'd stoop to blame
This sort of trifling? Even had you skill
In speech—which I have not—to make your will
Quite clear to such an one, and say, "Just this
Or that in you disgusts me; here you miss,
Or there exceed the mark"—and if she let
Herself be lessoned so, nor plainly set
Her wits to yours, forsooth, and made excuse,
—E'en then would be some stooping; and I choose
Never to stoop. Oh sir, she smiled, no doubt,
Whene'er I passed her; but who passed without
Much the same smile? This grew; I gave commands;
Then all smiles stopped together. There she stands
As if alive. Will't please you rise? We'll meet
The company below, then. I repeat,
The Count your master's known munificence
Is ample warrant that no just pretense
Of mine for dowry will be disallowed;
Though his fair daughter's self, as I avowed
At starting, is my object. Nay, we'll go
Together down, sir. Notice Neptune, though,
Taming a sea-horse, thought a rarity,
Which Claus of Innsbruck cast in bronze for me!
(1842)

Browning's use of the first-person point of view is especially intriguing because it allows the duke to reveal his personality directly through his own words. While his speech sounds colloquial, it is in the rigorous form of couplets. As the Duke of Ferrara describes the portrait of "my last duchess," he gradually reveals his pride, possessiveness, and brutality. Infuriated by his former wife's friendliness and warmth toward others, the duke gave orders that led to her death: "I gave commands; / Then all smiles stopped together." The brevity and vagueness of these words are especially effective, for they suggest the power and sinister cruelty of the speaker. Browning has carefully chosen accented monosyllables—"áll smíles stópped"—to emphasize the duke's action and its consequences.

This first-person speaker is fascinating not only as an individual personality but also as the representative of an historical period. Browning's Ferrara, like many dukes in the Italian Renaissance, is an absolute ruler—arrogant and dictatorial, all-powerful and merciless when contradicted. Even Ferrara's love of art, which is in keeping with his general possessiveness, is characteristic of Renaissance rulers, who were often great patrons of the arts.

The speaker's words also suggest a dramatic scene. As we realize toward the end of the poem, the duke has been addressing the emissary through whom he is arranging a new marriage. This revelation of his future plans creates an intensely ironic situation and brings to a climax the ironies inherent in the whole poem. The duke has revealed far more of his personal failings than is wise for a suitor. This first-person speaker has unwittingly shown more of himself than he realizes. Browning makes full use of dramatic irony here, for we can recognize so much more than the character. And at the conclusion of the poem we are aware of yet another irony: the future duchess may suffer the same fate as her predecessor, since the duke's nature is unlikely to change.

Browning is considered the master of this type of first-person narrative, called a **dramatic monologue**, in which the words of a single speaker are presented in what is a little theatrical scene. The emphasis is usually on the revelation of a complex character or an intriguing situation, expressed directly through one character's speech. The dramatic monologue also has other elements of a theatrical scene. It often has an implied second character to whom the words are addressed, and it also suggests a definite setting. Sometimes specific actions are indicated—the duke's drawing aside the curtain or preparing to go downstairs, for instance, in "My Last Duchess." All that is needed to turn dramatic monologue into actual drama is performance; but in poetry, the dramatic monologue is meant to be read, not impersonated by an actor.

Since the dramatic monologue concentrates on the thoughts of a single speaker, it can turn into stream of consciousness, the device we considered earlier in relation to prose fiction. In "The Love Song of J. Alfred Prufrock" (1917), T. S. Eliot (1888–1965) brilliantly reveals the character of a neurotic, aging bachelor through the character's seemingly random associations and even subconscious impulses. Another striking example can be found in "Moly," by Thom Gunn (b. 1929), which reveals the thoughts of one of Odysseus's followers who were turned into swine by the enchantress Circe. The speaker is seeking the herb moly, which is the only antidote for his transformation into a lowly animal.

Thom Gunn

MOLY

Nightmare of beasthood, snorting, how to wake.
I woke. What beasthood skin she made me take?

Leathery toad that ruts for days on end,
Or cringing dribbling dog, man's servile friend,

Or cat that prettily pounces on its meat,
Tortures it hours, then does not care to eat:

Parrot, moth, shark, wolf, crocodile, ass, flea.
What germs, what jostling mobs there were in me.

These seem like bristles, and the hide is tough.
No claw or web here: each foot ends in hoof.

Into what bulk has method disappeared?
Like ham, streaked. I am gross—grey, gross, flap-eared.

The pale-lashed eyes my only human feature.
My teeth tear, tear. I am the snouted creature

That bites through anything, root, wire, or can.
If I was not afraid I'd eat a man.

Oh a man's flesh already is in mine.
Hand and foot poised for risk. Buried in swine.

  I root and root, you think that it is greed,
It is, but I seek out a plant I need.

Direct me gods, whose changes are all holy,
To where it flickers deep in grass, the moly:

Cool flesh of magic in each leaf and shoot,
From milk flower to the black forked root.

From this fat dungeon I could rise to skin
And human title, putting pig within.

I push my big grey wet snout through the green,
Dreaming the flower I have never seen.

(1971)

Gunn presents one of Circe's victims as the speaker, so that the poem's viewpoint differs from Welty's "Circe," which presents the same incident from the enchantress's point of view. By assuming that the reader knows the episode in Homer, Gunn can omit all the details of the sailors' journey to the island and of their meeting with Circe. Instead, the poet can concentrate solely on the emotional experiences of one sailor, giving his responses as he awakens to discover his "beasthood." What really interests Gunn is the speaker's self-loathing ("I am gross"; "I am the snouted creature/ That bites through anything"); his awareness of the animal inside all human beings, where it cannot show ("I could rise to skin/ And human title, putting pig within"); and, finally, his longing for release through the magic of the herb ("Dreaming the flower I have never seen"). This example again demonstrates that the writer's decision about the voice or point of view is fundamental and crucial. Everything follows from this decision—both the few facts to be included and the many to be ignored, especially in an art form as highly compressed as poetry.

What, then, distinguishes Gunn's poem from a dramatic monologue such as Browning's, whose characteristics it shares? As the opening line reveals, the Gunn poem is far more disjointed. The sentences or fragments of sentences do not follow a logical order, but shift abruptly from one topic to another. Articles—"a," "the"—and connective words are sometimes omitted. Yet the poem has an internal logic, which comes from the speaker's private association of ideas. For example, the realization that his humanity is "buried in swine" leads the speaker immediately to mention his pig-like behavior—"I root and root"—as he tries to find the plant that will free him—"but I seek out a plant I need." Moreover, the seemingly haphazard list of animals in line 7 is puzzling, especially when followed by the reference to "germs" in line 8, until we understand that the speaker is using a typical stream-of-consciousness shorthand. He seems to be realizing—consciously or subconsciously—that he contains within himself the seeds or genes ("germs") not just of swine but of all animals. Through his speaker, Gunn seems to be alluding to the biological fact that the human embryo evolves through a series of animal-like stages. Gunn suggests that humanity has subsumed or absorbed these animal stages within it, so that a close relationship exists between the animal and the human in each of us. The point of view Gunn has chosen—the stream of consciousness of one of Circe's pigs—allows him to express this complicated idea in a fresh and richly suggestive way.

Third-Person Limited Speaker

The only point of view that we have not yet discussed in relation to poetry is the third-person limited. In poetry this point of view occurs far less frequently than in stories or novels. Only occasionally does a poet experiment with a speaker whose highly personal experiences are expressed by the third-person pronoun. Still, in his early collection *77 Dream Songs* (1959), John Berryman invented a character named Henry, whose anxieties and unhappiness "as he moves on in the world" are traced from the ages of 41 to 51.

Henry hates the world. What the world to Henry
Did will not bear thought

are the opening lines of one of these poems. Berryman insists that his work "is essentially about an imaginary character (not the poet, not me)." Even though Henry and Berryman have much in common, the speaker of the poem is to be considered a fictional character. Henry seems to have been created by Berryman to express the poet's own attitudes toward the world somewhat more objectively. Later, however, as we have seen in the poem "Of Suicide," Berryman simply adopted a first-person speaker. Perhaps the third-person limited point of view is rare in poetry because this voice can offer neither the immediacy of the first-person voice nor the flexibility of the omniscient narrator.

Theater

Not every art form can make use of all the points of view that are available. In the theater, the possibilities are more restricted than in either prose fiction or poetry.

First-Person Speaker

Basically, drama uses first-person presentations, for the characters in a play speak directly of their own experiences. Since the story is enacted by all those involved in it, all speak for themselves, reflecting their own concerns and their limited knowledge. Usually, the third-person limited point of view is not possible because drama is not restricted to a single point of view presented by someone else. Even an omniscient narrator is rare. Such famous plays as *Our Town* (1938) by Thornton Wilder (1897–1975) and *Antigone* (1944) by Jean Anouilh (b. 1910), with their all-knowing narrators, are nota-

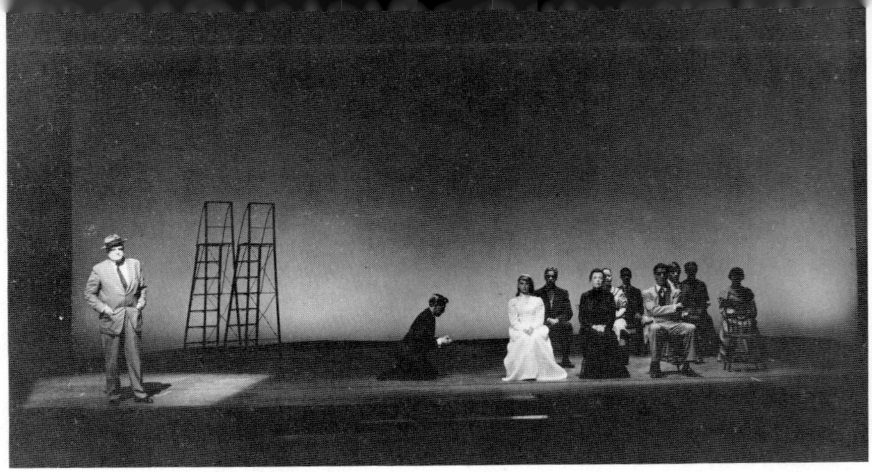

82 Scene from *Our Town* by Thornton Wilder, in the Williamstown Theatre Festival production, 1959. Directed by Nikos Psacharopoulos. Wilder, standing at the left, is playing the role of the Stage Manager.

ble exceptions. As the photograph from *Our Town* [82] reveals, the omniscient figure, here named the Stage Manager, stands spotlighted on one side of the stage, commenting on the action being played out by the actors spotlighted on the other side.

Because drama depends on first-person presentations, modern playwrights have experimented with direct stream of consciousness. Several plays by Samuel Beckett consist exclusively of characters revealing their innermost thoughts directly to an audience in a rambling, seemingly chaotic, but actually significant fashion. In Beckett's *Not I* (1974), which carries this point of view to the extreme, the language of the play is spoken entirely by a pair of disembodied lips, and the actress to whom these lips belong delivers the piece in a fluid, nonstop monologue. But Beckett is not the first to have experimented with stream-of-consciousness speeches. In *Strange Interlude* (1928), for instance, Eugene O'Neill (1888–1953) uses the device to striking effect in an otherwise conventional drama. Actually, this device is not so far removed from the technique used by earlier playwrights to express the thoughts of their characters. A **soliloquy** allows figures such as Hamlet to reveal their innermost selves to the audience while hiding their thoughts from the other characters in the play.

Identifying the genuine voice of a playwright is even more difficult than identifying the voice of an author in a fictional narrative or poem. Since the characters in a drama can reveal only their own personalities, none of these may be identical with the playwright's own. The exception is the **raisonneur**, whose function is to state the author's ideas explicitly. Yet we can never be sure to what degree even the *raisonneur* speaks for the author. The moderate and sensible Philinte in *The Misanthrope* (1666) by Molière (1622–1673) seems to be expressing the playwright's own moderate and reasonable attitudes, in contrast to the more extreme and unreasonable attitudes of the misanthropic Alceste. But few critics today would claim that Molière's own views are as simple as Philinte's. Significantly, too, among the hundreds of characters created by Shakespeare, none can be wholly identified with him. Even the great artist-magician Prospero of Shakespeare's last play, *The Tempest* (1610), who is sometimes identified with the playwright, cannot be simply equated with his creator.

Film

One might think that the points of view in film are similar to those found in drama, since both genres rely so heavily on characters revealing themselves in dialogue. But in fact more points of view are available in film, and many of them are similar to those we have observed in fictional narratives.

Omniscient Narrator

Insofar as the camera serves as the film director's eyes, taking us from character to character and from scene to scene, it functions like an omniscient narrator. As we saw in Chapter 3, film is free of restrictions of time and space in telling the story, and it can show in god-like fashion what various characters are experiencing. Moreover, just as in fiction, this point of view can be either unobtrusive or obtrusive. That is, smooth transitions or cuts between scenes can make the audience forget it is seeing through the eyes of a camera. On the other hand, devices that call attention to the camera at work are the equivalent of the obtrusive narrator. These more elaborate devices for changing from one shot to another include dissolves and fades (see Chapter 3); *iris-out* and *iris-in* (when a circular image fades into the center of the screen to be replaced by a new circular image, which first appears at the center of the screen); *wipes* (when a line erases one image and replaces it with another); or *turnabouts* (when the screen seems to turn over and continue on the other side). Such devices recall Fielding's chatty narrator in *Tom Jones,* who reminds us of what he is doing with his own art as he tells the story.

First-Person Narrator

The camera can also become the eye of an individual character, limiting the world to that character's perceptions. In this case, the camera functions like a first-person narrator. In *The Lady in the Lake* (1946), Robert Montgomery (b. 1904) lets us briefly see the detective who is the central character at the beginning to establish the flashback context for the rest of the film. From this point on, the entire action is recorded as seen through his eyes. But such a consistent first-person point of view is extremely rare in film. Most motion pictures use a combination of the omniscient and the first-person points of view. They enjoy the freedom of being able to show both the point of view of a character and the character whose point of view we are seeing.

Stream of Consciousness

Film can present the activity within a character's mind even more vividly than prose narrative or drama. The fluidity of film in capturing motion and its flexibility in capturing time make this art form especially good at presenting stream of consciousness, that is, presenting images that move freely backward and forward in time. For example, in *Hiroshima Mon Amour* (1959) [83] the director, Alain Resnais (b. 1922), uses the device of cross-cutting to link the heroine's perception of her current lover with her memory of a much earlier lover simply by juxtaposing images of their hands in similar positions.

Each of these images is presented for only a brief moment. We see the heroine, a French actress who has come to Japan to make a peace film, standing in the bedroom doorway and smiling (A); then, her sleeping Japanese lover, his naked arm and hand extended on the bed (B); then, a close-up of her face, now troubled and brooding (C); then, a close-up of another hand emerging from a uniform (D); then, a close-up of her at an earlier time bending over the bloodied face of an unknown man (E); and finally, another shot of the Japanese lover, his arm extended in the same position as before (F). This sequence of shots actually provides a momentary flashback to the actress's past, introducing her romance with a German soldier (D) in occupied France during World War II and its unhappy and violent termination by murder (E). Resnais demonstrates how quickly subconscious associations of two quite different moments can be made through mental images, and he brilliantly uses the camera to present the images in the character's mind. Since these images are the result of the heroine's private associations, the audience is baffled at first and only gradually comes to recognize the images' significance as the story unfolds.

The fluidity and flexibility of film are especially useful for presenting the psychological activity of dreams, for these are usually experienced in visual terms. Hitchcock makes a nightmare sequence in *Spellbound* ominous by presenting images of floating eyes, masked faces, an enormous scissors, and an oppressive, stylized landscape. These images were designed by Salvador Dali (b. 1904), a modern artist known for his paintings of frightening dream-like states. In this instance, the images not only express the hero's

below: 83 A series of scenes from *Hiroshima, Mon Amour,* with Emmanuèle Riva, Eiji Okada, and Bernard Fresson, 1959. Directed by Alain Resnais.

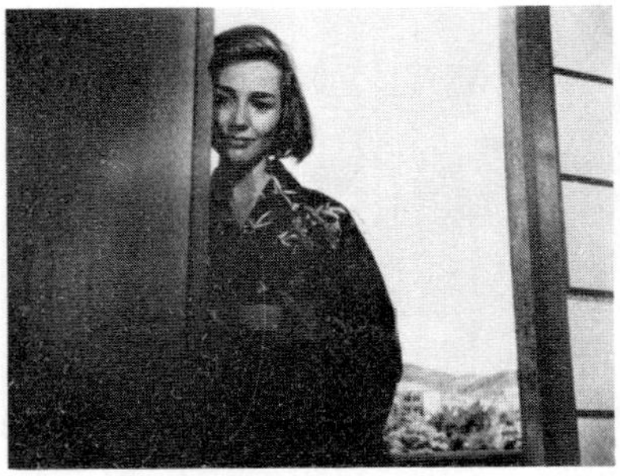

A

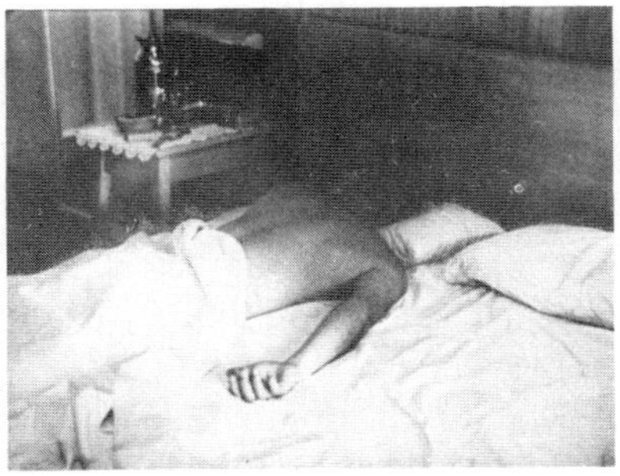

B

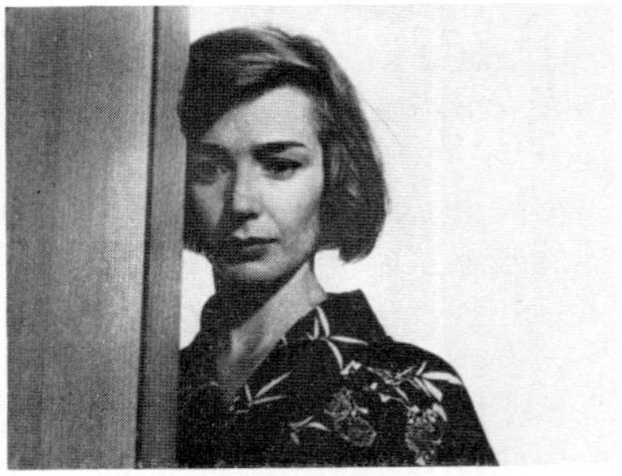

C

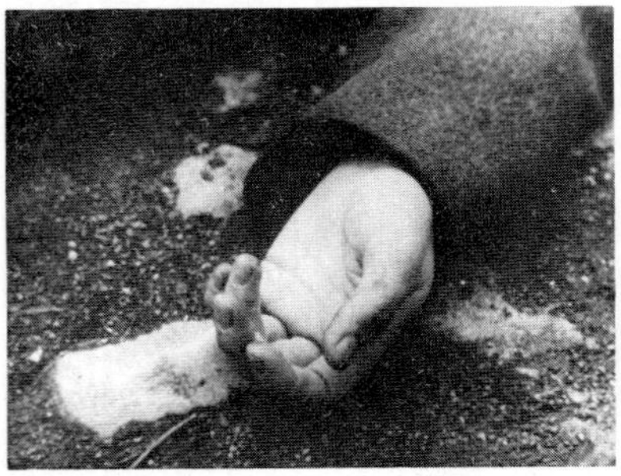

D

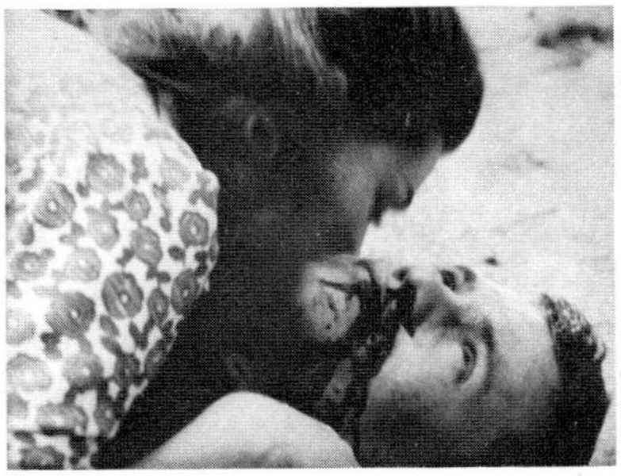

E

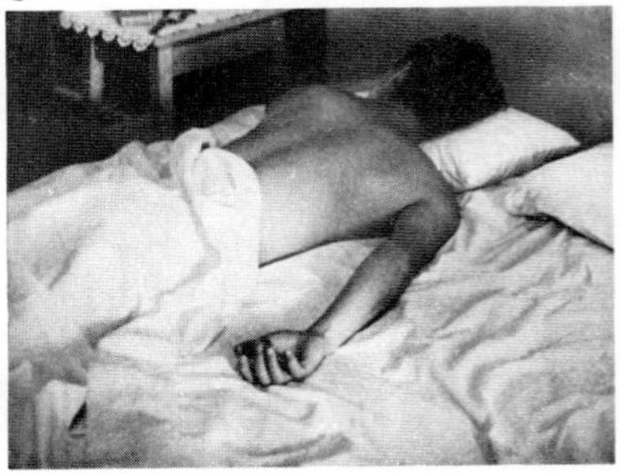

F

anxieties but also offer clues that can be interpreted to reveal the hero's past. We discover that the hero is a victim of amnesia who has suppressed his earlier history. As in the sequence from *Hiroshima Mon Amour,* we share the main character's experience in visual terms and only later come to appreciate its real meaning.

Altogether, film can match the points of view possible in drama and almost all the points of view possible in prose narratives and poetry as well. Yet film predominantly uses the perspective of the omniscient narrator. Perhaps this is true because restricted points of view such as the first-person or third-person limited viewpoint are not compatible with so flexible a medium, or because film-makers have not fully realized the other narrative possibilities of their medium.

To sum up, we can see that narrative points of view in fiction, poetry, drama, and film are similar in purpose to the various types of perspective in the visual arts. These viewpoints provide artists with the means of shaping their material. And they provide us, the audience, with a vantage point for perceiving and understanding the special world in each work of art.

Questions for Study and Discussion

1. From what vantage point—unitary, unitary-subordinate, and plural—do we see Rodin's *Thinker* [see Figure 6, page 9], the Im-Dugud plaque [see Figure 10, page 17], and the Crane Memorial Library [see Figure 14, page 19]?
2. How does the visual perspective invented in the Renaissance differ from that found in earlier works?
3. What devices has Rogier van der Weyden [see Plate 8, page 40] used to establish a sense of depth? Consider the bench, the floor, the rear wall, and the vista beyond. Do these elements achieve a unified three-dimensional effect?
4. In the Hogarth illustration [see Figure 78, page 123], what additional examples—beyond those mentioned in the text—can be found of the absurd violation of the rules of perspective?
5. Examine Galliari's stage design for *Didone* [see Figure 76, page 120] and find at least five ways in which the artist has achieved his three-dimensional effect. Consider the details in the drawing of the columns, arches, railings, and other architectural elements. Is there a single vanishing point, or are there several? To what degree would one's seat in the theater change the impression of three-dimensionality? Where is the best seat in the house?
6. How is the device of foreshortening consistent with the principles of perspective?
7. What type of perspective is achieved in Dürer's *Italian Mountains* [see Plate 6, page 38]? How has the artist created a sense of depth without the use of linear perspective?
8. In *Vanity Fair,* a novel about family life in the early 19th century, the young widow Amelia has just been forced to accept financial support from her unfriendly father-in-law.

So I must own that . . . with something akin to gratitude, Amelia took the crumbs that her father-in-law let drop now and then, and with them fed her own parent. Directly she understood it to be her duty, it was this young woman's nature (ladies, she is but thirty still, and we choose to call her a young woman even at that age)—it was, I say, her nature to sacrifice herself. . . . During what long thankless nights had she worked out her fingers for little Georgy [her son] whilst at home with her; what buffets, scorns, privations, poverties had she endured for father and mother! And in the midst of all these solitary resignations and unseen sacrifices, she did not respect herself any more than the world respected her; but I believe thought in her heart that she was a poor-spirited, despicable little creature, whose luck in life was only too good for her merits. O you poor women! O you poor secret martyrs and victims, whose life is a torture, who are stretched on racks in your bedrooms, and who lay your heads down on the block daily at the drawing-room table; every man who watches your pains, or peers into those dark places where the torture is administered to you, must pity you—and—and thank God that he has a beard. I recollect seeing, years ago, at the prison for idiots and madmen . . . near Paris, a poor wretch bent down under the bondage of his imprisonment and his personal infirmity, to whom one of our party gave a halfpennyworth of snuff. . . . The kindness was too much for the poor epileptic creature. He cried in an anguish of delight and gratitude: if anybody gave you and me a thousand a year, or saved our lives, we could not be so affected. And so, if you properly tyrannize over a woman, you will find a halfp'orth of kindness act upon her, and bring tears into her eyes, as though you were an angel benefiting her.

Chap. LVII (1848)

a. What type of omniscient narrator does Thackeray use in the above passage? What specific phrases reveal the narrator's personality?
b. By what specific phrases does the narrator suggest the conventional 19th-century male point of view toward women?
c. Does the narrator share this point of view? What is the narrator's attitude toward women, especially as revealed in the last sentence?

9. In the opening passage quoted from *Great Expectations,* (page 127) what evidence is there of the double first-person narrator—the young boy and the more mature Pip? Which phrases seem to belong to the child and which to the man?
10. In the opening passage quoted from *A Portrait of the Artist,* (page 128) what phrases are evidence of the first-person limited narrator? Why do we feel closer to little Stephen's experiences in *A Portrait* than to Pip's, even though Joyce uses the third-person pronoun?
11. In the first half of Edith Wharton's "Roman Fever," (see page 85), what three different points of view are presented? Whose are they and what is gained by giving all three? Are Mrs. Slade's thoughts presented as third-person limited or stream of consciousness here?
12. In Homer's Circe episode (see page 133), what are the interests of the narrator? How does he feel about his men, about Circe, and about his destined voyage?
13. How does Homer's point of view affect the presentation of Circe? To what extent are her feelings described or omitted at crucial moments such as when she invites Odysseus to bed and when he tells her he wishes to leave?

14. In Eudora Welty's "Circe" (see page 140) what are the chief interests of the narrator?
15. How do Welty's changes in point of view and central character permit a new and modern interpretation of the episode? To answer this question, consider the following:
    a. What are the stages in Circe's development? How does she feel about the visitors, especially Odysseus, at the beginning? When and how do her attitudes toward men change? What is her attitude when Odysseus and his men leave? In this context, what is the significance of the epitaph she suggests for young Elpenor?
    b. As an immortal, Circe's attitude toward mortals is condescending. Yet what are the signs that she also envies them? What is lacking in her life?
    c. In what respects does Circe represent a modern woman? How does she feel about her house, her cooking, her servants? What details reveal quite modern attitudes toward men, love, and abandonment?
    d. How does the author give Circe a sense of humor in addition to her many other traits? Is Circe ultimately a humorous or a poignant figure?
16. Can Welty's "Circe" be considered either an interior monologue or stream of consciousness? Does the story include patterns of subconscious as well as conscious associations?
17. In light of our earlier discussion of plot and character, is the plot of Welty's "Circe" tightly or loosely constructed? Are the characters of Circe and Ulysses types or individuals, flat or round? Why does Welty choose to present such a plot and such characters? How do these differ significantly from the plot and characters in Edith Wharton's "Roman Fever"?
18. What two different points of view are used in John Hollander's "Adam's Task" (see page 77) and how does this combination enrich the poem?
19. What is the point of view in W. H. Auden's "Musée des Beaux Arts" (see page 78) and how is it used to suggest the problems of 20th-century life as well as a particularly modern attitude toward them?
20. Frames are more immediately recognizable in paintings than in the other spatial arts, but they can be used to create different impressions in all these arts. To review the clearest examples of framing, consider what is achieved when artists include a frame as a part of their picture—for instance in the Ebbo Gospel [see Figure 21, page 26], Lichtenstein's *I Know How You Must Feel, Brad!* [see Figure 37, page 45], and Seurat's *Port-en-Bessin, Entrance to the Harbor* [see Figure 80, page 126]. Do equivalent frames exist in the theater? Do scenes staged in a proscenium theater differ from those staged in a theater-in-the-round?
21. Select a recent film that you have enjoyed and analyze how the director has treated the point of view. Through how many characters is the story seen by the audience? How does the visual point of view contribute to the film's presentation of plot and character?

CHAPTER 5

Performance: Interpreting the Work of Art

Unlike such art forms as painting and poetry, in which the creator alone decides how to shape the work, the performing arts require interpreters. Performance alone creates the work of art in music, drama, and ballet. Here, performing artists can be said to recreate the work with every performance, and they inevitably shape the material in their own special way. Composers, playwrights, and choreographers provide the script and directions, but the performers give the actual interpretation of the work of art, which exists fully only in performance.

Music

Performance in music can be presented in some instances by an individual and in others by a group. In both cases, the interpretation depends on at least three components: technique, musicianship, and personality.

Technique

The first component, *technique,* includes the ability to play or sing the notes accurately, with precision and ease, in order to produce the rhythm, melody, and harmony indicated in the score. In professional performances, such technical proficiency is often taken for granted, but to acquire it takes years of practice and study.

Each instrument presents its own challenge. A violinist must control the bow to produce a wide variety of dynamics as well as qualities of sound. At the same time, each note requires a precise coordination of the bow stroke with the finger placement of the left hand. This hand determines the pitch of the note with no guidance from any kind of mark or ridge such as the so-called fret that helps the guitarist. Accuracy in producing the pitch, known as *intonation,* is a crucial part of a violinist's technique. The left hand must also produce a slight waver in the sound, the *vibrato,* that gives to the tone of stringed instruments an expressiveness similar to the human voice. A pianist must coordinate both hands, which generally perform differing melodic patterns in different rhythms. To produce a musical effect, pianists must master many subtle shadings of sound and ways of connecting one note to the next, so that the essentially percussive instrument takes on some of the expressive possibilities of other instruments. Such nuanced playing requires not only considerable muscular development of the fingers and wrists but also considerable knowledge of the various possible interpretations.

A singer faces the more basic challenge of controlling the voice, which is not an instrument separate from the player, but an integral part of the body. The voice may not even seem beautiful to the singer when the sound is being produced because of the way the sound vibrates in the head. In any case, using the voice, whether to create lovely tone quality or to produce clear and distinctive notes or simply to find and hold the correct pitch, requires great technical skill. Mastery of technique is fundamental to all performance, and this mastery requires extraordinary proficiency as well as constant practice.

For professional musicians who have developed their technical prowess to the highest point, the term **virtuoso** is often used. Virtuosos are expected to master all aspects of their art, but from the 19th century on, the word has come to mean a performer whose technical achievement may overshadow all other qualities. Niccolò Paganini (1782–1840) astonished all Europe with his seemingly impossible technical achievements on the violin and inspired Franz Liszt (1811–1886) to similar feats on the piano. Today, James Galway (b. 1939) with his flute, Vladimir Horowitz (b. 1904) with his piano, and Zubin Mehta (b. 1936) with his baton are widely acclaimed virtuosos.

Musicianship

Since interpretation requires more than simply being able to execute the notes given in the score, *musicianship* is equally important. This refers to the intelligence of the performer in knowing how to convey the essential character of the material. Choices must be made about the tempo, which directly affects the expressive quality of the music. For instance, just how slow is the composer's *andante?* Is it intended to be languid or closer to a *moderato?* Choices must also be made about the phrasing—the pacing and shaping of the melodic line—and about **dynamics**—the loudness or softness of the sound. In some cases, composers have not marked their manuscripts. What is loud or soft, what increases or decreases in volume, what builds to a climax—all these questions of dynamics are left to the performer. In the vast quantity of Bach's keyboard works, scarcely five or six phrases bear the composer's dynamic markings. To take another example, in the performance of the Chopin *Ballade No. 1 in G minor* [Example 9] the pianist following Chopin's meager indications of *meno mosso* ("slower"), *sotto voce* ("softly"), and *pp* (*pianissimo,* "very softly") must decide which are the important notes, which of these notes should sound louder than others, and, finally, how to shape the entire **theme** into an expressive whole.

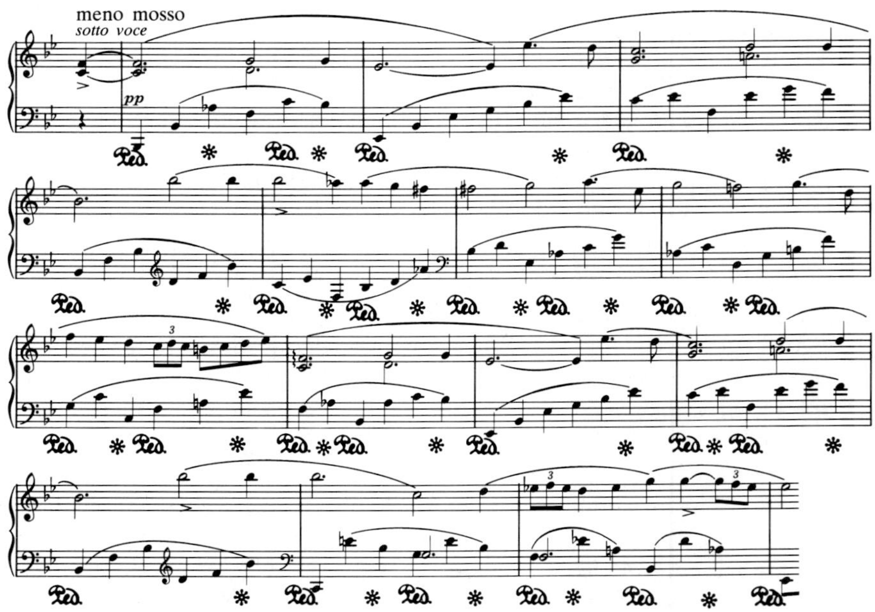

Example 9 Frédéric Chopin, *Ballade No. 1 in G minor,* Opus 23, second theme (Ped. = depress pedal; ✻ = release pedal; >=accent).

But such matters of tempo, phrasing, and dynamics are not decided arbitrarily by individual preference. Rather, the choice depends on what suits the composer and even the individual work being performed. For example, the piano damper pedal, which sustains the sound of the notes struck on the keyboard, is likely to be used sparingly for a Haydn piece, but fully and expressively for a Chopin work, thereby approximating on the modern piano the sound of the instruments for which these composers wrote. Musicianship requires a knowledge of music history and of the qualities of each composer.

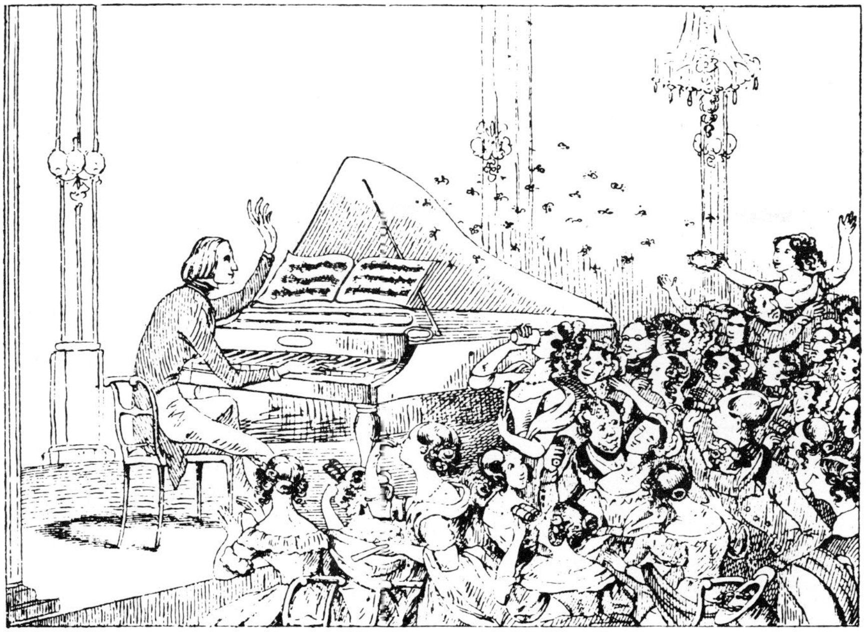

84 An anonymous caricature of Franz Liszt during one of his triumphal tours, being welcomed by the ladies of Berlin. 1846.

Personality

Finally, the *personality* of the performer, or rather the personality that the performer is able to project from the stage, plays an important part in the total interpretation. As audience, we respond not simply to the music but also to the person performing it. Concentration, intensity, spirit, poise, self-assurance—all communicate directly to us and affect our responses.

Some performers express their personalities more vividly than others. Not only do some have a more colorful temperament but they may choose to leave more of a personal imprint on the piece they are performing. Such charismatic performers were perceived as heroes by 19th-century audiences. Through their dramatic presentation and theatricality as well as their virtuoso technique, Paganini and Liszt [84] were among the first to attract an adoring public. Paganini was not merely an incredible technician. With his gaunt appearance, loose limbs, and long fingers, he seemed strangely demonic—an impression he emphasized by his clothing and gestures. Liszt, too, cultivated an image of wild, romantic enthusiasm together with what we would now call charisma and sex appeal. In opera a female singer with a charismatic personality is called a *prima donna* (first lady) or *diva* (goddess). The high praise suggested by these terms is similar to that implied by our use of *star* for certain stage or screen actors or actresses.

We should not lose sight of the fact that the performer's personality or temperament ought not to overshadow the work being performed. Although a few pieces are written merely as vehicles for the display of the performer's talent, serious performers recognize their responsibility to use their talents—their technique, musicianship, and personality—in the interpretation of the musical work.

Works composed for groups, such as symphonies and choral works, require a joint effort that draws on the skills and talents of all involved. In these instances, the performers are generally under the direction of a leader such as a conductor, who is charged with coordinating the group effort and shaping its contributions into a coherent interpretation. Here again, a sharp difference exists between conductors who limit their contribution to providing as exact a rendering as possible of the composer's directions in the music score, and conductors who prefer to impose the stamp of their own personality. Karl Boehm (1894–1981), for instance, tended to offer a restrained and scholarly interpretation, whereas Zubin Mehta generally gives a dynamic, exuberant reading of the score he conducts. Although all conductors naturally leave a mark on their work, some consciously allow themselves considerable freedom in expressing their own personality and point of view.

The importance of technique, musicianship, and personality in conveying an interpretation is widely recognized even when these terms are not used. The three characteristics are often either stated or implied, as in the following review of Christopher O'Riley's piano recital. Even if we did not hear the actual performance, reading such a review reminds us of the qualities that are demanded in musical performances.

Donal Henahan
RECITAL: CHRISTOPHER O'RILEY, PIANIST

In many of life's arenas, the magic letter is A, or even A-plus. Here and there, an E for Excellent is the one to shoot at. But for musicians, the alphabet sometimes seems to begin and end with T: their careers depend on how well they deal with the ever-evolving problems of technique, taste and temperament. Pianists, furthermore, must break down technique into a thousand little Tinker Toy parts bearing such labels as tone, touch or tension, not to forget for a moment the important techniques involved in touring. So you can see that the question of what makes one pianist different from another, let alone better, is altogether a ticklish one.

Anyone attending Christopher O'Riley's recital on Tuesday night at the 92nd Street Y, where the Young Concert Artists Series opened its 21st season, could have guessed in advance that the young pianist had technique to spare. He has been making the international contest rounds lately and doing well: fifth prize this year in both the Van Cliburn in Texas and the Leeds in England, and second in Montreal last year. His keyboard facility and solid musical schooling were clear in the opening piece, Bach's Toccata in E minor, which glistened under Mr. O'Riley's strong and fleet fingers. This is an episodic work that is hard to hold together, but Mr. O'Riley's mercurial approach was persuasive in suggesting an improvisatory style.

As the pianist worked his way through three Mendelssohn works, the individual profile of his temperament began to be more apparent. Two "Songs Without Words" and the rarely programmed Fantasy in F-sharp minor ("Scottish Fantasy") were played rather sternly and with a rhythmic tightness that could be felt during much of the evening. While the Fantasy's dancing finale was too heavy and hard-toned to be idiomatic Mendelssohn, the brilliance of execution could only be admired. Such intensity in Mendelssohn sounded odd, but peculiar enough to be interesting.

But how, you had to wonder, would Mr. O'Riley cope with Stravinsky's "Petrouchka," one of the real man-eating sharks of the repertory? The three pieces in this suite take the pianist beyond technical problems into aerobic feats of endurance and the kind of machine-driven frenzies that Stravinsky pretty well abandoned when he left his early ballet scores behind. Here temperament of a tense, extroverted sort had to come into play, and here again Mr. O'Riley could not be seriously faulted. True, he did not sustain the drive of the final movement as well as a more experienced "Petrouchka" pianist might. Little by little, the solid bases of tempo and rhythm began to waver. The image that came to mind was that of a house painter whose scaffolding and ladders have begun to shift under him: the excitement comes in wondering if he can finish this job before the whole shebang goes down, carrying him with it. Mr. O'Riley did, in fact, hold off collapse, and the audience rightly cheered him for it. The performance was a little less than magisterial technically, but then almost everybody's is.

Schumann's "Davidsbündlertänze" was as serious a test of the pianist as the Stravinsky, though in less obvious ways. This suite, actually a series of character studies, requires that the performer swing wildly from mood to mood, often within the space of a few pages or a few measures. Mr. O'Riley showed a close affinity with this fragmented work's more febrile pages, but the wool-gathering and day-dreaming that were the other side of Schumann's artistic personality were not so convincingly evoked. Mr. O'Riley struck this listener as a pianist who may have only recently begun to break out of the emotional straitjacket that professional disciplines impose on some young virtuosos-in-the-making. His playing generates tension, which all good performances must have, but sometimes it seems to be an inner tension that does not allow the music to breathe freely. One of these days soon he may remember that music is a joyful, life-giving force, and who knows what kind of artist he might become then.

N. Y. *Times,* November 5, 1981

Theater and Film

The other performing arts such as theater, opera, motion pictures, and ballet usually involve individual and group efforts and therefore require the same combination of individual and collective interpretation found in musical presentations. If we consider the individual's shaping of the material, we can say that, as in the case of a musical soloist, it is the result of technique, sensitive awareness of the spirit of the work (a counterpart to musicianship), and personality.

Technique, Sensitivity, and Personality in Acting

Actors require both skill and talent to master their craft. They need to develop techniques for voice production and stage movement as well as for impersonating characters of different ages and for using different speech dialects. As for the sensitivity to the text, actors must attune themselves to the spirit of both the play they are performing and the historical period to which

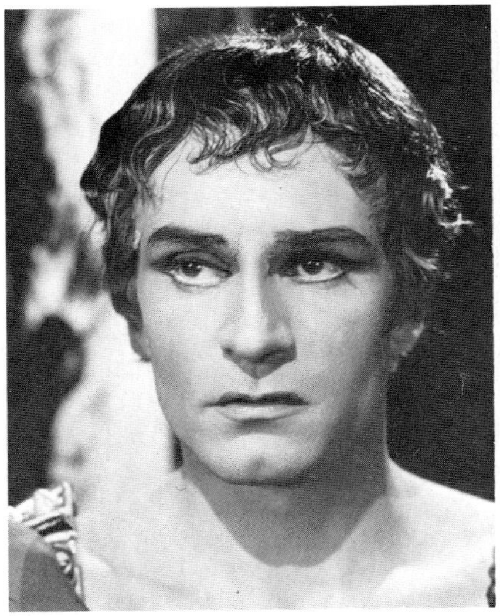
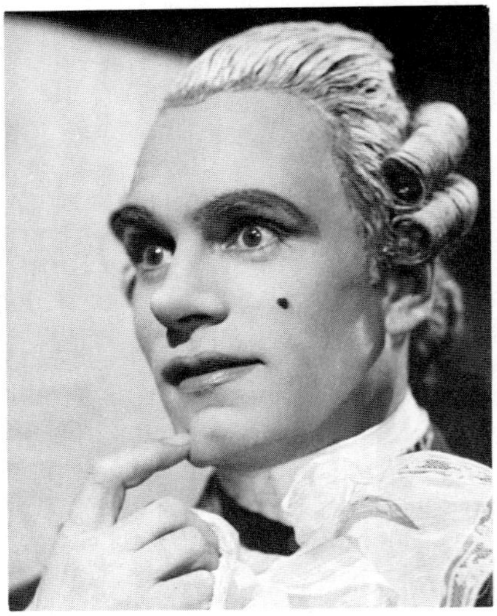

85, 86 Laurence Olivier in 1945 as the King in the Greek tragedy *Oedipus* and as Mr. Puff, the conceited dramatist, in the 18th-century comedy *The Critic.* Olivier acted these two widely differing roles on the same evenings during the 1945 season.

it belongs [85, 86]. Restoration comedy, with its elegantly dressed aristocratic characters engaged in clever wordplay, calls for graceful deportment, including perhaps even the expressive use of the lady's fan or the gentleman's snuffbox, and great facility in speaking the witty lines. In contrast, many modern plays, with commonplace figures speaking in ordinary colloquial terms, call for less mannered acting. Personality is also projected in varying degrees as actors leave their imprint on the roles they play. As we observed earlier, there are as many Hamlets as there are actors who have played the part.

Like some musicians and conductors, some actors also project their personalities in a more pronounced way than others on to the piece they are performing. The French actress Sarah Bernhardt (1844–1923)—with her powerful stage presence, declamatory style, and distinctive voice and manner—tended to dominate every play in which she appeared [87]. A similar phenomenon is familiar to us from motion pictures, in which personalities are often so striking that they lead to type casting, that is, the casting of an actor in roles that call for the display of the same personality. Always in dominant, tough-guy parts, Humphrey Bogart is invariably recognizable by his husky voice, steely gaze, and impassive manner—a cigarette perpetually dangling from his lips.

In contrast to this approach, a type of acting developed by the great actor-director Constantin Stanislavsky (1893–1938) emphasized the fictional characters being portrayed rather than the actors' own personalities. Stanislavsky spoke of the "building" of the dramatic character and developed special techniques for training actors. He also wanted productions to be as close to ordinary life as possible. The actors were to imagine themselves in the situation of the characters they were playing, to incorporate their observa-

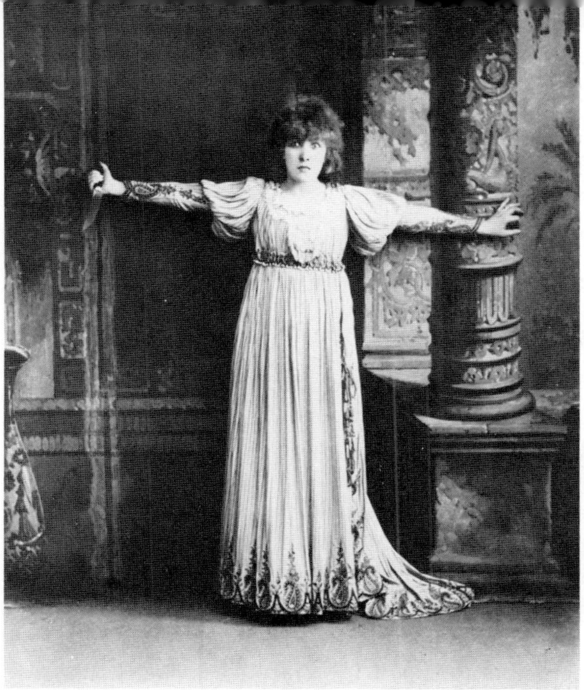

87 Sarah Bernhardt as Tosca (c. 1890). In the scene in which she confronts the villain of the play, Bernhardt demonstrates her powerful stage personality by her horrified expression and by her grand gestures.

tions of the people around them into their portrayals, and—unlike star personalities—to subordinate their roles to the work of the whole company. For his staging of *The Lower Depths* (1902) by Maxim Gorky, Stanislavsky actually visited a flophouse and, as Figure 88 shows, encouraged all the actors to become totally absorbed in their roles.

In New York, this approach was adopted by the Actors Studio. Here training is offered to actors in how to identify emotionally with the characters they are playing. They try to become aware of their character's entire life, beyond what is given in the script, and to use their own experience as a means of understanding and recreating each character. This **method acting**, instead of allowing actors to project their personalities, encourages them to understand and project the psychology of each character they play.

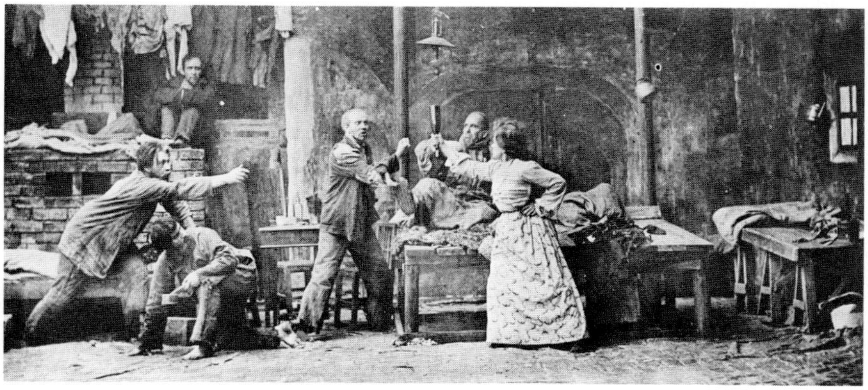

88 Scene from Maxim Gorky's *The Lower Depths*, staged by Constantin Stanislavsky at the Moscow Art Theater, 1902. The figure at the far left with his right arm extended is Stanislavsky.

Yet the contrast between star personalities and Method actors is not as sharp as might appear. On the one hand, an actor such as Marlon Brando is simultaneously a Method actor and a star with a distinctive personality. On the other hand, Sarah Bernhardt, whom we have considered as the epitome of a star, thought of her acting technique as a means of expressing the character she was portraying.

Technique, Sensitivity, and Personality in Directing

Since most plays are not solo but group performances, they must be coordinated like the music of an orchestra or chorus. The director who undertakes this task is usually a professional who is neither the playwright nor an actor, but a specialist who has the full responsibility for shaping the production. The all-embracing function of the director has developed only since the late 19th century, when powerful actor-managers began to run their own companies. But today we can hardly imagine a play that has not had the benefit of a strong director.

Like conductors of orchestras, directors of theatrical productions give coherence to the performance. To do so, directors must be able to interpret the script sensitively as well as to control the resources of the theater. For instance, they must make decisions about casting the various roles and then help the chosen actors to interpret their parts. With the set designer, directors must establish not only the general mood or atmosphere of the play but also the specific placement of walls, steps, furniture, and the movable objects known as *props.* Using a schematic diagram such as the one for *Death of a Salesman* [89], directors can prepare for the actors' stage movements, which cannot be left to chance. Such planning, or *blocking,* is essential if all the actors are to be visible to the audience and if their placement on stage is to contribute to the total effect. Moreover, directors must oversee the work of those who design the costumes and lighting. Some directors, in fact, take great care to prepare elaborate instructions in the *promptbooks.* Peter Brook (b. 1925), who is famous for his thoughtful and inventive stagings, carefully recorded everything that was to be seen and heard on stage in the promptbook for his production of Shakespeare's *A Midsummer Night's Dream* [90]. He included the blocking and gestures of the actors, as well as

1 Obe swings from trapeze SR to DSL, then up to C. Swings gently.

2 Puck out on rope from SL platform, and back.

3 Puck out on trapeze from SL, slowly down to ground.

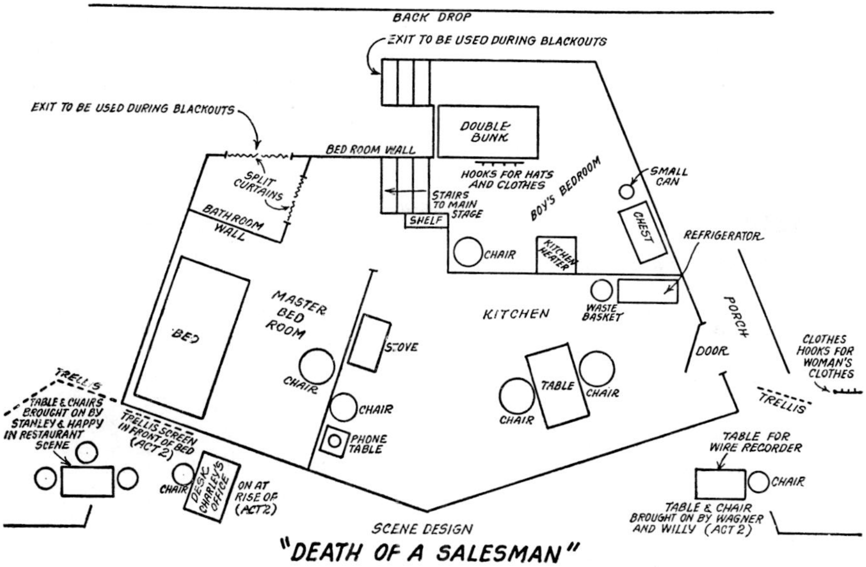

89 Scene design for *Death of a Salesman,* based on the original scene design by Jo Mielziner. This simplified plan for staging the play should be compared with the set designed for the original Broadway production [see Figure 62, page 103].

below: 90 Peter Brook's promptbook for the Royal Shakespeare Company production of *A Midsummer Night's Dream,* 1970. These pages give Brook's directions, originally in his own handwriting, for the scene shown in Figure 91. The left-hand page describes the movements of the actors; these are keyed with numbers in vertical ovals to the appropriate point in the text. The right-hand or text page includes instructions for the stage manager and the stagehands. On this page the words appearing in the rows of boxes are cues for the stage manager, who controls the automated light and sound board. The first row of boxes indicates "stand-by" and the second indicates "go." The numbers in the left margin, placed in horizontal ovals and accompanying the names of instruments, are keyed to the moment for particular music. These numbers, in turn, correspond to the numbers on the musical score, which was composed especially for this version of the play. The abbreviations used throughout mean: SR = Stage Right; DSR = Down Stage Right; DSL = Down Stage Left; C = Center Stage; SL = Stage Left; USR = Up Stage Right; USL = Up Stage Left.

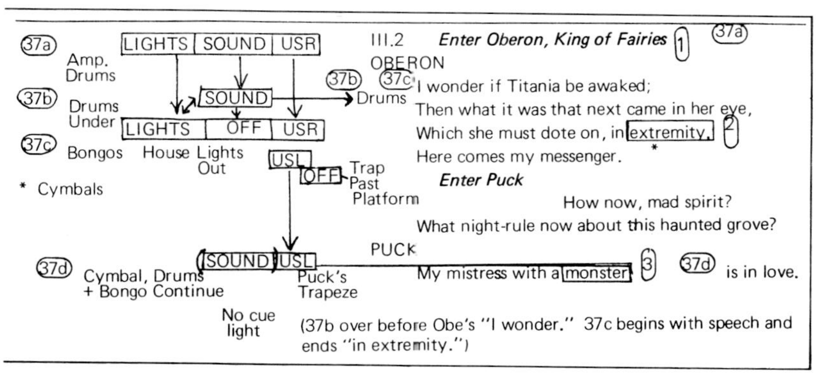

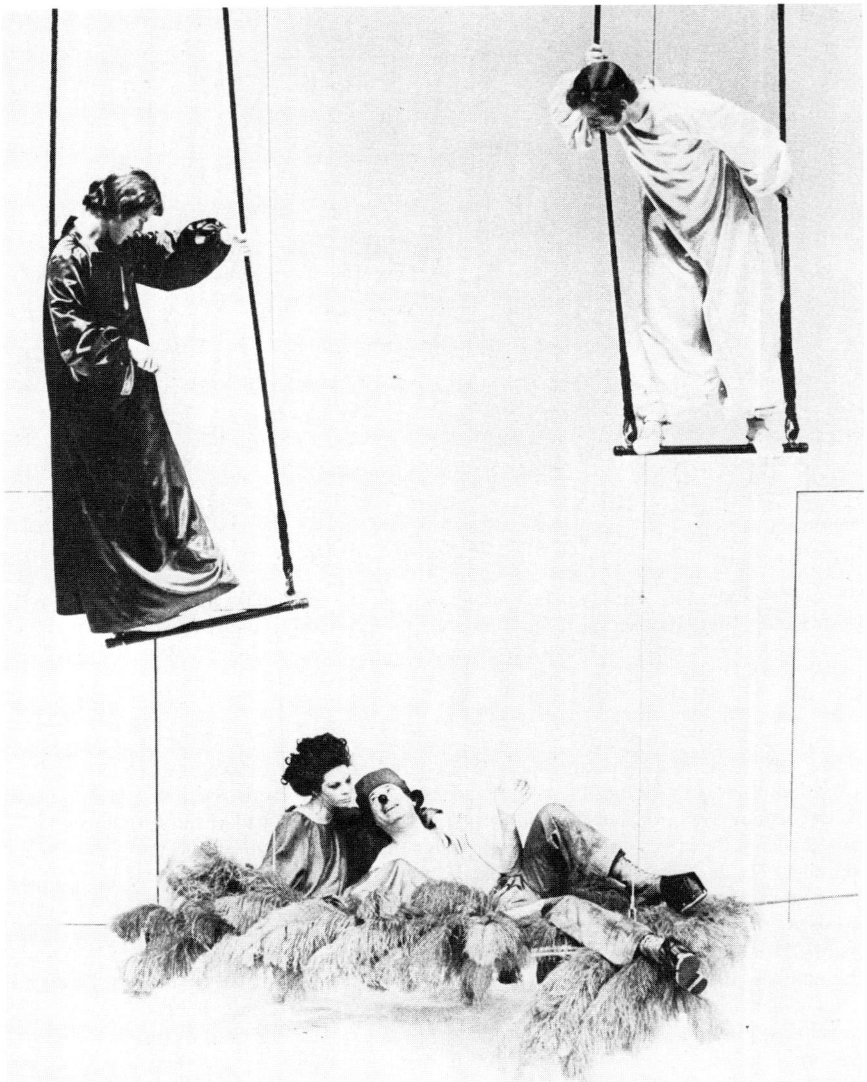

91 Peter Brook's Production of *A Midsummer Night's Dream* for the Royal Shakespeare Company at the Shakespeare Memorial Theatre, Stratford-on-Avon, 1970. Brook here uses his stark boxlike set to present the fairy king and his servant Puck on trapezes as they watch the absurdly infatuated fairy queen, Titania, with her rustic lover, Bottom. The huge feather on which the lovers rest suggests Titania's woodland bower.

the light cues and sound effects. In short, good directors exhibit the same qualities of sensitivity to the script and technical expertise as do the key interpreters of other art forms.

Like these other interpreters, many modern directors also leave the distinctive stamp of their personalities on their work. In his production of *A*

Midsummer Night's Dream [91], Brook turned the mischievous fairy Puck into a juggling acrobat and made the forest outside Athens into a bare white box in which all the action takes place. Brook used these devices to bring out the essential qualities of the piece—its joyousness and high spirits. Not all directors are so successful in their attempts to interpret a drama in their own way. Merely changing the look of a production—for instance, setting a Shakespearean comedy in a Mexican hacienda or in a futuristic space capsule—will do little to enrich the meaning.

All of the tasks of a stage director are also part of a film director's responsibilities. This fact explains why stage directors often become good film directors, and vice versa. One additional responsibility of a film director—and a responsibility unique to the film medium—is the technical process of editing, briefly discussed in Chapter 3.

Unlike stage performances, in which the scenes are acted consecutively, screen performances are recorded in small segments in whatever order is dictated by the location, weather, and availability of certain actors at certain times. Moreover, several versions of each scene are usually recorded, and far more film is shot than can be used. A director must choose which "takes" of a scene and even which scenes are to appear in the finished version. In addition, directors are usually in charge of such further manipulations of the film as *cutting* and *montage,* two terms that refer to the piecing together or assembling of the individual shots. Obviously, this assembling of the physical film is crucial to shaping the final version, for the editing can determine the mood and even change the emphasis of a motion picture. The first version of *Heaven's Gate* (1981), an ambitious four-hour epic treatment of the settling of the American West, was considered overly long and chaotic. It was recut by the director, Michael Cimino (b. 1940), but still found unsatisfactory by the critics. And so the studio took over the cutting process and simply reduced the work to a standard cowboy film of normal length. This example illustrates how profoundly the editing can affect a motion picture. It also makes us understand why all directors want to have exclusive control over the final editing.

Quite apart from their command over such technical resources, film directors have achieved even greater control over the other aspects of their medium than have musical conductors or stage directors. That is, they are often no longer interpreters of a film script created by someone else, but are instead the creators of a new work which reflects their own individuality. In short, the element of personality, which, we saw, is important in all interpreters of the performing arts, may easily become paramount in the film director.

Naturally, film directors can use quite different methods in creating their films. At one extreme, Alfred Hitchcock so completely visualized the individual shots and the work as a whole beforehand that he found the actual making of the film an anticlimax. At the other extreme, Jean-Luc Godard (b. 1930) began his *Breathless* (1959) with only a sketchy idea and improvised his shooting from day to day. In either case, however, the director is often more important than the screen writer or indeed any other contributor. In fact, according to one school of film criticism, the director should be recognized as the real author of the film. This so-called **auteur theory** suggests that the director should no longer be regarded as an interpreter but rather as a creator in his own right.

Dance

Another art form, the dance, links some of the arts we have been considering—music and the theater—with bodily movement. Dance has existed as part of religious ceremonies since recorded history, but became a special art form only in the Renaissance. It now assumes a variety of forms, from classical ballet to modern dance. All of these are particularly complex art forms because they require performers, both soloists and a supporting chorus of dancers known as the *corps de ballet;* musical accompaniment, often provided by a full orchestra under the baton of a conductor; and stage spectacle enhanced by sets, costumes, and lighting. These many contributions are coordinated by the artistic director of the company. Here again the three elements of technique, sensitivity to the work, and personality are of crucial importance in determining the qualities of the dancers.

Technique

Technique in ballet refers to the ability to perform a series of demanding physical movements. No less than in vocal and instrumental performances, mastery of dance technique is extremely difficult. It is achieved only after years of training and maintained only with constant practice. To appreciate a dancer's performance, we must have at least some knowledge of the basic steps and movements of the various kinds of dance.

In *classical ballet,* which developed from court dances in Renaissance Italy and 17th-century France and reached its high point in late 19th-century Russia, the dancer's movements are strictly prescribed. Such ballet is based on five positions [92]. In each of these positions, both feet are firmly on the ground and the legs are "turned out," that is, pointed outward so that the dancer can move as easily from side to side as to the front and back. Dancers

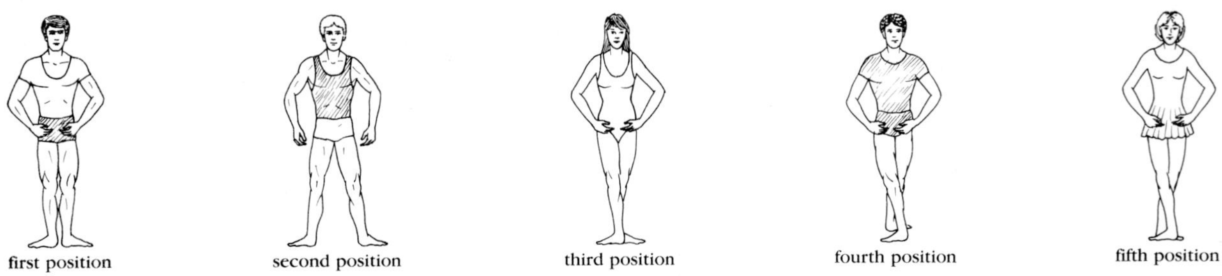

92 The five basic positions in classical ballet.

begin and end their movements—steps or leaps—in one of the five positions and thereby recapture their balance.

Starting from one of the basic positions, both male and female dancers can execute spectacular movements which may look spontaneous even though they are prescribed. To name only a few, a *grand jeté* [93*a*] is a leap in which a dancer tosses one leg forward, and holds this position for a moment in mid-air while turning the rear leg outward to create a graceful line. An *arabesque* [93*b*] is a pose in which the dancer stands on one leg with the body parallel to the floor and an arm stretched outward while extending the other leg behind. A *pirouette* [93*c*] is a complete turn of the body on one foot, with the toe of the other foot raised to the knee of the supporting leg. A *plié* [93*d*] is a bending of the knees to enable the dancer to spring into the air, perhaps into an *entrechat* [93*e*], in which the dancer crosses feet a number of times while in midair. The terms for all the steps for classical ballet are French because they were first named by the ballet master of the Paris Opera in about 1700.

Apart from the great skill necessary to execute the various steps, women dancers face the additional complication of performing many of them on their toes. They are helped with this *pointe* dancing by special shoes, which have a padded toe reinforced by layers of material glued together. Dancing on toes extends the line of the body and makes it appear especially graceful. Indeed, the object of these difficult movements is to give the impression of great lightness, delicacy, and ease while maintaining perfect balance and control.

Male dancers do not perform "on point," but specialize in leaps and spins in the air. For example, in the *tour en l'air* ("turn in the air") the dancer leaps into the air from fifth position, spins his body around once, twice, or even three times, and then returns gracefully to the fifth position. In addition, male dancers physically support the women, holding them as they execute *pirouettes* or actually lifting them or carrying them in graceful attitudes. Such acrobatic dancing again requires extraordinary balance and control.

Modern dance, which began in conscious opposition to classical ballet, has a dance vocabulary of its own. It can be quite free and individualized, as

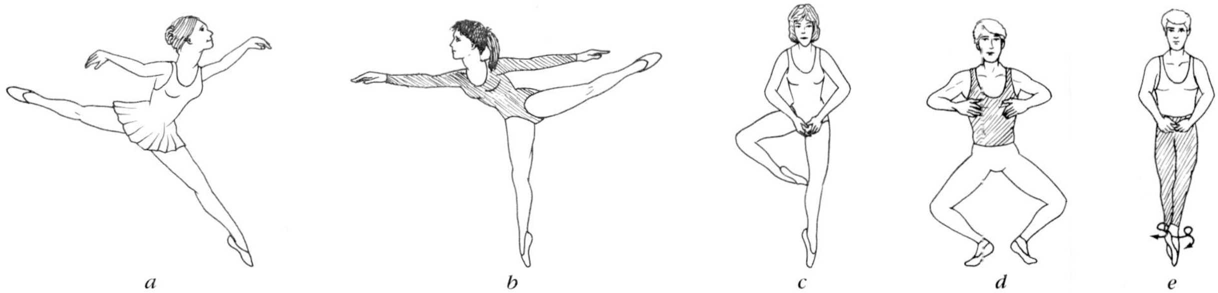

93 Some basic classical ballet movements.

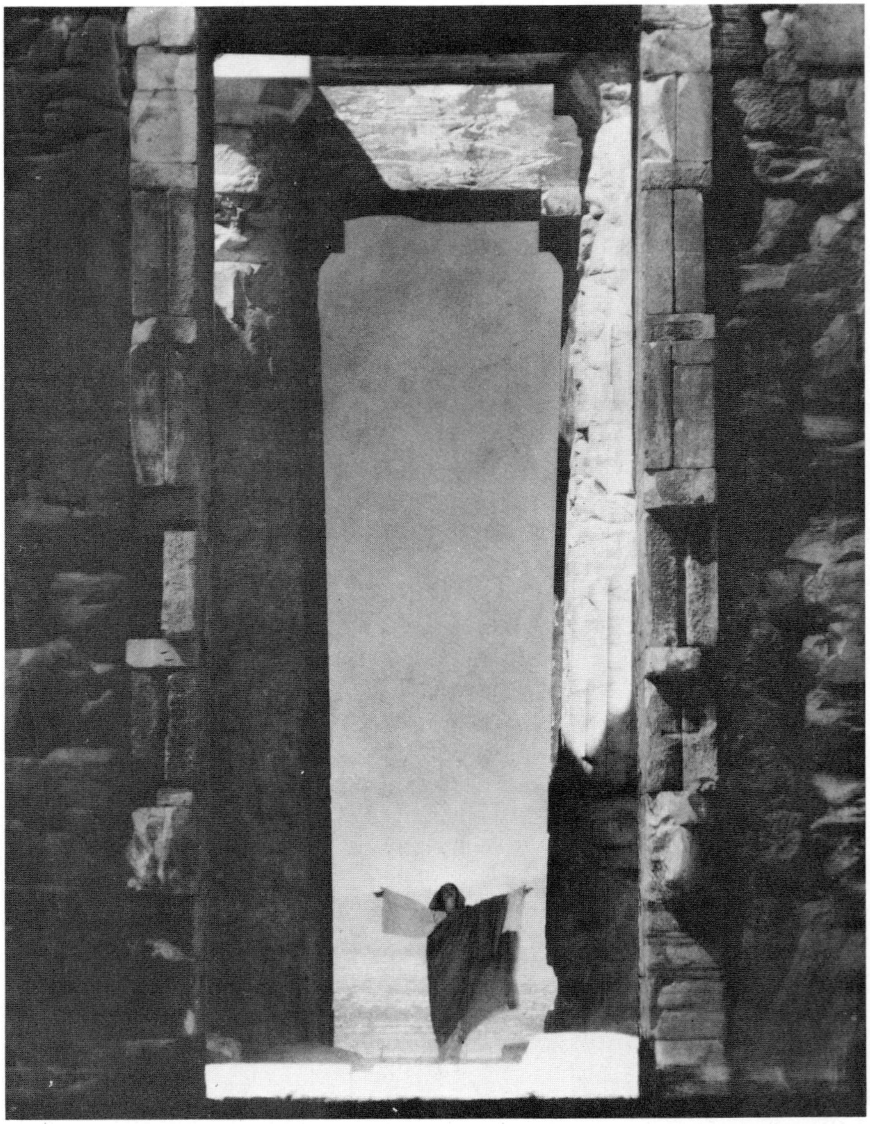

94 Edward Steichen.
Isadora Duncan at the Portal of the Parthenon. 1921.
Gelatin-silver print,
19⅝ × 15¼″ (50 × 39 cm).
Museum of Modern Art, New York (gift of the photographer).
The freedom and exuberance of Isadora Duncan's dance movement is contrasted with the quiet grace and solidity of the Parthenon. Duncan felt she was recapturing the purity of spirit of ancient Greece, but her highly emotional and idiosyncratic form of expression had little in common with Greek art. The photographer, Edward Steichen (1879–1973), demonstrates his skill by presenting the image dramatically and by capturing Duncan's personality.

in the lyrical dances of Isadora Duncan (1878–1927) [94], who rejected the steps and positions of classical dance, substituting natural, fluid movements that were highly personal and frequently improvised. Her work, she claimed, was based on nature and stressed self-expression rather than tradition and the dance heritage of the past. Alternatively, modern dance can be highly stylized, as in the distinctive angular movements of Martha Graham (b. 1894). Even though such modern dance forms no longer use the prescribed movements of classical ballet, the dancers must still develop their technical abilities. By taking classes and constantly practicing, they strive to perfect their coordination, balance, and control in order to perform with an appearance of ease.

Sensitivity to the Work

As in the other performing arts, sensitivity to the work is as important as the mastery of technique. The great Russian choreographer Mikhail Fokine (1880–1942) instructed his dancers not simply to perform his steps to the music, but additionally to move through and from the music. In other words, Fokine suggested that a great dancer expresses character and feeling by sensitively merging motion and music, by perfectly uniting the sequence of steps with the melodic line. According to Fokine, the dancer's movement is not dictated purely by the choreographer and composer, but arises out of the dancer's own response to the music and the situation.

Dancers may be asked to interpret a variety of ballets. In general, these consist of *narratives,* such as *Swan Lake* (1877/1895) or *Sleeping Beauty* (1890), and *abstract ballets,* which simply create patterns on the stage. The distinction between narrative and abstract ballet is not the same as that between classical ballet and modern dance. In fact, choreographers have used the vocabularies of both classical ballet and modern dance for narrative as well as for abstract works.

Sensitivity in narrative ballet is usually revealed in the creation of the characters. Such sensitivity is not easy, since only bodily movement can be used in the portrayal. Gesture, bearing, and movement must take the place of the language that actors have at their disposal. Yet with their movements, dancers can create distinctive personalities with seeming ease—whether serious lovers such as Prince Charming and Princess Aurora in *The Sleeping Beauty* or comic old women, sometimes even impersonated by male dancers, as in the case of the Ugly Sisters in the Royal Ballet's production of *Cinderella* [95]. The same dancer may perform contrasting parts. In *Swan Lake,* one of

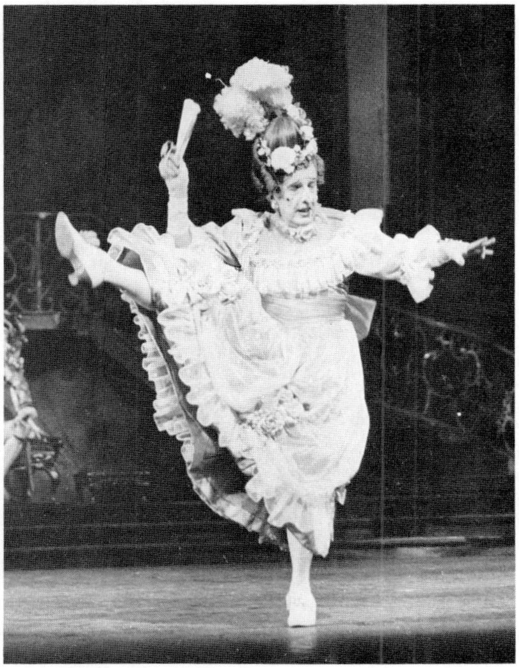

95 Frederick Ashton in his production of *Cinderella* for the Royal Ballet, 1965. Music by Sergei Prokofiev. Ashton thoroughly enjoys himself as the more bashful of the two Ugly Sisters in his production of the ballet.

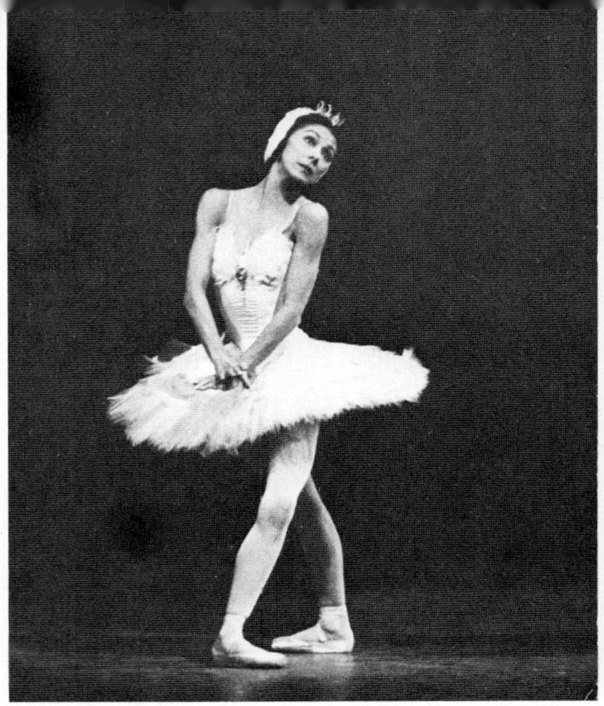

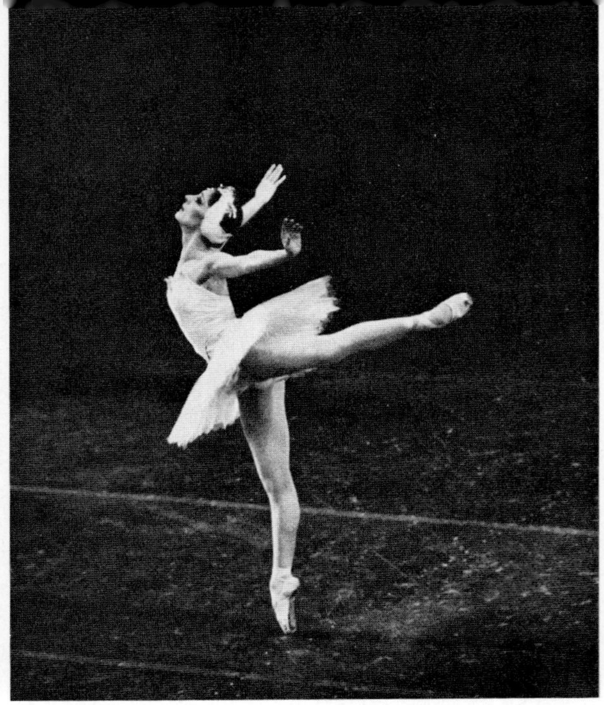

above left: 96 Margot Fonteyn in a Royal Ballet production of *Swan Lake.* Music by Peter Ilych Tchaikovsky.

above right: 97 Cynthia Gregory in the American Ballet Theater production of *Swan Lake,* 1978.

the great ballets in the classical idiom, the principal ballerina dances the roles of both Odette and Odile. According to the story, Prince Siegfried has sworn love and faithfulness to Odette, a princess who is periodically transformed into a white swan by a wicked magician. But the prince is tricked into breaking his oath by Odile, the magician's daughter, who takes the form of a black swan. As white swan, the ballerina must be pathetically innocent and fragile; as black swan, maliciously seductive and forceful.

Moreover, different dancers can make a distinctive imprint on a role, even though nearly every step is prescribed. In dancing *Swan Lake,* Margot Fonteyn (b. 1919) [96] and Cynthia Gregory (b. 1946) [97] offer strikingly different interpretations of the heroine. Margot Fonteyn, with her delicate features and slight, girlish figure, is a highly lyrical performer whose stage image projects a sense of fragility and pathos. Her characterization of Odette is generally distinguished by its delicacy, refinement, and helplessness. For example, when the sorcerer Von Rothbart transforms the princess back into a swan, her resistance is, at first, frantic but ineffectual, and as if against her will, her arms begin to move like wings. Fighting against the loss of her freedom and humanity, she expresses her anguish through her struggle against these involuntary movements. Slowly losing self-control and becoming again one of Von Rothbart's creatures, she parts in agony from Siegfried. As she makes her exit with the *corps de ballet,* Fonteyn faces upstage and moves diagonally across the stage, away from and with her back toward the audience. Through the motions of her upper arms, shoulders, and head, she poignantly communicates her grief in her separation from her lover. The audience watches this pained figure, almost broken in spirit, as she backs away, her limbs gradually resuming the swan-like movements that have now fully taken possession of the *corps de ballet.*

Cynthia Gregory's interpretation of the role, though totally unlike Margot Fonteyn's, is equally memorable. Taller than Fonteyn and with more aristocratic features, Gregory emphasizes not the helplessness and femininity of the princess, but her forcefulness and courage. For her the struggle and transformation from woman back into swan is more tense and dramatic. Rather than display a slow loss of self-control, Gregory marks the moment when Von Rothbart's power fully takes hold by snapping her entire body convulsively, freezing her expression, and then moving as in a trance. Gregory's interpretation is no less valid than Fonteyn's, for both do justice to the plight of the princess.

In narrative ballets that use the modern dance idiom, dancers must naturally be equally sensitive to the creation of character. In Martha Graham's *Appalachian Spring* [98], which celebrates a marriage and housewarming in a pioneer community, the two chief dancers must portray the young newlyweds who try to restrain themselves, but occasionally burst into expressions of their love and joy. Some of their excitement is shown in the fluttering motion of their hands as their fingers tap rapidly on their shoulders. Other dancers must portray a hellfire-and-brimstone preacher as well as assorted neighbors. All of the dancers, including Graham in the role of the bride, use the angular movements distinctive of Graham's modern dance idiom to suggest the courage and determination with which these Appalachian characters face the challenges of pioneer life. Throughout, the music—especially composed for the ballet by Aaron Copland (b. 1900)—vividly reinforces the dancers' moods and gestures.

Abstract ballet by its very nature has no named characters, so that the sensitivity required of the dancers is different from that in narrative dances. In

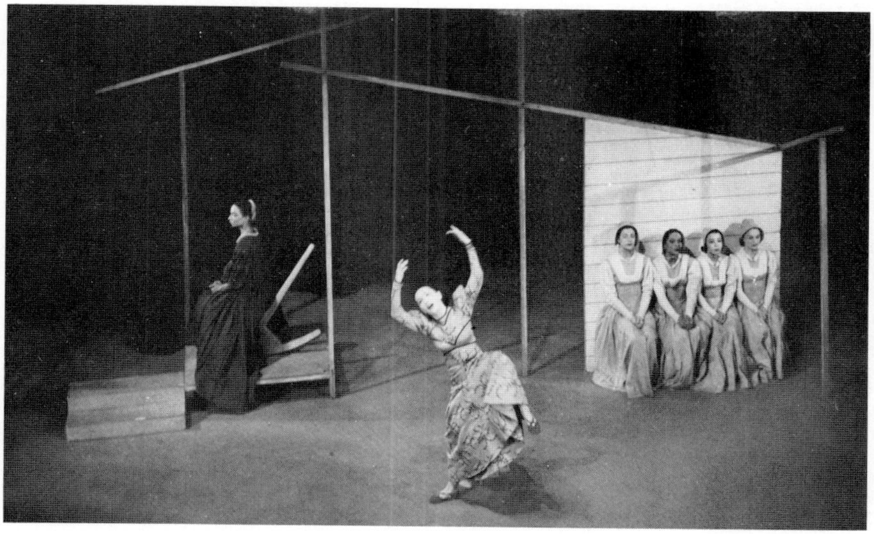

98 Martha Graham in the original production of her *Appalachian Spring,* 1944. Music by Aaron Copland.

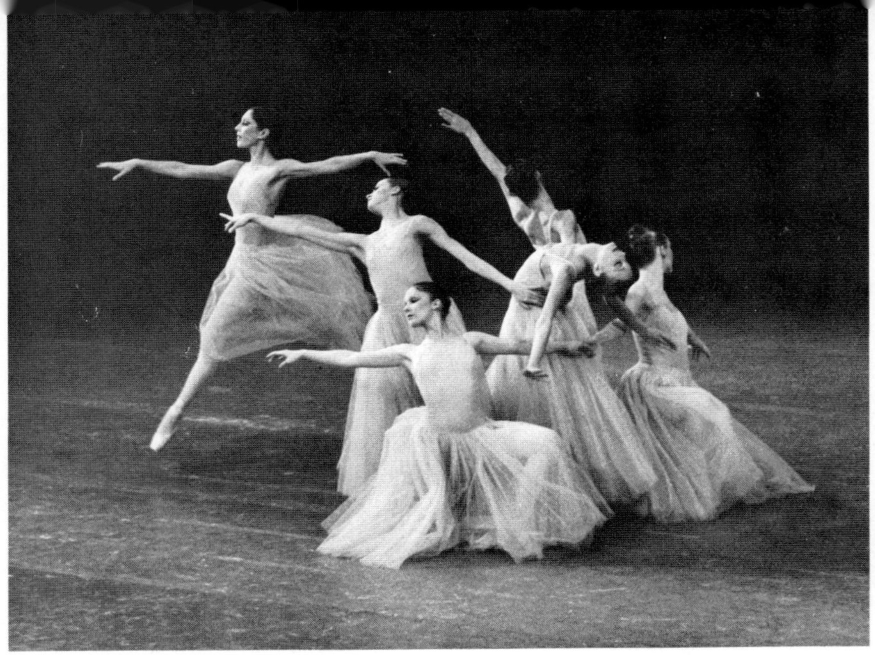

right: 99 The New York City Ballet in a 1978 performance at Lincoln Center, New York, of *Serenade* (1934), choreographed by George Balanchine. Music by Tchaikovsky.

below left: 100 Rudolph Nureyev in the Divertissement from *Napoli,* based on the choreography of August Bournonville. The Royal Ballet, 1963.

below right: 101 Mikhail Baryshnikov in *Romeo and Juliet,* choreographed by Kenneth MacMillan, 1975. Music by Sergei Prokofiev.

abstract ballets, whether in the classical or modern idiom, the sensitivity must be to the patterns and the mood called for by the choreographer as well as to the music the choreographer has chosen. For instance, in *Serenade* [99] by George Balanchine (1904–1983) the dancers form constantly shifting patterns that match the lyrical sweetness, tempo, and melodic grace of Tchaikovsky's music. Their unbroken, fluid movement becomes a visual expression of the orchestral score.

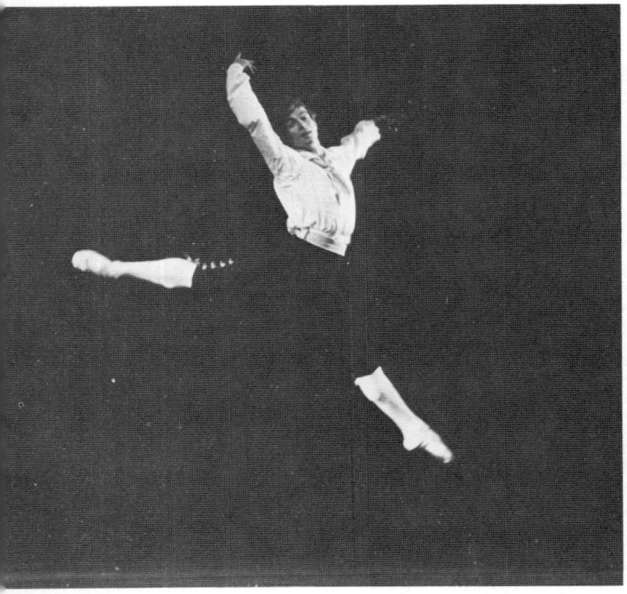

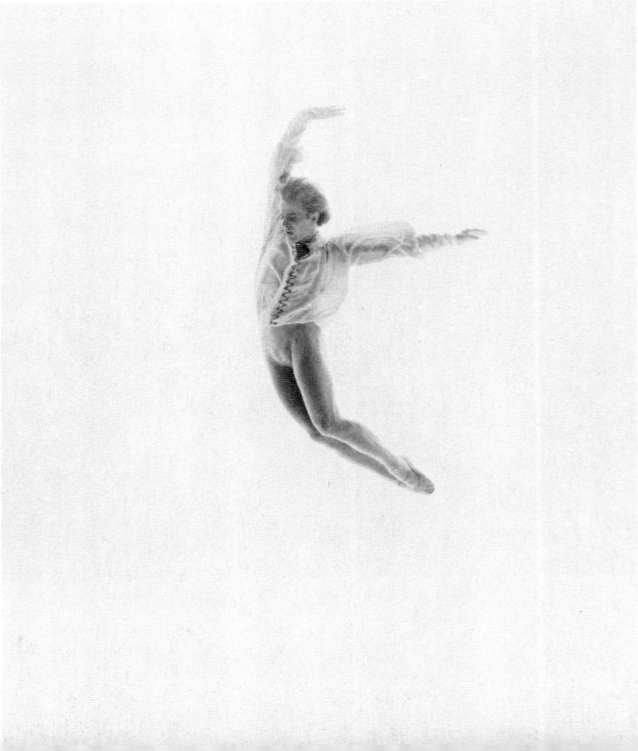

Personality

We might think that technique and sensitivity to the work are all that dancers need in an art form that is restricted to carefully prescribed bodily movements. However, personality is as important in dance as in the other performing arts, and great dancers can leave the imprint of their temperaments on a role. Quite different personalities are suggested when critics write "they dance as if a puff of wind had swayed them . . . and they would soar forever upwards" and "she dances with the power and precision of a steel trap." Just how the personality of the dancer can color a performance becomes clearer when we consider two of the great contemporary male dancers, Rudolf Nureyev (b. 1938) and Mikhail Baryshnikov (b. 1948). Nureyev [100] projects a sense of power and vigor. In contrast, Baryshnikov [101] projects a sense of lightness and ease. Neither of these personalities is better than the other, any more than are the contrasting stage personalities of Margot Fonteyn and Cynthia Gregory. All these dancers tend to have an electrifying effect on the audience.

Ballets rarely feature only one dancer, largely because of the strenuous physical exertion that is required. Usually ballets combine solos with dances by two or more performers *(pas de deux, pas de trois, pas de quatre).* Group dancing by a *corps de ballet* may also be included; these dancers, though they should not show distinct individual personalities, can project a collective personality appropriate to the piece they are dancing as well as to the style of their company. In *Swan Lake* [102], for instance, the group of swan maidens anticipates the impending separation of the royal lovers Prince Siegfried and Odette by turning their backs and poignantly moving their arms. Dancing in perfect unison, the dancers also demonstrate the lyricism for which the *corps de ballet* of the British Royal Ballet is famous.

All these dancers—along with the music, costumes, and scenery—must be coordinated as in the other performing arts by a company's artistic director. Often the director is also the chief choreographer and in that role is particularly sensitive to the subtleties of the work, as well as the abilities of the dancers. Balanchine, for example, took pains to teach Baryshnikov and

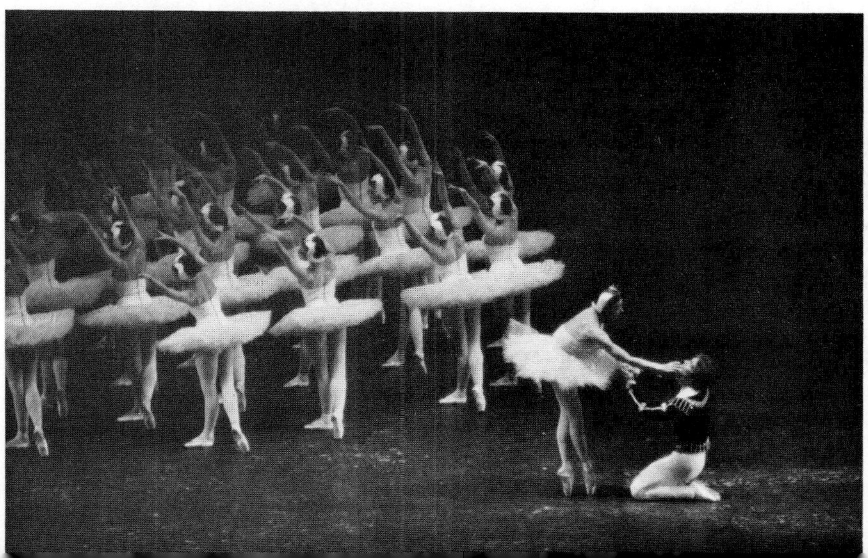

102 The *corps de ballet* turns from Margot Fonteyn and Rudol Nureyev in Act IV of The Royal Ballet production of *Swan Lake,* 1968, choreographed by Robert Helpmann. Music by Tchaikovsk

Nina Fedorova (b. 1958) their roles in his ballet *Harlequinade* [103], roles that had been performed earlier by other members of his company.

So important are directors that they can shape their group into distinctive companies with special dance styles and repertories. As artistic director, Balanchine made the New York City Ballet into the most influential dance company in the United States. Concentrating on abstract ballets such as *Serenade* [see Figure 99, page 176] and *Agon* [104], he freely adapted and reinterpreted classical dance movements. His ballets and the performances of his dancers are famous for their speed, intricacy, and often wit. Also in New York City, Alvin Ailey (b. 1931) has formed a company that specializes in modern ballet. His works draw heavily on the traditions of African, Caribbean, and other black dances. Ailey's *Revelations* [105] is set to black spirituals. These dances and the performances of Ailey's company are noteworthy for their energy and power.

Finally, a review of an actual performance can help us appreciate how widely recognized is the importance of a dancer's technique, sensitivity to the work, and personality. Such a review can also draw attention to the importance of the choreographer, director, and ballet company as a whole. As in the case of musical reviews, reading ballet criticism even if we have not seen the performance can increase our understanding of the qualities demanded of the dancers.

Anna Kisselgoff
BALLET: STEPS IN THE RIGHT DIRECTION

A recent, disturbing aspect of the New York City Ballet's performances has been the tendency of the younger principals and soloists to treat nearly all ballets as if they were the same.

below left: 103 George Balanchine rehearses Mikhail Baryshnikov and Nina Fedorova in the 1978 New York City Ballet production of *Harlequinade* (1965).

below right: 104 Heather Watts and Mel Tomlinson in a *pas de deux* from a 1981 New York City Ballet performance of George Balanchine's ballet *Agon* (1951). Music by Igor Stravinsky. At this dramatic moment, the ballerina is on point as in classical ballet, but the position of her head and body, bent over the right shoulder of her kneeling partner and resting against his stomach, is strikingly different from any posture found in a classical *pas de deux*.

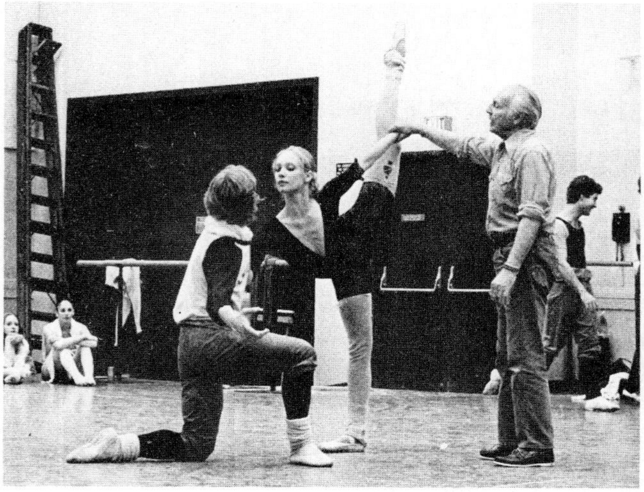

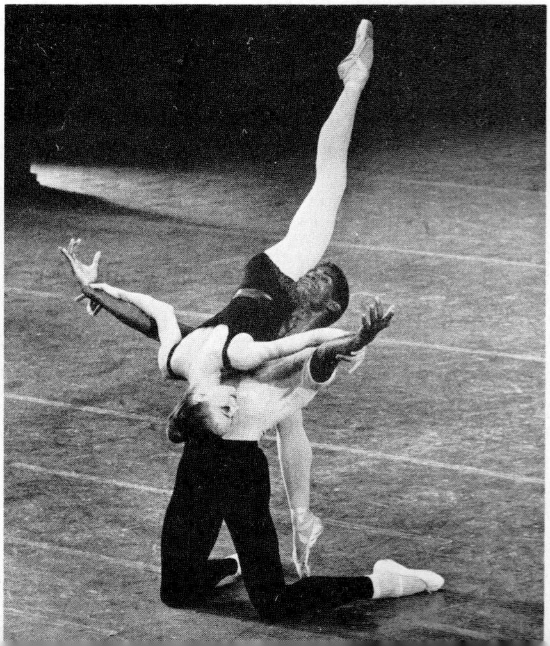

When these dancers appear in leading roles, they remain recognizably themselves. Little distinction is made between the style of one ballet and another. The reported dictum of George Balanchine, the company's artistic director, to "just dance the steps" seems to have been taken too literally lately. Even—or rather, especially—in the Balanchine plotless ballets, everything goes beyond steps. Phrasing, rhythm and musicality must be adjusted to each work.This is what the earlier generations of more versatile dancers in the City Ballet recognized in the 1950's and 60's and what made their performances so exciting.

Complaints that the current season, since November, has looked more dull than interesting are now heard about the theater, and they are not without foundation. It wouldn't hurt for some of the company's younger dancers to try a little harder, to work on each role as if it were the major one of the season.

A step in this direction was already visible on Thursday night's program at the State Theater. The veterans, including Suzanne Farrell, Adam Lüders and Stephanie Saland, set the best example in the Balanchine-Bizet "Symphony in C," and Ib Andersen made a magnificent debut in Jerome Robbins's "Opus 19/The Dreamer" by, in fact, making an effort to change his usual pure image.

The weak spot on the program was the season's first performance of "Ballo della Regina," one of Mr. Balanchine's most unusual ballets. Set to ballet music from Verdi's opera "Don Carlo," it is a plotless work that nonetheless refers in an abstract way to its discarded scenario—a tale of a fisherman seeking the most perfect of pearls. Four soloists now stand in for the other gems, while the opera's "Queen of Spain," allegorically represented as the most perfect pearl, is now the ballerina.

Kyra Nichols was that ballerina on this occasion, with Sean Lavery as her cavalier. Both danced well but with not enough of the clarity so special to this ballet. Too often they faded into the ensemble rather than glittered apart from it. Melinda Roy made a good debut as the third soloist, with the soaring variation, while Judith Fugate, Elyse Borne and Stephanie Saland rounded out this quartet. "Ballo della Regina" has a highly unconventional structure, shifting in tone with the music, from waltz to prance to Spanish anthem and processional. It needs sparkle and diamond-sharp dancing.

After Mr. Robbins created his Prokofiev ballet for Mikhail Baryshnikov in

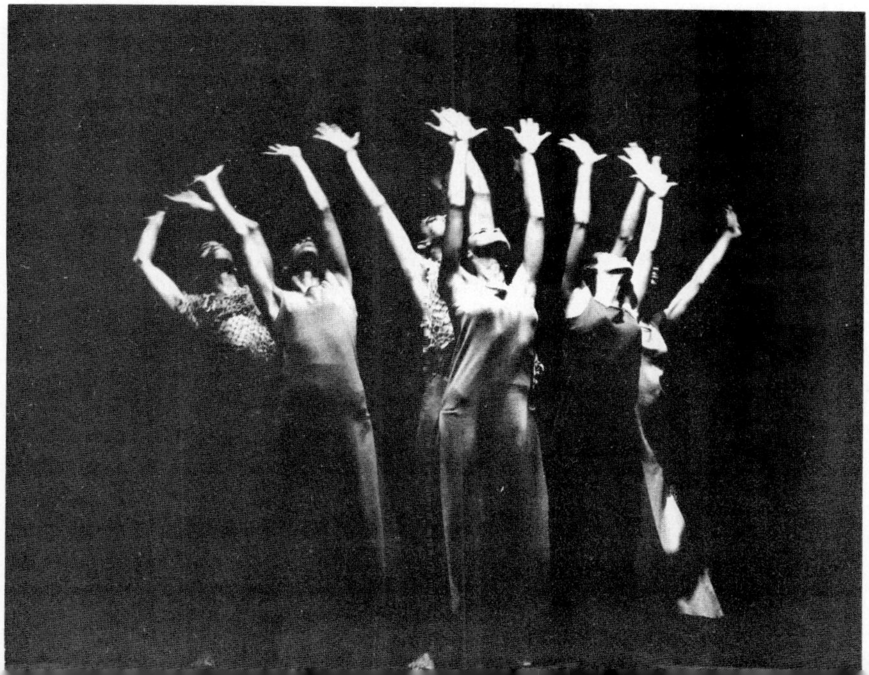

105 The Alvin Ailey American Dance Theater in *Revelations,* 1960.

1978, he clarified his intent by adding "The Dreamer" to the "Opus 19" title. Like his predecessors, Bart Cook and Helgi Tomasson, Mr. Andersen brought his own interpretation to the main role. He acted it out more than the others, imprinting an emotional shading upon each passage. All-suffering and vulnerable from the start, he seemed truly in the midst of some nightmare, and the effect was very strong. His encounter with his ideal, Heather Watts, recalled a boy subduing a wild animal.

As for the "Symphony in C," Miss Saland and Mr. Lüders, both very elegant, led the first movement. Miss Farrell, who received a huge ovation, and Mr. Lavery led the second while Christopher d'Amboise, much improved, was wonderful with Lourdes Lopez in the third, with Maria Calegari and Joseph Duell doing fine in the last section. Hugo Fiorato conducted.

N. Y. *Times,* January 9, 1982

In concluding this chapter on the performing arts, we must recognize that no amount of abstract discussion can substitute for the experience of participating in an actual performance, with its exciting interaction between the performers and the audience. Nonetheless, an awareness of technique, sensitivity, and personality will enable us to understand what is required of performers and what we as audience should expect.

Questions for Study and Discussion

1. What is meant in music by *technique, personality,* and *musicianship?* What comparable terms can be used for the other performing arts? In what sense are the three terms mutually exclusive and in what sense are they not?
2. In Donal Henahan's review of a piano recital (page 162), what key terms are used to describe the performance? How do these terms compare with those we have used in our consideration of the musical performer's role? What diction and images are used by Henahan to give an impression of the actual performance?
3. Find two or three reviews of the same play or film in newspapers and magazines. What aspects of acting and directing are considered in these reviews? How do the key terms used by the reviewer compare with those we have used in our discussion?
4. In what ways are the responsibilities of stage and film directors similar and in what ways are their responsibilities different? What is meant by the *auteur theory,* and in what sense could it also be applied to the theater?
5. What are the distinctive features of classical ballet and modern dance, of narrative and abstract ballet? Are these four types of ballet mutually exclusive?
6. In Anna Kisselgoff's review of a ballet performance (see page 178), what key terms are used and how do these compare with those we have used in our discussion? What kinds of ballets are being described? What point does the reviewer make about the dancing even of plotless ballets? How do her diction and images suggest the qualities she expects in a performance?

PART TWO

The Contexts of Tradition and Genres

We have been examining works of art as separate, independent creations. Although most of them can, indeed, be appreciated in and for themselves, they also inevitably reflect their culture—the distinctive beliefs, values, and behavior of the community that shaped them. Since all artists are likely to be profoundly influenced by their culture, we can understand a work of art more fully if we have some knowledge of its cultural context. For instance, we can enjoy the *Venus de Milo* [see Figure 4, page 5] not only as a magnificent female form but all the more if we know something about the cultural tradition that made her an embodiment of the goddess of love. Chapter 6, "Culture and Tradition," considers the influence of two main traditions, the Greco-Roman and the Judeo-Christian, on works of art created from ancient times to the present.

In addition, works of art tend to fall into groups or categories known as **genres,** which share recognizable characteristics. Since artists are usually conscious of the genres to which their work belongs and of the qualities of the genre they wish to adopt, we should be aware of the many different genres that exist in each of the arts. For example, we can gain more pleasure still from the *Venus de Milo* if we are aware of the genres of sculpture and can recognize this as a type of free-standing, larger-than-life-size nude. The various genres are discussed in Chapter 7, "Genres of the Arts of Space"; Chapter 8, "Genres of the Arts of Time"; and Chapter 9, "Genres of the Composite Arts."

CHAPTER 6

Culture and Tradition

Culture reveals the way in which a community tries to make sense of the world and can embrace everything from religion and politics to the affairs of everyday life. Works of art of our own civilization have been profoundly influenced by the culture of ancient Greece and Rome and by that of the Old and New Testaments of the Bible. To appreciate the broad impact of these cultures, we shall consider examples from several different art forms created over a long period.

All cultures are concerned with basic human experiences—birth, initiation into adulthood, love, marriage, the health and welfare of the community, death, and possibly afterlife or rebirth. Indeed, some of the arts, notably dance and drama, owe their origin to community responses to such basic experiences.

The Cultural Origins of Dance and Drama

Dance and drama originated from ceremonies that involved dancing and singing. These activities were performed by primitive agricultural societies to gain control over their environment—to ensure the proper weather for crops and cattle, health and fertility for the people and their animals. In their earliest phases, these ceremonies or *rituals* (repeated ceremonies) were often performed by all the members of the tribal community, so that actors and audience were identical.

Some ceremonies took the form of imitation to bring about a practical result. For instance, leaping and jumping after seeds were planted were intended to encourage the growth of crops: the higher the dancers leapt, the higher, they believed, their grain would grow. Similarly, rain dances imitated the fall of rain to encourage showers. These dances and the accompanying chants were performed in the belief that the imitation of an action (mimicking the falling of rain) could bring about that action (rainfall) in the physical world. These ceremonies prefigure, or pave the way for, the dance as art, since imitation is basic to this as well as to many other art forms.

Other ceremonies began as invocations, prayers calling upon a god or gods either to bring about a desired end or to prevent an undesired one. Once again these activities, such as animal sacrifices and feasts, had a practical purpose and could involve the entire community. Such ceremonies could also include narratives recalling events in the life of a particular god, and in this case prefigure drama.

The earliest Western drama grew out of the ancient Greek celebration of Dionysus, the god associated with spring, fertility, and intoxication. This celebration evolved in time, becoming more complex. A chorus of about fifty men, chanting an ode to the god in unison, was replaced by two smaller groups of men, who performed parts of the ode alternatingly. Soon a choral leader emerged to serve as moderator between these groups. In the 6th century B.C. one such leader, Thespis, identified himself with Dionysus and impersonated the god. We might say that Thespis recast his role from a third-person to a first-person narrator. The audience now no longer merely heard a choral ode, but witnessed scenes played out by the chorus with one actor, then two, and finally three actors. At this point, the chorus and actors became separated from the audience. And with these beginnings—chorus, actor, audience—the main elements of Greek drama were invented.

The continuity of the ceremonies celebrating Dionysus represents a cultural *tradition.* That is, succeeding generations repeated the same pattern of choral odes and dramatic dialogues in roughly similar ways. The term *tradition* comes from the Latin *traditio,* "something that is handed down." As with all traditions, subtle changes—in the number of actors or the size of the chorus—were also introduced over the course of time.

Traditions exist in social practices as well as in art forms. For instance, throughout the world the sharing of food is often a part of religious observances. A Thanksgiving dinner, a wedding feast, a Passover Seder, and the taking of bread and wine during the Mass are all traditional communal meals. Similarly, many aspects of the arts—both themes and treatments—are handed down from generation to generation. Moreover, just as social and artistic practices are slightly or even radically altered when they are passed on within a culture, so these can be not only absorbed but also adapted and changed when they are transferred from one culture to another.

The Greco-Roman and Judeo-Christian Traditions

Those of us who are part of Western European culture have been influenced to a large extent by the two great traditions we have already touched upon. These are our inheritance from ancient Greece and Rome as well as from the Judeo-Christian culture, particularly as expressed in the Old and New Testaments. The two traditions have not only influenced our philosophical and moral outlook but have also provided themes and recurring images for our arts. The continuity of these traditions can be vividly seen by tracing the varied representations of the Greek goddess Aphrodite and of the Biblical Abraham and Isaac. A similar continuity can be found by tracing the different visual representations of the halo and the changing musical settings of the Christian Mass.

Aphrodite-Venus

The figure of the goddess Aphrodite [see Figure 4, page 5, and Figure 12, page 18] inspired an especially rich tradition that began in ancient Greece. Greek religion was polytheistic, worshipping many gods. Each deity had a special function and was associated with some aspect of the universe. For instance, Zeus, the father of the gods, represented the elemental powers and was identified with thunder and lightning. His daughter Athena symbolized wisdom. Aphrodite was primarily the goddess of love, especially erotic love, and also to some extent of fertility.

Aphrodite is associated with one of the most fundamental human emotions. The many stories in which she, like the other Greek gods, is treated as if she were a human figure, show her in a variety of love relationships. She was supposedly married to the god Hephaistos; but tiring of him, she could not resist the dashing war god Ares. From her illicit union with Ares, Aphrodite had several children, the most important being Eros. Moreover, Aphrodite was said to have had affairs with several mortals. According to another old myth, Aphrodite entered a beauty contest—which she, of course, won—known as the judgment of Paris. Since the judge, Paris, was a Trojan prince, this contest involved her in the fate of Troy, a story that is brilliantly told in Homer's *Iliad* (8th century B.C.). In this great poem, Aphrodite functions both as the divine protectress of Paris and as the embodiment of physical love.

In Greek art and poetry, Aphrodite is often shown being born from the

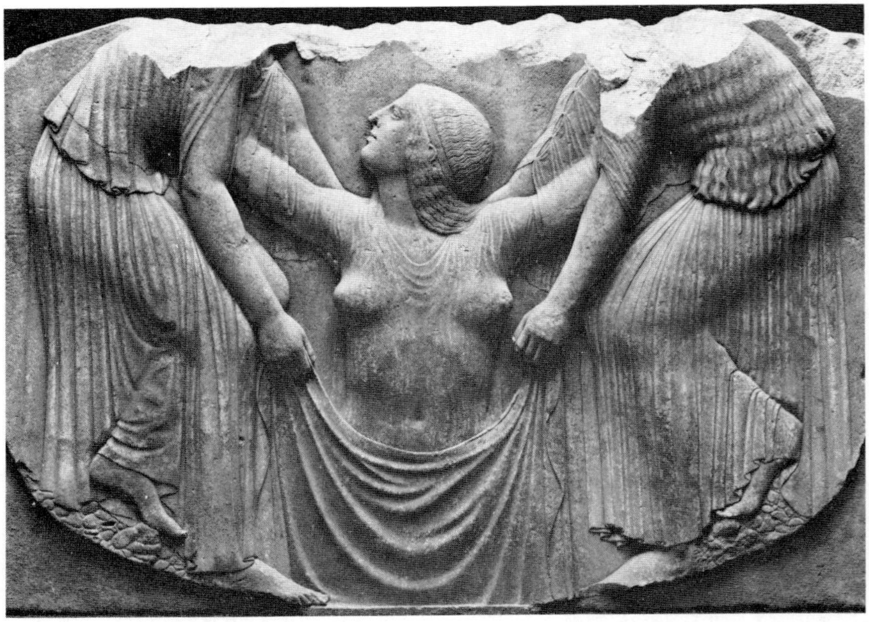

106 *Birth of Aphrodite,* from the Ludovisi Throne (low relief). Early 5th century B.C. Marble, width 4′8″ (1.4 m). Museo Nazionale delle Terme, Rome.

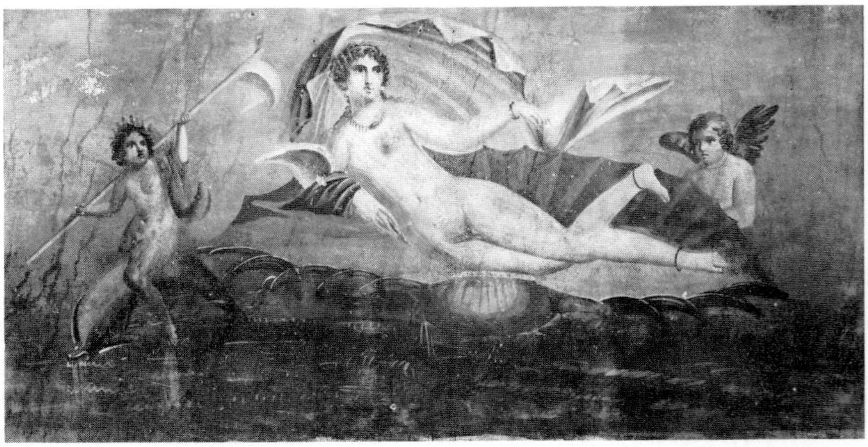

107 *Venus on a Seashell,* from Pompeii. 1st century. Fresco.

sea as in the Ludovisi Throne relief [106]. Modern historians believe that this story reveals that she was not originally a Greek goddess, but a continuation of the goddess Astarte or Ishtar, who was worshipped on the eastern shores of the Mediterranean. If so, she is an example of one culture's absorbing a deity from an earlier one. Aphrodite's ocean birth is frequently suggested in art by associating her with a shell, as in the Pompeian fresco [107] and Botticelli's painting [see Figure 12, page 18]. This shell is known as an **attribute**, a clue to the figure's identity, just as the thunderbolt is an attribute of Zeus or—to cite another familiar example—the lily is an attribute of the Virgin Mary. Insofar as an attribute identifies a particular aspect of a figure, it is a symbol. Aphrodite's shell symbolizes her sea origins, just as lilies next to the Virgin Mary symbolize her purity.

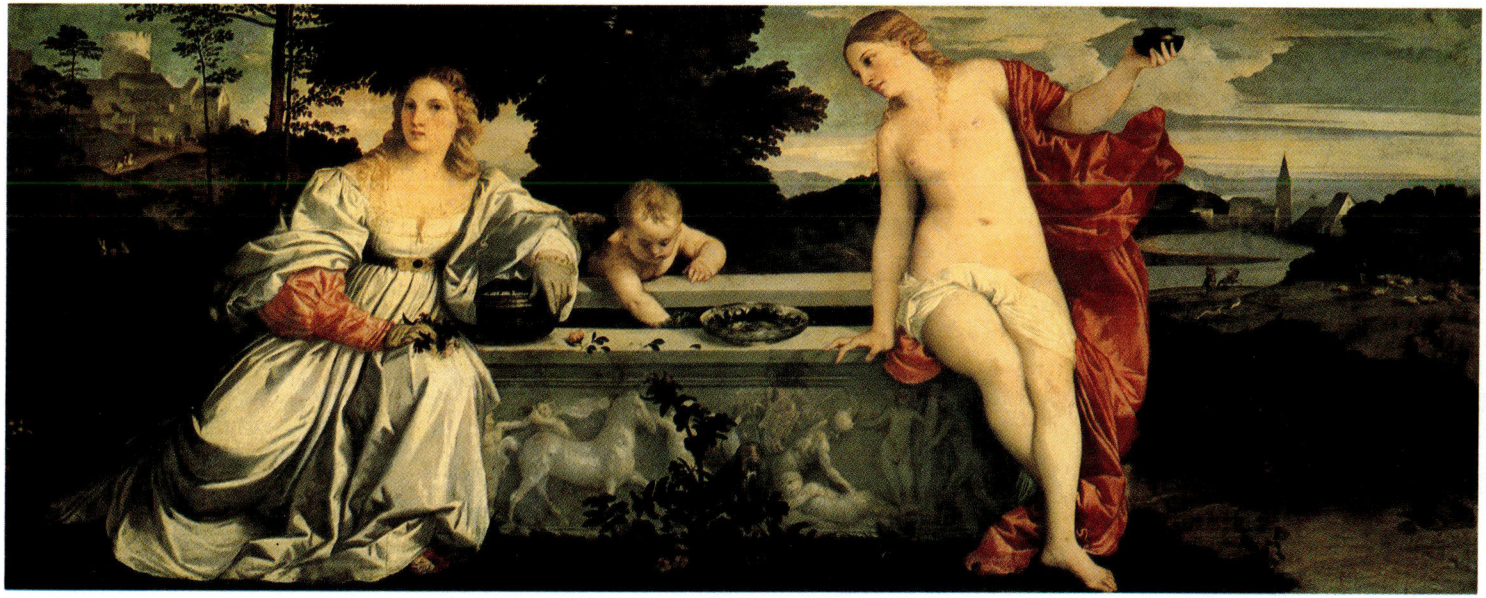

Plate 11 Titian. *Sacred and Profane Love*. c. 1515. Oil, approx. 3′6″ × 8′4″ (1.1 × 2.5 m). Borghese Gallery, Rome.

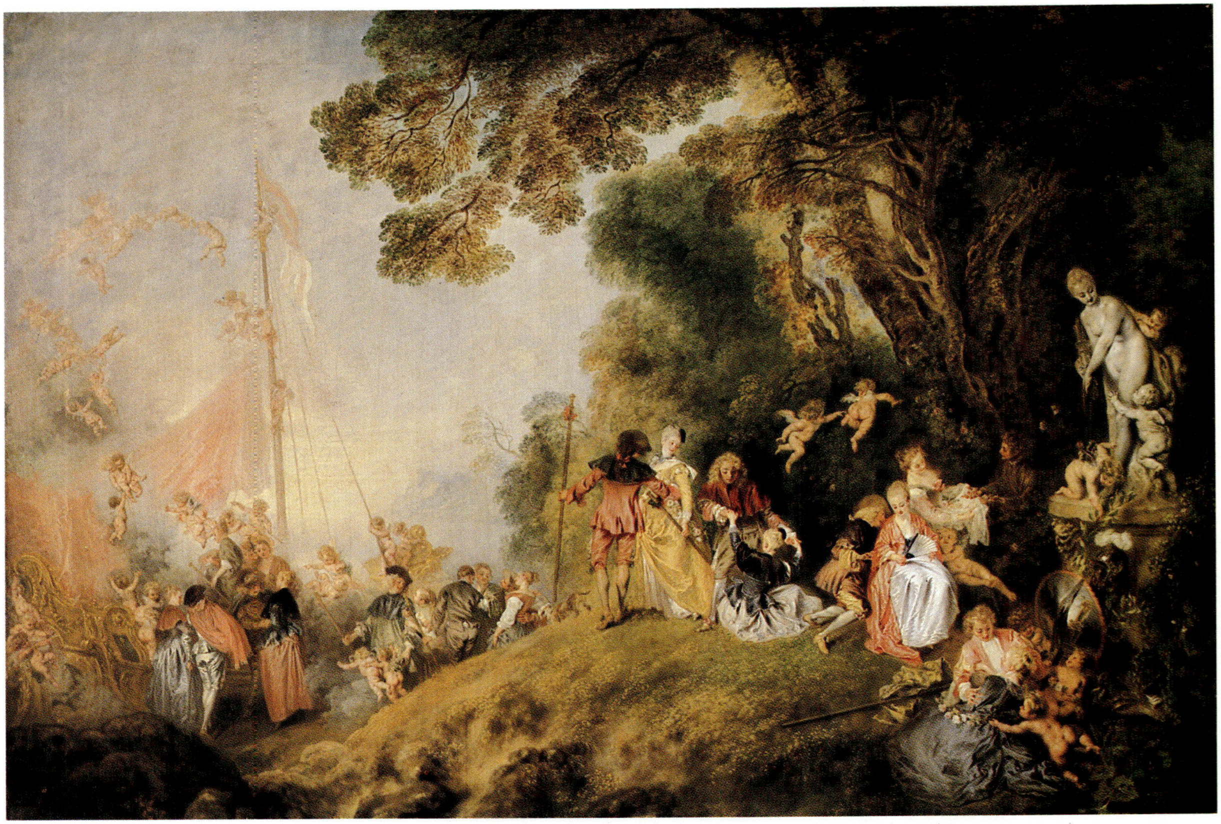

Plate 12 Jean Antoine Watteau. *Pilgrimage to Cythera.* 1717. Oil on canvas, 4′3″ × 6′4½″ (1.3 × 1.94 m). Staatlichen Schlösser und Gärten, Schloss Charlottenburg, West Berlin. .

In the Pompeian fresco, Aphrodite is also shown with a cloth or mantle billowing over her head. This attribute suggests her connection with the heavens. In addition to associating her with love and the sea, the Greeks identified Aphrodite with the Morning Star, the planet that we still call Venus after Aphrodite's Roman name. Astronomy and astrology provided material for art and literature, especially in the late Middle Ages and Renaissance, and Aphrodite-Venus gained the further association of great brightness from this identification with the most visible of the heavenly bodies after the sun and moon.

As the goddess of love, Aphrodite-Venus was worshipped throughout the ancient world. Within this world, however, she was associated with particular places, which she took under her protective mantle. These include the islands of Cyprus and Cythera, the cities of Troy and Corinth, and later Rome, where she was known as Venus. Through yet another love affair, this one with Anchises, the goddess was thought to be the mother of Aeneas, legendary founder of Rome, and therefore the ancestress of the Romans.

Aphrodite had both divine or cosmic qualities and more human, personal ones. Different aspects of her complex nature were emphasized during the many centuries of Greek civilization and its continuation under the Roman Empire. As early as the 5th century B.C., Greek philosophers began to rethink the religious ideas passed down from Homer and to bring these ideas into accord with their more rational and abstract conceptions. For example, Plato (427–347 B.C.), in his famous dialogue *The Symposium,* distinguishes between the heavenly Aphrodite, who presides over spiritual love, and the earthly Aphrodite, who is concerned with the physical passions. Later this distinction became important in Christianity as the contrast between sacred love and profane love. Still later, in the 15th century, the Italian thinker Marsilio Ficino (1433–1499) introduced the idea of "Platonic love" for the spiritual longing kindled by the Heavenly Aphrodite.

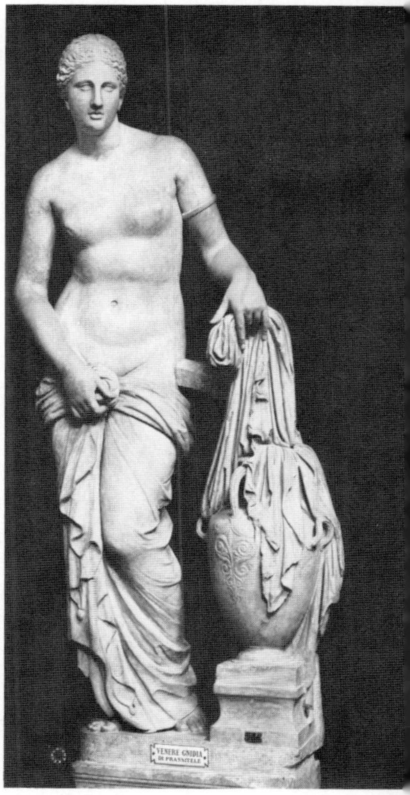

108 Praxiteles.
Aphrodite of Cnidos.
Roman copy after original of c. 320 B.C. Marble, height 6′8″ (2.03 m).
Vatican Museums, Rome.
A very similar pose can be seen in the *Venus de Milo,* Figure 4, page 5.

In the art of classical Greece, Aphrodite is presented as an image of supreme physical beauty. She is shown as such in the famous statue by the 4th-century B.C. sculptor Praxiteles which was kept in a special shrine in Cnidos. Although the bronze original has been lost, marble copies of the statue [108] still give a good idea of its appearance. The goddess is shown gracefully dropping her clothes onto a large jar, for she is about to take a ceremonial bath. The figure's nudity is not intended to incite lust, but to permit the viewer to contemplate the goddess in her full glory as a perfect figure of beauty. Her features are idealized, and the relative size of the parts of her body is governed by a system of proportion that Greek artists had evolved by trial and error over several generations. This statue, and similar Greek works, bequeathed to Western civilization the ideal of the *heroic nude,* somewhat larger than life, as a symbol of nobility and perfection. Still, not all images of Aphrodite were entirely nude, as the *Venus de Milo* [see Figure 4, page 5] also shows.

The Romans had a special affection for Aphrodite-Venus. In *The Aeneid* of Vergil, the Roman national epic, she plays an important political role as the ancestress and protector of the people. She also continues to function as the goddess of love, inflaming Vergil's Dido and Aeneas with physical passion. In

Roman art she is often shown with her mischievous son Eros, more commonly known as Cupid, ever ready to fire his arrows of passion at unsuspecting mortals.

In the Renaissance, Venus was no longer worshipped as a goddess. Yet, along with Cupid, she continued to appear as the embodiment of physical attraction, becoming an especially useful means of depicting love in all its variety and power. No longer divine, she and Cupid could now be treated playfully as well as seriously in the various mythological stories associated with them.

In "Cupid and My Campaspe," the English Renaissance poet John Lyly (1554–1606) presents a charming scene in which he imagines his sweetheart, Campaspe, playing at cards with Venus's son.

John Lyly

CUPID AND MY CAMPASPE

Cupid and my Campaspe played
At cards for kisses; Cupid paid.
He stakes his quiver, bow, and arrows,
His mother's doves and team of sparrows,
Loses them too; then down he throws
The coral of his lip, the rose
Growing on's cheek (but none knows how),
With these the crystal of his brow,
And then the dimple of his chin:
All these did my Campaspe win.
At last he set her both his eyes;
She won, and Cupid blind did rise.
  Oh Love! has she done this to thee?
  What shall, alas, become of me?

(1584)

Campaspe successively wins Cupid's various attributes—his quiver, bow, and arrows—and even his mother's doves. Eventually, Cupid stakes his eyes. Their loss becomes Lyly's way of gracefully suggesting that Campaspe is responsible for making Cupid into the blind god depicted in so many stories—that is, a symbol for the blindness of love. Considering how Campaspe has defeated Cupid, the lover asks what devastating effect Campaspe's beauty will have on him.

Venus and Cupid were popular not only in the poetry of the Renaissance but also in the visual arts. Perhaps the most famous depiction of the goddess in this period appears in Botticelli's *Birth of Venus* (1480) [see Figure 12, page 18], in which the painter presents Venus stepping from her shell as two winged gods scatter flowers and blow the gentle breezes of spring toward her. This idealized nude is an exquisite embodiment of love, while the flowers and water surrounding her reinforce her association with fertility.

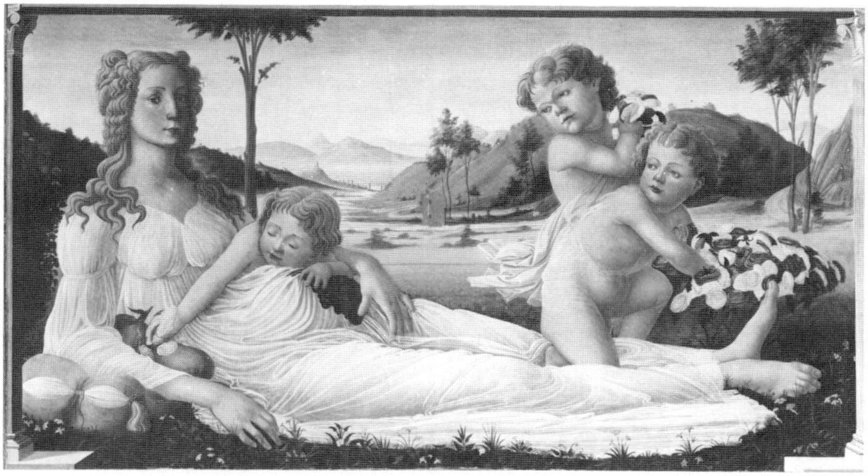

109 Follower of Botticelli. *Venus Reclining with Cupids.* 15th century. Oil on panel, 3′¼″ × 5′8″ (.92 × 1.73 m). National Gallery, London (reproduced by courtesy of the Trustees).

Cupid is absent in Botticelli's work, but he is featured prominently in most Renaissance paintings of Venus. For instance, in *Venus Reclining with Cupids* [109] by a follower of Botticelli, three chubby little boys climb over her. They are specifically identified as cupids and play with fruits and flowers. Similar little figures, often with wings, are sprinkled liberally in Renaissance paintings, where they are known as *amores,* or *putti.* Although these were originally derived from different sources, such as decorative and funerary painting in Roman art, they are clearly associated with Cupid and the love theme in the Renaissance.

Apart from these playful variations on the theme of Venus and Cupid, the Renaissance also revived and extended the Platonic distinction between Heavenly and Earthly Love. *Sacred and Profane Love* by Titian (c. 1488–1576) [Plate 11, page 187] is a case in point. Some viewers have been tempted to identify the elegantly dressed figure on the left as sacred love and the nude one on the right as profane love. But Titian, like Botticelli before him, adheres to the ancient Greek concept of the nude as an expression of purity and nobility. After all, the nude woman is holding a jar aloft in tribute to the heavens, whereas her fashionable companion seems content with earthly matters.

Indeed, the positioning of the figures in relation to the sarcophagus or stone coffin at the center of the painting is significant. Sacred Love, with her pensive expression, seems to be only temporarily perched on the rim of the coffin, as if ready to rise. On the other hand, Earthly Love, staring out directly at the world, is seated solidly on the coffin, suggesting her mortality. Moreover, the figure of Cupid next to her emphasizes her love of the physical rather than her interest in the otherworldly or spiritual.

By his use of color, Titian further stresses the contrast between these two figures. Earthly Love is dressed in an elaborate Renaissance gown of satiny texture, its richness conveyed by the play of light and shade as well as by the scarlet red at her sleeve and hem. Splendid though she is, Earthly Love is surpassed by her heavenly counterpart. The billowy drapery—in the brilliant red for which 16th-century Venetian painters are famous—sets off her nude body in a highly dramatic way. Finally, the subdued landscape, with its delicate blue sky on the sacred side, provides a subtle contrast for these two glowing Venus-like figures who embody two very different kinds of love.

Some artists gave the idea of sacred love a purely Christian meaning, as did Otto van Veen (1556–1629) in his *Emblems of Divine Love (Amorum Emblemata)* [110]. This illustrated book contains sixty images of Love as a benign child guiding another child, who represents the human soul. Van Veen's transformation of the Cupid type seems to be based on the Gospel admonition "Except ye be converted, and become as little children, ye shall not enter into the kingdom of heaven" (Matthew xviii:3).

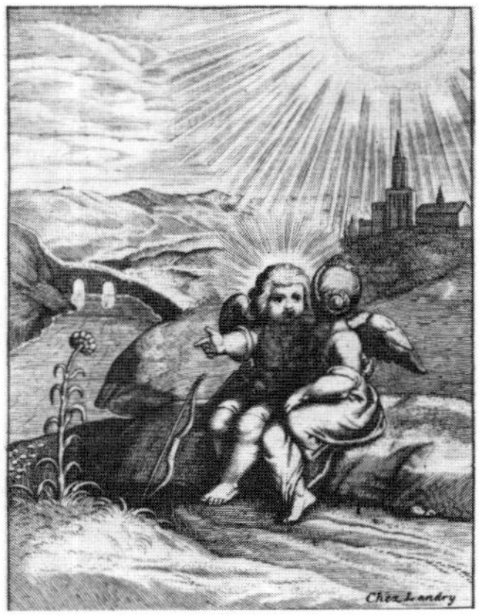

110 Otto van Veen (O. Vaenius). Divine Love, emblem from *Amorum Emblemata.* Antwerp, 1608. Engraving, 3½ × 2⅝" (9 × 7 cm). British Library, London (reproduced by courtesy of the Trustees).

Post-Renaissance art and literature have continued to use Aphrodite-Venus and Cupid for a wide range of purposes. For instance, Watteau (1684–1721) uses these figures in his *Pilgrimage to Cythera* [Plate 12] to present an image of love as both enchanting and ephemeral. The title is misleading, since the painting depicts a group of courtiers not journeying to, but actually leaving, the island associated with the goddess of love. Presiding over the landscape is a statue of Venus appropriately surrounded by plump little cupids. Two of these are still inspiring the lovers in the right foreground while two others, having apparently accomplished their mission, are flying away. In addition, the cupids on the left are far more diaphanous, suggesting the transience of love's pleasures.

To create his interpretation of love, Watteau makes the most of all the possibilities of oil painting. He is equally skillful in presenting the solidity of

111 Antonio Canova. *Maria Paulina Bonaparte Borghese as Venus Victorious.* 1808. Marble, length 6′6″ (1.98 m). Borghese Gallery, Rome.

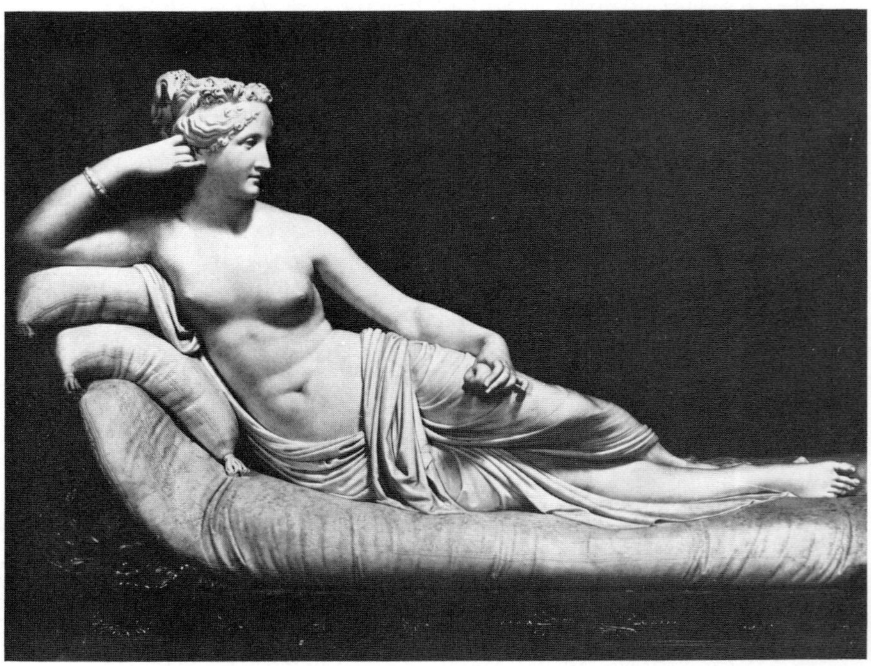

the stone statue at the right and the translucence of the ship's sails at the left. The whole of his picture is suffused with delicate colors—subdued greens and browns to suggest autumn and subtle pinks to suggest sunset. Watteau introduces highlights and some shading to produce the jewel-like brilliance and satiny sheen of the courtiers' clothing. He also employs a wide variety of brushwork—swirling strokes for the rich gowns of the ladies; long, gliding strokes for the sails; tiny specks of color for the delicate carpet of flowers in the foreground; and diffused wash-like applications in the sky. The whole painting, with its autumnal colors, sunset glow, and the backward glances of the departing figures, suggests Watteau's emphasis on the short duration of love, beauty, and happiness even for the privileged few.

But in the 18th century the figure of Venus was also used to suggest less melancholy and nostalgic themes Matthew Prior (1664–1721) used it in a witty and satirical little poem typical of the period.

Matthew Prior

THE LADY WHO OFFERS HER LOOKING-GLASS TO VENUS

Venus, take my Votive Glass;
  Since I am not what I was;
What from this Day I shall be,
  Venus, let me never see.
(1718)

The "votive glass" in the first line refers to the mirror which the lady is offering to Venus because it reflects the aging face the speaker no longer wants to see. By implication, the lady has been worshipping her own face in the mirror!

The Venus figure could be used not only for purposes of **wit** but also for flattery. Antonio Canova (1757–1822) complimented Napoleon's sister, the beautiful Maria Paulina Bonaparte Borghese, by representing her as Venus Victrix, or the Victorious Venus [111], holding the prize apple awarded her by Paris of Troy in his famous judgment. Highly idealized, the Princess Borghese is shown to be aloof and serene—her head in profile turned away with indifference. The allusion to her goddess-like nature is strengthened by her classical hairstyle, her perfect body, and even her couch, which is fashioned in the style of ancient Rome.

In contrast to Canova's serene and dispassionate tribute, the "Venus Victrix" poem of Dante Gabriel Rossetti (1828–1882) is very personal and passionate. Rossetti begins by alluding to the beauty contest, in which Paris, acting as judge, gave the prize to Aphrodite-Venus rather than to her rivals, the goddesses Juno and Pallas Athena. At the end of the poem, Rossetti also alludes to the Greek princess Helen, reputed to be the most beautiful woman in the world, whom Aphrodite gave to Paris as a reward for his choice.

Dante Gabriel Rossetti

VENUS VICTRIX

Could Juno's self more sovereign presence wear
  Than thou, 'mid other ladies throned in grace?—
  Or Pallas, when thou bend'st with soul-stilled face
O'er poet's page gold-shadowed in thy hair?
Dost thou than Venus seem less heavenly fair
  When o'er the sea of love's tumultuous trance
  Hovers thy smile, and mingles with thy glance
That sweet voice like the last wave murmuring there?

Before such triune[1] loveliness divine
  Awestruck I ask, which goddess here most claims
The prize that, howsoe'er adjudged, is thine?
  Then Love breathes low the sweetest of thy names;
And Venus Victrix to my heart doth bring
Herself, the Helen of thy guerdoning.[2]

(1881)

[1]triple
[2]reward

In reworking the legend of the judgment of Paris, Rossetti lets his speaker proclaim that his beloved deserves the prize for supreme beauty more than any of the original three goddesses. In the complicated last two lines the speaker suggests that his loved one is so beautiful that her name alone brings Venus Victrix to his heart. The intensity of the lover's experience is conveyed by the heightened language and especially by the elaborate sea-wave images appropriate for Venus.

A remarkable musical example of the Venus tradition can be found in the opera *Tannhäuser* (1845) by Richard Wagner (1813–1883), in which the contrast between profane and sacred love is once more powerfully reworked. The opera dramatizes the experiences of the knight Tannhäuser, who has fallen prey to the temptations of Venus. The goddess, representing physical love, is contrasted with a second figure, Elizabeth, who represents pure love and sacred duty.

Act I is set in the realm of Venus, the Venusberg. To suggest the physical pleasures associated with the goddess, Wagner creates a bacchanal, or orgy, presented in the form of a ballet. The music, with its quick tempo, driving rhythms, and surging melodic line vividly suggests the ecstasy of love. This music builds to a climax; and as it subsides, new musical themes are introduced to suggest the lulling of passion and the exhaustion of the bacchanalians. Wagner's rich and lush music, combined with the writhing of the dancers, brilliantly expresses the sensuous, erotic qualities long associated with Aphrodite-Venus. Later in the opera, Wagner's music emphasizes the contrasting sacred love, personified by Elizabeth, which ultimately saves Tannhäuser.

As both Rossetti's poem and Wagner's opera suggest, the treatment of Venus could be infused with a passionate intensity not found in Renaissance or 18th-century art and poetry. In the 20th century, on the other hand, Robert Graves (b. 1895) treats Aphrodite-Venus in still another way, with the ironic detachment typical of modern art.

Robert Graves
JUDGMENT OF PARIS

What if Prince Paris, after taking thought,
Had not adjudged the apple to Aphrodite
But, instead, had favoured buxom Hera,
Divine defendress of the marriage couch?
What if Queen Helen had been left to squander
Her beauty upon the thralls of Menelaus,
Hector to die unhonoured in his bed,
Penthesileia to hunt a poorer quarry,
The bards to celebrate a meaner siege?
Could we still have found the courage, you and I,
To embark together for Cranae[1]
And consummate our no less fateful love?

(1964)

[1]the island where Paris and Helen first made love

The speaker raises the question of what might have happened if Paris had chosen not to give his prize, an apple, to Aphrodite but rather to Hera-Juno, the goddess of married love. In this case, none of the consequences of Paris's decision would have occurred. Helen would have remained with her husband, Menelaus, instead of running off to Troy with Paris; Hector, the leader of the Trojans, would not have died defending his city; and none of these great events would have been commemorated in verse. Focusing on the speaker's own feelings, the poem ends with the question of whether, without these passionate deeds, he would have been capable of consummating his own great love. The poem is modern in that it raises an unanswerable question and uses a matter-of-fact tone. At the same time, by invoking the great myths of the past, the poem shows how powerful the classical tradition has remained.

Abraham and Isaac

The second great tradition that has profoundly influenced Western European culture has its roots in the Bible. Like the Greco-Roman tradition we have traced in the figure of Aphrodite-Venus, the biblical tradition also concerns the relationship between the human and the divine. But the Judeo-Christian God is very different from the classical gods, for he lacks the human traits of Aphrodite and the others who live on Mount Olympus.

The well-known story of Abraham and Isaac, an episode in the life of the first great Jewish patriarch as told in Genesis, serves as a good example of the continuing imaginative appeal of the Old Testament. This story touches on relationships that are fundamental to our culture, particularly those between human beings and God, as well as between father and son. The King James Version account (Genesis 22:1–18) is as follows:

And it came to pass after these things, that God did tempt Abraham, and said unto him, Abraham: and he said, Behold, here I am.

And he said, Take now thy son, thine only son Isaac, whom thou lovest, and get thee into the land of Moriah; and offer him there for a burnt offering upon one of the mountains which I will tell thee of.

And Abraham rose up early in the morning, and saddled his ass, and took two of his young men with him, and Isaac his son, and clave the wood for the burnt offering, and rose up, and went unto the place of which God had told him.

Then on the third day Abraham lifted up his eyes, and saw the place afar off.

And Abraham said unto his young men, Abide ye here with the ass; and I and the lad will go yonder and worship, and come again to you.

And Abraham took the wood of the burnt offering, and laid it upon Isaac his son; and he took the fire in his hand, and a knife; and they went both of them together.

And Isaac spake unto Abraham his father, and said, My father: and he said, Here am I, my son. And he said, Behold the fire and the wood: but where is the lamb for a burnt offering?

And Abraham said, My son, God will provide himself a lamb for a burnt offering: so they went both of them together.

And they came to the place which God had told him of; and Abraham built an altar there, and laid the wood in order, and bound Isaac his son, and laid him on the altar upon the wood.

And Abraham stretched forth his hand, and took the knife to slay his son.

And the angel of the Lord called unto him out of heaven, and said, Abraham, Abraham: and he said, Here am I.

And he said, Lay not thine hand upon the lad, neither do thou any thing unto him: for now I know that thou fearest God, seeing thou hast not withheld thy son, thine only son from me.

And Abraham lifted up his eyes, and looked, and behold behind him a ram caught in a thicket by his horns: and Abraham went and took the ram, and offered him up for a burnt offering in the stead of his son.

And Abraham called the name of that place Jehovah-jireh: as it is said to this day, In the mount of the Lord it shall be seen.

And the angel of the Lord called unto Abraham out of heaven the second time.

And said, By myself have I sworn, saith the Lord, for because thou hast done this thing, and hast not withheld thy son, thine only son:

That in blessing I will bless thee, and in multiplying I will multiply thy seed as the stars of the heaven, and as the sand which is upon the sea shore; and thy seed shall possess the gate of his enemies;

And in thy seed shall all the nations of the earth be blessed; because thou hast obeyed my voice.

What makes the Abraham and Isaac episode so powerful is its succinctness; characters and events are at a minimum. The cast is limited to the figures of God, Abraham, Isaac, two servants, an angel, and a ram. The plot is simple: Abraham hears God's command and immediately submits. He takes Isaac to the designated spot, places him on the altar, and seizes the knife. At the last possible moment the angel of the Lord intervenes, and Abraham is able to substitute a ram. Few other details are given. Nothing is said of the psychological anguish of Abraham, asked to sacrifice his only son, or of Isaac, whose single question reveals that he senses his father's intention. Time and place are vague. All is stark and to the point.

Even more powerful than the story's succinctness are its implications. The episode touches on profound themes involving basic human experiences. In their relation to God, human beings are asked to show complete obedience. This demand is especially difficult in Abraham's case, because Isaac is the only and much loved son of his old age and also because Isaac represents Abraham's only hope of continuity for his people. Yet the old man fulfills God's command unquestioningly. Isaac, in turn, shows total obedience to his father, apparently uttering not a single word of protest. The story ends with the point that obedience to the divine will is rewarded. Having passed God's test—"now I know that thou fearest God, seeing thou hast not withheld thy son"—Abraham is allowed not only to keep Isaac but also to hear that the future of his tribe is assured.

The simplicity and directness of the language in this excerpt add to its memorable quality. The English translation we are reading is justly famous as the King James Version of the Bible, translated by a group of Anglican bishops working under the direction of King James (1603–1625), who completed their task in 1611. Their style is unadorned yet evocative, often introducing repetitions—"Here am I," "thy son, thine only son." It is enriched by only an occasional simile such as "I will multiply thy seed as the stars of the heaven, and as the sand which is upon the sea shore." The whole episode is a terse and moving demonstration of the need for absolute obedience and its rewards.

Long before the King James translation, the Abraham and Isaac episode was kept current through the study of other versions of the Old Testament. It also inspired artists to create a series of remarkable visual representations of the story. Although spanning the centuries, these tend to remain close to the text in the Bible. Often they show the servants as well as the main characters, the animals as well as the climactic moment on the altar. Perhaps this similarity of treatment is due to the fact that the story is part of a sacred text. As such, it may have retained a kind of sanctity or inviolability. The treatment of the Abraham and Isaac material differs sharply from the much more varied and flexible treatment of the Aphrodite-Venus stories we have just considered. Radically reworking a story may be easier and only possible for some artists when it is no longer considered sacred material.

An early visual interpretation of the Abraham and Isaac story, dated about the 6th century A.D., can be found in the floor **mosaic** of a synagogue in

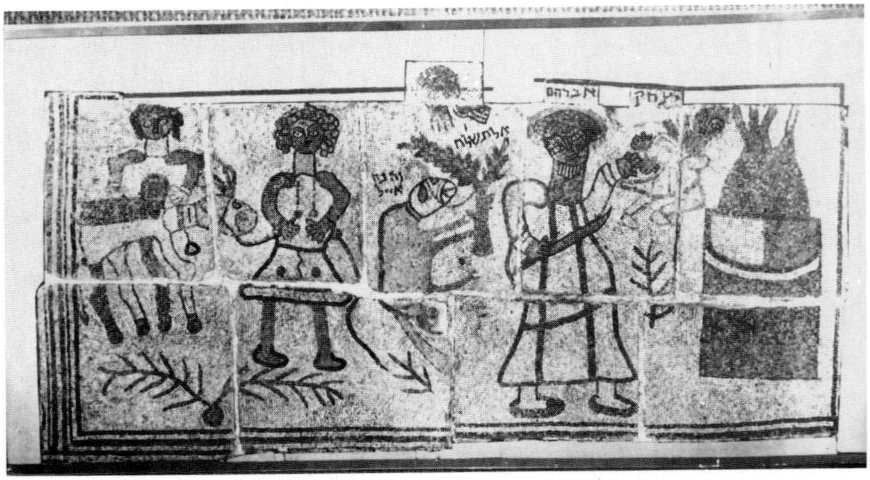

112 *The Sacrifice of Isaac,* from a synagogue in Beth Alpha, Israel. 6th century. Floor mosaic.

Beth Alpha, Israel [112]. Mosaics are composed of tiny cubes or tiles, known as **tesserae**, which are selected for their color and fitted together into a kind of gigantic jigsaw puzzle. The Beth Alpha design is engaging because of its almost child-like simplicity. No attempt is made to have the figures appear life-like. Their bodies, indicated only by strong, dark outlines, are contorted. The hands of God, shown at the top center, are also drawn as if by a child. In keeping with the prohibition in Judaism against the worship of idols, the deity is never shown.

The naive quality of the presentation is primarily the result of its lack of perspective. Objects and figures are placed haphazardly. Isaac seems to float in space. Abraham's face and hands are viewed from the front while his feet and rear are drawn as if in profile. Moreover, although the flesh tones are brightly colored, the clothing of the figures is the same cream color as the background of the mosaic. In other words, the artist has made little distinction between figure and ground. In spite of the flatness of the presentation, the mosaic as a whole expresses both the emotions of the participants—woefulness in Abraham's face, dismay in Isaac's—and a general feeling of innocence through the naive style the artist has adopted.

The Abraham and Isaac episode gained new importance at the hands of Christian artists because the Old Testament not only continued to be valued for itself but came to be read as prefiguring the events of the New Testament. This practice of reinterpreting Old Testament stories as symbolic **foreshadowings** of the life of Christ is known as **typology.** As an especially rich kind of symbolism, it was widely adopted by artists as well as theologians, particularly in the Middle Ages. The Abraham and Isaac story, with its emphasis on willing sacrifice in obedience to God's commands, was seen as prefiguring the sacrifice of Christ on the Cross. Abraham's willingness to sacrifice his only son was also seen as a parallel to God's sacrifice of his son. Even the mercifulness displayed toward Abraham and Isaac by the usually wrathful God of the Old Testament could be regarded as a foreshadowing of the still more merciful and loving New Testament God, who sacrificed his son for the salvation of humanity.

The typological interpretation of the Abraham and Isaac episode explains why Christian artists often placed this scene in close proximity to the Crucifixion. In the elaborate Klosterneuburg Altarpiece, which consists of more than fifty **panels**, the sacrifice of Isaac is placed directly above the image of Christ on the Cross [113]. The two scenes are linked by the identical framing devices, which create a distinctive shape with a triple arch at the top. The upper panel presents the dramatic scene of Isaac lying bound on the altar while an angel stops Abraham from completing his sacrifice. The complementary panel below shows the broken body of Christ on the Cross—his sacrifice completed—flanked by the grieving Virgin Mary and Saint John. In contrast to the complicated Abraham and Isaac scene, in which several figures and objects are arranged in a pattern of dynamic balance, the Crucifixion is severely simple and symmetrical, dignified and moving. The chief figure is centered, and each of the three participants is framed by a little arch. Taken together, these panels demonstrate how Christian artists, even while subordinating the Abraham and Isaac story to their own concerns, clearly recognized its power as a human drama.

In the Renaissance, the Abraham and Isaac story remained popular. In fact, it was the assigned subject for a famous competition in 1401 for the doors of the Baptistry in Florence. This competition called for small gilded bronze reliefs (21″ × 17½″) in the shape of a quatrefoil, or four-leafed clover. Two of the entries have survived, both by major artists.

The panel [114] by Filippo Brunelleschi (1377–1446) is notable first for its full use of the space available. The area is divided horizontally. The top half

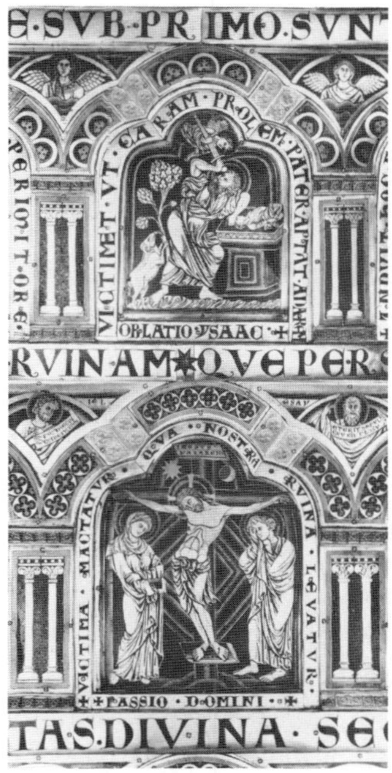

113 Nicholas of Verdun. *The Sacrifice of Isaac* and *The Crucifixion*. 1181. Enamel on copper, each 8 × 6½″ (21 × 17 cm). Museum, Klosterneuburg, Austria.

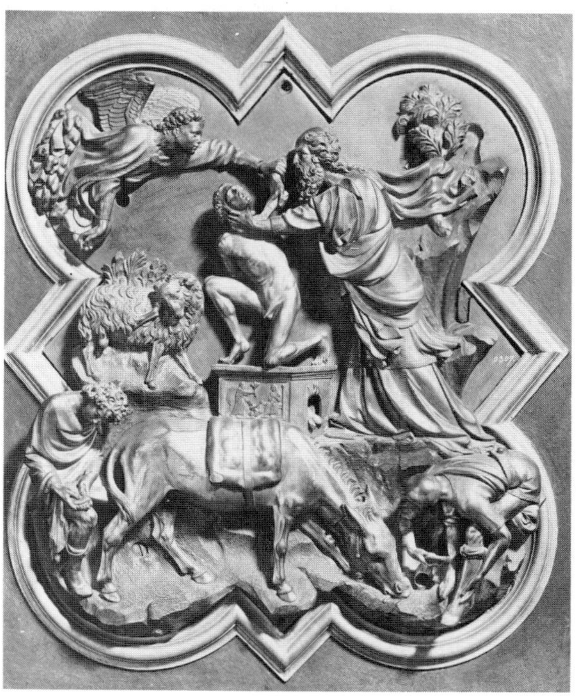

114 Filippo Brunelleschi. *The Sacrifice of Isaac*. 1401–1402. Gilded bronze, 21 × 17½″ (53 × 44 cm). Museo Nazionale del Bargello, Florence.

shows the main characters in the upper center; the bottom half, the subordinate figures of the two servants at the sides and the donkey filling out the middle. In this way, Brunelleschi is contrasting those engaged in an action ordered by the Divinity with those involved in the everyday world.

The main figures are presented in a highly dramatic way. Abraham has seized Isaac's head, forcefully twisting it around in preparation for the fatal blow. At the same moment, the angel is clutching Abraham's arm to stop him. As their flowing garments suggest, both the father and the angel seem to be rushing at the kneeling figure from opposite directions. The ram, part of the divine scheme, stands in readiness directly below the angel. In contrast, the lower half of the panel depicts each servant involved in a mundane activity. The one on the right feeds the donkey; the one on the left is removing a thorn from his foot. As in Brueghel's *Fall of Icarus* [see Figure 59, page 79], Brunelleschi gives the impression that even during the most momentous occasions, ordinary life continues.

These details suggest that the artist is interested in giving a fuller depiction of the scene than his predecessors. Other realistic or life-like details are also included. For instance, a thin stream of water drips from the mouth of the drinking ass. The ram is scratching itself. And Isaac has upturned toes that seem to reflect his fear. The whole conception of this figure is significant, for unlike earlier depictions, Brunelleschi's Isaac is naked, reflecting the renewed interest of Renaissance artists in the human body.

In spite of its forcefulness and dramatic power, Brunelleschi's design

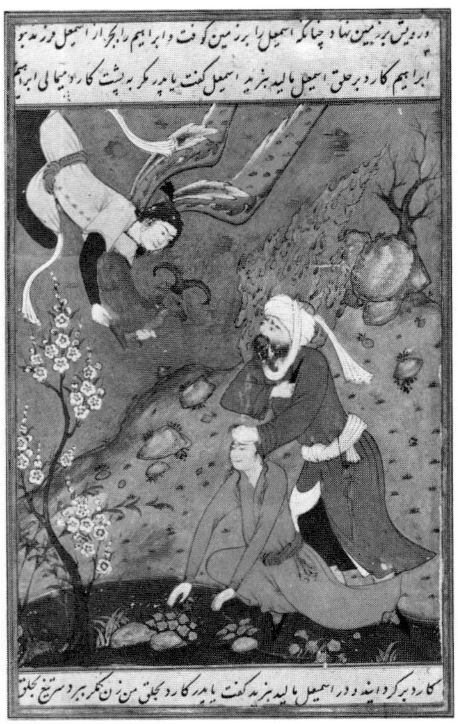

below left: 115 *Angel Bringing the Ram to Abraham,* from a Persian manuscript. c. 1590. Manuscript illumination, 8⅝ × 5½" (22 × 14 cm). Bibliothèque Nationale, Paris.

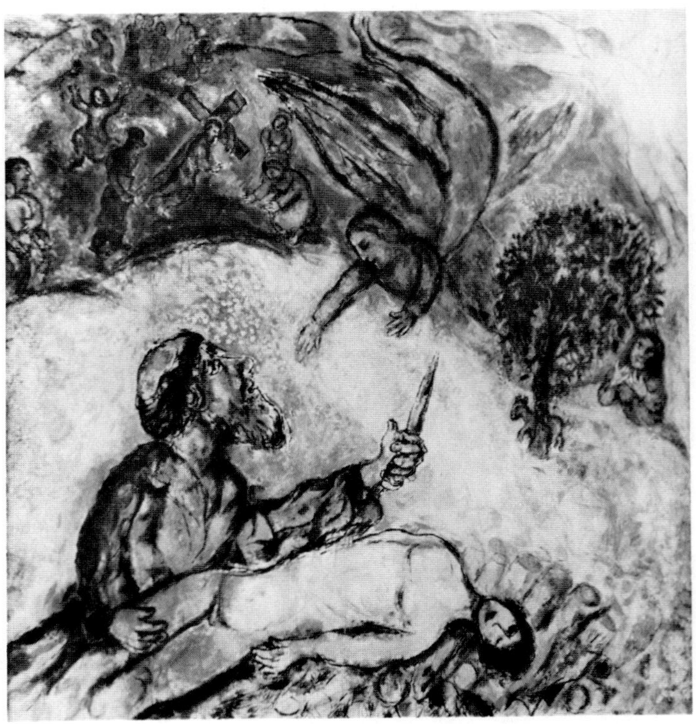

below right: 116 Marc Chagall. *The Sacrifice of Isaac.* 1954–1967. Musée Nationale, Message Biblique Marc Chagall.

lost the competition. Instead, the winning treatment, which used the same component figures, was created by Lorenzo Ghiberti (1381?–1455). In making their decision, the judges surely considered the general organization and the placing as well as the shaping of the figures, which (as we shall see in Chapter 14) reveal Ghiberti's even greater artistic and technical mastery.

Abraham and Isaac were important not only in Judaism and Christianity but also in the Muslim religion. In fact, the two were honored, along with other Old Testament prophets, as precursors of Muhammed (A.D. 570–632), regarded as the greatest prophet and God's final messenger. A Persian **manuscript** [115] shows the usual Abraham and Isaac scene, but with a distinctively Near-Eastern appearance. Abraham is in Islamic dress and turban. The angel, who prevents him from completing the sacrifice and actually offers the substitute ram to him, wears an Oriental headdress. Even the perspective attempted in the picture uses a device popular in Oriental art, for it works by strong diagonal lines. The outline of the hill crosses from the lower left to the upper right, and the blossoming tree at the bottom is appropriately larger than the bare tree at the top. The features as well as the dress of the figures and the characteristic Near Eastern landscape all show how thoroughly the Abraham and Isaac story has been absorbed into a totally different cultural tradition.

The presentation of Abraham and Isaac has remained relatively unchanged over the centuries, as we can see in the recent version by Marc Chagall (b. 1887) [116]. But some modern artists, given to questioning traditional values, have felt free to offer quite different interpretations. A strikingly novel reworking was provided by the British poet Wilfred Owen (1893–1918), who suffered in the trenches of World War I and was killed shortly before the 1918 Armistice.

Wilfred Owen
THE PARABLE OF THE OLD MAN AND THE YOUNG

So Abram rose, and clave the wood, and went,
And took the fire with him, and a knife.
And as they sojourned both of them together,
Isaac the first-born spake and said, My Father,
Behold the preparations, fire and iron,
But where the lamb for this burnt-offering?
Then Abram bound the youth with belts and straps,
And builded parapets and trenches there,

And stretched forth the knife to slay his son.
When lo! an angel called him out of heav'n,
Saying, Lay not thy hand upon the lad,
Neither do anything to him. Behold,
A ram, caught in a thicket by its horns;
Offer the Ram of Pride instead of him.
But the old man would not so, but slew his son,
And half the seed of Europe, one by one.

(pub. 1920)

In this brief but devastating poem, published in 1920, the traditional figures of Abraham, Isaac, the angel, and the ram are retained, but with significant changes in meaning. Isaac has come to symbolize all the young men sacrificing themselves in the war; Abraham, the old men who have sent them to the trenches. The father-son relationship has been converted into a conflict between generations. The theme is no longer willing obedience but bitter reproach that the old make wars in which the young must fight and die. The ram here is not just a sacrificial animal, miraculously provided to replace Isaac, but a symbol of pride—the pride the old men refuse to sacrifice in place of the young men they are sending to battle. Most shocking is the ending, for the command of the angel to spare the young men is ignored; the young are really sacrificed; and with them the seeds of future generations, whose continuity was promised to Abraham in the Bible, are irretrievably lost.

The haunting effect of Owen's poem depends on our knowledge of the Old Testament story. Because we are familiar with the Abraham and Isaac episode and because we have always seen it as a story of unquestioning obedience that is tested, proved, and rewarded, we are startled to find it reinterpreted to show the opposite—a questioning of obedience, blaming of those who demand it, and feeling of loss at the end. In short, using a tradition in order to reverse its usual meaning can be more powerful than reworking it in customary ways.

The Halo

Not only specific characters but particular attributes or symbols have also been reinterpreted in the course of time. A fascinating example is the

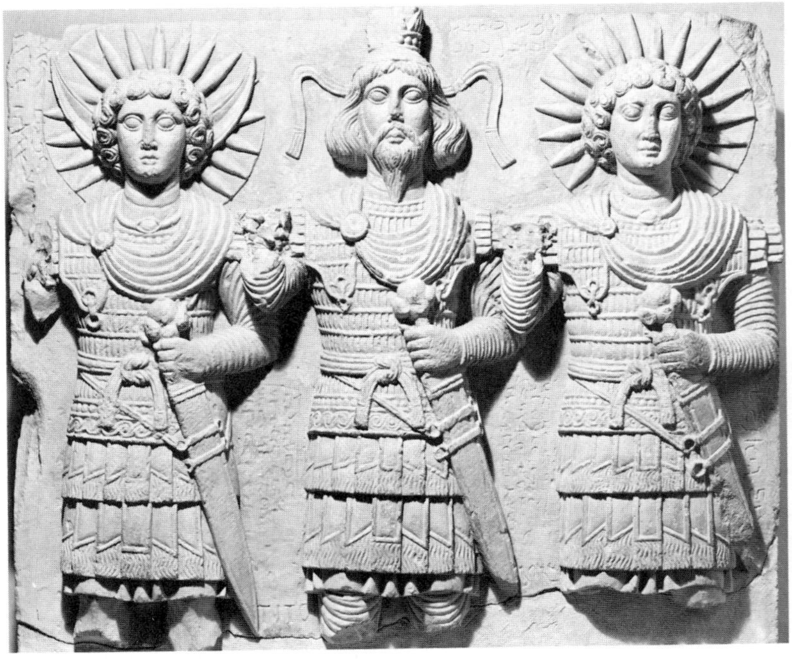

117 The divine triad Ba'alsamin, Aglibôl, and Malakbel, from Palymra. 1st century B.C. Relief, height 21⅞" (56 cm). Louvre, Paris.

halo, sometimes called a **nimbus**. This is a circle of light radiating from the head of an idealized figure, suggesting its holiness or power.

In general, we associate the halo with Christian saints, but it seems to have originated in the ancient Near East. The halo is another instance of transmission from one culture to another. In what is now Syria and Iraq, the halo was first used in images of cosmic deities. In the Palymra relief carving [117], a kind of altar, the head of Aglibol, the moon god, is surmounted by a crescent and the head of Malakbel, the sun god, by rays; these symbols show who the gods are. The halo as we know it is a simplification of these symbols, reducing them to a single disk. Variations of these forms—sometimes simple, sometimes complex and flaming—made their way all across Asia to the medieval Buddhist art of China [118], Korea, and Japan.

The use of the halo also spread west to Rome, where something extraordinary happened: during the Roman Empire the simple disk or circle of the halo appeared in paintings of a living person. However, the only individual who could be so honored was the emperor, who was considered divine even in life. This use of the halo to honor a ruler, rather than a god, continued in early Christian art. That is why the evil King Herod is shown with it in a mosaic in the church of Santa Maria Maggiore in Rome.

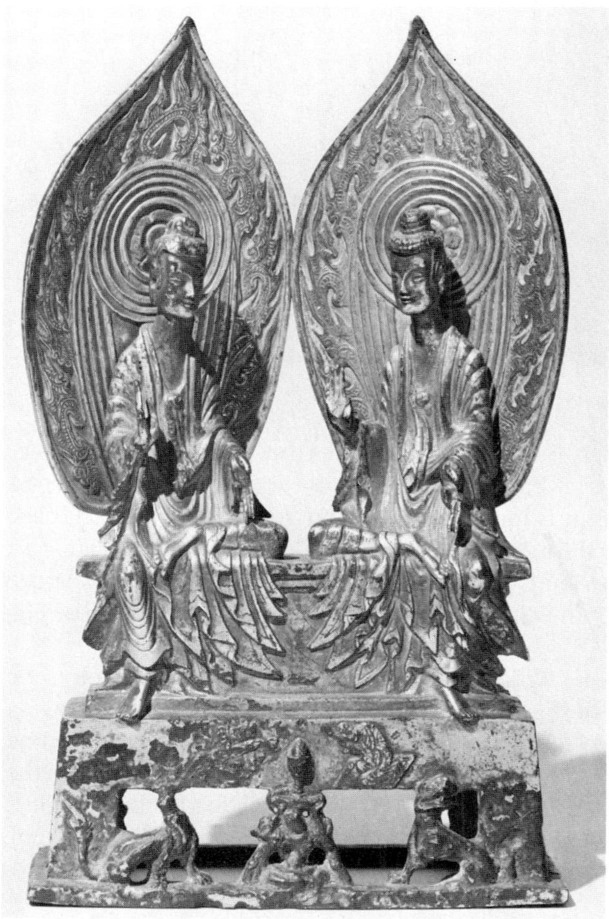

118 Conversation between the Buddha Śākyamuni and Prabhūtaratna (altar relief). 518. Gilded bronze, Musée Guimet, Paris.

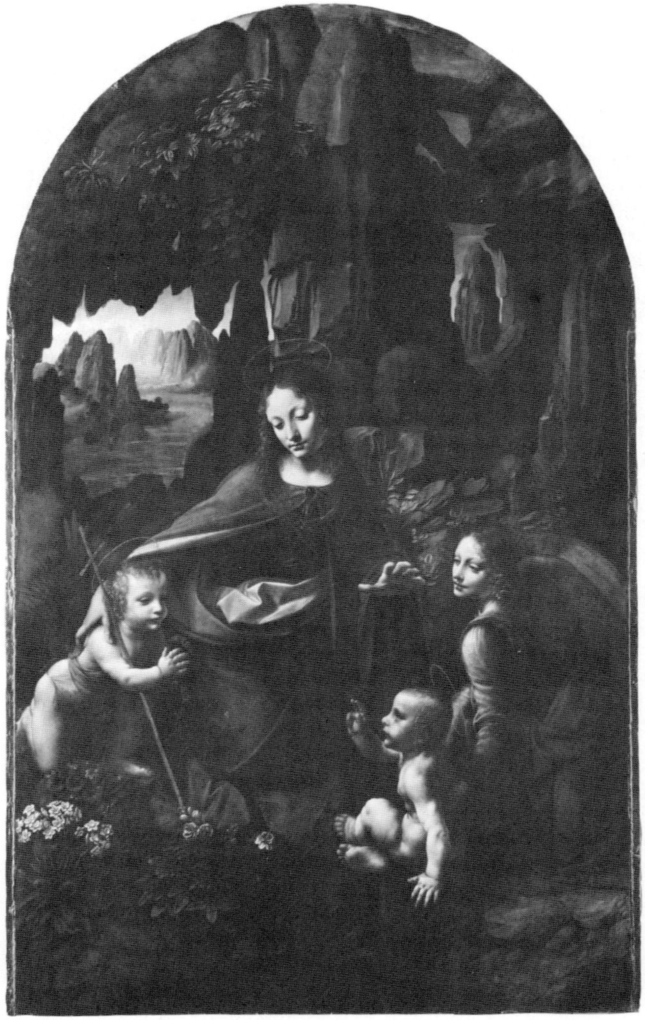

119 Leonardo da Vinci. *The Virgin of the Rocks.* c. 1485. Oil on panel, 6′2⅝″ × 3′11¼″ (1.9 × 1.2 m). National Gallery, London (reproduced by courtesy of the Trustees). The holiness symbolically conveyed by the halos is reinforced by Leonardo's dramatic lighting, the serene mysteriousness of the faces, and the gesturing of the Madonna, who holds her hand in benediction over the Christ child.

Eventually, Christian art settled on the use of the halo to mark the saints, including the Virgin Mary. Christ often received a special halo with a cross inscribed. Such halos appear throughout the Middle Ages [see Plate 3, page 35] and also, in simpler form, in the Renaissance [119]. Moreover, Islamic art continued to use this attribute, as we can observe in the flaming halo above Abraham's head in the 16th-century Persian manuscript illumination [see Figure 115, page 201].

In more recent times, halos are less common, for they were felt to be out of keeping with the new realism demanded of art, the interest in showing only what can be seen in real life. Ironically, just as sacred halos were going out of fashion, a brief bid for the revival of their secular use was made in the 17th century. The artists of Louis XIV's time followed the lead of his courtiers in flattering him as the Sun King, complete with a halo of cosmic rays [120].

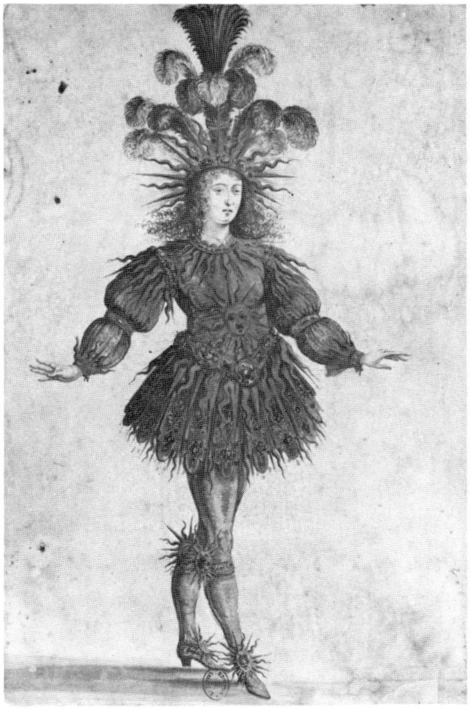

above: 120 Benserade's designs for the *Ballet de la Nuit.* 1653. Pen and ink. Bibliothèque Nationale, Paris. This lively sketch is an artist's rendering of the costume Louis XIV wore when he danced the role of the Sun King in a court ballet—an art form he actively encouraged. His elaborate headgear incorporates the sun's rays, creating a halo-like effect.

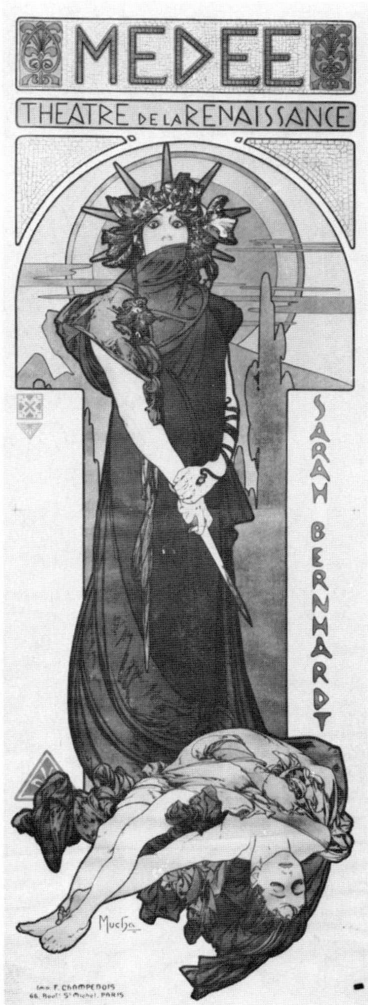

right: 121 Alphons Mucha. Poster of Sarah Bernhardt in *Medea,* 1898. Lithograph, 6′6½″ × 2′3″ (2.0 × .7 m). Museum of Modern Art, New York (gift of Joseph H. Heil).

In the 19th century, charismatic performers—musical virtuosos, opera divas, great actors and actresses—became to some degree the counterparts of the kings and saints of earlier times. Sarah Bernhardt, who consciously encouraged public adulation, promoted her image through the striking posters of the Czech artist Alphonse Mucha (1860–1939). One of these shows her as Medea [121], the savage princess who killed her children to punish her unfaithful husband. It depicts Bernhardt in a violent pose, wearing a spike-like headdress that suggests solar rays. Behind this, Mucha has also drawn what appears to be a halo-like disk. These attributes suggest that Medea was no ordinary murderess and Bernhardt no ordinary actress.

Sarah Bernhardt was not the only figure of the recent past to get away with assuming such attributes of canonization in her lifetime. When John Singer Sargent (1865–1925) painted a portrait of Mrs. Isabella Stewart Gard-

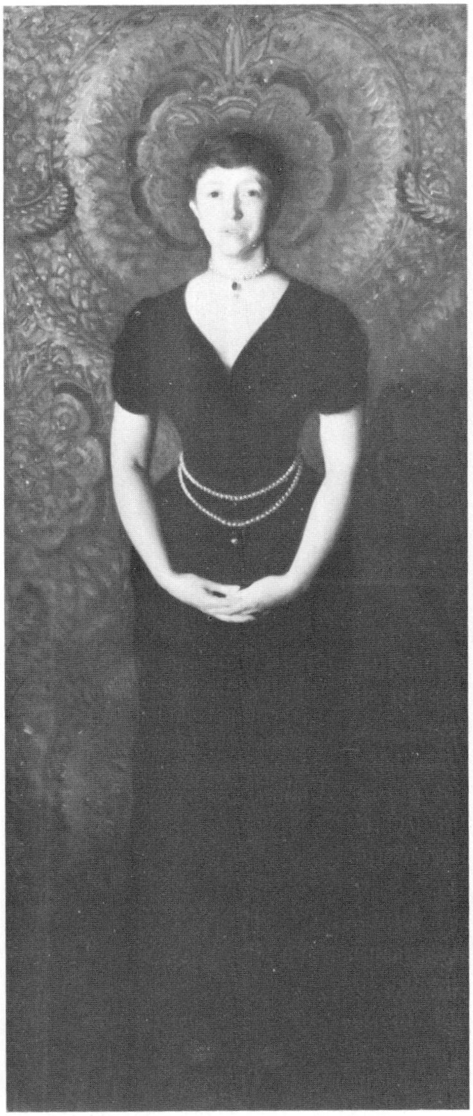

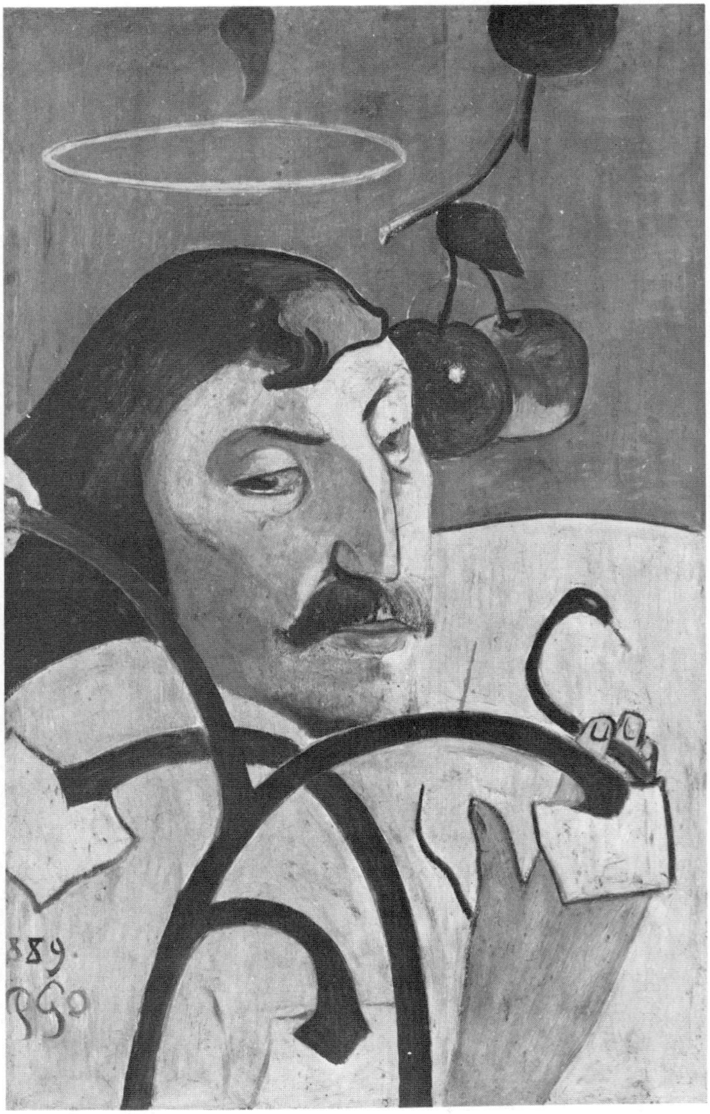

above: 122 John Singer Sargent. *Mrs. Isabella Stewart Gardner.* 1888. Oil on canvas, 6′2⅛″ × 2′7⅝″ (1.9 × .81 m). Isabella Stewart Gardner Museum, Boston.

above right: 123 Paul Gauguin. *Self-Portrait.* 1889. Oil on panel, 31¼ × 20¼″ (79 × 51 cm). National Gallery of Art, Washington (Chester Dale Collection, 1962).

ner [122], the Boston art patron and collector whose home is now a museum, he used the pattern on a small piece of material as a halo to set off her face. The rich fabric and intricate beauty of its design enhance the aura of wealth, dignity, taste, self-assurance, and perhaps even strong-willed determination suggested by Sargent.

On the other hand, Paul Gauguin (1848–1903) includes an unmistakable halo in his self-portrait [123] for ironic purposes. A self-acknowledged scoundrel, he juxtaposes the halo with his own features, exaggerated to appear almost devilish. He thereby sharply rejects the traditional association of the halo with saintly or otherwise admirable figures. Such a reversal of the halo's established significance no doubt startled the public of Gauguin's time.

For artists of our own less religious age, the halo seems to have lost its symbolic power. Unlike the story of Abraham and Isaac, which has remained relatively the same, the halo illustrates a tradition that has changed radically in its passage from one cultural situation and century to another.

The Christian Mass

Since music is the most abstract art, it offers fewer opportunities for reworking characters such as Aphrodite or Abraham and Isaac. Nor can music present visual attributes such as the halo. Music can, however, rework a subject by variations in treatment.

A prime example of an extensive musical tradition can be found in the settings of the Christian **Mass.** The Mass uses music to accompany the prayers and ritual actions that recall the sacrifice of Jesus Christ. During these ceremonies, worshippers share food and drink, a practice that is a cultural tradition. Composers have concentrated on writing musical settings for the prayers of the Mass that are always presented—known as the *Ordinary*—rather than for the prayers that vary with the day or festival—known as the *Propers.* The Ordinary consists of the following five sections, each with its own unvarying text;

THE MASS

KYRIE Kyrie eleison. Christe eleison. Kyrie eleison.	KYRIE Lord, have mercy on us. Christ, have mercy on us. Lord, have mercy on us.
GLORIA Gloria in excelsis Deo, et in terra pax hominibus bonae voluntatis. Laudamus te. Benedicimus te. Adoramus te. Glorificamus te. Gratias agimus tibi propter magnam gloriam tuam. Domine Deus, Rex caelistis, Deus Pater omnipotens. Domine Fili unigenite, Jesu Christe. Domine Deus, Agnus Dei, Filius Patris. Qui tollis peccata mundi, miserere nobis. Qui tollis peccata mundi, suscipe deprecationem nostram. Qui sedes ad dexteram Patris, miserere nobis. Quoniam tu solus sanctus, Tu solus Dominus, Tu solus altissimus, Jesu Christe, cum Sancto Spiritu in gloria Dei Patris. Amen.	GLORIA Glory to God in the highest. And on earth peace to men of good will. We praise Thee. We bless Thee. We adore Thee. We glorify Thee. We give Thee thanks for Thy great glory. O Lord God, heavenly King, God the Father almighty. O Lord Jesus Christ, the only-begotten Son. Lord God, Lamb of God. Son of the Father. Who takest away the sins of the world, have mercy on us. Who takest away the sins of the world, receive our prayer. Who sittest at the right hand of the Father, have mercy on us. For Thou alone art holy. Thou alone art Lord. Thou alone, O Jesus Christ, art most high. Together with the Holy Spirit, in the glory of God the Father. Amen.

CREDO

Credo in unum Deum, Patrem omnipotentem, Factorem caeli et terrae, visibilium omnium et invisibilium. Et in unum Dominum Jesum Christum, Filium Dei unigenitum, et ex Patre natum ante omnia saecula. Deum de Deo; Lumen de Lumine; Deum verum de Deo vero; genitum non factum; consubstantialem Patri, per quem omnia facta sunt. Qui propter nos homines, et propter nostram salutem, descendit de caelis. Et incarnatus est de Spiritu Sancto, ex Maria Virgine; et homo factus est; crucifixus etiam pro nobis; sub Pontio Pilato passus et sepultus est. Et resurrexit tertia die secundum scripturas; et ascendit in caelum; sedet ad dexteram Patris: et iterum venturus est cum gloria judicare vivos et mortuos; cujus regni non erit finis. Et in Spiritum Sanctum, Dominum et vivificantem; qui ex Patre Filioque procedit; qui cum Patre et Filio simul adoratur et conglorificatur; qui locutus est per prophetas. Et unam Sanctam, Catholicam et Apostolicam Ecclesiam. Confiteor unum Baptisma in remissionem peccatorum et expecto resurrectionem mortuorum, et vitam venturi saeculi. Amen.

CREDO

I believe in one God, the Father almighty, Maker of heaven and earth, and of all things visible and invisible. And in one Lord, Jesus Christ, the only-begotten Son of God. Born of the Father before all ages. God of God, light of light, true God of true God. Begotten, not made; of one being with the Father: by whom all things were made. Who for us men, and for our salvation came down from heaven. And was made flesh by the Holy Spirit, of the Virgin Mary: and was made man. He was also crucified for us, suffered under Pontius Pilate, and was buried. And on the third day He arose again, according to the Scriptures. And ascending into heaven, He sitteth at the right hand of the Father. And He shall come again with glory to judge the living and the dead: and of His kingdom there shall be no end. And in the Holy Spirit, the Lord and Giver of life, who proceedeth from the Father and the Son. Who together with the Father and the Son is adored and glorified: who spoke by the prophets. And in one, holy, catholic and apostolic Church. I confess one baptism for the remission of sins. And I look for the resurrection of the dead. And the life of the world to come. Amen.

SANCTUS AND BENEDICTUS

Sanctus, sanctus, sanctus Dominus Deus Sabaoth. Pleni sunt caeli et terra gloria tua. Hosanna in excelsis. Benedictus qui venit in nomine Domini. Hosanna in excelsis.

SANCTUS AND BENEDICTUS

Holy, holy, holy, Lord God of hosts! Heaven and earth are filled with Thy glory. Hosanna in the highest! Blessed is He that comes in the name of the Lord. Hosanna in the highest!

AGNUS DEI

Agnus Dei, qui tollis peccata mundi, miserere nobis. Agnus Dei, qui tollis peccata mundi, miserere nobis. Agnus Dei, qui tollis peccata mundi, dona nobis pacem.

AGNUS DEI

Lamb of God, who takest away the sins of the world, have mercy on us. Lamb of God, who takest away the sins of the world, have mercy on us. Lamb of God, who takest away the sins of the world, grant us peace.

As the text shows, a basic characteristic of the traditional Latin Mass is its repetition of familiar words from the liturgy. The first section, the *Kyrie,* uses the Greek phrases for "Lord have mercy on us" and "Christ have mercy on us," drawing on the Greek version of the New Testament. The remaining sections use the Latin of the later versions of the New Testament.

Another basic element of the Mass is its use of threefold divisions in some parts. Not only does the *Sanctus* repeat the Latin word *sanctus* three times, but the *Kyrie* has an ABA structure, with the third part repeating the opening. A threefold division can be found in many art forms, but it serves as a tribute to the Trinity when it appears in such a Christian context.

Although the wording used in the Ordinary of the Mass remains unchanged, the musical settings have developed markedly over the centuries. Ranging from the severely simple to the extraordinarily elaborate, they always reflect the musical vocabulary and culture of their time.

The earliest settings of the Mass are to be found in the *Gregorian chants,* so called because they were collected under the direction of Pope Gregory I (540?–604). These are the most important body of religious music in Western Christianity. Sung collectively by priests, nuns, or choir members, the music could fill even the vast spaces of the great Gothic cathedrals.

The Gregorian chants give a powerful impression of both purity and simplicity because they are **monophonic**, consisting of a single melodic line. Moreover, the melody moves in an orderly progression by steps or half-steps, rarely skipping or leaping. The simplicity—indeed the austerity—of this music can be felt merely by looking at a brief transcription of the *Sanctus* from *Mass II,* the mass setting *Kyrie fons bonitatis* [Example 10] believed to have been composed in the 12th century. As we listen to this passage, we are

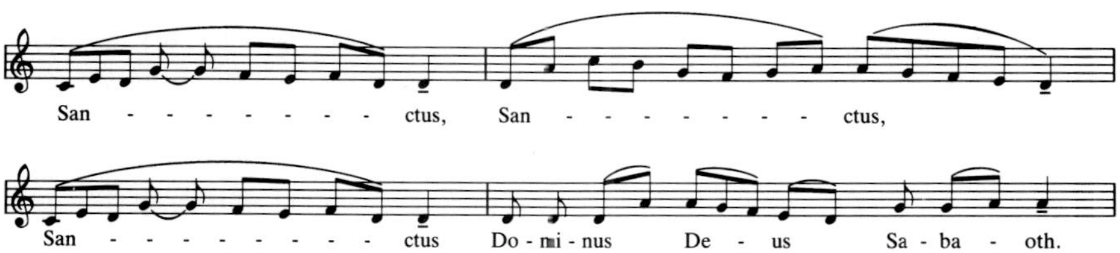

Example 10 *Sanctus* from *Mass II (Kyrie fons Bonitatis).*

struck by several other distinctive features that make Gregorian chants sound medieval. The music has a very limited dynamic range; that is, it has little variation in loudness and softness. In addition, most notes are held for the same length of time, allowing little rhythmic variation. And since the chants are monophonic, they are sung without any harmony.

Another characteristic of Gregorian chants that contributes to their distinctive medieval quality is their use of special **modes**. These are sequences of whole and half-tones or melodic steps that differ somewhat from the major and minor scales to which we are accustomed. (In fact, the eight traditional modes are the ancestors from which our modern scales are derived.) The mode of the *Sanctus* from *Mass II,* known as mode I, or the Dorian mode, characteristically repeats the notes D (the tonic) and A (the dominant).

The difference between the opening of the *Mass II Sanctus,* in its original modal form, shown in Example 10, and the similar pitches written using either of the modern scales can be seen in Examples 11 and 12. The absence of sharps (♯) or flats (♭) in the original points to one of the major differences between the older mode and our modern scale.

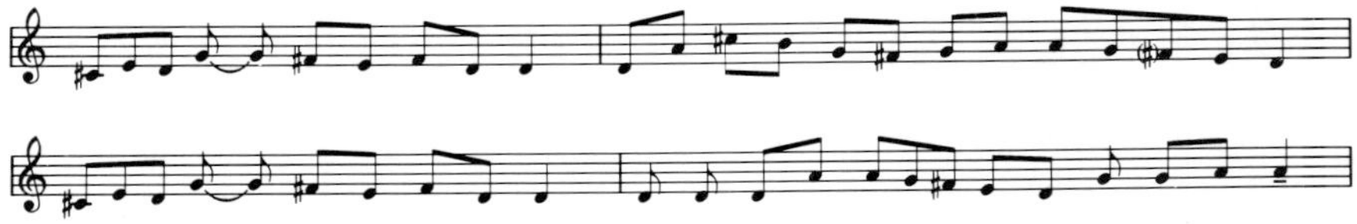

Example 11 The same *Sanctus,* in modern D-Major transcription.

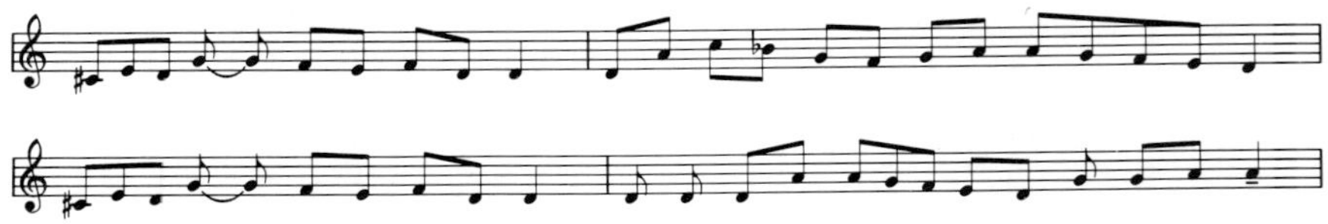

Example 12 The same *Sanctus,* in modern D-minor transcription.

The next major development in the musical tradition of the Mass comes with the writing of **polyphonic** music. As its name suggests, polyphonic music consists of several melodic lines composed to be heard simultaneously. One of the earliest polyphonic masses, the *Messe de Notre Dame* (c. 1350), was composed by Guillaume de Machaut (1304?–1377). This work provides a musical setting in four parts, probably intended for two groups of boys and two groups of men. It also provides for some musical accompaniment. Example 13 makes clear that the music is still close to that of the Gregorian chants, for the melody moves, for the most part, in an orderly step-by-step or half-step progression of notes and has a narrow range of pitches. Like the Gregorian chants, too, it presents few changes in loudness or softness. Nonetheless, the *Messe de Notre Dame* sounds quite different from the earlier austere examples, since its four groups of voices naturally create a richer, fuller musical effect than the single melodic line of the Gregorian setting. As the score shows, the *Messe* is also metrical music because of its definite beat and variety of rhythmic note values.

After Machaut, composers continued to write in the polyphonic style, but by the 16th century musical settings of the Mass had greatly increased in complexity. The *Pope Marcellus Mass* (*Missa Papae Marcelli,* 1555?) by Giovanni da Palestrina (1525–1594) was written largely for six separate groups of male voices. In fact, Palestrina's *Mass* is distinguished by much more than the number of voices. In contrast to our earlier examples, Palestrina's melody uses more skips and leaps [Example 14]. Moreover, the long, soaring phrases cover almost the entire range of the human voice. And this increase in the range of the melodic line brings greater changes in dynamics. Although the dynamics are not marked in the manuscript, variations in loudness and softness are naturally created as a group of voices rises to a high note; the higher

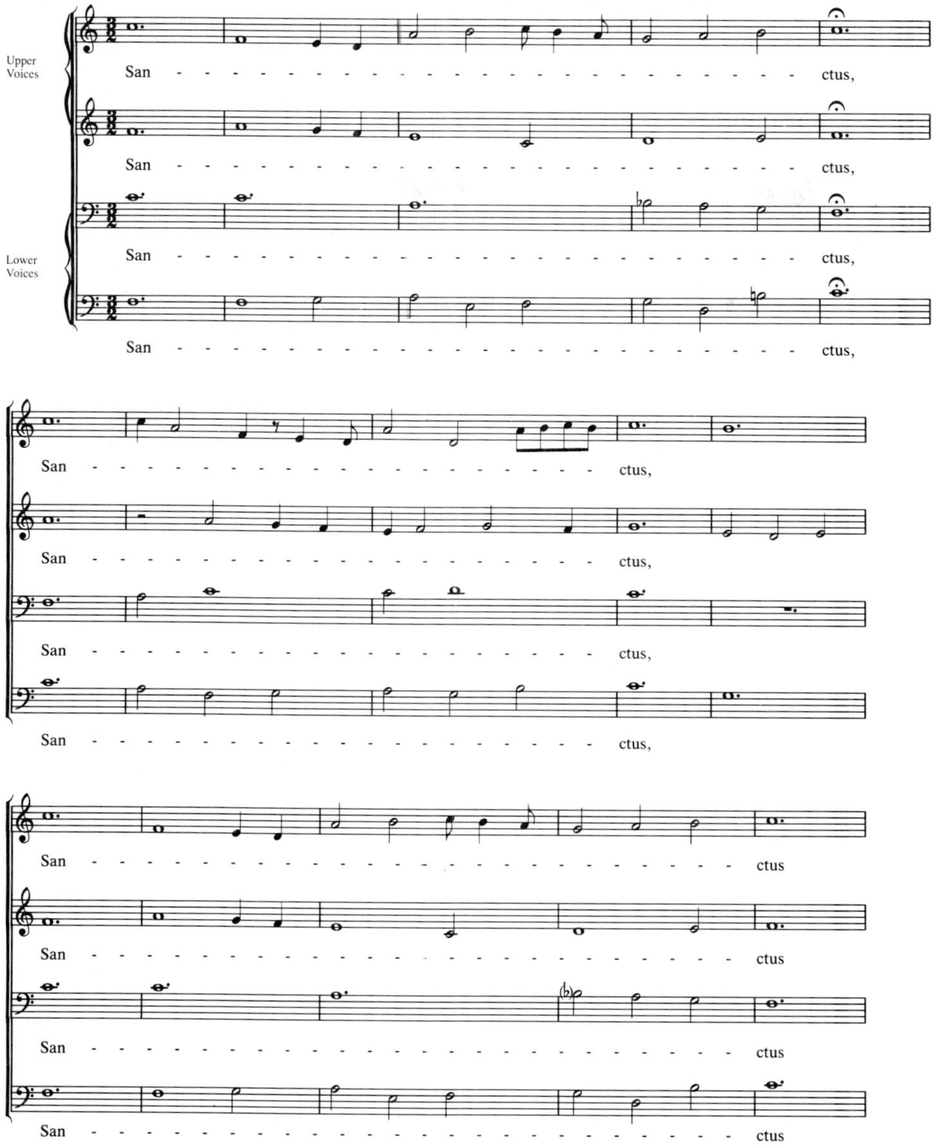

Example 13 Guillaume de Machaut, *Messe de Notre Dame, Sanctus.*

pitch produces a louder sound or climax. These traits make the music for the Palestrina *Mass* far more emotionally expressive and dramatic than earlier settings of the Mass.

Perhaps the most celebrated of all settings of the Mass is the *B-minor Mass* (1733–1738) by Johann Sebastian Bach (1685–1750). This work incorporates a number of older conventions. Bach uses the much earlier Gregorian chants for certain melodic themes, especially in the *Credo* section, and he also draws on the techniques of Renaissance polyphony by writing for a chorus in six parts.

But Bach goes beyond the earlier Mass settings by drawing on newer musical forms such as the *opera* and the *oratorio,* which had become popular in his time. Both of these forms dramatize religious or secular stories through voices and orchestral accompaniment, the opera being a full-scale stage performance and the oratorio a concert recital. By using elements from these musical forms, Bach's *Mass* presents far wider dramatic contrasts than earlier musical settings of the Mass. Such contrasts juxtapose solo voices with the chorus, as well as individual instruments with groups of instruments.

The *Sanctus* from Bach's *B-minor Mass* [Example 15] reveals the richness and complexity of his treatment. It is scored for a chorus of six parts, which is later redivided into eight parts, as well as a solo tenor voice. The

Example 14
Giovanni da Palestrina,
Missa Papae Marcelli, Sanctus.

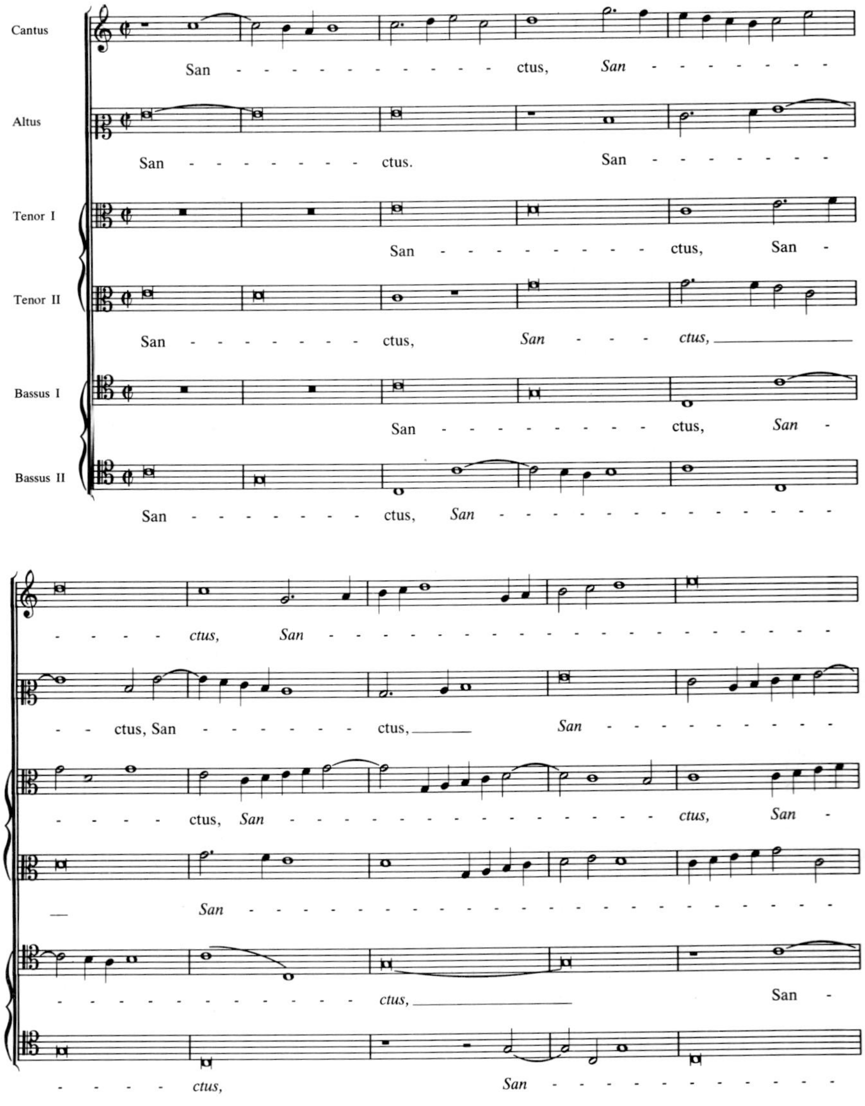

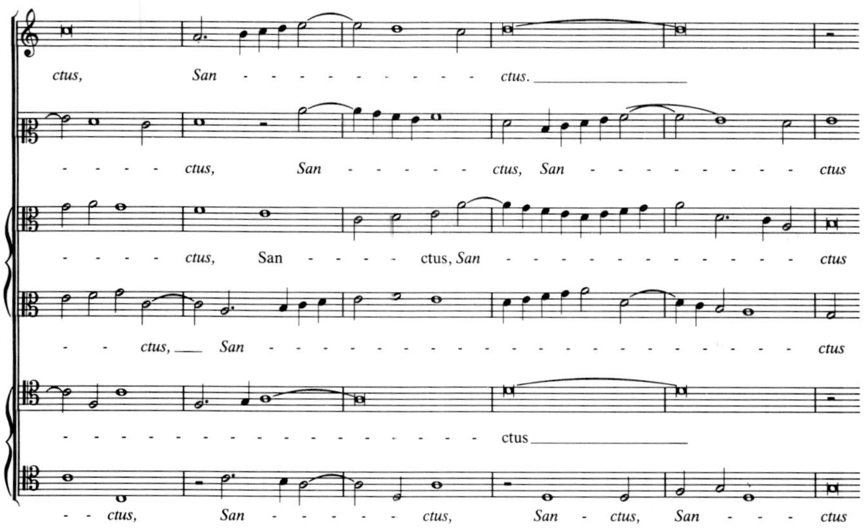

instrumental forces include two sections of violins; violas, celli, and double basses; three trumpets, three oboes, two flutes, two bassoons; an organ, and kettledrums. The various sections of the *Sanctus* provide a maximum of variety. Some are performed by an unaccompanied voice or voices, others by the instruments without singers, and still others by the full complement of voices and instruments. With his increased resources, Bach presents an extraordinarily great range of dynamics from *pianissimo* (softest) to *fortissimo* (loudest).

Furthermore, Bach writes in a much freer and more varied style, with a melodic line consisting of more dramatic skips and leaps than in the masses of earlier periods. Bach makes enormous demands on the skill and talent of both singers and instrumentalists. Finally, no longer using the medieval modes, Bach exploits the contrast between our modern major and minor scales. More flexible and dramatic than earlier masses in all these respects, Bach's *B-minor Mass* is truly a virtuoso piece—one that dazzles with its brilliance.

To explain why Bach's *Mass* is unexcelled, we must recognize the perfect balance he maintains between the polyphony created by the separate groups of voices, on the one hand and, on the other hand, the harmonic structure—the chords created when these various groups merge their sounds. Both the horizontal sequence of the melodic lines and the vertical interrelationship of the notes flawlessly follow the technical rules governing such matters as counterpoint and chord progression. At the same time, the sounds that strike the listener are emotionally rich and varied. Bach's achievement can be compared to a perfect poem in which the meter, rhyme, verse form, and other technicalities ideally suit the themes being expressed.

Going beyond these elaborate interrelationships, Bach manages to use the convention of threefold divisions more elaborately than any other composer. Especially in the *Sanctus,* he repeatedly organizes the elements at his disposal into patterns of three that serve to pay tribute to the Trinity. At the beginning of the *Sanctus,* for instance, the orchestra uses three sets of instruments, each set consisting of three: three trumpets form one unit, three oboes a second, and two sections of violins a third. The voices, too, form a unit of three as two sopranos are joined by an alto. Not only do these voices repeat

Example 15 J. S. Bach, *Mass in B minor, Sanctus.*

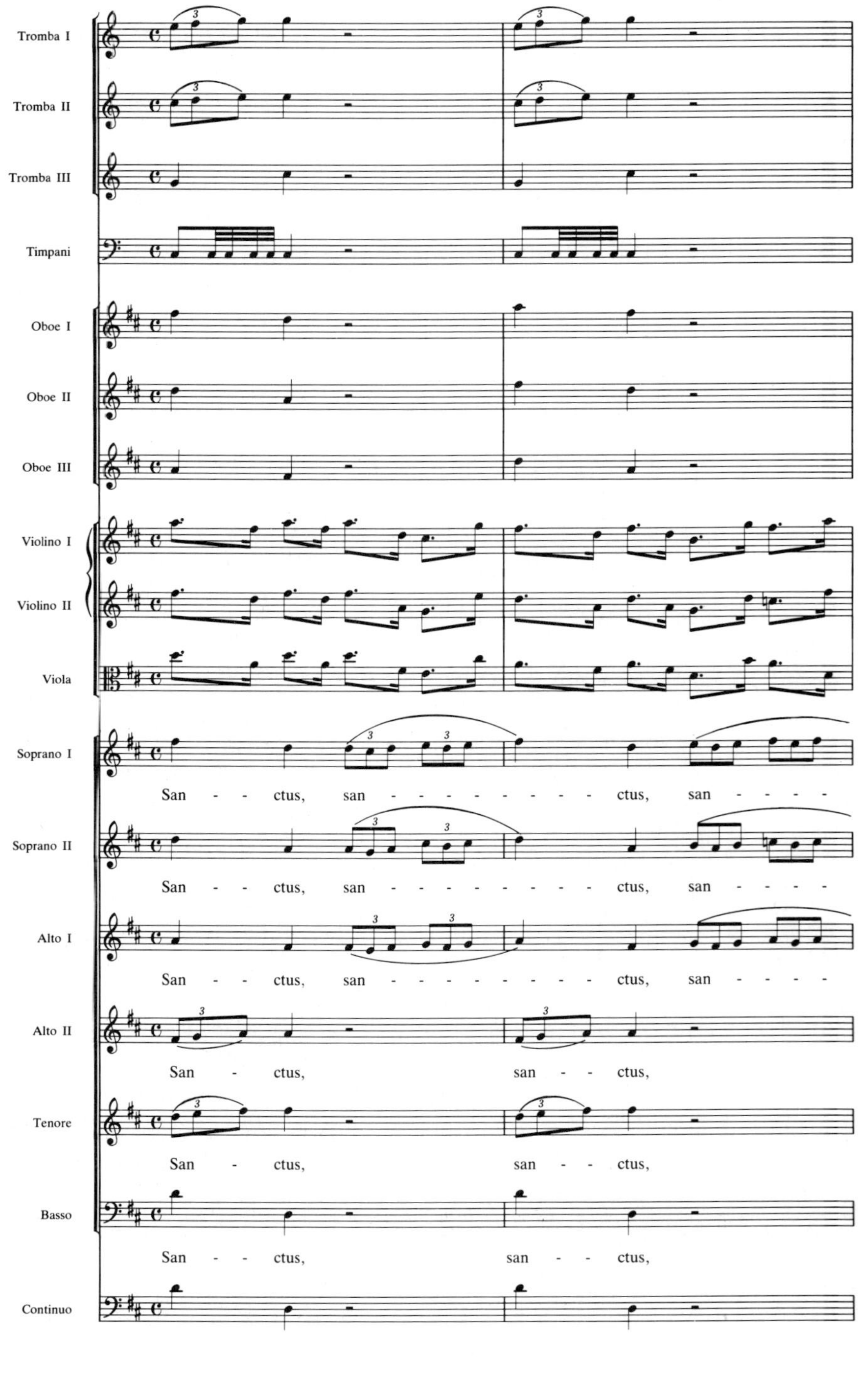

the word *sanctus* three times, but they do so in triplets, three notes sounded in the time of one beat. And these voices form a series of complete chords, each one consisting, as usual, of three notes. The more we study the score, the more examples we can find of this symbolic use of the sacred number three.

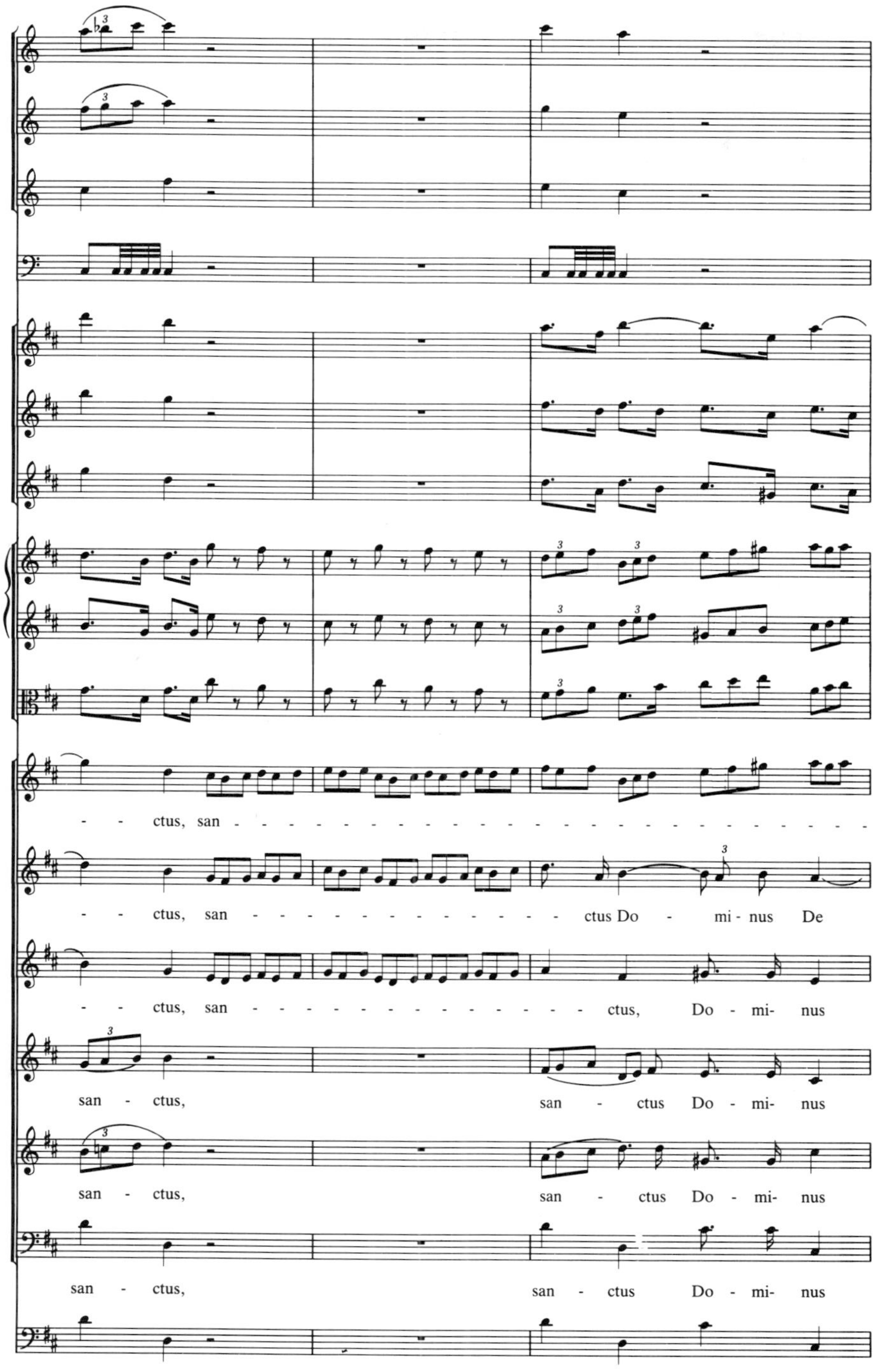

So great is the complexity of the *B-minor Mass* that this work transcends the original purpose of the musical settings we have been studying. Instead of accompanying the celebration of the Mass, Bach's music becomes the center of attention. Indeed, the *B-minor Mass* is far too long for performance at a church service and is usually presented as a musical work in its own right.

Bach's work represents a high point in the evolution of music for the Mass, but composers certainly did not give up writing masses in awe of the *B-minor Mass.* Beautiful Mass settings were created in the late 18th and 19th centuries by Haydn, Mozart, Schubert, and other major composers. Indeed, Beethoven's *Missa Solemnis* (1824) is thought by some to come the closest to equaling the emotional power and musical complexity of Bach's *B-minor Mass.* Generally, these Mass settings, like the Bach example, are too ornate for the church services that provided their original reason for being. To complicate matters, in the 19th century, the public taste for grandiose, operatic styles of composition clashed with a desire for musical reform in the Roman Catholic Church. Many within the Church wished to restore the earlier, simpler types of composition and to return to the use of unaccompanied voices which they associated with Palestrina and his contemporaries. The result was that the best musical settings were generally excluded from church use, while the music regarded as suitable for Sunday morning services rarely rose above mediocrity.

In our own century, the problem of writing music that is both functional and artistically valid persists. Perhaps the most interesting 20th-century examples of the Mass are those that try to break away from the traditional style of serious Western music. Leonard Bernstein (b. 1918) in his *Mass* (1971) has attempted to combine popular and jazz styles with more traditional music. He has also incorporated theatrical settings and dance.

Another striking departure from the traditional idea of religious music is the *Missa Luba* of the African Congo (1950s). Improvised by members of a tribe with the assistance of a Catholic priest, this work unites the form of the Mass with the traditions of African music. In particular, it makes full use of percussion instruments, notably drums. Creating the *cross-rhythms* that are typical of African music, the drummers play different rhythms with strong beats that do not coincide. Although the rhythmic patterns appear to be disorganized and even frenzied, they are actually coordinated by the beating of a master drummer.

In contrast to these complex rhythms, the voices in the *Missa Luba* harmonize in relatively simple ways. Solo singers and chorus answer each other in a so-called *litany.* In the *Sanctus* this litany, or answering pattern, is created by pairs of voices. Their tempo increases wildly in the "Hosannah" passage that concludes the *Sanctus.* Here the voices seem to shout rather than sing, in a joyous outburst that resembles the frenzy of certain North American revival meetings. The *Missa Luba* represents a remarkable union of music with the emotional and religious life of the group.

As the preceding examples from art, literature, and music suggest, working within a tradition can lead to creations that have clear links with the past but are also distinctive in their own right. The conscious decision to use a definite tradition allows artists to draw on recognized patterns, whether visual, verbal, or musical. In doing so, artists face the challenge of equaling, if not surpassing, the ways in which their predecessors used this established vocabulary. At the same time, artists face the additional challenge of reworking traditions and thereby reinterpreting the material for themselves and for their society.

Questions for Study and Discussion

1. To become aware of cultural differences, describe how two different cultures mark such basic human events as a wedding, funeral, or initiation into adulthood (e.g., communion, bar mitzvah).
2. To demonstrate the continuity of community traditions, describe how your community commemorates events that are part of its history such as the Signing of the Declaration of Independence, the end of World War I, and possibly the founding of the community itself.
3. How do communal rituals such as agricultural ceremonies and prayers foreshadow the artistic forms of dance and drama? What similar foreshadowing can be found in the cave drawings shown in Figure 16, page 20, which were not meant to be decorative but to bring success to the hunt?
4. Which contemporary actresses of stage and screen continue the Aphrodite-Venus tradition and in what specific ways?
5. In how many different ways is the Aphrodite-Venus figure reinterpreted in the examples offered in this chapter?
6. What is the symbolic significance of the larger-than-life-size nude in the classical tradition as seen not only in the Greco-Roman statues of Aphrodite-Venus [see Figure 4, page 5, and Figure 108, page 189] but also in Titian's *Sacred and Profane Love* [see Plate 11, page 187]? In what ways do Michelangelo's *David* [see Figure 36, page 44] and Rodin's *The Thinker* [see Figure 6, page 9] belong to the same tradition?
7. What recurring details can be found in the treatments of Abraham and Isaac offered in this chapter? Why have fewer changes been introduced in the treatments of Abraham and Isaac than in those of Aphrodite-Venus? Why could Wilfred Owen's version (see page 201) probably have been written only in the 20th century? Why is it nonetheless shocking?
8. What is the difference between monophonic and polyphonic music?
9. Why has the text of the Christian Mass remained unchanged throughout different periods? What changes in the musical settings of the Mass have occurred in the same periods? What is the importance of Bach's *B-minor Mass?*
10. What features of the Mass setting demonstrate Christian symbolism?
11. What musical qualities in the masses discussed in this chapter or in other religious music seem religious (as opposed to secular) to you?
12. How are some traditional Christian conceptions of God and humanity expressed in the wording of the *Gloria* and *Credo* reflected in George Herbert's "Easter Wings" (see page 83)?

CHAPTER 7

Genres of the Arts of Space

Just as artists in every field gain inspiration by drawing on recognizable cultural traditions, they often also find strength in shaping their work in accordance with the established artistic traditions known as genres. The term *genre,* taken from the French, is derived from the Latin *genus,* or "type," and suggests a classification of works that are linked by similar subject matter, treatment, or organizational pattern. Generic categories exist in each of the arts, and each genre—whether portrait painting or chamber music or tragedy—has distinctive characteristics.

Moreover, many of these categories use recognizable conventions, that is, arbitrary features that are commonly accepted. The word *convention* comes from the Latin *convenire,* "to come together" or "to agree." A convention may pertain not simply to the individual parts of a work of art but also to entire structures. We have already seen examples in the halo, the little luminous disk that we agree to interpret as a symbol of holiness or special power. We also accept conventions quite easily in the case of the omniscient narrator, who knows more than normal human beings, or in the stage settings which present a room as if its fourth wall were removed.

By working within traditional genres and their conventions, artists gain a framework for organizing their material. As audience, we need to know the principles of the various genres if we are to gain not only a more thorough understanding of a work but also a basis for comparing it with others of the same type.

Painting

The genres of painting are recognizable either by their subject or by a distinctive treatment of their subject. History painting, portraiture, landscape, still life—each is a separate genre with its own subject matter.

History Painting

Through much of Western art the genre of **history painting** has enjoyed high status. As the term suggests, such painting presents scenes of historical significance, such as the death of Socrates or Washington crossing the Delaware. The esteem accorded such paintings stems from the conviction that they show the accomplishments of great personalities. After being highly regarded for over two thousand years, history painting began to decline in reputation in the 19th century. At this time people increasingly voiced doubt about the importance of heroic leaders, particularly since the more anonymous contributions of social forces were coming to be recognized.

Like much else in our tradition, history painting began among the Greeks and Romans. At first the Greeks approached the subject indirectly, preferring to depict stories chosen from the legendary lives of their heroes. The Greeks developed true history painting only in their later centuries, bequeathing the genre to the Romans. The *Battle of Alexander and the Persians* is a Greek story executed in mosaic by Roman artists in Pompeii, probably in the 1st century B.C. [124]. The rectangular space teems with the bodies

below: 124 *Battle of Alexander and the Persians.* 1st century B.C. Mosaic copy from Pompeii of a Hellenistic painting, 8′11″ × 15′1½″ (2.72 × 4.91 m). Museo Nazionale, Naples.

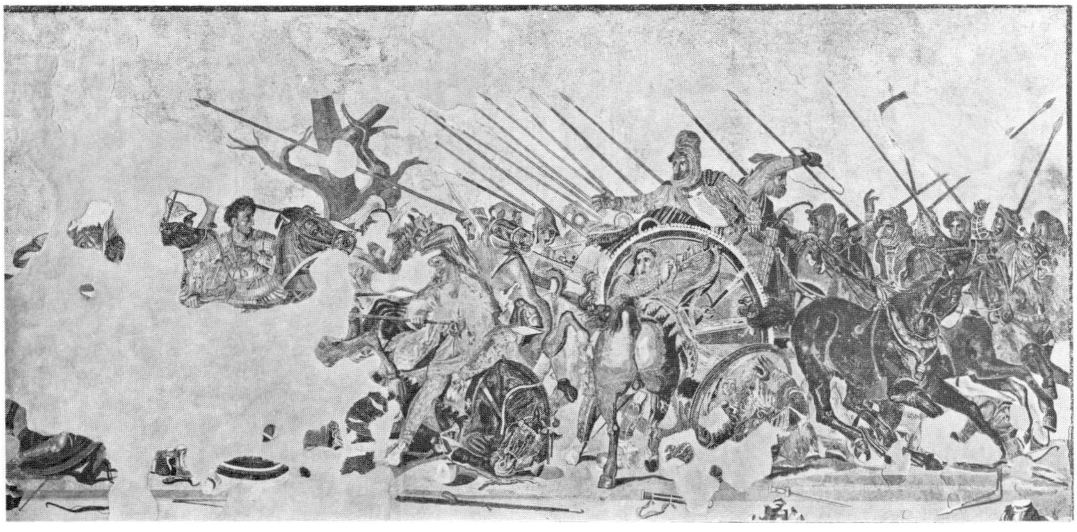

of horses and men, projecting the turbulent excitement of one of the decisive encounters between West (the Greeks) and East (the Persians). Even though the left-hand side has been damaged, the head of Alexander commands attention with his lion-like mane and imperious eye. Rising from the mass on the right side, the Persian king Darius is caught offguard by his enemy's impetuous rush and is only saved by the sudden turning movement of his chariot. In this work we feel a great sense of immediacy because the brilliant lights and the fore-shortening of the figures make them seem very close to us. The natural setting consists of only one object, the tree rising behind the head of Alexander's horse.

The German Renaissance painter Albrecht Altdorfer (c. 1480–1538) created his own *Battle of Alexander* [125] without knowing the Pompeian

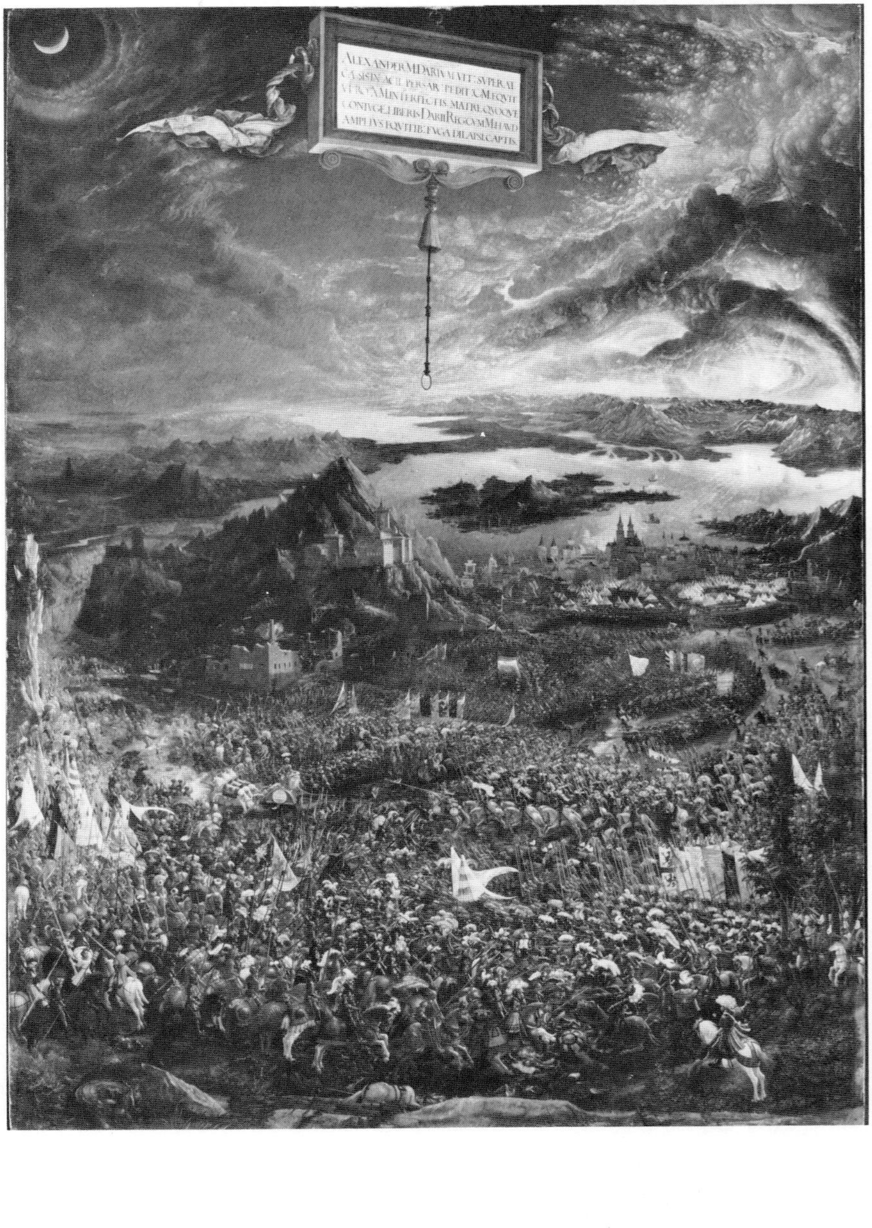

125 Albrecht Altdorfer. *The Battle of Alexander*. 1529. Oil on panel, 5′2″ × 3′11″ (1.57 × 1.19 m). Alte Pinakothek, Munich. The Latin inscription, not painted by Altdorfer, gives details of Alexander's victory over Darius and his Persian troops.

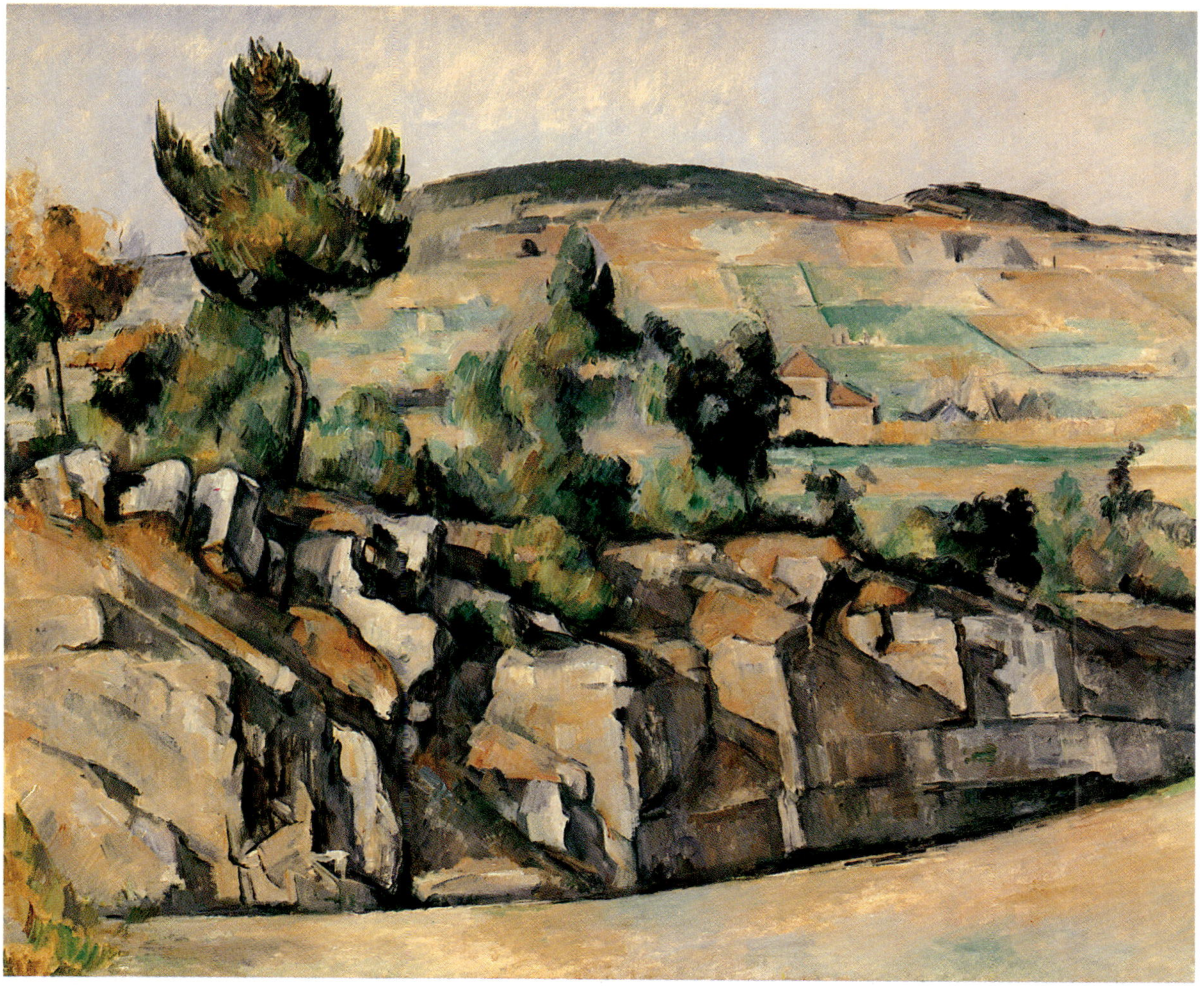

Plate 13 Paul Cézanne. *Mountains in Provence.* c. 1886–1890. Oil on canvas, 25 × 31¼″ (63 × 80 cm). National Gallery, London (reproduced by courtesy of the Trustees).

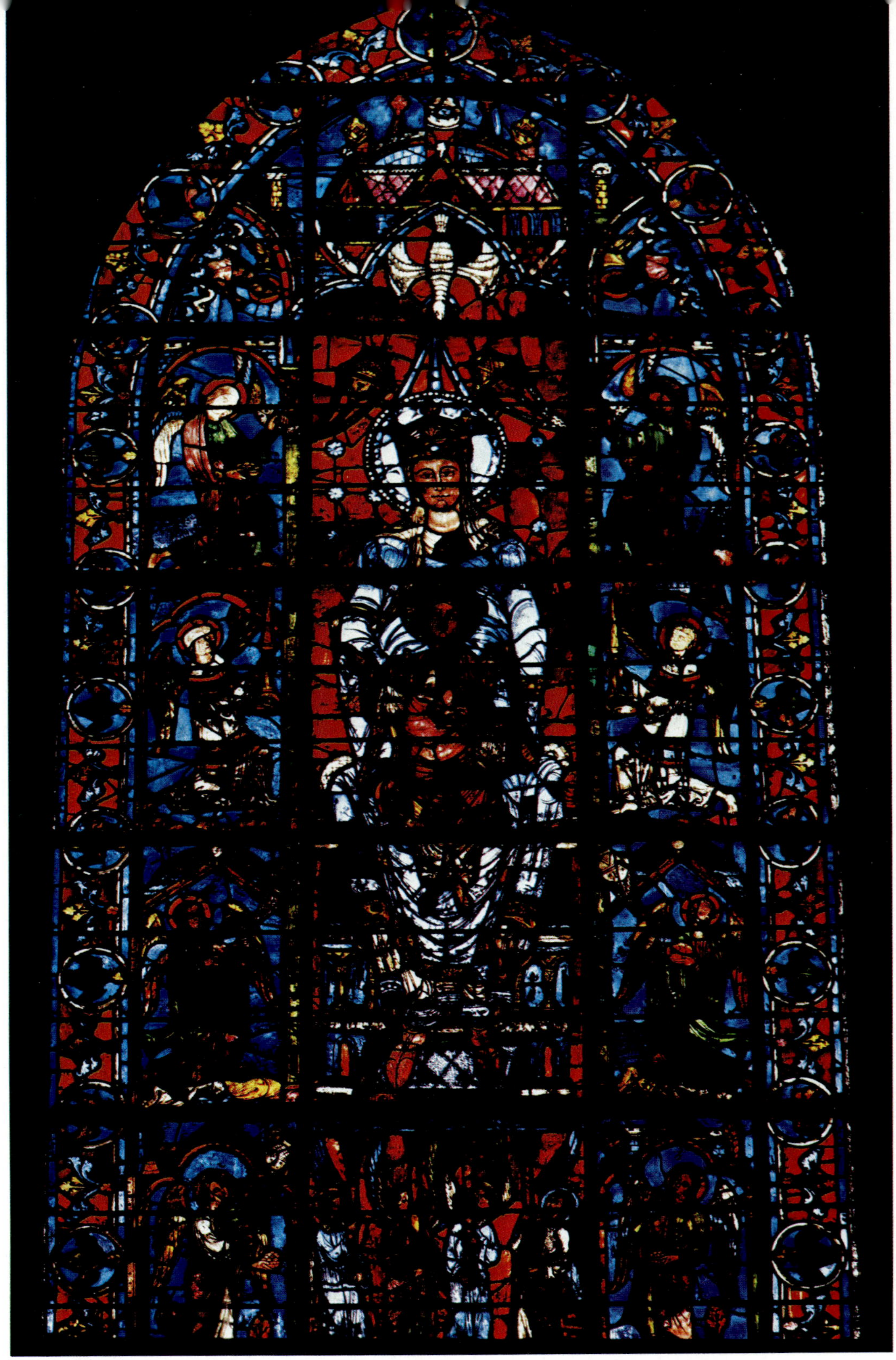

 Plate 14 *Notre Dame de Belle Verrière,* Chartres Cathedral. Early 13th century.

mosaic. His was an entirely different conception. The choice of a vertical format permitted Altdorfer to devote the top half of his picture to a brilliant landscape extension with sea and clouds. Over the whole image floats an inscription describing the epochal significance of the event. The lower half is filled with swirling masses of tiny figures. With his "long-shot" composition, the painter has chosen to stress not so much the individual combatants as the collective meaning of the whole. The depiction of the scenery in the upper half—above all the sun breaking through the clouds and outshining the pale moon in the upper left corner—trumpets forth the cosmic significance of the battle as a turning point in the history of the world.

Altdorfer does not try to show Alexander's troops in ancient armor, even though a good deal was known about this subject at the time the picture was painted. Instead, he presents his figures in the armor and equipment of his own day. Such modernizations were a recognized convention in the Renaissance.

The Portrait

Another major artistic genre, the **portrait**, is an image of a human being that captures the main characteristics of the personality. A portrait may present the whole body or confine itself to the face or to the head and shoulders. In any case, some revelation of the sitter's personality is essential.

Such an impression of character is charmingly created in the portrait of Henry Pelham, known as *Boy with a Squirrel* [126] by John Singleton Copley (1738–1815). The painter highlights the boy's face, seen in profile, against a dark curtain. The presence of the sitter's pet squirrel emphasizes what the two have in common—their liveliness and curiosity—as well as what they do not share—the boy's vastly greater sensitivity and intelligence. The youth-

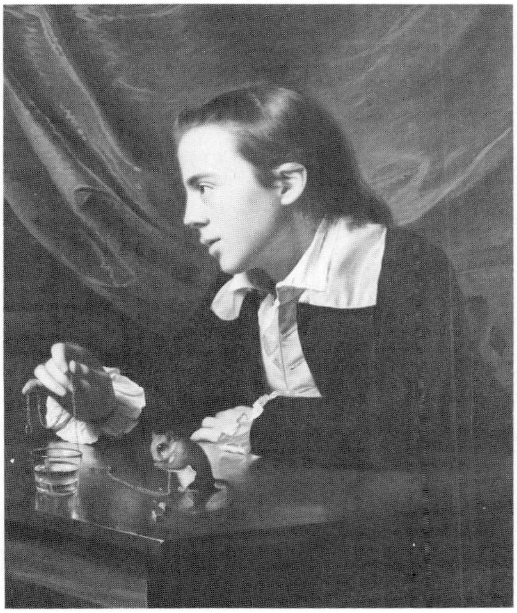

126 John Singleton Copley. *Boy with a Squirrel (Henry Pelham).* c. 1765. Oil on canvas, 9¾" × 11¾" (25 × 30 cm). Museum of Fine Arts, Boston (anonymous gift).

ful exuberance of the boy is conveyed also by the dynamic balance of the composition. Copley has deliberately chosen not to place his sitter stiffly in the center of the canvas. Rather, Master Pelham dominates the right side and center, while the left is counterbalanced by the jutting table on which rests the sitter's hand, the squirrel, and the glass of water.

Some Western European artists have also cultivated a special type of portraiture in which they depict themselves. Two *self-portraits* by Dutch artists of different periods show how very different personalities can be revealed in such paintings. Judith Leyster (1609–1660) shows herself taking a short break from creating one of her characteristic pictures, a merry fiddler, which is visible to the right [127]. This work belongs to the 17th-century **Baroque** style, with its emphasis on dramatic presentation, elaborate ornament, and extravagant form. Leyster's head is turned sharply, and the textures of the ruff and sleeves are deliberately contrasted. She appears as the successful professional who clearly enjoys practicing her craft. Leyster's self-portrait exudes the solid contentment that comes from being at ease with one's self and one's work.

In contrast, the self-portrait of Vincent van Gogh (1853–1890) [128] reveals a deeply troubled personality. In this painting, executed just a year before the artist's suicide, the long furrow-like strokes of the shirt and the background set off the anxious but luminous features of the face. By including his palette, van Gogh, like Leyster, emphasizes his craft. But unlike Leyster's face, van Gogh's is gaunt, tormented, and despairing. Indeed, the suggestion of a halo produced by the strokes that curve around the head may

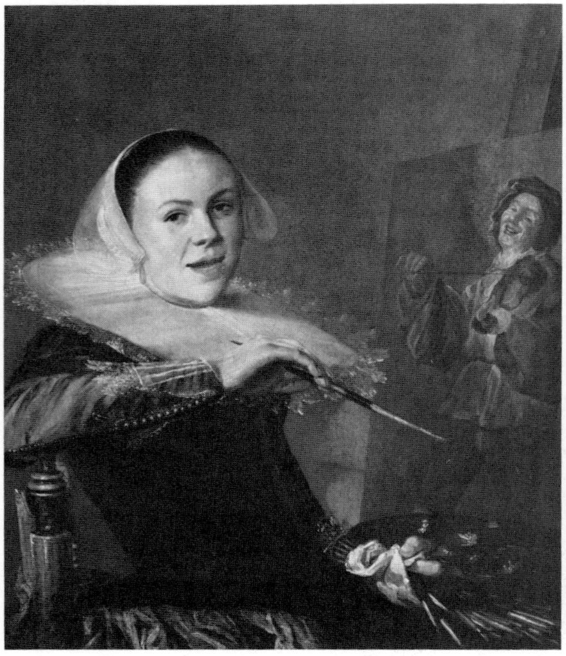

below left: 127
Judith Leyster. *Self-Portrait.* c. 1635. Oil on canvas, 29⅜ × 25⅝" (72 × 65 cm). National Gallery of Art, Washington (gift of Mr. and Mrs. Robert Woods Bliss, 1949).

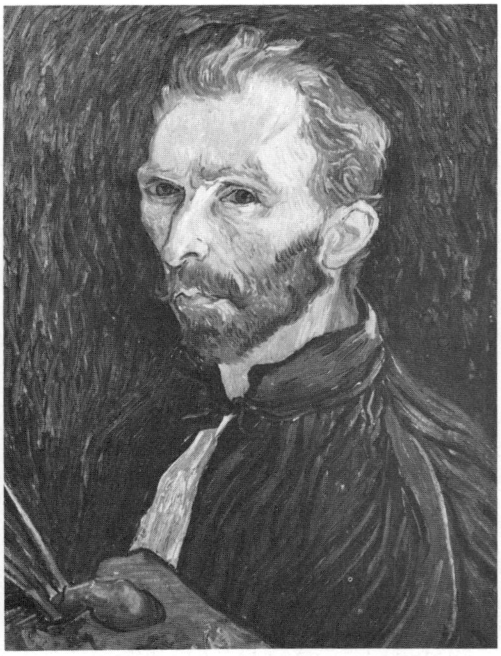

below right: 128
Vincent van Gogh. *Self-Portrait.* 1889. Oil on canvas, 22½ × 17¼" (57 × 44 cm). Collection of Mrs. John Hay Whitney.

imply the artist's intense dedication to his art, even a feeling of martyrdom. At their best, then, portraits can capture not only the likeness but also the temperament of the subject.

Landscape Painting

Another artistic genre, the presentation of natural scenes, appeared occasionally among the Greeks and Romans and in the Middle Ages. But as a special genre, **landscape painting** came into its own only in the 16th century, when the Renaissance had reawakened powerful curiosity about the environment. Interest in presenting landscape dominates Pieter Brueghel the Elder's *Fall of Icarus* [see Figure 59, page 79]. The artist carefully included the tilled field in the left foreground as well as the wonderful twists and turns of the seacoast and its bordering towns, fields, and hills in the background. The chief purpose of this painting was to present a story from classical mythology, yet the panoramic landscape upstages the myth.

In the 17th century many Dutch artists yielded completely to the seductions of the natural world. These painters created some of the finest of all pure landscapes, pictures without the pretext of some other formal subject. Jacob van Ruysdael (1628–1682) in his *View near Haarlem* [129] shows the gently rolling countryside of the Netherlands, modified by the patient toil of many generations of farmers and builders. Dominating the upper two-thirds of the canvas is the dramatic sky, an area as yet uninvaded by modern science and technology, and therefore still capable of symbolizing the supremacy of

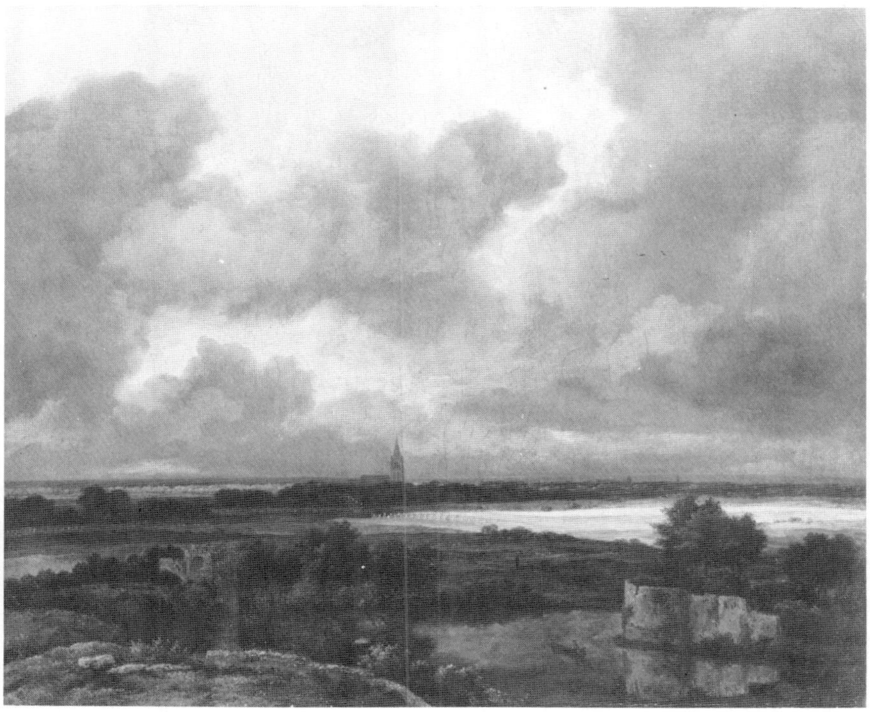

129 Jacob van Ruysdael. *View near Haarlem.* 1665–1675. Oil on canvas, 13⅜ × 15¾" (34 × 40 cm). National Gallery, London (reproduced by courtesy of the Trustees).

the natural order. Van Ruysdael's mastery of technique enables him to interweave both linear and aerial perspective, creating a subtle and harmonious scene.

A second high point in the history of landscape painting was reached by the 19th-century movements of **Impressionism** and **Postimpressionism** in France. Paul Cézanne (1839–1906) celebrated his native countryside in the south of France with a series of landscape paintings that present the strong patterns created by fields, mountains, and rocks baked in the sun. *Mountains in Provence* [Plate 13, page 221] is painted in warm earth colors—brown, orange, red, gray, and green. Some of these colors merge or flow into each other through subtle shading—for instance, the greens, yellows, and grays of the trees at the center. Other small color patches are separated from each other by definite outlines, particularly the grays of the rocks in the foreground. The jagged contours of these outcroppings verge on the geometric and abstract. They establish a feeling of the inner solidity of nature, of the underlying structure of the world—a structure that lies, so to speak, just beneath the skin of reality. While the fluid merging of the colors in the trees hints at the changes or flux in nature, the sharply defined contours of the rocks convey an even greater sense of the fundamental permanence and integrity of nature—qualities that Cézanne sought to enshrine in his art.

Paradoxically, then, although landscape is seemingly concerned solely with the outside world, with "objective reality," it often expresses a great deal about the feelings of the artist. No less than history paintings or portraits, landscapes are a reinterpretation of reality.

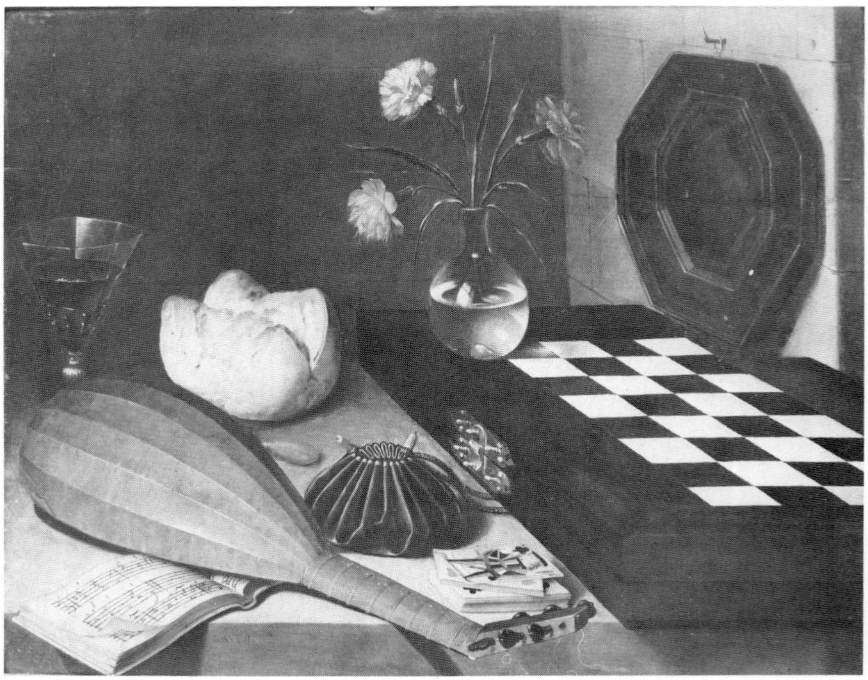

130 Baugin. *Still Life with Chessboard.* c. 1640. 21⅝″ × 28¾″ (54 × 72 cm). Louvre, Paris.

Still Life

The genre of **still life** focuses exclusively on objects of everyday life. As in many landscapes, human figures do not appear at all. But instead of offering us a great panorama of nature's bounty, still life deliberately restricts itself to narrow confines. We might say that still lifes are the piano sonatas, as distinct from the symphonies, of art.

The *Still Life with Chessboard* by a French artist of the 17th century known to us only as Baugin (c. 1610–1663) is richer than some [130]. Except for the flowers, all the objects shown are made by human agency. Some are forms of nourishment—the bread and the wine—and others are amusements—the lute and the music, the cards and the chessboard. Perhaps these objects were chosen because they all relate to the five senses—sight, hearing, taste, touch, and smell. This is a characteristic still life, a subtle glorification of modest objects which contrasts various shapes, colors, and textures, and which contributes to our enjoyment of daily life.

The genre of still life has also appealed to modern artists. Since the intrinsic interest of the subject matter is not strong, artists can concentrate on the formal manipulation of the shapes and colors of the objects on the canvas. *Still Life: The Table* [131] by Georges Braque (1882–1963) shows, clockwise from the lower center, two pieces of fruit on a plate, a glass, a guitar, an open book, a bottle, a pitcher, and a napkin. These objects appear on a table that is tilted forward, though it is standing upright in a room suggested by the vague shapes around the edges of the canvas. True to the Cubist style in which

below: 131 Georges Braque. *Still Life: The Table.* 1928. Oil on canvas, 2′8″ × 4′3½″ (.8 × 1.3 m). National Gallery of Art, Washington (Chester Dale Collection).

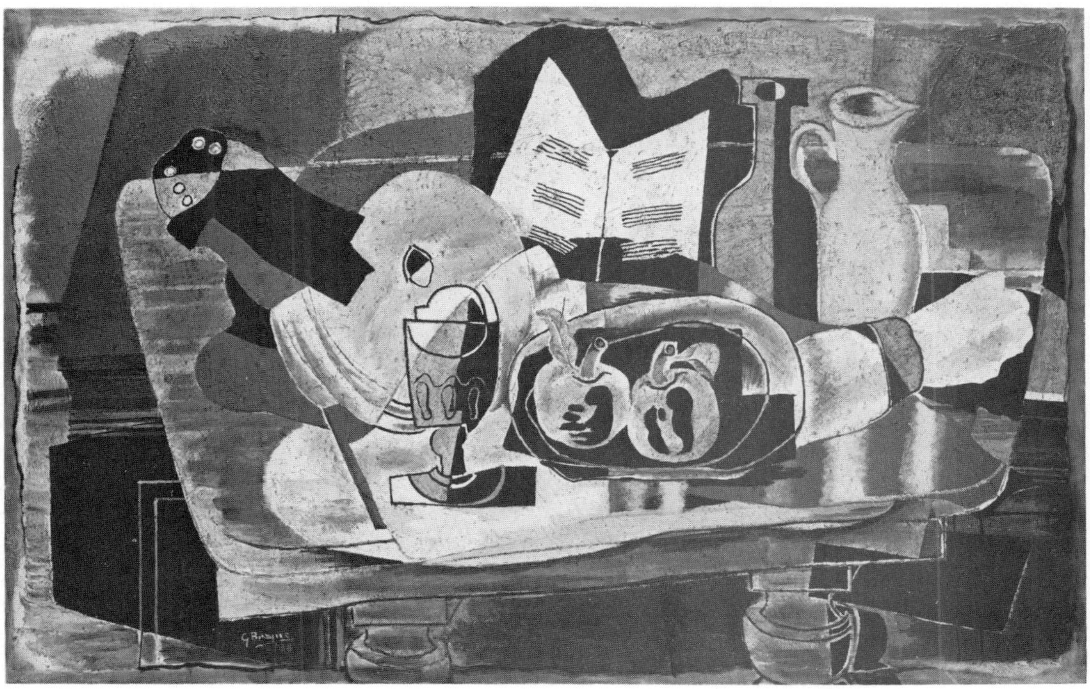

Braque was working, the painting stresses the interplay of formal shapes, especially geometric ones. The painting may, in fact, be regarded primarily as a study in the contrast of sinuous, curving elements—ovals or parts of ovals—which dominate the central area, with angular elements that become more important as the eye moves toward the four sides of the canvas.

Photography

As might be expected, some genres of photography closely resemble those of painting. A counterpart to history painting is photojournalism or social documentation, while portraits, landscapes, and still lifes are also genres of photography. However, other genres, such as performance and fashion photography, are distinctive to this art form.

Photojournalism and Social Documentation

Among the earliest types of photography, *photojournalism* uses the camera to record local, national, or world events. Though we take such pictures for granted whenever we open a newspaper or magazine, they can be regarded as a separate genre. One of the first major photojournalists, Mathew Brady (1823–1896) captured images of the Civil War in the United States with great skill and immediacy. So intimately was he involved in the military action he was photographing that he was nearly killed in the Battle of Bull Run. And so overwhelmed was he by the task he had set for himself that he hired teams of other photographers, including the talented Timothy H. O'Sullivan (1840–1882), with whom he produced over seven thousand negatives. Their work is

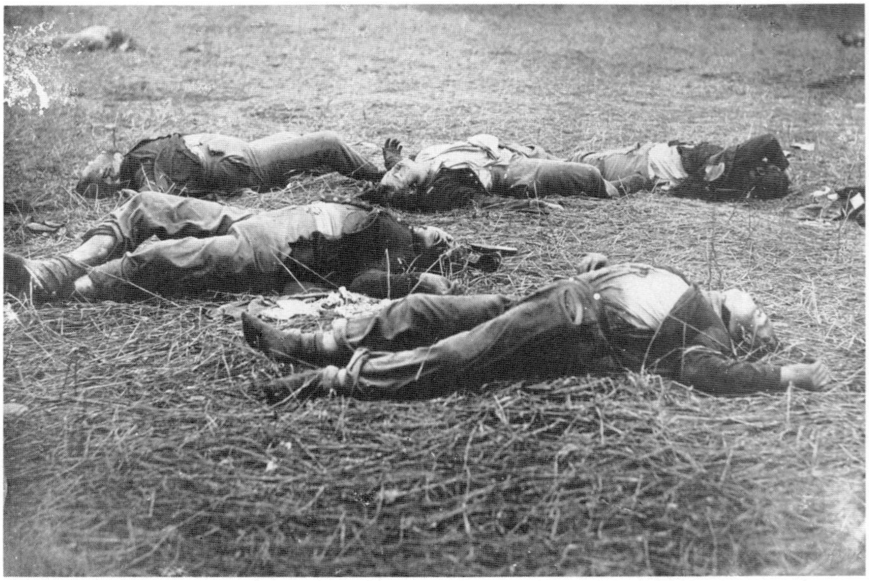

132 Timothy H. O'Sullivan. *Federal Dead After First Day of Gettysburg*. 1863. Photograph. Library of Congress, Washington.

exemplified by the picture of the battle scene [132], in which the corpses on the field give a vivid impression of the brutality and waste of warfare.

After 1897, when advances in technology made possible the printing of photographs on high-speed presses, a wider public became accustomed to seeing photographs. Most newspaper pictures tend to be records of fact rather than works of art. Yet artistic skill is involved in the creation of certain powerful images—the half-starved faces of children who survived the concentration camps of World War II, the anguished expressions of both the Asians and the United States soldiers fighting in Vietnam. The choice of moment, composition, and lighting contributes to the effectiveness of the whole.

Photojournalism and other photographs that make social conditions their subject are known as *social documentation.* In the Depression of the 1930s, United States government agencies commissioned pictures of the deplorable living conditions of sharecroppers, migrant workers, and farmers, who were suffering both from a terrible drought and from the collapse of the economy. The best of these photographers succeeded in doing more than simply recording reality. Dorothea Lange (1895–1965), for example, hauntingly presents the human suffering of the Depression in her *Migrant Mother* [133] by emphasizing the intense worry and stoic dignity of the farm worker and the pathos of the two small children who cling to her for comfort. With a remarkable eye for composition, Lange has concentrated on the three figures—the mother full-face in the center and the two children at her shoulders, heads turned away, in dynamic balance at either side. Other photographers have given similar attention to urban scenes—to the deprivation and despair in slums and factories. Fulfilling what we have called the gadfly role of art, they appeal to the conscience of the viewer. Indeed, much social documentation has as its aim the improvement of society.

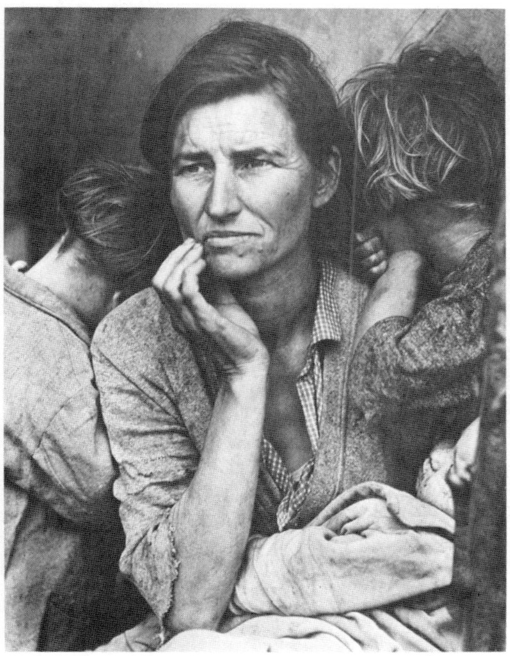

133 Dorothea Lange. *Migrant Mother, Nipomo, California.* 1936. Photograph. Oakland Museum, Oakland (Dorothea Lange Collection, 1985).

Portrait Photography

We tend to think of photographs as giving a highly accurate rendering of their subject. But the choice of pose and gesture, the lighting and camera angle, as well as the developing and printing are all means of shaping the image, emphasizing some aspects and understating others. With such variables available, portraits of the sitter depend on the artist's interpretation of the subject's personality.

The noted British photographer Cecil Beaton (1904–1980), who specialized in pictures of theatrical and social celebrities, idealized the actress Greta Garbo [134] by the angle as well as the dramatic lighting of his shot, making her far more glamorous and intriguing than a mere mortal could possibly be. In contrast, the Canadian portrait photographer Yousuf Karsh (b. 1908)—far from idealizing his subject—concentrated on the dominant but not entirely attractive qualities of Winston Churchill's personality [135]. In order to capture the former Prime Minister's characteristic gruffness and belligerence, Karsh, so the story goes, snatched Churchill's habitual cigar and then quickly shot his subject's disgruntled scowl.

below left: 134 Cecil Beaton. *Greta Garbo.* 1946. Photograph. Courtesy Sotheby's, London.

below right: 135 Yousuf Karsh. *Winston Churchill.* 1941. Photograph. © Karsh, Ottawa.

Nature Photography

The equivalent of landscape and still life in painting, nature photography can present both natural scenes and close-ups of selected objects such as fruit and flowers. Here again, not the recording of reality but its interpretation is important. In his *Monolith, the Face of Half-Dome, Yosemite* [136], Ansel

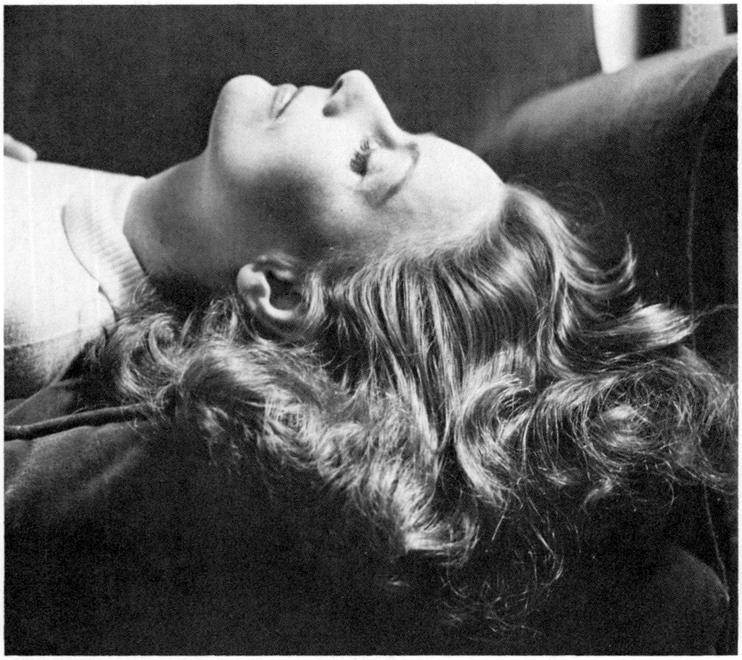

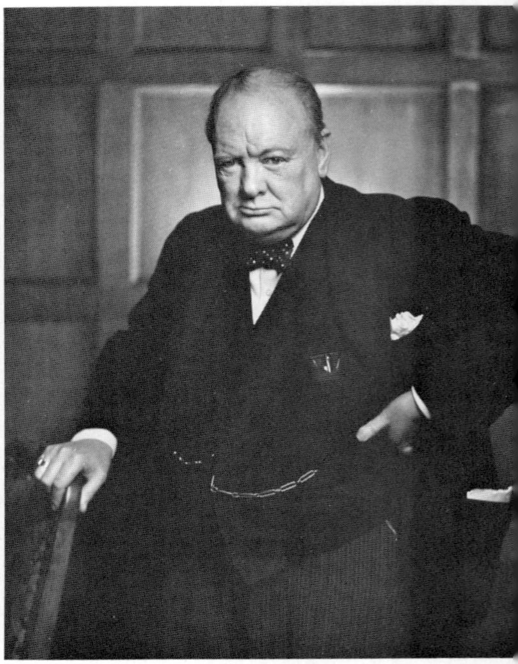

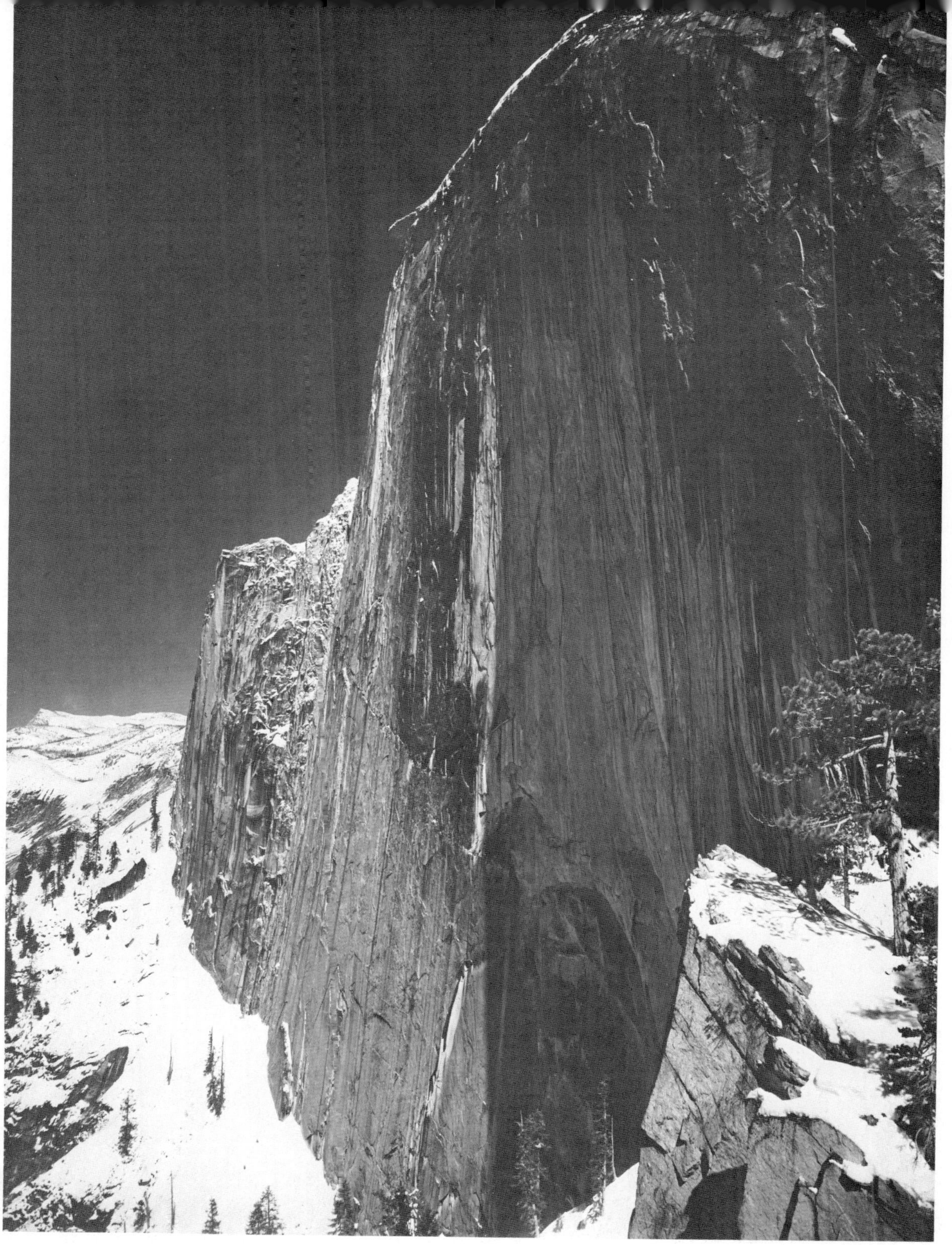

136 Ansel Adams. *Monolith, the Face of Half-Dome, Yosemite National Park.* 1927. Photograph.

Adams (1902–1984), who is famous for capturing the beauty of unspoiled nature, conveys the power and magnificence of the mountain by the composition of the picture. The mountain dominates the photograph, filling it from top to bottom, and the two sides of Half-Dome come together at the precise center. In focusing the image, Adams achieves subtle contrasts between the sharpness of the vertical striations on the central rock and the slight blurring of the rocks near the top. In addition, Adams uses both the exposure and the development of the film to vary the shading, which ranges from black to white, with intermediate grays. So concerned was Adams with controlling the image that he even devised a special system to determine how to achieve exactly the desired light and shade in the finished print.

Performance and Fashion Photography

Together with social scenes, portraits, and nature, certain other subjects such as performances and fashion have become special genres of photography. Those who concentrate on such pictures are sometimes called *professional photographers,* but this term is misleading because all the photographers we have considered so far are professionals who have made a career of their art and may well benefit financially from their work.

Photographing a performance—whether a play, dance, or opera—

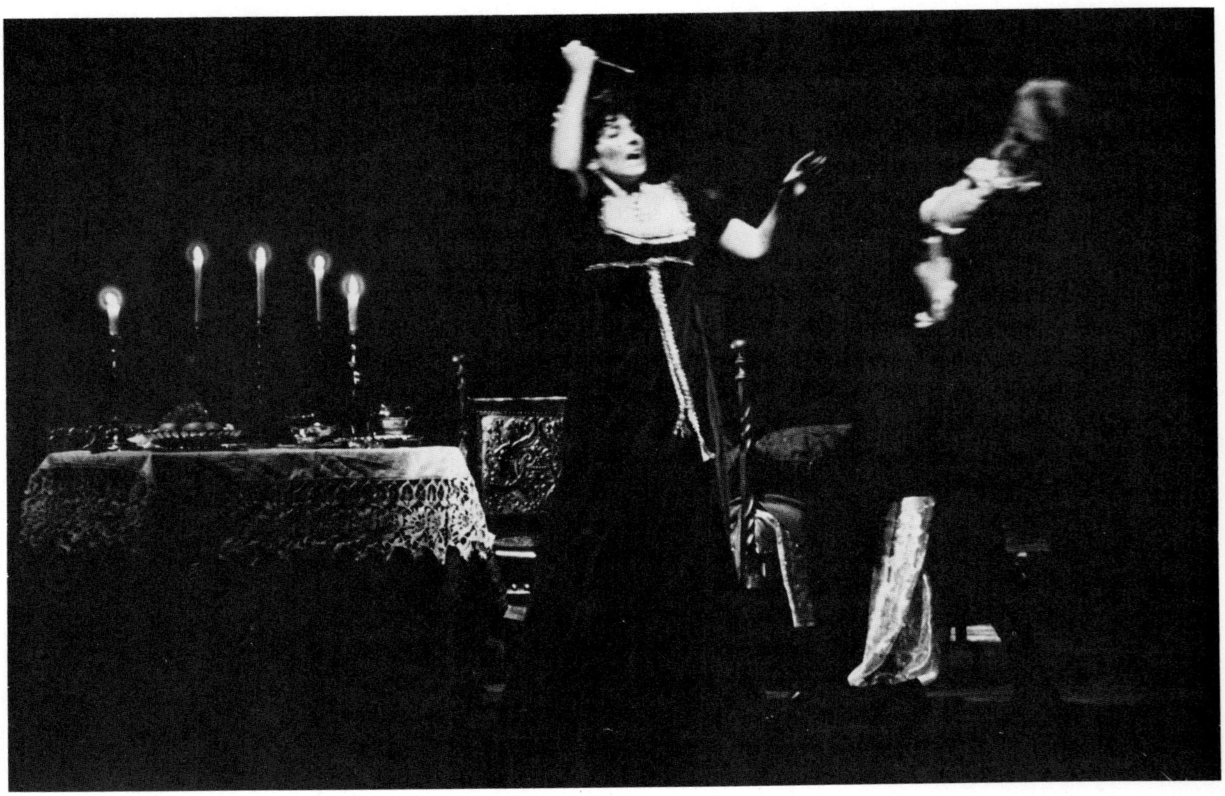

137 Anthony Crickmay. Maria Callas and Tito Gobbi in *Tosca,* at the Royal Opera House at Covent Garden, London. 1964. Photograph.

presents a particular challenge: the essence of the whole performance must be caught in a single image. Consequently, the best of such photographs are, again, more than records; they convey the spirit of the work. In his photograph [137] of the opera *Tosca* (1900) by Giacomo Puccini (1858—1924), Anthony Crickmay has carefully chosen not the climactic moment when the heroine actually thrusts a knife into her tormentor, nor the subsequent great one when he lies writhing at her feet, but the moment after she has struck him and he is reeling backwards. Moreover, the photographer has brilliantly conveyed the fiery temperament of the soprano Maria Callas (1923–1977), who was an extraordinarily powerful actress as well as singer. Finally, he has deliberately blurred the figure of her victim to suggest the rush of movement in this highly charged scene. Altogether, this performance photograph gives a vivid impression both of the opera's plot and of the personality of the opera star.

Certain photographers specialize in such commercial subjects as automobiles, food, cosmetics, and clothing. Often their pictures do little more than promote the sale of these goods. However, the work of some fashion photographers has been recognized as having definite artistic merit. What distinguishes such photographs is the special interpretation of the subject and the imaginative use of technical resources. A delightful and complex example can be seen in *Monique Knowlton and Babies* [138] by Bert Stern (b. 1929), which appeared in *Vogue* magazine to advertise a formal black gown.

Instead of focusing on the dress, Stern has created a study in contrasts. A tall, slender, elaborately dressed woman is contrasted with small, pudgy, naked children. In addition, the dignified, formal pose of Monique Knowlton is contrasted with the charmingly spontaneous positions of the babies. Implied are further contrasts between femininity and masculinity (or asexuality), sophistication and naiveté, fashion and nature. These contrasts are unified by the strong dynamic balance of the composition. The figure of the woman, not quite at the center of the picture, is balanced by three children on her right and two on her left, while one lies prone directly in front of her. Together, the woman and children form a distinct triangle, whose two long sides are in part defined by the woman's extended arms.

The photograph demonstrates careful attention not only to the composition but also to the distinctive expressions of the figures. Each reveals a different personality, as if this were a group portrait. From the gracious, restrained smile of Monique Knowlton to the coy, outraged, quizzical, and self-absorbed looks of the children, the photographer has suggested a whole gamut of human reactions.

Finally, as an added twist, the photograph reminds us subtly of earlier images of a beautiful woman surrounded by chubby, naked babies. These echoes of Venus with cupids [see Figure 109, page 191] cleverly reinforce the glamour of the whole.

The types of photography we have just considered do not exhaust the possible categories of this medium. Still, enough has been said to make clear that photographs, like paintings, do not merely mirror real life but shape and interpret it according to the vision of the artist.

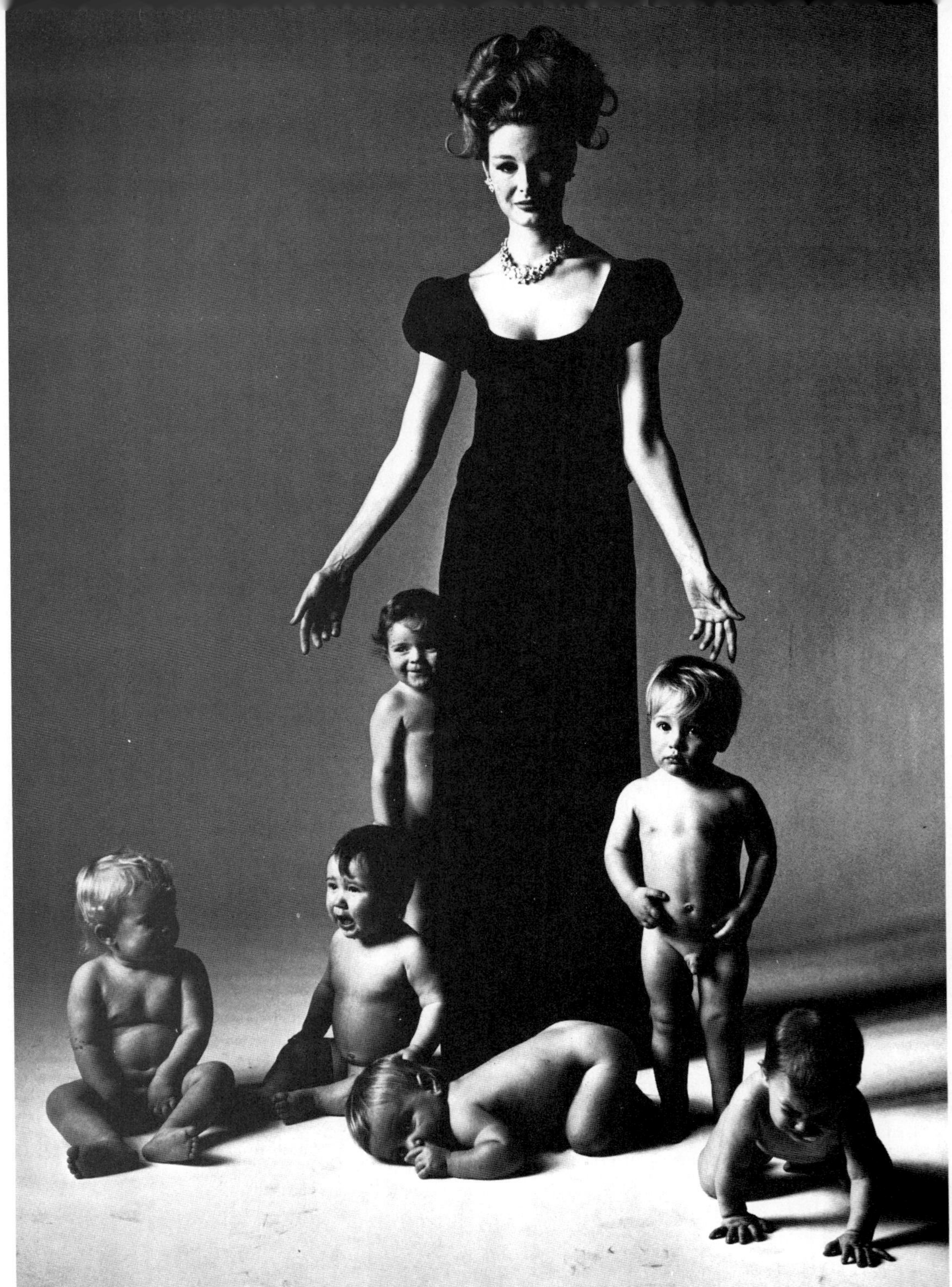

138 Bert Stern. *Monique Knowlton and Babies.* 1962. *Vogue.*

Sculpture

The genres of sculpture do not coincide exactly with those of painting or photography, perhaps because sculpture is less able to present the many details required by such genres as history painting, photojournalism, and landscape. Yet the durability and imposing character of sculpture make it especially suitable for certain kinds of portraiture, for religious figures, and for civic monuments.

Portraiture: The Bust and Full-Figure Sculpture

Like painting and photography, sculpture can present portraits. A sculptured portrait that is restricted to the head and upper torso of a figure is known as a **bust.** Presenting the head and shoulders, severed from the rest of the body, has become a convention of sculpture that may seem strange, but is understandable when we consider that the face is the most distinctive and expressive part of the anatomy. Indeed, like any other portrait, the bust seeks to express the personality of the original. Bernini's portrait of Louis XIV of France [139] clearly captures the arrogant personal style of the monarch. The sculptor has dispensed with the attributes of royalty—the scepter, crown, and elaborate robes—preferring to convey the ruler's power by the extravagant curls of the hair and the upswept drapery.

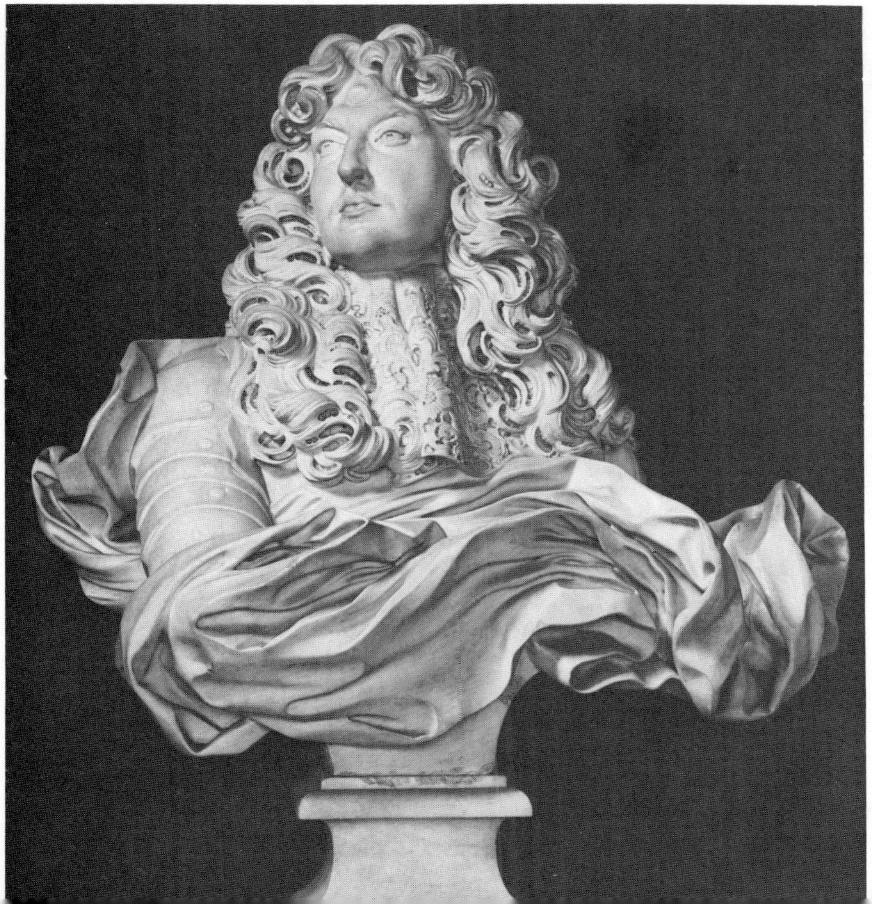

139 Gian Lorenzo Bernini. *Louis XIV.* 1665. Marble, height 33 1/8" (84 cm). Palace of Versailles.

As important as the bust is the *full-figure sculpture,* which shows all of the body, whether naked or clothed. In this genre, the sculptor can further express the personality of the subject by the posture of the body. For example, in his *David* [see Figure 36, page 44], Michelangelo presents the muscular grace and strength of the young hero through the body as much as a calm self-assurance through the face. In its relaxed pose, this figure gives a harmonious, idealized image of the masculine figure. Bernini, in his *David* [see Figure 34, page 43] uses the tension and vigorous movement of the body to reinforce the intense concentration of the face. This is a study in motion—all the more remarkable because it is frozen in stone.

Religious Sculpture

Because the statues of David represent an Old Testament figure, they also belong to the genre of religious sculpture. However, Michelangelo's and Bernini's *Davids* are types of humanity rather than sacred figures. Works that are more clearly intended as religious statues often have special attributes and conform to particular conventions.

In ancient civilizations, some sculptors were so successful in representing a god or goddess that the statue came to be worshipped. Such a statue, associated with a specific place, is known as a *cult image.* The Aphrodite of Praxiteles [see Figure 108, page 189], also called the *Aphrodite of Cnidos,* is an example, for it was revered in a special shrine at Cnidos. The *Venus de Milo* [see Figure 4, page 5] may also have been a cult image. Both figures are, appropriately, larger than life and idealized in their beauty. Cult images were

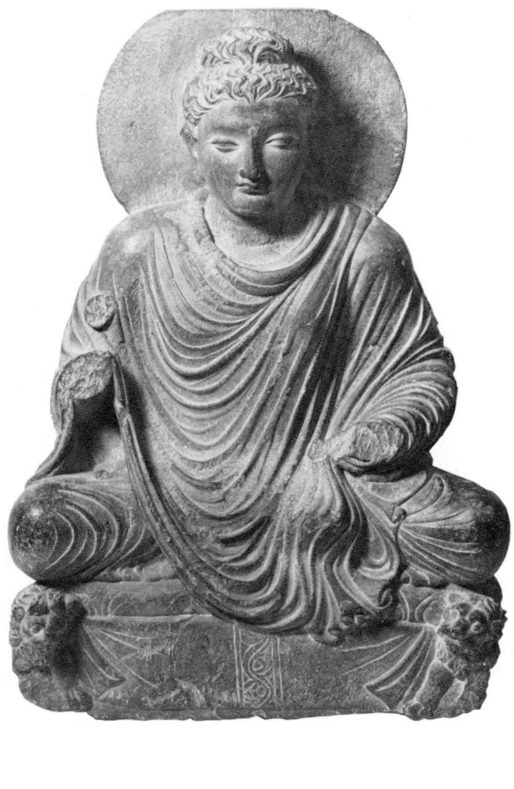

140 Seated Buddha, from Takht-i-Bāhi, Gandhāra. A.D. 100–200. Schist, height 20 ¼″ (52 cm). Museum für Indische Kunst, West Berlin. Staatliche Museen Preuszischer Kulturbesitz.

frequently the focus of the temples that housed them and are, therefore, examples of sculpture intimately related to architecture.

Whether or not such statues are regarded as sacred, they represent a key figure of their religion and try to express some of its fundamental beliefs. The statue of the Buddha from Afghanistan [140] of about the 3rd century A.D., created for a temple niche, shows the revered teacher who lived in India in the 5th century B.C. In a position traditionally associated with him, he is seated in calm repose, with his eyes half-closed. His serene and meditative expression suggests the blissful absence of individual feeling that is the goal of Buddhism. His holiness is further conveyed both by a kind of halo and by the turban-like bump at the top of his head, which symbolizes his more-than-mortal knowledge. This swelling at the top of the cranium, together with the small circular mark between his brows, is not a deformity nor an individual trait, but a convention repeated in many carvings of the Buddha.

Christian religious sculpture also has its recurring figures and conventions. The Virgin Mary and Jesus are the most familiar, whether presented separately or together. Indeed, the most frequent subjects of Christian sculpture are this mother with her infant son, often called the "Madonna and Child"; Christ on the Cross, or the "Crucifixion"; and Mary holding the body of the crucified Christ, or the **"Pietà"** (Italian for "pity" and "piety"). In sculptures of the Virgin and the child Jesus, she is usually seated while her son can be either an infant in her arms or a slightly older boy, seated on her lap or standing near her, as in the medieval *Madonna and Child* [141]. In the modern version [142] by Sir Jacob Epstein (1880–1959), the Christ child, standing between his mother's knees, is still close to and, in a sense, sheltered

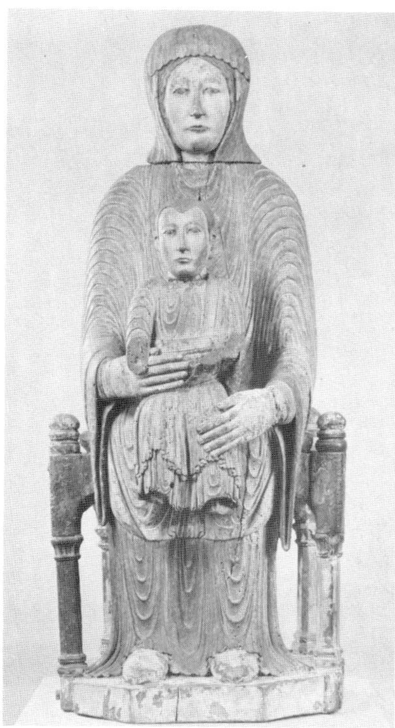

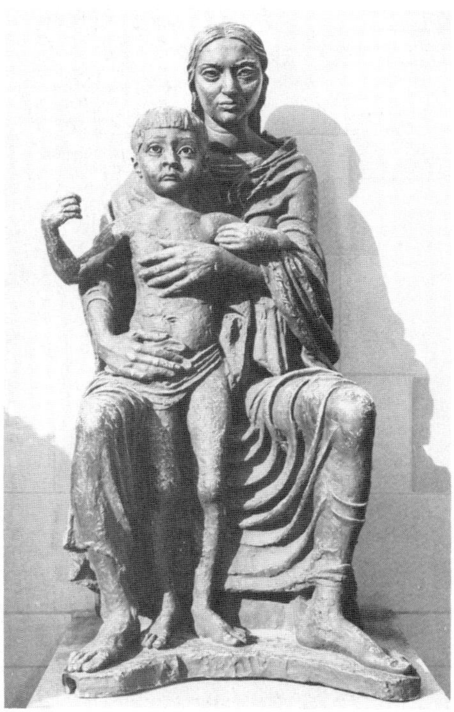

far left: 141 School of Auvergne. *Virgin and Child.* 12th century. Polychromed oak, height 31″ (79 cm). Metropolitan Museum of Art, New York (gift of J. Pierpont Morgan, 1916). This image of the Virgin and Child achieves a special solemnity and formality through the frontal placement of the figures and the symmetrical patterning of the garments. Seated on a throne, Mary provides a throne for her son, reflecting the great importance of the Virgin in medieval Christianity.

left: 142 Jacob Epstein. *Madonna and Child.* 1927. 66″ high and 31″ at base (165 × 77.5 cm). Riverside Church, New York.

by her. A poignant humanity is suggested not only by the warm relationship between the two figures but also by the human scale of the work. At the same time, something of the divinity of the child is indicated by the fact that he stands unsupported, facing outward, with his arms extended in a formal beckoning gesture. This formal gesture, together with a certain stiffness in both figures, deliberately recalls the formality and stiffness of earlier treatments of the subject, particularly in the Middle Ages. The Epstein statue reminds us that religious sculpture continues to use time-honored patterns, maintaining its vitality through its strong link with tradition.

Monumental or Civic Sculpture

Unlike religious works, which tend to be similar because they are shaped by a particular tradition, civic monuments take different forms because they can commemorate a variety of events in the life of a community.

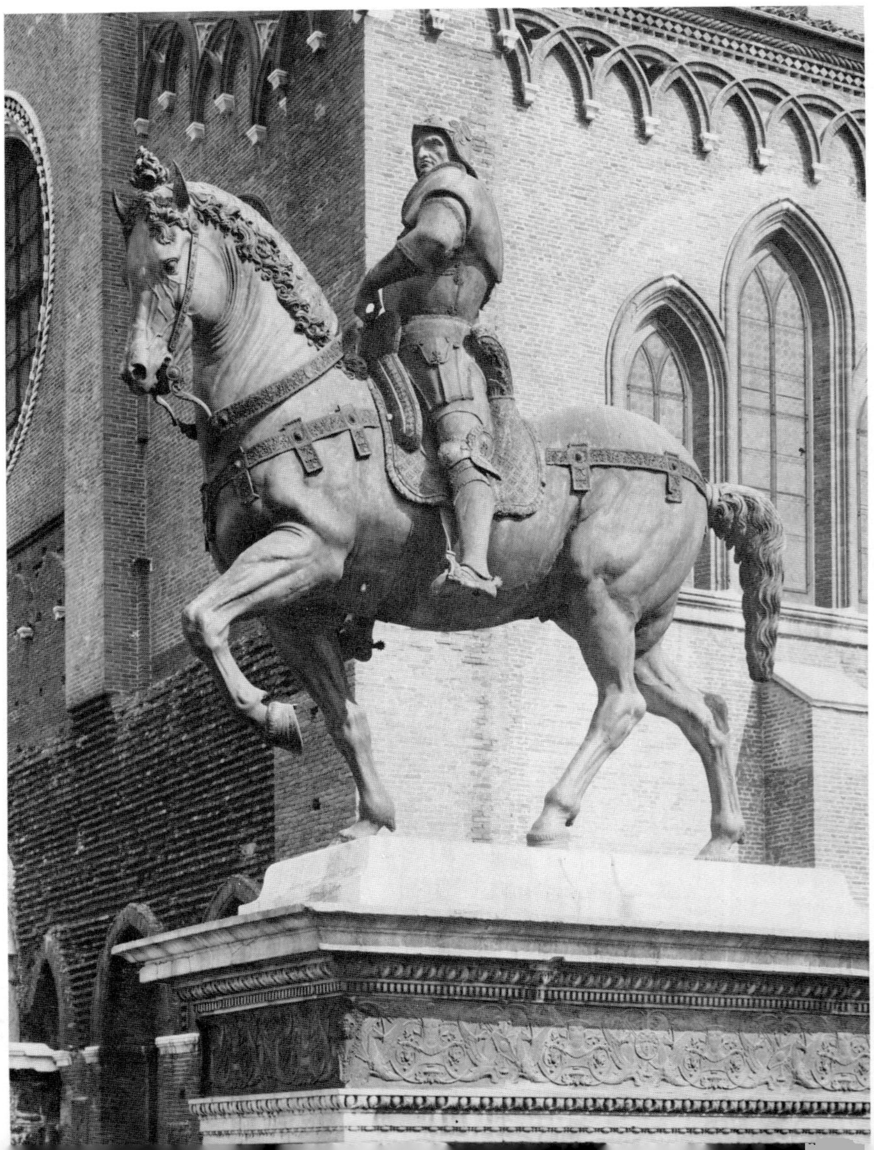

143 Andrea del Verrocchio. *Bartolomeo Colleoni.* c. 1483–1488. Bronze, height approximately 13′ (3.96 m). Campo dei Santi Giovanni e Paolo, Venice.

They may take the form of individual figures, groups, triumphal arches, and even gigantic, abstract constructions. They may commemorate civic leaders, military victories or defeats, and acts of heroism or self-sacrifice. In beautifying their surroundings, all such works are symbols of civic pride.

Nearly all civic monuments are placed outdoors. In order to be visible and imposing, they are large in scale and usually raised above the viewer on a pedestal or column. In order to withstand the weather, they are made of durable material such as marble or bronze.

A significant civic monument is the **equestrian statue**, showing a figure on horseback. In such a work, the power of the leader is emphasized by the size, strength, and nobility of the horse. Great artistic and technical skills are required to create so large and complex a piece. Artists of ancient Rome already knew how to cast memorable equestrian statues in bronze, and their work inspired several artists of the Italian Renaissance.

One of the liveliest equestrian statues is that of the Venetian military commander Bartolomeo Colleoni [143] by Andrea del Verrocchio (c. 1435–1488). The sculptor, though taking over the figure of a rider on horseback, has deliberately broken with the Roman tradition in one important respect: instead of presenting a likeness of the subject's face, he has distorted and exaggerated the features. Here the commander's eyes are wide and fiercely glaring, the nostrils are flared, and the mouth is turned down in disdain. This is a forceful image of the pride, not to say arrogance, of a leading personality of the Renaissance, an era known for its affirmation of the individual.

The *Colleoni* meets one of the greatest challenges of equestrian statues by conveying a remarkable sense of motion. This is achieved by the placement of the rider, who is turned so that his left shoulder is thrust energetically forward. In addition, the left foreleg of the horse is sharply bent and raised as if taking a step, while the hind legs seem about to make a sudden start. This dynamic presentation has been rarely surpassed, although some of Verrocchio's successors tried to outdo him. Leonardo da Vinci is known to have planned, but never executed, a colossal equestrian statue of the Duke of Milan, with both forefeet of the horse off the ground. The tradition of equestrian statues continues to our own day, as can be seen in many city squares, but few exhibit the dynamism and energy of Verrocchio's piece.

Civic leaders may be presented even more elaborately than on horseback. A widely known example is the statue [144] by Daniel Chester French (1850–1931) in the Lincoln Memorial in Washington, D.C. Unlike the *Colleoni,* with its exaggerated facial expression, the statue is remarkably true to life. Not only does it look like the Lincoln we know from photographs but it also conveys the kindness and humility associated with him. On the other hand, the larger-than-life size of the figure makes Lincoln appear heroic.

Surprisingly, this man, dressed in a 19th-century suit, sits in what is clearly a temple, a building designed by Henry Bacon (1866–1924). As such, he recalls the cult images we observed earlier, which were also housed in special shrines. The temple of the Lincoln Memorial is, in fact, a classical one, with rows of columns that bring to mind the architecture of ancient Greece and Rome [see Figure 44, page 50]. This choice of setting was, no doubt,

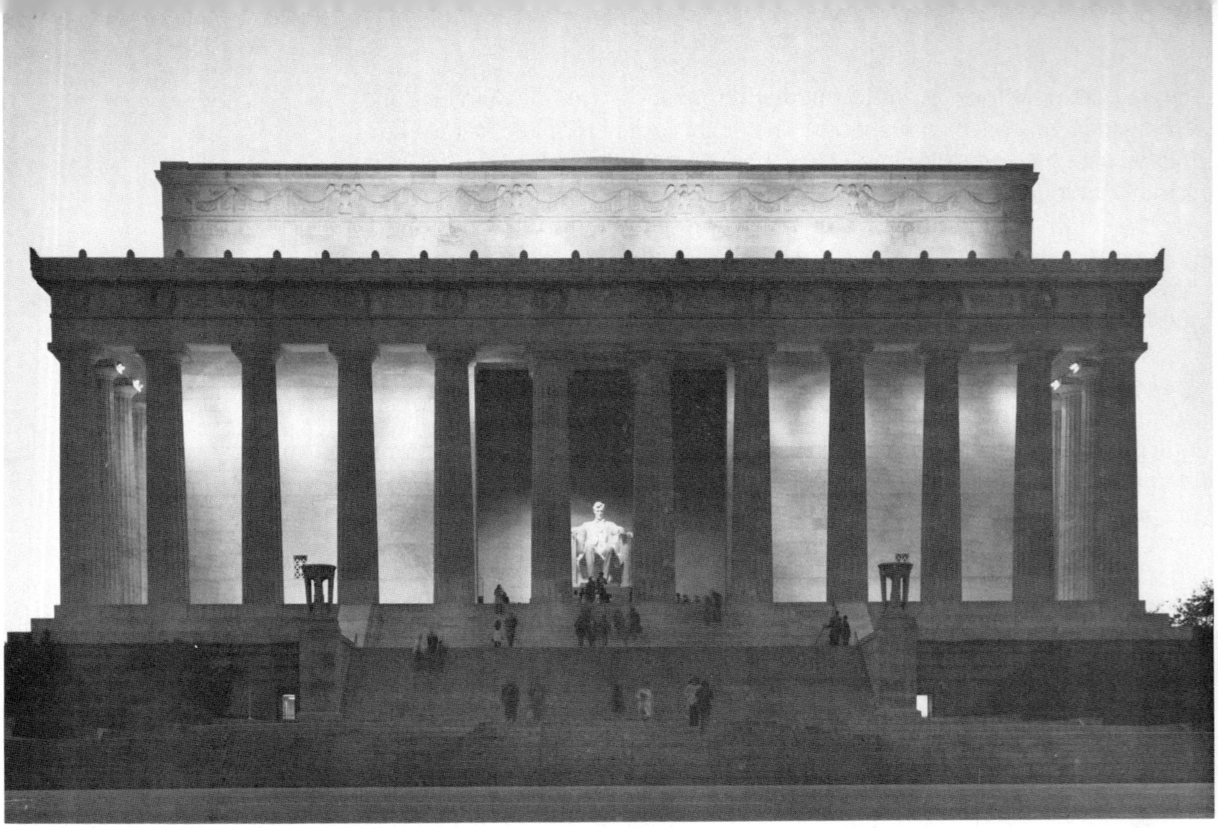

above: 144 Daniel Chester French. *Abraham Lincoln.* 1922. Lincoln Memorial. 1923. Washington, D.C.

intended to link the Republic of the United States, which Lincoln fought to preserve, with the great democracies of the ancient world. Here again, a work tries to draw symbolic significance from earlier traditions.

Civic sculpture continues to be created both on a local and a national level. Modern monuments tend, however, not to be equestrian statues or elaborate monuments such as the Lincoln Memorial. Rather, paralleling developments in modern painting, they are likely to be abstract and geometric.

In conclusion, we should recognize that unlike the genres of painting and photography, the genres of sculpture are not mutually exclusive. For instance, the *Colleoni* and French's *Lincoln* are both portrait sculptures and civic monuments. Nonetheless, a knowledge of the different genres of sculpture makes us aware of important traditions and of the distinctive ways in which each sculptor has worked within these traditions.

Architecture

The genres of architecture are not as universally recognized as those of painting and sculpture. Yet works of architecture can also be profitably subdivided into categories or *building types* such as churches, theaters, and railway stations. As we have seen, genres in painting and sculpture are determined by the subject matter of the work or its treatment. In architecture, however, building types are determined by function or use, for this affects such fundamental elements as the shape and size. We shall find that the designs of churches and theaters, for example, change over time, influenced by differing conceptions of their functions as well as by newly developed construction techniques. Consequently, although we can classify churches or theaters as genres of architecture, these are not as constant as, for instance, the genres of landscape painting or the sculptured bust.

Churches

Churches have often followed a particular design, for they must provide an appropriate setting for religious ceremonies and also accommodate large numbers of worshippers. A long-established design in church architecture is the **basilica**, which features a wide central aisle called the **nave**, a lower aisle on each side, and a semicircular alcove, or **apse**, that can occur at either or both ends. This design was adapted from the Roman forums, law courts, and other public buildings. Indeed, the general organization goes back to ancient Egypt, as we have seen in the Temple of Khonsu at Karnak [see Figure 43, page 49] with its rectangular passage flanked by columns.

Because of its capacity to hold large crowds, the basilica was adopted by the early Christians for major churches and cathedrals. One of the most notable examples is Old Saint Peter's Basilica [145, 146], the predecessor of the

below left: 145 Old Saint Peter's Basilica, Rome. c. A.D. 333. Reconstruction study by Kenneth J. Conant. Length of grand axis 835′ (255 m), width of transept 295′ (87 m).

below right: 146 Groundplan of Old Saint Peter's Basilica.

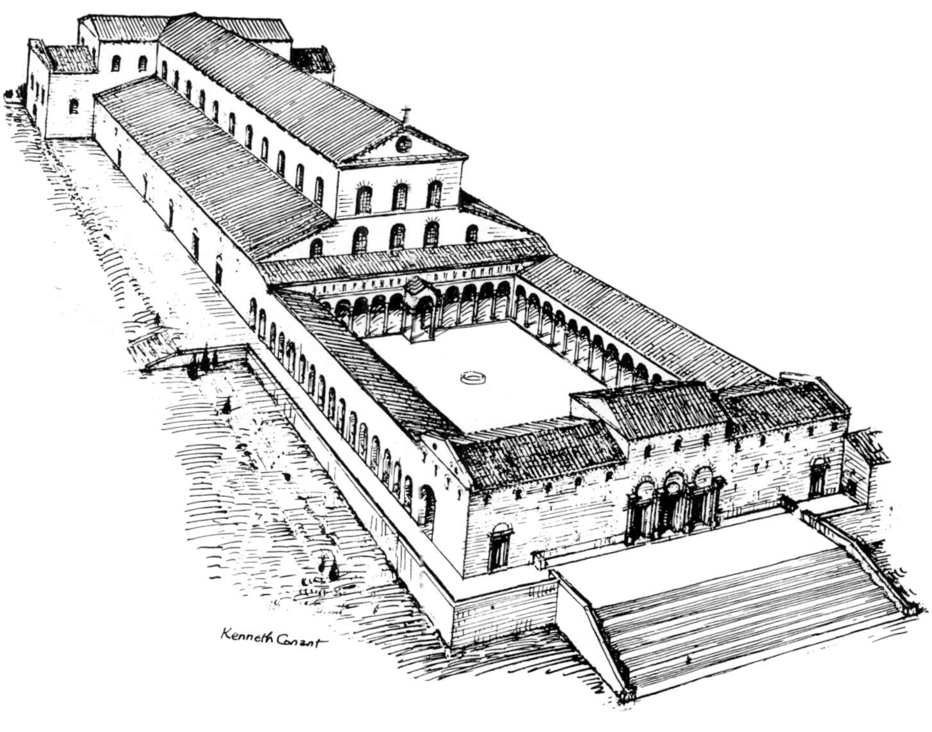

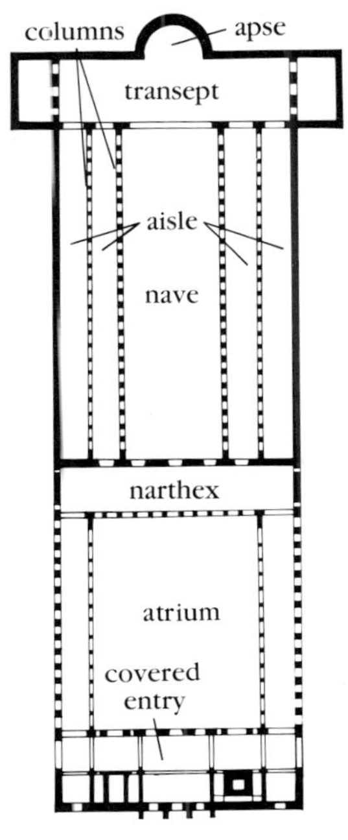

great Saint Peter's in Rome. Although we now know Old Saint Peter's only through drawings and descriptions, its plan was widely known and imitated in subsequent churches. The building complex was approached by a monumental flight of steps leading to a covered entryway. This, in turn, gave access to an open courtyard, the **atrium**, which led to the vestibule, or **narthex.** Only here did the basilica proper begin. The typical broad central nave was flanked, in this elaborate version of the basilica, by not one but two aisles on either side. Rows of columns separated the nave from the aisles and the aisles from each other. The main axis, which moved from east to west, was then interrupted by a large hall set perpendicular to both the nave and the aisles. This **transept**, which held the altar, formed a secondary north-south axis. The building ended in the semicircular apse that marked the conclusion of the main east-west axis. The apse, surmounted by a half-dome, served as an impressive backdrop to the altar.

The basilica design underwent significant changes and elaborations during the Middle Ages. The Gothic cathedrals, built largely from the 12th to the early 16th centuries and characterized, as we have seen, by pointed arches and flying buttresses [see Figures 50 and 51, pp. 54, 55], were even more spacious than the basilicas. Their transept is much broader, and their apse is expanded enormously. These enlarged spaces could accommodate a great number of worshippers at a time when the whole community attended religious services. The groundplan also resembles a cross, a central symbol of Christianity.

At Notre Dame of Chartres, one of the greatest Gothic cathedrals, the main façade is distinguished by two towers [147] that are not symmetrical because they were constructed over centuries. One enters through an elaborate triple doorway [148] that displays richly varied statuary, mainly of Old and New Testament figures. Inside, the nave [149] reaches the remarkable height of 122 feet, or 37.2 meters, giving a soaring quality to the whole. This nave is separated from the side aisles, which are less high, by rows of **piers**; each pier consists of what looks like a cluster of five columns.

As the groundplan of Chartres [150] reveals, the middle of the building is expanded by the great transept at right angles to the main axis, which forms a secondary north-south axis. This transept resembles the nave in that it has the same height and side aisles. Moreover, each end of the transept has its own entrance with elaborate sculpture similar to that of the main entrance, thereby increasing its nave-like appearance. The building is further complicated by the vast **choir**, which encompasses the whole area beyond the transept and has a nave-like central space where the original altar was placed. The central space of the choir is flanked by two side aisles. These merge into an open area at the end of the building, and here the exterior wall curves outward, forming five small semicircular chapels, each with its own altar.

The interior of Chartres is especially famous for its magnificent stained-glass windows. These tell various stories based on the Bible, saints' lives, and even secular legends such as the *Song of Roland.* One of the most beautiful, known as *Notre Dame de Belle Verrière* ("Our Lady of the Beautiful Window") [Plate 14, page 222], celebrates the Madonna to whom the cathedral is dedi-

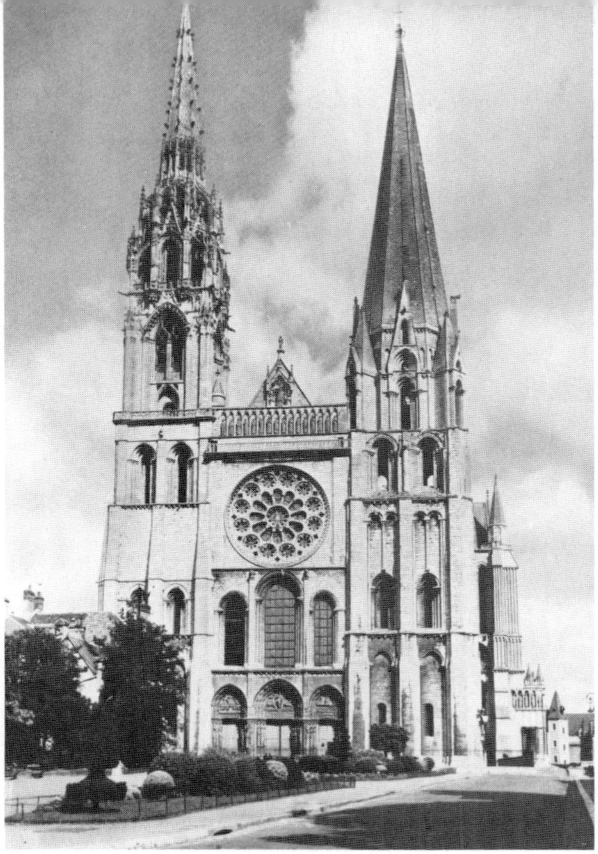

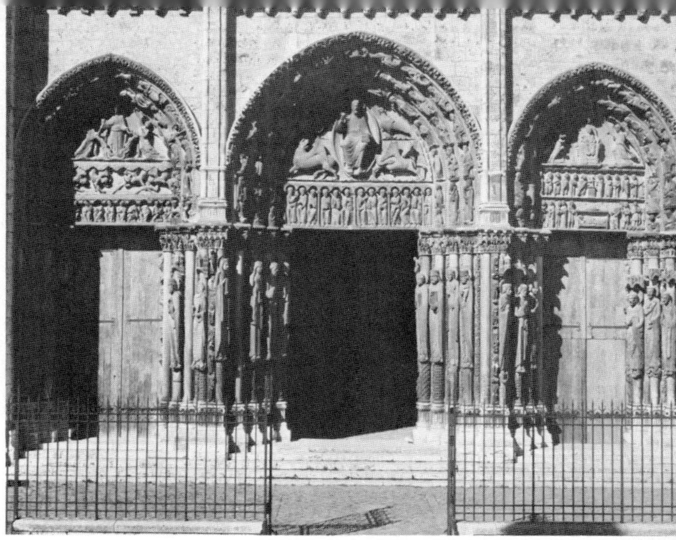

left: 147 West façade, Chartres Cathedral. 1194–1240.

above: 148 The Royal Portal, west façade, Chartres Cathedral. This highly decorated entrance presents, in the panels above the doors, three scenes central to the life of Christ: in the middle, Christ in majesty surrounded by the symbols of the four Evangelists; on the right, the Virgin holding the Christ child and other scenes of Christ's early life; on the left, the Ascension of Christ into heaven and other scenes of his last days on earth. Below, on the columns flanking the doors, are prophets and kings, probably from the Old Testament.

below: 149 Interior of Chartres Cathedral, showing side aisles and piers.

right: 150 Groundplan of Chartres Cathedral.

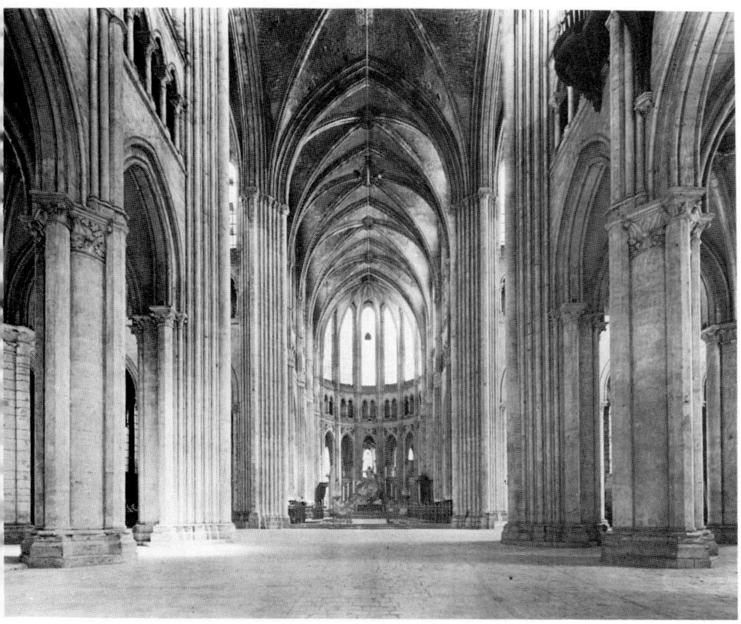

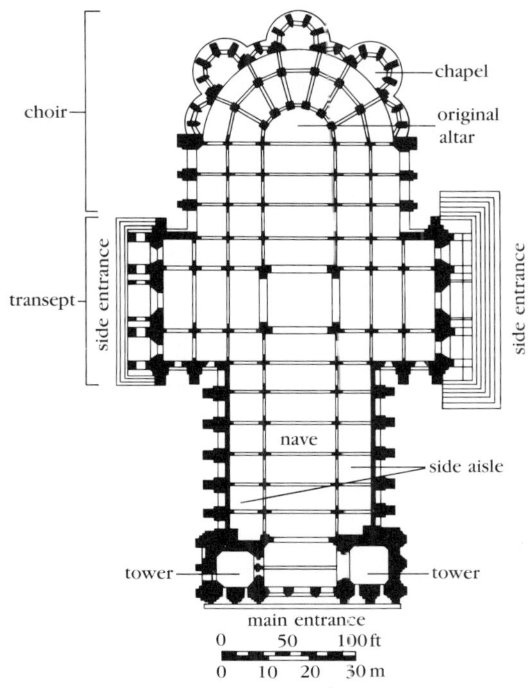

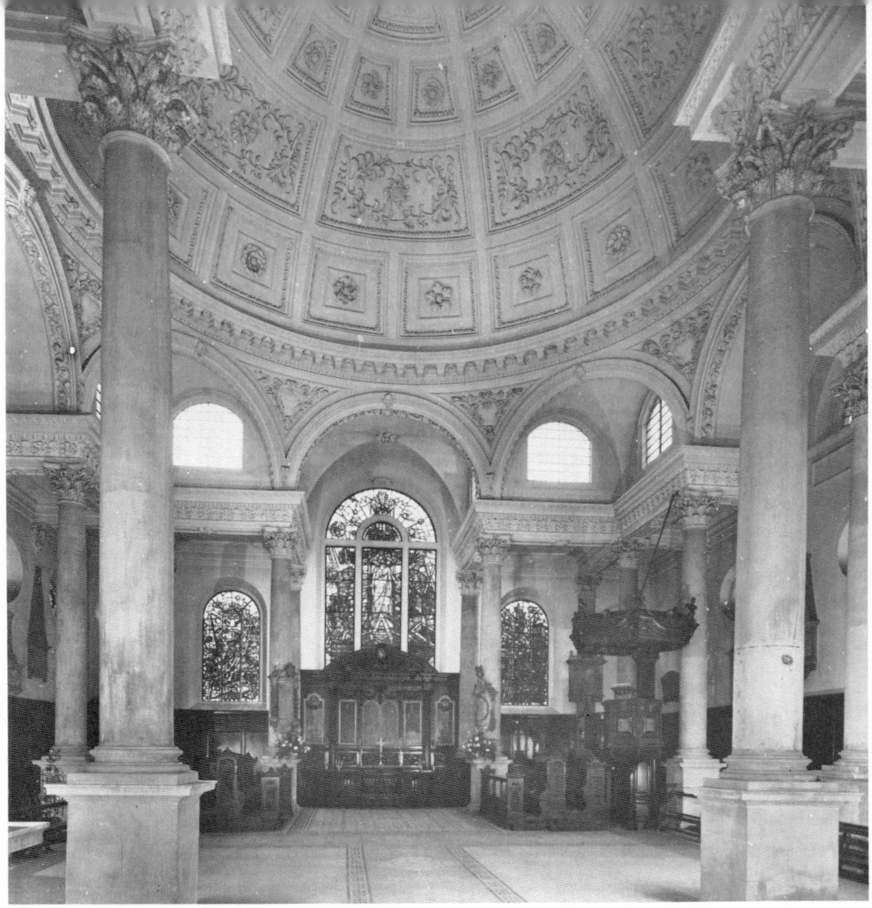

151 Christopher Wren.
Church of Saint Stephen Walbrook, London. 1672–1679.

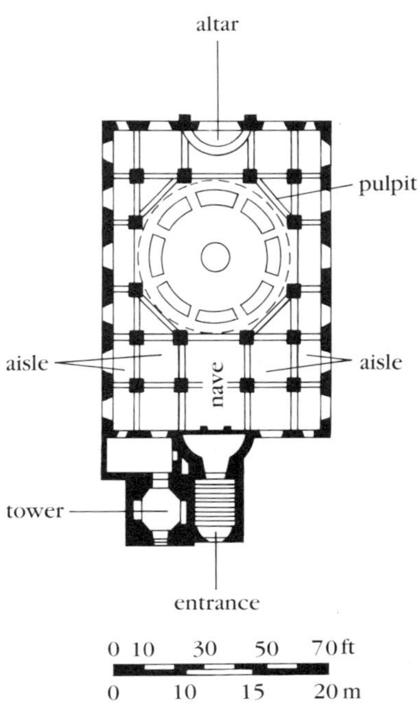

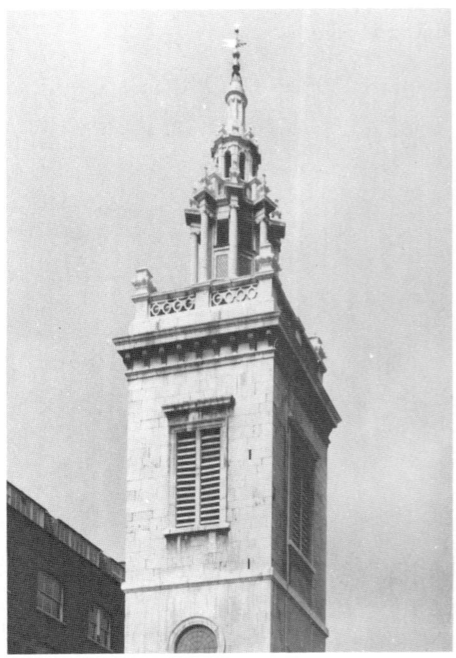

right: 152 Groundplan of Church of Saint Stephen Walbrook, London. Courtauld Institute of Art (Conway Library), London.

far right: 153 Christopher Wren. Steeple of Saint Michael Paternoster, London. 1713.

cated. Her head appropriately surrounded by a white halo, the Virgin is shown in her traditional pose holding the Christ child [see Figures 141 and 142, page 237]. The window's brilliant reds and blues are produced by chemicals within the glass; the actual details of the face and drapery are painted onto the surface. Representing definite figures, the small pieces of glass also create geometric patterns defined by the leading that holds the pieces in place. Still other geometric patterns are formed by the thick vertical and horizontal cross-bars that reinforce the entire window. Viewed from inside, the many stained glass windows in the cathedral appear especially glorious and vibrant when the sunlight outside illuminates them. Indeed, the radiant windows, contrasting with the generally subdued light of the vast, soaring interior space, create a profoundly religious atmosphere.

Just as the cathedral form is the architectural design most characteristic of Roman Catholicism, so a smaller, much simpler type of church building is most distinctive of Protestantism. Especially in England, Anglican churches usually consist of a unified space, rectangular or semicircular in shape. Since Protestant services emphasize the sermon, the pulpit tends to rival the altar in importance, and all parishioners are seated within earshot of the minister. The addition of galleries provides further seating without enlarging the overall floor space. Sir Christopher Wren (1632–1723), the greatest architect of Protestant churches, insisted that the congregation "should hear the service and both hear and see the preacher." Wren's domed Church of Saint Stephen Walbrook (1672–1679) [151, 152] is a fine realization of this ideal. The slender columns are arranged to offer a minimum interruption of the sightlines, and the whole is surmounted by a hemispherical dome, which shelters the parishioners like a heavenly canopy.

Following the neoclassic tastes of his time, Wren greatly admired the designs of ancient Greece and Rome. Accordingly, he adapted the classical columns and basic post-and-lintel style, especially in his façades and his interior spaces. Wren also created distinctive **steeples**, often made up of various geometric elements stacked one on top of another and surmounted by a thin tapering spire [153]. This steeple has become a distinctive feature of Protestant churches, which continue to be built, especially in the United States, according to the basic 18th-century English design.

Theaters

Perhaps the closest secular counterpart to cathedrals and churches is the theater. In ancient Greece and Rome, theaters were usually in the open air, reflecting their origins in gatherings of spectators on hillsides. Built in curved descending tiers around an open playing space, these early designs are known as *amphitheaters.* In ancient Greece the open playing space, or *orchestra,* was circular and often contained an altar to the god Dionysus. Behind it was a stage house, called a *skene,* through which the actors could enter or exit. The *skene* also provided a background for the action and a place for costume changes. The largest of the Greek theaters could hold more than fifteen thousand spectators. Figure 154 shows a typical Greek amphitheater.

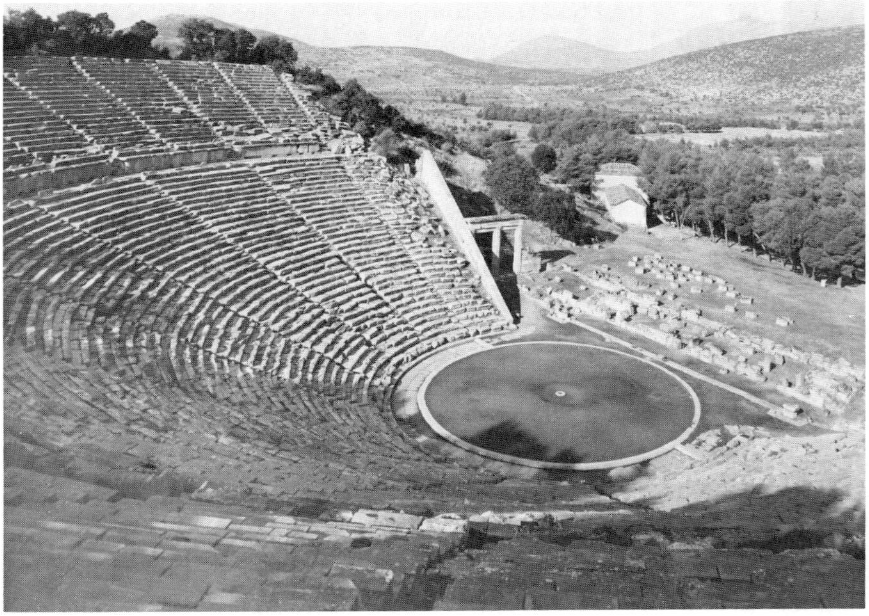

154 Polyclitus the Younger. Theater, Epidaurus. c. 350 B.C. Diameter 373′ (114 m), width of orchestra 66′ (20 m).

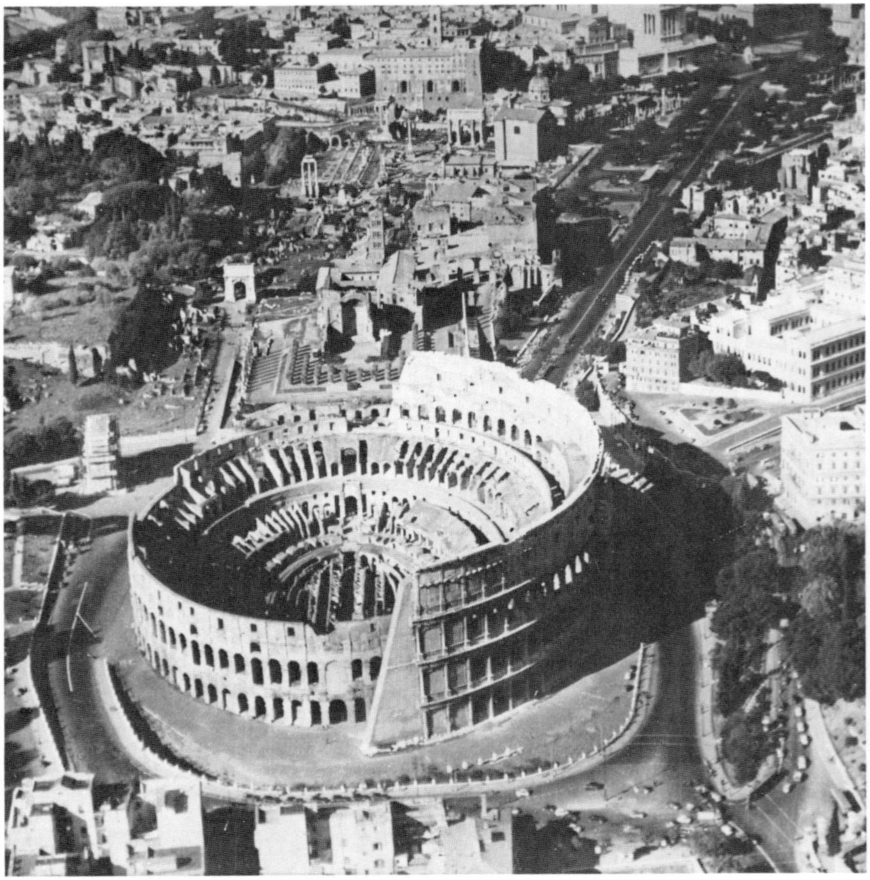

155 Colosseum, Rome. A.D. 72–80. Concrete; long axis 620′ (189 m), short axis 513′ (156 m), height 160′ (49 m).

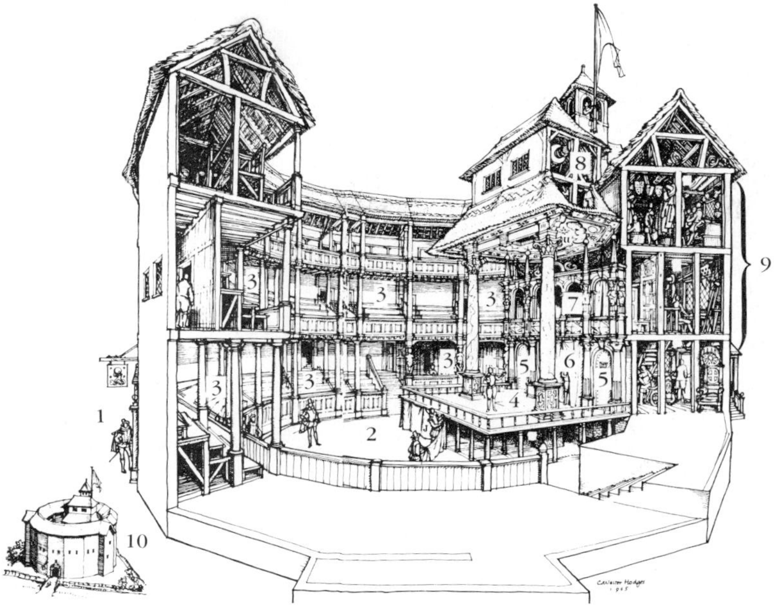

156 Globe Playhouse, London. 1599–1613. Conjectural reconstruction drawing by C. Walter Hodges. *1* Main entrance. *2* The Yard with standing room. *3* Covered galleries for seated audience. *4* Thrust stage. *5* Entrance doors for actors. *6* Curtain and "discovery space." *7* Balcony. *8* The "hut," with machinery for sound effects and raising or lowering actors playing gods, angels, etc. *9* Backstage area with dressing rooms. *10* The exterior of the Globe.

In ancient Rome the same basic design continued to be used, but the theaters were built on flat ground rather than into hillsides. Furthermore, the stage house was joined to the seating area, changing the orchestra into a semicircle. Most of the action took place on a long narrow platform in front of the stage house. Some Roman theaters even had a curtain that could be dropped into a trough at the front of the stage.

The Romans also created arena theaters such as the Colosseum [155, see also Figure 60, page 89], in which the audience fully surrounded the playing area. Because of the number of people it could hold, the arena theater was especially suitable for public spectacles. Wild animal fights and gladiatorial combats were staged there, and even mock naval battles were performed on the flooded Colosseum floor.

The basic stage design of the ancient Greek and Roman theater is the forerunner of the **thrust stage.** Here, as its name suggests, the playing space is projected into what would be the seating area of our conventional theaters. The Globe Playhouse [156], in which some of Shakespeare's plays were presented, used this design, for the stage jutted into the midst of the spectators. The audience either stood on the ground on three sides of the raised stage or sat in covered galleries which also surrounded the stage on three sides. In the Globe, a polygonal building, the stage was partially covered as well. Actors made their entrances and exits from two doors in the rear wall or from a curtained area in this wall called the "discovery space." The upper part of the wall also provided a balcony that could be used in the performance. But the main playing area was the large thrust stage.

Some modern theaters still use a thrust stage. Others have even gone back to the arena of ancient Rome, appropriately calling themselves "theater

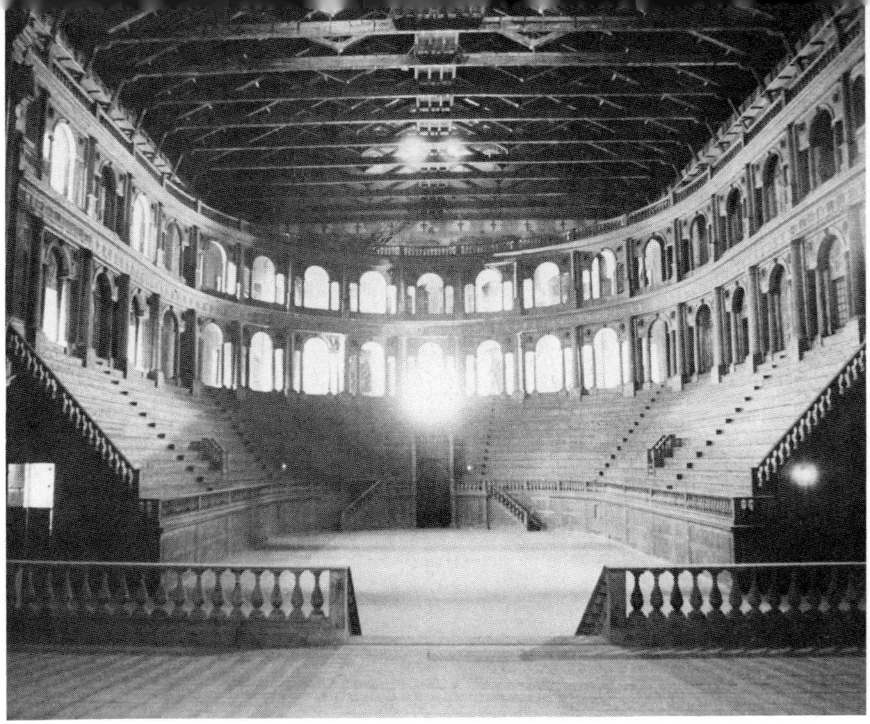

157 Giambattista Aleotti.
Teatro Farnese, Parma. 1618–1628.

in the round." The advantage of both the thrust and the arena stage is that all the spectators are brought into close proximity with the playing area.

Still another type of theater evolved from the Roman stage, though it underwent considerable modification. In western and northern Europe in the 15th and 16th centuries, the climate required covered or—as in Shakespeare's theater, semicovered—spaces. At first, existing halls in palaces and public buildings were temporarily outfitted for performing, but the increasing popularity of plays—and soon of the allied art of opera—led to the

158 Teatro Farnese, proscenium arch.

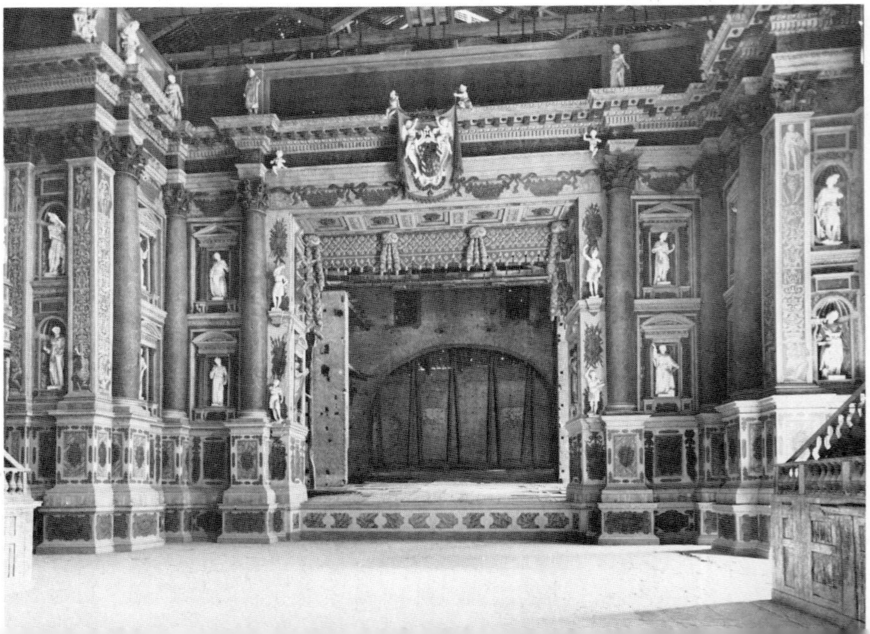

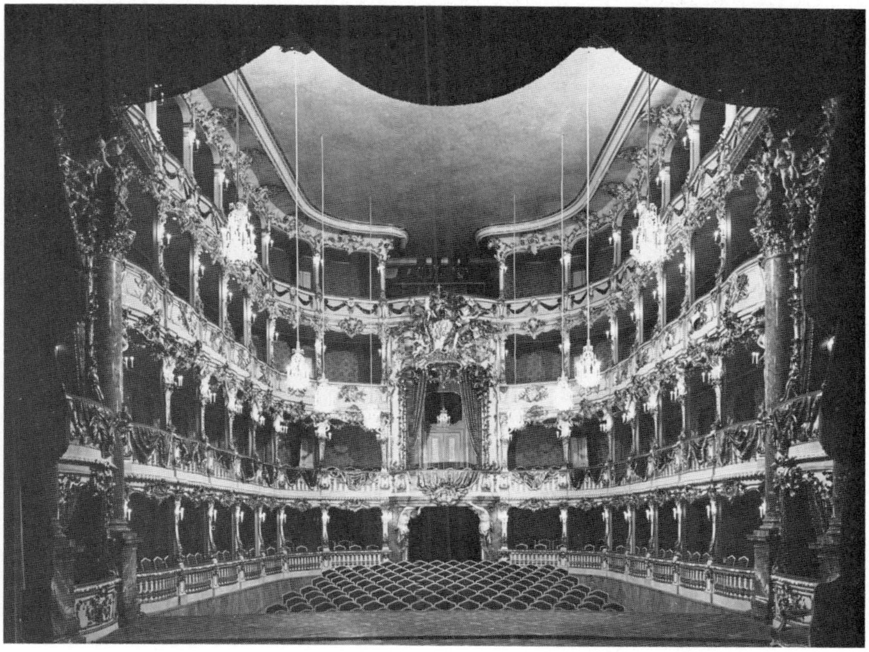

159 François Cuvilliés. Residenztheater, Munich. 1752.

construction of permanent theaters. In these, a horseshoe-shaped auditorium was combined with a *proscenium arch stage*—a playing area framed by a pronounced arch. Moreover, a wide curtain could be drawn across the stage area. In the Teatro Farnese [157, 158], the earliest example of this kind of construction, three general areas were created: a space for the scenery, another for the performers, and a third for the 3,500 spectators who could be accommodated. This arrangement was flexible. The semicircular orchestra could be used either for further spectacles—it could even be flooded—or for additional seating. In any case, the spectators were always seated on the benches rising along the walls.

The proscenium stage encourages the illusion that we are looking into a room with one wall removed (see page 100). Indeed, this stage permits the use of scenery painted in perspective and is, therefore, also appropriately known as the *picture-frame stage*. Both the proscenium and the curtain prove useful in concealing the machinery for changing the settings as well as in storing settings not being displayed.

Later theaters that combined a proscenium arch with a horseshoe-shaped auditorium became increasingly elaborate. In the 18th century, they range from the small, highly ornate Residenztheater [159], designed by François Cuvilliés (1698–1767), to the huge magnificent La Scala Opera House (1778) in Milan. In fact, the horseshoe auditorium with its boxes remained typical for all theaters into the 19th century and is still standard for opera houses today. Modern theaters, however, tend to be smaller and to have one or two balconies instead of rows of boxes.

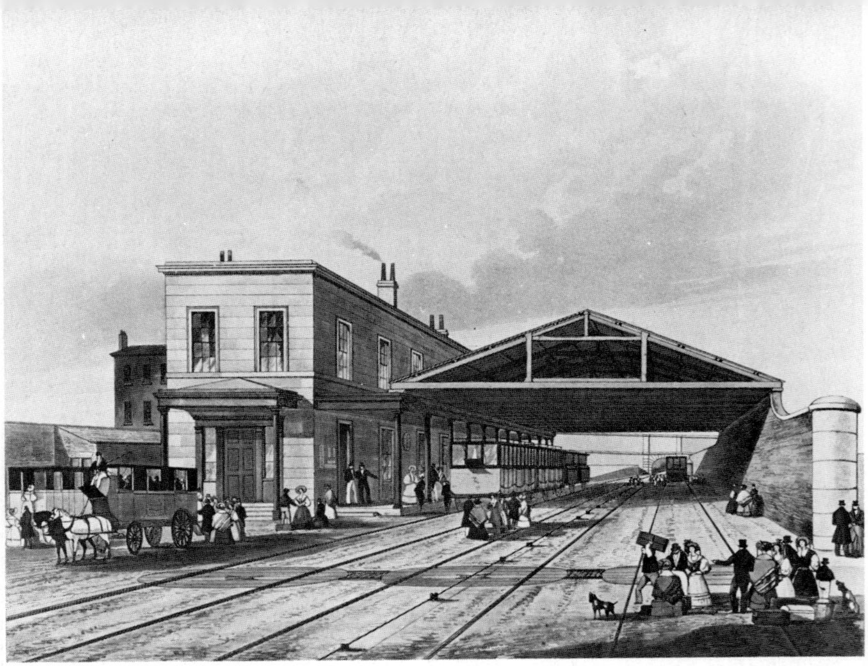

160 Crown Street Station, Liverpool. 1830.

Railroad Stations

Unlike the theater, the *railroad station* is a public building without a long history. In this case, a new building type was created only 150 years ago to serve the needs of a new means of transportation. One of the first of these structures is the Crown Street Station [160] in Liverpool, England. Although modest compared to later examples, this station already has the standard elements, for it joins a covered platform to a structure containing a waiting room and offices.

As passenger traffic increased, stations naturally became larger and more imposing. They also copied the ornate decorations characteristic of other public buildings in the 19th century, as if to claim that despite their recent lineage, they, too, had social standing. In the larger centers, such as New York and London, the terminals were often connected to luxury hotels so that travelers could go directly to their rooms without a fatiguing cab ride.

The great days of railroad station design and construction in the United States occurred at the end of the 19th century and the first forty years of the 20th century. Especially opulent are Union Station in St. Louis (1891–1896), Union Station in Washington, D.C. (1903–1907), and Grand Central Terminal in New York City [161]. All are built in the classical Roman style with huge arches, domes, and columns. The arrival area of Grand Central is particularly imposing, for its vaulted ceiling is 116 feet high and spans 125 feet. This spaciousness is combined with extraordinary efficiency in the arrangement of the tracks. Two subterranean levels under Park Avenue bring nearly seventy tracks into midtown Manhattan.

In some other regions of the United States, local traditions have prevailed. For instance, the Santa Fe Passenger Depot in San Diego (1914–1915) and the Union Passenger Terminal in Los Angeles (1934–1939) [162] are built

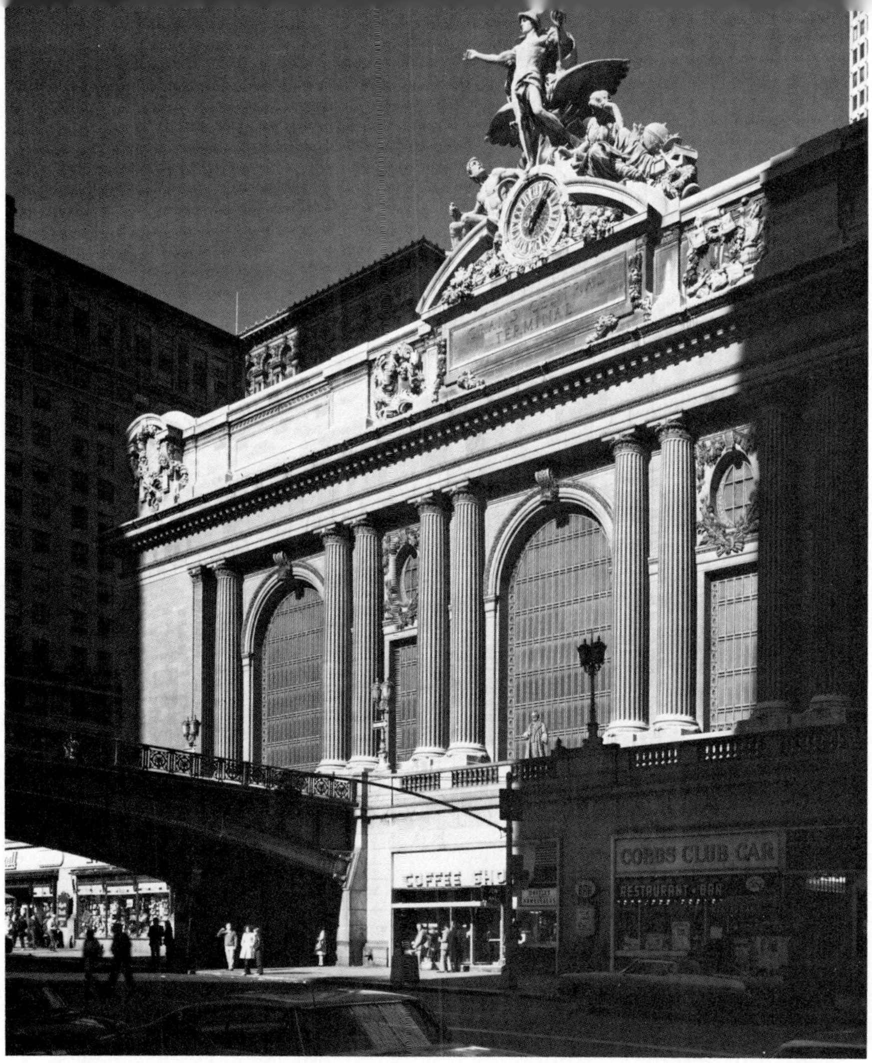

161 Charles Reed and Allen Stem, succeeded by Whitney Warren and James Wetmore. Grand Central Terminal, New York. 1903–1913.

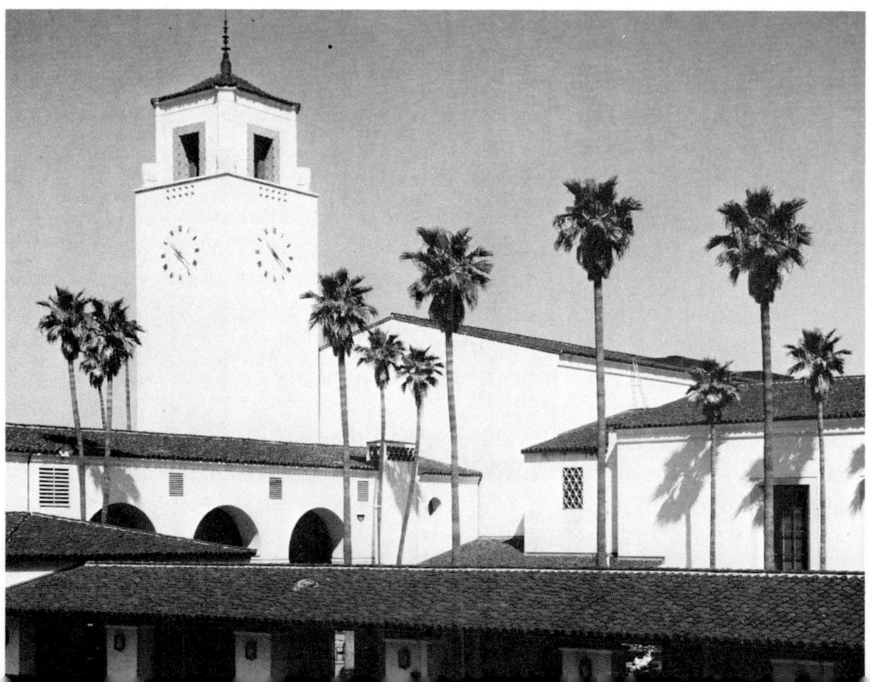

162 H. L. Gilman, J. H. Christie, and R. J. Wirth, with Donald B. Parkinson and John Parkinson. Union Passenger Terminal, Los Angeles. 1934–1939.

in Mission style, adapting the austere hacienda design with its emphasis on horizontal lines and its use of adobe or stucco instead of stone or brick. Such large and imposing buildings, however, are no longer being constructed because of the declining use of passenger trains. Still, many threatened examples have been successfully converted and given new life as restaurants and stores. Their continuing use is a tribute to their value as architecture.

High and Low Culture

The genres examined in the spatial arts—from history painting to the still life, from portrait busts to civic monuments—belong to the mainstream of Western civilization, the respected, traditional forms that are often called "high culture." Counterparts to these genres have flourished in other complex societies, notably the Far Eastern civilizations of China and Japan. There we find such additional distinctive genres as landscape scrolls (see Figure 38), bird-and-flower painting, and calligraphy (decorative handwriting).

Complex civilizations also develop genres outside the realm of high culture, especially in what are known as the **folk arts** (or crafts) and the **commercial arts.** Objects of the various branches of the folk arts are made by nonprofessionals in peasant or farming communities for local consumption. Vigorous folk art traditions have flourished in all Western countries, from Sweden to Albania and from Russia to Mexico. Despite some superficial similarities, works of folk art must not be confused with the objects produced among tribal peoples—sometimes called **primitive art**—since the latter objects constitute the mainstream in tribal societies. The existence side by side of folk art and high-culture art is characteristic only of complex societies.

below: 163 Samuel Dwight. Walker Stillson grave marker, Hillside Cemetery, Sandgate, Vt. 1796. White marble, 24 × 28″ (61–71 cm).

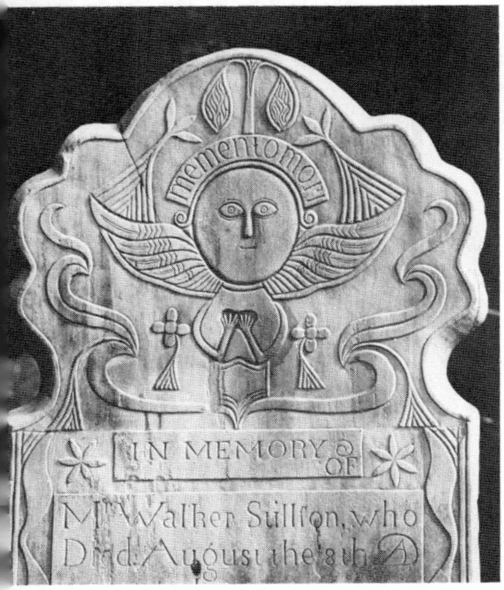

Folk Art

Works of folk art vary greatly from country to country and from genre to genre. Still, common features can be identified. Their lack of professional training means that folk artists tend to avoid sophisticated techniques such as perspective and shading. Folk art pieces are often highly schematic, using flat patterns and repeated standard motifs—almost as if the democratic circumstances of their production were matched by a democracy of motif. The proportions of the human body may be modified or even distorted for expressive effect. A case in point is the gravestone [163] of Walker Stillson in Sandgate, Vermont. Since the winged figure dominating the upper part of the stone represents not the earthly form of the deceased but his soul, the artist has appropriately carved the image in an almost schematic fashion. The design also emphasizes such decorative motifs as leaves, scrolls, and stars, as well as the quaint dignity of the lettering. The many surviving gravestones of this kind, which contrast with the elegant funerary monuments being made then in Europe—and occasionally in North America—constitute an important branch of North American folk art. Other genres found in North American folk art are scrimshaw (carving on whalebone), commemorative pottery, samplers, and quilts.

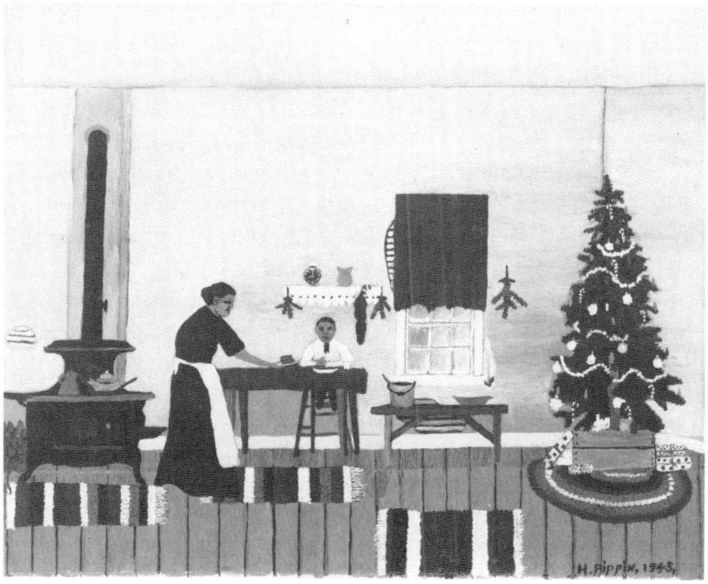

164 Horace Pippin. *Christmas Morning, Breakfast.* 1945. Oil on canvas, 21 × 26¼″ (53 × 67 cm). Cincinnati Art Museum (Edwin and Virginia Irwin Memorial).

Naive Painting

Work recalling folk art in its directness has been produced by more sophisticated artists active in a tradition that is sometimes called **naive painting.** Such naive artists as Henri Rousseau [see Figure 1, p. 3] have had contact with mainstream art, but deliberately choose to retain the freshness associated with the folk tradition.

Christmas Morning, Breakfast [164] is by the black painter Horace Pippin (1888–1946), a self-taught artist who completed his first painting at the age of 43. Pippin's scene, so clearly laid out, probably does not represent an actual room as much as a memory image in which the elderly painter recalled his childhood home. Without giving any impression of depth, Pippin distributes the four pieces of furniture, including the temporary adornment of the Christmas tree, and the four rugs almost as separate units in sequence across his canvas. The individual furnishings are like keepsakes, remembered mental data fixed forever in the still forms of the painting.

Commercial Art

Unlike folk art objects, which are individually produced, unique, and distinctive, *commercial art objects* are mass-produced in great numbers. In spite of superficial resemblances, the two art forms are mutually exclusive. Unhappily, modern means of distribution and advertising have given commercial works a competitive edge, narrowing the sphere in which folk art flourishes. Still, some forms of commercial art, such as photojournalism and fashion photography [see Figure 133, page 229, and Figure 138, page 234], have made use of modern technology to produce significant works.

The poster The genre of *posters*—large-scale advertisements—has also inspired major works of art. Extensive poster-making became possible only after 1800, with the invention of color **lithography**. In this process, stone or zinc plates are used to produce almost unlimited numbers of posters in sizes unattainable by other methods. Since lithography favors broad areas of color, its striking effects are suited not only to attracting the attention of a busy urban public but also to inspiring designs of artistic merit.

The first posters publicized newly released books, but in the late 19th century theatrical posters became popular, drawing on and expanding the possibilities of the new technique of lithography. Such well-known artists as Henri de Toulouse-Lautrec (1864–1901) and Alphonse Mucha (1860–1939) [see Figure 121, page 205] rely heavily on either shading or line. James Pryde and William Nicholson, who did their best work in 1894–1895 under the pseudonym "Beggarstaff," simplify their drawing, presenting arresting images defined almost entirely by color. As their Hamlet poster [165] demonstrates, their visual images are powerful while the text is minimized—to the dismay of the advertiser. Striking posters that continue the simplification of form and the forceful use of color and line are still being created today, as for instance in the advertisement by Paul Davis (b. 1938) for the New York production of *The Threepenny Opera.* This poster [166] admirably captures the tough spirit of the Bertolt Brecht play by concentrating on a stocky figure, Mack the Knife, and even having this figure break the frame.

Posters have also served political purposes. World War I saw the rise of the propaganda poster. A familiar example in the United States is the recruiting poster with the caption "Uncle Sam Wants You!" in which a figure wearing stars and stripes points an accusing finger. Other countries, including fascist Italy, the Soviet Union, and Maoist China, have used equally strong posters for

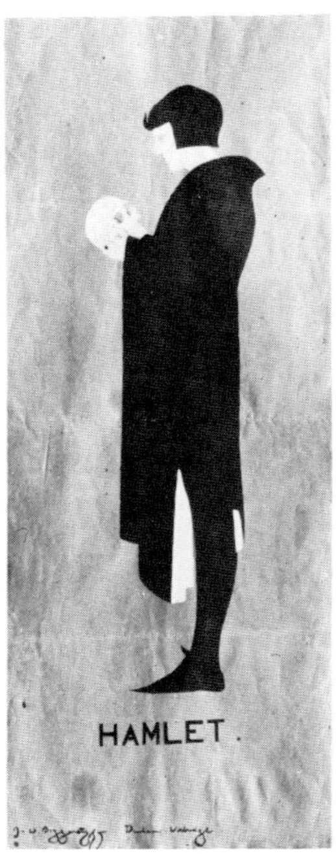

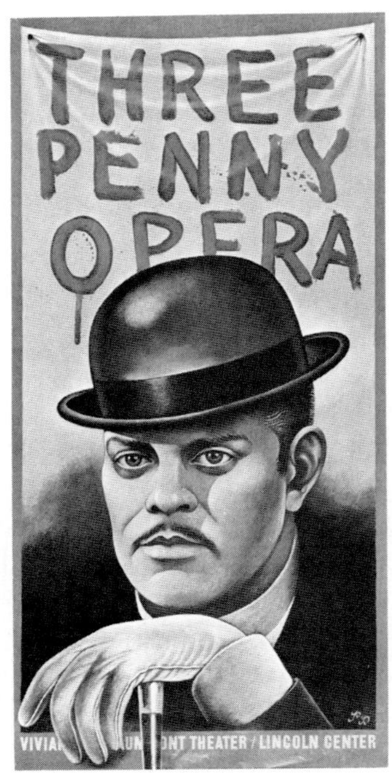

right: 165 "J. T. Beggarstaff" (James Pryde and William Nicholson). *Hamlet.* 1921. Stencil, 5′4½″ × 2′3½″ (1.64 × .7 m). Victoria and Albert Museum, London (Crown Copyright). The artists used not a brush, but cut-outs of colored pieces of paper to create the simplified forms of this poster. The design was then lithographed.

far right: 166 Paul Davis. *The Threepenny Opera.* 1976. Offset lithograph, 46 × 23″ (117 × 58 cm). Museum of Modern Art, New York (gift of New York Shakespeare Festival).

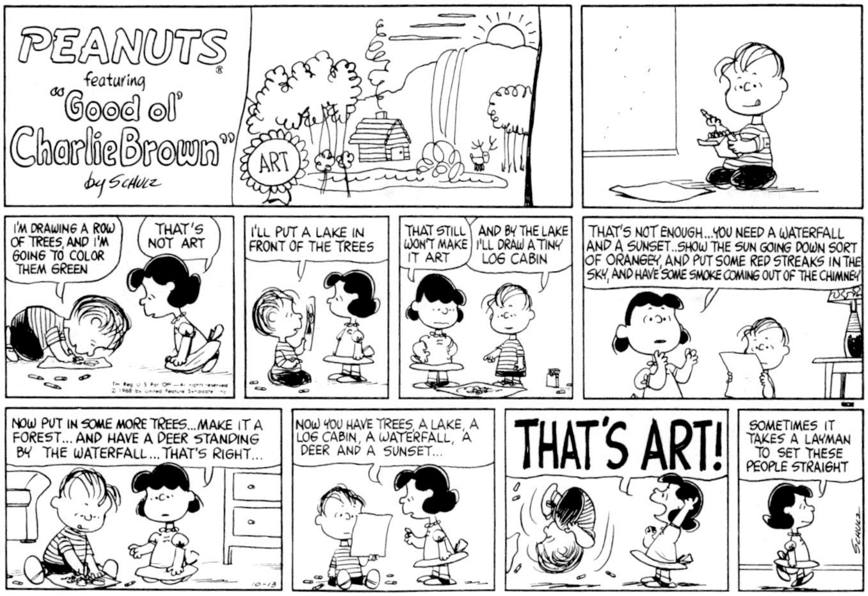

167 Charles M. Schulz. *Peanuts.* © 1968 by United Feature Syndicate, Inc.

propaganda. We should bear in mind, however, that the purposes for which these posters were first designed do not determine their artistic merit.

The comic strip The comic strip is another genre that is linked to modern commercial art, since it was introduced as a promotional device in newspapers at the end of the 19th century. To increase sales, the creators of the strips invented continuing characters such as Krazy Kat, the Katzenjammer Kids, and Winnie Winkle, who could capture the reader's interest in the strip and in the newspaper in which it appeared. Today such figures as Superman, as well as Snoopy, Charlie Brown, and Lucy of *Peanuts* [167], have become household words. Comic strips are a prime example of *popular art,* as opposed to high culture. Their appeal is simple and immediate, and they are widely enjoyed by mass audiences.

A basic feature of the comic strip is the panel, a rectangular unit in which a single scene is shown. Several panels are linked to form strips and rows that present a continuous narrative. The drawings in these panels, which may be either in black and white or in color, tend to be schematic, relying heavily on line and on simplification of outline. Often they present startling shifts of perspective or striking close-ups of the speakers. But cartoonists differ in their techniques, for some also provide highly detailed drawings which suggest texture as well as light and shade.

Another distinguishing feature of the comic strip is the balloon, a small inset enclosing the words of a speaker. The inclusion of language within a panel enables the genre to combine verbal effects (dialogue and narrative) with visual ones. Because of this combination, cartoonists find the comic strip a considerable challenge. Since they must work within a limited space and with a minimum of words to tell an exciting or amusing story, they often use such shorthand terms as "ZOOM!" or "C-R-R-R-ASH." They even have special symbols that express feelings in a highly concentrated way—a rain cloud to suggest depression, a light bulb to suggest the dawning of a bright idea. These devices are conventions of the comic strip. Perhaps the challenge of working in such a compressed form, along with the great popularity of the genre, explains why serious modern painters such as Roy Lichtenstein have adopted comic strip devices [see Figure 37, page 45].

From our discussion, we can well understand that considerations of genre frequently play an important part in helping artists give shape or organization to their work. Whether they are creating portraits or religious sculptures or even cartoons, artists often deliberately follow established patterns or introduce widely accepted conventions. By directly or indirectly acknowledging that their work belongs to the same category or genre as earlier ones, artists not only hold their own efforts up for comparison with what has already been accomplished but also share in the cultural tradition that unites works of the same genre.

Questions for Study and Discussion

1. What features—subject matter, form, treatment, or a combination of these—determine each of the genres described in this chapter? Are these features the same for all genres of the arts of space? Can one say that some genres are better than others?
2. To show the different ways in which artists can work within a particular genre, find contrasting examples of portrait painting, landscape, and still life in art books of your school library.
3. Using a current newspaper or magazine, find examples of various genres of photography. What aspects of the image are emphasized by the photographer's technique, and is this emphasis typical of the particular photographic genre?
4. Locate and identify a religious or civic sculpture in your vicinity. In what ways has the artist given distinctive treatment to the subject? If the treatment is not distinctive, what does this suggest about the work?
5. Compare and contrast the groundplans of the Temple of Khonsu at Karnak [see Figure 43, page 49], Old Saint Peter's Basilica [see Figure 146, page 241], Chartres Cathedral [see Figure 150, page 243], and Saint Stephen Walbrook [see Figure 152, page 244]. What differing religious conceptions and ceremonies account for the different organizations of the interior space?
6. What elements of the church buildings described in this chapter can be seen in the churches of your community?
7. How do the seating and view of the stage differ in the Greek theater, the Elizabethan theater, and the 18th-century theater? What socioeconomic differences among the theatergoers might account for these differences in design?
8. How are folk art, naive painting, and commercial art related, and what are the differences among them?
9. Choosing a representative comic strip, show how it exemplifies the features of the genre.

CHAPTER 8

Genres of the Arts of Time

Music

Major musical genres include such familiar categories as the **symphony**, **concerto**, **sonata**, and **song**, the latter encompassing both the **art song** and the **folk song**. The broader term **chamber music** includes different genres, such as the trio and quartet, characterized by the small number of players involved. Indeed, most of the musical genres are distinguished primarily by the number and types of performers called upon by the composer.

Symphony

Characteristic of a *symphony* is its use of a large number of musicians, generally between thirty and one hundred, playing a variety of instruments that make up the symphony orchestra (see Chapter 2). Today, major symphony orchestras generally comprise nearly one hundred players, although before the middle of the 19th century, composers had a smaller group at their disposal. Another characteristic of a symphony is that it is a long work. Haydn's and Mozart's last about twenty minutes; but the *Third Symphony,* known as the *Eroica* (1806), by Ludwig van Beethoven (1770–1827) takes about forty-five minutes to perform, and some symphonies are longer. Moreover, a symphony is divided into contrasting parts, called **movements.** These are often virtually complete pieces in themselves, coming to a clear final cadence. In performance, each movement usually is separated from the next by a substantial pause. The division into movements separated by a pause is one of the conventions of the symphony as well as of other long works.

The basic pattern of a symphony can be clearly seen in Beethoven's *Eroica.* Like the majority of symphonies, this has four movements, each designated by its principal tempo marks:

1. *Allegro con brio*
2. *Marcia funebre: Adagio assai*
3. *Scherzo e Trio: Allegro vivace*
4. *Allegro molto: Poco andante: Presto*

The key words for an understanding of the symphonic structure here are: *allegro,* "fast"; *adagio,* "quite slow"; *scherzo,* "joke," and *allegro vivace,* "fast and lively"; *allegro molto,* "very fast." In other words, the overall scheme follows the conventional pattern of fast, slow, fast, fast. In the *Eroica,* however, we will hear many changes in emotional character and many different melodic ideas (themes), without which we would scarcely want to keep listening for five minutes—let alone forty-five minutes.

In general terms, the first movement can be characterized as heroic, epic, noble, and grand. The second movement, as the heading *Marcia funebre* indicates, is a funeral march, slow and somber, with a contrasting major key section that suggests consolation for the tragedy expressed in the opening and closing sections of the movement. The "joking" character of the third movement is vigorous and humorous in a down-to-earth, hearty way, and the music has an infectious swing, partly as a result of its rapid $\frac{3}{4}$ meter. The last movement varies widely in mood, but ultimately expresses a feeling of heroic triumph. Here Beethoven uses the theme and variations form, in which a basic melodic idea is stated as a whole and then repeated with increasing elaboration and embellishment. Thus, the *Eroica,* like most symphonies, embraces a wide range of musical themes, fully developed in varying tempi in the course of four separate movements.

Concerto

Another type of long composition combines the symphony orchestra with a solo instrument. Such a work is called a *concerto* (plural *concerti*) and is quite similar to the symphony, though it commonly has only three movements (fast, slow, fast) rather than four.

To its basic symphonic nature, the concerto adds a dramatic element that comes from a kind of struggle or competition between the solo instrument and the accompanying mass of instruments. Moreover, the concerto generally features the solo instrument playing completely alone in a special section called the **cadenza**. Originally, this section was improvised, enabling the performer to display skill both in executing difficult passages and in composing them on the spot. But in the late 18th and early 19th centuries, composers grew increasingly dissatisfied with the soloist's improvisation and wished to control the length and quality of this part of their composition as well. Accordingly, composers began to write the cadenza themselves.

Most concerti are written for violin or piano as the solo instrument. Among the most beautiful and challenging examples are Beethoven's *Fifth Piano Concerto,* known as the "Emperor," and Tchaikovsky's *First Piano Concerto* (in B-flat minor). Both composers also wrote lyrical and passionate violin concerti in D major. The fact that both these violin concerti are composed in the same key is no accident, for the instrument is most brilliant in keys that take advantage of the open strings (G, D, A, E).

The concerto is a particularly attractive genre because it combines the rich sounds of the orchestra with the virtuoso performance of the soloist.

Sonata

A longer work for a solo instrument, the *sonata* may be written for one instrument, for two, or occasionally even for three instruments. In contrast to the concerto, a sonata never calls for a full orchestra.

Among the best-known examples are the *Sonata No. 23 in F minor* (the "Appassionata") (1804) for solo piano by Beethoven and the *Sonata No. 3 in D minor* for violin and piano by Johannes Brahms (1833–1897). The most popular sonatas feature the piano, violin, or cello, although composers have also written for almost every other orchestral instrument. In form, the sonata is usually similar to the concerto, with three movements that are fast, slow, fast.

The sonata as a genre featuring the solo instrument should not be confused with the *sonata-form,* which is an organizational structure frequently used in the first movements of symphonies and other musical works. Although it is also known as *sonata-allegro form* or *first-movement sonata form,* neither of these terms accurately describes it, for its tempo need not be *allegro* and it is used not only in the first movement. Its essential principle is a carefully organized dramatic contrast of themes and keys. A sonata-form movement must have three principal sections, traditionally called the *exposition, development,* and *recapitulation.* These correspond in a general way to the parts of a three-part form ($A–B–A^1$), with the recapitulation (A^1) restating most of the exposition (A) and with the development section (B) providing contrast. Sonata-form movements may also have an additional introduction and/or a concluding **coda**.

Song

A *song* can be defined as a relatively short composition for one or more voices, generally accompanied on one instrument, but occasionally also by a full orchestra. The genre of song can be subdivided into two categories: the art song and the folk song. Both consist of musical settings of brief poems that either tell stories or express distinctive emotions. At their best, songs represent a perfect union of music and poetry, each reinforcing the other.

Art songs The distinctive feature of art songs is that they are written by identifiable composers. Many were intended to be sung to the accompaniment of a lute or guitar, for the plucked string instruments set off the sustained timbre of the human voice more effectively than other backgrounds. Still, most art songs performed today were created originally for piano accompaniment. Major composers such as Franz Schubert (1797–1828), Robert Schumann (1810–1856), and Hugo Wolf (1860–1903) have written this kind of song, known by the German term **Lied** (plural, *Lieder*). Such songs form one of the most important and enjoyable bodies of serious music.

A delightful example of the art song is Schubert's *"Die Forelle"* ("The Trout"), based on a poem about a fisherman trying to catch a trout.

DIE FORELLE

In einem Bächlein helle,
Da schoss in froher Eil
Die launische Forelle
Vorüber wie ein Pfeil.
Ich stand an dem Gestade
Und sah in süsser Ruh
Des muntern Fischleins Bade
Im klaren Bächlein zu.

Ein Fischer mit der Rute
Wohl an dem Ufer stand,
Und sah's mit kaltem Blute,
Wie sich das Fischlein wand.
So lang dem Wasser Helle,
So dacht ich, nicht gebricht,
So fängt er die Forelle
Mit seiner Angel nicht.

Doch endlich ward dem Diebe
Die Zeit zu lang.
Er macht das Bächlein tückisch
  trübe,
Und eh ich es gedacht,
So zuckte seine Rute,
Das Fischlein zappelt dran,
Und ich mit regem Blute
Sah die Betrogne an. (c. 1817)

In a clear little brook
In merry haste
A playful trout
Shot by like an arrow.
I stood on the bank
And watched in sweet calm
This lively little fish's bathing
In a clear little brook.

A fisherman with his rod
Happened to stand on the bank
And coolly watched,
How the little fish darted to and fro.
As long as the clearness of the water
Does not break, I thought,
So long he will not catch
The trout with his rod.

But finally the thief
Found that it took too long.
Maliciously he made the brooklet
  muddy,
And before I thought of it,
His rod twitched,
The little fish squirmed on it,
And I with quickened blood
Gazed at the betrayed one.

The first two stanzas of the poem give the scene, but relatively little action. Here Schubert presents a simple melodic setting against a rippling background of chordal notes in the piano part, suggesting the motion of water in a stream. Since these opening two stanzas describe no activity, the music repeats the same melody. Only in the third stanza (strophe), when the fisherman muddies the water in order to trick the fish, does the musical line change, becoming more agitated. The arrangement here is a "modified strophic form," which is distinct from a simple strophic arrangement, in which each stanza of the poem is set to exactly the same tune. Schubert has modified the pattern in order to provide a musical climax that corresponds to the increasingly energetic action described in the poem.

Many art songs concentrate on expressing emotions, particularly love and grief. Both of these figure prominently in "Flow My Tears" by John Dowland (1563–1626), a setting of a poem by an unknown author.

FLOW MY TEARS (LACRIME)

Flow my tears, fall from your springs,
Exiled forever, let me mourn
Where night's blackbird her sad infamy sings,
There let me live forlorn.

Down vain lights, shine no more!
No nights are dark enough for those
That in despair their lost fortune's deplore,
Light doth but shame disclose.

Never may woes be relieved,
Since pity is fled,
And tears, and sighs, and groans my weary days
Of all joys have deprived.

From the highest spire of contentment,
My fortune is thrown;
And fear, and grief, and pain for my deserts,
Are my hopes, since hope is gone.

Hark you, shadows, that in darkness dwell,
Learn to contemn[1] light.
Happy, happy they that in hell
Feel not the world's despite. (1600)

[1] Despise

Dowland's music exquisitely expresses the love and grief of the rejected lover. The song is set in the minor mode, with the melodic line repeatedly descending to suggest the falling tears. The slow rhythm and plaintive, almost monotonous harmonies contribute greatly to the emotional effect.

Moreover, a kind of dissonance called **suspension** is introduced in "Flow My Tears." This dissonance occurs when a note is held, but the underlying chord changes. The contrast between the sustained note and the new chord produces the dissonant sound. Dowland frequently uses the dissonance of suspension, particularly in the high notes, to emphasize the speaker's poignant grief. Suspension and similar dissonances have been in continual use since the 16th century to convey pathos. The expressive use of dissonance is, in fact, one of the fundamental conventions of Western music.

Composers have expressed intense emotions not only in individual songs but also in more elaborate *song cycles* of loosely connected songs that trace a whole sequence or history of emotional experiences. Schubert's *Die Schöne Müllerin* ("The Miller's Beautiful Wife"), for example, presents the varying moods of a young wanderer ranging from happiness to heartbreaking sorrow. And Schumann's *Frauenliebe und Leben* ("Woman's Love and Life") follows the events and accompanying moods experienced in the life of a woman from love and courtship through marriage and widowhood.

Folk songs In contrast to art songs, folk songs are anonymous, having no identifiable single author. Virtually every people has its own store of such songs, whose melodies and words are passed on from one generation to the next. Folk songs can take the form of love songs, work songs, play songs, sea chanties, or **ballads** that tell a brief story—all dealing with the common events of life. In musical terms, they most often consisted originally of a pure melody, intended to be sung without accompaniment. Yet in some cases, traditional accompaniment on the guitar or banjo has also been handed down.

Some of the most memorable and popular folk songs are ballads—longer, narrative songs with many stanzas sung to the same tune (strophic form). The anonymous "Frankie and Johnny" is an example widely known in the United States.

FRANKIE AND JOHNNY

Frankie and Johnny were lovers,
Oh Lordy, how they could love,
Swore to be true to each other,
True as the stars above,
He was her man, but he done her wrong.

Frankie went down to the corner,
To buy her a bucket of beer,
Frankie says "Mister Bartender,
Has my lovin' Johnny been here?
He is my man, but he's doin' me wrong."

"I don't want to cause you no trouble
Don't want to tell you no lie,
I saw your Johnny half-an-hour ago
Making love to Nelly Bly.
He is your man, but he's doin' you wrong."

Frankie went down to the hotel
Looked over the transom so high
There she saw her lovin' Johnny
Making love to Nelly Bly.
He was her man; he was doin' her wrong.

Frankie threw back her kimono,
Pulled out her big forty-four;
Rooty-toot-toot: three times she shot
Right through that hotel door,
She shot her man, who was doin' her wrong.

"Roll me over gently,
Roll me over slow,
Roll me over on my right side,
'Cause these bullets hurt me so,
I was your man, but I done you wrong."

Bring all your rubber-tired hearses,
Bring all your rubber-tired hacks,
They're carrying poor Johnny to the burying ground
And they ain't gonna bring him back,
He was her man, but he done her wrong.

Frankie says to the sheriff,
"What are they going to do?"
The sheriff he said to Frankie,
"It's the 'lectric chair for you.
He was your man, and he done you wrong."

"Put me in that dungeon,
Put me in that cell,
Put me where the northeast wind
Blows from the southeast corner of hell,
I shot my man, 'cause he done me wrong." (19th century)

The many versions of "Frankie and Johnny" are vividly described by the poet Carl Sandberg (1878–1967) in his *American Songbag* (1927):

If America has a classical gutter song, it is the one that tells of Frankie and her man. Josie, Sadie, Lillie, Annie are a few of her aliases; she has many. Professor H. M. Belden of the University of Missouri showed me sixteen Frankie songs, all having the same story though a few are located in the back country and in bayous instead of the big city. Then I met up with R. W. Gordon; he has 110 Frankie songs, and is still picking up new ones. . . . The Frankie and Albert song . . . was common along the Mississippi river and among railroad men of the middle west as early as 1888. It is a simple and mournful air, of the short and simple annals of the poor. The Frankie and Johnny song is of later development, with notes of violence and flashes of exasperation. The Frankie Blues came still later, and with its "blue" notes is, of course, "meaner" as a song. In many colleges are groups who sing Frankie songs in ragtime manner, with lackadaisical verses. As our American culture advances, it may be that classes will take up the Frankie song as seriously as a play by Molière or a Restoration comedy or the Provençal ballads of France.

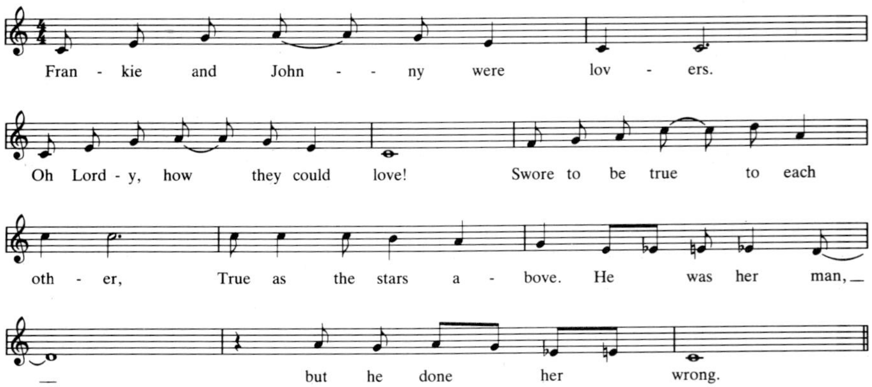

Example 16 "Frankie and Johnny."

In the musical excerpt from "Frankie and Johnny" [Example 16], the flat signs before the note E represent the "blue" note, which occurs in the melody whenever the word *her* appears in the last line of each stanza. The pitch is actually between E-flat and E-natural and is sung as a slide or "bent" note. These blue notes, which lie outside traditional Western European scale systems, are generally thought to have entered North American music from the singing of Southern blacks, who preserved some non-Western elements of their native African music. Also characteristic of this blues influence is the syncopated rhythm found in ragtime. "Frankie and Johnny," like many folk melodies, uses a small group of notes, primarily those that constitute the "pentatonic" scale (C, D, E, G, A).

The great popularity of folk music has led to the development of a contemporary form of popular song that combines many stylistic features of the traditional folk song with the care and craft we associate with the art song. One of the better popular songs of the late 1960s is "Bridge Over Troubled Water," whose words and music are by Paul Simon. From the folk idiom comes its mainly pentatonic melody. Most of the chords derive from black spiritual and Gospel singing, as does the syncopation, which is also characteristic of black African music. Yet the chord progression that underscores the title phrase each time it recurs as a refrain is highly sophisticated and places this song very much in the tradition of Brahms and Schubert.

Popular songs today borrow from many sources. Like art songs, they are creations of a single, identifiable composer, who uses the traditions of Western music as part of the material. Like folk songs, too, they are generally restricted melodically in order to be easily remembered and sung, even by someone without musical training.

Popular songs, like the examples of popular art we have already discussed, tend to be simple and immediate in their appeal as well as widely accepted by mass audiences. As such, they remain a somewhat suspect genre for the serious, traditionally trained musician. Yet a few popular songs of our own time hold a place in the mind's ear that make one feel they will one day be as widely appreciated as Dowland's or Schubert's.

Chamber Music

As a refreshing respite from the dramatic demands of genres such as the symphony and concerto, musicians often turn to chamber music, music meant to be played in chambers rather than large concert halls. Ironically, chamber music is so popular today that chamber music concerts are often performed in large halls, destroying the intimacy that the form is meant to provide.

Chamber music may be played by many different types of groups. The defining characteristic of chamber music is that each individual player has a unique part to play—unlike the symphony, in which the violins, for example, play as a section. Normally, chamber music groups have from three to seven or eight members. The most popular grouping is the *string quartet,* consisting of first and second violin, viola, and cello. Also fairly common are the *piano trio,* consisting of piano, violin, and cello; and the *string trio*—violin, viola, and cello. Although chamber music groupings are predominantly string instruments, the *wind quintet,* consisting of flute, oboe, clarinet, bassoon, and the French horn, is gaining popularity.

To get some sense of the qualities of chamber music, we can listen to the fourth movement of Schubert's *Trout Quintet* (1819), cast in the form of a theme and variations. Scored for piano, violin, viola, cello, and double bass, this is delightfully melodic music with many sections full of energy and brilliance. In the fourth movement, Schubert obliged some of his friends, who wanted an arrangement of the song "*Die Forelle,*" which we have just discussed. The setting for strings alone at the beginning states the "Trout" melody in simple four-part harmonic setting, presenting it as the theme to be varied. This theme is an example of binary form (A–A–B–B), and the variations maintain this formal structure. At the same time, each successive variation introduces some new element, whether change of instrumental texture, melodic embellishments, or mood:

- Variation 1: The piano plays the theme, ornamented by trills, while the strings accompany it.
- Variation 2: The violin has the ornamental part while the viola sounds the theme.
- Variation 3: The cello and double bass play the theme while the piano plays cascades of notes.
- Variation 4: A dramatic episode is presented in the minor key; the melodic interest shifts back and forth between the piano and the violin.
- Variation 5: Principally a lyrical solo for the cello, this section is in still another new key (B-flat Major).
- Variation 6: *(Allegretto finale)* By returning to the rippling chordal notes of accompaniment of the original song, "The Trout," Schubert comes full circle. The original melody is now played by the violin and cello, alternating phrases.

By convention, the last variation can take two possible forms. The one exemplified here repeats the original theme with little or no variation. The other possibility is a lengthy, brilliant expansion of the theme with virtuoso embellishments and new material composed to create a larger form. Although Schubert did not choose this more elaborate finale, his *Trout Quintet* with its six variations admirably demonstrates how a composer of genius can create a rich and varied work of chamber music with a limited number of players.

When listening to a chamber music work in actual concert performance, we have the additional enjoyment of observing the animated interplay between different members of the group. Chamber music has no conductor, no one leader; interpretation is decided democratically. In the best performances, we can hear the imaginative ideas of each member of the group blend into a satisfying unified whole.

Poetry

Genres in poetry, like those in the other arts, can be determined either by subject matter or by treatment or, in some cases, by a combination of the two. The **epic**, **lyric**, **ballad**, and **sonnet** are among the most frequently encountered, and some of these, such as the epic, make use of especially elaborate conventions.

Epic

Among the genres that exist in poetry, the oldest and most highly respected is the *epic.* This is recognizable by its special themes and characters as well as by its characteristic poetic devices. It was a favorite type of writing from Homer (c. 800 B.C.) on, and its distinguished examples are among the most powerful poems in world literature, even though modern versions are rare.

Homer's two great epics, *The Iliad* and *The Odyssey,* were so influential that they established many of the characteristics of later epics. Both epics show great heroes engaged in tasks that test the limits of their abilities. The heroes of *The Iliad* prove their prowess in the battle over the city of Troy. Although Homer does not return to the original cause of the war—the Judgment of Paris—he vividly shows not only the individual combats between Greek and Trojan warriors fighting over Helen of Troy, but also the dissension between Greeks when their chief fighter, Achilles, temporarily withdraws from battle. Recurring scenes depict the arming of heroes and their combat. In contrast, the heroes of the *Odyssey* prove their prowess by overcoming many obstacles on their way home from Troy to Greece.

In his *Aeneid,* the Roman poet Vergil, the next great writer of epics, combined the themes of heroes in battle with heroes on significant journeys as he traces the hardships involved in the founding of Rome. Vergil makes explicit an idea already suggested by Homer, namely that the fate of a nation depends on the success of his hero, Aeneas.

Both Homer and Vergil interweave their stories with the great legends of the past. Consequently, the action takes place not only among human beings but also among the gods and other superhuman figures. Indeed, the gods in both Homer and Vergil play an active role. The deities either protect or plot against the heroes, suggesting the precariousness of human existence. *The Odyssey,* especially, is peopled with strange figures such as the immortal sorceress Circe, who can change men into beasts (see Chapter 4). Clearly, the characters include more than this-worldly figures. Moreover, the action of the epics takes place not simply on earth and on Mount Olympus, the home of the gods, but even in the underworld. This descent, described briefly in *The Odyssey* and more extensively in book VI of *The Aeneid,* becomes another major convention of the epic.

Along with the themes, characters, and key scenes, the narrative style of the epic is governed by well-established conventions. These are found especially in the openings of epic poems. The very first lines often announce the major theme. *The Iliad,* for instance, begins with a reference to the anger of Achilles and its consequences for the Greeks. The next lines present an *invocation to the Muse,* a calling upon the divine patroness of poetry for inspiration. Such an invocation, together with the lofty tone typical of the opening, emphasizes the seriousness of the poet's undertaking. Only then does the *epic question,* asking how the main events came about, lead into the narrative. This narrative does not begin at the beginning of the story, but *in medias res,* "in the middle of things." *The Iliad,* for instance, begins in the ninth year of the Trojan War, and *The Aeneid* opens with Aeneas already in Carthage, halfway on his journey to Rome. An awareness of these conventions enables us to appreciate what later poets—Milton in *Paradise Lost* and Pope in the **mock epic** *The Rape of the Lock*—do at the beginnings of their poems.

Some of the stylistic conventions result from the fact that the first epics were *oral;* that is, they were recited and heard rather than written down and read. Indeed, Homer's poems were retold entirely from memory for many generations before they were set down in writing. Later epics such as the Anglo-Saxon *Beowulf* (8th century) and the medieval French *Song of Roland* (11th century) have a similar history. To make them easier to remember, epics tend to use stirring repetitions. Whole sequences of lines are repeated to emphasize a scene and to draw out the narrative. In addition, brief phrases are also repeated, usually to describe the characters. These *epithets*—"swift-footed Achilles" or "pale-gold Aphrodite"—recall the characters and also help keep the rhythm of the poetic line.

Perhaps the most distinctive stylistic convention of the epic is the elaborate, extended simile, which has come to be known as the *Homeric simile.* In the following example from *The Iliad,* Homer offers a detailed comparison of two youthful warriors to young lions:

> Like two lions on the mountain top, reared by their mother in the thickets of a deep wood, who seize cattle and fine sheep and ravage the farms of men until they in turn are killed with sharp bronze by the hands of men, so were these two [warriors] vanquished at the hands of Aeneas and fell like tall pine trees.
>
> (V, 554–560)

The similes of the lions and the pine trees emphasize both the strength of the young men and the poignancy of their deaths.

Finally and most importantly, epics are characterized by their length. So extensive are they that they are often divided into separate books—twenty-four in *The Iliad* and twelve in *The Aeneid.* This length enables the epic poets to follow the experiences of their heroes over an extended period, and to incorporate mythic and folklore material that reminds their own ages of the rich traditions of their past. When we praise other art forms such as novels or films for their "epic sweep," we are acknowledging the expansiveness and panoramic quality of the epic.

Lyric

Unlike the elaborate epic, another genre of poetry, the lyric, is usually brief. The term *lyric* comes from "lyre," a stringed, harp-like instrument, and suggests a pronounced musical quality. In addition, lyrics also tend to express emotional states. Unlike the epic, which presents a lengthy narrative with many characters, the lyric concentrates on feelings. Such short poems as Nikki Giovanni's "Kidnap Poem" and W. H. Auden's "Look, stranger" in Chapter 2 are lyrics because they have a musical quality and express emotion in a loose and flexible form.

Even as brief a poem as the anonymous "Western Wind" demonstrates the essentials of a lyric:

WESTERN WIND

Western wind, when will thou blow,
The small rain down can rain?[1]
Christ, if my love were in my arms,
And I in my bed again!

(14th century)

[1] so that the fine rain can begin to fall

The emphasis is on the speaker's emotions of loneliness and longing. Obviously far from home, he is yearning for a reunion with his beloved amidst the comforts of his own house. Significantly, the poet omits any explanation of the speaker's background and current situation, any narrative concerning what led up to this separation from the beloved and the homeland. Neither the speaker's identity nor the reasons for his plight are made explicit.

The poet does not, however, omit the details that emphasize the speaker's emotions. The poem begins with an invocation of the western wind and of the gentle rain that usually comes with it—natural forces that the speaker regards as responsive to his feelings. His invocation suggests that the forces of nature may bring relief from his sterile existence.

Throughout, the poet uses the simplest possible language to express emotions in a hauntingly powerful manner. Having presented general images of nature—wind and rain—in the first two lines, he introduces a heartfelt exclamation of a single charged monosyllable, "Christ," which serves as a transition to the more specific as well as more personal last lines. In these, great emphasis is given to the speaker's desolation by the repetition of "in my," first for the arms with which he longs to enfold his beloved and then for the bed, which suggests not only love but also comfort, rest, and security. The whole is a pained outcry as well as a nostalgic expression of the feelings of someone far from all he holds dear.

Ballad

In some respects, "Western Wind" also belongs to a special type of lyric called a *folk ballad* because it has no identifiable author and has been passed on by word of mouth from one generation to the next. Such ballads usually tell a story with great concentration, though few are as terse as this one. Their themes vary widely from the adventures of knights and ladies to the exploits of cowhands, miners, and railroad workers. Folk ballads are parallel to folk songs, and many are identical with these songs. In other words, ballads can be known and valued both as the lyrics to songs and as literary works in their own right.

As poems, ballads often use a special verse form known as the *ballad stanza.* This consists of iambic tetrameter (a four-foot line) alternating with iambic trimeter (a three-foot line) and an abcb rhyme scheme. "Western Wind" follows this metrical scheme. In addition, ballads often have a *refrain,* a line that is repeated at the end of each stanza. "Frankie and Johnny" uses such a refrain to emphasize the central situation of a woman who finds that her lover has been unfaithful: "He was her man, but he done her wrong." A careful reading of the poem shows that this refrain is not always repeated in exactly the same words at the end of each stanza. Actually, the variations adjust the sense to the incidents being described. This *incremental repetition,* a refrain with significant variations, is another well-known characteristic of the ballad.

Although the great age of folk ballads in English was the 15th century, when many were inspired by the conflict between English and Scottish barons living in the border counties, the genre has remained popular. Imitations of folk ballads, known as *literary* or *art ballads,* have been written since the 19th century, the most famous being "The Rhyme of the Ancient Mariner" (1798) by Samuel Taylor Coleridge (1772–1834) and "La Belle Dame Sans Merci" (1819) by John Keats (1795–1821). Modern poets have continued to experiment with this form, but it now appears most frequently in popular music. Since most folk ballads were originally sung, this format of sung narrative as practiced by the Beatles or Simon and Garfunkel marks a fitting return to the beginnings of the genre.

Sonnet

A much more precisely defined type of lyric is the *sonnet,* which conforms to a specific structure. In this case the meaning must be shaped to fit into fourteen lines of iambic pentameter with a definite rhyme scheme.

One of the most popular forms in English is the *Elizabethan,* or *Shakespearean,* sonnet, which is named from the masterful sequence of love sonnets Shakespeare wrote in this genre. The Shakespearean sonnet is easily recognizable because the ideas are divided into three groups of four lines, or *quatrains,* which are followed by a pithy concluding *couplet.* In the following sonnet, the speaker presents three separate comparisons for his beloved to suggest that her beauty is not only greater than any beautiful thing in nature but also more lasting.

William Shakespeare

SONNET 18

Shall I compare thee to a summer's day?
Thou art more lovely and more temperate.
Rough winds do shake the darling buds of May,
And summer's lease hath all too short a date.
Sometime too hot the eye of heaven shines,
And often is his gold complexion dimm'd;
And every fair from fair sometime declines,
By chance or nature's changing course untrimm'd.
But thy eternal summer shall not fade
Nor lose possession of that fair thou ow'st;
Nor shall Death brag thou wand'rest in his shade,
When in eternal lines to time thou grow'st.
So long as men can breathe or eyes can see,
So long lives this and this gives life to thee.

(pub. 1609)

Each unit of four lines ends in a period, signifying the completion of one comparison, and each of these four-line groups has its own rhymes: abab; cdcd; efef; with the couplet gg as culmination. Within this scheme the lover makes comparisons that involve increasingly larger units of time. First, he likens his beloved to a day in May, then to the season of summer, and, finally, to "eternal summer." The concluding couplet develops the idea emerging in the last quatrain that she will be granted a kind of immortality. Unlike the beauty of nature, which fades, the beloved's beauty will live on in the lines of this poem.

A more elaborate version of the sonnet—again with its own special structure and rhyme scheme—is known as the *Italian,* or *Petrarchan,* sonnet, named after Francesco Petrarca (1304–1374), one of the greatest Italian lyric poets of the early Renaissance. In this kind of sonnet, the sense is divided between a unit of eight lines, the *octave,* and a second unit of six lines, the *sestet.* Both sections have their own complicated intertwining rhymes—usually abba, abba—followed by cde, cde, or some variation of three rhymes.

In the following sonnet, Henry Constable (1562–1613), a contemporary of Shakespeare's, clearly follows the Petrarchan pattern:

Henry Constable
from DIANA

My lady's presence makes the roses red,
Because to see her lips they blush for shame.
The lily's leaves, for envy, pale became,
And her white hands in them this envy bred.
The marigold the leaves abroad doth spread,
Because the sun's and her power is the same.
The violet of purple colour came,
Dyed in the blood she made my heart to shed.
In brief: all flowers from her their virtue take;
From her sweet breath their sweet smells do proceed;
The living heat which her eyebeams doth make
Warmeth the ground, and quickeneth the seed.
The rain, wherewith she watereth the flowers,
Falls from mine eyes, which she dissolves in showers.

(1594)

As is typical of the Petrarchan sonnet, the octave uses only two rhymes: abba, abba. In the first eight lines the speaker explains how his beloved's beauty accounts for the color or behavior of various flowers—roses, lilies, marigolds, and violets. Each flower receives two lines of the speaker's attention. The turning point of the sonnet occurs, as usual, in line 9 with the words "In brief" and introduces a new group of rhyme sounds: cdcdee. In the sestet, the speaker points out what beneficial qualities flowers derive from his beloved. Finally, the couplet involves the speaker, for among the benefits his sweetheart contributes to nature are the showers she makes from his tears of rejection.

As in the sonnet by Shakespeare, Constable has contrived an extravagant and fanciful expression of love by comparing his mistress to objects of natural beauty—Shakespeare's "the darling buds of May," the sun, and the summer function in the same way as Constable's flowers, their perfume, and the spring showers. Shakespeare's thoughts and phrases may strike us as more powerful and expressive than Constable's, but Constable has demonstrated his talent by writing an unforced and pleasant sonnet in a difficult form that demands a high degree of skill and control.

A poet faces no easy task in observing all the conventions of a sonnet, especially the complex rhyme scheme. Writing Petrarchan sonnets is particularly difficult because only five rhymes are permitted, requiring the poet to make sense while using a limited number of sounds. Indeed, in the Petrarchan octave only two rhymes are available. By contrast, the Shakespearean sonnet is easier to write, requiring only two lines to rhyme on the same sound and allowing seven rhymes to be used in the poem. Since the English language offers a limited number of words that end in the same sound, both forms of the sonnet, but especially the Petrarchan, present a great challenge. We might ask why a poet would care to write in this genre with its strict conventions. Perhaps the answer is that a definite framework and other restrictions can serve as a spur rather than an obstacle to poetic inspiration. To paraphrase the poet Robert Frost (1874–1963), working without rules in poetry is like playing tennis without a net.

Prose Narrative

Prose narratives are more loosely categorized than poems. But such narratives, too, can be subdivided by treatment or, more usually, by subject matter.

Short Story, Novella, Novel

Length and complexity generally determine whether a prose narrative belongs to the genre of short story, novella, or novel. The *short story*—as we have seen in Edith Wharton's "Roman Fever" (see Chapter 2) and Eudora Welty's "Circe" (see Chapter 4)—tends to be brief and concentrated. It often presents a single action with a surprise twist, a character study, or a mood piece. A *novella,* also known as a *long short story,* develops any one of the possibilities of the short story more fully, as does Joseph Conrad's *Heart of Darkness.* The *novel,* finally, is distinguished by its considerable length, ranging from a hundred to a thousand pages. Using all the elements of prose narrative—plot, character, setting, and the like—novels can develop their themes with great detail and complexity.

The genre of the novel can be divided into subcategories. *Epistolary novels,* such as *Pamela* (1740) and *Clarissa* (1749) by Samuel Richardson (1689–1761), are written as a series of letters. With this device, the author can present the states of mind as well as the differing points of view of several characters as they send letters to one another. Other types of novels are recognizable by their subject matter. Those telling the adventures and misadventures of a rogue-hero through a series of loosely linked episodes are **picaresque novels**, a term derived from the Spanish word *pícaro,* "rogue." Such a hero, innocent at the beginning, soon becomes worldlywise and learns how to survive in a harsh and often brutal society. With the increase in the reading public in the 18th century, this kind of novel, like the epistolary, became popular. Henry Fielding's *Tom Jones* won a wide audience. The genre continues to be practiced by modern novelists such as Saul Bellow (b. 1915) in *The Adventures of Augie March* (1953) and John Barth (b. 1930) in *The Sot Weed Factor* (1960).

Another genre that originated in the mid-18th century and still enjoys popularity with some modern readers is the *Gothic novel.* This deliberately avoids the depiction of everyday life and offers, instead, supernatural and other extraordinary, thrilling incidents—mysterious strangers, graveyard meetings, midnight shrieks. The earliest and most influential example of this kind is *The Castle of Otranto* (1764) by Horace Walpole (1717–1797), which established many of the conventions designed to arouse "delicious horror" in the reader. Elements of the Gothic novel have found their way not only into modern pulp novels but also into the work of major writers. Charles Dickens in *Great Expectations* has the terrifying convict suddenly return to a lonely and frightened Pip during a fierce midnight thunderstorm in a scene that epitomizes the Gothic strain. And William Faulkner, along with other 20th-century southern writers in the United States, liked to incorporate macabre elements into his novels.

Still, the mainstream of the novel is to be found in works that offer a realistic view of life. The term **realism** refers both to the choice of subject and to technique. The subjects of realistic novels are usually middle-class and lower-class characters engaged in commonplace activities. Moreover, in technique these novels emphasize specific details—the sights and sounds of everyday life and the speech patterns of ordinary people. Realism may set out to report haphazard, unstructured experience, but an author's choice of material inevitably involves selectivity and therefore a shaping or interpretation of life.

Realistic novels included the epistolary and picaresque novels popular in the 18th century, but became even more important in the 19th century. At that time, the dominant genre became the *social novel,* which portrays characters facing problems in family life and society and which provides concrete details that reveal the manners of different social classes. In *Pride and Prejudice* (1813) Jane Austen (1775–1817) concentrates on the varied behavior of young women in a small, tightly knit English community as they experience the pleasures and pains of courtship. Austen gives attention to such minor matters as the choice of dancing partners and the conversation at dinner parties, which actually reveal each character's social standing and values. Many other realistic social novels since the 19th century have focused not on the usually amusing incidents leading up to marriage, but on its less happy consequences—problems of adjustment, marital conflict, and even adultery.

Closely related to the social novel, and often combined with it, is the *psychological novel.* Here the emphasis is on the complexity of the main character, usually a young person who is developing as an individual and who may also be trying to rise in society. The thought processes of such a character are usually presented in great detail. To increase the realism, the device of stream of consciousness (see Chapter 4) may be used in an attempt to capture the workings of the mind as thoughts or images come into consciousness. When the focus is on the maturing of the central character, the novel is also called a *Bildungsroman—Bildung* being the German word for the formation of a personality. How greatly these classifications overlap can be seen in Dickens' *Great Expectations,* which can be regarded as a social novel, a psychological novel, and a *Bildungsroman,* with occasional Gothic touches.

Other categories of the novel abound. As their names make clear, they emphasize different kinds of subject matter. The *historical novel,* made popular by Sir Walter Scott (1771–1832), tells a story set in an historical period and gives a strong sense of the social realities of that time. Unlike history painting, which tends to focus on the leading historical figures of the event being depicted, this kind of novel usually presents fictional characters as the central figures. The *political novel* places its characters in the arena of contemporary government or international affairs. The *detective novel* is distinguished by its main character and, together with the *mystery novel,* by a plot that is organized in terms of a search for the solution of a mystery. The *Western* and *science-fiction* are distinguished by their settings. In addition to such primary features, each of these genres has its own conventions. These include particular kinds of heroes in detective novels, standard conflicts in Westerns, and futuristic technology in science-fiction.

Now that we have reviewed some of the genres in the arts of time, we can see that these range from categories that are loosely united by subject matter to others that have definite conventions. Until recently, artists tended to pay close attention to the traditional elements of the genre in which they were working. Poets, for instance, deliberately submitted to the tight requirements of the sonnet, and composers closely followed the standard structure of the symphony. If we, as audiences, become familiar with the characteristics of the various genres, we can better appreciate the skill of artists who work within these genres while imposing their own stamp upon their creations. Knowledge of the genres will help us even when we find works, usually modern ones, that seem not to belong to any established genre. We will be better able to understand and appreciate such works if we realize that the artist may be deliberately combining elements from several genres or deliberately refusing to accept any of the conventions of the traditional genres.

Questions for Study and Discussion

1. What features—such as subject matter, form, treatment, or a combination of these—determine each of the genres described in this chapter? Are these features the same for all genres of the arts of time? Can one say that some genres are better than others?
2. When hearing an unfamiliar piece of music, how can one know whether the work is a symphony, concerto, sonata, or chamber music? What are the chief characteristics of each of these genres?
3. What is the difference between the sonata as a genre and sonata-form composition?
4. What are the differences between the art song and the folk song?
5. Analyze the lyrics of a popular song. What devices of images, sound effects, and stanza form are used? Does the emotion expressed in the words find comparable expression in the musical setting? Is the music in strophic form?
6. What human experiences presented in the epic cannot be as readily shown in the other poetic genres described in this chapter? What distinctive treatment is given to these experiences in the epic?
7. To show the different ways in which poets can work within a genre, find contrasting examples of the lyric, ballad, and sonnet.
8. How does the Shakespearean, or English, sonnet differ from the Petrarchan, or Italian, sonnet? How does the structure of each type of sonnet affect the way the ideas are organized? What do the last two lines contribute?
9. Why do many artists—whether they work in the arts of time or space—choose to create within the established genres of their field? Why do modern artists tend to pay less attention to the requirements of these genres?
10. Among modern novels, which genres are still frequently used, and why are these genres more popular today than the others?

CHAPTER 9

Genres of the Composite Arts

Theater

Plays are categorized basically by their view of life and by how the plot and characters are presented. **Tragedy**, **comedy**, **tragicomedy**, the **problem play**, and **melodrama** tend to reveal different conceptions both of the individual and of society, and these genres range widely from the serious to the frivolous in their treatment.

Two of the oldest and most complex genres of drama are tragedy and comedy. These represent fundamentally different views of life. As Horace Walpole observed, "This world is a comedy to those who think, and a tragedy to those who feel."

Tragedy

Perhaps the single most characteristic element of tragedy is that it deals with serious and usually unresolvable problems of human existence. It dramatizes basic conflicts between individuals and forces beyond their control—the gods, or the state, or even powerful emotions within themselves. All of these can be seen in the tragedies of 5th-century B.C. Athens when the genre first flourished. In *Oedipus the King* by Sophocles (496–406 B.C.) the hero slowly discovers that he has failed to avoid a terrible curse placed on him by the gods—he has murdered his father and married his mother. In *Antigone,* again by Sophocles, the spirited daughter of Oedipus defies the state and accepts death as the price for giving honorable burial to her brother. In *Medea* by Euripides (484–407/406 B.C.) the savage princess is so overwhelmed and tormented by the infidelity of her husband, Jason, that she murders their sons in revenge. Similar unresolvable conflicts can be found in the tragedies of the Renaissance, the second great flowering of this genre. The ambitious hero in Christopher Marlowe's *Dr. Faustus* mistakenly thinks he can challenge God by selling his soul to the devil in return for infinite power and knowledge. And Hamlet is asked to fulfill a duty that places him in conflict with the state and with his own inner nature.

As these summaries of plot reveal, the characters in tragedy whose downfall is relentlessly traced tend to have considerable *stature* not only socially but also in other ways. They are superior to ordinary people—whether morally, intellectually, or in the intensity of their feelings—in that they are capable of carrying on a struggle in a conflict they cannot win.

Still, the tragic hero is generally defined as someone who has not only great stature but also a *tragic flaw.* This flaw or weakness, first discussed by Aristotle (384–322 B.C.) in his *Poetics,* is usually pride or, to use the Greek term, **hubris** or **hybris.** This failing is found in Oedipus, Antigone, and Faustus, to name only a few. Even if their pride is a fault, it is also an essential and positive quality, since they must endure against tremendous odds.

Whether the flaw is actually the cause of the tragic hero's downfall, as is often thought, depends on the playwright's view of life. Macbeth's pride or ambition, for instance, is directly related to his defeat, suggesting an orderly universe that functions in terms of cause and effect. But Oedipus's pride is not the primary cause of his ultimate suffering, which is due to the will of the gods. In Oedipus's case, the playwright is emphasizing the precariousness of human existence in an ultimately indifferent or irrational universe.

The general pattern of the tragic plot consists of the *reversal* of the hero's fortune from good to bad. In classical Greek tragedy, as Aristotle pointed out, this reversal is most successful when it occurs simultaneously with another element of dramatic structure: *recognition* on the part of the hero. Oedipus experiences a series of such reversals and recognitions as various messengers bring him news that is meant to reassure him of his innocence, but actually makes him increasingly conscious of his guilt. At the climactic moment, his most profound recognition—his insight into the enormity of what he has done—coincides with the greatest reversal. He who was most fortunate is now a self-cursed man, guilty of killing his father, the former king of Thebes, and of committing incest with his mother. In other tragedies the reversals and recognitions may not be so closely intertwined, but both are likely to be present.

As a consequence of their recognition, tragic heroes eventually come to a greater understanding of themselves and of the human situation. This *moment of insight* often occurs at the lowest point of their worldly fortunes and paradoxically serves to make them more admirable than they were at the height of their power. Attaining this insight into the human condition—Oedipus's acceptance of the full truth about himself, Hamlet's quiet resignation before the duel he senses will be fatal to him—is a special mark of tragedy, of its ability to dramatize the most serious and profound human experiences. After this final recognition, some tragic heroes may experience a rebirth or regeneration. Still, tragedies generally conclude with the death or at least the banishment of the hero, giving a sense of the ending of a great period and the beginning of a lesser one. The last words spoken over the body of Shakespeare's King Lear are, appropriately, "We that are young/ Shall never see so much, nor live so long."

Although we have been considering classical and Elizabethan tragedies together, these are actually two different subgroups, each with its own conventions. *Classical tragedies* are noteworthy for their tight construction. No more than three speaking characters appear at one time in the main scenes, which are separated by a chanting *chorus.* The plot is highly unified. It concentrates on one main action, with no subplot, and this action usually occurs in less than twenty-four hours and in only one location. These three characteristics—later called the *unities of action, time,* and *place*—are prominent in *Oedipus,* which focuses on the hero's search for the truth during his last day as king and which takes place entirely in front of the palace of Thebes. Moreover, in classical tragedies, the tone or mood of the whole is consistently serious and dignified [168]. Scenes of broad comedy are absent, and violent

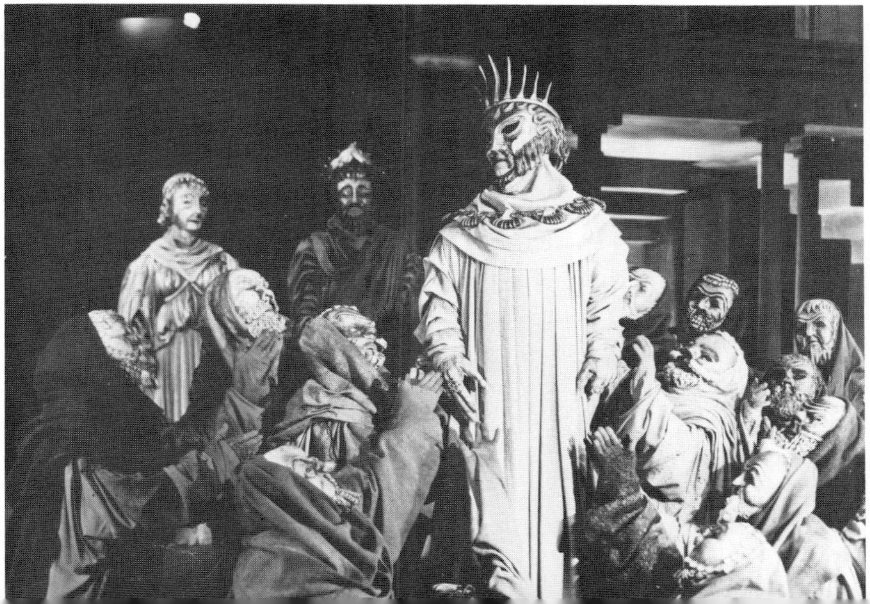

168 Scene from *Oedipus the King* in a production by the Shakespearean Festival Foundation of Canada, 1955. In this modern staging the actors are wearing costumes and masks in the style of the ancient Greek theater.

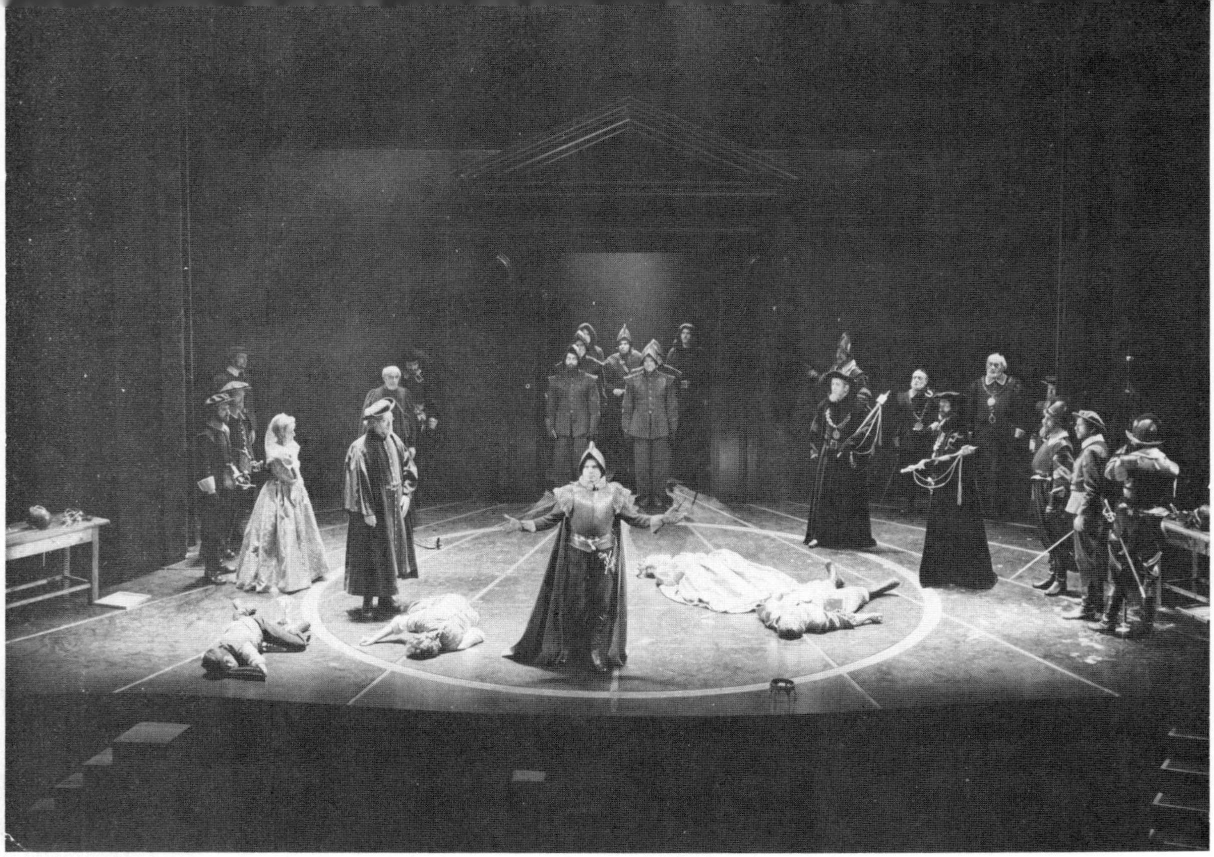

above: 169 Scene from a production of *Hamlet* at the National Theatre at the Old Vic, 1975. Directed by Peter Hall. This scene, at the close of the play, shows Hamlet and Laertes dead from wounds inflicted on each other with a poisoned rapier, the Queen dead from drinking poisoned wine intended for Hamlet, and King Claudius dead at Hamlet's hands. The Norwegian Prince Fortinbras has just arrived to restore order to the land.

action is never shown on stage but reported by a messenger. From the Renaissance on, all these characteristics came to be regarded as essential for tragedies. In Italy and later in France during the 17th century, those characteristics derived from ancient Greek tragedy became unbreakable rules and had to be scrupulously observed.

In contrast, Elizabethan tragedies are much more loosely constructed. These plays use many speaking roles to develop a highly complicated story. *Subplots,* which usually parallel the action of the main plot, are common. The time span and location of the action are unrestricted, so that years can pass and places can change between the events that are dramatized. Shakespeare's *Hamlet* has several subsidiary actions involving Polonius and his children, as well as the Norwegian Prince Fortinbras; its time span covers many months; and the scene shifts from the palace to the fields and graveyard. The generally serious tone or mood is occasionally varied by comic scenes, and violent scenes are also vividly enacted. The scene of Hamlet's conversation with the gravediggers provides broad comedy, and violence is shown on stage not only in Hamlet's stabbing of Polonius but also in the final duel, which leaves the stage littered with bodies [169]. Unlike Greek tragedy, which has intense concentration and unity, Elizabethan tragedy has great sweep and variety.

Even within Elizabethan tragedy, various subgroups can be distinguished. *Hamlet* belongs to the special genre of the *revenge tragedy,* which has its own conventions. These include dramatizing the revenger's problem in carrying out his task, his temporary madness, and even a play within a play in which the actual revenge is usually accomplished. Knowing the conventions of the genre, we can better appreciate the skill with which Shakespeare has not only adopted these in *Hamlet* but has also expanded their meaning to raise profound questions about life.

Comedy

Perhaps the single most characteristic element of *comedy* is that it deals with the less serious and ultimately resolvable problems of human existence. Comedy usually presents conflicts that individuals experience within themselves or their society, rather than forces beyond human control. Love and courtship, succeeding in spite of the lovers' blindness or parental and social opposition, is a frequent theme. So is the testing of moral worth, such as the unmasking of characters who seem to be good but are hypocrites. Shakespeare's *Twelfth Night* (1600) traces the experiences of two sets of lovers who are at cross-purposes because the Duke thinks he loves Olivia, and she, in turn, thinks she loves the Duke's page, who is really Viola in disguise. Molière's *Misanthrope* (1666) is largely a character study of someone whose uncompromising outspokenness in a fundamentally hypocritical society reveals the shortcomings of everyone concerned.

These two examples suggest that characters in comedies lack the stature or heroism of tragic figures. Unlike Oedipus or Hamlet, who arouse our admiration, the Duke, Olivia, and Molière's Alceste arouse our laughter and sometimes even our scorn.

Comic figures tend to be type characters rather than individuals, perhaps because comedy dramatizes social relationships rather than the struggle of a single hero. Eager lovers—often in pairs—clever or meddling servants, and angry parents belong to a tradition of comedy that goes back as far as the plays of Plautus (c. 254/3–184 B.C.) and Terence (c. 190–159 B.C.) in ancient Rome. Moreover, social types based on nationality, profession, or background appear frequently—foreigners with accents, doctors and lawyers with their jargon, hayseeds out of place in the drawing room. The weaknesses of these figures, which are displayed at every opportunity, are far less serious than the tragic flaw of pride. Their flaws are also more varied, ranging from foibles or minor eccentricities to follies or major failings to vice or wickedness.

Not only do the characters of comedy tend to be the same basic types, but the plots in which they function also frequently use similar devices. Many comedies rely on *disguises* or the introduction of identical twins whose presence leads to *mistaken identities*. After the causes of confusion have been established, the plot often creates increasingly intricate complications. All of these complications are eventually unraveled so that the misconceptions are clarified and the truth is revealed. The Duke in *Twelfth Night* ultimately discovers that his page is really Viola, an eligible young woman, and at that moment realizes that he truly loves her rather than Olivia, who, in fact, has just married Viola's twin brother, Sebastian. Here Shakespeare's comedy uses

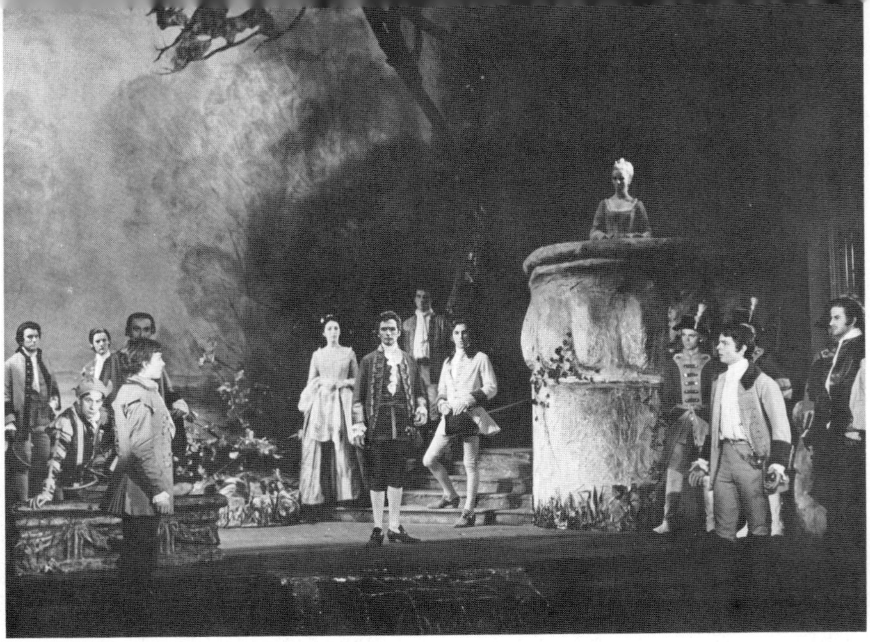

170 Scene from Shakespeare's *Twelfth Night* from the Old Vic production, 1958. The moment of recognition between Barbara Jefford as Viola (left), still dressed as a boy, and Gerald Harper as her twin brother, Sebastian (right) is emphasized by their positions at opposite sides of the stage.

the same pattern of reversal and recognition [170] observed in tragedy, but the general movement is from bad to good fortune. Even comedies with less intricate plots use striking reversals and recognitions. In *Candida* (1894) and *Major Barbara* (1905), George Bernard Shaw (1856–1950) delights in unexpectedly changing the balance of power between the major characters in each act.

The ending of comedy usually brings not only clarification but also suitable rewards and punishments. Generally, the good are allowed to marry one another, and the wicked are punished appropriately. This ideal resolution, which is known as **poetic justice**, implies that the universe is just and more orderly than appears in most tragedies. The happiness that dominates the conclusion also suggests that comedy celebrates life—the continuity of human existence and the health of society.

Comedy consists of many more subgroups than tragedy, ranging from **high comedy** to **farce** and from *comedy of manners* to *comedies of character, situation,* or *ideas.* These terms, as we shall see, are not mutually exclusive. Elements of one subgroup frequently appear in combination with those of another. The category to which a comedy is assigned depends largely on what aspect of the play is being considered.

Comedies are often grouped according to their subject matter or theme, and the terms used to describe these genres are often self-explanatory. *Romantic comedy*—such a play as *Twelfth Night*—concentrates on love relationships. *Comedy of character* makes fun of special character types—the miser, the hypocrite, or the hypochondriac. *Comedy of manners* emphasizes the idiosyncratic behavior of groups in society, for instance that of the scandalmongers in *The School for Scandal* (1777) [171] by Richard Brinsley Sheridan (1751–1816). *Comedy of ideas* features characters who serve as advo-

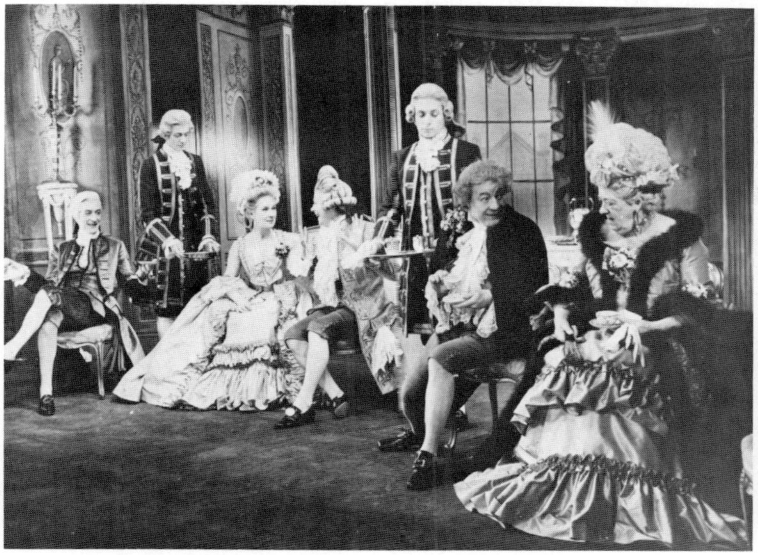

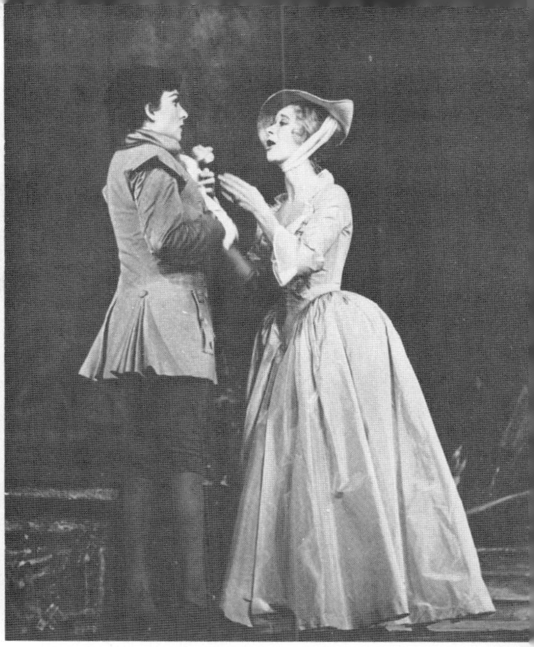

cates of differing philosophies that are played off against each other. In *Major Barbara,* Shaw, the playwright most famous for such comedy, has the heroine, Barbara, begin by believing in the values of traditional religion, while her father, Undershaft, represents atheism and the values of modern capitalism. In the course of the play Shaw paradoxically shows Barbara's ideas to be less valid than Undershaft's and makes us, as audience, reexamine our normal preconceptions. What prevents such plays from becoming propaganda pieces—which try to indoctrinate their audience with one special message or idea—is the skill of the playwright in dramatizing the conflict between important but conflicting ideas, giving equal force to both sides of the argument and thereby avoiding oversimplification.

Comedies can also be classified according to their treatment of plot, character, and language. The most sophisticated type is known as *high comedy.* This usually features upper-class characters of elegance and astuteness who prove their intelligence by their dazzling control over language. In one of the complicated wooing scenes of *Twelfth Night* [172], Viola, dressed as the Duke's page, realizes that Olivia, thinking her a young man, has fallen in love with her. Unable to reveal her identity, Viola manages to speak the truth without revealing it.

OLIVIA Stay.
I prithee tell me what thou think'st of me.
VIOLA That you do think you are not what you are.
OLIVIA If I think so, I think the same of you.
VIOLA Then think you right. I am not what I am.
OLIVIA I would you were as I would have you be!
VIOLA Would it be better, madam, than I am?
I wish it might; for now I am your fool.

(III, i)

above left: 171 Scene from *The School for Scandal* at the Theatre Royal Haymarket, London, 1962. Directed by John Gielgud. John Neville as Joseph Surface (far left), Muriel Forbes as Lady Sneerwell (third from left), and Margaret Rutherford as Lady Candour (far right). The superficial values of upper-class English society, as well as the malicious character of the gossipmongers, are revealed in this elaborately staged scene.

above right: 172 Olivia woos Viola in this scene from the 1958 Old Vic production of *Twelfth Night.*

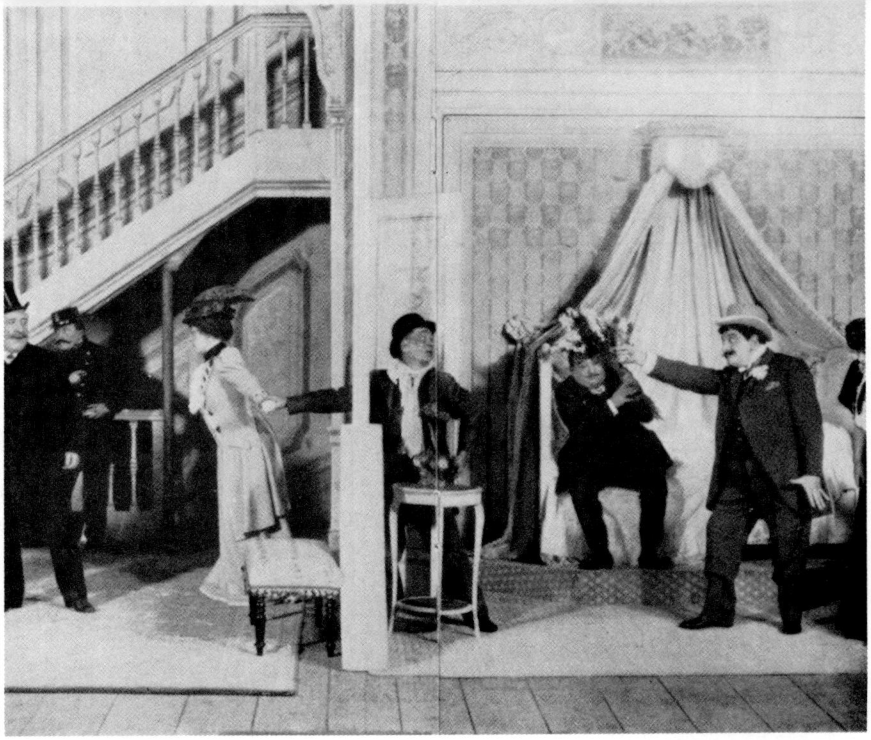

173 Scene from Act II of *A Flea in Her Ear* in the original production at the Théâtre des Nouveautés, Paris, 1907. The action is at the height of confusion. In a hotel of scandalous reputation, an irate husband wildly fires a pistol; his wife mistakenly leads off the drunken hotel porter; and a revolving bed, which has turned when a bullet hit the switch, unexpectedly reveals still another participant, who was hiding in the next room.

Viola is simultaneously teasing Olivia and mocking her own predicament. Indeed, Viola is intelligent enough to see the absurdity not merely of others but also of herself. She expresses this complicated response by her adroit manipulation of language. In her retorts she repeats Olivia's verbs in a quick, duel-like exchange known as *repartee.* Elsewhere, she uses *double entendre* in speeches that have different meaning to different people. For instance, when Viola tells the Duke

My father had a daughter lov'd a man,
As it might be perhaps, were I a woman,
I should your lordship, (II. iv.)

she is leading him to assume that she is speaking hypothetically, although the audience knows that she is describing her real emotions. Such rhetorical devices as repartee and double entendre are signs of *wit,* the intellectual agility that usually reveals itself in clever, highly polished language. And wit is a key characteristic of high comedy.

With its sophisticated, articulate characters, high comedy is often combined not only with romantic comedy but also with *comedy of manners.* In the late 17th century and the 18th century, plays such as *The Way of the World*

(1700) by William Congreve (1670–1729) as well as Sheridan's *The School for Scandal* [see Figure 171, page 281] united their survey of social types with brilliant, witty dialogue. So closely are *high comedy* and *comedy of manners* intertwined in these plays that the two terms are used interchangeably to describe them, again demonstrating how the categories of comedy overlap.

At the other extreme from high comedy is *low comedy,* or *farce.* Broadly funny, exaggerated, and improbable, farce often features slapstick or horseplay. Its characters tend to be flat, that is, distinguished by only one or two traits, which are often physical qualities such as a large nose or cleft palate. The action tends to be highly complicated and full of coincidences. Especially in bedroom farces, husbands, wives, and lovers rush in and out of each others' rooms in implausible sequences. The language tends to rely on coarse jokes and is less important than sight gags that may use stage devices such as disappearing beds. Entire plays may take the form of farce, as does *A Flea in Her Ear* (1907) [173] by Georges Feydeau (1862–1921). More commonly, elements of farce are introduced into other types of comedy. *Twelfth Night* has two low-comedy characters, Sir Toby Belch and Sir Andrew Aguecheek, whose names suggest their nature or appearance. They engage in raucous drinking bouts and absurd duels that culminate in their being thrashed. In contrast to the highly refined central characters, these farcical figures introduce moments of earthiness that greatly broaden the range of human experiences presented in the play. By incorporating elements from different types of comedy—romantic comedy, high comedy, and farce—*Twelfth Night* provides remarkable variety within a single play and therefore greatly extends our enjoyment.

Tragicomedy

Some plays combine not simply various types of comedy but radically different types of drama. An important example is *tragicomedy,* which is not merely an alternation of tragic and comic elements but a blending of the two that results in a distinctive genre. In tragicomedy, the characters are placed into situations that are intensely serious, yet the resolution is noncatastrophic. Shakespeare works in this form in *Troilus and Cressida* (1602), set during the period of the Trojan War. His young lovers, the title characters, are separated by this war and by the flaws of their own natures—Troilus's immaturity and Cressida's promiscuity. Furthermore, Hector, Ulysses (Odysseus), and the other warriors on both the Greek and Trojan sides are shown fighting for egotistical, cynical, or foolish reasons. But these serious issues lead neither to a fully tragic nor to a comic resolution. At the end, the lovers remain separated and the fighting resumes. The bitter and cynical attitude expressed in *Troilus and Cressida* reveals a highly complex view of life. In this instance, Shakespeare must have wished to write neither a tragedy, with its consistent emphasis on the insoluble problems of life, nor a comedy, with its final happy solution.

Perhaps the possibility of presenting such a complex view of life has attracted modern playwrights to the genre of tragicomedy. In *Who's Afraid of*

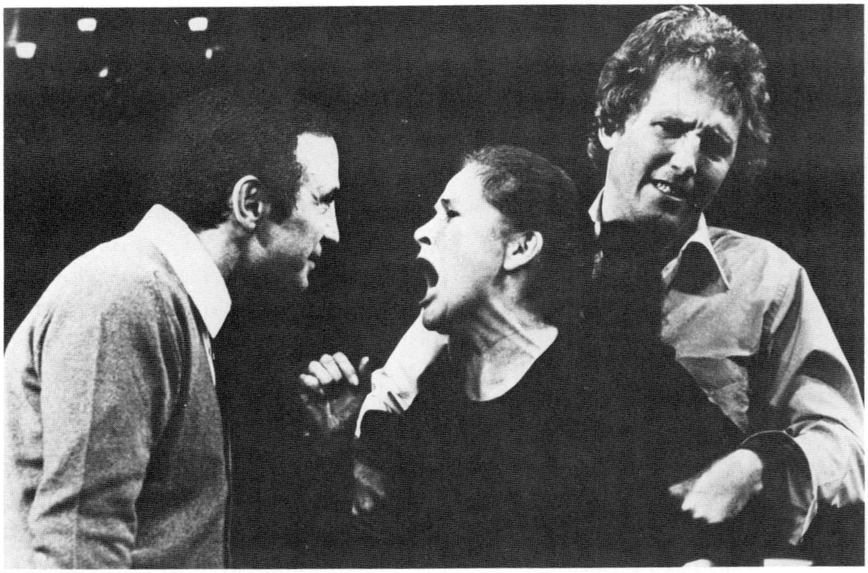

174 Scene from *Who's Afraid of Virginia Woolf?* In this 1976 revival at the Music Box Theatre, New York, Martha (Colleen Dewhurst) quarrels with her husband, George (Ben Gazzara), as she is restrained by their dinner guest (Richard Kelton.).

Virginia Woolf? (1962) [174], Edward Albee (b. 1928) dramatizes the intense love-hate relationship in a modern marriage, uniting near-tragic self-deceptions with witty dialogue. And, as we shall see in Chapter 12, Samuel Beckett in his *Waiting for Godot* conveys a similarly ambivalent attitude toward profound questions about the meaning of human existence.

Problem Play

Another popular 19th-century genre, one using realistic rather than sensational situations, is known as the *problem* or *thesis play*. As its name suggests, this genre focuses on contemporary social problems such as alcoholism and class conflicts. Some plays by John Galsworthy (1867–1933) such as *Strife* (1909), dealing with the problems of labor and management, and *Justice* (1910), dealing with the problems of legal and penal systems, are typical examples. Perhaps the most famous play of this genre may be *A Doll's House* (1879), in which Ibsen dramatizes the experience of a woman who is frustrated by her roles of wife and mother, and who finally walks out on her family, symbolically slamming the door as she leaves. In addition, such plays usually provide a vivid impression of ordinary life in all its details as background for the central problems. In this respect, these plays are closely related to realistic social novels (see Chapter 8).

Melodrama

Unike the genres we have just considered, *melodrama* makes no effort to provide a serious interpretation of life. It presents flat characters in exaggerated situations chosen for their sensational or sentimental effects. *Sensa-*

tionalism refers to the arousing of thrills or other strong emotions, often by scenes of violence. *Sentimentalism* refers to the excessive arousing of pity or sympathy, often by scenes of endangered innocence. In the play *La Tosca* (1887), Victorien Sardou (1831–1908), presents the sympathetic heroine Floria Tosca, a famous actress, being blackmailed into agreeing to give herself to the sadistic chief of police, Scarpia. Sardou develops this exciting situation through a series of thrilling scenes, many with an unexpected reversal. Scarpia has Tosca's lover, Mario Cavaradossi, tortured to persuade her to yield; she pleads for her own and her lover's safety, but then agrees to submit to Scarpia in return for a passport for herself and Mario. Once she has gained this safe conduct, she seizes the unexpected opportunity to stab Scarpia to death. Then she witnesses what she was told would be the mock shooting of Mario to effect his release from prison, but finds to her horror that she has witnessed his actual execution. Finally, Tosca, pursued by the police who have discovered Scarpia's body, hurls herself off the prison roof. These reversals are created to provide the maximum emotional impact. Significantly, they are not combined with recognition scenes, since these would not be appropriate for the flat characters of melodrama, who never develop or change.

In spite of the limitations of melodrama, *La Tosca* was the perfect vehicle for Sarah Bernhardt [see Figure 87, page 165], for whom it was written. So powerful was the material and what Bernhardt did with it that—although she spoke only in French—she enthralled audiences on her world tours even though they could not understand what she was saying. Her expressive gestures and stage movements, together with the broad effects she was communicating, made words almost unnecessary. This broad interpretation was characteristic of Bernhardt's acting only in melodrama and not in the tragedies for which she was also famous.

Opera, Operetta, and the Musical

Fundamentally, an *opera* is a play set to music, and it has all the elements described earlier in relation to the theater. An opera is performed on stage with actors who impersonate different characters in the story. And the actors are costumed and made to appear as much like the characters as the director chooses to make them.

Still, opera differs in major and obvious ways from a play. All the characters sing, rather than speak, their lines. Consequently, operatic performers must be trained as singers before they develop as actors, and their singing is more important than their acting. Likewise the quality of the music of the opera, far more than the quality of the words, provides the principal enjoyment for the operagoer.

For many people, opera is an extremely difficult form to appreciate because it seems stilted, artificial, unbelievable, and hard to follow. Who of us confronted with a spouse's infidelity or a loved one's murder could react by singing for ten or fifteen minutes accompanied by a symphony orchestra? Moreover, who of us normally enjoys performances in a language we do not know or with sung dialogue that can hardly be understood above the orchestra? We can respond to this genre only if we accept the premise that opera is highly stylized, depending on many conventions which are understood and accepted by the composer, director, performers, and audience. For maximum enjoyment, the audience must set aside the expectation of "realism" and recognize that the opera will not present experiences as we know them in life.

In spite of these difficulties, opera is one of the most exciting art forms. Many powerful works continue to attract huge, enthusiastic audiences in major opera houses throughout the world. One of the earliest operas to remain truly popular today is *The Marriage of Figaro* by Wolfgang Amadeus Mozart (1756–1791), first given in Vienna, on May 1, 1786.

Mozart must share some of the credit with the writers who contributed to the work. Pierre Augustin Caron de Beaumarchais (1732–1799) wrote the play *Le Mariage de Figaro* (1784), which forms the basis for the plot and which is a lively comedy still read and performed in its original version. Lorenzo da Ponte (1749–1838) rearranged the words of the play as text for the opera (called the **libretto**). His clever and witty lines, coupled with his imaginative sense of comic and dramatic confrontations, provided Mozart with a perfect vehicle for an opera.

The Marriage of Figaro is set in the castle and grounds of Count Almaviva (baritone) near Seville, Spain. He is represented as continuing some of the traditions of a feudal lord. Tired of his wife, the Countess (soprano), Almaviva wants to make love to her pretty maid Susanna (soprano), who is, however, betrothed to Figaro (bass-baritone), the Count's valet. These are the chief characters of the drama, along with Cherubino (soprano), the Countess' page, who is perpetually in love with every woman he sees. Although Cherubino is a young man's role, it is always sung by a woman—a convention used frequently in opera, since the composer is usually more interested in the combination of singing voices than in the gender of the actors.

The plot complication arises when the Count tries to revive the ancient privilege of the *droit du seigneur,* the right of the feudal lord to replace the bridegroom on the wedding night of any bride on his estate. Although Count Almaviva likes to think of himself as an enlightened modern gentleman and has abolished the *droit du seigneur,* he is now eager to revive the custom with Susanna! After many hilarious twists and turns of the plot, the Count is finally outwitted by both his wife and Susanna, whereupon Susanna and Figaro are happily married. This resolution of the plot implies that the Count is both immoral and foolish. The anti-aristocratic nature of the piece was not lost on the audiences of Beaumarchais' and Mozart's day. Indeed, the French Revolution (1789), with its violent overthrow of the aristocracy, was soon to begin.

Mozart uses all available devices of traditional operatic structure to tell his story. The musical events are divided into sections called *set pieces,* in which the singing is accompanied by the orchestra and the voice parts are quite elaborate. When these set pieces are sung by solo voices, they are called **arias**; when they are sung by two, three, four, five, or even six voices, they are known as *duets, trios, quartets, quintets,* or *sextets.* The set pieces are separated by stretches of sung dialogue that seem almost to be spoken. This sung dialogue, accompanied only by a harpsichord, is called **recitative.** During the recitatives, not very much happens musically, but we have a chance to hear the characters hatching plots and plans, and the action of the opera moves forward quickly. During the set pieces, the reverse is true: all interest is in the music. The singer is often content to face the audience, standing in one place and expressing a variety of emotions through the musical line as well as through gestures of face and hands.

In spite of this conventional alternation between set pieces or arias and recitatives, Mozart's music vividly conveys the quality of each character and situation. In the opening act, Figaro's aria *"Se vuol ballare"* ("If you wish to dance") establishes his cleverness and his confidence that he can outwit his master, the Count. The sorrow of the Countess as she reflects on the loss of her husband's affection is expressed in the poignant lament *"Porgi amor"* ("Bring some relief, love, to my sorrow"), the aria that opens Act II. Mozart's music, beautiful and sad, conveys a sense of mature dignity and grief. Shortly thereafter, the excitement and turbulent emotions of youth are expressed by Cherubino [175] in an entirely different kind of song, *Voi che sapete* ("You who know what love is"), which he performs for the Countess while Susanna mimes an accompaniment on the guitar.

Going far beyond the traditional alternation of set pieces and recitative, Mozart also creates dazzling organic scenes of considerable length—full of dramatic action, comic twists, contrasting voices, and appropriate orchestral accompaniment. For instance, toward the end of Act II, the Count, suspecting that the Countess is secretly meeting Cherubino, demands that she open the door to her dressing room. When she refuses, the Count returns with the necessary tools to break open the door, for he expects to find Cherubino in hiding. Instead, he is confronted by Susanna, who emerges from the room nonchalantly pretending not to know why the Count is furious. Next, Figaro

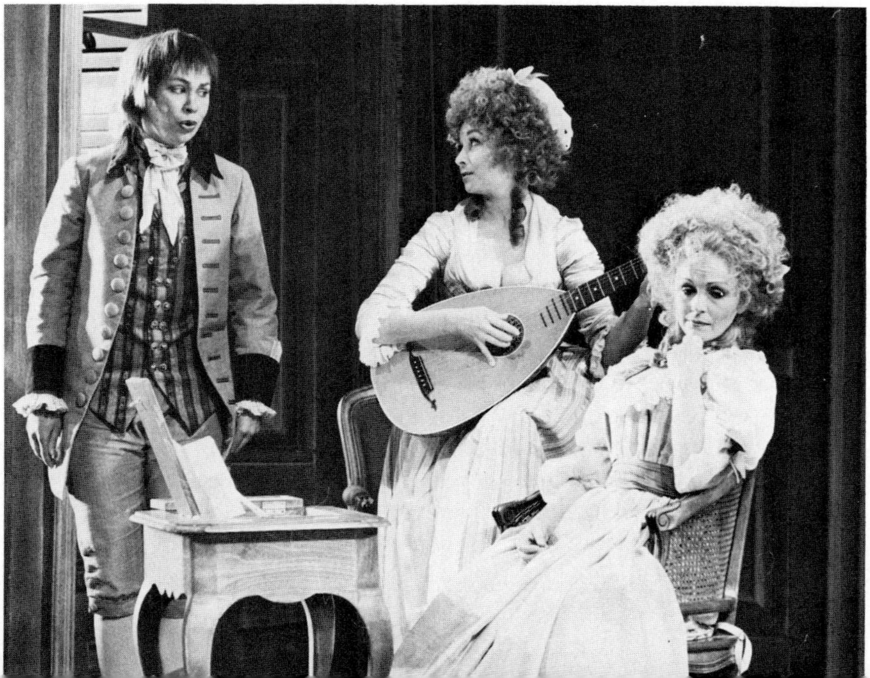

175 Scene from Mozart's *The Marriage of Figaro* in the 1978 production by the English National Opera, with Sally Burgess as Cherubino, Lillian Watson as Susanna, and Valerie Masterson as the Countess.

arrives and attempts to confuse the Count even more. But the gardener totters onto the scene, complaining that someone—Cherubino—has jumped out of the Countess' window and has destroyed the flowerbeds.

Throughout this scene, Mozart uses a wide variety of musical themes, keys, and tempi to keep the dramatic interest high. Each entrance of a new character not only provokes a new confrontation but also brings a corresponding change in the musical substance and mood. The whole section is unified by the use of closely related keys (E-flat Major is the central tonality) and, above all, by the gradual building to a climax. This is achieved by adding voices until Mozart has six characters, a sextet, energetically singing different words to different music at the same time. The sequence of scenes presenting several characters who sing together in various combinations is known as *ensemble-finale* (*ensemble*-"together"; *finale*-"ending") and creates a brilliant closing for the act.

Plays other than comedies were also reworked as opera librettos. Not surprisingly, melodrama proved to be a perfect vehicle for an opera. In his *Tosca* (1900), Giacomo Puccini (1858–1924) took full advantage of the emotion-charged conflicts in Sardou's play to create powerful vocal music. Tosca's moving plea to Scarpia *"Vissi d'arte"* ("I lived for art") and her vengeful cry *"Muori! Muori!"* ("Die! Die!") over the writhing body of her stabbed tormentor are unforgettable moments. [See Figure 137, page 232.] Not only is music a natural medium for expressing basic powerful emotions and sentimental effects, but the sensational plots also lend themselves to being understood even if the audience cannot grasp every word.

In the 19th century, many composers tried to avoid some of the older conventions, particularly the alternation of recitative and aria. The unity of Mozart's ensemble-finales served as inspiration. The constant striving for organic unity in opera reached its high point in the operas of Richard Wagner (1813–1883). In these, no recitative, no dialogue unaccompanied by the full orchestra, and no obviously separate set pieces appear. Since Wagner's harmonic style avoids clear-cut cadences, his music gives the effect of what has been called a "seamless web." In addition to composing the music, Wagner wrote his own librettos so that his operas are unified by one man's words and music.

Wagner also unified his operas by the use of repeated phrases or motives that identify particular characters, situations, or ideas. His name for a phrase of this kind is **Leitmotiv** ("leading-motive"). The repeated brief phrases take on great emotional and musical significance. Wagner often uses them to illuminate a psychological state through music in a way that would otherwise be impossible. For example, the orchestra plays a *Leitmotiv* that symbolizes fate or death while the character whose fate is foreshadowed ironically sings about his glorious plans.

An outgrowth of opera, in which all parts are usually sung and great technical skill is required of the vocalists, the operetta and musical comedy make lesser demands on the singers. In addition, operetta and musical comedy combine spoken dialogue with singing. *Operetta,* like opera, flourished in the 19th century. In France, this genre was popular in the hands of Jacques

Offenbach (1819–1880). His *La Belle Hélène* (1864) amusingly reinterprets the events following the abduction of Helen of Troy in a way that mocks the manners and morals of mid-19th-century France. In Austria, Johann Strauss (1825–1899) and Franz Lehar (1870–1948) set charming though sentimental love stories to music. They are remembered today especially for their delightful waltzes. In England, the greatest masters of the operetta, William S. Gilbert (1836–1911) and Sir Arthur Sullivan (1842–1900), spoofed social and political issues of Victorian England in witty songs with intricate rhymes. In *H.M.S. Pinafore* (1878), Gilbert lets his Sir Joseph, First Lord of the Admiralty, recount his rise to the top from the lowly positions of window cleaner, officeboy, and junior clerk in a law office:

SIR JOSEPH
As office boy I made such a mark
That they gave me the post of a junior clerk.
I served the writs with a smile so bland,
And I copied all the letters in a big round hand—
CHORUS
He copied all the letters in a big round hand.
SIR JOSEPH
I copied all the letters in a hand so free,
That now I am the Ruler of the Queen's Navee!
CHORUS
He copied, &c.
SIR JOSEPH
In serving writs I made such a name
That an articled clerk I soon became;
I wore clean collars and a bran-new suit
For the pass examination at the Institute.
CHORUS
For the pass examination at the Institute.
SIR JOSEPH
That pass examination did so well for me.
That now I am the Ruler of the Queen's Navee!
CHORUS
That pass examination, &c.
SIR JOSEPH
Of legal knowledge I acquired such a grip
That they took me into the partnership.
And that junior partnership I ween
Was the only ship that I ever had seen.
CHORUS
Was the only ship he ever had seen.
SIR JOSEPH
That kind of ship so suited me,
That now I am the Ruler of the Queen's Navee!
CHORUS
But that kind, &c.
SIR JOSEPH
I grew so rich that I was sent

By a pocket borough[1] into Parliament.
I always voted at my party's call,
And I never thought of thinking for myself at all.

CHORUS

He never thought of thinking for himself at all.

SIR JOSEPH

I thought so little, they rewarded me
By making me the Ruler of the Queen's Navee!

CHORUS

He thought so little, &c.

SIR JOSEPH

Now landsmen all, whoever you may be,
If you want to rise to the top of the tree,
If your soul isn't fettered to an office stool,
Be careful to be guided by this golden rule—

CHORUS

Be careful to be guided by this golden rule.

SIR JOSEPH

Stick close to your desks and never go to sea,
And you all may be Rulers of the Queen's Navee!

CHORUS

Stick close, &c.

[1] a borough whose representative is chosen by the political party rather than by popular vote

Sullivan's spirited music accompanies these satirical lines, which are always delivered at top speed in more of a speaking than a singing voice.

The 20th-century American version of the operetta has become known as *musical comedy,* or, simply, *the musical.* At its best, it is distinguished by its total integration of spoken drama, song, and dance, requiring performers to be proficient in all three of these art forms. *Oklahoma!* (1943), with music by Richard Rodgers (1902–1979) and book and lyrics by Oscar Hammerstein (1895–1960), is often regarded as the first great modern musical comedy in that it fuses characteristically American-sounding music and a serious love story with exuberant dancing, choreographed by Agnes de Mille (b. 1905). Like *Oklahoma!,* two more recent and equally distinguished musicals are reworkings of plays. *My Fair Lady* (1956), with music by Frederick Loewe (b. 1904) and book and lyrics by Alan Jay Lerner (b. 1918), closely follows the plot and witty dialogue of George Bernard Shaw's *Pygmalion.* Not surprisingly, dialogue and songs are more important here than dance. *West Side Story* (1957), with music by Leonard Bernstein and lyrics by Stephen Sondheim (b. 1930), freely adapts Shakespeare's *Romeo and Juliet,* transposing the action to the conflict between youth gangs in 20th-century New York City. Here the synthesis among the art forms is bolder, for dance is incorporated more successfully with dialogue and song. Indeed, a French critic has rightly called *West Side Story* "total theater." Finally, *A Chorus Line* (1975) [176] by Michael Bennett (b. 1943), Marvin Hamlisch (b. 1946) and James Kirkwood, Jr., (b. 1930), the musical that has had the longest run on Broadway, cleverly continues this integration of story, music, and dance by focusing on a group of dancers auditioning for a place in the chorus line of a new musical.

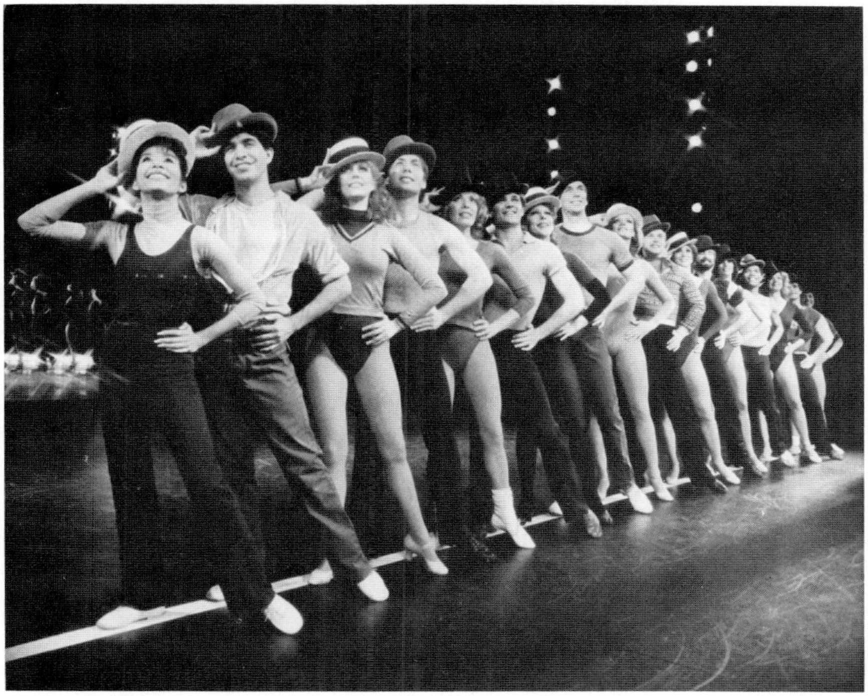

176 Scene from *A Chorus Line,* 1975. Book by James Kirkwood and Nicholas Dante. Music by Marvin Hamlisch. Directed by Michael Bennett.

Film

Because film is so closely related to most of the art forms we have just considered, it works within some of the same genres as these other art forms. The Western, zany and musical comedies, epic spectacle, and the thriller are popular and easily recognizable types. Their nature is usually determined by the subject matter and, in the case of epic films, by elaborate treatment. In addition, genres such as **film noir** are determined by their cinematographic techniques. In examining these categories in turn, we should bear in mind that, as in the other arts, genres in film are not mutually exclusive and several may be combined within a single motion picture.

The Western

Usually set in the period following the Civil War and located in the West or Southwest of the United States, the Western tends to present characters who are clearly either good or evil and who are shown in situations that involve physical conflict and other forms of violence. Typically, the good characters—cowhands, farmers, sheriffs, and schoolteachers—represent the forces of order, law, and civilization. They oppose the representatives of disorder, lawlessness, and savagery such as train robbers, rustlers, and renegades. The confrontation between these two opposing factions leads to stand-

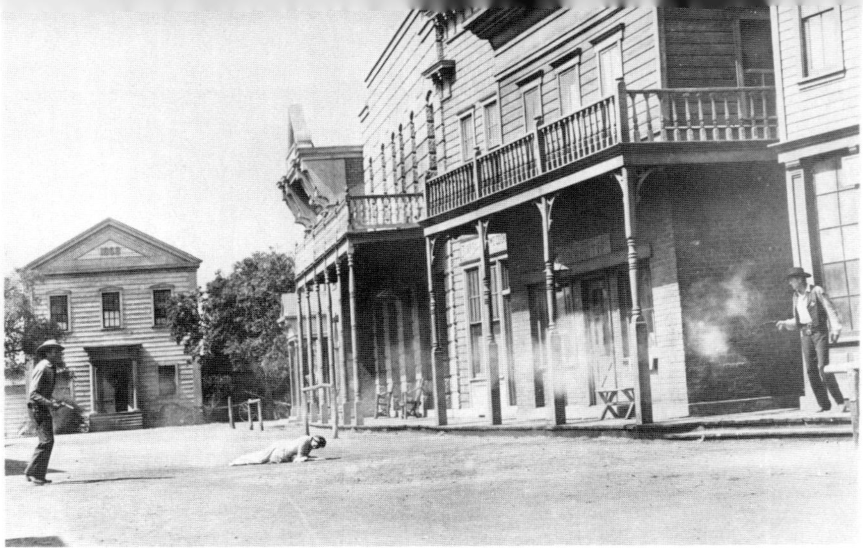

177 The final shootout scene from *High Noon,* 1952. Directed by Fred Zinnemann. In the last moments of the showdown, the sheriff's wife (Grace Kelly) has just broken free of the outlaw (Ian MacDonald) on the left, who had been holding her hostage. She has fallen in the street as her husband (Gary Cooper) kills the last member of the outlaw gang.

ard scenes including a chase and a final showdown [177]. Visually, these films—often shot in Monument Valley, Arizona—present immense open spaces which are contrasted with tiny outposts of civilization. The ability of film to capture motion by tracking and panning can make the chase and showdown scenes especially exciting.

The simple conflict between the forces of good and evil or civilization and lawlessness which is the theme of the ordinary Western has been treated with great subtlety in such outstanding examples of the genre as *My Darling Clementine* (1946), directed by John Ford (1895–1973), *High Noon* (1952), directed by Fred Zinnemann (b. 1907), and *The Wild Bunch* (1969), directed by Sam Peckinpah (1926–1984). In *High Noon,* members of the supposedly civilized community are shown to be weak and cowardly as they refuse to help the heroic sheriff in his struggle against a group of outlaws. Not only the community's but also the hero's behavior is atypical. At the end, although he has been successful, the disillusioned sheriff throws down his badge, leaving the town to its fate. In addition, this film is much more tightly constructed than the usual Western, for it strictly observes the unities of both action and time. Everything is directly related to the central conflict and takes place within a few hours. Its disillusionment with civilization and the concentrated action make *High Noon* far more thought provoking and powerful than most Westerns.

Comedy

Like drama, film can successfully present a great range of comedies. *Zany* or *screwball* comedies, popular in the 1930s and 1940s, offer very broad, farcical situations, often brought about by obvious incongruities. For instance, the directors Frank Capra (b. 1897) and Preston Sturges (1898–1959) liked to link a working-class hero and an aristocratic heroine, as in Capra's *It Happened One Night* (1934). The happy marriage that ends such films suggests a utopian or ideal society, in which class differences are eliminated. At the other extreme, *high comedy* offers sophisticated misunderstandings, witty dialogue, and upper-class settings. In *Roman Holiday* (1953), directed by William Wyler (b. 1902), a clever reporter and a high-spirited princess, having fallen in love, both try to conceal their identities. As a result, their conversation is full of double meanings, and their meetings are made more glamorous by the beauty of the Roman setting.

Farce is an especially old type of film comedy, going back to the days before sound recording was invented. Pratfalls, horseplay, and other types of slapstick were emphasized by accelerating the speed of the film, as in the chases of Mack Sennett's Keystone Cops. The outstanding actor of such farce, both in silent films and in those with sound, was Charlie Chaplin (1889–1977), who became famous in *City Lights* [178] and *Modern Times* (1936) for his portrayal of the little man—at once resilient and pathetic—standing up to modern society with its callousness and cruelty.

After the development of sound, the *musical* became one of the most popular types of comedy in film. Closely related to musical comedy in the theater and often adapted from it, such films benefit from the special capacities of the camera. Busby Berkeley (1895–1976), a former director of Broadway musicals, is famous for elaborate production numbers [179] and also for using the camera to move among the singers and dancers instead of remaining static at the front of the stage. The result, a dynamic, fluid impression, has distinguished film from stage musicals ever since. Although early musicals tended to separate the simple plot from the production numbers, later films such as *Swing Time* (1936), with Fred Astaire and Ginger Rogers, directed by George Stevens (1904–1975), and *The Wizard of Oz* (1939), with Judy Garland, directed by Victor Fleming (1883–1949), integrated the story and music

below left: 178 Scene from *City Lights,* 1931. Written, produced, and directed by Charles Chaplin, with his music. With his bowler hat, moustache, and cane, Charlie Chaplin appears here in his famous impersonation of a timid, naive tramp. In this scene he is unexpectedly offered a large sum of money by a rich man (Harry Myers) who is brutal when sober but generous when drunk. Charlie's tramp, who is often greeted by such erratic behavior, is understandably bewildered.

below right: 179 Scene from *Footlight Parade,* 1933. Directed by Busby Berkeley. In this production number entitled "By a Waterfall," the dancers are positioned on a revolving carousel and their image is reflected in the water below.

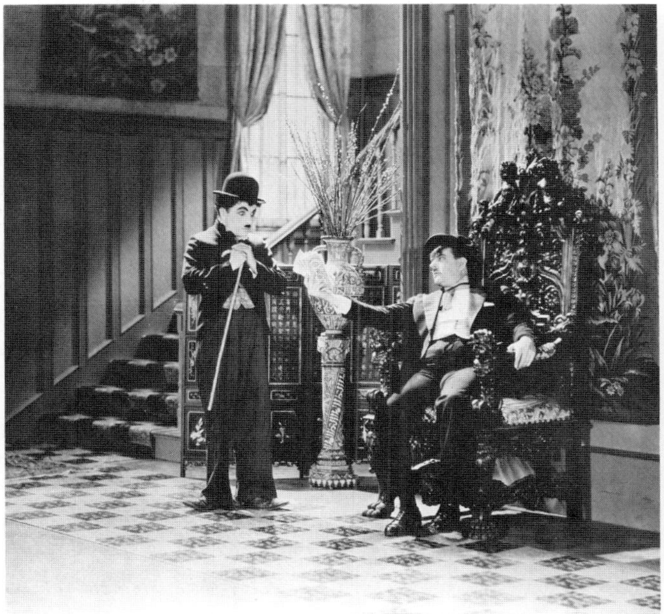

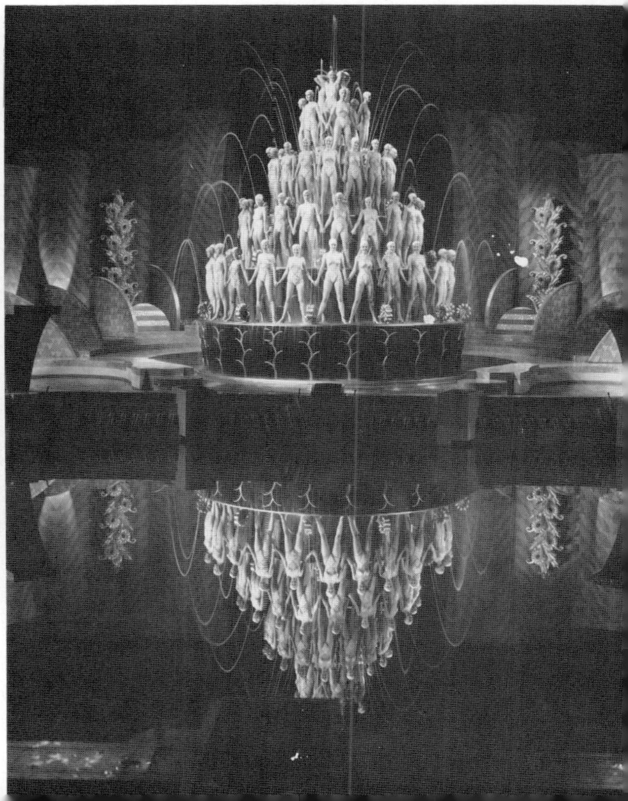

more effectively. Musicals flourished especially in the 1950's, when the use of color increased their appeal. *Singin' in the Rain* [180], directed by Stanley Donen (b. 1924), is memorable for the vigorous dancing by Gene Kelly and Donald O'Connor integrated into an amusing story set in Hollywood at the time when sound was revolutionizing the film industry. Today, musicals are still produced, but with far less frequency, perhaps because of changing tastes as well as increased costs.

Epic

The Hollywood *epic* has no connection with the literary epic we considered earlier, except for its scope. Its breadth is its key characteristic and one that is unique to film. For film can show far more actors, scenery, and action than is possible on a theater stage. Cecil B. DeMille (1881–1959) is famous for directing casts of thousands in elaborate spectacles with lavish costumes and gigantic sets. Often such films take place in earlier historical periods—ancient Egypt in DeMille's *The Ten Commandments* (1923 and 1956); the Civil War South in *Gone with the Wind* (1939), produced by David O. Selznick (1902–1965) and directed by Victor Fleming; and Imperial Rome in *Cleopatra* (1961–1963), directed by Joseph Mankiewicz (b. 1909) and starring Elizabeth Taylor and Richard Burton. More recent periods have also been treated with epic sweep, notably in *Lawrence of Arabia* (1962), directed by David Lean (b. 1908), and *Gandhi* (1982), directed by Richard Attenborough (b. 1923). Both of these films present not only the remarkable careers of the heroes but also elaborate physical, historical, and political background.

A new version of the film epic that has recently emerged substitutes the future or otherworldly settings for historical ones. Space epics such as George Lucas's *Star Wars* and Stanley Kubrick's *2001: A Space Odyssey* (see Figure 66, page 109) make full use of the camera's special capacity to make fantasy worlds appear real.

below left: 180 Donald O'Connor and Gene Kelly performing "Fit as a Fiddle" from *Singin' in the Rain,* 1952. Screenplay by Betty Comden and Adolph Green. Songs by Nacio Herb Brown and Arthur Freed. Directed and choreographed by Stanley Donen and Gene Kelly.

below right: 181 *Citizen Kane,* 1941. This scene shows the confrontation between Kane (Orson Welles), his wife (Ruth Warrick), and a political enemy (Ray Collins), while Kane's mistress (Dorothy Comingore) looks on. Screenplay by Herman J. Mankiewicz and Orson Welles. Produced and directed by Orson Welles.

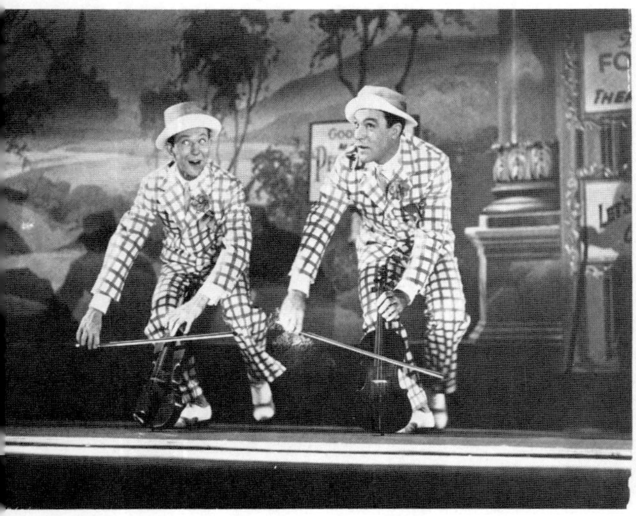

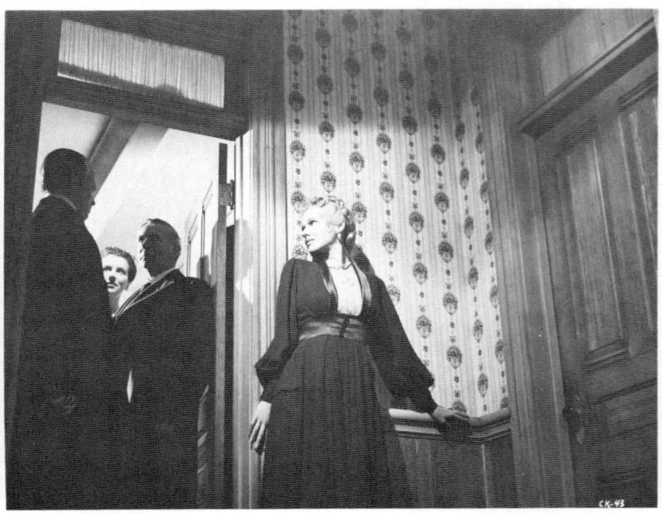

The Thriller

As its name suggests, the thriller has as its first objective the titillating or scaring of the audience. The James Bond series illustrates many characteristics of the type, particularly the implausible action, which provides a thrill a minute. The hero, an agent of the British government, usually faces powerful and malevolent political opponents. His weapons are his own intelligence, resilience, luck, and the latest scientific gimmicks. Without attempting any profound interpretation of life or society, such films as *Goldfinger* (1964) or *Diamonds Are Forever* (1972), directed by Guy Hamilton (b. 1922), are content simply to offer excitement.

The genre of thrillers actually embraces such subtypes as the *spy thriller,* whose hero is involved in international intrigue; the *psychological thriller,* which motivates the action through the disturbed personality of one of the characters; the *detective film,* which features either hard-boiled professionals or amateur sleuths; the *gangster film,* which frequently portrays hoodlums as rebel heroes in some ways superior to the society they prey upon; and the horror film, which often creates suspense by pseudoscientific inventions. In the hands of a great director, such films can present fascinating psychological complexities and, above all, make full use of all possible cinematographic devices. Alfred Hitchcock, whose work we have often referred to in our earlier discussion of film, is the acknowledged master of various types of thrillers.

Film Noir

Closely related to the thriller because it often uses similar plots and characters is the genre known as *film noir* ("black film"). This genre is determined not by its subject matter, but by its distinctive cinematographic techniques and special images. Usually shot in black and white, it uses subtle lighting techniques that contrast light and shade, often keeping large portions of the screen in darkness. Great attention is paid to the settings, many of which are shown at night. Moreover, some of the shots are taken at exaggerated angles, stressing oblique or vertical lines [181]. These techniques, which intentionally distort reality, are used to convey a pessimistic view of life, stressing feelings of alienation and isolation.

Citizen Kane is probably the most influential example of *film noir.* Showing the unsuccessful efforts of a reporter to understand the life of a recently dead newspaper tycoon Orson Welles, the director, uses disturbing angle shots and strongly contrasting black-and-white shading. The complicated story line, involving a series of flashbacks in which different narrators give their view of Kane, gradually reveals Kane's empty and unhappy life. Other examples of *film noir* feature criminals, psychopaths, and lonely people, usually in urban settings. For example, *Taxi Driver* (1976), directed by Martin Scorsese (b. 1942), shows the brutality of city life through an angry, disoriented, psychologically disturbed central character.

A great range and variety of genres can be found in the composite arts of theater, opera and other forms of musical theater, and film. Many of these genres—tragedy, comedy, melodrama, the Western, the thriller, and even *film noir*—are characterized by a distinctive view of life and a special tone. Some genres—notably tragedy, opera, and even musical comedy—have distinctive conventions as well. Like the genres of the spatial and the temporal arts, those associated with the composite arts provide a definite framework for organizing material. Often we can fully appreciate the qualities of an individual work only when we are familiar with the conventions and other characteristics of its genre.

Questions for Study and Discussion

1. How is the personality of the tragic hero directly related to what happens to the character in the course of the tragedy and how the hero changes at the end?
2. If one were seeing a tragedy without knowing its period or country of origin, what features would reveal whether it was written in classical Greece or Elizabethan England?
3. What distinguishes the tragic hero from the chief character of other genres of drama such as melodrama and farce?
4. Tragedy and comedy have been called opposite sides of the same coin. Support this statement by considering such elements as plot, character, language, and world view.
5. How does the use of reversal and recognition affect plot and character development? Why are reversal and recognition equally important in tragedy and comedy?
6. How do high comedy and farce differ in the means they use to arouse laughter? What is meant by *wit* and why is it particularly associated with a certain genre of comedy?
7. What are the chief characteristics of tragicomedy, the problem play, and melodrama? Are these three genres mutually exclusive?
8. Of all the genres of drama mentioned in this chapter, which ones are still frequently written today, and why are these more popular than the others?
9. On the basis of the operatic structure used and without knowing whether an opera was written by Mozart or by Wagner, how can one identify which of these two composed the work?
10. What is the distinctive feature of the musical, and in what sense is it an outgrowth of other performing arts?
11. What films that you have seen exemplify each of the genres described in this chapter? What traits of a film determine the genre to which it belongs?
12. What is meant by *film noir,* and how does the basis for determining this genre differ from what determines the other genres of film?
13. Which genres of film discussed here match the genres of poetry, prose narrative, or theater described earlier?

PART THREE

The Context of Historical Periods

Artists are profoundly influenced not only by traditions and genres but also by the assumptions and tastes of their own time. Consequently, a knowledge of its historical context can often increase our understanding and appreciation of a work of art. A study of three relatively recent historical periods in the next three chapters—Chapter 10, "Neoclassicism"; Chapter 11, "Romanticism"; and Chapter 12, "Modernism"—will reveal striking resemblances among works in different art forms created at the same time. These similarities include not only characteristic techniques but also a distinctive view of life. Although the qualities of neoclassicism and romanticism can be found at various other times, neoclassicism is closely associated with the 18th century, and romanticism with the 19th century. Modernism is associated with the 20th century.

CHAPTER 10

Neoclassicism

In ordinary usage, the term *classic* refers to something that is excellent of its kind. When we refer to a book, song, or film as "a classic," we do not relate it to a particular period, but when we identify artistic works as examples of **classicism** or **neoclassicism**, we have a more specific meaning in mind. Strictly speaking, classicism refers to the art and civilization of classical antiquity in Greece and Rome. Neoclassicism refers to most of the arts of 17th-century and 18th-century Europe and suggests that these returned to or allowed themselves to be influenced by the classical civilization of ancient times. Indeed, the 18th-century admiration for classical art is vividly shown in *Charles Towneley and His Friends in the Park Street Gallery* by Johann Zoffany (1734–1810) [182]. Here the collector, in the company of his dog and his

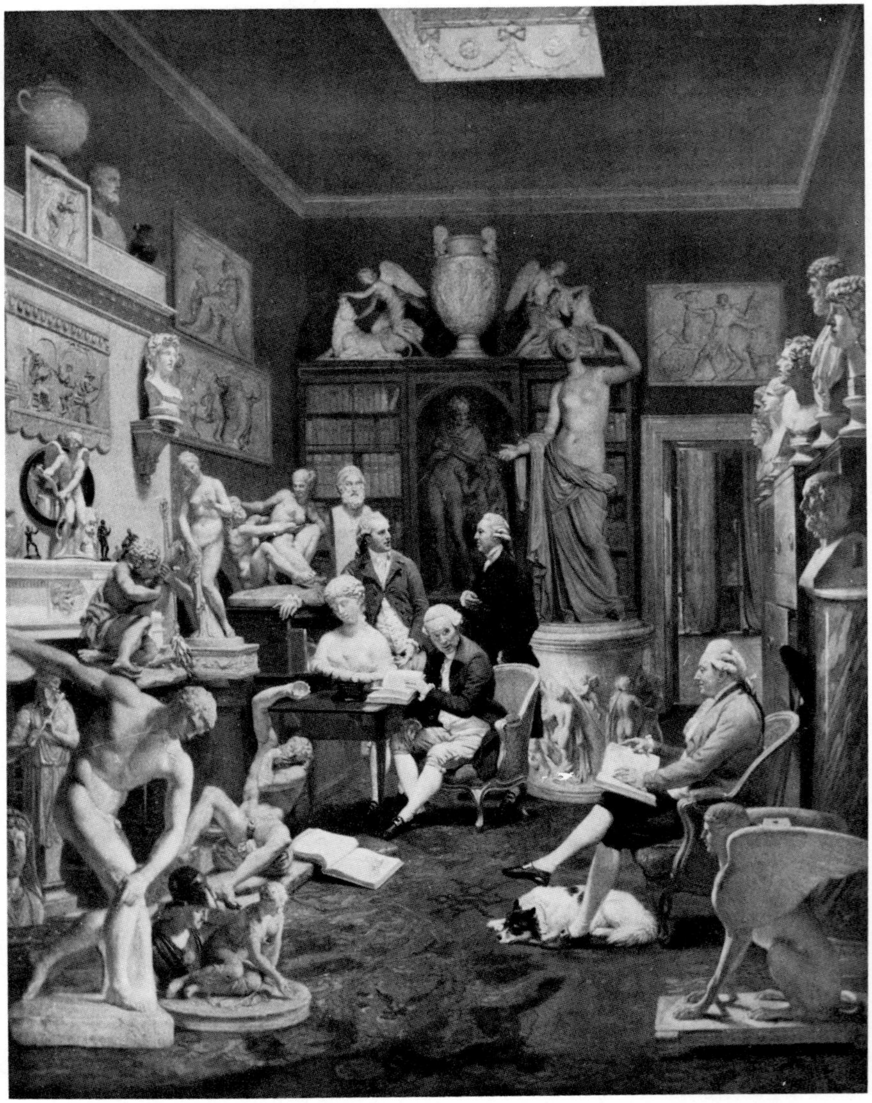

182 Johann Zoffany.
Charles Towneley and His Friends in the Park Street Gallery, Westminster. 1790.
Oil on canvas, 4′2″ × 3′3″ (1.2 × .9 m). Towneley Hall Art Gallery and Museums, England: Burnley Borough Council.

friends, has surrounded himself with casts of famous Greek and Roman sculptures.

The terms *classicism* and *neoclassicism* are also used more loosely. They are sometimes used interchangeably and the former is even applied to works of any period that share the characteristics of ancient classicism. As for music, 18th-century composers are known only as classical—and never as neoclassical—because they do not harken back to the music of classical antiquity, about which little is known.

The essential characteristic of both classicism and neoclassicism is their confidence in the power of the human intellect. Affirming the validity of the mind and of reason, they hold that almost everything in the universe and in life is comprehensible, order in the world can be discerned, and most problems can be solved. Clear thinking, good sense, and moderation are highly valued.

Classicism and neoclassicism are associated with a distinctive approach to life—a life conducted according to the dictates of reason. A direct consequence of this attitude is the notion of social responsibility, since our capacity for living reasonably is closely bound up with the behavior of others. The resulting political ideas may be either conservative, upholding the existing order as rational and well founded, or revolutionary, favoring the creation of a new and better order.

Closely related to confidence in the intellect is the emphasis that neoclassical artists, like the classical, place on *order*. Their works tend to be clear and definite. Nothing is confused or blurred in their presentation. They tend to exhibit a principle of *balance*, one that is often, though not necessarily, symmetrical. Little ambiguity exists about which are the principal elements and which are the subordinate ones—a separation that is sometimes called the principle of hierarchy. What is included in the work has been selected with great care in order to achieve *unity* and *coherence*. Nothing can be added or subtracted but for the worse. Finally, although these works arise in particular times and places, they strive to have a *universal* quality that enables them to transcend the limitations of time and place.

From this description we might conclude that classical and neoclassical art is cold, remote, and deadly serious. But such failings occur only in lesser works. Humor and playfulness are also found in the work of neoclassical artists, for they value the kind of mental astuteness or intellectual cleverness known as *wit*. For instance, in the cartoon by James Gillray (1757–1815) entitled *The Great South Sea Caterpillar, Transform'd into a Bath Butterfly* [183], the famous botanist Sir Joseph Banks (1743–1820) is gently ridiculed

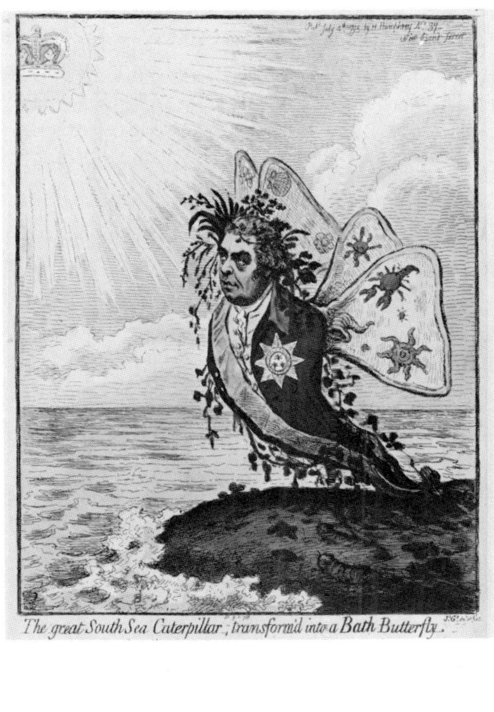

183 James Gillray. *The Great South Sea Caterpillar, Transform'd into a Bath Butterfly.* 1795. Engraving, 12⅛ × 9⅜" (31 × 24 cm). British Museum, London (reproduced by courtesy of the Trustees). The subject, Sir Joseph Banks, had accompanied Captain Cook on his first South Sea voyage to collect specimens and later became president of the Royal Society for the Advancement of Learning. An advisor and friend of George III, Banks was honored with a knighthood as well as membership in the Order of the Bath. Gillray, in this early example of a witty political cartoon, suggests that Banks owed his rise to royal favor.

by being shown as one of the creatures he was known to collect. To represent Banks as a magnificent butterfly was not only appropriate but also timely because King George III had just made Banks a knight of the Order of the Bath, which had as its insignia a golden starburst. Similar unexpected comparisons or juxtapositions can be found in neoclassic writing, where they are usually expressed in polished, elegant phrasing. Such witty effects are often delightful and surprising, and they are intended to show the artist's intelligence and control over the material.

The qualities of neoclassicism will become even clearer as we examine three major works, each from a different art form: David's painting *The Death of Socrates,* Haydn's *Sonata in E-flat,* and Pope's "Bufo" from the *Epistle to Dr. Arbuthnot.* A detailed analysis will also show how powerful and pervasive were the dominant attitudes and artistic principles of the time.

Painting: David's *Death of Socrates*

In the painting *The Death of Socrates* [Plate 15, page 319] the seriousness of the subject does not allow the French artist Jacques Louis David (1748–1825) to demonstrate his wit or playfulness. But his work provides a fine example of the other characteristics of neoclassicism.

David's painting tells the story of the death of the great Greek philosopher Socrates in 399 B.C. After the defeat of Athens in a long war, an arbitrary government came to power. In their search for scapegoats, the leaders settled on Socrates, falsely accusing him of impiety, of doubting the reality of the gods. After a trial, he was condemned to death and ordered to drink a cup of poisonous hemlock. We can still read the moving account of his last days in the dialogue *Phaedo,* written by his pupil Plato (c. 472–347 B.C.). David's decision to paint an event that took place two thousand years before in a distant country shows that he felt the theme to have abiding value. Not surprisingly for a neoclassical painter, David chose an historical event of ancient Greece. At the same time, the incident could be interpreted as a revealing instance of the clash between state power and the ethical values of the individual—a theme significant for David and his public in view of their own experiences with the often despotic monarchy in 18th-century France.

We can easily locate Socrates in the painting. He is the central figure, contrasted with the clusters of despairing disciples on either side. The philosopher occupies a dominant position, and in this manner the artist heightens the pathos of the scene: Socrates, who now dominates, will soon be gone; his pupils, who are downcast, will live. With one hand, he gestures toward the heavens, eloquently refuting the false accusation that he has mocked the gods, while with the other he reaches for the fatal potion. Although offered a chance to escape, Socrates has decided that he should accept the decree of the government, however unjust. His actions are therefore not taken on the spur of the moment—caprice and willfulness are generally foreign to the spirit of classicism—but are the outcome of a lifetime of reflection and reasoning. David's work is a didactic picture—one that teaches a lesson. It instructs us in the value of reason in all of human life.

The formal qualities of this painting also make its neoclassicism evident. First, the figures are arranged so that despite the variety of poses, we notice the main actor immediately. The individual human forms are crisply and precisely executed, so that they seem to be almost like statues. Indeed, the precision of sculpture was often admired by neoclassical artists. No important aspect of the action is left obscure. In the far distance at the left, we see the departing figure of Socrates' wife, who is being led away. Even the setting is carefully presented: the precise shape of the blocks of stone in both the floor and walls define the space clearly. The great arch at the left lends an air of finality to the scene, suggesting that an irrevocable decision has been made here.

David's brushwork is unusually smooth and self-effacing, so that we have the illusion of gazing at an actual scene through a window. This tendency of the artist to underplay his means, a technique sometimes called *transparency,* is fundamental to classicism in the visual arts. In addition, the colors are deliberately muted. Against a somber background, painted in shades of gray, the marble-like figure of Socrates emerges in strongly highlighted flesh tones and white drapery. The highlighting of some of the disciples, together with the recurring use of red and blue, contributes to the unified impression of the whole.

Altogether, David's picture has been planned with great skill. Its organization, brushwork, and use of color unite to produce a single effect. Nothing is left to chance. The elements are presented in such a coherent manner that the painting teaches the supremacy of reason not only in its subject but also in its style and organization.

Music: Haydn's *Sonata in E-flat*

The elements of clarity and proportion in David's painting of Socrates can readily be found in music as well. Classical composers, who flourished from about 1760 to 1820, attempt to make their music appealing, uncomplicated, and clear. To do so, they tend to write tuneful, singable melodies, and they make these memorable by setting them against a relatively simple chordal accompaniment. Their compositions are, then, predominantly **homophonic**, in contrast to the polyphonic, richly contrapuntal writing of an earlier composer such as Bach, whose *Mass in B minor* we considered in Chapter 6.

The *Piano Sonata in E-flat Major* (1794) by Franz Joseph Haydn—traditionally numbered 52—brilliantly combines singable melodies, varied rhythmic patterns, and limited modulations. The piece demonstrates these classical characteristics from the very start. The phrases in the first bar are continued in the second with a contrast of chords but nearly identical rhythm. The third bar provides the balancing contrast of an "echo"; the second bar is repeated in exactly the same melodic contour and rhythm, but at a pitch

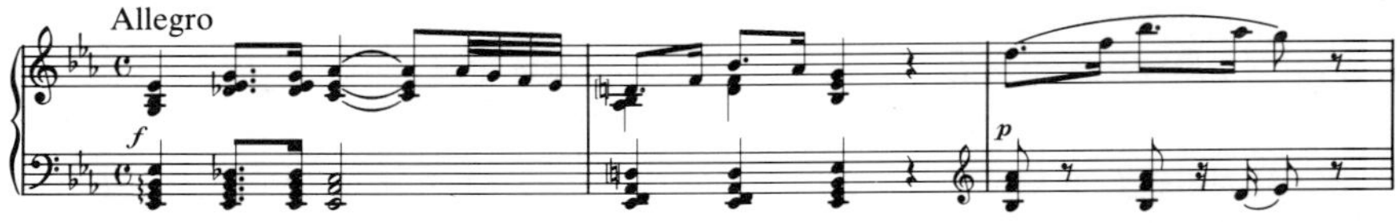

Example 17 Franz Josef Haydn. *Piano Sonata in E-flat Major,* Hob. XVI:52, I (bars 1–3).

register one octave higher and in a much softer dynamic [Example 17]. Such a repetition with its unexpected variation pleases yet surprises us. This kind of delight lies at the heart of classical music. By altering the pattern established by the repetition, the composer can create surprising or even dramatic developments.

To organize the piece as a whole, Haydn uses a clearly ordered structure. He begins with the *sonata-form,* also known as *sonata-allegro* form or *first-movement sonata* form, frequently found in the first movements of works by classical composers. This type of organization, as we have seen in Chapter 8, consists of three principal sections traditionally called the exposition (A), the development (B), and the recapitulation (A^1). Haydn's exposition begins with the majestic first theme and ends after about two minutes with a clear cadence (at bar 43). The exposition, here as in other sonatas and symphonies, is frequently repeated in performance. Then comes the development which extends from this point to where the opening chords return, about two minutes later, signaling the start of the recapitulation (at bar 79). Within each of these sections, variations in themes and modulations in key create variety, giving the impression of "going away" from the home key. The recapitulation ultimately returns to the tonic chord in the original key, creating the comforting feeling of arriving "back home."

In Haydn's exposition, the transitions from one key to another are sharply stated. The first of these transitions occurs early, when the work moves decisively into the key of B-flat, the dominant of E-flat [Example 18]. The contrast with the opening is emphasized by repeating the first three chords of the theme virtually unchanged, except that the pitch level is now a fifth higher. Following this change in key, a contrast in theme begins to assert itself, and a genuinely new theme, the "skipping" melody in the upper register of the piano, is soon clearly heard [Example 19]. Still in the dominant key, this leads to a closing theme—often called the **codetta**—for the first section.

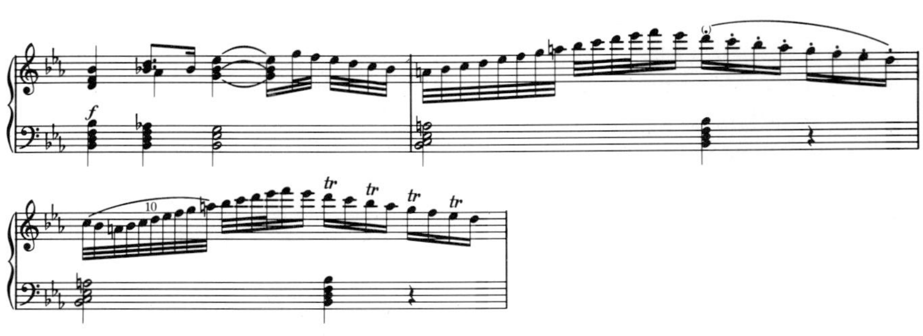

Example 18 Haydn. *Piano Sonata* (bars 17–19).

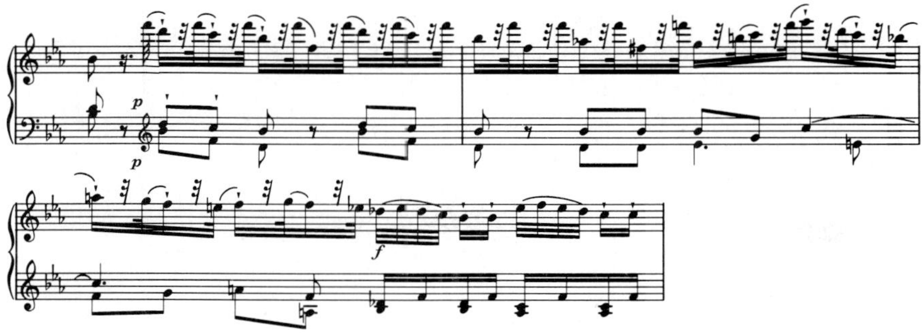

Example 19 Haydn. *Piano Sonata* (bars 27–29).

Haydn's exposition deserves close attention not only for its formal organization but also for its clever, witty details of theme and phrase. Characteristically, Haydn's themes are chosen for their divisibility—they divide easily into the small segments called *motives.* In Example 17, as we have just noticed, the first three bars show some of the classical penchant for balanced question-and-answer phrasing: bar 2 nearly repeats the rhythm and three-chord motive of bar 1; bar 3 echoes bar 2 an octave higher and in a softer *(piano)* dynamic. But the combination of these two balancing motives is a subtly unbalanced whole. The phrase is three bars long rather than the typical two or four: two answers, in effect, to the single question of bar 1. So Haydn toys with our sense of formal balance at the same time as he works within its bounds.

A witty self-awareness underlies the surprise of what follows almost immediately (bar 9). Here Haydn begins as though he would repeat the theme an octave higher, yet the four descending 32nd notes used at the end of bar 1 now seem to run out of control, becoming a 32nd-note scale that runs from nearly the top of the shorter keyboard of Haydn's day to the bottom. Then, as if no interruption had occurred, Haydn continues with a variation of an earlier lyrical phrase. On closer inspection, this lyrical variation consists of the right-hand melody transposed an octave higher, but played in the left hand, with a right-hand accompaniment above it—instead of the usual accompaniment in notes lower than the melody. This proves to be a bridge serving to modulate into the dominant key and preparing the second key group.

Throughout the exposition, subtle thematic relationships abound. The countermelody in the left-hand thumbs (the tenor line) in Example 17 (bar 1) consists of three notes—another motive—descending à la "Three Blind Mice" that later become an important theme (bar 27) [Example 19]. Here the "skipping" rhythm of the right hand gives an entirely new character to the motive. In fact, the entire piece creates its spirited effects in part by just such economy of musical motives. These same three notes will later signal the opening of the development section, where they form part of three chords that provide a harmonic surprise.

As the development continues, Haydn takes bits and pieces of the original themes and reworks them in new keys and new harmonic contexts until, somehow, he arrives at the very distant key of B minor (bar 72). At this point, he must invent some device to return to E-flat (three flats) from B minor (two sharps). By a kind of musical sleight-of-hand, Haydn slips smoothly down a chromatic half-step (from an F-sharp seventh chord to an F seventh) (bar 76) in a resolution at once exotic and inevitable. Soon the original tonic returns, marking the start of the third and last major section of the whole movement, the recapitulation. Both the modulations into distant keys and the dramatic preparation for the return to the tonic are typical of the development section in the classical sonata-form.

Amid all this harmonic wizardry, a constant rhythmic interest is maintained by a basically simple 4/4 meter kept refreshing and suspenseful by varied note rhythms. Haydn uses all note values from whole notes to 32nd notes as well as dotted and triplet rhythms in varied combinations. He also skillfully introduces pauses to highlight the dramatic effects. Despite the somewhat limited resources of the piano of Haydn's day, the composer makes use of all it has to offer in dynamic color—with shifts of *forte* and *piano,* swells, *diminuendi,* and register changes. The changes in register are particularly noticeable in this movement, as Haydn states certain themes in only the high or only the low range of the keyboard, while he introduces other themes that skip quickly back and forth across several octaves.

With its abundant material, Haydn's sonata-movement remains wedded to the resources of classical form, and never more so than at the close of the recapitulation, just fifteen seconds before the movement ends. Here, in a witty alteration of the exposition, Haydn inserts an extra bar of mysterious, tonally misleading slow octaves. Then, in the ensuing triumphant E-flat outburst—Haydn's way of saying, "Aha, you see! I never seriously intended to abandon the home key!"—we hear a quick trumpet fanfare, bravura scales, a sound like giggles in the higher register, and finally staccato grace-note chuckles as Haydn laughs with both performer and listener at his series of witty jokes.

Poetry: Pope's "Bufo" from *Epistle to Dr. Arbuthnot*

Many of the qualities we have observed in David's painting and Haydn's music can also be found in the poems of Alexander Pope. These neoclassical qualities are apparent in the brief description of Bufo, which Pope seems to have written as a separate piece and later incorporated into his *Epistle to Dr. Arbuthnot* (1735). Pope is describing a patron, a protector who gives encouragement and financial help to artists. At a time when poets as well as painters and composers had extreme difficulty in earning a living by their work, such sponsors often provided the only financial support available to artists. Although Pope was not dependent on specific patrons, because a number of subscribers subsidized his publications, he was fully aware that some patrons enjoyed the prestige of encouraging artists while keeping their actual support to a minimum.

Proud as Apollo on his forkèd hill
Sat full-blown Bufo, puffed by every quill;
Fed with soft dedication all day long,
Horace and he went hand in hand in song.
His library (where busts of poets dead
And a true Pindar stood without a head)
Received of wits an undistinguished race,
Who first his judgment asked, and then a place;
Much they extolled his pictures, much his seat,
And flattered every day, and some days eat;
Till grown more frugal in his riper days,
He paid some bards with port, and some with praise,
To some a dry rehearsal was assigned,
And others (harder still) he paid in kind.
Dryden alone (what wonder?) came not nigh,
Dryden alone escaped this judging eye;
But still the great have kindness in reserve,
He helped to bury whom he helped to starve.

In creating the figure of Bufo, Pope seems to have had two of his contemporaries in mind. George Bubb Dodington (1691–1762) was known as a vain but niggardly patron; and Charles Montagu, Earl of Halifax (1661–1715), may have withheld support from the great poet John Dryden (1631–1700) but later offered to have a monument erected in Dryden's memory in Westminster Abbey. Significantly Pope did not focus on the individual personalities of these two noblemen but combined the characteristics of each to create a general type. Pope was interested in the phenomenon of the patron as a social force, and he was also interested in the demeaning position of those dependent on a patron. Neoclassical artists were concerned with the problems of society, and they liked to present easily recognizable types in order to achieve universality.

The name *Bufo* not only makes the typical patron sound ridiculous but also has a definite sting. In Latin, it means "toad." Nor is the association with ancient Rome accidental, for Pope was deliberately following the model of the classical poet Horace, who liked to introduce character sketches—set descriptive pieces—in many of his poems. Before Horace, the Greek writer Theophrastus (c. 371–c. 287 B.C.) had also written brief character sketches of general types, so that Pope was drawing on a long tradition going back to classical literature. This conscious alignment with the classical past becomes explicit in Pope's opening lines, in which Bufo is linked with the god Apollo as well as with the poets Horace and Pindar.

Pope is not serious in linking Bufo to these great figures of the past. Rather, Pope introduces these comparisons for purposes of **satire**, the ridiculing of follies and foibles. Pope is mocking the outrageous vanity of the patron as well as the exaggerated compliments offered by his fawning dependents. Only in their hypocritical dedications is Bufo the equal of the Roman poet: "Horace and he went hand in hand in song." Pope goes on to ridicule the ostentation and lack of good taste of the patron, whose library is full of sculptured busts, including a headless one of Pindar. Here Pope is making fun not only of the patron's mania for collecting antique statues but also of his lack of discrimination, since he seems not to care that his Pindar has lost the most vital part—mentally as well as physically.

In the opening two lines, Pope uses an especially clever device of satire, the *mock heroic.* This is an heroic or solemn treatment of an unworthy subject. The term *mock heroic* does not refer to a mocking of the heroic, but to the mocking of something unheroic by presenting it in an inappropriately elevated way. By likening the vain Bufo to "Apollo on his forkèd hill," the Greek god of light and poetry associated in mythology with the twin-peaked mountain of Parnassus, Pope raises Bufo to such undeserved heights that he seems all the more ridiculous. Indeed, the second line, "Sat full-blown Bufo, puffed by every quill" suggests that Bufo is not so much raised as inflated, puffed up with false pride and with false praise. In addition, "to puff" in 18th-century speech meant to give inflated commendation, especially in advertising, and so "puffed by every quill" emphasizes that the praise coming from the poets' pen ("quill") is exaggerated and insincere. The result of all this inflating is that Bufo is amusingly deflated—punctured like an overblown balloon.

Even the few lines just examined reveal that Pope's satire is sophisticated and has a primarily intellectual appeal. In keeping with the general interest in the intellect or reason during the neoclassical period, satire was a favorite literary genre of the time. Moreover, satire is strongly dependent on *wit,* the intellectual agility or astuteness required of the writer in creating the ridicule and also, we should notice, of the reader in recognizing its finer points. *Wit* is a favorite term of the 17th and 18th centuries. Often, it referred to the writer's ability to create unexpected similarities, in contrast to *judgment,* the ability to discern differences. And certainly the likening of Bufo to Apollo is both unexpected and amusing. Wit could also be applied to people who aspired to belonging to the intelligentsia or to fashionable society. Pope uses it in this sense in line 7, when he describes those who come to Bufo's library as "an undistinguished race" of wits. More broadly, wit applies to the ability to express oneself in elegant and polished phrasing, often with a surprise twist, as we observed in considering high comedy (see Chapter 9). Pope excels in such concise, polished, and amusing expression.

Pope's phrasing is especially witty when he describes what the dependent poets do or hope for and what they actually gain. They ask first for Bufo's "judgment" and then for a "place" but the implication of this concise statement is that though they ostensibly ask for Bufo's opinion of their work, they actually want a position in his household. They praise Bufo's possessions—his pictures and his country house ("his seat")—all the time, but they eat only some of the time. Indeed, although they see that Bufo is "fed with soft dedication all day long"—a witty image that suggests the pap with which they bolster his ego in the insincere dedications at the beginning of their works—they ultimately receive less and less nourishment for all their efforts (lls. 10–14).

Pope is not just being clever and amusing, but is criticizing serious moral flaws. He is presenting two extremes: the patron who wants credit for gifts he does not provide, and the poets who prostitute their gifts for an unworthy cause. Implied is the double notion that patrons should not indulge in ostentatious display or demand absurd flattery, especially if they are willing to do so little in return, and that poets should not abase either themselves or their profession. Between the two extremes, the proper sort of behavior is also implied—one governed by integrity, moderation, and good sense or reasonableness. This behavior is briefly suggested in line 15 by the figure of Dryden, who "came not nigh"; even though he lacked material support, Dryden refused to lower himself before a potential patron. By the end, we have a deeper impression of what is wrong with the world of the arts and which standards ought to prevail. This concern for social and moral questions as well as the rational standards that are being invoked are characteristic of neoclassicism.

Just as characteristic is the strong sense of order that permeates the whole passage. Although it consists of only eighteen lines, it has a remarkably clear and well-defined structure. It begins with Bufo at his height, surrounded by fawning poets, all behaving badly, and it ends with Dryden, the one poet who, though at a low point financially, behaves properly. Moreover, the passage is unified by the recurring food images. At the beginning, Bufo is being "fed"; in the middle, his poets get decreasing rations; and at the end, Dryden is said to "starve," but is clearly more admirable than the rest. The pattern is one of balance and contrast—the kind of symmetry we observed earlier in David's neoclassic painting [see Plate 15, page 319].

Not only the passage as a whole but the verse form Pope has chosen also has order, balance, and symmetry. The couplets—two lines that rhyme—balance one line with the next, sometimes even one half-line with the other half. Usually, the half-line or whole-line units are not only parallel but also form an *antithesis,* or contrast. For instance, in line 12, "He paid some bards with port, and some with praise," *port* and *praise* are in parallel positions and also linked by the alliteration of the *p* sound, but they are antithetical, since port is still a tangible nourishment whereas praise leaves the recipients hungry and thirsty. In the couplet "To some a dry rehearsal was assigned,/ And others (harder still) he paid in kind," the two lines are parallel—both show the continuing decline in Bufo's favors—but they are also slightly antithetical in that the first shows Bufo offering no sustenance ("a dry rehearsal") while the next shows him reading his own writings to the disappointed poets ("paid in kind"), presumably adding insult to injury. The expression of so much satire within each couplet is another manifestation of Pope's wit.

The description of Bufo is, then, carefully crafted and polished. It is a very finished piece of work, the result of a clear conception of the whole and meticulous attention to details. Yet the impression is one of high-spirited ease. This ease comes from a skill that Pope brilliantly describes in his *Essay on Criticism* (1711):

True ease in writing comes from art, not chance,
As those move easiest who have learned to dance.

(362–363)

Such polish, along with the delight in surprising the audience with witty juxtapositions, certainly recalls the classical music of Haydn.

Indeed, the neoclassical painting and poem as well as the classical music we have been considering share a firmness of structure or organization—unity, clarity, coherence. David's *Death of Socrates* and Pope's "Bufo" also show a concern for universal experiences, whether by presenting a great scene from the classical past or an easily recognizable type. In addition, our examples from music and poetry show considerable wit—the intellectual cleverness that provides for surprising turns of phrase or points out unexpected similarities. The power of human reason to understand and order experience underlies all the efforts of the artists who share this approach to art.

Questions for Study and Discussion

1. To what historical periods do we apply the terms *classicism* and *neoclassicism?* How does the terminology differ for music?
2. What aspects of *The Death of Socrates* [see Plate 15, page 319] link it with such works of classical antiquity as the Parthenon [see Figure 44, page 50] and the Pantheon [see Figure 48, page 53]?
3. What characteristics of neoclassicism can be found in the Petit Trianon [see Figure 13, page 19] and in Canova's sculpture *Maria Paulina Bonaparte Borghese as Venus Victorious* [see Figure 111, page 192]?
4. Where in his *Sonata in E-flat* does Haydn include the classical elements of orderly structure, repetition, and witty surprise?
5. What other characteristics of classicism in music found in Haydn's sonata also occur in his minuet from the *Symphony No. 104 in D Major* discussed in Chapter 2 (see page 71)?
6. What characteristics of neoclassicism in poetry found in Pope's "Bufo" also occur in his description of the cycle of life in *Essay on Man,* quoted on page 80? What other aspects of neoclassicism can be found in Matthew Prior's "The Lady Who Offers Her Looking-Glass to Venus," quoted on page 193?
7. What characteristics of neoclassicism found in Pope's "Bufo" can also be found in both of Haydn's compositions?
8. In what ways is Gillray's *The Great South Sea Caterpillar Transform'd into a Bath Butterfly* [see Figure 183, page 301] an example of neoclassic wit?

CHAPTER 11

Romanticism

Like *classicism* and *neoclassicism, romanticism* is a complex term. As an artistic mode, it suggests an approach that is opposed to the classical. Rather than emphasize the rational powers of the mind, romanticism stresses the primary role of feeling—even to the extreme of expressing unbridled or emotionally excessive responses. In this sense, we will find elements of romanticism in most art, since artists of every age have actively concerned themselves with shaping works of emotionally expressive power.

But as a specific historical period, one in which the traits of the romantic attitude were most strongly developed and explored, the romantic age coincides very nearly with the 19th century. As with all such artistic movements, we can offer neither a precise beginning nor ending date for romanticism; nor can we provide what would be even more fascinating, a precise explanation for the profound change in artistic sensibility that characterizes the shift from one style to the other.

Nevertheless, we can describe some of the effects of this change in sensibility on works of art. First, we shall discover that romantic works exhibit less interest in the classical virtues of moderation, balance, and restraint than in unusual states. For example, in an etching significantly entitled *The Sleep of Reason Produces Monsters* [184], Francisco Goya (1746–1828) depicts a sleeping student haunted by grotesque creatures. Since the Spanish word *sueño* means both "sleep" and "dream," the title Goya has included in the work suggests that when reason slumbers, the mind is possessed by a dream of monsters. Such nightmares exemplify the romantic interest in the unconscious or in the mysterious powers of the mind. Indeed, the romantic impulse originates in the sensitive—sometimes hypersensitive—individual.

Some romantic creators as well as the heroes of their works may be rebels who actively seek to pull down the existing social order even though they have no detailed plan for a new society. But other romantic artists have less interest in society than in nature. Indeed, some of these, such as Caspar David Friedrich (1774–1840), feel themselves in accord with a divine and mystical power that is suffused throughout the natural world. In Friedrich's *Monk at the Sea* [185] the vagueness and absence of specific details in the earth, sea, and sky suggest not only the grandeur but also the mystery of nature and of the divine in nature. The tiny figure in the middle distance, though nominally a monk, has been interpreted as a symbol of the isolated romantic artist communicating with nature. Such communication in romantic

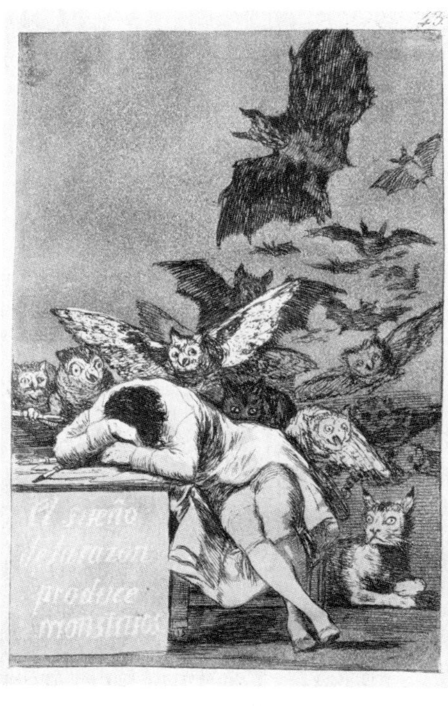

184 Francisco Goya. *El Sueño de la razon produce monstruos (The Sleep of Reason Produces Monsters),* from *Los Caprichos (Caprices),* Plate 43. 1797–1799. Etching and aquatint, 8½ × 6″ (22 × 15 cm). Metropolitan Museum of Art, New York (gift of M. Knoedler & Co., 1918).

art is achieved not through traditional religion or the intellect, but through personal feeling and intuition.

Furthermore, romantic heroes often long to escape from the banal and the ordinary. They not only experience dreams and nightmares but also seek drug-induced states of consciousness. Some romantic artists suggest estrangement by remoteness in space and time; the biblical Near East and the Middle Ages are both favorite settings. A high value is placed on strange, mysterious, and exotic events, as in the horror stories of Edgar Allan Poe (1809–1849).

In the visual arts, romantic works tend to prefer soft outlines to the crisp, precise, and clearly defined shapes of neoclassicism. Forms and space frequently shade into a vague blur. Night scenes are often chosen because in a dim light not everything can be presented simply and baldly. Romantic artists seem to be saying that what is of the highest value is ineffable or inexpressible: we can sense its presence but cannot expect to do justice to intuitions in concrete words and forms. At best, the artist can hint at these supreme values in the hope that we will translate inadequate approximations into our own special language of feeling. Perhaps we will appreciate romanticism more if we realize that this striving to convey something of the hidden and ineffable anticipates the 20th-century psychoanalytic explorations of the unconscious.

To understand the characteristics of romanticism more fully, we shall again focus on three major works, each from a different art form: Delacroix's painting *Death of Sardanapalus,* Chopin's *Ballade in G minor,* and Keats's "Ode to a Nightingale." In these cases, a detailed analysis will show not only how the artists reflect their age but also how they maintain their individuality.

185 Caspar David Friedrich. *Monk at the Sea.* 1808–1809. Oil on canvas, 3′7¼″ × 5′7½″ (1.11 × 1.73 m). Schloss Charlottenburg, Berlin.

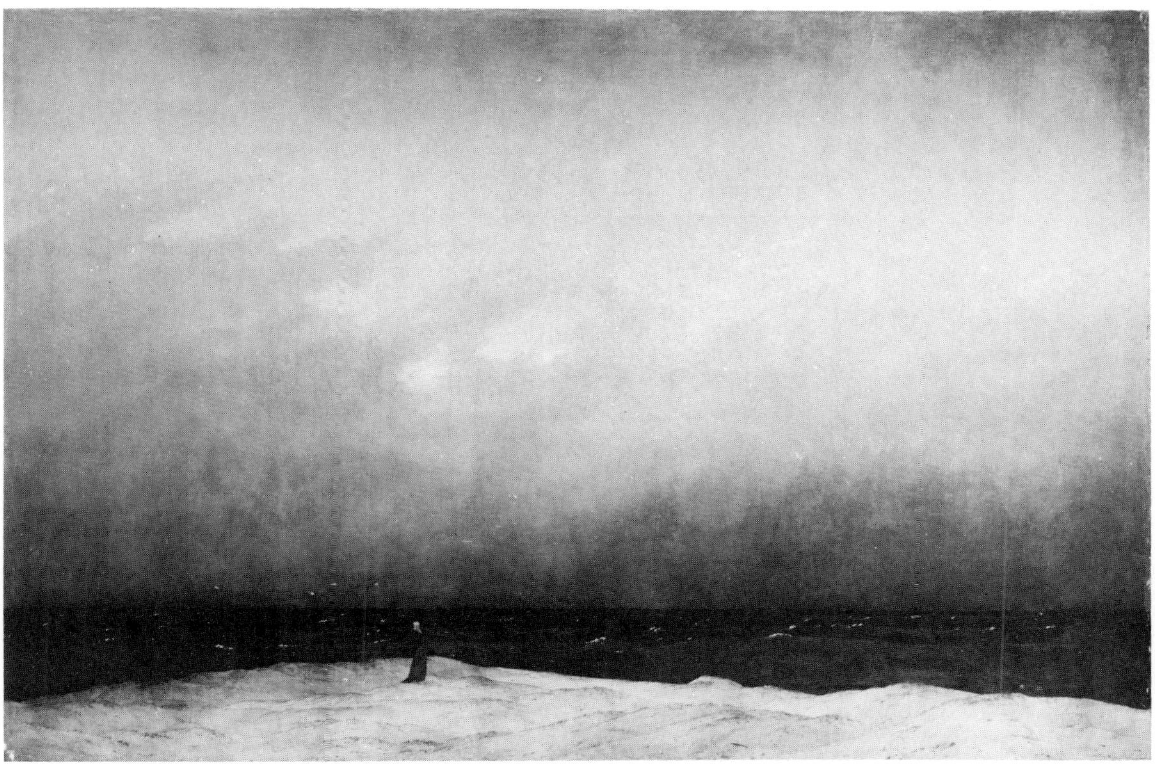

Painting: Delacroix's *Death of Sardanapalus*

More than three times as high and two-and-a-half times as wide as *The Death of Socrates* [see Plate 15, page 319], the vast *Death of Sardanapalus* (1826) [Plate 16, page 319] by Eugène Delacroix (1799–1863) is a highly romantic work that provides a clear contrast to David's neoclassic painting. Whereas David focuses on a historical figure, realistically depicting the final moments of Socrates in 399 B.C., Delacroix fantasizes about the death of a king who may never have lived. Sardanapalus is a shadowy figure in history. Possibly he was a Near Eastern ruler of about the 7th century B.C. According to legend, he neglected his kingdom to gratify sensual pleasure. When his besieged Nineveh was about to fall to a savage enemy, he decided to commit suicide, taking with him his most precious possessions, the ladies of his harem.

This exotic story of passion and death may well have been suggested to Delacroix by another great romantic artist, George Gordon, Lord Byron (1788–1824), who wrote a highly intense and imaginative play about this hero. In the painting as in the play, Sardanapalus is an individual and not a type. Delacroix is fascinated by the doomed king, who is self-absorbed and melancholy, detached from the world, and unmoved by the demands of social responsibility. Seen in a moment of splendor, violence, and mystery, he is the perfect embodiment of the romantic hero—in every respect unlike the heroes of neoclassicism.

Sardanapalus is not immediately apparent to the viewer of the painting; this will come as a surprise to those who have been studying the principles of classicism and neoclassicism. But we can locate him in the upper left, reclining pensively, seemingly unmoved by the violent scenes taking place in the foreground. Beside him is the jeweled cup into which he will pour the drugged wine in the pitcher. This figure of the indolent king is the starting point of a funnel-like diagonal that ends in the execution group in the lower right. The great number of figures and objects in Delacroix's crowded canvas makes this main sweep of the painting a kind of cornucopia, or horn of

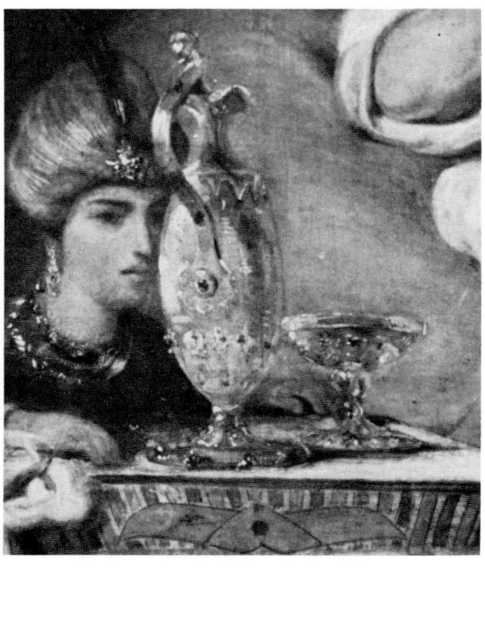

186 Eugène Delacroix. *The Death of Sardanapalus,* detail [see Plate 16, page 319].

plenty. By encircling the unperturbed ruler with several violent figures—for example, the horse being tamed in the lower left and the woman being stabbed in the lower right—the artist has created a scene full of fluid movement, quite different from the static poses of the figures in David's *Death of Socrates.* Delacroix furthermore prefers dynamic balance to perfect symmetry.

Apart from this general organization, the details in the picture suggest an excessive sensuousness that is often found in romantic painting. Everywhere Delacroix has tried to capture a great variety of textures, from cloth, metal, and braid to animal skin and human flesh. The king's cup [186] is elaborately decorated and intricately wrought—totally different from the plain cup that Socrates holds in David's neoclassical work.

But the primary means of creating the romantic sensuousness of *The Death of Sardanapalus* is the color shading. Delacroix knew and admired such acknowledged masters of coloring as Titian [see Plate 11, page 187] and Rembrandt [see Plate 2, page 34]. As a romantic painter, Delacroix applied what he learned from them to subject matter that was much less socially acceptable. Delacroix's shading is especially remarkable in the nude female bodies, which range from bright flesh tones to muted browns and which seem to merge into the shadows. The bodies are set off against the sumptuous reds of the bed covers and other indistinct draped materials. The threatening shadows and blurred forms in the corners and background introduce an additional note of the undefined and undefinable. Moreover, the general impression of violence and sensuality is enhanced by the artist's energetic, free brushwork.

The setting also contributes to the sensuousness and the indeterminacy and ambiguousness of the scene. The king lies stretched out on an enormous ornate bed—he was reputed to be the inventor of the featherbed. Although beds are customarily found indoors, this one seems to be part of an exterior setting at the upper right that includes the wall of the city. The spatial ambiguity, together with the general exoticism, increases the visionary, dream-like, even nightmarish quality of the whole. Like so much in romanticism, the painting goes beyond logic and reason, stimulating a large complex of responses that remain beyond our rational grasp.

Music: Chopin's *Ballade in G minor*

Just as the romantic painter Delacroix has chosen a disturbing and dramatic scene to achieve a powerful emotional effect, so romantic composers prefer unusual key relationships and increasingly dramatic shifts in the tonal center of their music. Frédéric Chopin (1810–1849) does so in his piano composition, the *G-minor Ballade.* The opening themes here are stated in G minor (two flats) and E-flat Major (three flats), keys that are closely related in traditional harmony. But the next large section of the piece begins in A minor (no sharps or flats) and modulates suddenly to A Major (three sharps), a key about as far from G minor as one can find in the traditional harmonic scheme. The sudden A Major tonality, combined with a *fortissimo* dynamic, sounds like an unexpected triumphal reentrance of a theme (formerly in E-flat) transformed from the quiet nocturnal musing it seemed at first hearing. This new freedom in treating the traditional tonal relationships can be so extreme that at times we can hardly be sure in what key a romantic piece is written—something that never happens in the works of the classical period.

In their search for new and different orchestral timbres, or tone colors, romantic composers were also aided by improvements in the production of more sophisticated wind instruments such as the oboe and the trumpet, as well as by improvements in the mechanism of the piano. And their willingness to experiment encouraged players and manufacturers to make further advances in instrumental design. In fact, one of the most obvious consequences of all these developments was that the symphony orchestra increased the number of both traditional and new instruments. The art of instrumentation and orchestration really begins with 19th-century music; indeed, such major romantic composers as Hector Berlioz (1803–1869) and Nikolai Rimsky-Korsakov (1844–1908) wrote books on the subject.

The impulse to find new orchestral tone color and to expand the harmonic language did not stop with theorizing. Composers exceeded what their friends and audiences could readily grasp. In the seventh measure of Chopin's *G-minor Ballade* the upper note of the left-hand chord is an E-flat, strongly dissonant and poignantly expressive in the context of its phrase. Chopin's friends urged him to change it to a D, a consonant, neutral-sounding harmony, and some editions of the *Ballade* were published in Chopin's lifetime with this change. But the original version is more powerful. Franz Liszt and Richard Wagner, two other romantic composers, also used harmonies that were repeatedly condemned for being too dissonant. As it turned out, Wagner was right to call his compositions the "music of the future," for his harmonic innovations eventually led to the dissonance we take for granted in modern music.

The Chopin *Ballade* can demonstrate other characteristics of romantic music in addition to its heightened tone color and untraditional harmonic sequence. Although key and dynamic contrasts clearly distinguish the various sections, the piece as a whole is unlike a classical work in that it does not use pauses or clear cadences to indicate the division between sections. Moreover, these sharp key and dynamic contrasts create a fluid impression that is less unified and coherent than the impression left by a classical work. Indeed, clarity of form and structural coherence are less important for Chopin than the expression of emotional force. No longer are themes valued either for their simplicity ("singability") or divisibility (aptness for use as separate motives), two qualities of great importance to composers of the classical period. Rather, Chopin is interested in complex and flowing themes that are intense and charged with emotion—expressing deep, unsatisfied yearning or emotional turmoil. Chopin's melodic line is typically romantic: sensuous and lyrical.

Chopin is also an appropriate example of a romantic composer since he is the quintessential writer for the piano, the preeminent musical instrument of his time. Actually, most important romantic composers were themselves pianists, and some, like Chopin [187] and Liszt [see Figure 84, page 161], were brilliant virtuosi. The piano owes its dominance among romantic musicians to two factors already mentioned: new musical capabilities brought about by changes in design and manufacture, and the notion of the highly individualistic romantic hero. By the 19th century the piano had become an imposing instrument. It could create melody and harmony at the same time, permitting great range in nuance and expression, yet remain under the control of one performer. With these advantages, the piano and the piano recital became a central part of European musical life.

In his piano music Chopin is not only typically romantic but also quite distinctive. For example, his melodies are full of *flourishes,* rapid notes that have a virtuoso effect. Moreover, Chopin developed a new style of writing for the performer's left hand. The notes of the accompanying chords are spread over the lower and middle register. By sustaining the sound of the accompanying chords with the damper pedal, the performer can create a rich, resonant background for the melody. This, added to the unusual harmonic progressions, produces the "Chopinesque" effects we recognize in such works as the *Nocturnes* and the *Ballades.* Chopin's *Ballades,* like literary ballads, are brief, each lasting about ten minutes, and each is believed to have been inspired by a poem.

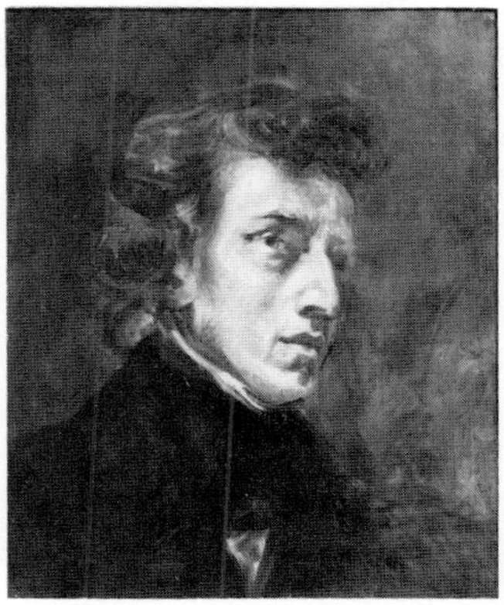

187 Eugène Delacroix. *Frédéric Chopin.* 1838. Oil on canvas, 18 × 15" (46 × 38 cm). Louvre, Paris. Chopin's brooding, noble face, dramatically highlighted in Delacroix's painting, conveys a strong impression of the sensitive romantic genius.

Music that is based on some sort of literary or nonmusical program, as many romantic compositions are, is known as **program music**. The composer's interest in writing music that "tells a story" led to the development of the **tone poem** or *symphonic poem,* terms that are generally used to describe a large-scale orchestral composition in which a specific story, poem, painting, or even historical event serves as subject matter. The opposite of program music is *absolute music,* which has no nonmusical source. Although the difference between the two seems to be clear-cut, in practice the distinction is not always easy to make. Chopin, for example, never revealed the specific poems he had in mind when he wrote the *Ballades,* so that these pieces hover between absolute and program music. In any case, these works share that most fundamental trait of romantic music—emotional intensity.

Poetry: Keats's "Ode to a Nightingale"

Our literary example of romanticism, the "Ode to a Nightingale" (1819) by John Keats (1795–1821) shares this characteristic emotional intensity. Despite its title, Keats's poem is not about a nightingale, nor even primarily about a nightingale's song. The central concern of Keats is a personal reaction to the bird and its music. The speaker's powerful response—esthetic, emotional, and imaginative—to the experience of hearing the bird is at the heart of the matter. And here the contrast with the neoclassical poetry of Alexander Pope is extreme. For the neoclassic poet, poetry is seen as social and intellectual, rational, impersonal, highly structured, and traditional. For the romantic poet, poetry is seen as intensely personal, highly charged, richly suggestive, even experimental.

The actual writing of the poem is a fine example of a romantic artist's immediately recording his own responses. Keats often heard a nightingale sing in a near-by grove of trees, and one morning within two or three hours jotted down the poem substantially as it exists today. But, of course, the composition was not entirely spontaneous, for Keats had already given much thought to the themes he was developing [188].

In addition, Keats was no doubt aware that the nightingale, famous for the beauty and pathos of its song, was a traditional subject for poetry. Moreover, Keats had already begun experimenting with the special genre of the **ode**, an elaborate kind of lyric. Two classical poets served him as models. The Greek Pindar (c. 522–443 B.C.) was known for expressing powerful feelings in seemingly irregular strophes; the Roman Horace, for presenting more controlled feelings in polished, regular stanzas. Keats deliberately combined these two models by casting a Pindaric outburst of feeling into Horatian

188 Claude Lorrain. *The Enchanted Castle,* or *Psyche Outside the Palace of Cupid.* 1664. Oil on canvas, 2′10″ × 4′10⅞″ (.87 × 1.51 m). National Gallery, London (reproduced by courtesy of the Trustees). Keats owned an engraving of this painting. It inspired some lines in an early poem that combined the fantasies of magic casements, perilous seas, and sweet music with "dreamings all of wake and sleep." These details reappear in the "Ode to a Nightingale" in evocative and memorable phrases.

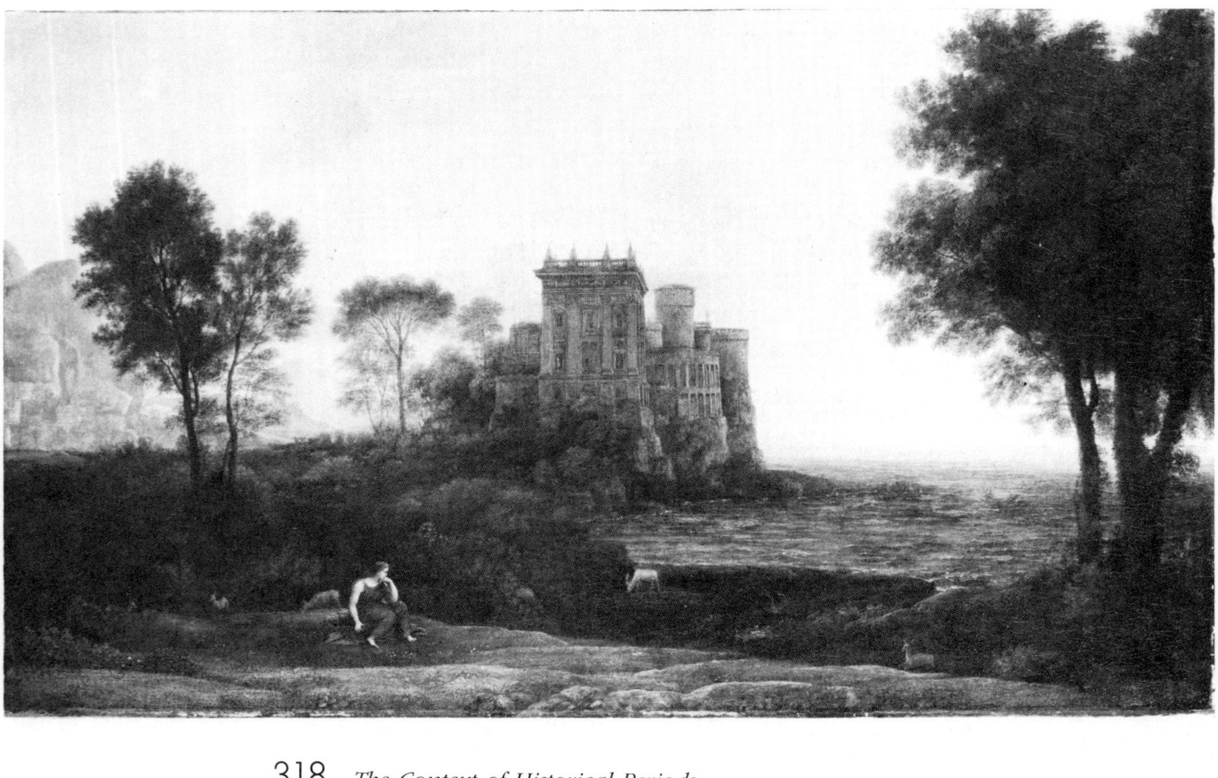

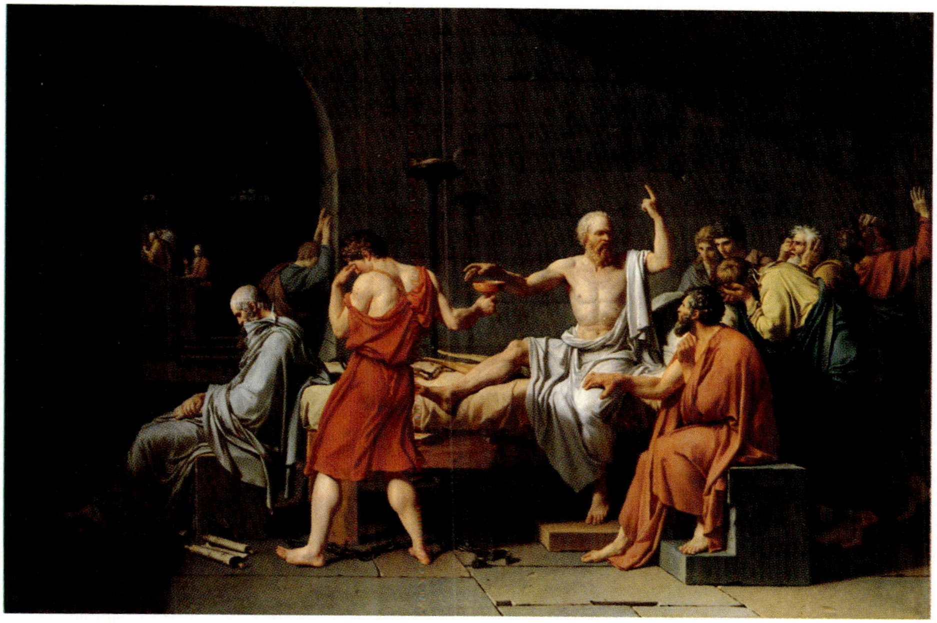

Plate 15 Jacques Louis David. *The Death of Socrates.* 1787. Oil on canvas, 4′3″ × 6′5¼″ (1.3 × 1.96 m). Metropolitan Museum of Art, New York (Wolfe Fund, 1931).

Plate 16 Eugène Delacroix. *The Death of Sardanapalus.* 1826. Oil on canvas, 12′1″ × 16′3″ (3.68 × 4.95 m). Louvre, Paris.

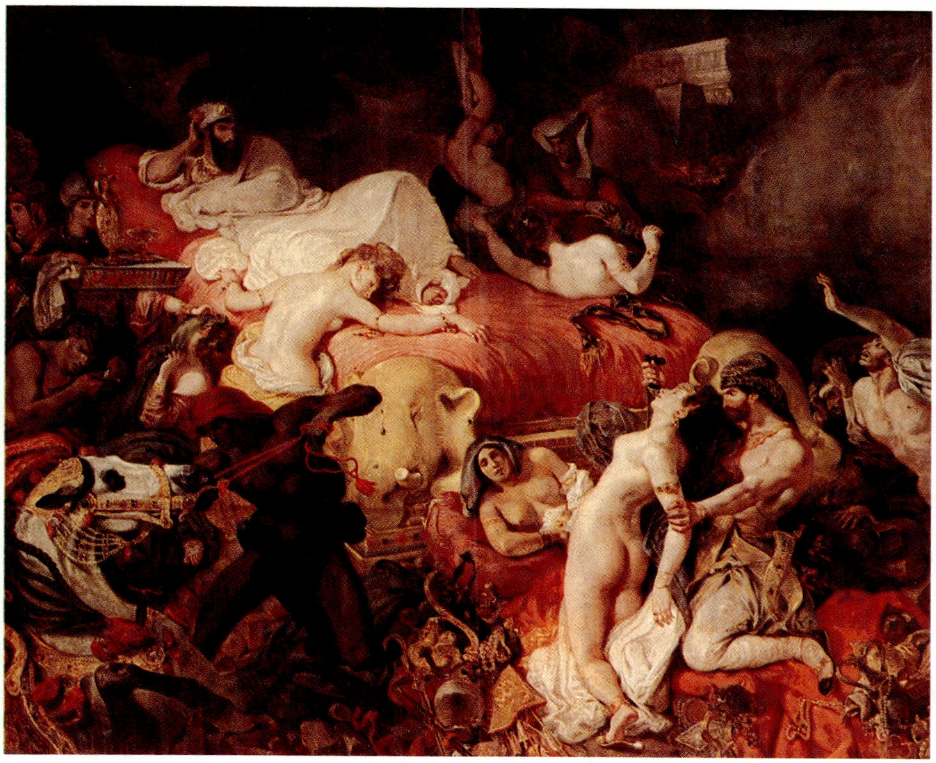

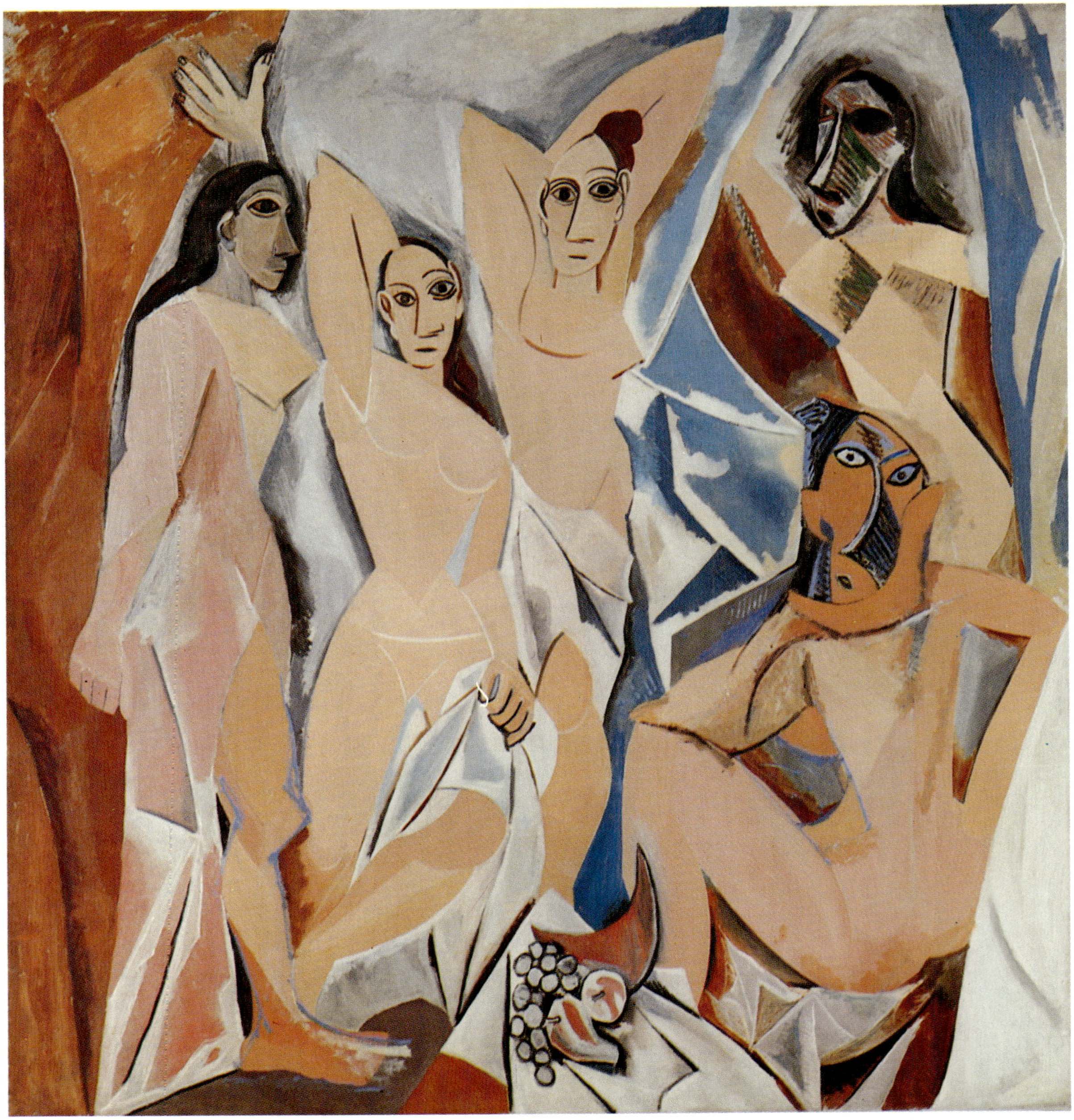

Plate 17 Pablo Picasso. *Les Demoiselles d'Avignon.* 1907. Oil on canvas, 8′ × 7′8″ (2.44 × 2.34 m). Museum of Modern Art, New York (acquired through the Lillie P. Bliss Bequest).

stanzas. Like many artists, then, he was drawing on established literary traditions and genres, but like romantic artists in particular, he was using these in innovative ways to express his own profoundly personal feelings.

John Keats
ODE TO A NIGHTINGALE

I

My heart aches, and a drowsy numbness pains
  My sense, as though of hemlock[1] I had drunk,
Or emptied some dull opiate to the drains
One minute past, and Lethe-wards[2] had sunk;
'Tis not through envy of thy happy lot,
  But being too happy in thine happiness,—
    That thou, light-wingèd Dryad[3] of the trees,
        In some melodious plot
  Of beechen green, and shadows numberless,
    Singest of summer in full-throated ease.

II

O, for a draught of vintage, that hath been
  Cooled a long age in the deep-delvèd earth,
Tasting of Flora[4] and the country green,
  Dance, and Provençal song, and sunburnt mirth!
O for a beaker full of the warm South,
  Full of the true, the blushful Hippocrene,[5]
    With beaded bubbles winking at the brim,
        And purple-stainèd mouth;
  That I might drink, and leave the world unseen,
    And with thee fade away into the forest dim:

III

Fade far away, dissolve, and quite forget
  What thou among the leaves hast never known,
The weariness, the fever, and the fret
  Here, where men sit and hear each other groan;
Where palsy shakes a few, sad, last gray hairs,
  Where youth grows pale, and spectre-thin, and dies;
    Where but to think is to be full of sorrow
        And leaden-eyed despairs,
  Where Beauty cannot keep her lustrous eyes,
    Or new Love pine at them beyond to-morrow.

[1] poisonous shrub
[2] the river of forgetfulness (or death)
[3] wood nymph
[4] goddess of flowers
[5] fountain of the Muses

IV

Away! away! for I will fly to thee,
  Not charioted by Bacchus[6] and his pards,[7]
But on the viewless[8] wings of Poesy,
  Though the dull brain perplexes and retards;
Already with thee! tender is the night,
  And haply the Queen-Moon is on her throne,
    Clustered around by all her starry Fays;[9]
        But here there is no light,
  Save what from heaven is with the breezes blown
    Through verdurous glooms and winding mossy ways.

V

I cannot see what flowers are at my feet,
  Nor what soft incense hangs upon the boughs,
But, in embalmèd darkness, guess each sweet
  Wherewith the seasonable month endows
The grass, the thicket, and the fruit-tree wild;
  White hawthorn, and the pastoral eglantine;
    Fast fading violets covered up in leaves;
        And mid-May's eldest child,
  The coming musk-rose, full of dewy wine,
    The murmurous haunt of flies on summer eves.

VI

Darkling I listen; and, for many a time
  I have been half in love with easeful Death,
Called him soft names in many a musèd rhyme,
  To take into the air my quiet breath;
Now more than ever seems it rich to die,
  To cease upon the midnight with no pain,
    While thou art pouring forth thy soul abroad
        In such an ecstasy!
  Still wouldst thou sing, and I have ears in vain—
    To thy high requiem become a sod.

VII

Thou wast not born for death, immortal Bird!
  No hungry generations tread thee down;
The voice I hear this passing night was heard
  In ancient days by emperor and clown:[10]
Perhaps the self-same song that found a path
Through the sad heart of Ruth,[11] when, sick for home,
  She stood in tears amid the alien corn;
      The same that oft-times hath
Charmed magic casements, opening on the foam
  Of perilous seas, in faery lands forlorn.

[6] god of wine
[7] leopards
[8] invisible
[9] fairies
[10] a low-born rural figure
[11] biblical heroine (Ruth 2) who left her homeland to live with the family of her dead husband

VIII

Forlorn! the very word is like a bell
  To toll me back from thee to my sole self!
Adieu! the fancy cannot cheat so well
  As she is famed to do, deceiving elf.
Adieu! adieu! thy plaintive anthem fades
  Past the near meadows, over the still stream,
    Up the hill-side; and now 'tis buried deep
      In the next valley-glades:
  Was it a vision, or a waking dream?
    Fled is that music:—Do I wake or sleep?

In the first three stanzas we learn the initial response of the speaker to the nightingale and its music. The beauty and joy aroused by the unseen singer heighten the speaker's awareness of the sorrow, suffering, and death that are conditions of human life. To the speaker, the bird's seeming ability to sum up the happiness of its existence in a melodious song of "full-throated ease" is enviable. Its unthinking joyfulness makes him even more conscious of his pain and increases his longing to escape from the burden of self-awareness. Either through the drowsiness of near-death, or through drugs or drink, he would willingly merge identities with the bird and "fade away into the forest dim" (line 20). By such a loss of self and total immersion into nature, the speaker hopes to forget this world, "where men sit and hear each other groan" (line 25) and where every conscious thought reminds him only "to be full of sorrow" (line 27).

The intensity of the speaker's desire to escape the pain of the human condition leads to the outburst that opens the fourth stanza. Here, at the midpoint of the poem, he determines that the means of escape will be provided not by the god of wine but by the "viewless wings of Poesy" (line 33), the inner world of the poetic imagination, supralogical, transcending the limits of the rational, the visual and tangible. And at this point, the texture of the poem changes: the abundant references to classical mythology ("Lethe," "Dryad," "Flora," "Hippocrene") give way to points of reference that are more sensuous, highly charged, and suggestive. The use of synaesthesia—the mingling of sense experiences—and of sensory imagery heightens the emotion: the moonlight and starlight is "blown" through the darkness by heavenly breezes; the perfume of the spring flowers is like "soft incense [that] hangs upon the boughs" (line 42). The delights of life and nature are to be experienced now as one must "guess each sweet" encountered in the darkness of the wood. The conscious, logical reasoning process that had made one so aware of the pain of existence is yielding to a sensory and intuitive apprehension of life: "the murmurous haunt of flies on summer eves" (line 50).

Listening in the darkness to the ecstatic song of the bird, the speaker acknowledges his readiness to lose his own sensibility in the rapture of the music: "Now more than ever seems it rich to die" (line 55). In fact, he has always been aware of the attraction death has held for him. The very darkness is "embalmèd," a word that suggests two meanings: filled with soothing balm and readied for burial. With the beauty of the music as accompaniment, he would willingly give himself up to "easeful Death" and "cease upon the midnight with no pain." But in this moment of ecstatic surrender, his own death would deny him the delight that he is seeking, for he would then have "ears in vain" and to the "high requiem" of the bird's melody he would "become a sod"—no more than lifeless earth.

The song of the bird remains the same, unchanged throughout eternity. The conditions of its existence—its permanence and immortality—are distinct from those of the speaker. The music of the nightingale is a constant in the cycle of living things, and the song's timelessness and beauty express the freshness, vitality, and strength of nature. Appropriately, the bird finds a place in the world of both history and fancy. According to the next to last stanza, the song is immortal because it could have been heard "In ancient days by emperor and clown" [rustic], in the legendary or Biblical past—by "Ruth, when sick for home,/ She stood in tears amid the alien corn"—and even "in faery lands forlorn," the realm of the imaginative and invented, where "charmed magic casements [open] on the foam/ Of perilous seas."

But to the speaker's mind these facts only emphasize the great separation between his existence and the event he describes. The imaginative life cannot be sustained for long. Impending death or the tread of "hungry generations" are realities that distinguish the world in which human beings must live from that of the unthinking and untroubled bird. And as the nightingale's music recedes in the distance, across the stream at the far edge of the meadow, over the hill on the other side, and finally "buried deep/ In the next valley-glades," the speaker is left to inquire into the ultimate value of his experience. Did his moment of nearly total identification with a pure and natural beauty allow him to glimpse a profounder reality? Moreover, did Keats, the poet, in the process of creating a poem achieve a heightening of experience, a "vision" (line 79) that reveals something true and lasting about the nature of existence? Or was this simply a "waking dream," a second caught between consciousness and sleep in which the mind indulges in an evasion of the hard facts of life? In any case, "Fled is that music"—the moment has passed. The pressure of daily life reasserts its imperatives.

We began our discussion of this poem by trying to focus on its central concern, and we quickly realized that, unlike Pope, Keats has no interest in writing poetry about society. Public manners and morals are of no concern to him. He is interested not in types, but in an individual with personal feelings. And by analyzing these personal feelings, Keats considers more fundamental and philosophical questions. He asks not only whether escape is possible but also what value can be found in works of art and in artistic creation. Although Keats does not answer these questions directly, he implies that for those of us responsive to the language of poetry, art alone can unlock "magic casements" into charmed realms of the imagination and uniquely enrich our understanding of life.

Although Keats and Pope agree on the importance and value of poetry, they have quite different conceptions of its nature. The personal, subjective, and sensuous responses expressed in Keats's writing are in sharp contrast to the social, rational, and witty lines in Pope. Indeed, Keats's celebration of the individual temperament could not be more opposed to Pope's concern with the ridicule of a type. Pope's work is highly refined, polished, sophisticated, reflecting the belief that art is an ordering of life. In contrast, Keats suggests that art is superior to life, and his poetry is a direct and immediate response to the emotions that generate it. Perhaps we can sum up these differences by observing that Pope presents us with a meticulously prepared, finished product, while Keats takes us with him in the process of creation.

To close our discussion of romanticism, we should stress that painting, music, literature, and the other arts share not only common themes but also similar techniques for expressing these. Color, rhythm, and form, for example, are all treated in similar fashion. At the same time, we should realize that the most talented artists can take standard elements and give them a highly personal character. The mysterious and disturbing aspects of the Delacroix painting [see Plate 16, page 319], the exceptionally expressive lyrical quality of Chopin's melody, and the philosophic questions that concern the relation of art and life in Keats's "Ode," raising it above an escapist fantasy, make these three works highly individualized. They are more than good examples of romanticism. Like all excellent art, they exhibit the characteristics of an historical and artistic age, but transcend the limitations of that age by their personal and distinctive qualities.

Questions for Study and Discussion

1. How does the attitude toward life—and death—in Delacroix's *Death of Sardanapalus* [see Plate 16, page 319] differ from that expressed in David's *Death of Socrates* [see Plate 15, page 319]? What difference in treatment makes Delacroix's a characteristically romantic work and David's a characteristically neoclassical work?
2. What characteristics of romanticism can be seen in Turner's *Rain, Steam, and Speed* [see Plate 10, page 122], and how do these differ from those found in Delacroix's *Death of Sardanapalus?*
3. What do Goya and Friedrich have in common as romantic artists? How do they differ?
4. Elements of romanticism can be seen in works of periods other than the 19th century. What romantic elements can be found in Altdorfer's *The Battle of Alexander* [see Figure 125, page 220] and Claude Lorrain's *The Enchanted Castle* [see Figure 188, page 323]?
5. How do the romantic characteristics of Chopin's *Ballade in G minor* differ from the neoclassical characteristics of Haydn's *Sonata in E-flat?*
6. In what respects is Chopin a quintessentially romantic composer?
7. Romantic poetry has been described as "intensely personal, highly charged, highly suggestive, even experimental." Cite examples from Keats's "Ode to a Nightingale" for each of these characteristics.
8. In what sense is the ballet *Swan Lake* a "classical ballet," and in what sense is its story [page 174] typical of romanticism?

CHAPTER 12

Modernism

As artistic movements, neoclassicism and romanticism can be described with relative ease, perhaps because they are far enough removed in time that we can see their characteristics clearly. *Modernism,* in contrast, is more difficult to describe because we are in its midst. Nevertheless, some of its elements can be singled out.

Unlike neoclassical artists with their notion of a universal order that is largely comprehensible to the human mind, and unlike romantic artists with their sense of a mysterious universe accessible only through feeling or intuition, modern artists tend to be tormented by a sense that the universe is bafflingly complex and probably even meaningless and indifferent. Many influences have led to such a general feeling of uncertainty. These include the effects of modern science and technology, which are to some extent responsible for the loss of religious faith as well as for the increasingly destructive weapons used in 20th-century warfare. Modernism is, in fact, chiefly characterized by an attitude of insecurity and, beyond that, by a kind of cosmic anxiety, known by the German term *Angst.* Not surprisingly, modernism is also typified by a questioning of all accepted values.

In their rejection of older values, modern artists have frequently looked for novelty. They have turned to unexpected sources of inspiration. The Dada painters, whose name is meant to suggest an infant's first nonsense syllables, tried to demonstrate the meaninglessness of life by creating art based on irrationality and chance. The title "Squares Arranged According to the Laws of Chance" (1922), a work by the French painter-sculptor Jean Arp (1887–1966), speaks for itself. Similarly, some of the musical compositions of the North American John Cage (b. 1912) were written according to chance and may be performed in any order desired. The aim of such art is to reflect the disorder of modern life and often to shock the audience.

The modern questioning of accepted values has led some artists to reject high culture, the serious art inspired by the Greco-Roman and Judeo-Christian traditions we have been considering. The great themes of earlier art are no longer meaningful to these artists. They turn instead to images of their own commercial society. Roy Lichtenstein, as we have seen, based some of his art on the comic strip, Andy Warhol (b. 1930) created paintings of soup cans, and Claes Oldenburg (b. 1929) made a sculpture in the shape of a giant lipstick. All these suggest, not without irony, how greatly consumer culture has replaced high culture.

Other artists have turned to modern technology for their images as well as for new techniques. The French painter Fernand Léger (1881–1955) [189]

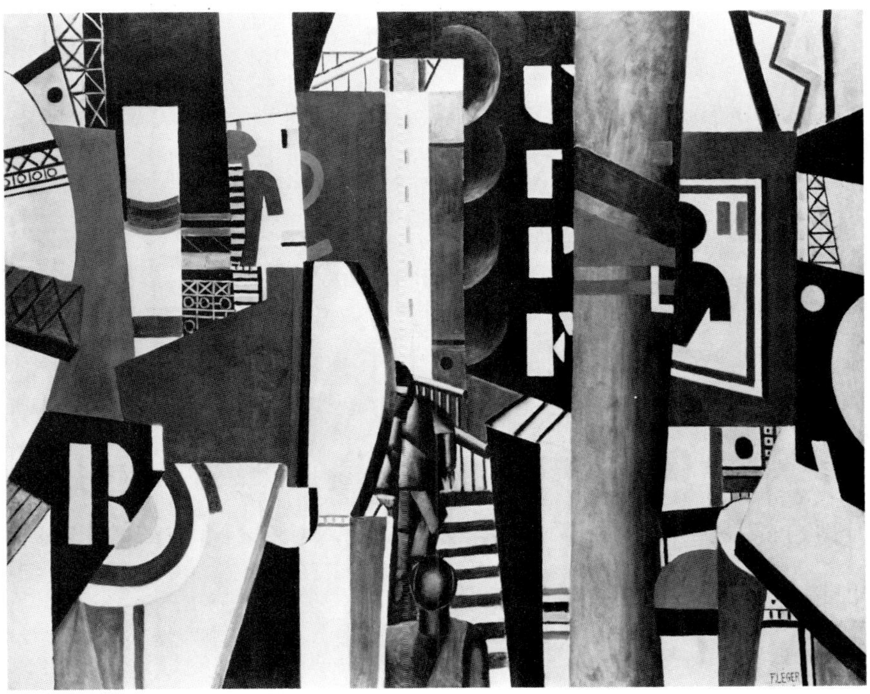

189 Fernand Léger. *The City.* 1919. Oil on canvas, 7′7″ × 9′8½″ (2.31 × 2.96 m). Philadelphia Museum of Art (A. E. Gallatin Collection).

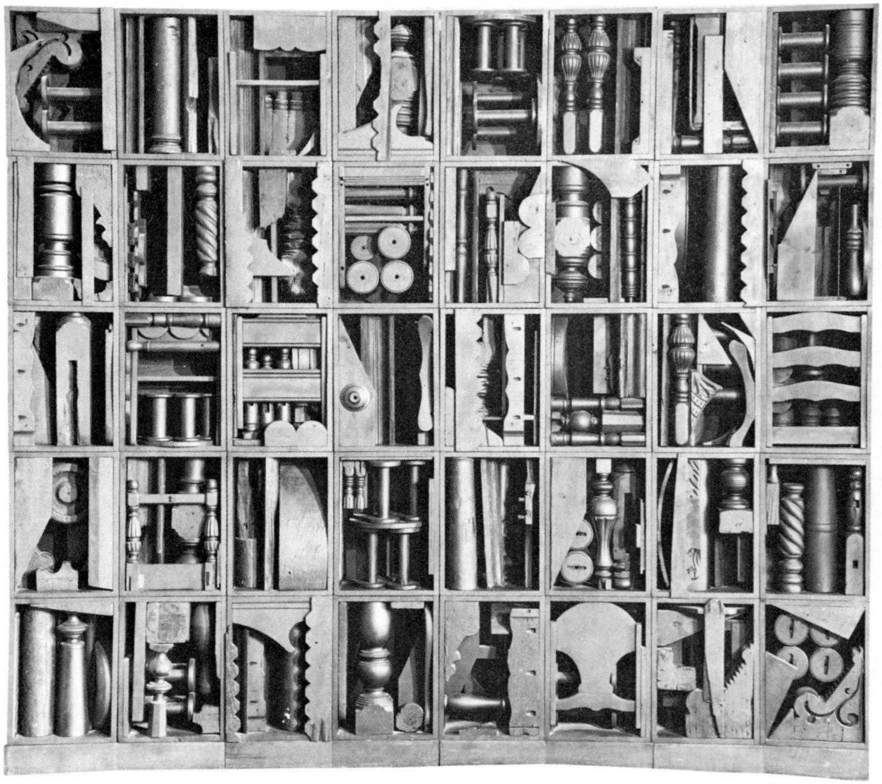

above: 190 Louise Nevelson. *Tide I, Tide.* 1963.
Wood construction, approx. 9 × 12′ (2.74 × 3.66 m).
Albert A. List Family Collection, Byram, Conn.

has created human figures that look like machines, emphasizing the impact of the modern factory with its assembly line. The New York sculptor Louise Nevelson (b. 1900) [190] uses "found objects," bits and pieces of wood designed for commercial use, to create her works. In her intricately designed structures, she seems to be trying to make order out of the discards of our technological society. More recently, artists have discovered that the new technology can provide them with new and striking techniques. Painters are beginning to use computers to experiment with colors and three-dimensional effects, while composers are taking advantage of electronic synthesizers. In rejecting traditional themes of Western culture, other modern artists have turned not to 20th-century technology, but to non-European sources and even to primitive anthropological or archeological material.

These distinctive qualities of modernism will become even clearer when analyzed in three major works of different art forms: Picasso's painting *Les Demoiselles d'Avignon,* Stravinsky's ballet music *Le Sacre du printemps,* and Beckett's play *Waiting for Godot.*

Painting: Picasso's *Les Demoiselles d'Avignon*

Perhaps the most important painting to express some of these new influences, as well as to embody other characteristics of modernism, is *Les Demoiselles d'Avignon* ("The Young Ladies of Avignon") [Plate 17, page 320], by Pablo Picasso. This work marks a significant turning point in the history of 20th-century painting.

At first, the figures on the canvas seem strange and unattractive. Picasso has given his quintet of naked women a menacing air of violence and brutality. These young women challenge us with faces that are either coldly appraising or fiercely hostile. Limbs akimbo, they are assembled of harshly angular shapes. The dominant colors are a liverish pink in the bodies and a related orange-brown in the curtain, as well as an icy blue in the areas that separate the figures from each other.

The characters, mood, and setting can be better understood when we realize that Picasso has transported us to the interior of a Spanish brothel and brought us face to face with those who work there. Indeed, the title of an earlier study [191] for the work, *Le Bordel d'Avignon* ("The Avignon House of Prostitution"), was even more direct and less ironic. As several preparatory studies show, Picasso removed the figures of two male clients from the final version, thereby placing the viewers in the role of customers. The artist has not only chosen a shocking subject but has also presented it in an aggressively shocking manner. And yet the choice of subject for this painting is not surprising, but typical of modernism. For 20th-century art is often concerned with outsiders, with the alienated who reject or are rejected by society. If romantic artists had presented Picasso's scene, they might have portrayed the women as victims and encouraged us to sympathize with them. But Picasso uncompromisingly forces us to remain detached and to see his figures purely as tough representatives of a hard and brutal existence.

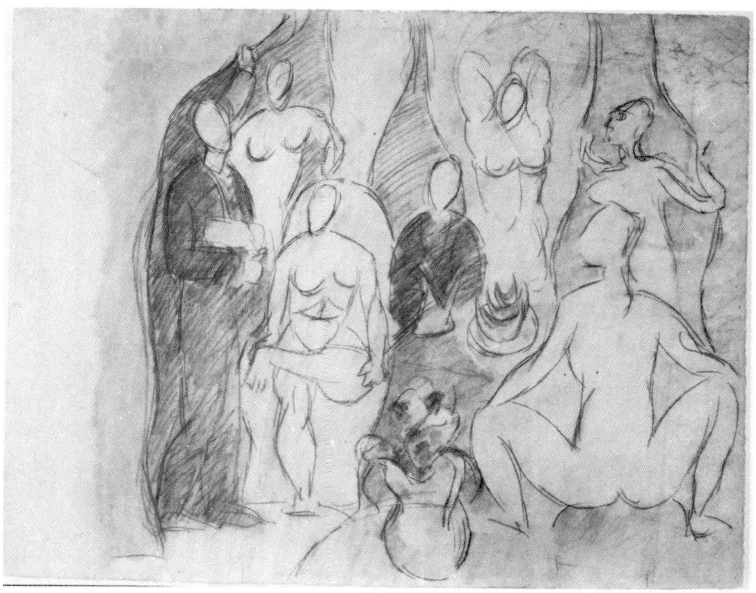

191 Pablo Picasso. Study for *Les Demoiselles d'Avignon*. 1907 [see Plate 17, page 320]. Charcoal and pastel, 18⅞ × 25″ (48 × 66 cm). Kupferstichkabinett, Öffentliches Kunstmuseum, Basel.

Les Demoiselles d'Avignon reveals the characteristics of modernism not only in its choice of subject matter and mood but also in its use of primitive material. Picasso actually uses two separate sources, combining images derived from prehistoric Spanish sculpture [192] with those derived from African sculpture. The three left-hand figures reveal Picasso's admiration for the carving of his native Spain, which attracted him by the bold simplification of its forms. This source is reflected in the immobility of the expressionless faces and especially in the elongated eye of the woman on the far left. The two figures on the right-hand side, in contrast, reflect the impact of African sculpture [193], which was just beginning to be known in Paris. These have bodies as starkly drawn as the other three, but they appear twisted in space, as if denying the laws of our physical world. In turning to such prehistoric or non-European sources, Picasso is seeking a new kind of artistic expressiveness, elemental or primordial, and therefore remote from the comforting familiarity of the European tradition.

Picasso's interest in these new sources also led him to experiment with the treatment of space. His experiment resulted in the revolutionary modern movement known as Cubism [see Figure 79, page 124]. In trying to transfer the three-dimensional forms of his Spanish and African sculptural models to two-dimensional space on his canvas, Picasso came to treat space as a series of faceted elements connected to one another but not coordinated within an overall scheme. This treatment is best seen to the right of the center of the painting, where the background is presented only as contiguous blue wedges. Picasso's approach provides no consistent illusion of depth. Indeed, Picasso's manner of dealing with space departs radically from the tradition of linear perspective accepted by painters from the time of the Renaissance.

Finally, Picasso breaks with tradition in still another way by the treat-

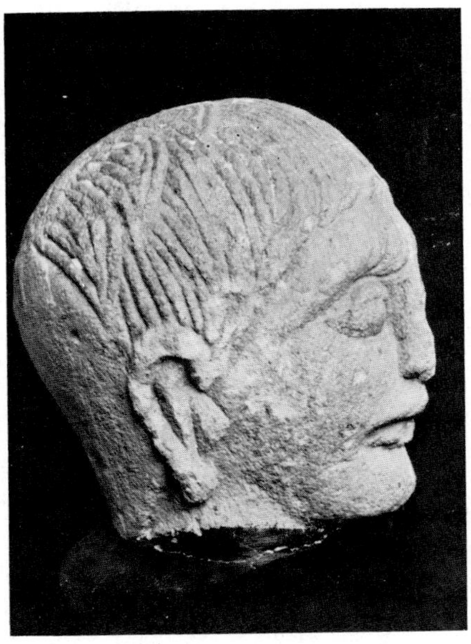

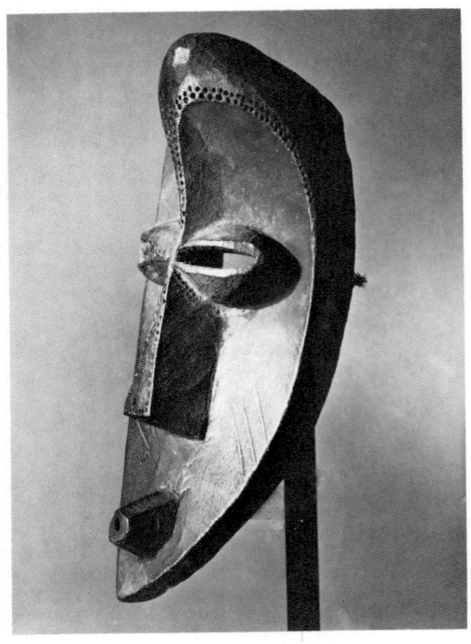

right: 192 Head of a Man. Perhaps first century B.C. Iberian. Museo Arqueológico Nacional, Madrid. This primitive Spanish sculpture was owned by Picasso. Its stylized and impassive features influenced the presentation of the three women at the left of *Les Demoiselles d'Avignon*.

far right: 193 Mask. Etoumbi region, People's Republic of the Congo. Wood, height 14″ (35.6 cm). Musée Barbier-Müller, Geneva.

ment of his nudes. As we observed in our discussion of the Aphrodite-Venus figure (see Chapter 6), the nude has been an enduring subject since classical Greece. Usually, it presents an ideal of beauty, and it can suggest not merely physical but also spiritual beauty, as in Titian's *Sacred and Profane Love* [see Plate 11, page 187]. By depicting a group of nudes, Picasso is linking himself with a great tradition that includes many major artists. But he rejects the idealized representation of the human body. Instead, he presents a new concept of the human figure, stripped of its beauty and reduced to angular shapes. This deliberate reduction of the human form to interlocking planes corresponds to a conscious reduction of the art of painting. Through the emerging idiom of Cubism, painting is stripped to its most fundamental components of lines, planes, and masses of color.

Music and Dance: Stravinsky's *Le Sacre du printemps*

No less than Picasso's *Les Demoiselles d'Avignon, Le Sacre du printemps* ("The Rite of Spring") (1913) by Igor Stravinsky (1882–1971), marks a startling break with tradition and reveals many of the elements of modernism. Indeed, this ballet, set to savage music, outraged its first audience and critics.

The riot that occurred at the opening performance in Paris is a notorious example of the shock effect created by many modern works. So infuriated were the spectators that they hissed, booed, threw objects, and fought among themselves until the police were called in. Stravinsky escaped through a back-

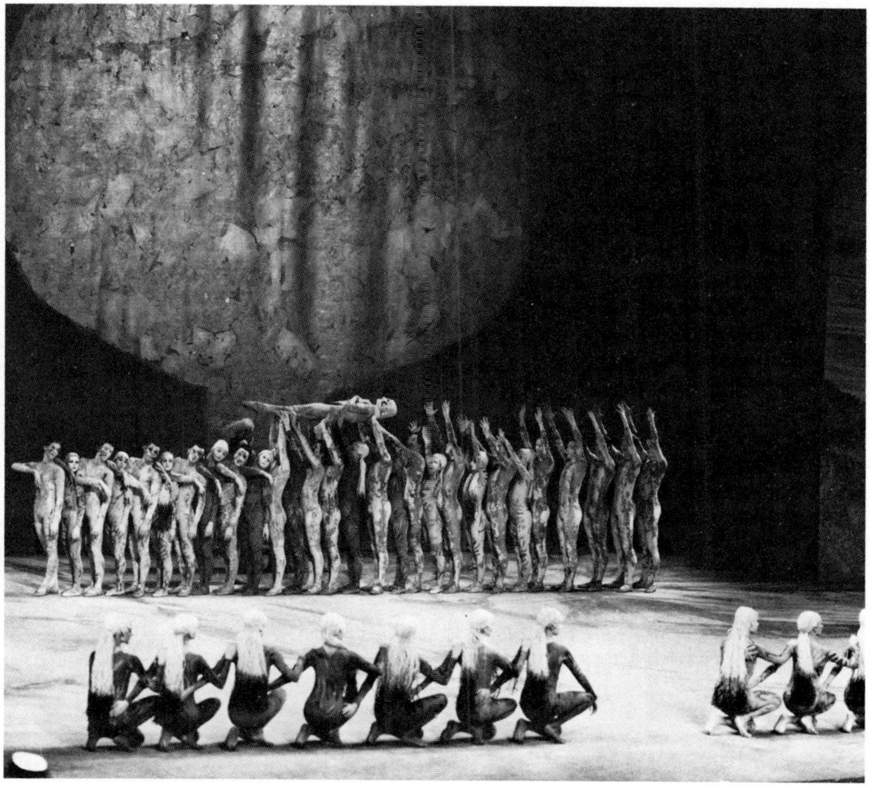

194 Scene from revival by the Royal Ballet of the original production of *Le Sacre du printemps,* 1979. Choreography by Kenneth MacMillan. Set design by Sidney Nolan. The dancer (Monica Mason) being lifted is the Chosen Maiden. She is about to be sacrificed.

stage window. Although we no longer find the piece outrageous, we can understand the first audience's reaction.

Part of the shock effect of the piece comes from its subject, which is primitive, pagan, and barbaric. Stravinsky's music was written for what he called a "fleeting vision" of a tribal ceremony in which a young girl is chosen to dance to death as a sacrifice to the god of spring [194]. No doubt inspired by recent anthropological studies, Stravinsky dramatizes the ritual sacrifice of a scapegoat—a widespread practice among pagan tribes in their effort to bring renewed fertility to the community. In choosing this subject, he is returning to the very origin of dance (see Chapter 6). Moreover, Stravinsky's work reflects the growing interest in the primitive encouraged by contemporary psychology. Both Freud and Jung, the two leading psychiatrists of the early 20th century, stressed the importance of the past. Freud drew attention to the primitive creative forces of the unconscious within the individual, while Jung emphasized the link between the individual and the collective primitive experience of the human race.

The ballet is divided into two major sections. In the first part, called "The Fertility of the Earth," an eerie introduction is followed by the "Dance of the Youths and Maidens," performed by several tribal groups. The "Dance of Abduction" is a play-acted rape; the "Games of the Rival Towns," a dance substitute for war. Toward the end of this part, the priestly Celebrant, or Wise Man, is ushered in to perform a "Kiss to the Earth" and "Dance to the Earth," in which the other groups join. In the second part, called "The Sacrifice," one of the adolescent girls is selected as The Chosen One. The ancestors are called on for a ritual dance; then, in the final climactic scene, the chosen girl dances to death. The various choreographies that have been created for the ballet—all of which make dramatic use of writhing and twisting bodies—express the primitive and sensual experience at the heart of the work.

The enactment of this savage story is a far cry from the traditional fairy-tale ballets such as *Cinderella, Sleeping Beauty,* and *Swan Lake* (see Chapter 5), popular in the 19th century. Musically, too, *Le Sacre du printemps* marks a break with 19th-century traditions. Expanding the resources of a large symphony orchestra with its many players, Stravinsky calls for special instruments such as the alto flute, two bass clarinets, two double bassoons, and a piccolo trumpet. The score also requires a much larger percussion section than normal, with three players rather than one for the kettledrums. The expanded wind and percussion sections enable Stravinsky to introduce extremes in the range of sounds and in dynamics.

With this imposing orchestra, Stravinsky gives much greater emphasis to rhythm than did his 19th-century predecessors. To create intense excitement, he does not hesitate to contrast simple, regular rhythmic patterns with irregular and surprising interruptions of these patterns. For instance, in the early "Dance of the Youths and Maidens," the meter specified in the score is a simple 2/4 time. But Stravinsky creates a throbbing, irregular beat by combining the constant repetition of eighth-notes with surprising and unpredictable accents from the French horns, eight of which are required. Sometimes two distinct rhythms are heard simultaneously; at other times, the regular meter is totally disrupted by irregular patterns of notes. In the "Sacrificial Dance" that concludes the work, both these effects are heard. The most striking pattern, played at the beginning of this section and repeated later, consists of a few distinct rhythmic motives separated by short rests and repeated irregularly with sharp accents. Here we can hardly distinguish any regular rhythm. The effect is savage, primitive, and arousing.

Stravinsky's melodies are also quite unlike those written by earlier composers. Some listeners consider his music unmelodic, but actually a great deal of melodic material is included. Unlike the lyrical outpouring of the romantics, however, the melodies in *Le Sacre du printemps* generally consist of short, repeated units of only a few pitches. The section "Spring Rounds" [Example 20] provides a particularly clear example. The inspiration for this type of melody comes from Russian folk songs. Sometimes the melodies have an eerie, almost medieval flavor resulting from their use of the older system of scales called *modes* (see Chapter 6).

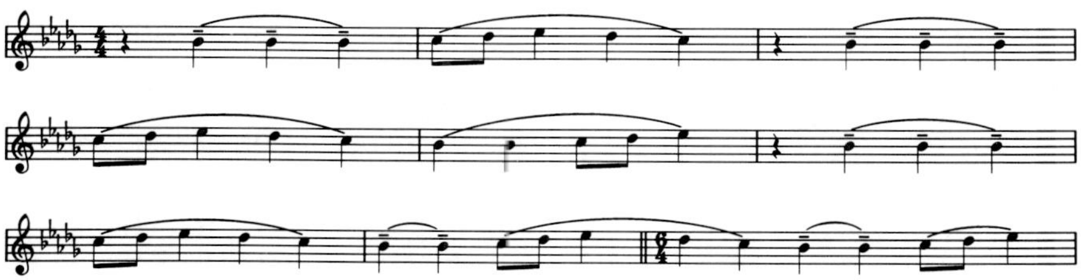

Example 20 Igor Stravinsky. *Le Sacre du printemps,* "Spring Rounds."

As for Stravinsky's harmonies, they are dissonant, but tonal—harsh and clashing, but nearly always in a recognizable key. Other modern composers such as Arnold Schoenberg (1874–1951) have written music totally without reference to a key center—music therefore known as *atonal.* But many of Stravinsky's most striking harmonic effects are created simply by juxtaposing two normal chords that clash when played together. In the "Dance of the Youths and Maidens," Stravinsky combines an E major with an E-flat seventh chord to create such a dissonant chord structure. Often the primitive effect of the work is created by the insistent repetition of such chords. At other times, frenzy is expressed by chords that shift rapidly in a fast tempo. We should notice that these experiments with harmony and also with rhythm and dynamics are similar to the experiments with line, angles, and color we observed in *Les Demoiselles d'Avignon* [see Plate 17, page 320]. Like Picasso, Stravinsky is interested in drawing attention to the most basic elements of his medium.

Perhaps we should ask why Stravinsky's extraordinary work, with its primitive rituals and savage rhythms, is considered typical of modernism. No simple answers can be given. But the clashing, dissonant music echoes some of the disturbing complexities that musicians, no less than other artists, find typical of the 20th century. At the same time, the powerful primitive myth serves as a contrast to—even a protest against—the vapid, uncommitted, sterile attitudes that many artists have diagnosed as a modern malady.

Theater: Beckett's *Waiting for Godot*

Many of the elements of modernism that we have observed in the work of Picasso and Stravinsky are also prominent in *Waiting for Godot* (1952) by Samuel Beckett (b. 1906). First written in French, this play was translated into English by its author and has been acclaimed for its importance throughout the world.

The opening with its puzzling speeches and ridiculous actions seems to be insignificant, even meaningless, but serves to introduce a major theme in many modern works: the meaninglessness and indifference of the universe. The entire action of the play consists of the efforts of two tramps to fill the time while waiting for a mysterious stranger called Godot, who in some way may be able to give meaning to their lives. But Godot never comes; his messages are unclear; and neither the characters nor we, the audience, are ever sure who Godot is. Feelings of insecurity and anxiety are the inevitable result, as the main characters vividly demonstrate.

The characters, few in number, are all types, but they are more difficult to define than the type character we have seen in Pope's satire, for nothing in this modern play is clear and simple. The two tramps, Vladimir and Estragon, by their very way of life, are outsiders, with no place in established society. Moreover, they are old-time comedians of the sort found in films and vaudeville, performing hackneyed routines with their baggy pants and bowler hats. In this respect, they were probably inspired by such slapstick comedy teams as Stan Laurel and Oliver Hardy and, even more importantly, by Charlie Chaplin, the epitome of the "little man" [see Figure 178, page 293] and affectionately known in France as *Charlot.* Like Chaplin's tramp, Vladimir and Estragon stand not just for social types but for all of modern humanity.

Perhaps Vladimir and Estragon seem so human because Beckett has endowed each with personal idiosyncrasies. Estragon suffers from his boots, Vladimir from his bladder. More importantly, they are immensely talkative, expressing opinions on countless subjects and exhibiting a wide range of unexpected emotions. Although they are type characters, they are presented very much in the round.

Pozzo and Lucky, the two other chief characters, appear grotesque at first. But they, too, are types, though they embody psychological rather than social traits. Representing the aggressive master and the passive slave, they engage in confrontations that reveal the more brutal and self-destructive aspects of humanity.

These figures, strange and yet somehow universal [195], are not involved in the kind of plot we have come to expect in drama. They perform none of the actions typical of characters in classical tragedy nor in traditional comedy nor even in melodrama. The play in which they appear has no climax and no resolution. Its unusual division into two, rather than three or five, acts emphasizes its basically repetitive nature, for the second act more or less replays the first. Beckett draws further attention to the circular structure through Vladimir's song, a "round" that ends where it begins so that it can begin all over again. Through this structure, Beckett demonstrates that the members of modern society lead endlessly repetitive, meaningless lives.

While nothing much happens on stage in one sense, a great deal happens in another sense. In their seemingly aimless conversations, Vladimir and Estragon are asking fundamental questions about the search for truth and the meaning of life. And, unobtrusively, they are reviewing some of the great answers that have traditionally been given to these questions.

One of the first questions raised in the discussion is whether personal salvation is possible. Vladimir reminds Estragon that according to the best-known account of the Crucifixion, one of the two thieves crucified with Christ was saved and the other damned. But Vladimir points out that this version is given by only one of the four Evangelists. We cannot, then, be sure that this particular version has any validity. So the Bible, the most basic document of Western morality and religion, is shown to be inconsistent and even contradictory—certainly no reliable guide.

A question raised more indirectly is whether human reason can provide a definitive answer about the meaning of existence. But when Lucky is told to "think," all he can provide is gibberish. The neoclassical faith in the power of human reason is shown to be entirely misplaced. In his great speech in Act I, Lucky reviews the opinions of a series of scholars who have spent their lives in study and in the application of their reason. In a rare lucid passage, Lucky quotes Puncher and Wattmann on the subject of a white-bearded God, who "loves us dearly with some exceptions for reasons unknown" but who plunges others into torment and hellfire, also for reasons unknown. Academic authority, then, is ultimately unilluminating and maddening. The names of some of the scholars—Fartov and Belcher, for instance—also suggest what we are to think of such pedants. Neither human reason nor scholarship can provide certainty.

Another question that is implied is whether nature can offer a means of feeling at one with the universe. Such a romantic view of life is quickly dispelled. When Estragon says, "We should turn resolutely towards Nature," Vladimir answers laconically, "We've tried that" (p. 41b). Earlier, Pozzo becomes "lyrical" about the beauties of the twilight. But his poetic flights end in anticlimaxes, as each is undercut by a return to the prosaic or the ordinary. Eventually, "his inspiration leaves him," and Pozzo's hymn in praise of nature and twilight ends with the observation that night inevitably follows—"That's how it is on this bitch of an earth." (p. 25b) So nature, the great solace for the romantics, offers no consolation.

The all-pervasive uncertainty leads Vladimir and Estragon to question whether their life is worth living and makes them repeatedly consider suicide, whether by leaping from the Eiffel Tower, jumping into the river Rhône, or hanging themselves. But even such drastic action is no solution for their anxiety. They cannot decide who should go first, and on a second try at hanging, the rope breaks. The implication is that one must go on, even though the universe seems to offer no meaning.

Although Beckett is introducing profoundly philosophic and abstract issues, he presents them in language that is remarkably simple and colloquial.

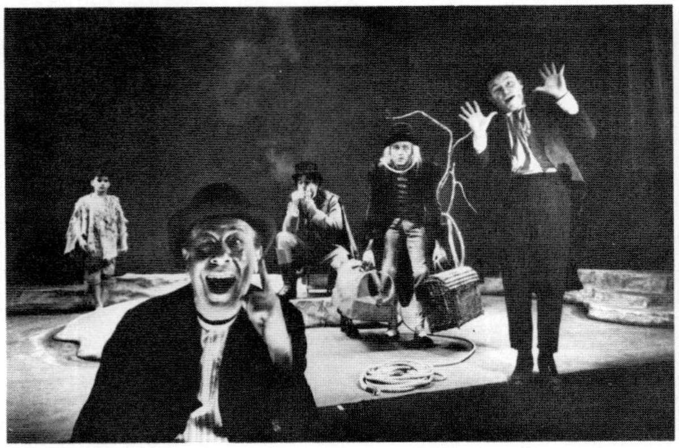

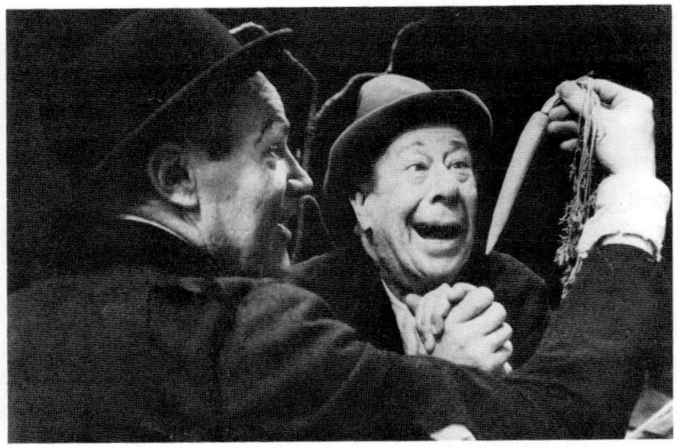

above left: 195 Scene from *Waiting for Godot* by Samuel Beckett, in a 1956 production. Bert Lahr as Estragon, E. G. Marshall as Vladimir, Alvin Epstein as Lucky, Kurt Kaznar as Pozzo, Luchino Solito De Solis as the boy. Production supervised by John Paul. Costumes by Stanley Simmons. Scenery by Louis Kennel. Directed by Herbert Berghof.

above right: 196 Scene from *Waiting for Godot,* 1956 production. Bert Lahr is at right.

In short phrases bandied back and forth, Vladimir and Estragon often seem to imitate the patter or set routines of professional comedians. They are even aware of this similarity, occasionally congratulating themselves on their successes:

ESTRAGON That wasn't such a bad little canter.
VLADIMIR Yes, but now we'll have to find something else.

(p. 42)

In a very different vein, Beckett has cast Lucky's think-piece as a dazzling stream-of-consciousness passage. Poured forth in a rapid, nonstop outburst that grows progressively more hysterical, this speech strings together loosely related ideas interspersed with nonsense words. Although it may sound like disjointed raving, it is actually a pointed attack on academic thinking.

Occasionally, Beckett makes his dialogue unexpectedly poetic. Still using a minimal vocabulary enriched only by the simplest similes and repetition, Vladimir and Estragon evoke the dead voices of the past which they cannot avoid hearing.

VLADIMIR They make a noise like wings.
ESTRAGON Like leaves.
VLADIMIR Like sand.
ESTRAGON Like leaves. (p. 40b)

Here Beckett seems to acknowledge that even though all past ties with culture and tradition—the Bible, classicism, romanticism—have been broken, this heritage remains as a background murmur. And although Beckett sharply breaks with earlier traditions throughout the play, he invokes them almost with nostalgia even in the process of rejecting them.

With its complexity of meaning as well as eloquent simplicity of language, Beckett's play gains immeasurably from performance. The staging reinforces the bareness of the universe and the sparseness of the characters' existence. The only object on the empty playing space is a tree, barren in Act I but with "four or five leaves" in Act II. Despite the bleakness of the setting, the play can be surprisingly lively. Vladimir and Estragon not only perform their comic routines but also tease the audience, which they address sarcastically as "an inspiring prospect" or rudely as "a bog." In fact, the performance can radically change the mood of the work. The original French director of the play, Roger Blin (b. 1907), emphasized its pessimism. In contrast, the New York production, directed by Herbert Berghof (b. 1909), suggested a more positive view of life through the irrepressible vitality of the comic actor Bert Lahr (1895–1967) [196].

Two such different interpretations are possible because *Waiting for Godot* is at times intentionally ambiguous. Although not a desirable quality when it merely reflects an unclear meaning, ambiguity can be a useful means of expressing the complexities and contradictions of modern life. The ending of the play offers a striking example, for it is both positive and negative. At Vladimir's insistence, Estragon pulls on his trousers and both agree to get on with living:

VLADIMIR Well? Shall we go?
ESTRAGON Yes, let's go. (p. 60b)

But the positive actions and words are belied by the final stage direction: "They do not move." No attempt is made to resolve this contradiction.

Contributing to the play's complexity is the fundamental contrast between the seeming pessimism of Beckett's view of life and the humor of his presentation. Modern life, as Beckett shows it, has no philosophic justification nor clear cause-and-effect relationships. His world is bare and cruel. In Act II Lucky has become dumb and Pozzo blind without any explanation for these catastrophes. Consequently, the universe seems utterly meaningless. Yet instead of gloom and tears, a certain black or gallows humor prevails. Beckett's characters make us laugh, although their situation is desperate. Perhaps this is why he has subtitled the play a tragicomedy. But Beckett's work also belongs to a modern type of drama called the **theater of the absurd** because it greets the meaninglessness of the universe with bitter laughter. The jarring combination of discordant elements—here of theme and tone—can be likened to the dissonance found in other modern art forms. The faces of Picasso's women with their clashing colors and harsh markings as well as the strident chords of Stravinsky's *Le Sacre du printemps* suggest that dissonance is a characteristic of modern life and hence of modern art.

Finally, Beckett displays another of the characteristics we have noticed in the works of modern artists. *Waiting for Godot* is self-conscious in its use of the elements of drama, reminding us always that its existence as a work of art depends on language, action, and performance. The characters draw attention to their use of language by their obvious enjoyment of their verbal "canters." They emphasize their existence as stage figures when they indirectly and amusingly acknowledge the presence of the audience. They even play-act incidents and engage in role playing "I'll do Lucky, you do Pozzo." By deliberately mimicking vaudeville stage business involving hats, boots, and falling trousers, Beckett further stresses the theatrical nature of the action. Rather than mask the resources at his command, Beckett draws attention to them in the same conscious manner we have noticed in Picasso and Stravinsky. Perhaps because modern civilization has failed to find a meaningful basis for understanding human experience, art has come to stress its self-sufficiency by emphasizing the very elements through which it comes into being.

Not surprisingly, *Waiting for Godot* and all its peculiarities shocked the audience when it was first performed. Indeed, each of the modern works we have been considering had a profound shock effect on its audiences. For the themes of these works question accepted values and conventional ways of viewing the individual, society, and the universe. And the techniques used tend to be highly experimental, playing with the possibilities of each medium—Picasso breaks the illusion of three-dimensionality and perspective, Stravinsky introduces harsh dissonances, and Beckett uses stark, minimal staging. Gone are the clarity, order, and emphasis on reason of neoclassicism. Gone, too, are the mysteriousness, suggestiveness, and emphasis on feeling of romanticism. Instead, modern works offer baffling questions, deliberate disorder, and frequent emphasis on impulses that are hostile, primitive, and subconscious.

Questions for Study and Discussion

1. In what ways is *Les Demoiselles d'Avignon* [see Plate 17, page 320] shocking in both theme and treatment, and how does that account for its importance in 20th-century art?
2. What elements of Cubism can be found in *Les Demoiselles d'Avignon?* How is Cubism developed further in Picasso's *Girl With a Mandolin* [see Figure 79, page 124], his *Girl Before a Mirror* [see Figure 41, page 47], and Braque's *Still Life: The Table* [see Figure 131, page 227]?
3. What elements of primitivism are included in both *Les Demoiselles d'Avignon* and Stravinsky's *Le Sacre du printemps?* Why are modern artists, who belong to an urban society, attracted to such material?
4. How do the musical aspects of *Le Sacre*—rhythmic patterns, melodies, use of orchestra—differ from those of earlier works?
5. What characteristics of modernism can be found in Wilfred Owen's "Parable of the Old Man and the Young" (see page 201)?
6. In how many different ways does Beckett dramatize the typically modern view of the universe, which we have described as "bafflingly complex and probably even meaningless and indifferent"?
7. In what ways do the characters in Beckett's play resemble the figures in Picasso's *Les Demoiselles d'Avignon,* especially in their place in society and their attitude toward it?
8. If you were asked to direct *Godot,* what aspects would you emphasize if you wanted to draw attention to its elements of farce, social comedy, melodrama, and serious philosophical questioning?
9. In what ways does Beckett break with the conventions of traditional playwriting and why is his rejection of tradition typical of modernism?
10. In what specific ways does each of the modern works considered here draw attention to the fundamental components of its medium? Why is this self-conscious presentation of the work of art typical of modernism?

PART IV

Approaches to Appreciating and Evaluating the Arts

Now that we have considered the elements of the various art forms and some of the contexts that enrich them, we should ask how we can bring such knowledge to bear on our experience of particular works. How can we appreciate and enjoy any work of art to the full? And how can we evaluate it? What principles can lead us toward a more knowledgeable response that may supplement our initial impression? Chapter 13, "Fully Experiencing a Work of Art," and Chapter 14, "Forming a Judgment," should help us to answer these questions.

CHAPTER 13

Fully Experiencing a Work of Art

After considering the importance of both first impressions and reexamination, we will give some attention to how our appreciation of a work of art can be affected by additional background information about the creator's life, about the immediate social and political context, and even about the relation of the particular work to others created before and after it, known as **intertextuality.** Such knowledge will contribute to the development of an informed judgment.

Naturally, we cannot overlook the importance of our personal responses. If we are bored or thoroughly annoyed, we may not make the effort necessary to know a work of art fully and thereby to respond to it intelligently. But we must remember that training and experience with works of art can change our response. They can help us to avoid the boredom or confusion that may come from being unfamiliar with the techniques or traditions of the various arts. In short, our response is likely to vary with our knowledge and experience.

Moreover, we should realize that our reactions to the same work may vary. For instance, our mood may differ, making us more observant and receptive at one time than another. Our ideas may change as we grow older, making us more responsive to some works and impatient with others. More fundamentally, our experience of a work of art will differ depending on whether we are encountering it for the first time or returning to it later.

First Impressions and Reexamination

Our first impression of a work of art is likely to be vivid and unexpected as we will experience the excitement that comes from discovering something new. Viewing Delacroix's *Death of Sardanapalus* [see Plate 16, page 319] for the first time, we cannot help being almost overwhelmed by its size, the profusion of exotic figures and details, the glowing colors, and above all the horror of the scene. As we first look at Dürer's *Italian Mountains* [see Plate 6, page 38], on the other hand, we will probably be charmed by the delicacy of color and the suggestive haziness of the images. This watercolor painting gives us the impression of seeing the world afresh.

In the temporal arts, our first experience often involves suspense, an eager expectation of what is to come. How will Haydn in his *Sonata in E-flat* (see Chapter 10) lead us back to the tonic after the varied wanderings in the development section? How do the two placid matrons in Edith Wharton's "Roman Fever" (see Chapter 2) outmaneuver each other, and which one will have the last word? In performing arts such as theater, opera, and ballet, the element of suspense may be even stronger as we are caught up in the action.

In some instances, we already know the whole story. Most theatergoers know from the start that the murderer whom Oedipus seeks is himself and that however much he struggles to evade the outcome, he is doomed. All Greek tragedies are based on stories well known to most audiences and certainly known to the original audience. In these cases, we still experience an initial excitement—wondering not what will happen next, but rather how the author will shape and interpret the familiar material, and how the director and actors will present the scenes.

But when we come back to a work, after a first encounter, we are likely to have a more complicated experience. Repeated encounters may make us much more aware of the complexities, the numerous interrelationships and subtleties of detail that contribute to the whole—all the elements, in short, that we have considered in our earlier discussions. In other words, we will be much more conscious and appreciative of the skillful artistry that has gone into the creation of the work.

In the arts of time especially, a reexamination is usually essential. Only once we have experienced the ending can we fully appreciate what has led up to it and how carefully it has been prepared. In extended pieces of music such as sonatas and symphonies, we need several hearings to grasp the total organization. We need to become familiar with the various themes and their development and resolution in order to appreciate the work more fully. After we have gained such familiarity, we have the pleasure on rehearing it that comes from reacquaintance with an old friend.

Just as rehearing a piece of music is likely to lead to a richer experience, so the rereading of a literary text can be more meaningful and enjoyable than a first reading. Once we know the outcome of the plot in "Roman Fever," for instance, we can reread the story with an awareness of all the clues that foreshadow the series of reversals at the end. Only when we realize how the two matrons have behaved in their youth can we appreciate how carefully Edith Wharton has created their personalities, making them capable of such surprising behavior. Because character and plot action are inseparable, we cannot fully understand one or the other until we know the entire story. Rereading, then, provides a pleasure of its own.

Moreover, longer works such as novels can be reread in part. To understand how Pip in *Great Expectations* has been misled about the identity of his benefactor, for example, we will want to go back to several earlier scenes with the lawyer Jaggers and his various clients. Some modern critics have even suggested that novels should be read "backwards" as well as forwards, meaning that the earlier sections can be fully understood only if we read them after finishing the whole text.

In performances, we have a special pleasure when we see the same role interpreted differently by various artists or even by the same artist on different evenings in the same production. We can delight in Derek Jacobi's thoughtful and sensitive Hamlet, quite different from Richard Burton's energetic and powerful Hamlet; and in Cynthia Gregory's forceful Odette, the bewitched Princess of *Swan Lake,* quite different from Margot Fonteyn's fragile delicate Odette (see Chapter 5). Coupled with the sense of discovering a new interpretation in these cases is the pleasure of experiencing a familiar work again as it unfolds before us.

Actually, our second or later encounter with a work is usually not so different from our first as the foregoing discussion may have implied. As spectators, we are likely still to be thrilled by the violence in *The Death of Sardanapalus* [see Plate 16, page 319], even as repeated visits make us more aware of Delacroix's artistry. We are likely to relive the fate of a tragic hero whenever we see a performance, even as repeated viewings enable us to appreciate the playwright's skill and the production's merits more fully. In effect, at later encounters we can experience a work of art from both the inside and the outside.

Understanding the Background

Although most works of art can be understood and enjoyed on their own terms, in some cases our appreciation will be enriched when we have background information. Such information may concern the artist's biography, that is, details of the artist's character and life. It may also involve history, or the relation of the work of art to its own time or even the appearance of historical material within the work itself.

Biography

Knowledge of the creator's life and character is often interesting in itself, but whether it helps us to understand a work will differ from case to case. To know that Van Gogh was suffering from nervous exhaustion and was on the brink of a mental breakdown when he painted his self-portrait [see Figure 128, page 224] is surely valuable background information. But knowing these facts is not absolutely essential, for we can recognize the overtones of violence and tension in the harshly contrasting colors and the erratic brushstrokes of the painting itself.

Beethoven, about whose life a great deal has come to light, presents a more complicated case. Knowledge of his character and personal experiences is sometimes irrelevant, but in other instances can heighten our appreciation of his music. For instance, we need not know that Beethoven's unhappy private life included a childhood marred by an abusive, drunken father; a painful love relationship; and later disappointment with an ungrateful nephew whose affections he tried to win. More significant, however, is our knowledge that from the age of 26 Beethoven was confronted with the terrifying problem of increasing deafness, which no physician of the time could cure. In a heart-rending letter called the *Heiligenstadt Testament* (1802), intended to be read only after his death, Beethoven explained to his brothers:

> For 6 years now I have been hopelessly afflicted, made worse by senseless physicians, from year to year deceived with hopes of improvement, finally compelled to face the prospect of *a lasting malady*. . . . I was soon compelled to withdraw myself, to live life alone. If at times I tried to forget all this, oh how harshly was I flung back by the doubly sad experience of my bad hearing. Yet it was impossible for me to say to people, "Speak louder, shout, for I am deaf." Ah, how could I possibly admit an infirmity in the *one sense* which ought to be more perfect in me than in others, a sense which I once possessed in the highest perfection, a perfection such as few in my profession enjoy or ever have enjoyed. . . . But what a humiliation for me when someone standing next to me heard a flute in the distance and I heard nothing, or someone heard a *shepherd* singing and again *I heard nothing*. Such incidents drove me almost to despair, a little more of that and I would have ended my life—it was only *my art* that held me back. Ah, it seemed to me impossible to leave the world until I had brought forth all that I felt was within me.

Clearly, Beethoven spent years in silence, embarrassment, and the worst kind of fear and suffering that a musician could endure.

The intensity and poignancy of some of Beethoven's music—such as the *F-minor Piano Sonata,* which is appropriately known as the "Appassionata" ("impassioned")—may be all the more understandable in light of his personal experiences. But such music cannot be regarded merely as a direct expression of the composer's personal unhappiness. Instead, this and other works written at the same time reveal how a strong personality responds to unhappiness. We should beware of concluding that intense emotions inevitably lead to great artistic works, for deep feeling may prevent the creation of controlled and complex works of art. Still, we can say that Beethoven's character and genius enabled him to translate his private experiences into art. Moreover, he was composing at a time when romantic ideas about individuality and self-expression were becoming popular. Indeed, the highly personal element in Beethoven's music made him one of the foremost exponents of the romantic idea that artists should express their personalities in their art.

In addition, a knowledge of Beethoven's political views can also contribute to our understanding of his music. In an age when the aristocracy was still powerful, he favored democratic principles and believed strongly in the freedom and equality of the individual. Accordingly, he wrote his one opera *Fidelio* (1814) about a man imprisoned unjustly because of his political opinions and rescued by his heroic loyal wife. Furthermore, Beethoven concluded his last, *Ninth Symphony* (1824) by setting to music the great "Ode to Joy" of the German poet Friedrich Schiller (1759–1805). That poem celebrates universal brotherhood. These and other works by Beethoven are grandiose and heroic, reflecting both the composer's deep convictions and his indomitable spirit.

Interesting as biographical details may be, they are not absolutely essential to our understanding of Beethoven's music. We should realize that these works are self-sufficient entities; our experience may be enriched by a knowledge of the composer's personal history, but his music is certainly comprehensible in and of itself.

Yet occasionally, biographical information is necessary if we are to understand a work fully. For example, the knowledge that the poet Nikki Giovanni is black makes us more sensitive to some of the images in "Kidnap Poem" (see page 72). Not only is *black* the only word that is capitalized in this lyric, but the colors in line 16 "wrap you in the red Black green" refer to those used in the Afro-American flag. The speaker is proudly insisting on a certain racial identity in the course of her joyous expression of love.

History

Like biographical information, knowledge of historical facts can shed light on individual works of art to varying degrees. Such knowledge can encompass not only information about the work in its own time—its commission and standing—but also about historical material incorporated in the work.

Both kinds of historical background can enhance our appreciation of Michelangelo's *David* [see Figure 36, page 44]. On the one hand, recalling the Old Testament story of David will help us to understand Michelangelo's resolute but vulnerable figure. On the other hand, knowing that his *David* was commissioned for the city of Florence will also enable us to understand why Michelangelo made this figure so noble and heroic. The biblical youth David who slew the giant Goliath had become a traditional symbol of Florence in its struggle against the larger and more powerful rival city-states of Milan and

Venice. So enthusiastic were the Florentines about Michelangelo's sculpture that, discarding earlier plans for its location, they gave it a place of honor in the central square. This background information, though not crucial for appreciating the statue as an idealized image of heroic youth, enriches our response.

In literature, too, knowledge of historical background may be helpful and sometimes essential. Writers who incorporate references to historical events into their works usually provide sufficient explanation so that these references are self-explanatory. In *A Tale of Two Cities* (1859), for instance, Charles Dickens presents scenes of the French Revolution that may be more interesting to us if we know about the Reign of Terror that engulfed France in 1793–1794. Yet we can certainly sympathize with Dickens' characters even without such additional knowledge.

On the other hand, modern writers especially may present historical events only in brief allusions. In *Portrait of the Artist as a Young Man,* James Joyce refers to key personalities of modern Irish politics such as James Parnell and his mistress Kitty O'Shea without further explanation, for he is interested in presenting only the emotional reaction of his fictional characters. To understand these passages fully, we must bring our own knowledge of history to the work or rely on either a lengthy footnote or a well-informed teacher.

Relation to Other Works—Intertextuality

In addition, we should bear in mind that although art works are independent entities, they are also related to one another. As we have seen in our analysis of traditions and historical periods, works of art may express similar themes and use similar images. Moreover, works belonging to the same art form tend to become part of a chain, whether they adopt or deliberately reject elements of earlier works. Recent critics have spoken of *intertextuality* to signify the close relationship whereby one work is illuminated by an earlier or later work.

Artists have, in fact, always drawn freely on their predecessors. In music, for example, the Mass settings of the late Middle Ages or the Renaissance incorporated phrases from earlier Gregorian chants. Furthermore, even simple quotations illustrate this kind of interrelationship. Mozart provides a brilliant example in his opera *Don Giovanni* (1787) when the orchestra plays two melodies from rival operas and then an immediately identifiable melody from his own *Marriage of Figaro.* At this point, the servant Leporello winks at the audience and says, "This one I know only too well."

The identifiable allusion to other themes is put to serious use in *Madama Butterfly* (1904) by Giacomo Puccini. Here one or two phrases from "The Star-Spangled Banner" are heard from the orchestra when the action, set in Japan, refers to the distant United States. This use of musical quotation is, in fact, rather like Wagner's *Leitmotiv* technique (see Chapter 9).

Often, artists allude to or quote from older works in order to ring significant changes on their themes. Eudora Welty also draws profoundly on an earlier work in her "Circe" (see Chapter 4). But in recasting an episode from Homer's *Odyssey,* she gives it a poignant meaning concerning the plight of both immortals and women.

In film, directors may quote from earlier examples of their art. Steven Spielberg (b. 1947) has the extra-terrestrial creature of his *E.T.* (1982) mistakenly greet a child in Hallowe'en costume dressed as Yoda, a kindred extra-terrestrial being who appeared in another recent science fiction film. Here Spielberg is wittily linking his new film with an earlier one. In another scene, E.T. accidentally turns on a television set which is showing John Ford's *The Quiet Man* (1952). E.T. actually shares some of the traits of Ford's hero—both are displaced in a strange country and utter few words. These similarities make the reference apt, while the difference between the vulnerable little E.T. and the strong John Wayne adds an amusing contrast. Spielberg's choice of *The Quiet Man* is a tribute to John Ford, whom he clearly admires. Indeed, when modern film directors repeat scenes or sequences from earlier films, they are usually expressing their admiration for their predecessors.

In painting, some artists have echoed the figures or even the whole composition of earlier established works, at times in tribute and at other times in contrast. In *The Turkish Bath* (c. 1852–1863) [197], J. A. D. Ingres (1780–1867) creates a sensuous scene of nude women in an indoor bath, possibly attached to a harem. The woman in the foreground, who turns her back to us, plays an oriental instrument while around her other women are seen in sensual poses. One of these, voluptuously reclining on the right, stares shamelessly at us, breaking the painting's implied "fourth wall" by offering an erotic challenge that anticipates the pin-ups of our own day. Ingres was actually reworking the well-known theme of women bathing that had been popular at least since the Renaissance. For instance, Diana, the Roman goddess of chastity, and her nymphs are shown bathing in a beautiful landscape in *Women Bathing* [198] by Palma Vecchio (1480–1528). Idealized in their grace and beauty, they are modest and absorbed in their activities, unaware of any watchers. Such nudes are part of the great tradition of idealized female figures exemplified in the *Venus de Milo* and various paintings of Venus rising from the sea. But whereas Palma Vecchio and his predecessors present their women as coolly remote, distanced by their mythological identity, and placed in an outdoor setting, Ingres daringly paints his sensuous harem women in a sultry indoor setting. Far from being remote and distanced, they seem to be aware of our watching them. In this instance, the contrast between Palma Vecchio's and Ingres's paintings makes us sharply aware of the special qualities of each.

An even more startling example of intertextuality—the mutual illuminating of similar works—can be found in *The Turkish Bath* by Sylvia Sleigh [199]. The title suggests that the artist is deliberately echoing Ingres' painting. The placing of her figures confirms her conscious reference to the earlier work, as does the inclusion of the musical instrument played by a nude figure whose back is turned. What makes Sylvia Sleigh's painting so arresting is that she has changed the sex of her nudes and that she has presented them in a startlingly realistic way. Since the setting is not the woods of ancient Greece nor the indoor baths of imperial Turkey, but a New York City apartment, the

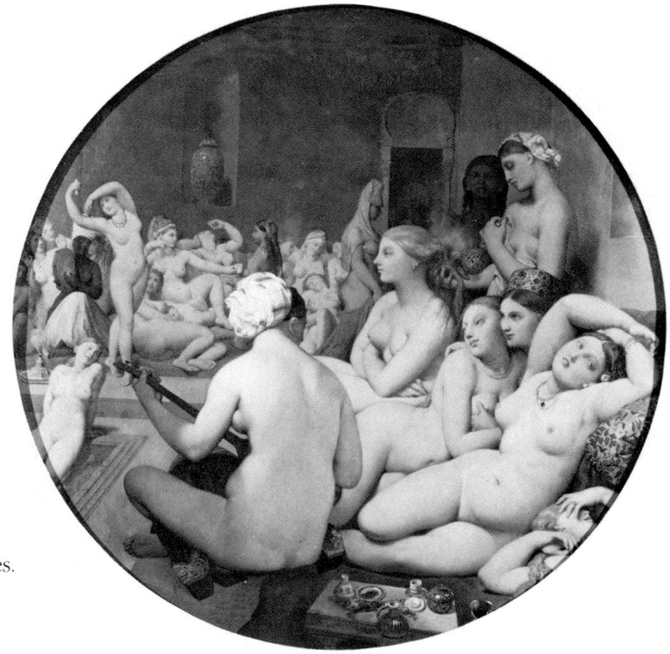

197 Jean Auguste Dominique Ingres. *The Turkish Bath.* c. 1852–1863. Oil on canvas, diameter 42½″ (108 cm). Louvre, Paris.

scene has a blunt immediacy. In addition to the unexpected conversion of female nudes to males, the artist has made a telling point that becomes clear when we realize that all her figures are in some sense art critics, including her husband, Lawrence Alloway, in the right foreground. As they stare out at us, perhaps in the same unresponsive way in which they have examined her paintings, we are allowed to stare back and examine them. The artist has turned the tables not only in mocking the tradition of female bathers but also in subjecting her critics to a searching critical examination.

Certainly, we could not understand Sylvia Sleigh's painting fully if we had never seen Ingres's *Turkish Bath.* Conversely, we are likely to view In-

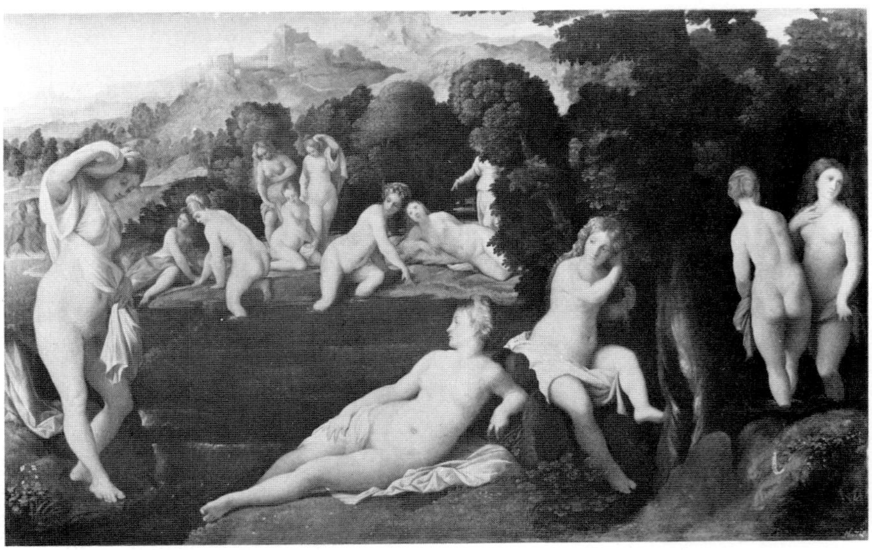

198 Palma Vecchio. *Women Bathing.* or *Diana and Callisto.* c. 1525. Oil on canvas mounted on wood, 2′6¼″ × 4′⅜″ (.78 × 1.24 m). Kunsthistorisches Museum, Vienna.

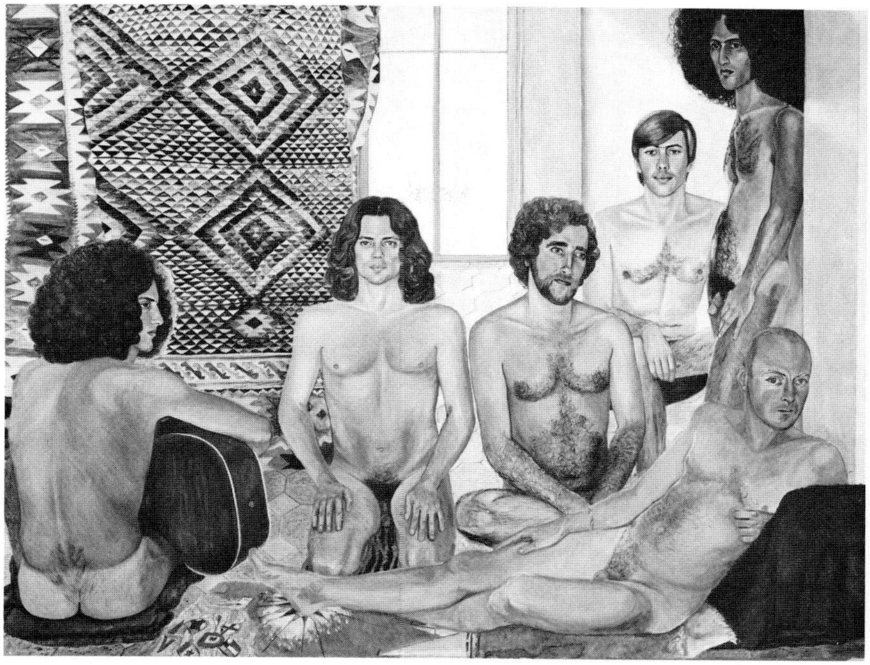

199 Sylvia Sleigh. *The Turkish Bath.* 1973. Oil on canvas, 6′4″ × 8′6″ (1.93 × 2.59 m). Private collection, New York.

gres's painting differently now that we have seen Sleigh's reinterpretation, for we realize that if male artists can depict passive naked women, then female artists can depict impassive naked men. This example of intertextuality shows how more recent works can affect our response to older ones. Such an awareness of intertextuality—of influences not bound by chronology—differs from an awareness of traditions—the cumulative influence of earlier works on later ones.

Questions for Study and Discussion

1. How are first impressions and reexaminations of a work equally important but different experiences? If possible, describe how a subsequent encounter with a painting, sculpture, story, play, or film differed from your first impression of this work.
2. To what varying extent does a knowledge of the artist's life increase our understanding of the works discussed in this section? How does the knowledge of Wilfred Owen's death affect our response to "The Parable of the Old Man and the Young" [see page 201]?
3. To what extent does a knowledge of the historical context increase our understanding of the works discussed in this chapter? How does such knowledge affect our response to Schmidt-Rottluff's *The Way to Emmaus* [see Figure 26, page 29]?
4. What is meant by *intertextuality*? How does this differ from the notion of influence? In what ways is Thom Gunn's "Moly" [see page 149] an example of intertextuality?

CHAPTER 14

Forming a Judgment

Once we have tried to understand a work of art as fully as possible, analyzing it closely and bringing to bear on it all the relevant background information, we will want to consider how to weigh its merits. To do so, we can draw on a number of criteria that are traditionally used. This trying out of various criteria on individual works of art can heighten our sensitivity and help us to recognize the special qualities of each work.

Some Widely Accepted Criteria

To help us weigh the usefulness of the commonly held criteria, we can group these according to whether they are related to the creator—originality and sincerity—or to the audience—easy comprehensibility and relevance—or to the work itself—beauty of subject matter, complexity, and coherence. Naturally, these criteria should not be regarded as *absolutes.* Rather, they are guides that may help us appreciate and evaluate a work of art. Some of these criteria are more helpful than others and some, as we shall see, are not helpful at all. Nevertheless, an awareness of the most commonly used criteria will enable us to keep more clearly in mind the basis on which we and others are passing judgment. In any case, we should realize that knowing which criterion—or combination of criteria—is appropriate for a particular work comes mainly with experience.

Originality

We might assume that in gauging a creator's talent, we should look for originality, for we usually expect a painter, musician, or writer to offer something new. However, total novelty is probably unattainable; artists must create within the limits imposed by their medium and their awareness of the traditions established by their predecessors. Even when a sharp break with a tradition occurs, the first example of the new approach is difficult to identify. For instance, despite the fact that abstract painting is a recent innovation, we cannot establish precisely who created the first canvas of this sort. Similarly, we cannot name with any certainty the originator of the narrative device of stream of consciousness.

In the rare instances when considerable originality—in the sense of total novelty—has been achieved, this may not really contribute to the greatness of the work. For example, the Milanese artist Giuseppe Arcimboldo (1527–1593) enjoyed great but momentary success by his paintings of grotesque human heads composed of the shapes of vegetables, flowers, or inanimate objects. That is, he used still-life elements to mimic the parts of the human body. The portrait entitled *Fire* is made up of burning sticks of wood, candles, a lamp, steel, flints, and cannons [200]. Around the neck appears the

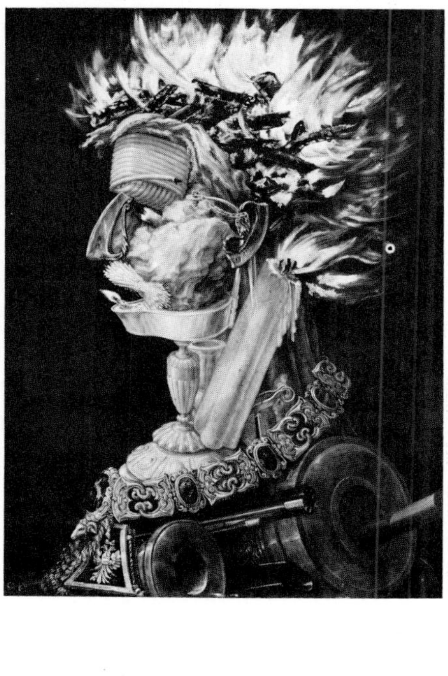

200 Giuseppe Arcimboldo. *Fire.* 1566. Oil on panel, 26 × 19⅞″ (67 × 51 cm). Kunsthistorisches Museum, Vienna.

collar of the Hapsburg Order of the Golden Fleece, suggesting that the image was intended to portray an aristocrat who seems also to have had a fiery temperament. As far as is known, this method of patching together an approximation of a human figure out of inanimate objects was an invention of Arcimboldo's that is without precedent in Western art. It is also, however, so specialized and bizarre that its range of application is severely limited.

Nonetheless, originality can be a useful criterion if we understand it not as total novelty, but as a fresh approach to an existing tradition. Shakespeare can certainly be credited with originality in reworking material taken from earlier plays or stories. *King Lear* is based on an earlier play that has many of the same characters and incidents, yet only Shakespeare gives this essentially folktale material a profound significance. Indeed, by introducing great scenes of human suffering, a double plot that generalizes the problematic father-child relationship, and a tragic ending, Shakespeare gives a much more serious interpretation of human life than can be found in the anonymous play *King Leir.* Beethoven, too, can be credited with originality when he takes the form of the symphony as it had evolved in the works of Haydn and Mozart, and expands it in both length and emotional power. And in both these instances, the artists' originality consists not only of reworking earlier stories or genres, but also of adding their distinctive personal voice, tone, or attitude toward life.

To take a more recent example, Eudora Welty in her "Circe" (see Chapter 4) might be accused of lacking originality, for she returns to one of the earliest narratives in Western literature, Homer's *Odyssey.* Yet her reinterpretation of the Circe episode, from the point of view of the woman, giving it modern significance, is surely as original as if she herself had invented the plot and characters.

Sincerity

Another principle sometimes used to gauge a creator's talent is *sincerity.* Some people expect artists genuinely to feel the emotions they are expressing in their work. Yet such sincerity is not easily ascertainable, for we cannot really measure to what extent, if any, the feelings expressed in an artistic work were felt by the artist. Conversely, deeply felt emotions do not necessarily aid in the creation of masterpieces. Emotions may prevent artists from doing the best work possible because their art may become overly personal and embarrassing.

Perhaps the best example of the irrelevance of sincerity as a criterion can be found in judging the work of John Milton (1608–1674). He was able to write a powerful poem of mourning, the elegy "Lycidas" (1637), about the death of a young minister he hardly knew. On the other hand, after he had lost his sight, he was inspired to write eloquently about blindness both in his epic *Paradise Lost* (1667) and in his last work, *Samson Agonistes* (1671). "Dark, dark, dark amid the blaze of noon" is an unforgettable expression of the suffering of someone who, like the hero Samson, must exist in total darkness. And yet neither "Lycidas" nor the later works should really be

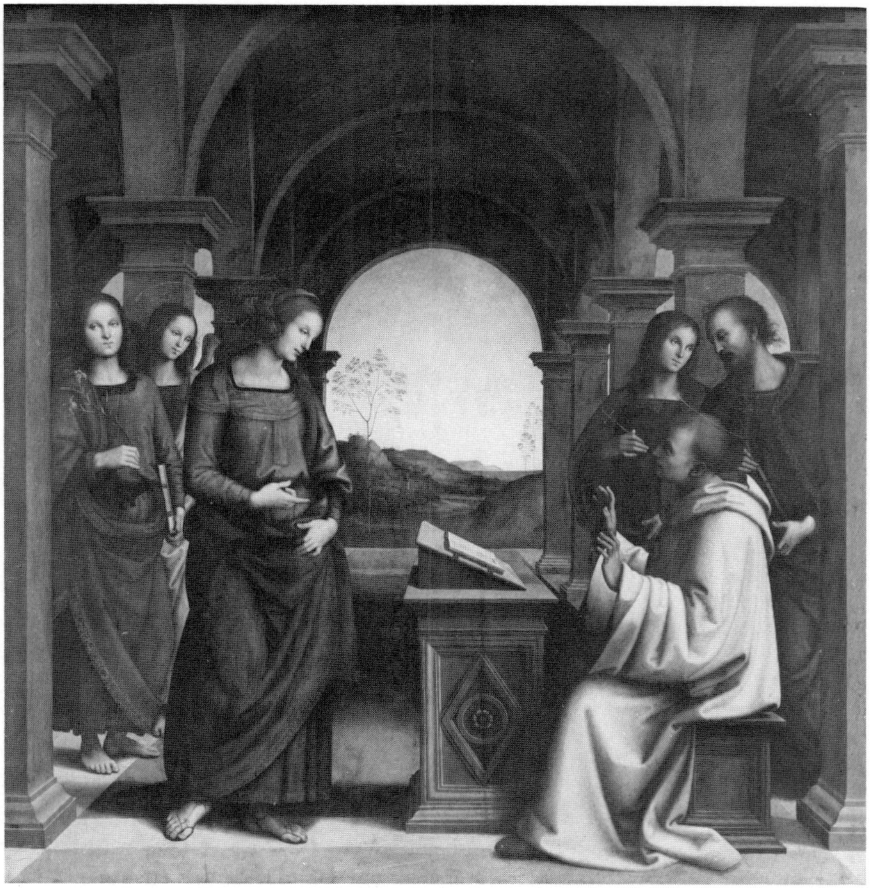

201 Pietro Perugino. *The Vision of Saint Bernard.* 1494. Oil on canvas, 5′8″ × 5′7″ (1.73 × 1.70 m). Alte Pinakothek, Munich. Saint Bernard, seated in his study, looks up, surprised at his unexpected holy visitors. Perugino has organized the whole composition to convey a sense of dignity and repose. The architectural background complements the disposition of the figures in two groups.

judged in terms of Milton's possible sincerity, but simply as literary creations in their own right.

Alternatively, some naive members of an audience expect artists to be sincere in honestly believing the ideas they express in their work. Yet the artist's sincerity of belief cannot be ascertained any more accurately than the artist's feelings. We know of artists who did not believe what they depicted. For instance, the painter Pietro Perugino (c. 1445–1523) created magnificent frescoes and oils on religious subjects, yet was a radical for his time and did not fully accept all the doctrines taught by the Catholic Church. For instance, Perugino is known not to have believed in the immortality of the soul. However, his *Vision of Saint Bernard* [201] includes long-dead saints who appear in bodily form to Saint Bernard. In spite of Perugino's doctrinal doubts, his work was valued so highly that he was commissioned to paint one of the frescoes in the Sistine Chapel in the Vatican. Clearly, the artist's emotional or intellectual sincerity is not a helpful criterion for determining the excellence of the work.

The two criteria related to the creator's talent are, then, of varying usefulness. Originality in the sense of total novelty is a highly questionable criterion, but originality in the sense of a fresh and distinctive approach is a legitimate one. Sincerity, whether emotional or intellectual, is indeterminable and irrelevant to the value of the work. No less than these criteria that focus on the artist, those related to the audience's response have serious limitations.

Easy Comprehensibility

As audience, we may be tempted to find a work good when it is easily understandable and to reject a work that seems difficult to comprehend. However, the criterion of *easy comprehensibility* is also not an adequate means of judging artistic worth. The fact that a work is easily understandable does not make it good. We may enjoy such accessible entertainments as soap operas, but know that they are not great art. Their very simplicity of character types and character motivation may make them momentarily enjoyable but usually also quickly forgotten.

Better works that may appear to be simple on first acquaintance are often actually quite complicated. The four-line lyric "Western Wind" (see Chapter 8) needed extensive analysis. Brilliant as it is at first sight, Michelangelo's *David* [see Figure 36, page 44] gains considerably when we bring some knowledge of its historical background to bear on it. Alternatively, a work that is difficult, such as Thom Gunn's poem "Moly" in Chapter 4, can with some background knowledge and close attention to the words be understood as a fascinating character study. Similarly, Rogier van der Weyden's *Christ Appearing to His Mother* [see Plate 8, page 40], confusing at first sight, can be appreciated—once we recall the story of the Virgin and look attentively at the details—as a remarkably unified presentation of the key events of her life following the Crucifixion.

Relevance

According to another criterion directly related to the experience of the audience, art is often judged by its *relevance:* the more relevant, the better. Actually, this term has two applications. *Immediate relevance* refers to specific problems of current interest; *universal relevance* refers to concerns that remain unchanging over time. We may admire works of immediate relevance—for instance, those dealing with women's rights or nuclear arms—especially when these works correspond to our personal views. But if we insist that art must have topical significance, we restrict its range unnecessarily; we may praise works that will be forgotten once the issues they present are resolved, and we may reject other works, especially of earlier periods, that seem to be removed from our current interests.

Although works of art should not be judged on the basis of their immediate relevance, we can certainly expect to find some universal relevance in them. *King Lear,* for instance, with its far-from-contemporary characters and setting, seems not to be relevant to modern life. But in showing the complex interactions between parents and children as well as the possibility of both cruelty and forgiveness in human relations, Shakespeare's play has undeniable universal relevance. And such works of earlier periods may challenge our preconceptions, expanding our sympathy and understanding in more fundamental ways than the immediately relevant can do.

In looking for either immediate or universal relevance, we should be careful not to assume that works of art have readily identifiable and extractable ideas. As we have seen throughout our discussion, most works of art cannot be reduced to any simple meaning.

Ultimately, the most fruitful criteria for judging works of art relate not to the talents of their creators nor to the responses of the audience, but to the qualities of the works themselves. Even here, however, not every commonly held criterion is valid.

Beauty of Subject Matter

We may be tempted to judge a work by the attractiveness or *beauty* of its subject; alternatively, we may be tempted to reject a work if its subject matter is repulsive or ugly. Yet mere pleasantness is no guarantee of artistic value, and many works of art have intrinsically disturbing or distressing subjects. Pablo Picasso's prostitutes in *Les Demoiselles d'Avignon* [see Plate 17, page 320], with their brutish faces, and the art critics in Sylvia Sleigh's *The Turkish Bath* [see Figure 199, page 349] with their blank expressions, might well be considered intrinsically unattractive. Or we might find fault with works of art whose components are jarring or harsh—the color combinations of a painting, the sound patterns of a poem or piece of music. The strident dissonances and savage rhythms of *Le Sacre du printemps* (see Chapter 12) were sufficient to make this work repellent to many in the first audience.

If we consider only the subject matter or the component parts, our judgment is likely to be too limited. We ought to take into account how the subject matter or the components have been transformed in the work. That is, we should focus on how these have been shaped or organized into complex interrelationships that form a coherent whole. Indeed, we cannot really separate the subject matter or parts from their treatment, any more than we can separate the characters from the action of a story or, to paraphrase Yeats, the dancer from the dance.

Having found fault with so many ways of judging art, we may wonder whether acceptable criteria can be found. Whatever principles we ultimately adopt are likely to be very general, for they have to be applicable to the various arts and to the productions of many ages. Such principles cannot be regarded as simple or mechanical rules, but must always be applied in a sensitive and flexible manner.

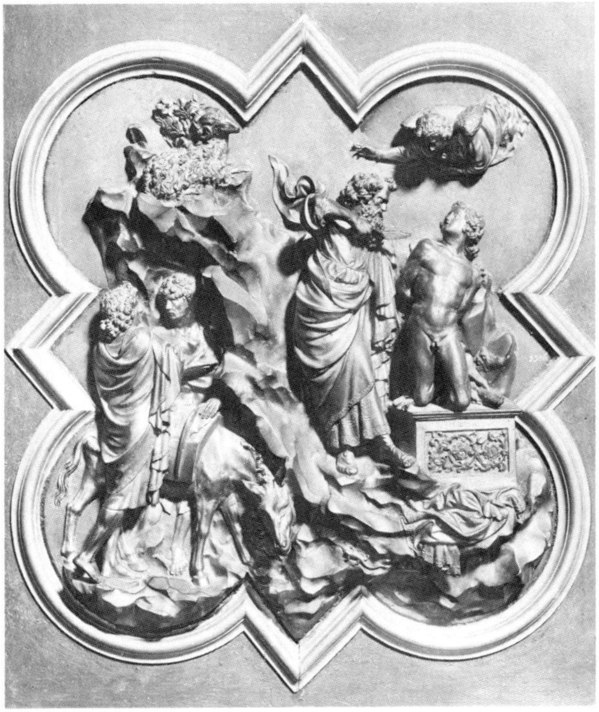 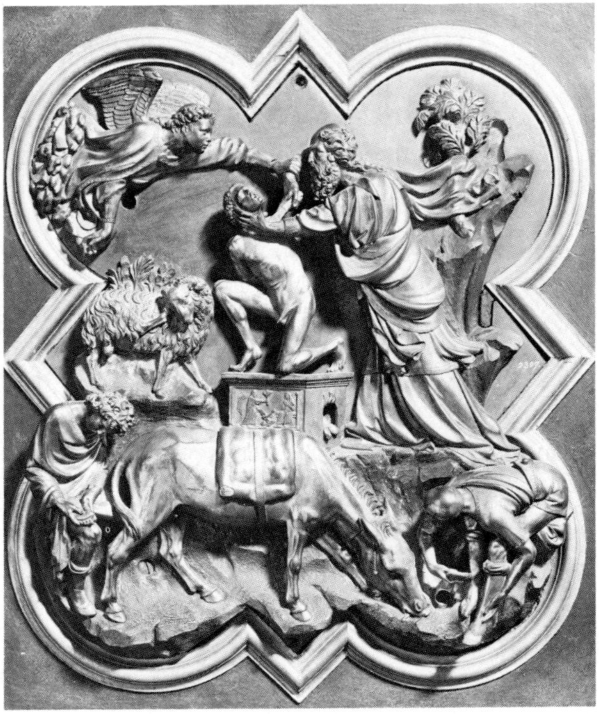

above left: 202 Lorenzo Ghiberti. *The Sacrifice of Isaac.* 1401–1402. Gilded bronze, 21 × 17½″ (53 × 44 cm). Museo Nazionale del Bargello, Florence.

above right: 203 Filippo Brunelleschi. *The Sacrifice of Isaac.* 1401–1402. Gilded bronze, 21 × 17½″ (53 × 44 cm). Museo Nazionale del Bargello, Florence.

Complexity and Coherence

Perhaps the most valid criteria are the related ones of *complexity* and *coherence.* When we judge a work in terms of its complexity, we are considering the many interrelationships within it. When we judge it in terms of coherence, we are focusing on the ways in which the parts form a unified whole. Our earlier discussions should have made us aware of the various aspects that contribute to the complexity of a work of art—especially its basic components and shaping point of view—aspects that must be pulled together to create a coherent entity.

If we consider two treatments of the same subject, we can, perhaps, more easily understand how the criteria of complexity and coherence can help us to form a judgment about each work's relative merit. Two that lend themselves to such a comparison are Brunelleschi's and Ghiberti's panels, both entitled *Sacrifice of Isaac.* They are comparable because, as entries in the competition for the Baptistry doors in Florence in 1401, they depict the assigned subject in a predetermined quatrefoil shape and in the same medium of gilded bronze [202, 203]. Although both works are outstanding, the Florentine judges preferred Ghiberti's panel, and we might now ask ourselves why.

Looking at the composition of Ghiberti's panel we can appreciate the remarkable complexity and coherence of its organization. The work is arranged in terms of dynamic balance. Abraham, Isaac, and the angel on the right are loosely separated from the servants and the ass on the left by a diagonal line suggested by the rocky outcropping. Moreover, the ram at the top left with its highly patterned wool is counterbalanced by the solid rectangular altar near the bottom right with its intricate ornamentation. Within this complex scheme, unity or coherence is maintained as almost all the subsidiary figures face the central ones of Abraham and Isaac.

Brunelleschi's panel also reveals considerable complexity of organization. Using symmetrical balance, the artist has placed Isaac and Abraham in the upper center, has balanced the flowing garments of the angel on the left with those of Abraham on the right, and has juxtaposed the two servants at the lower corners. But Brunelleschi has sharply divided his panel horizontally into two nearly equal parts. Perhaps he has done so (as suggested in Chapter 6) to show that ordinary life continues while momentous actions take place. Fascinating as this theme may be, it hardly deserves as much space as the main theme of the sacrifice. Moreover, the ass is inordinately large, for no better reason, one feels, than the need to fill out the space. We might conclude, then, that while Brunelleschi's panel is complex, it lacks the coherence or unity that Ghiberti achieves by retaining a clear emphasis on the central figures.

Turning now to the use of line and volume to shape the figures—the **modeling** of three-dimensional forms—we can again admire Ghiberti's extraordinary skill and talent. He achieves a variety of surface textures in depicting wool, hair, cloth, rock, and flesh. Such complexity, difficult to accomplish in any medium, is especially noteworthy in this panel, most of which was cast as a single unit. More importantly, Isaac is presented as a youth of such great beauty that the mere thought of sacrificing him becomes all the more painful. Ghiberti has carefully observed the proportions of Isaac's body, emphasizing its harmony and smoothness. The figures with draped garments are also distinguished by their grace. Indeed, the harmoniousness, grace, and elegance contribute to the general impression of dignity, which is appropriate for the religious theme. Since all aspects of the work are so carefully integrated, the panel is remarkable for its coherence.

Brunelleschi's surface texture also exhibits considerable variety. But the modeling of his central figure is rather crude. Isaac is less fully developed than the other figures, and his body, with its wrenched head, though it conveys violence and pain, looks clumsy. The servants are more fully and skillfully modeled than Isaac. Moreover, the panel was cast in sections with some of its seams visible—a common practice that is far less demanding than a single casting.

The various components of the two Abraham and Isaac panels contribute to their complexity and coherence in yet another way. The component parts provide what may be called an interpretation of life, and this, too, can be evaluated in terms of its complexity and coherence.

That is not to say that works of art mirror the world in any simple or predictable way and that they should be judged by how accurately they reflect the outside world or human existence. As we have seen, all the parts require selectivity and arrangement, and can therefore present only a particular view of life. The two Abraham and Isaac panels, after all, are highly selective in focusing only on the figures found traditionally in the Bible material. And the arrangement of these figures in the quatrefoils does not mirror real life; for instance, the human figures are much more prominent than the suggested scenery.

Yet Ghiberti's and Brunelleschi's panels offer fascinating interpretations that can indeed be evaluated by the principles of complexity and coherence. The grace and harmony of Ghiberti's work imply a universe overseen by a God who may give cruel commands, but who ultimately brings all to a harmonious and orderly conclusion. In contrast, the vehemence of Brunelleschi's version, in which Abraham has the knife directly at Isaac's throat, stresses the harshness of the divine command. Moreover, the indifference of the servants, absorbed in their own trivial concerns, suggests that such insensitive individuals may be untouched by the divine drama so near them. Here the universe is clearly not so unified. Consequently, the interpretation of life provided in Brunelleschi's panel is more complex than that in Ghiberti's.

To sum up, we may well argue that Brunelleschi's lesser technical skill, less successful modeling, questionable composition, and less orthodox interpretations of life probably contributed to his losing the competition. Yet his view of life can be appreciated for its complexity, and a perceptive judge must have found it difficult to choose between two such different entries. In any case, Brunelleschi's loss led him to an unexpected success in an allied field. Disappointed by the rejection of his panel, he gave up his career as a sculptor and became an architect. As such, he gave Florence one of its most magnificent structures, the dome (1420–1436) of its cathedral.

The criteria of complexity and coherence are also useful in helping us make judgments about modern works. Perhaps the most challenging test of these criteria is to apply them to abstract paintings—for instance, to *Twelfth Station* [204] by Barnett Newman (1905–1970) and *Painting I* or *Composition in White and Black* [205] by Piet Mondrian. These two works are rather similar and can be judged fairly when reproduced in black and white, since neither uses color. We should notice, however, that Mondrian's painting is about a quarter of the size of Newman's work, which stands over six feet high and challenges us much more forcefully than the illustration can show.

Since these are abstract works, we must give great attention to their formal qualities—the arrangement of lines and shapes created by the areas of black and white. As Newman's title indicates, his is a religious work. It is, in fact, part of a series of fourteen paintings, each representing in abstract terms one of the Stations of the Cross—places where significant events occurred during Christ's tortured journey to his execution. Appropriately, the division of the canvas into three rectangular areas recalls the format of the religious triptych, the sort of altarpiece common in medieval and Renaissance art that consists of a large central panel and two identical smaller side panels, often hinged to the main one. But Newman introduces an unexpected complexity in making his side sections differ in width. Moreover, the left section is linked to the middle by their common black pigment. This black also gently spills over into the third section (on the right)—which is otherwise entirely white—

above: 204 Barnett Newman. *Twelfth Station* (from *Fourteen Stations of the Cross).* 1965. Acrylic polymer on canvas, 6′6″ × 5′ (1.98 × 1.52 m). Collection of Annalee Newman, New York.

right: 205 Piet Mondrian. *Painting, I,* or *Composition in White and Black.* 1926. Oil on canvas, diagonal measurements 44¾ × 44″ (114 × 112 cm). Museum of Modern Art, New York (Katherine S. Dreier Bequest).

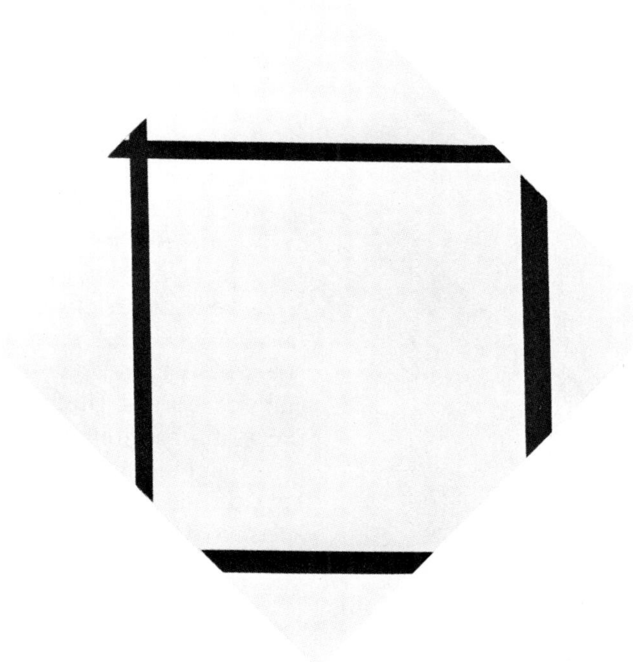

just enough to show up the vertical white boundary line. In addition, tension is created between two types of division—broad in contrast to narrow and dark in contrast to bright. In keeping with these contrasts, the three sections can be described from left to right either as A–B–A in terms of their width or as A–A–B in terms of their coloration. In spite of its sparse and sharply limited means, *Twelfth Station* has greater complexity than might at first appear.

Mondrian's *Painting I* also uses precise lines to delimit its areas of black and white. Instead of three, five such fields are demarcated. Four of them are triangular, or nearly so, and one is a square with three corners lopped off. At first sight, Mondrian's work, too, seems austere, perhaps even dull and banal, suggesting the exercise of doodling whereby we may try to fill a diamond with a square. Yet closer attention will reveal a subtle and complex balancing of elements. The inner square is not complete within the boundary of the canvas. We must use our imagination to complete it by extending the fields on the upper and lower right as well as the lower left. In making this series of extensions, we will notice that in the upper left, where the inner square is actually complete on the canvas, the lines extend farther to the left and above than is necessary to create the square. From this clue we can gather that we are dealing not with a simple square but with part of a grid or lattice. If such is the case, we must imagine the other lines also continuing beyond the point needed to complete the remaining three corners of the square. In effect, we seem to be looking through a diamond window at a lattice pattern that might—if we could see it all—consist of many squares. Such a pattern could exist independently of any relation with the diamond format.

At the same time, the lines within Mondrian's diamond are of varying thicknesses: the shorter they are, the thicker they are. Indeed, the width of the lines varies in inverse proportion to their length, which is determined by the boundaries of the diamond. Mondrian has used precise mathematical calculations to determine the thickness of each line. He has thereby added another principle of organization that increases the complexity of his work. Viewed purely in terms of formal structure, then, Mondrian's painting is more complex than Newman's.

On the other hand, Newman's painting has an added dimension because of its religious theme. Using the clue provided by the title, we must ask ourselves what the Twelfth Station represents. In fact, it marks Christ's death on the Cross and, as such, also prepares for the Resurrection. With this knowledge, we may well see symbolic significance in the relationship of the black and white areas. The black that dominates not only the center but also the preceding section on the left might be associated with the final agony of Christ and the trials preceding this—with mourning and suffering. The following white section could then be associated with the Resurrection, and the spilling over of the black into the white field could even suggest Christ's transition from matter to spirit and from suffering to release. With astonishingly minimal means, Newman is suggesting highly complex themes.

Although both paintings clearly merit intensive analysis, making value judgments about them is far from easy. Both have an elegant simplicity of means and obvious coherence, but unexpected complexities. Yet distinctions between them can still be drawn. Mondrian's painting is a purely abstract work with no subject beyond the patterns created by the geometric shapes. Newman's also works with abstractions, but has in addition a thematic significance—its religious frame of reference. As so often in dealing with works of art, we cannot say that one is good and one is bad. These paintings are fundamentally different, and each must be understood in its own terms to be appreciated properly.

Turning now to poetry, we will consider how our criteria can be used in judging two short poems. "Remember" by Christina Rossetti (1830–1894) and "Go! Forget Me" by Charles Wolfe (1791–1823) both deal with the serious theme of separation from the beloved and can easily be compared.

Christina Rossetti

REMEMBER

Remember me when I am gone away,
   Gone far away into the silent land;
   When you can no more hold me by the hand,
Nor I half turn to go yet turning stay.
Remember me when no more day by day
   You tell me of our future that you planned:
   Only remember me: you understand
It will be late to counsel then or pray.
Yet if you should forget me for a while
   And afterwards remember, do not grieve:
   For if the darkness and corruption leave
   A vestige of the thoughts that once I had,
Better by far you should forget and smile
   Than that you should remember and be sad.

(1849)

The speaker in the Rossetti poem is clearly dying and urgently wishes to be remembered. The moment of parting is conjured up with great poignancy: "Nor I half turn to go yet turning stay." With deceptively simple diction, this line, contrasting "go" with "stay" and repeating "turn" as "turning," emphasizes the speaker's reluctance to leave. The next four lines (5–8) restate the wish to be remembered after death has occurred: "when no more . . ./ You tell me of our future." Here the repetition of the simple, understated phrase "Remember me" emphasizes the intensity of the feeling. With line 9, the speaker suggests an alternative—the beloved may, indeed, forget for a time. In this case, the beloved is urged not to feel guilty. Rather than be remembered always with sadness, the speaker would prefer to be remembered only occasionally, but with fondness and joy. The whole is, then, a preparation for a final parting but also ultimately a consolation. The speaker is acknowledging that however much one may wish to be remembered, human beings cannot be expected to devote themselves exclusively to memories of past life.

The speaker in Wolfe's poem, although also addressing a beloved, is less clear about the reasons for their separation.

Charles Wolfe

GO! FORGET ME

Go! forget me, why should sorrow
  O'er that brow a shadow fling?
Go! forget me—and to-morrow
  Brightly smile, and sweetly sing.
Smile—though I shall not be near thee;
Sing—though I shall never hear thee.
  May thy soul with pleasure shine,
  Lasting as the gloom of mine.

Like the sun, thy presence glowing
  Clothes the meanest thing in light;
And when thou, like him, art going,
  Loveliest objects fade in night.
All things looked so bright about thee,
That they nothing seem without thee.
  By that pure and lucid mind
  Earthly things were too refined.

Go! thou vision, wildly gleaming,
  Softly on my soul that fell,
Go! for me no longer beaming,
  Hope and beauty, fare ye well!
Go! and all that once delighted
Take—and leave me, all benighted,
  Glory's burning gen'rous swell,
  Fancy and the poet's shell.

(c. 1815)

A momentous parting is suggested by the diction: her soul will "with pleasure shine" while his will remain in "gloom"; she is a "vision wildly gleaming" while he is left "benighted." But these elaborate light-dark images apparently describe her simply leaving him—by no means as absolute or profound an experience as the one in the Rossetti poem. Moreover, some of the diction and especially the syntax or word order are confusing. "By that pure and lucid mind/ Earthly things were too refined" makes no sense, for if her mind is so pure and lucid, earthly things should be too *little* refined for her. The second line from the end (line 23) is also unclear, for just what is "Glory's burning gen'rous swell" and is the loved one leaving a positive, creative gift or a negative, empty one? In short, Rossetti treats a complex experience in simple, direct, clear language, while Wolfe treats a slighter subject in more elaborate, overstated, and sometimes muddy terms.

Furthermore, Rossetti compresses rather complicated ideas into the tight form of a Petrarchan sonnet (see Chapter 8). The octave, rhyming abbaabba, emphasizes how much the speaker wants to be remembered. But then the sestet, with a significant "Yet" to mark the turn in thought, contemplates the possibility that the beloved may for a time forget. And the last two lines offer a touching, sensitive resolution which shows less concern for the speaker's desire to be remembered after death than for the beloved's continuing happiness in life.

Wolfe sets down less complicated feelings in a much longer and easier form. The emotion, already intense in the first stanza, continues at the same pitch in the second and reaches its high point in the last, which closes with the speaker's sense of loss and emptiness. Yet in spite of this slight intensification, Wolfe provides no development of either the theme or the images. He merely repeats his complaint and continues to contrast brightness and darkness throughout. Furthermore, Wolfe's rhymes—"near thee"/"hear thee," "about thee" "without thee"—are obvious and obtrusive unlike Rossetti's subtle rhymes woven into an intricate pattern.

Then, too, instead of the touching repetition of Rossetti's "Remember me," Wolfe's fivefold repetition of "Go!" sounds petulant. Although the speaker is supposedly filled with deep regret, he seems, especially at the beginning, merely to be saying, "Go, forget me—see if I care!" Above all, the pronounced, bouncy rhythm is too obtrusive. This rhythm, with its strong beat and its feminine endings ("sorrow," "to-morrow"; "glowing," "going"; "gleaming," "beaming"), is hardly appropriate for the solemn theme.

To sum up, Rossetti's poem is distinguished by a profound theme movingly expressed in the intricate form of a Petrarchan sonnet. Wolfe's poem neither offers a particularly illuminating theme nor gives it memorable expression. In short, this poem has little complexity, and even occasionally lacks sense or coherence.

We should now raise the more fundamental question of why complexity and coherence have come to be regarded as useful general principles for judging works of art. A possible answer might be that we value in art the complexity that we also know to be true of life. For this reason, we especially admire works that introduce *irony,* such as the discrepancy between appearance and reality or between expectation and actual result, and *paradox,* a contradiction that actually expresses a profound insight. Realizing that life is full of unexpected reversals and contradictions, we expect some of these in art, even though we do not expect art to mirror life in any simple and direct way.

Moreover, even though life often seems chaotic and pointless, we look in art for some sort of order and coherence. These may be more or less prominent, depending on whether the work suggests a chaotic universe, as does *Waiting for Godot* (see Chapter 12) or an orderly one, as does the "Bufo" selection from Pope (see Chapter 10). Yet even when the world shown in a work of art is essentially chaotic, we can expect a certain coherence. *Waiting for Godot,* for instance, presents an aimless, seemingly meaningless existence, summed-up in Pozzo's bitter speech in Act II:

> One day, is that not enough for you, one day he [Lucky] went dumb, one day I went blind, one day we'll go deaf one day we were born, one day we shall die, the same day, the same second, is that not enough for you?
>
> (p. 57b)

However, the continual emphasis on the meaninglessness of life unifies the play, and the deliberate parallel between the first and second acts, though it suggests the impossibility of resolving anything, also becomes an organizing principle that brings coherence to the whole.

To recapitulate, the most useful criteria are related not to the creator's talent nor to the audience's response, but to the quality of the work. The two criteria we have found to be most helpful—complexity and coherence—will enable us to understand why certain works of art are excellent. These criteria have the added advantage that they will make us fully aware of the diversity and richness as well as of the unity to which all the various components of a work contribute.

Yet we should remember that complexity and coherence are not rigid and inflexible principles. The kinds of complexity and coherence found in the works of sculpture, painting, and poetry just considered are not exactly the same. In every case, knowing what to look for and how to apply these criteria can come only from training, sensitivity, and experience. Using these criteria will clarify our thinking about art and enhance our appreciation.

Questions for Study and Discussion

1. In what sense is originality a valid criterion for judging a work of art, and in what sense is it not? Why is a knowledge of the genre of a work, or, in the performing arts, of previous interpretations often essential in order to establish the originality of a work? How is the criterion of originality used in Anna Kisselgoff's ballet review [see page 178]?
2. Why are sincerity, easy comprehensibility, and immediate relevance of doubtful value in judging a work? Why are these often advanced as reasons for liking or disliking a work?
3. To show that beauty of subject matter is not a valid criterion, describe a film that you consider successful in spite of its disturbing subject.
4. In judging a work of art, why are complexity and coherence preferable to the other principles we have discussed? How do complexity and coherence complement each other?
5. Analyze the ways in which complexity and coherence are used in our discussion as criteria for judging the panels by Brunelleschi and Ghiberti [see Figures 202, 203] and the paintings by Mondrian [see Figure 205, page 359] and Newman [see Figure 204, page 359]. What aspects of each work receive particular consideration—the technical, thematic, or structural?
6. Analyze how complexity and coherence are used in our discussion as criteria for judging the poems by Christina Rossetti and Charles Wolfe. What aspects of each work receive particular consideration?
7. Refer again to the discussion of the Haydn *Sonata in E-flat* [see page 303] or to the Chopin *G-minor Ballade* [see page 315]. How are complexity and coherence used as criteria in explaining and judging these works? How can these criteria be applied to a familiar piece of contemporary music?
8. To clarify the relative merits of the statue of *Venus de Milo* [see Figure 4, page 5] and the photograph of Marilyn Monroe [see Figure 5, page 5], apply the criteria of complexity and coherence to each.

Conclusion: The World Beyond the Classroom

Our explorations in the arts, far from being completed, have only just begun. We should now apply what we have learned to the world immediately around us. Regardless of whether we live near or far away from a great cultural center, we can find many opportunities to continue our experience with the spatial arts, music, literature, theater, film, opera, and dance.

We should bear in mind that works of art can be found in almost all inhabited locations. Indeed, even an ordinary manhole cover [206], as the New York photographer Mark Feldstein (b. 1937) has demonstrated, can be decorative and worth our notice. Moreover, works of art can be created by people in all walks of life, as is vividly shown by the extraordinary Watts Towers [207]. These were designed and constructed over a period of thirty-three years by an otherwise unknown eccentric, Sam or Simon Rodia (c. 1875–1965), in his Los Angeles backyard.

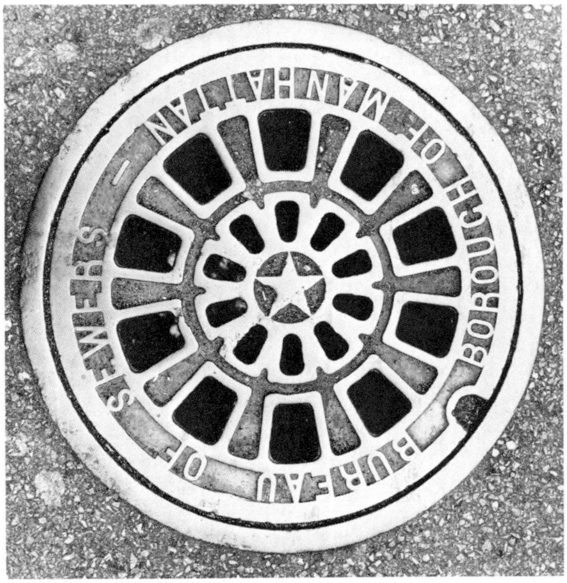

left: 206 Mark Feldstein. *Manhole Cover.* Photograph. 1975.

below: 207 Simon Rodia (Rodilla). Watts Towers, Los Angeles. 1921–1954 (now partially destroyed). This complex of several towers and other structures, the tallest almost 100 feet (30½ meters) high, consists of reinforced concrete openwork encrusted with colorful bits of refuse—stones and shells as well as broken glass, tile, and pottery. A highly personal architectural sculpture, it has only recently come to be recognized as an artistic creation. It is now listed on the National Register of Historic Places and protected as a Los Angeles City Monument.

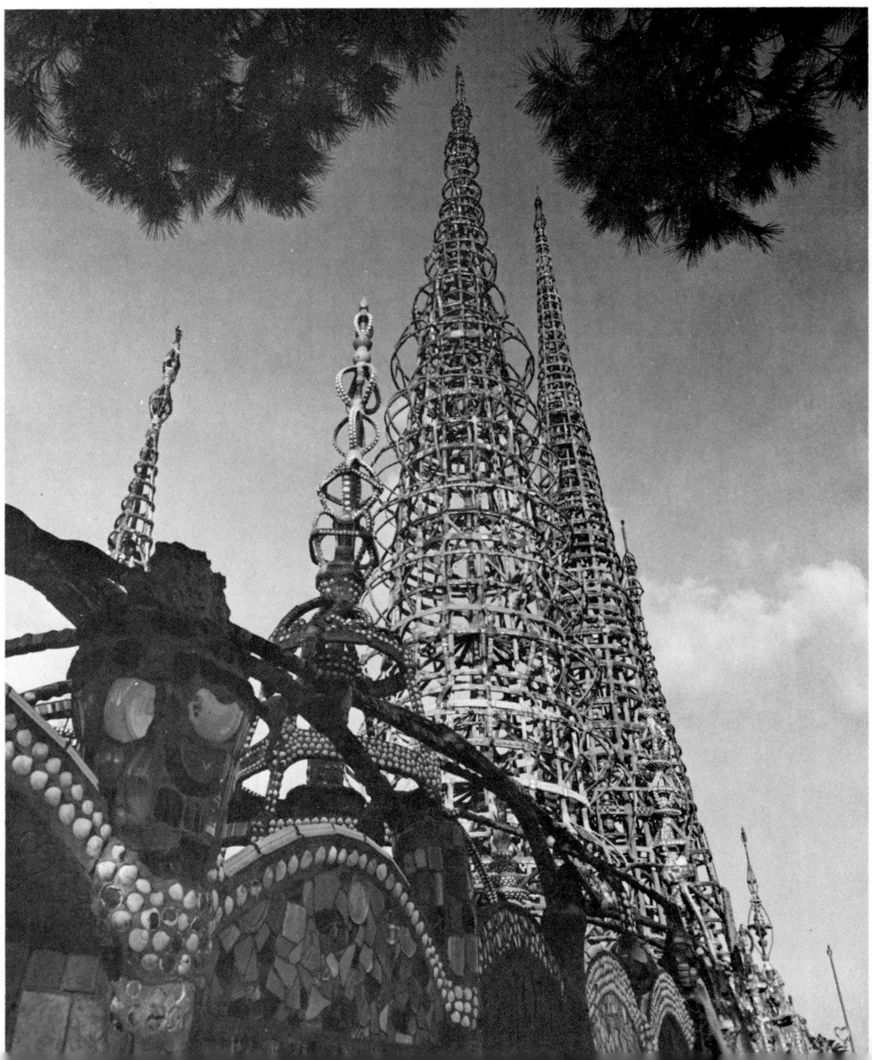

As the illustration of the Watts Towers reveals, studying works of sculpture or architecture in two-dimensional reproductions is far less satisfactory than experiencing them in their original state. When we actually see a sculpture, we can become aware of the importance of its material and scale as well as its location. When we actually see a painting, we also can observe not only its size and colors—neither of which may be accurately represented in a copy—but the very brushstrokes that contribute to the impression of texture. As for architectural works, which surround us everywhere, we can train ourselves to observe the various elements used in the types of buildings considered in our discussions, as well as other types such as banks, schools, and hospitals. Buildings are, in fact, especially difficult to appreciate from photographs. We must walk through them and see them from various sides if we are to have a full sense of the whole.

On the other hand, the reproductions that are now widely available allow us to become acquainted with many works that are not within easy reach. For instance, we can find reproductions of paintings of all ages, and we may want to acquire some of these for our own surroundings. Better still, we may be able to purchase at little cost original works such as posters, woodcuts, and engravings. Once we are aware of the varied possibilities, we will have to face the difficult but enjoyable challenge of deciding which works we would most like to live with—a first step in recognizing and developing our own taste.

Now that photography is fully accepted as an art form, the works of master photographers can be seen in exhibitions as well as in publications. As amateur photographers, we can train ourselves to take into account the composition of the scene, the play of light and shade, and the character and mood of what is being photographed. Those who are also able to develop their negatives can exercise even greater control over their visual effects.

In music, hearing actual performances is as important and unique a pleasure as seeing the originals of paintings. Concerts by orchestras, chamber groups, and soloists, though more frequent in urban areas, are likely to be available everywhere. We should seek them out in order to experience the excitement shared by the audience at the performance and to become acquainted with unfamiliar works or to hear a distinctive interpretation of a work we already know.

Recordings of music offer great convenience, for they can be played whenever and wherever we wish. In addition, they enable us to hear a complicated piece often enough to become thoroughly familiar with it and so to appreciate the subtleties that escape us at first or second hearing. Indeed, such repeated hearings can greatly develop our musical taste.

Literature, too, is widely accessible. Even the greatest masterpieces are available in paperback. And literature in such inexpensive forms is as authentic as in the original edition. However, as with the other arts, our experience of literature will become more rewarding as it increases. We know that literary works are usually highly complex and may also be linked to other works of literature. The more we read, the more we will gain from our reading.

We may find an additional pleasure if we take the risk of reading aloud.

As we have seen, poems in particular draw on the sounds of the language. And when spoken, the prose rhythms of novelists may also become more evident. But even if we only mentally "read aloud," our appreciation of literature will expand as we increase our attentiveness in reading.

In the performing arts such as theater, opera, and dance, we should again, as with music, seize every opportunity to go to actual productions. The excitement of a live performance cannot be matched by a mere reading of the script or score. Although we may be able to see filmed versions of operas and dance performances on television, these two art forms can hardly be appreciated fully except in actual performance.

In addition, we might try to participate more actively in the production of a play, opera, or ballet. If not as actors, singers, or dancers, we can take part in local efforts by joining the technical crew—building sets, working on lighting and costumes, moving scenery. In doing so, we will become increasingly aware of the complexities of each production as well as of the risks entailed in every performance.

We probably need no encouragement to go to films, which are perhaps the most popular art form of our age. Since film is also possibly the most flexible and creative of the arts, we should not be content with unimaginative examples. Having become more conscious of many of the resources of film, we can be more perceptive and critical as audiences and try to support works that use the medium in complex and distinctive ways.

Closely related to film and seemingly replacing it in popularity is television. With its ability to record events instantly on tape and to rebroadcast these immediately from any part of the globe, it is the medium par excellence for keeping us informed about politics, sports, and the world at large. Television is also outstanding in its ability to transmit performances in the established arts, especially theater, opera, and film. It can provide close-up views that are not available to an audience in a theater or concert hall. It can also present multiple views of stage performances while they are in progress simply by shifting from one camera to another. Miraculously, it can bring the performances into our very homes.

Although its impact on the lives of most of us is undeniable, we will probably agree that television has not yet found its own identity as a distinctive art form. Perhaps this failing explains why so many of its programs are disappointing. Yet television has great artistic potential and may soon develop in new and exciting ways. Still, in relation to the arts, it serves best at present as a means of transmitting other art forms to us.

We are extremely fortunate to live in a technological age when not only television but also art reproductions, records, and tapes enable us to experience art forms that were rarely accessible to the vast majority of people only a few years ago. Not only are the arts much more available to us now but we are also fortunate to have far more leisure time to give to them.

As we have seen, to come to understand and appreciate any work of art fully requires concentration, training, and experience. This effort is surely repaid by the lifelong satisfactions we will gain as we continue our explorations in the arts.

Appendix: Musical Notation

With practice, understanding music in printed form becomes far easier than we might suppose. That is not to say that reading a few pages of explanation will enable someone who has no experience on a musical instrument to go to a piano and play a Beethoven sonata. Expertise in playing an instrument takes years of practice. But the ability to read music to the point of grasping musical examples in a textbook of this kind is within the reach of nonmusicians and is ultimately very rewarding.

Probably the clearest aspect of musical notation is the system for designating *pitch*. Each different pitch is shown by a different position on the five-lined grid called the *staff*. Notes printed higher on the staff are higher in pitch [Example A1].

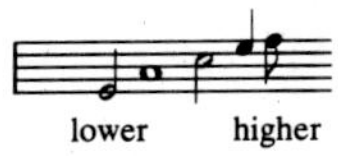

Example A1 Rudimentary system for designating pitch.

Notes may be on a line or in a space between two lines. Each successive note is a step away from the next. These steps correspond to the white keys of the piano. There are essentially seven original or "natural" notes. They may be designated by letter or syllable [Example A2]. The next C (or do) is precisely one octave above the first, or "middle," C [Example A3]. Two notes an octave apart sound very similar, although we can easily hear that one is higher in pitch than the other. The similarity is the result of the vibration ratio of the two tones, which is exactly 2 to 1. If middle C is tuned to 256 Herz (256 vibrations per second), the C an octave above vibrates at 512 Herz. The A in between, to which the orchestra tunes, is "440-A," that is, a pitch of precisely 440 Herz.

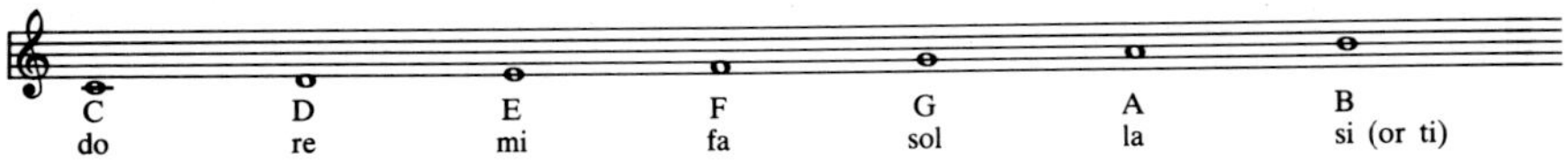

Example A2 The seven notes of the diatonic major scale.

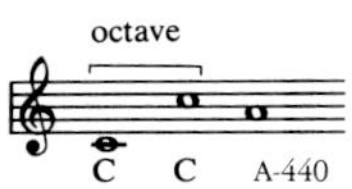

Example A3 Octave.

A clef sign such as the treble clef (𝄞) is needed to show what range of notes is designated by the staff. The lower pitches are normally indicated with the bass clef (𝄢). The two staves are related as shown in Example A4:

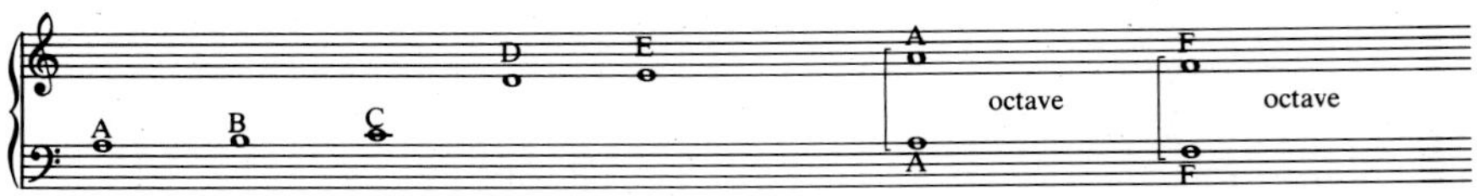

Example A4 The two staves (the grand staff).

Besides the seven natural pitches, five additional notes appear as black keys on the piano. They have a double notation, as sharps or flats, according to the musical context. Thus, the black key between C and D may be written as C-sharp or D-flat [Example A5], but it is the same pitch. The sharp-sign shows that the pitch of the natural note has been raised by a half-step (see Chapter 2), while the flat lowers the pitch by the same amount. Thus C-sharp lies a half-step above C and a half-step below D. A sharp or flat is canceled by a natural sign (♮). These symbols of altered pitch are together called *accidentals.*

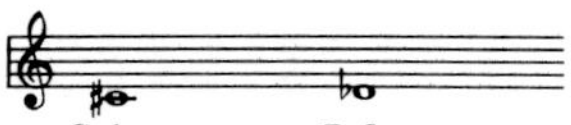
C-sharp D-flat

Example A5 Accidentals.

The notation of *rhythm,* while not complicated in theory, is more difficult to master in practice. The principle is that the shape of the note symbolizes its duration. Example A6 shows the principal rhythmic note values:

Each note is twice as long as the next below it.
𝅝 = whole note
𝅗𝅥 or 𝅗𝅥 = half note
♩ or ♩ = quarter note
♪ or ♪ = eighth note
𝅘𝅥𝅯 or 𝅘𝅥𝅯 = sixteenth note
2 eighth notes joined = ♫ or ♫
4 sixteenth notes joined = ♬♬ or ♬♬

𝅗𝅥. or 𝅗𝅥. ("dotted half note") = duration of 3 quarter notes, i.e., half + quarter

Example A6 Musical note values.

A silence of a given duration is shown by a *rest.* Each rest corresponds to a note of the same length [Example A7]:

𝄻 = whole rest
𝄼 = half rest
𝄽 = quarter rest
𝄾 = eighth rest
𝄿 = sixteenth rest

Example A7 Rests.

These symbols give only the relative length of the notes. How long they sound in absolute terms depends on two other aspects of rhythm: the tempo and the meter.

Tempo, the speed of the beat, can be readily understood even without reference to musical notation; it is discussed in Chapter 2.

Meter, also discussed in Chapter 2, is shown in the musical notation by the *time signature.* This consists of a pair of numbers, often written as a fraction, such as 2/4, 3/4. In a musical score, the two numbers are printed one over the other with no line between: $\genfrac{}{}{0pt}{}{2}{4}$, $\genfrac{}{}{0pt}{}{3}{4}$. The upper number (or numerator of the fraction) sets the number of beats to each measure of music; the lower number (denominator) indicates which note value is to be counted as equal to one beat. Most commonly, the quarter-note receives one beat (2/4, 3/4, 4/4 time), but there are other possibilities, of which the most common are 6/8 and 2/2 time. 4/4 time may be symbolized by a half-circle (like the letter *C*), and 2/2 is most often printed as a half-circle with a vertical line through it [Example A8]. These symbols are vestiges of medieval musical notation.

$\genfrac{}{}{0pt}{}{2}{2}$ = 𝄵 $\genfrac{}{}{0pt}{}{4}{4}$ = 𝄴

Example A8 Time signatures.

To give an idea of the absolute duration of musical notes, we can consider a typical tempo and meter such as a *moderato* tempo in 4/4 time. In this case, a quarter-note would be slightly faster than one per second, or about 72 per minute. This corresponds approximately to the normal adult heartbeat. In an *allegro* tempo, still in 4/4 time, the same quarter-note would be faster, typically between 112 and 144 per minute. In waltz time (3/4 time), the quarter-note is even faster, so that an *allegro* tempo 3/4 meter would imply a quarter-note of about 184 per minute! The musician must exercise careful judgment in order to establish the correct tempo for a given piece of music. Regardless of the meter and tempo, the relative values of the notes remain fixed—a half-note is always twice as long as a quarter-note.

Besides the time signature, the musician is aided by the grouping of the notes into measures by bar lines, the vertical lines through the staff. The beginning of the song "Long, Long Ago" is given in notation to illustrate the coordination of pitch and rhythmic notation [Example A9].

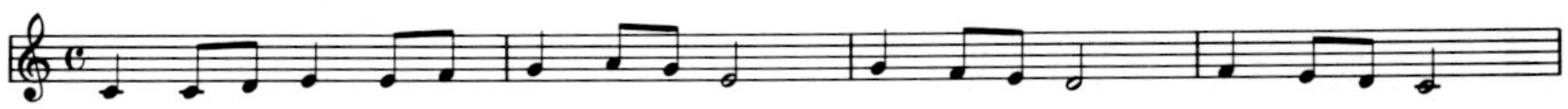

Example A9 "Long, Long Ago."

Notes that are to be played simultaneously are lined up vertically one over another. The stems may be separate or connected [Example A10].

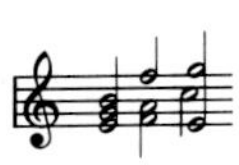

Example A10 Notes to be played simultaneously are written one above the other.

In a musical score for several instruments, one or two parts are normally printed on each staff. The vertical alignment of the several staves allows the reader to see which notes are played together [Example A11]. Consequently, it is possible to follow the rhythm and the changes in instrumentation in an orchestral score without actually reading the individual pitches.

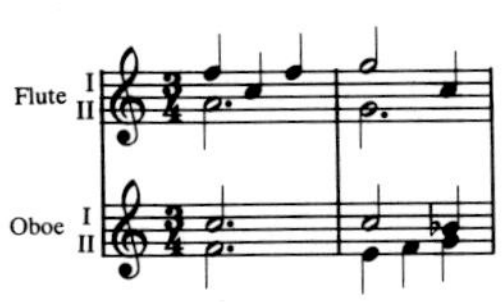

Example A11 When several instruments sound together, their notation is aligned vertically on the staves.

Dynamics

The dynamic markings are easy to read and follow. Normally, they are printed below the notes to which they apply and are either graphic symbols or abbreviated Italian words. Here is a table of the most common dynamics:

ff	= *fortissimo,* very loud
f	= *forte,* loud
mf	= *mezzo forte,* medium loud
mp	= *mezzo piano,* medium soft
p	= *piano,* soft
pp	= *pianissimo,* very soft
cresc. (<)	= *crescendo,* getting gradually louder
dimin. (>)	= *diminuendo,* getting gradually softer
decresc.	= *decrescendo,* same as *diminuendo*
sfz	= *sforzando,* suddenly, sharply louder
>	= accent, gentler version of sfz

Most of these can be modified by words such as *molto* (very), *poco* (a little), or *più* (more).

This brief review of musical notation does not deal with every refinement of the system. Still, it provides a basis for understanding the musical examples in this and other books.

Glossary of Terms

Terms *italicized* within the definitions are themselves defined in the Glossary.

acrylic A recently developed, fast-drying medium for painting in which a plastic substance, acrylic polymer, is combined with the pigment.

aerial perspective See *perspective.*

aisles In a Roman *basilica* and Christian church, the longitudinal spaces flanking the *nave.*

alliteration The repetition of consonants at the beginning of nearby words.

amphitheater An oval or circular space surrounded by rising tiers of seats for spectators.

apse The semicircular space at one end of a Roman *basilica* and Christian church. In a church, the apse, with its surmounting half-dome, generally serves as a backdrop for the altar.

arch A curved structural support, often constructed of wedge-shaped blocks, used to span an opening. Arches are either round (when the profile consists of half or part of a circle) or pointed (when the profile consists of the two parts meeting in a point at the top); the latter type is used in *Gothic architecture.*

architrave In a Greek temple the lowest section of the *entablature,* resting on the *capital* [see Figures 45 and 46, page 51].

aria An elaborately worked-out musical composition that is a part of most operas. An aria is sung by one of the leading characters in the opera with the accompaniment of the full orchestra.

art song A song written by an identifiable composer to express the thought or emotion of a short poem that serves as its text.

aside A device, primarily in plays, in which a character expresses private thoughts while, by convention, those present cannot hear the words spoken.

assonance The repetition of a vowel sound in nearby words.

atonality The quality of music that has no key-center or *tonic.*

atrium In architecture, an open court located in front of a Christian church.

attribute A visual property, such as the thunderbolt of Zeus or the keys of St. Peter, which traditionally accompanies a figure and serves as an aid to identification.

***auteur* theory** The French film theory whereby the director is regarded as the chief creator of a motion picture.

axis In architecture, an imaginary line or pathway through the building.

axis of symmetry In the visual arts, an imaginary line which bisects the object so as to facilitate understanding of the composition.

ballad A type of short narrative poem, often set to music, that celebrates folk heroes or common people. It frequently uses a special verse form of alternating three- and four-foot lines.

Baroque A style that flourished in Europe in the 17th and 18th centuries, characterized by striking, elaborate, and dramatic effects calculated to enlist the emotional participation of the observer.

basilica A rectangular building with an *apse, nave,* and *aisles.*
bas relief See *relief.*
Bildungsroman A novel that traces the growth of the central character to maturity and self-awareness.
blank verse Unrhymed iambic pentameter (not to be confused with *free verse*).
box set A stage set with three walls and often a ceiling.
broken chord A *chord* whose individual pitches are sounded in close succession rather than simultaneously. Broken chords are characteristic of accompaniment patterns played by such instruments as the piano and guitar.
bust A type of sculpture that presents only the figure to the head and shoulders of a human figure.
cadence A resting-place or pause in the musical line that marks the end of a *phrase.*
cadenza A musical passage intended for ornament or *virtuoso* display, at one time improvised by the performer at the moment of performance but now usually written out in advance. Most often heard near the close of the first movement of a *concerto* before the full orchestra plays for the final time.
caesura A pause within a line of poetry.
cantilever In architecture, a horizontal projection, such as a balcony, that extends beyond its vertical supports and appears to be self-supporting.
capital The decorated top of a column [see Figure 45, page 51].
cella The windowless inner shrine of a Greek temple that housed the statue of a god.
chamber music An intimate form of music performed by few players, each taking a separate part.
choir In architecture, the part of a church beyond the *transept* that may include an *apse* and chapels.
chord A group of three or more pitches that sound together as a unit; an element of *harmony.*
classicism The style of classical Greece and Rome. In music, the dominant style of the late eighteenth century. See *neoclassicism.*
coda The closing section of a piece of music.
codetta A short *coda;* also, the closing section of a *sonata-form* exposition.
columns Rounded vertical supports in *post-and-lintel construction.* In the classical architecture of Greece and Rome as well as in the later styles, they were known as Doric, Ionic and Corinthian, each with distinctive *fluting* and *capitals* [see Figure 45, page 51]. The three types of columns are known as the classical *orders.*
comedy Dealing with the less serious aspects of life and arousing smiles or laughter in the audience. This type of drama amusingly considers the weaknesses or failings of individuals and usually ends happily.
commercial art Standardized production for mass consumption that is characteristic since the early 19th century of industrial society.
concerto Usually a musical composition in which a single instrument joins with or is accompanied by the orchestra. It normally has three movements.
cornice A molding that outlines or frames the top of a building; the top section of the *entablature* that in Greek temples extends beyond the wall of the building [see Figure 45, page 51].
couplet Two lines that *rhyme.*
cross-cutting A film technique of shifting alternately between different shots to suggest that various events are occurring simultaneously.
cubism A style of painting developed in the early 20th century that, breaking with traditional three-dimensional *perspective,* showed figures and objects as geometric shapes and presented their various planes simultaneously.

cutting A film technique of splicing one shot to another, thereby creating an immediate transition. Used also as a term for editing a film.

diction In literature, the choice of words.

dissolve A transitional device whereby the image on the screen slowly disappears (a *fade-out*) as a new image replaces it (a *fade-in*).

dissonance In *harmony,* those combinations of tones which produce a sense of restlessness or need for further *resolution* rather than of rest or finality.

dome A half-sphere covering a building or portion of a building.

dominant In the Western key system, the fifth note of the *scale* or key, which is the note second in importance to the *tonic.* Thus, in the key of A, the dominant is E. The term *dominant* may refer not only to a particular note but also to a key located a fifth higher (the dominant key) or to the fifth chord of a key (the dominant *triad*).

dramatic monologue A type of poem in which a single character reveals his or her nature, often unwittingly, by words spoken alone or to someone else.

duration A length of time; in music, the time value of a particular note or rest.

dynamic balance In the visual arts, the compositional principle whereby a marked contrast exists in the elements on either side of the axis of symmetry.

dynamics The loudness or softness of musical sounds; also used to refer to the written symbols for the level of volume, and to the use of varied levels of loudness in performance.

elevation A graphic representation of a building showing its arrangement vertically, complementing the *plan.*

engraving A technique of the graphic arts in which the artist cuts a pattern of lines into the surface of a metal plate with a special tool, the burin. The plate is then inked to make a print.

entablature That section of a Greek temple supported by the columns, usually composed of *architrave, frieze,* and *cornice* [see Figure 45, page 51].

epic A long narrative, told in an elevated style, that usually presents national heroes and their gods in a series of exploits.

equestrian statue A portrait or statue of a figure, often a ruler or military leader, on horseback.

etching A technique of the graphic arts in which the lines of an engraved metal plate are softened by suspending it in a series of acid baths before printing.

façade Usually the front or main side of a building.

fade-in, fade-out See *dissolve.*

farce A type of comedy in which laughter is aroused more by slapstick action than by character analysis or witty language.

film noir A type of film that normally uses black-and-white photography to present violent scenes of urban life. Its pessimism is conveyed by exaggerated lighting, emphasis on darkness, and sharp angle shots.

flashback A narrative device in novels, plays, and films that interrupts the time sequence by presenting an earlier moment of the action as if it were happening at that moment.

fluting Vertical grooves in a *column* [see Figure 45, page 51].

flying buttress A support on the outside of a Gothic cathedral that carries the thrust of the vaulted roof to another support away from the building.

folk art A type of art created by simple people working with their own traditional themes and motifs.

folk song A song without identifiable composer but arising out of the traditions of a people.

foreshadowing In narratives, preparation for future action.

foreshortening In painting, a method of representing objects as if they recede into space; the more distant parts take up a proportionally smaller area than the parts presented as being closer to the observer.

framing Composing an image—a picture, photograph, or still shot—so that it appears as if in a border or frame.

free verse Poetry, usually modern, that is unrhymed and irregular in rhythm.

fresco A wall painting in which the pigments are applied to the plaster as it dries, forming a permanent bond with it.

frieze Any band of painted or carved decoration; in a Greek temple the middle section of the *entablature,* often decorated with designs or carving [see Figure 45, page 51].

fugue An elaborate musical composition in which a melodic phrase (the *theme* or subject of the fugue), after sounding in one part or voice, is imitated by other parts in succession.

genre A type or category in any art form.

Gothic architecture A style of building that flourished in Europe from the mid-12th century to the early 16th century, employing *pointed arches, flying buttresses,* and other engineering resources to create a sense of lightness, space, and height.

halo An aura of light, generally around the head of a figure, to denote its sanctity or special importance.

harmonics The component pitches, normally not separately distinguishable, that comprise a single musical tone.

harmony Any simultaneous combination of sounds; a *chord;* also, the movement and structure of chords in a musical composition.

high comedy A kind of *comedy* in which sophisticated characters and witty language provide insight into human nature and society.

high relief See *relief.*

history painting Representations, often large in scale, of important historical events.

homophonic Describing music whose *texture* consists of a melodic line supported by a secondary chordal element; *melody* plus accompaniment.

hubris (or **hybris**) Arrogant pride, often considered the flaw of tragic heroes.

hue The property of color that distinguishes one color from another; for example, yellow or blue.

imagery In poetry or prose, vivid sensory details as well as figurative language such as similes and metaphors.

impressionism A style of painting that developed in the second half of the 19th century in France, rendering the effects of light and color through patterns of small dots of pigment.

in medias res "In the middle of things"—the characteristic opening of the *epic* in the midst of the action rather than at the beginning.

intensity In painting, the degree of saturation of color particles so that one red, for example, is "redder" than another; in music, the softness or loudness of a sound, also known as *dynamics.*

interior monologue In prose fiction, the expression in private of a character's inner thoughts; in film, the expression of inner thoughts that are heard while the character is not seen speaking.

intertextuality The modern critical concept that artistic works are interrelated in such a way that later works may not only draw on earlier ones but can also illuminate earlier ones.

interval The distance between two musical pitches. The interval between two adjacent pitches is called a step; larger intervals are skips or leaps.

intonation In music, creating accurate *pitch.* The term is used for the voice and for instruments that do not predetermine the pitch.

landscape painting A scene of nature depicted in art.

Leitmotiv A repeated theme, phrase or *motive* used in the operas of Wagner and many later composers to represent a character, situation, recurrent idea, or physical object.

libretto The text of an opera.

Lied The German word for *song,* referring to the repertory of German art songs created by such composers as Schubert, Schumann, Brahms, and Wolf (plural: *Lieder*).

lithography A graphic technique in which the print is reproduced from a design drawn on a limestone slab.

lyric A short poem expressing emotion that is or might well be accompanied by music.

manuscript A handwritten book, sometimes decorated with illuminated (painted) miniatures.

Mass A choral composition, which may have instrumental accompaniment, whose movements are the repeated segments of the Roman Catholic liturgical service: *Kyrie, Gloria, Credo, Sanctus,* and *Agnus Dei.*

melodrama A type of drama specializing in excessive emotions, violence, and other sensational effects. Usually the characters are either purely good or purely evil, and the resolution tends to reward all according to their just deserts.

melodic curve The rise and fall of *melody* as well as its *rhythm.*

melody A fundamental element of music referring to the sequence of notes that is heard as the musical line.

meter In music, the pattern established by stressed and unstressed beats, and in poetry, the pattern of rhythmic beat established by accented or unaccented syllables. Traditional metrical patterns in poetry consist of iambs (˘′), trochees (′˘), dactyls (′˘˘), anapests (˘˘′), spondees (′′), and pyrrhic (˘˘) feet.

method acting A technique whereby the actors try to make their portrayal of characters authentic by drawing on their own emotional experiences.

metopes In a Greek temple, square blocks of stone decorated with sculptures that are part of the *frieze* [see Figure 45, page 51].

mock epic A satirical narrative technique that elevates subject matter not deserving of such treatment by the use of devices associated with traditional *epics.*

mode In general, a choice of musical *pitches,* arranged in a *scale* that, by the character of its *intervals,* establishes the nature of a piece of music. It often refers to the medieval Church modes, the ancestors of the major and minor scales. Major and minor are also modes.

modeling In painting, the suggestion of the three-dimensional character of a body through the use of light and shade; in sculpture, the shaping of the forms.

modulation The transition from one *tonality* (key) to another in the course of a musical composition.

monophonic Describing music whose texture consists solely of a single melodic line. Contrasted with *homophonic* and *polyphonic textures.*

montage A film technique for combining or juxtaposing a series of images.

mosaic A method of decorating walls, floors, or vaults with patterns composed of small pieces of colored stone, glass, or other permanent materials (known as *tesserae*), which are cemented in place.

motive In music, a melodic or rhythmic fragment, shorter than a *phrase,* which assumes importance through repetition.

movement A principal section of a musical composition, normally set off by clear pauses and characterized by its own *meter, tempo,* key, and thematic material.

naive painting Work by artists who have not been formally trained (sometimes called "Sunday painters"). Such paintings are often characterized by simplified forms and strong color.

narthex In architecture, the porch or vestibule of a church.

nave The great central space of a church or secular basilica, flanked by *aisles.*

neoclassicism The style or period of the later 17th and 18th centuries, harking back to classical Greece and Rome, that values reason, order, symmetry, balance, and often *wit.*

nimbus See *halo.*

notes In music, individual sounds characterized by their *pitch, duration, intensity,* and *tone color;* the written symbol or notation of such sounds that identifies their *pitch* and *duration.*

ode A type of lyric poem that is elaborate and usually elevated in tone.

opus A work or composition. Opus numbers normally are assigned when a work is published, not when it is composed, so that they are of limited value in understanding a composer's chronology.

order The combination of *column, capital,* and *entablature* in Greek temple architecture. The three classical orders are the Doric, Ionic, and Corinthian [see Figure 45, page 51].

overall patterning A type of design, such as a geometric pattern on wallpaper, that can continue indefinitely in any and all directions.

panel A rigid flat support, usually rectangular, for a painting, or the material out of which a *relief* sculpture has been carved.

panning The film technique of pivoting the camera from a fixed position to photograph a wide area.

pediment In a Greek temple, the triangular gable above the *entablature* [see Figure 45, page 51].

perspective In the spatial arts, a means of suggesting depth on a two-dimensional surface. In aerial perspective, the blurring of distant objects so that they seem to be enveloped in atmosphere. In linear or *single-point perspective,* the use of an underlying pattern of straight lines meeting at a *vanishing point* as a guide for presenting objects as progressively smaller, the further away they are.

phrase A unit of musical structure that corresponds to a line of poetry and is of about the length that can be sung in a single breath.

picaresque novel The type of fiction that relates the adventures of a rogue-hero who becomes more worldly through experience.

piers In architecture, a vertical support or pillar.

Pietà In Christian art, the image of the sorrowing Virgin holding the dead Christ.

pitch A fundamental quality of a musical tone; each pitch is produced by a different frequency of vibration and is designated by letter name (A, B, C, D, E, F, G), syllable *(do, re, mi),* or, most generally, as "high" or "low."

plan A graphic representation of a building showing its arrangement horizontally, complementing the *elevation.*

poetic justice The exact distribution of rewards to the good and punishments to the wicked according to what each deserves.

point of view In the spatial arts, the angle from which the scene is presented; in the temporal arts, the "voice" through which the events are narrated. In painting, it often involves *perspective,* which provides the illusion of three-dimensional space on a two-dimensional surface. In prose fiction, it involves the writer's choice of narrator, such as an omniscient or first-person storyteller.

polyphonic Describing music that consists of two or more relatively independent melodic lines, as contrasted with *homophonic* or *monophonic textures.* The *fugues* of J. S. Bach are an excellent example of polyphonic composition.

portrait An image of a human being that captures the distinctive characteristics of a personality.

post-and-lintel construction A type of architecture employing uprights (posts or columns) surmounted by horizontal slabs (lintels).

postimpressionism A style of painting, created toward the end of the nineteenth century, which grew out of *Impressionism,* but stresses firmer contours and often more emotional content.

pregnant moment In the spatial arts, depicting the episode just before the climax.

primitive art The art of the tribal peoples of Africa, the Americas, Asia and Oceania.

problem play A type of drama that presents a serious treatment of contemporary social or moral problems by means of realistic plot development and staging.

program music Instrumental music that attempts to translate a poem, story, or painting into musical terms.

proscenium stage A playing space sharply separated from the audience, usually by an *arch* or frame.

raisonneur A character, usually in a play, who argues for reason, moderation, and good sense. Often such a character is thought to be voicing the author's own position.

realism An artistic style that tries to recreate life as it really is, usually by showing typical people involved in ordinary events and by presenting details of everyday life.

recitative A style of composition in opera designed to imitate normal speech. Passages of recitative are usually less elaborate or musically developed than set pieces such as *arias.*

relief A type of sculpture in which the background *panel* is pared away, leaving the figures. When these emerge only slightly from the background, the work is called *bas relief* ("low relief"); when they project more fully, the work is called *high relief.*

resolution In music, the combination of sounds that provides a release or harmonious conclusion after the tension of *dissonance.*

rhyme Echoing of sound, usually of the last one or two syllables in nearby lines of poetry. Internal rhyme occurs within, rather than at the end of, poetic lines.

rhythm In music and poetry, a fundamental element, the pattern of sounds in time. In music, it is determined by the length of tones, meter, and tempo; in poetry, by accented and unaccented syllables.

satire A work that ridicules the major or minor flaws of individuals or society.

scale The step-wise arrangement of the principal *pitches* of a *melody* or composition in ascending or descending order.

shade A nontechnical term for the combination of *value* and *intensity,* especially in color.

single-point perspective See *perspective.*

soliloquy A stage and film device whereby a character expresses private thoughts with no one else present but the audience (see *aside*).

sonata a large-scale work for solo instrument or for two instruments, generally in three or four *movements.* In music written before the classical period, the term often means simply "sounding-piece" and hence any instrumental composition.

song See *art song* and *folk song.*

sonnet A type of lyric poem in fourteen lines of iambic pentameter following a definite rhyme scheme. The Elizabethan, or Shakespearean, sonnet organizes its material into three quatrains and a concluding couplet; the Italian, or Petrarchan, sonnet, into an octave and a sestet.

steeple The top part of a church tower.

still life A type of painting that depicts objects of daily life such as flowers, fruit, food, or tools.

stream of consciousness The technique of presenting a character's direct sense impressions, reactions, and spontaneous thoughts as these arise in the mind. Whether in novels, plays, or poems, such passages are often presented without normal grammatical structure or clear, logical sequence.

suspension A kind of dissonance produced by sustaining a *pitch* while the underlying *harmony* changes. The sustained pitch thus becomes dissonant with respect to the underlying *chord.*

symbol An object or image that conveys a further meaning.

symmetrical balance In the spatial arts, the compositional principle whereby the elements are the same, or nearly the same, on each side of the axis of symmetry.

symphony A large-scale composition for orchestra (the "symphony orchestra"). Most symphonies have three or four distinct *movements* and last at least twenty minutes.

synaesthesia In poetry or prose, a type of *image* that describes one sense experience in terms of a different sense, as in Keats's "pale and silver silence."

syncopation A rhythmic device that emphasizes the normally unaccented beat or fraction of a beat.

tempera A painting technique using colors suspended in an egg-based medium.

tempo The speed of a musical piece.

tesserae Small cubes of stone, glass, or other solid material used to make up a *mosaic.*

texture In the spatial arts, the treatment of the surface to give the impression of roughness or smoothness; in music, the degree of complexity achieved by the number and arrangement of voices or instrumental parts in a composition.

theater of the absurd A type of drama, popular since the mid-20th century, which emphasizes the apparently inescapable futility and frustration in the lives of the characters trapped in an incomprehensible universe. Highly experimental, it avoids conventional realistic staging. Its predominant tone tends to be bitter, ironic humor.

theme A segment of a composition used as a basic musical statement. Themes are generally recognized by their *melodies.*

thrust stage A playing space projecting into the auditorium which enables the audience to view the action from two or three sides of the stage.

timbre Term of French origin, used as a synonym for *tone color.*

tonality The fundamental *pitch* center of a composition or portion of a composition; key.

tone color Also called *timbre,* one of the fundamental qualities of a musical sound. Determined by the intensity of the different *harmonics* that comprise each tone, tone color is heard as that characteristic quality or "flavor" of sound that permits one to distinguish different instruments or voices.

tone poem *Program music* written for orchestra, generally in one movement; also called symphonic poem.

tonic The fundamental note of any key. For example, the tonic of the key of C is C; the tonic of E-flat is E-flat. The term *tonic* is also used to refer to the key in question, or to the fundamental *chord* of the key (the tonic *triad*).

tracking The film technique of moving the camera while photographing an action.

tragedy Dealing with the serious and problematic aspects of life in a dignified manner and arousing a deep emotional response in the audience. This type of drama usually traces the downfall of a hero, whose abilities and efforts are often frustrated by forces beyond that hero's control or understanding.

tragicomedy A type of drama in which a serious plot is brought to a near catastrophe but then ends more or less happily.

transept In a cross-shaped church, the rectangular arm that crosses the *nave.*

triad A three-note *chord.*

trompe l'oeil The artist's attempt to deceive the eye by employing simulated volume, perspective, and other devices.

typology In theology, a method of interpretation whereby events are paired so that the earlier one is said to *foreshadow* the later. Thus, the sacrifice of Isaac is held to foreshadow the passion of Christ.

value The property of color that makes it appear light or dark.

vanishing point In linear *perspective,* the point at which parallel lines—whether actual or theoretical—moving away from the viewer seem to converge [see Figure 75, page 119].

virtuoso A musical performer who excels in technical ability.

voice-over A film technique in which the voice of an unseen narrator is heard.

watercolor A technique of painting that uses pigments mixed in water-soluble gum.

wit Mental agility expressed in clever and polished language.

woodcut A graphic technique whereby the artist cuts away the background of the wooden surface, leaving a network of lines that are inked to produce the print.

Index

Boldface numbers indicate illustrations and literary selections. Works are listed under the names of their creators, when known, otherwise under their titles. Architectural works and the art associated with them are listed under the cities where they are located. Many technical terms are included in the Index, with references to their text definitions. For a more complete list of terms, consult the Glossary.

Photographic credits: The authors and publisher wish to thank the custodians of the works of art for supplying photographs and granting permission to use them. Photographs have been obtained from sources listed in the captions, unless otherwise listed below.

AC: Anthony Crickmay, London
AF: Alison Frantz, Princeton
A/AR: Alinari/Art Resource, New York
BVS: Bayerische Verwaltung der Staatl. Schlösser, Gärten und Seen, Munich
BM: British Museum, London
BN: Bibliothèque Nationale, Paris
BPK: Bildarchiv Preussischer Kulturbesitz, West Berlin
BS: Bayerische Staatsgemäldesammlungen, Munich
CAISSE: Caisse Nationale des Monuments Historiques et des Sites, Paris
FU: Fototeca Unione, Rome
G/AR: Giraudon/AR, New York
H: Hirmer, Munich
M: Bildarchiv Foto Marburg, Marburg/Lahn
NYPL: New York Public Library
PR: Photo Researchers, New York
S/AR: Scala/Art Resource, New York
WS: Wim Swaan, New York

References are to **boldface** figure numbers.

Color **Plate 1:** Christie, Manson & Woods, International. **Plate 3:** A. C. Cooper, London. **Plate 9:** S/AR. **Plate 11:** S/AR. **Plate 14:** WS. **Plate 16:** G/AR.

Introduction **1:** CAISSE. **5:** Tom Kelley Studios, Inc., Los Angeles.

Chapter 1 **11:** Tass from Sovfoto, New York. **12:** A/AR. **13:** GIR/AR. **14:** Wayne Andrews, Grosse Pointe. **15:** AC. Achille B. Weider, Zurich. **21:** GIR/AR. **23:** A/AR. **27–29:** A/AR. **30:** BVS. **34:** A/AR. **36:** A/AR. **37:** Leo Castelli Gallery, New York, New York. **38:** Guy A. Weill, New York. **39:** A/AR. **42:** Oriental Institute of the University of Chicago. **44:** AF. **46:** AF. **48:** A/AR. **50:** Jean Roubier/PR. **51:** WS. **52:** Hedrich-Blessing, Chicago. **53:** George Holton/PR.

Chapter 2 A.C.L., Brussels. **60:** Robert Emmett/PR.

Chapter 3 **61:** Theatre Collection, Museum of the City of New York. **62:** Eileen Darby, Point Lookout, New York. **63:** Kobal Collection, London. **64:** Museum of Modern Art/Film Stills Archive, New York. **66:** MPG Collection, New York/MGM. **67:** Theatre Collection, Museum of the City of New York.

Chapter 4 **68–69:** H. **73:** S/AR. **74:** A/AR. **82:** Williamstown Theatre Foundation. **83:** From *Into Film* by Laurence Goldstein and Jay Kaufman, E. P. Dutton & Co., Inc. New York © 1976.

Chapter 5 **84:** Bettman Archive, New York. **85–86:** John Vickers Archives, London. **87:** Bettmann Archive/BBC Hulton. **88:** MPG Collection, New York. **89:** Dramatists Play Service, Inc., New York. **90–91:** Royal Shakespeare Theatre Collections, the Shakespeare Centre Library, Stratford-upon-Avon. **94:** Reprinted with permission of Joanna T. Steichen. **95–96:** AC. **97:** Martha Swope, New York. **98:** Bettman Archives/BBC Hulton. **99:** © Paul Kolnik, New York. **100–101:** AC. **102:** MIRA, New York. **103:** Stevens Caras, New York. **104:** © Paul Kolnik, New York. **105:** AC.

Chapter 6 **106:** A/AR. **107:** Deutsches Archäologisches Institut, Rome. **108:** A/AR. **111:** A/AR. **112:** Courtesy of the Israel Department of Antiquities and Museums, Jerusalem. **114:** A/AR. **116:** Art Resource, New York. **118:** GIR-Lauros/AR.

Chapter 7 **124:** A/AR. **125:** BS. **130:** GIR/AR. **135:** Woodfin Camp & Associates, New York. **137:** AC. **139:** A/AR. **142:** Russell Dian, New York. **143:** A/AR. **144:** Gene Ahrens/Freelance Photographers Guild, New York. **147:** Marburg/Art Reference Bureau, Pittsfield, Mass. **148:** Sonia Halliday Photographs, Weston Turville, Buckinghamshire. **149:** M. **151:** A. F. Kersting, London. **153:** A. F. Kersting, London. **154:** M. **155:** FU. **156:** Reprinted by permission of Coward-McCann, Inc. from *Shakespeare and the Players* by C. Walter Hodges. Copyright 1968 by C. Walter Hodges. **157:** Raoul Fornezza, Milan. **158:** A/AR. **159:** BVS **160:** Science Museum, London. **161:** Cervin Robinson, New York. **162:** William D. Middleton, Charlottesville. **163:** Francis Y. Duval, Brooklyn.

Chapter 9 **168:** Donald McKague, Courtesy of the Stratford Festival, Ontario. **169–170:** AC. **171:** Angus McBean/Harvard Theatre Collection, Cambridge. **172:** AC. **174:** Billy Rose Theatre Collection, New York Public Library. **175:** AC. **176:** Martha Swope, New York. **177:** John Cocchi/United Artists Corporation. **178:** Phototeque, New York/RKO-Radio. **179:** Culver Pictures, Inc., New York. **180:** MPG Collection, New York/MGM. **181:** Phototeque, New York/RKO-Radio.

Chapter 11 **187:** GIR/AR.

Chapter 12 **190:** Pace Gallery, New York. **194:** Dominic Photography, London. **195–196:** Theatre Collection, Museum of the City of New York.

Chapter 13: **197:** GIR/AR. **199:** Geoffrey Clements, New York.

Chapter 14: **201:** BS. **202–203:** A/AR.

Conclusion: **206:** Mark Feldstein, New York. **207:** American Stock Photos, Los Angeles.